KJ–KKZ

Law of Europe

Library of Congress Classification
2008

Prepared by the Cataloging Policy and Support Office
Library Services

LIBRARY OF CONGRESS
Cataloging Distribution Service
Washington, D.C.

0819

This edition cumulates all additions and changes to class KJ-KKZ through Weekly List 2008/11, dated March 12, 2008. Additions and changes made subsequent to that date are published in weekly lists posted on the World Wide Web at

<http://www.loc.gov/aba/cataloging/classification/weeklylists/>

and are also available in *Classification Web*, the online Web-based edition of the Library of Congress Classification.

Library of Congress Cataloging-in-Publication Data

Library of Congress.
    Library of Congress classification. KJ-KKZ. Law of Europe / prepared by the Cataloging Policy and Support Office Library Services. — 2008 ed.
        p. cm.
    "This edition cumulates all additions and changes to class KJ-KKZ through Weekly List 2008/11, dated March 12, 2008. Additions and changes made subsequent to that date are published in weekly lists posted on the World Wide Web ... and are also available in *Classification Web*, the online Web-based edition of the Library of Congress classification."
    Includes index.
    ISBN-13: 978-0-8444-1206-1
    ISBN-10: 0-8444-1206-6
    1. Classification, Library of Congress. 2. Classification—Books—Law. 3. Classification—Boooks—Europe. 4. Law—Europe—Classification. I. Library of Congress. Cataloging Policy and Support Office. II. Title. III. Title: Law of Europe.
    Z696.U5K64 2008   025.4'63494—dc22   2008014100

For sale by the Library of Congress Cataloging Distribution Service,
101 Independence Avenue, S.E., Washington, DC 20541-4912.
Product catalog available on the Web at **www.loc.gov/cds**.

PREFACE

The first edition of subclasses KJ-KKZ, *Law of Europe*, was published in 1988. A 2000 edition cumulated additions and changes that were made during the period 1988-2000. This 2008 edition cumulates additions and changes made since the publication of the 2000 edition.

Classification numbers or spans of numbers that appear in parentheses are formerly valid numbers that are now obsolete. Numbers or spans that appear in angle brackets are optional numbers that have never been used at the Library of Congress but are provided for other libraries that wish to use them. In most cases, a parenthesized or angle-bracketed number is accompanied by a "see" reference directing the user to the actual number that the Library of Congress currently uses, or a note explaining Library of Congress practice.

Access to the online version of the full Library of Congress Classification is available on the World Wide Web by subscription to *Classification Web*. Details about ordering and pricing may be obtained from the Cataloging Distribution Service at

<http://www.loc.gov/cds/>

New or revised numbers and captions are added to the L.C. Classification schedules as a result of development proposals made by the cataloging staff of the Library of Congress and cooperating institutions. Upon approval of these proposals by the weekly editorial meeting of the Cataloging Policy and Support Office, new classification records are created or existing records are revised in the master classification database. Weekly lists of newly approved or revised classification numbers and captions are posted on the World Wide Web at

<http://www.loc.gov/aba/cataloging/classification/weeklylists/>

Jolande Goldberg, law classification specialist in the Cataloging Policy and Support Office, and Paul Weiss, senior cataloging policy specialist, are responsible for coordinating the overall intellectual and editorial content of class K and its various subclasses. Kent Griffiths, assistant editor, creates new classification records and their associated index terms, and maintains the master database.

This printed edition of KJ-KKZ must be used in conjunction with the separately published K Tables: Form Division Tables for Law, available for purchase from the Cataloging Distribution Service. This classification schedule includes references to form division tables within the range K1 to K24, which are found only in that publication.

Barbara B. Tillett, Chief
Cataloging Policy and Support Office

March 2008

OUTLINE OF SCHEDULE

OUTLINE OF SCHEDULE

OUTLINE OF SCHEDULE

OUTLINE OF SCHEDULE

KJG	Albania
KJH	Andorra
KJJ	Austria
	Belarus, see KLF
KJK	Belgium
KJM	Bulgaria
	Corsica, see KJW
KJN	Cyprus
KJP	Czechoslovakia (to 1993)
KJP	Czech Republic (1993-)
KJQ	Slovakia (1993-)
KJR	Denmark
KJS	Estonia
KJT	Finland
	France, see KJV-KJW
	Germany. West Germany. East Germany, see KK-KKC
	Gibraltar, see KRY
	Great Britain. United Kingdom, see KD
KKE	Greece
KKF	Hungary
KKG	Iceland
	Ireland, see KDK
KKH	Italy
KKI	Latvia
KKJ	Liechtenstein
KKJ	Lithuania
KKK	Luxembourg
KKK	Malta
	Moldova, see KLM
KKL	Monaco
KKM	Netherlands
KKN	Norway
KKP	Poland
KKQ	Portugal
KKR	Romania
	Russia, see KLA
KKS	San Marino
	Soviet Union, see KLA
KKT	Spain
KKV	Sweden
KKW	Switzerland
KKX	Turkey
KKY	Ukraine

Vatican City, see KB

KKZ   Yugoslavia

OUTLINE OF SUBJECT DIVISION TABLES

Commercial law. Commercial transactions
Banking. Stock exchange - Continued

KJ-KKZ1 961.5	Investments
KJ-KKZ1 970	Maritime law
KJ-KKZ1 998	Insurance law
KJ-KKZ1 1040	Business associations. Personal companies. Stock corporations
KJ-KKZ1 1155	Intellectual and industrial property
KJ-KKZ1 1160	Copyright
KJ-KKZ1 1194	Patent law and trademarks
KJ-KKZ1 1234	Unfair competition
KJ-KKZ1 1261	Labor law
KJ-KKZ1 1347	Labor-management relations
KJ-KKZ1 1376	Collective bargaining and labor agreements
KJ-KKZ1 1440	Labor courts and procedure
KJ-KKZ1 1468	Social legislation
KJ-KKZ1 1472	Social insurance
KJ-KKZ1 1520	Social services. Public welfare
KJ-KKZ1 1552	Social courts and procedure
KJ-KKZ1 1572	Courts and procedure
KJ-KKZ1 1580	Court organization
KJ-KKZ1 1600	The legal profession
KJ-KKZ1 1650	Procedure in general
KJ-KKZ1 1695	Civil procedure
KJ-KKZ1 1834	Non-contentious (ex parte) jurisdiction
KJ-KKZ1 1846	Notaries. Notarial practice and procedure
KJ-KKZ1 1850	Registration. Recording
KJ-KKZ1 1870	Domestic relations procedure
KJ-KKZ1 1885	Insolvency
KJ-KKZ1 1888	Execution
KJ-KKZ1 1942	Bankruptcy
KJ-KKZ1 2000	Public law
KJ-KKZ1 2010	The State
KJ-KKZ1 2050	Constitutional law
KJ-KKZ1 2064	Sources. Individual constitutions
KJ-KKZ1 2101	Constitutional history
KJ-KKZ1 2400	Foreign relations administration
KJ-KKZ1 2429	Individual and state
KJ-KKZ1 2500	Organs of national government. Supreme organs of state power and state administration
KJ-KKZ1 2504	The people. Election law
KJ-KKZ1 2510	The legislature. Legislative power
KJ-KKZ1 2530	Heads of state

KJ-KKZ2 1	Bibliography
KJ-KKZ2 1.5	Official gazettes
KJ-KKZ2 1.8	Legislation
KJ-KKZ2 2.2	Court decisions and related materials
KJ-KKZ2 2.6	Law dictionaries
KJ-KKZ2 3.4	Trials
KJ-KKZ2 4.2	Legal research. Legal bibliography
KJ-KKZ2 5	Legal education. Law schools
KJ-KKZ2 5.5	Bar associations. Law societies
KJ-KKZ2 5.53	Public registers. Registration
KJ-KKZ2 5.8	Congresses. Conferences
KJ-KKZ2 5.9	Academies
KJ-KKZ2 8.5	History of law
KJ-KKZ2 44	Philosophy, jurisprudence, and theory of law
KJ-KKZ2 47	Law reform and policies
KJ-KKZ2 47.5	Private law
KJ-KKZ2 48	Private international law. Conflict of laws
KJ-KKZ2 49	Civil law
KJ-KKZ2 50	General principles
KJ-KKZ2 51	Persons
KJ-KKZ2 53	Juristic persons of private law. Associations. Foundations. Endowments
KJ-KKZ2 54	Domestic relations. Family law
KJ-KKZ2 58.3	Consanguinity and affinity. Parent and child
KJ-KKZ2 63	Property. Law of things. Ownership and possession
KJ-KKZ2 68.3	Real property
KJ-KKZ2 72	Hypothecation
KJ-KKZ2 73	Pledges
KJ-KKZ2 74.4	Land register and registration
KJ-KKZ2 76	Inheritance. Succession upon death
KJ-KKZ2 78.5	Wills. Testaments
KJ-KKZ2 80	Obligations
KJ-KKZ2 83.5	Delicts. Torts
KJ-KKZ2 87.5	Unjust enrichment
KJ-KKZ2 87.6	Contracts and transactions
KJ-KKZ2 89.75	Individual contracts and transactions
KJ-KKZ2 97	Commercial law. Commercial transactions
KJ-KKZ2 97.2	Merchant and business enterprise
KJ-KKZ2 97.5	Commercial sale
KJ-KKZ2 98.2	Freight forwarders and carriers
KJ-KKZ2 99	Negotiable instruments. Titles of credit
KJ-KKZ2 99.5	Banking. Stock exchange
KJ-KKZ2 100.5	Loans. Credit

OUTLINE

National defense. Military law - Continued

KJ-KKZ4 9.2	Military criminal law and procedure
KJ-KKZ4 9.3	Criminal law
KJ-KKZ4 9.34	Punishment
KJ-KKZ4 9.35	Individual offenses
KJ-KKZ4 9.4	Criminal courts and procedure

	History of law (Europe)
	Class here general and comprehensive works on legal and constitutional history of the region including the legal history of ancient/early nations of the region
	For legal history of an individual jurisdiction, see the jurisdiction
	For common law in Europe see KJA1935+
	For history of an individual branch of the law see KJC2+
2	Bibliography
<6>	Periodicals
	For periodicals consisting chiefly of articles on the history and development of the law in Europe see K1+
	For periodicals consisting predominantly of articles on Germanic law see KJ166
	For periodicals consisting predominantly of articles on Roman law see KJA6
54	Encyclopedias
56	Law dictionaries. Terms and phrases. Vocabularies
	Methodology see KJ195+; KJA190+
	Auxiliary sciences
74	General works
75	Diplomatics
76	Paleography
	Papyrology see KJA190+
77	Linguistics. Semantics
78	Archaeology. Symbolism in law
	Class here general works on various manifestations of legal symbolism
(80)	Inscriptions. Epigraphy
	see KJ195; KJA190+
83	Heraldry. Seals. Flags. Insignia. Armory
100	Proverbs. Legal maxims. Brocardica. Regula juris
(102)	Symbolism in law
	see KJ78
	Formularies (History of law) see KJ615+
	Formularies (Roman law) see KJA105
	Law and lawyers in literature
	see subclasses PB-PZ
	Biography of lawyers
	Collective
	For collective national biography, see the subclass for the country
122	General biography
124	Collections of portraits
	Individual
	see the subclass for the country of the biographee
135	Congresses. Seminars. By date of the congress

The Celts
  Sources
    Individual sources and groups of sources
      By region or nation
        Gaul
          Texts. Unannotated and annotated editions --
            Continued

155.A33A-.A33Z	Iconography. By title or location
155.A4A-.A4Z	Novellae (Amendments). By ruler or title
155.A5A-.A5Z	Glosses. Summae (Summulae). Monographic-systematic commentaries on the source
155.A6A-.A6Z	Translations. By language
155.A7A-.A7Z	Treatises. Textual criticism. Controversies
	Including early (contemporary) works
155.A8A-.A8Z	Special topics, A-Z
	Ireland (Éire). Brehon law see KDK145
158.A-Z	Special topics, A-Z
158.A88	Associations
158.B55	Blood covenant
158.C65	Consanguinity and affinity
	Crimes see KJ158.C74
158.C74	Criminal law and procedure
	Descent see KJ158.C65
	Divorce see KJ158.D65
158.D65	Domestic relations. Family
158.D68	Dowry
	Family see KJ158.D65
158.I53	Inheritance and succession
	Kinship see KJ158.C65
	Lineage see KJ158.C65
158.M37	Marriage
158.O73	Ordeal
158.P85	Punishment
	Succession see KJ158.I53

  Germanic law
    Bibliography
      For bibliographies of special topics, see the topic

160	Bibliography of bibliography
162	General bibliography
163	Indexes to periodical literature, society publications, etc.
	Indexes to festschriften see KJ185
	Subject indexes (early). Repertoria see KJ609
166	Periodicals
167	Encyclopedias
168	Law dictionaries. Terms and phrases. Vocabularies
	Including early works
	Methodology see KJ195

Germanic law
Sources
Individual sources and groups of sources
East and West Germanic
Leges Barbarorum. Folk laws (Volksrechte)
Visigoths and Ostrogoths. Leges Gothorum --
Continued
222.2-227   Codex Eurici (Euricianus, ca. 469-475) (Table K20a
modified)
Add number from table to KJ220
Text. Unannotated and annotated editions
Including facsimiles or originals; and including
typographical reproductions of the text entirely
in non-Roman or ancient type, or transliterated
in Roman characters
223.A-Z   Particular manuscript editions. By title or
location, A-Z
223.P37   Paris fragmenta codicis Euriciani (early 6th
cent.)
Lex Romana Visigothorum (Breviarium Alarici;
Codex Theodosianus, 506) see KJA592.2+
242.2-247   Codex Eurici (Antigua; revision by King Leovigild,
572-586) (Table K20a modified)
Add number from table to KJ240
Text. Unannotated and annotated editions
Including facsimiles or originals; and including
typographical reproductions of the text entirely
in non-Roman or ancient type, or transliterated
in Roman characters
243.A-Z   Particular manuscript editions. By title or
location, A-Z
243.G38   Gaudenzi Nuovi Frammenti (Fragmenta
Gaudenziana)
252   Lex Visigothorum Reccesvindiana: Liber judicorum
(revision by King Reccesvind, ca. 654) (Table
K20b)
258   Lex Visigothorum renovata (Ervigiana; revision by
King Ervig, 681) (Table K20b)
259   Lex Visigothorum: Novellae (by King Egika, 687-
701) (Table K20b)
260   Lex Visigothorum vulgata (8th cent.) (Table K20b)
Fuero de Córdoba (Fuero juzgo, 13th cent.)
see KKT
Edictum Theoderici (ca. 512) see KJA612.2+
272.2-277   Edictum Athalarici (526-534) (Table K20a)
Add number from table to KJ270
Variae of Cassiodor see KJ212

Germanic law
  Sources
    Individual sources and groups of sources
      East and West Germanic
        Leges Barbarorum. Folk laws (Volksrechte) --
          Continued
          Burgundians

290	General works
292	Collections. Compilations
302.2-307	Lex Burgundionum (Liber constitutionum; Lex Gundobada, 5th cent.) (Table K20a)
	Add number from table to KJ300
	Including Novellae King Gundobads and Sigismunds
	Lex Romana Burgundionum (Papianus; early 6th cent.) see KJA632.2+

          Franks

320	General works
322	Collections. Compilations
	e.g. Benedict of Mainz (Benedictus Levita; spurious compilations, 848-850); Capitularia regum Francorum; Legiloquus liber (Ansegisus, Saint, Abbot of Fontanelle, ca. 770-833)
332.2-337	Lex Salica (508-511) (Table K20a modified)
	Add number from table to KJ330
	Text. Unannotated and annotated editions
	Including facsimiles or originals; and including typographical reproductions of the text entirely in non-Roman or ancient type, or transliterated in Roman characters
333.A-Z	Particular manuscript editions. By title or location, A-Z
333.L48	Lex emendata
334.A-Z	Novellae. By ruler or title, A-Z
	e. g.
334.C37	Capitula Legis Salicae (Louis I, the Pius, 818-820)
334.E34	Edict of Chilperich (561-584)
334.P32	Pactus pro tenore pacis (Childebert I and Chlotar I, 511-558)
335	Glosses. Summae (Summulae)
	e.g. Malberg Gloss
351	Decretio of Childebert II, 591-595 (Table K20b)
355	Edict of Chlotar II, 614 (Table K20b)
372.2-377	Lex Ripuaria, 741-747 (Table K20a modified)
	Add number from table to KJ370
384.A-Z	Novellae. By ruler or title, A-Z
	e. g.

Germanic law
　Sources
　　Individual sources and groups of sources
　　　East and West Germanic
　　　　Leges Barbarorum. Folk laws (Volksrechte)
　　　　　Franks
　　　　　　Lex Ripuaria, 741-747
　　　　　　　Novellae. By ruler or title, A-Z -- Continued

384.K37	Nova legis constitutio Karoli imperatoris qua in lege Ribuaria mittenda est, 803
384.S25	Recapitulatio legis Salicae
390	Lex Francorum Chamavorum, 802-803 (Table K20b)
	Capitulatio de partibus Saxoniae see KJ507
	Capitulare Saxonicum see KJ512
	Capitula ad legem Baiuvariorum addita see KJ494.A+
398	Capitulare de villis Karoli Magni (Table K20b)

Langobards. Leges Langobardicae. Lombard law

399	General works
400	Collections. Compilations
	e.g. Capitulare Langobardorum, ca. 774-11th cent.
402.2-407	Liber edictus (Edictus; Edictum) (Table K20a)
	Add number from table to KJ400
	Text. Unannotated or annotated editions
402.22.A-Z	Individual parts or sections. By title, A-Z
	e. g.
402.22.E44	Edictum Luitprandi, 713-735
402.22.E47	Edictum Rothari, 643
402.22.L32	Leges Aistulfi, 755
402.22.L34	Leges Grimoaldi, 668
402.22.L37	Leges Ratchis, 745-746
404.A-Z	Novellae. By ruler or title, A-Z
	e. g.
404.N67	Notitia Luitprandis, 733
406	Translations. By language
	e.g. Greek: Fragmenta versionis Grecae legum Rotheris (Benvento, 9th cent.)
412	Recensio of the Edictus (Benvento, 774) (Table K20b)
412.A4A-.A4Z	Novellae. By ruler or title, A-Z
	e. g.
412.A4A33	Adelchis, 866
412.A4A73	Aregis, 774-787

	Germanic law
	Sources
	Individual sources and groups of sources
	East and West Germanic
	Leges Barbarorum. Folk laws (Volksrechte)
	Langobards. Leges Langobardicae. Lombard law
	Recensio of the Edictus (Benvento, 774) --
	Continued
412.A5	Glosses. Summae (Summulae)
	e.g. Eberhard of Rezia and Friuli (Capitula legis regum Langobardorum seu concordia di singulis causis, 829-832)
422.2-427	Liber legis Langobardorum Papiensis, 1019-1037) (Table K20a modified)
	Add number from table to KJ420
425	Glosses. Summae (Summulae)
	e.g. Ariprandus, early 12th cent.; Expositio ad librum Papiensem, 1070; Gualcausus of Pavia (Valcausiana, 1019-1037); Lombarda (Liber Langobardae [Liber Lombardae], 12th cent.); Lombarda vulgata; Quaestiones ac monita, 11th cent.; De regulis juris Langobardorum; Summa legis Langobardorum
	Libri feudorum see KJC4434.5
	Alamanni
438	General works
439	Collections. Compilations
440	Pactus Alamannorum, late 6th cent. - early 7th cent. (Table K20b)
452.2-457	Lex Alamannorum, early 8th cent. (Table K20a)
	Add number from table to KJ450
463	Lex Alamannorum, emendata (Table K20b)
	Bavarians
470	General works
472	Collections. Compilations
482.2-487	Lex Baiuvariorum (Odiloniana, 744-748) (Table K20a)
	Add number from table to KJ480
494.A-Z	Novellae. By ruler or title, A-Z
	e. g.
494.C45	Charlemagne (Capitula ad legem Baiuvariorum addita, 801-813)
494.T38	Tassilo III (Decreta Tassilonis III, 756-772)
497	Capitulum Bawaricum, ca. 810
499	Epitome legis Alamannorum (Table K20b)
	Saxons
505	General works

Germanic law
Sources
Individual sources and groups of sources
East and West Germanic
Leges Barbarorum. Folk laws (Volksrechte)
Saxons -- Continued

507	Collections. Compilations
510	Capitulatio de partibus Saxoniae (Charlemagne, ca. 785) (Table K20b)
512	Capitulare Saxonicum, 797 (Table K20b)
522.2-527	Lex Saxonum, early 9th cent. (Table K20a)
	Add number from table to KJ520

Angli and Warni

538	General works
540	Collections. Compilations
545	Lex Angliorum et Werinorum (hoc est Thuringorum, early 9th cent.) (Table K20b)

Frisians

552	General works
555	Collections. Compilations
562.2-567	Lex Frisionum, late 8th cent. (Table K20a modified)
	Add number from table to KJ560
565	Glosses. Summae (Summulae)
	e.g. Wulemar and Saxmund (Additio sapientum)

Curic Rhaetia (Churratien)

575	General works
578	Collections. Compilations
580	Capitula remedia (Remedius of Chur, bsp.) (Table K20b)
	Lex Romana Curiensis see KJA1582

Anglo-Saxon law
see KD
Contemporary legal literature

600	Documents
	Class here general collections
	For collections or individual documents on a particular subject, see the subject
609	Compends. Indexes. Digests
	Including repertoria, remissoria, registra, regesta, etc. (e.g. Chunnas)

Formularies

615	General works
619	Collections. Compilations
	Individual formularies
	Subarrange by date
623	Formulae Wisigothicae, 7th cent.

Germanic law
Sources
Individual sources and groups of sources
East and West Germanic
Contemporary legal literature
Formularies
Individual formularies -- Continued

North Germanic. Scandinavian

Bibliography see KJ160+

For source collections of an individual Scandinavian country, see the subclass for the country (e.g. Iceland, KKG)

For source collections as well as treatises on a particular topic (e.g. North Germanic marriage law), see the topic

Germanic law -- Continued
> Germanic nations and their constitution
>> Class here works on the organization and constitution of the
>> Germanic nations
>> Including early Germanic periods, the period of the Frankish
>> empire, and the period of the Lombard empire (Regnum
>> Langobardorum) to ca. 1000 A.D.
>> For works on the history of political institutions and public
>> administration in Europe, see subclass JN

700	General (Table K22)
703	Concepts and principles. The State (Table K22)
	Including Germanic and Christian theories of state
	The estates
707	General (Table K22)
	Particular estates
709	Nobiles. Etheling (West Germanic). Jarl (North Germanic) (Table K22)
	Including kings, princes, and priests
711	Ingenui. Fulcfree. Frihals (Freie) (Table K22)
	Commoners. Freemen (Gemeinfreie)
713	General (Table K22)
715.A-Z	Classes of commoners or freemen, A-Z
715.C45	Censuales (Zinshorige)
715.L52	Libertini (Freigelassene)
718	Servi. Skalks. Slaves (Unfreie) (Table K22)
720.A-Z	Special topics, A-Z
722	Formation and expansion of the Germanic empires. Territorial divisions (Table K22)
	Including provincia, ducatus, regio, pagus, comitatus (go), etc.
	Systems of church and state relationships
724	General (Table K22)
726	Carlovingian state church (Table K22)
	Feudal law see KJC4432+
	Rural land tenure
742	General (Table K22)
744	Mark communities. Village communities (Table K22)
	Including commons (Allmende)
746	Free tenures (Table K22)
748	Allod. Odal (Table K22)
	Kings and kingdom
752	General (Table K22)
753	Title (Table K22)
	Succession
755	General (Table K22)
757	Election (Table K22)
759	Imperium. Bannum (Table K22)

Germanic law
  Criminal law and procedure
    Punishment
      Individual offenses, A-Z -- Continued
        Magic see KJ985.W58

985.S48	Sexual integrity, Offenses against
	Including works on legal implications of sexual behavior in general
985.W58	Witchcraft. Magic

    Criminal procedure

988	General works (Table K22)
1000	Accusation principle (Table K22)
1002	Inquisition principle (Table K22)
1004	Parties to action (Table K22)
1006	Compulsory measures against the accused (Table K22)
1010	Right of asylum (Table K22)

      Trial

1012	General (Table K22)

        Evidence. Burden of proof

1014	General (Table K22)
1016	Oath. Witnesses. Purgative oath (Table K22)
	Including compurgators

         Ordeal

1018	General (Table K22)
1020.A-Z	Particular ordeals, A-Z
1022	Torture. Confession (Table K22)

        Particular proceedings

1024	Anefang. Intertiatio (Table K22)
1026	Juries and jurors (Table K22)
1028	Proceedings for slaves (Table K22)
1030	Vestigii miatio (Spurfolge) (Table K22)
1032	Sentence (Table K22)
1034	Remedies (Table K22)

      Execution of sentence
        For individual penalties see KJ982.A+

1038	General (Table K22)
1040	Capital punishment (Table K22)

  Slavic nations
    For the history of Russia, including Russian Central Asia, see subclass KLA

1102	Bibliography
1106	Periodicals
1154	Encyclopedias
1156	Law dictionaries. Terms and phrases. Vocabularies
	Including early works

    Auxiliary sciences

1175	General works

	Slavic nations
	Auxiliary sciences -- Continued
1176	Paleography
1177	Linguistics. Semantics
	Archaeology. Folklife studies
1178	General works
	By place or nation
1179	Czechoslovakia
1220	Congresses. Seminars. By date of the congress
1225	General works
	Class here works on Slavic law in Europe as a region
	Including compends, essays, festschriften, etc.
	For development of national legal systems compared
	with Slavic law see KJC472
1230	Influence of other legal systems on Slavic law
	e.g. Roman law; Greek law
	Sources
1233	Studies on sources
	Including history of sources and methodology
	For non-legal sources, see PG
	Collections. Compilations
1235	General
1237	Indexes
	Individual sources and groups of sources
(1250)	Russkaia Pravda. Rus'ka pravda
	see KLA125
	By nation or ethnic group
1350	Bulgars
1400	Croats
1500	Czechs
1600	Ruthenians
1700	Serbs
1800	Slovacs
1820	Slovenes
2000.A-Z	Special topics, A-Z
2000.D65	Domestic relations. Family
	Family see KJ2000.D65
2000.L35	Land grants
2000.L36	Land tenure
2000.P75	Property
2000.S37	Serfdom
	Greece. Archaic and Hellenistic periods
	see subclass KL
	For medieval law see KJA1350+

Roman law
    Including Byzantine law
    For works on a specific province of the Roman Empire see the
        province or jurisdiction, e.g. Gaul, KJ155; Egypt, KL2814.5;
        Syria, KL6901+
    Bibliography
        For bibliographies of special topics, see the topic
2   Bibliography of bibliography
3   General bibliography
4   Indexes to periodical literature, society publications,
            collections, etc.
        Subject indexes (early). Repertoria
            see the author in the appropriate period
4.3   Personal bibliography
            Including bio-bibliography
        Catalogs, inventories, and guides to manuscripts and early or
            rare book collections in public libraries or archives. By
            name of the library or archive
            Including university, museum, or mosque libraries, and other
                institutional libraries or archives
4.4   General (Collective)
4.5   European
6   Periodicals
56   Encyclopedias. Law dictionaries. Terms and phrases.
            Vocabularies
            Including early works
            For encyclopedias and law dictionaries of both Roman and canon
                law, see KBR56, e. g. Vocabularius utriusque juris; Albericus
                de Rosate, 1290-1360 (Dictionarium juris tam civilis, quam
                canonici)
64   Directories
        Methodology see KJA190+
        Auxiliary sciences
75   General works
            Diplomatics see KJ75
            Paleography see KJ76
            Papyrology see KJA190+
78   Archaeology. Symbolism in law
                Class here works on various manifestations of legal symbolism
                For early works including schemata, stemmata, arbores, etc.,
                    see the author
(80)   Inscriptions. Epigraphy
                see KJA190+
83   Coins
92   Seals. Insignia. Armory, etc.

100   Proverbs. Legal maxims. Brocardica juris. Regulae juris. By
                   author or title, A-Z
                   Including early works
(102)   Symbolism in law
                   see KJA78
105   Formularies. Clauses and forms
                   Class here general and unnamed formularies and comparative
                       works about formularies. For individual or collected
                       formularies, see the author in the appropriate period. For
                       formularies for trial lawyers, court practice, etc. in a particular
                       country, see the subclass for the country
                   For works on libelli, actiones, ordines judicorum see
                       KJA2784+
               Law and lawyers in literature
                   see subclasses PB - PZ
               Biography of jurists
                   Collective
122   General
124   Collections of portraits
                   Individual
                       see the jurist in the appropriate period; for the biography of a
                           modern writer, see the subclass for the country of the
                           biographee
                   Trials
                       Including civil and criminal trials
127   Collections
128.A-Z   Individual. By defendant, plaintiff, or best known (popular)
                       name, A-Z
               Legal research. Legal bibliography. Methods of bibliographic
                   research
130   General
132   Systems of citation. Legal abbreviations. Modus legendi
                       abbreviaturas
                       Including early works
               Legal education. Study and teaching
                   For works on study and teaching of both Roman and canon law
                       comparatively, e. g. Johannes Jacobus Canis (d. 1490), De
                       modo studendi in utroque iure, 1485, see KB133+
133   General
134.A-Z   By school, A-Z
147   General works
                   Including compends, essays, festschriften, etc.
                   For early works, see the author in the appropriate period
               Roman law compared with other legal systems
160   General works
162   Common law

Roman law compared with other legal systems -- Continued

164 National legal systems

Class here comparisons of Roman law with more than one other legal system

For comparisons of subjects of Roman law with subjects of two or more other legal systems, see the appropriate subject in KJA

For comparisons of Roman law with a particular national system, see the subclass for the country, e.g. KK941

For comparisons of subjects of an individual national system with Roman law, see the subclass of the country

(166) Canon law (Traditio juris utriusque)

see KB or KBR

Other ancient legal systems

For comparisons of subjects, see the appropriate subjects in KJA

168 General works
170 Egyptian
171 Germanic
172 Greek
(174) Jewish

see KB

(180) Works on diverse aspects of a particular subject and falling within several branches of law

see KJA2170

Sources

Studies on sources

Including history of sources and methodology (i.e. epigraphy, papyrology, etc.)

190 General works
192 Classification of sources

Collections. Compilations

Including translations

Class here all periods of Roman law

195 General
195.5 Indexes. Chronology. Concordances

For indexes, chronologies, etc., to a particular work, see the author or title

By period

Pre-Justinian periods. Fontes antejustiniani

Including early and classical legal writings

(200) General works

see KJA190

Collections. Compilations. Selections

201 General
202 Fragmenta Vaticana juris antejustiniani (4th or 5th cent. A.D.)

Sources
  By period
    Pre-Justinian periods. Fontes antejustiniani
      Individual sources and groups of sources
        Provincial laws. Laws of particular regions or districts.
          Municipal laws -- Continued

520	General works
525	Collections. Compilations
	Individual laws
527	Tarentum (Law of) (Table K20b)
530	Lex Coloniae Genetivae (Urso in Andalusia) (Table K20b)
533	Lex Malacitana (80-84 A.D.) (Table K20b)
537	Lex Lauriacensis (212-217 .A.D.) (Table K20b)
540	Lex metalli Vipascensis (Table K20b)
552	Other decrees. Decrees of praetorian prefects
	Including collections and individual decrees

Leges Romanae barbarorum. Roman law of the
    Germanic nations

580	General works
582	Collections. Compilations
	Cf. KJA390+ Constitutiones principum

By nation

592.2-597	Lex Romana Visigothorum (Breviarium Alarici, 506) (Table K20a)
	Add number from table to KJA590
	Cf. KJ210+ Leges Visigothorum
612.2-617	Edictum Theoderici, ca. 512 (Table K20a)
	Add number from table to KJA610
	Cf. KJ210+ Leges Visigothorum
632.2-637	Lex Romana Burgundionum (sometimes Responsum Papiani) (Table K20a)
	Add number from table to KJA630
	For Lex Burgundionum (Liber constitutionum; Lex Gundobada) see KJ302.2+

Public documents other than laws

662	Privilegia veteranorum
664	Juris jurandi in principem formulae
670	Private legal documents and instruments. By title or location
	Including editions, commentaries, textual criticism, translations, etc.

Jurists' law. Jus
    Including oriental and occidental

690	General works
692	Collections. Compilations

Sources
By period
Pre-Justinian periods. Fontes antejustiniani
Individual sources and groups of sources
Jurists' law. Jus
Individual jurists or titles
Individual jurists and titles are interfiled and arranged
alphabetically

798	C. Ateius Capito, d. 22 A.D. (Table K3)
805	Sextus Caecilius Africanus (Table K3)
808	Celsus, Publius Juventius, fl. 2nd cent. A.D. (Table K3)
810	Marcus Tullius Cicero (Table K3)
812	Consultatio veteris cuisdam iurisconsulti, 5th-6th cent. A.D. (Table K20b)
814	Ermogeniano (Table K3)
816	Florentinus (Table K3)
	Fragmenta de jure fisci, 2nd or 3rd cent. A.D. see KJA204
	Fragmenta Vaticana juris antejustinianei, ca. 320 A.D. see KJA202
822.2-827	Fragmentum Dositheanum (Pseudo-Dositheus), 2nd cent. A.D. ? (Table K20a)
	Add number from table to KJA820
842.2-847	Fragmentum de formula Fabiniana (Table K20a)
	Add number from table to KJA840
862.2-867	Fragmentum de judiciis (Table K20a)
	Add number from table to KJA860
882	Gaius, fl. 117-192 (Table K3)
885	Hermogenianus, fl. 4th cent. A.D. (Table K3)
	Codex Hermogenianus see KJA432.2+
885.3	Epitome juris, 3rd cent. A.D.
887	Javolenus Priscus, 60-125 A.D. (Table K3)
889	Salvius Julianus, fl. 150 A.D. (Table K3)
892	Papirius Justus (Table K3)
895	M. Antistius Labeo, fl. 18 B.C. (Table K3)
897	Liber Syro-Romanus (Syro-Roman law book), 5th cent. A.D. (Table K20b)
	For comparative works of the Liber Syro-Romanus with other sources, e.g. Code of Hammurabi, see KB
	For comparative works of the Liber Syro-Romanus with other sources, e.g. Code of Hammurabi see KB206
899	L. Volusius Maecianus (Table K3)
905	Aelius Marcianus, fl. 198-211 (Table K3)
910	Arrius Menander, fl. 193-217 (Table K3)

KJA

Sources
  By period
    Pre-Justinian periods. Fontes antejustiniani
      Individual sources and groups of sources
        Jurists' law. Jus
          Individual jurists or titles -- Continued

915	Herennius Modestinus, fl. 212-217 (Table K3)
	Mosaicarum et Romanarum legum collatio, 398-438 A.D. see KB200
918	Neratius Priscus, Lucius (Table K3)
919	Aemilius Papinianus, d. 212 (Table K3)
924	Julius Paulus, fl. 180-235 (Table K3)
929	Sextus Pedius (Table K3)
933	Pegasus (Table K3)
937	Sextus Pomponius, fl. 117-180 A.D. (Table K3)
942	Proculus, Licinius (Table K3)
946	Servius Sulpicius Rufus, d. 43 B.C. (Table K3)
950	Massurius Sabinus, fl. 14-68 A.D. (Table K3)
954	Q. Mucius Scaevola, 140-82 B.C. (Table K3)
959	Q. Servitius Scaevola (Table K3)
963	Scholia Sinaitica on Ulpians Libri ad Sabinum, 439-533 A.D. (Table K3)
967	C. Trebatius Testa, fl. 54 B.C. (Table K3)
972	Tractatus de gradibus cognationum (Table K3)
976	Tribonianus, d. 546 A.D. (Table K3)
982	Claudius Tryphoninus, fl. 211-212 (Table K3)
986	Q. Aelius Tubero (Table K3)
990	Domitius Ulpianus, fl. 212-217 (Table K3)
994	P. Alfenus Varus, fl. 39 B.C. (Table K3)

          Literary (non-legal) sources see PA6202+
    Justinian, 527-565 A.D.

1030	General works
1042.2-1047	Codex Justinianus, 529 (Table K20a)
	Add number from table to KJA1040
1062.2-1067	Corpus Iuris Civilis (Table K20a modified)
	Add number from table to KJA1060
	Exceptiones. Excerpta. Flores
	see the author or title in the appropriate period, e.g. Ashburnham law book, 11th or 12th cent., see KJA1602; Exceptiones legum Romanorum Petri, 12th cent., see KJA1600, Liber juris Graeciensis (Graz law book, 12th cent.), see KJA1603; Liber juris Tubingensis, 12th cent., see KJA1589
1082.2-1087	Institutiones, 533 (Table K20a modified)
	Add number from table to KJA1080

Sources
By period
Justinian, 527-565 A.D.
Corpus Iuris Civilis
Institutiones, 533 -- Continued
Glosses. Summae (Summulae)
 see the author or title in the appropriate period, e.g.
  Brachylogus juris civilis (Corpus legum, 12th cent.),
  see KJA1604; Turin Gloss (Glossa Torinese, 6th
  cent.), see KJA1575

1112.2-1117   Digesta (Pandectae, 533) (Table K20a modified)
 Add number from table to KJA1110
Text. Unannotated and annotated editions
 Including facsimiles or originals; and including
  typographical reproductions of the text entirely in
  non-Roman or ancient type, or transliterated in
  Roman characters

1113.A-Z   Particular manuscript editions. By title or location,
 A-Z
1113.C34   Codex Florentinus, 6th or 7th cent.
1113.C72   Codex S(ecundus)
1132.2-1137   Digestum Vetus (Liber 1-24.3.2) (Table K20a)
 Add number from table to KJA1130
1152.2-1157   Infortiatum (Liber 24.3.38) (Table K20a)
 Add number from table to KJA1150
1161   Tres partes (Liber 35.2.82-83) (Table K20b)
 For commentaries on the source, see the author in
  the appropriate period, e.g. Angelo degli Ubaldi
  de Perusia. Super prima Infortiati KJA1785
1172.2-1177   Digestum Novum (Liber 39-50) (Table K20a)
 Add number from table to KJA1170
 For commentaries on the source, see the author in the
  appropriate period, e.g. Rainerius de Forlivio.
  Lectura super digesto novo KJA1778.A3L4
1192.2-1197   Codex Justinianus (repetitae praelectionis, 534) (Table
 K20a modified)
 Add number from table to KJA1190
Text. Unannotated and annotated editions
 Including facsimiles or originals; and including
  typographical reproductions of the text entirely in
  non-Roman or ancient type, or transliterated in
  Roman characters
1193.A-Z   Particular manuscript editions. By title or location,
 A-Z
1193.E84   Epitome codicis (Codex epitomatus, 11th or 12
 the cent.)

Sources
  By period
    Justinian, 527-565 A.D.
      Corpus Iuris Civilis
        Codex Justinianus (repetitae praelectionis, 534) --
          Continued
          Glosses. Summae (Summulae)
            see the author or title in the appropriate period, e.g. Lo
              codi, 1149 or 1170, see KJA1617; Pistoia gloss,
              12th cent., see KJA1609; Rogerii Summa codicis,
              see KJA1652, Summa codicis Londiniensis, see
              KJA1612; Tractatus de aequitate, see KJA1614

1212.2-1217	Novellae constitutiones (Table K20a)
	Add number from table to KJA1210
	Including works in Greek as well as bilingual (Latin/ Greek) editions
1232.2-1237	Juliani epitome novellarum, ca. 570 (Table K20a)
	Add number from table to KJA1230
1252.2-1257	Authenticum (Autentica; Liber authenticorum). Versio vulgata (Table K20a)
	Add number from table to KJA1250
1272.2-1277	Volumen parvum (Table K20a)
	Add number from table to KJA1270
1292.2-1297	Institutiones (Table K20a)
	Add number from table to KJA1290
1312.2-1317	Tres Libri (Table K20a)
	Add number from table to KJA1310
1332.2-1337	Authenticum (Table K20a)
	Add number from table to KJA1330
1345	Individual constitutiones. By date
	Provincial laws. Laws of special districts see KJA520+

Post-Justinian periods
  Orient. Byzantine Empire
    Including Isaurian, Macedonian, and Post-Macedonian
      periods

1350	General works
	Collections. Compilations
	Individual works are arranged by date
	Including codifications
1355	General
1362.2-1367	Eclogē (Eklogē tōn nōmon, ca. 726); (Leo III, 717-ca. 741) (Table K20a)
	Add number from table to KJA1360
1375	Nomos geōrgikos kat' eklogēn ek tōn Ioustinianou bibliōn (Table K20b)
1378	Nomos rhodiōn nautikos kat' eklogēn ek tou id' bibliou tōn digestōn (Table K20b)

27

	Sources
	By period
	Post-Justinian periods
	Orient. Byzantine Empire
	Collections. Compilations -- Continued
1380	Nomos stratiōtikos (Table K20b)
1382	Eparchikon biblion (Liber praefecti); (Leo VI, Sapiens, 886-911) (Table K20b)
1392.2-1397	Prochiron (Procheiros nomos, ca. 870-879); (Basilius I, Macedo, 867-886) (Table K20a)
	Add number from table to KJA1390
1405	Epanagoge tou nomou (Basilius I, Macedo, 867-886) (Table K20b)
1412.2-1417	Basilica (Anakatharsis tōn palaiōn nomfonikon); (Leo VI, Sapiens, 886-911) (Table K20a)
	Add number from table to KJA1410
1432.2-1437	Synopsis Basilicorum, 10th cent. (Table K20a)
	Add number from table to KJA1430
1442	Epanagogē aucta, 10th cent. (Table K20b)
1444	Ecloga ad Prochiron mutata, 11th cent. (Table K20b)
1446	Prochiron auctum, ca. 1300 (Table K20b)
1452.2-1457	Hexabiblos (Konstantinos Harmenopoulos, d. 1380?) (Table K20a)
	Add number from table to KJA1450
	Private collections and compilations
1462	Epitome novellarum (Theodorus Hermopolitanus, Scholasticus, fl. ca. 600) (Table K20b)
1464	Epitome novellarum (Athanasius of Hemesa, Scholasticus, 565-578) (Table K20b)
1466	Epitome fragments (Anonymos) (Table K20b)
	Collectio XXV capitulorum see KBR198.3
	Collectio LXXXVII capitulorum (Joannes Scholasticus) see KBR198.4
	Collectio constitutionum ecclesiasticarum (c. tripartita) see KBR198.6
	Nomocanon L titulorum see KBR199
	Nomocanon XIV titulorum see KBR199.2
	Recension Theodorus Bestes, 11th cent. see KBR199.7.B47
	Hexabiblos see KJA1452.2+
1475	Individual constitutiones
1480	Provincial laws. Laws of particular regions or districts. Municipal laws
	For modern adaptations or reception of the law, see the law of the jurisdiction
	Jurists' law
1484	General works

KJA

	Sources
	By period
	Post-Justinian periods
	Orient. Byzantine Empire
	Jurists' law -- Continued
1486	Collections. Compilations
	By period
	6th and 7th centuries
	Including Antecessor literature
1488	General works
1490	Collections. Compilations
	Individual jurists or titles
	Individual jurists and titles are interfiled and arranged by date
1492	Anatolius (Table K3)
1492.A3A-.A3Z	Individual works. By title, A-Z
	e.g. Index on Digesta (Fragments in Stephanus and Theodorus)
	Athanasius (of Hemesa, Scholasticus) see KJA1464
1494	Cyrillus (Table K3)
1494.A3A-.A3Z	Individual works. By title, A-Z
	e.g. Extract from Digesta
1499	Thalelaeus (Table K3)
1499.A3A-.A3Z	Individual works. By title, A-Z
	e.g. Index on Codex, ca. 535
1502	Dorotheus (of Berytus) (Table K3)
1502.A3A-.A3Z	Individual works. By title, A-Z
	e.g. Index fragments on Digesta, ca. 542
1510	Isidorus (Table K3)
1510.A3A-.A3Z	Individual works. By title, A-Z
	e.g. Index on Codes, ca. 542
1514	Stephanus (Antecessor)
1514.A3A-.A3Z	Individual works. By title, A-Z
	e.g. Index on Digesta
1518	Anonymos (Enantiophanes)
1518.A3A-.A3Z	Individual works. By title, A-Z
	e.g. Index and Paragraphai on Digesta, 565-578)
	Theodorus Hermopolitanus see KJA1462+
	Theophilus (Antecessor)
1524	Index fragments on Digesta
1525	Paraphrasis institutionum (supposed authorship)
1527	Hai Rhopai (Peri chronon kai prothesmion; Libellus de temporibus ac dilationibus, 7th cent. (Table K3)

Sources
By period
Post-Justinian periods
Orient. Byzantine Empire
Jurists' law
By period
6th and 7th centuries
Individual jurists or titles -- Continued

1529	Peri Pekoulion (Tractatus de peculiis) (Table K3)
1531	Hai agogai (Peri idikon agogon; De actionibus, 7th cent. (Table K3)
1533	Peri enantiophaneion (Ton Enantiophanon monobiblion; Anonymos or Enantiophanes, 7th cent.) (Table K3)
1535	Paragraphai to the Summa of Anonymus (Table K3)

8th to 14th centuries

1540	General works

Individual jurists or titles
Individual jurists and titles are interfiled and arranged by date

1543	Demetrius Chomatenus (Table K3)
1543.A3A-.A3Z	Individual works. By title, A-Z

e.g. Responsa
Ecloga ad Prochiron mutata see KJA1444
Epanagogē aucta see KJA1442

1545	Epitomō tōn nomōn (Epitomē legum, 929) (Table K20b)
1547	Glossae verborum juris (Table K20b)
1549	Meletē peri psilōn symphōnōn (Meditatio de nudis pactis, 11th cent.) (Table K20b)
1552	Michael Attaliates (Table K3)
1552.A3A-.A3Z	Individual works. By title, A-Z
1552.A3P64	Poiēma nomikon (Opus de jure, 1074) (Table K20b)
1554	Michael Psellus (Table K3)
1554.A3A-.A3Z	Individual works. By title, A-Z
1554.A3S95	Synopsis tōn nomōn (Synopsis legum, 11th cent.) (Table K20b)
1556	Nomimon kata stoicheion (Mikra synopsis; Liber juridicus alphabeticus, 13th cent.) (Table K20b)

Prochiron auctum see KJA1446
Synopsis Basilicorum see KJA1432.2+

Occident

1560	General works

Sources
  By period
    Post-Justinian periods
      Occident
        Jurists' law. Legistic
          By period
            6th to 15th centuries. Jus Romanum Medii Aevi
              Individual titles -- Continued

	Lex Romana canonice compta, 9th cent. see KBR1270
1583	Notae juris a Magnone collectae, early 9th cent. (Table K20b)
1584	Bamberg Gloss (Codex Bamberg, 9th to 10th cent.) (Table K20b)
1589	Liber juris Tubingensis, 12th cent. (Table K20b)
1600	Exceptiones legum Romanorum (Exceptiones Petri, 12th cent.)
1602	Ashburnham law book, 11th or 12th cent. (Table K20b)
1603	Liber juris Graeciensis (Graz law book, 12th cent.) (Table K20b)
1604	Brachylogus juris civilis (Corpus legum, 12th cent.) (Table K20b)
	Libri feudorum, 12th cent. see KJC4434.5
1606	Epitome exactic regibis, 12th cent. (Table K20b)
1608	Epitome codicis, 10th to 12th cent. (Table K20b)
1609	Pistoia Gloss, 12th cent. (Table K20b)
1610	Summa codicis, Trecensis (Troys MS., 1140-1157) (Table K20b)
1612	Summa codicis Londiniensis (Table K20b)
1614	Tractatus de aequitate, 12th cent. (Table K20b)
1615	Questiones de juris subtilitatibus, ca. 1160 (Table K20b)
1617	Lo codi (Province, 1149 or 1170) (Table K20b)
1618	Compendium juris, 12th cent. (Table K20b)
1620	Summa institutionum Vindobonensis, 12th cent. (Table K20b)
1622	Liber juris Florentinus, 13th cent. (Table K20b)

              Individual jurists
                Individual jurists are listed in chronological order

1630	Peter Damian, Saint (Petrus Damianus), 1007?-1072 (Table K3)
1631	Marbode, Bishop of Rennes, 1035?-1123 (Table K3)
1632	Ivo, Saint, Bishop of Chartres, ca. 1040-1116 (Table K3)

Sources
By period
Post-Justinian periods
Occident
Jurists' law. Legistic
By period
6th to 15th centuries. Jus Romanum Medii Aevi
Individual jurists

Ivo, Saint, Bishop of Chartres, ca. 1040-1116 --
Continued
Panormia see KBR1347
Decretum see KBR1349

1633	Gualcausus (Galgosius; Gualcoxius), 11th cent. (Table K3)
1634	Pepo (of Bologna), fl. 1075-1099 (Table K3)
1636	Irnerius, 1085-1125 (Table K3)
1640	Vacarius, fl. 1149 (Table K3)
1652	Rogerius (Frogerius), d. 1162 (Table K3)
	Quattuor doctores
1653	Bulgarus, d. 1166 (Table K3)
1654	Martinus Gosia, d. ca. 1166 (Table K3)
1655	Hugo, de Alberico (Ugo da Portanavegnana), d. 1171 (Table K3)
1657	Jacobus, d. 1178 (Table K3)
1658	Alabericus de Porta Ravennata, fl. 1165-1194 (Table K3)
1660	Aldericus (Table K3)
1662	Odericus de Bonconsiliis, fl. 1166-1200 (Table K3)
1663	Pillius, Medicinensis, fl. 1169-1207 (Table K3)
1664	Henricus de Baila, fl. 1170 (Table K3)
1666	Cyprianus (Cilianus) Florentinus (Table K3)
1667	Obertus de Orto, d. 1175 (Table K3)
1667.A3A-.A3Z	Individual works. By title, A-Z
1667.A3B4	De beneficiis
1669	Accursius, glossator, ca. 1182-ca. 1260 (Table K3)
1670	Lotharius, fl. 1191-1212 (Table K3)
1672	Placentinus, Petrus, d. 1192 (Table K3)
1673	Burgundio (Johannes), d. 1194 (Table K3)
1674	Cacciavillanus, fl. 1199 (Table K3)
1676	Johannes Bassianus, 2nd half 12th cent. (Table K3)
1678	Otto, 2nd half 12th cent. (Table K3)
1679	Gratia, fl. 1206-1224 or 1236 (Table K3)
1680	Albertus Papiensis, fl. 1211-1240 (Table K3)

Sources
By period
Post-Justinian periods
Occident
Jurists' law. Legistic
By period
6th to 15th centuries. Jus Romanum Medii Aevi
Individual jurists -- Continued

1682	Pontius de Ylerda (Catalanus; Hispanus), fl. 1213 (Table K3)
1682.A3A-.A3Z	Individual works. By title, A-Z
	e. g.
	La Summa arboris actionum see
	KJA1682.A3A+
1683	Bandinus Familiatus, d. 1218 (Table K3)
1685	Guizardinus, d. 1222 (Table K3)
1686	Lanfranco (of Milan), d. 1229 (Table K3)
1688	Nicolaus Furiosus (Table K3)
1690	Azo, Portius, d. ca. 1231 (Table K3)
1692	Hugolinus (Ugo; Ugolinus), d. after 1233 (Table K3)
1693	Jacobus Columbi (Table K3)
1695	Jacobus Balduini, d. 1235 (Table K3)
1696	Tancred (Tancredus Bononiensis), ca. 1185-1236? (Table K3)
1698.3	Ubertus de Bonacurso, fl. 1231 (Table K3)
1699	Bernardus Dorna, fl. 1240 (Table K3)
1700	Bagarottus de Coradis (processualist), d. ca. 1242 (Table K3)
1702	Damasus (Damaseus) fl. 1210-1215 (Table K3)
	Cf. KBR100.D36 Canon law
1704	Karolus de Tocco (Beneventanus) (Table K3)
1706	Martino, da Fano (Cassaro), fl. 1229-1272 (Table K3)
1708	Rainerius, de Perusio, fl. early 13th cent. (Table K3)
1708.A3A-.A3Z	Individual works. By title, A-Z
	e.g. Ars notariae
1709	Vivianus Tuscus, 13th cent. (Table K3)
1709.A3A-.A3Z	Individual works. By title, A-Z
	e.g. Casus longi
1710	Alberto Gandino, 13th cent. (Table K3)
1710.A3A-.A3Z	Individual works. By title, A-Z
	e.g. Super codice
1712	Beneventanus Roffredus (Roffredus de Epiphanio), ca. 1170- 1243? (Table K3)
1713	Ubertus de Bobio, d. ca. 1245 (Table K3)

KJA

	Sources
	By period
	Post-Justinian periods
	Occident
	Jurists' law. Legistic
	By period
	6th to 15th centuries. Jus Romanum Medii Aevi
	Individual jurists -- Continued
1714	Pier, delle Vigne (Petrus de Vineis), 1190? - 1249 (Table K3)
1715	Johannes de Blanosco, fl. ca. 1250 (Table K3)
1715.A3A-.A3Z	Individual works. By title, A-Z
1715.A3A2	De actionibus
1715.A3F4	De feudis et homagiis
1717	Nepos, de Monte Albano, 13th cent. (Table K3)
1718	Bonaguida (of Arezzo) (Table K3)
1719	Guilelmus Pansonus (Panthonius), fl. 1241-1252 (Table K3)
1720	Pascipoverus, fl. 1249-1252 (Table K3)
1722	Vincentinus Bellovacensis, d. ca. 1261 (Table K3)
1723	Odofredo Denari (Odofredus Bononiensis, d. 1265 (Table K3)
1725	Accursius Reginus (of Reggio), fl. 1266-1273 (Table K3)
1726	Albertus Galeottus, fl. 1251-1272 (Table K3)
1727	Thomas de Piperata, fl. 1272 (Table K3)
1729	Salathiel, d. ca. 1275 (Table K3)
1729.A3A-.A3Z	Individual works. By title, A-Z
1729.A3S8	Summa artis notariae
1730	Rolandinus de Romanciis, d. 1284 (Table K3)
1730.A3A-.A3Z	Individual works. By title, A-Z
1730.A3O7	De ordine maleficiorum
1732	Hugelinus Fonatana, fl. 1285 (Table K3)
1734	Johannes Fasolus (Fasilus, Fazeolus, Fagelus), d. 1286 (Table K3)
1736	Cervottus Accursius, ca. 1240-1286 (Table K3)
1738	Cursinus Accursius, 1254-1288 (Table K3)
1740	Aegidius Fuscararius, d. 1289 (Table K3)
1742	Andreas de Barulo, fl. 1250-1291 (Table K3)
1743	Guido da Suzzara (di Suzarre), 13th cent. (Table K3)
1745	Franciscus Accursius, 1225-1293 (Table K3)
1747	Jacobus de Arena, d. 1296 (Table K3)
1748	Durand, Guillaume (Guilelmus Durante, Speculator), 1230-1296 (Table K3)
1749	Eilbertus Bremensis, fl. ca. 1300 (Table K3)

Sources
  By period
    Post-Justinian periods
      Occident
        Jurists' law. Legistic
          By period
            6th to 15th centuries. Jus Romanum Medii Aevi
              Individual jurists -- Continued

1805	Lancellotto Decio (Lancellotus Decius; Desio), d. 1503 (Table K3)
1806	Bartholomaeus Raimundus, fl. 1506 (Table K3)
1807	Bartholomaeus Socinus (of Siena), 1436-1507 (Table K3)
1808	Ludovicus Bologninus, 1447-1508 (Table K3)
1809	Giasone dal Maino (Iason de Mayno), 1435-1519 (Table K3)
1810	Aelius Antonius Nebrissensis (of Lebrica), 1442-1522 (Table K3)
	Juris civilis Lexicon (1506) see KJA56
1811	Alexander ab Alexandro, 1461-1523 (Table K3)
1812	Nicolaas Everaerts (of Gripskerke/Holland), 1462 or 3-1532 (Table K3)
1813	Petrus Aegidius, 1486-1533 (Table K3)
1814	Filippo Decio (Philippus Decius), 1454-1536 or 7 (Table K3)
1814.5	Agostino Beró, 1474-1554 (Table K3)
1815	Marianus Socinus (junior), 1482-1556 (Table K3)
	By nationality
	Class here individual jurists writing on Roman law as compared with, or influencing, their national legal systems
	For consilia collections and consilia of an individual author see KJA2150.A+
	English
	see KD
	French
1822	General works
1823	Collections. Compilations. Selections
	e.g. Quaestiones doctorum Tholossanorum, 13th cent.
	Individual jurists
	Individual jurists are listed in chronological order
1828	Jacques de Révigny (Jacobus de Ravennis), d. 1296 (Table K3)
1830	Guido de Cumis, 13th cent. (Table K3)

Sources
  By period
    Post-Justinian periods
      Occident
        Jurists' law. Legistic
          By period
            6th to 15th centuries. Jus Romanum Medii Aevi
              By nationality
                French
                  Individual jurists -- Continued

1832	Simon de Paris, 13th cent. (Table K3)
1834	Jean Monchy, 13th cent. (Table K3)
1836	Pietro Peregrossi, 13th cent. (Table K3)
1838	Odo Senonensis (de Senonis) (Table K3)
1840	Petrus de Bellapertica, d. 1308 (Table K3)
1842	Petrus Jacobi, fl. 1311 (Table K3)
1844	Guilielmus de Cuneo (Guillaume da Cunh), fl. first half 14th cent. (Table K3)
1846	Joannes Faber (Jean Faure), d. 1340 (Table K3)
1847	Nicolas de Bohier, 1469-1539 (Table K3)

                Spanish

1850	General works
1852	Collections. Compilations. Selections

                  Individual jurists
                    Individual jurists are listed in chronological order

1854	Martinez de Zamora, d. 1275 (Table K3)
1856	Jacobo de las Leyes, d. 1294 (Table K3)
1857	Gonzalo Gonzales Bustamente, d. 1392 (Table K3)
1859	Jaime de Vallseca, 14th cent. (Table K3)
1860	Jaime de Montjuich (Jacobus de Montejudaico), 14th cent. (Table K3)
1861	Arias de Balboa, d. 1414 (Table K3)
1862	Jaime Callis, 1364?-1434 (Table K3)
1863	Bonifacio Garcia, 15th cent. (Table K3)
1864	Alonso Diàz de Montalvo (Alphonsus Didaci), 1405-1499 (Table K3)
1867	Juan de Socarrats, 15th cent. (Table K3)
1868	Martinus de Pertusa, d. 1485 (Table K3)

                Portuguese

1870	General works
1872	Collection. Compilations

                  Individual jurists
                    Individual jurists are listed in chronological order

Sources
　By period
　　Post-Justinian periods
　　　Occident
　　　　Jurists' law. Legistic
　　　　　By period
　　　　　　6th to 15th centuries. Jus Romanum Medii Aevi
　　　　　　　By nationality
　　　　　　　　Portuguese
　　　　　　　　　Individual jurists -- Continued

1874	João de Deus (Deogratia), fl. 1247-1256 (Table K3)
1876	Luiz Teixeira Lobo, 14th/15th cent. (Table K3)
1878	Joao das Regras (Johannes ab Aregis), d. 1404 (Table K3)

　　　　　　　　German

1882	General works
1884	Collections. Compilations

　　　　　　　　　Individual jurists
　　　　　　　　　　Individual jurists are listed in chronological order

1886	Johann von Buch, d. after 1356 (Table K3)
1888	Hermann von Schildesche, d. 1357 (Table K3)
1890	Nicolaus Wurm, d. after 1401 (Table K3)
1892	Henricus Brunonis (de Piro), d. 1473 (Table K3)
1894	Nicasius de Voerda, d. 1492 (Table K3)
1896	Jodocus, middle 15th cent. (Table K3)
1898	Ulrich Tengler, d. ca. 1510 (Table K3)
1900	Hermann Langenbeck, d. 1517 (Table K3)
1902	Sebastian Brant, 1458-1521 (Table K3)

　　　　　　　　Dutch

1905	General works
1907	Collections. Compilations

　　　　　　　　　Individual jurists
　　　　　　　　　　Individual jurists are listed in chronological order

1910	Jehan Boutillier, 14th cent. (Table K3)
	Somme rural (1393-1396) see KJV258; KJV258
1912	Guillaume van der Tanerijen, 14th cent. (Table K3)
1914	Jean de Hocsem, d. 1384 (Table K3)
1914.A3A-.A3Z	Individual works. By title, A-Z
1914.A3F46	Flores utriusque juris

Sources
  By period
    Post-Justinian periods
      Occident
        Jurists' law. Legistic
          By period
            6th to 15th centuries. Jus Romanum Medii Aevi
              By nationality
                Dutch
                  Individual jurists -- Continued

1916	Jean de Ham, 14th cent. (Table K3)
1916.A3A-.A3Z	Individual works. By title, A-Z
1916.A3F67	Formularium
1918	Arnold Gheilhoven, d. 1442 (Table K3)
1918.A3A-.A3Z	Individual works. By title, A-Z
1918.A3R45	Remissorium utriusque juris
1920	Johannes de Turnhout, d. 1492 (Table K3)
1920.A3A-.A3Z	Individual works. By title, A-Z
1920.A3C38	Casus breves
1925.A-Z	Jurists of the 14th and 15th cent.
1925.A35	Matthaeus de Afflictis, 1448-1528 (Table K4)
1925.A39	Albericus, de Maletis (Table K4)
1925.A4	Alessandri, Antonio, d. 1499 (Table K4)
1925.A43	Joannes Baptiste Alfanus (of Perugia), fl. 1446 (Table K4)
1925.A48	Alvarotti, Jacopo, (Jacobus Alvarothus), 1385-1453 (Table K4)
1925.A52	Andrea Alferi, d. 1422 (Table K4)
1925.A54	Andreas (Ciaffi) Pisanus, first half 14th cent. (Table K4)
1925.A57	Antonio, da Cannara, d. 1451 (Table K4)
1925.A96	Johannes de Aurbach (Urbach), 15th cent. (Table K4)
1925.B33	Bartolus Baldinottus (of Pistoia), fl. 1479-1480 (Table K4)
1925.B34	Bartholus Baratterius, fl. 1421-1442 (Table K4)
1925.B35	Baldus Bartolinius (Novellus), 1408-1490 (Table K4)
1925.B36	Andrea Barbazza (Barbatia; de Bartholomeo; Siculus), ca. 1410-1480 (Table K4)
1925.B364	Jean Barbier (Johannes Berberius), 15th cent. (Table K4)
1925.B37	Bartholomaeus a Novaria (Table K4)
1925.B375	Benedetto Barzi, d. 1410 (Table K4)
1925.B38	Thomas Basin (abp.), 1412-1491 (Table K4)
1925.B47	Giovanni Bertachini, (Bertachinus, of Fermo), b. ca. 1448 (Table K4)

Sources
By period
Post-Justinian periods
Occident
Jurists' law. Legistic
By period
6th to 15th centuries. Jus Romanum Medii Aevi
Jurists of the 14th and 15th cent. -- Continued

1925.B48	Bertrandus de Monte Faventino, d. 1348 (Table K4)
1925.B63	Bonaccursius (Bonus Accursius), 15th cent. (Table K4)
1925.B65	Bonicontius (Bonincontrus), d. 1350 (Table K4)
1925.B78	Bernardus Brunswicensis (Table K4)
1925.B84	Bulgarinus de Bulgarinis, 1441-1497 (Table K4)
1925.B85	Antonius de Butrio, 1338-1408 (Table K4)
1925.C32	Vitalis de Cambanis, 15th cent. (Table K4)
	Giovanni Battista Caccialupi, d. 1496 see KJA1802
1925.C35	Giovanni Campeggi, 1448-1511 (Table K4)
1925.C36	Joannes Jacobus Canis (a Canibus), d. 1490 or 1494 (Table K4)
1925.C37	Benedictus Capra, fl. 1515-1576 (Table K4)
1925.C38	Philippus de Cassolis, d. 1391 (Table K4)
1925.C39	Cato Saccus (Table K4)
1925.C47	Petrus de Cernitis, d. 1338 (Table K4)
1925.C49	Cervarius Tubero, Ludovicus, 1455-(ca)-1527 (Table K4)
1925.C65	Contes (Comes) de Perusio, fl. 1364 (Table K4)
1925.C67	Petrus Philippus Corneus (della Corgna; Pier Filippo Corneo), 1420-1492 (Table K4)
1925.C68	Antonio Corsetti, ca. 1450-1503 (Table K4)
1925.C7	Corte, Francesco, d. 1495 (Table K4)
1925.C74	Giovanni Crispo de' Monti (Joannes Crispus de Montibus), 15th cent. (Table K4)
1925.C74A3-.C74A39	Individual works. By title
	e. g.Termini omnium actionum cum arbore
1925.C76	Joannes Crotus (Grotus; of Casale), fl. 1513 (Table K4)
1925.C85	Raphael Cumanus (de Raimundis; da Como), d. 1427 (Table K4)
1925.C87	Franciscus Curtius (Corti), d. 1495 (Table K4)
1925.D44	Del Monte, Pietro, d. 1457 (Table K4)
(1925.E93)	Nicolaus Everardi, 1462 or 3-1532 see KJA1812
(1925.F37)	Jean Faure, d. 1340 see KJA1846

Sources
  By period
    Post-Justinian periods
      Occident
        Jurists' law. Legistic
          By period
            6th to 15th centuries. Jus Romanum Medii Aevi
              Jurists of the 14th and 15th cent. -- Continued

1925.F47	Giovanni Pietro Ferrari (Joannes Petrus de Ferrariis; of Parma), fl. 1400 (Table K4)
1925.F48	Johannes Ferrarius, 1485 or 6-1558 (Table K4)
1925.F54	Filippo Franchi, d. 1471 (Table K4)
1925.F67	Philipus de Formaglinis (of Bologna) (Table K4)
1925.F68	Thomas de Formaglinis, 1st half 14th cent. (Table K4)
1925.F73	Franciscus Albergotus (Table K4)
1925.G35	Angelo Gambiglioni, 1422-1451 (Table K4)
1925.G47	Gerardus Monachus (Table K4)
1925.I83	Andrea d'Isernia (de Rampinis), ca. 1220-1316 (Table K4)
1925.J62	Johannes, Monachus, d. 1313 (Jean, le Moine) (Table K4)
1925.L35	Ubertus de Lampugnano (Table K4)
1925.L4	Leonardus, de Utino, 15th cent. (Table K4)
1925.L65	Joannes de Londris Pictaviensis, fl. ca. 1350 (Table K4)
(1925.L83)	Ludovicus Pontanus (Romanus), 1409-1439 see KJA1925.P65
1925.M36	Hippolytus de Marsiliis (of Bologna), 1450-1529 (Table K4)
1925.M37	Matthaeus de Matthesilanis (of Bologna), b. 1381 (Table K4)
1925.M38	Petrus de Matthesilanis, fl. 1412 (Table K4)
1925.M65	Joannes Petrucchi de Montesperello (of Perugia), 1390-1464 (Table K4)
(1925.N52)	Nicasius de Voerda (of Mecklenburg) see KJA1894
1925.O93	Ozeri, Giovanni Francesco (Table K4)
1925.P33	Joannes Pagliarensis (of Siena) (teacher of Baldus) (Table K4)
1925.P36	Guy de La Pape (Guido Papa; Guipapa), ca. 1402-ca. 1487 (Table K4)
1925.P46	Franciscus Pepius Quirici, fl. 1476-1505 (Table K4)
1925.P47	Federicus Petruccius (de Senis), fl. 1321-1343 (Table K4)

Sources
By period
Post-Justinian periods
Occident
Jurists' law. Legistic
By period
6th to 15th centuries. Jus Romanum Medii Aevi
Jurists of the 14th and 15th cent. -- Continued

1925.P48	Petrus Ravennas (Petrus Tomasi, Tomai), d. 1502 (Table K4)
1925.P52	Paulus Picus a Monte Pico, fl. 1439 (Table K4)
1925.P55	Joannes de Platea (of Bologna) (Table K4)
1925.P65	Lodovico Pontano, 1409-1439 (Table K4)
1925.P67	Joannes Christophorus Portius (Porcius; Parcus), fl. 1434 (Table K4)
1925.P87	Jacobus de Puteo (of Alessandria), d. 1453 (Table K4)
1925.P88	Paris de Puteo (del Pozzo), ca. 1413-1493 (Table K4)
1925.R35	Franciscus Raimundi de Ramponis (of Bologna), d. 1401 (Table K4)
1925.R38	Raymundus, fl. 1506 (Table K4)
1925.R42	Jacobus Rebuffi (of Monpellieri), d. 1428 (Table K4)
	Ridolfi, Lorenzo, fl. 1395-1439 see KJA2066.5
1925.R55	Johannes Maria de Riminaldis of Ferara, fl. 1559-1579 (Table K4)
	Rolandinus, de Passageriis see KJA1750
1925.R64	Rolandinus de Placiola (Piazzola), fl. 1303-1323 (Table K4)
1925.R68	Antonius Rosellus (of Arezzo), d. 1466 (Table K4)
1925.R84	Carolus Ruinus, fl. 1530 (Table K4)
1925.S24	Jacobus de Saliceto (of Bologna), d. 1418 (Table K4)
1925.S25	Richardus de Saliceto (of Bologna), d. 1379 (Table K4)
1925.S26	Florianus de Sancto Petro, d. 1441 (Table K4)
1925.S27	Felino Maria Sandeo, 1444-1503 (Table K4)
1925.S38	Claude de Sayssel (of Aix), 1450-1520 (Table K4)
1925.S53	Signorolus (Signorinus) de Homodeis (of Milan), fl. 1414 (Table K4)
1925.S55	Harynghus Sifridus Sinnama (of Frisia) (Table K4)
1925.S63	Nicolaus Spinellus (de Napoli), d. 1394 (Table K4)

Sources
By period
Post-Justinian periods
Occident
Jurists' law. Legistic
By period
6th to 15th centuries. Jus Romanum Medii Aevi
Jurists of the 14th and 15th cent. -- Continued

1925.S85	Joannes de Stynna, fl. 1511 (Table K4)
1925.T55	Tindarus (Alfanus), fl. 1450 (Table K4)
1925.T67	Hieronymus Tortus, 1427-1484 (Table K4)
1925.U215	Niccolo degli Ubaldi (Table K4)
1925.U22	Pietro degli Ubaldi (Petrus de Ubaldis), d. ca. 1499 (Table K4)
1925.V52	Vianesius Pascipoverus (of Bologna), early 14th cent. (Table K4)
(1925.V82)	Nicasius de Voerda see KJA1894

16th to 18th centuries. Common law in Europe
Class here general comprehensive and comparative
works
For works on a particular subject, see the subject in
KJC or in the subclass for the country

1935	General works
1937	Collections. Compilations

Including quaestiones, decisiones, observationes,
responsae, etc.
For collections, opera omnia, and selections of an
individual jurist, see the jurist
For consilia (opinions) of an individual law faculty,
see the subclass for the country
For decisiones of a particular court or jurisdiction,
see the subclass for the country
For consilia of an individual jurist see
KJA2150.A+
By nationality
Class here individual jurists writing on Roman law
as compared with, or influencing, their national
legal systems
English
see KD
French

1942	General
1944	Collections. Compilations

Individual jurists
Individual jurists listed in alphabetical order

Sources
 By period
  Post-Justinian periods
   Occident
    Jurists' law. Legistic
     By period
      16th to 18th centuries. Common law in Europe
       By nationality
        French
         Individual jurists -- Continued

1950	Andre Alciat (Andreas Alciatus), 1492-1550 (Table K3)
	Antonio Augustin (Abp, of Tarragon) see KJA2000
1952	Bernard Automne, d. 1666 (Table K3)
1953	Pierre Ayrault, 1536-1601 (Table K3)
1954	Francois Baudouin (Balduinus), 1520-1573 (Table K3)
1956	Barnabe Brisson, 1531-1591 (Table K3)
	De verborum significatione see KJA56
	De formulis et solemnibus populi Romani verbis see KJA105
1958	Guillaume Bude (Budaeus), d. 1540 (Table K3)
1958.5	Claudius Cantiuncula, d. 1560? (Table K3)
1959	Jean Chappuis, fl. 1500 (Table K3)
1959.5	Claude Chifflet, 1541-1580 (Table K3)
1960	François Clapiers (de Claperiis), 1524-1585 (Table K3)
1962	François de Connan, 1508-1551 (Table K3)
1963	Antoine LeConte (Contius), 1517-1586 (Table K3)
1963.5	Jean de Coras, 1513-1572 (Table K3)
1964	Thomas Cormier (Sieur de Beauvais), ca. 1523-1600 (Table K3)
1965	Pierre Coustau, fl. 1554 (Table K3)
1966	Jacques Cujas (Cujacius), 1522-1590 (Table K3)
1968	Jean Domat, 1625-1696 (Table K3)
1970	Hugo Doneau (Donellus), 1527-1591 (Table K3)
1970.A3A-.A3Z	Individual works. By title, A-Z
1970.A3C65	Commentarius juris civilis
1970.5	François Douaren, 1509-1559 (Table K3)
1970.8	Nicolas, Du Bois, ca. 1620-1696 (Table K3)
1972	Charles Dumoulin (Molinaeus), 1500-1566 (Table K3)

Sources
  By period
    Post-Justinian periods
      Occident
        Jurists' law. Legistic
          By period
            16th to 18th centuries. Common law in Europe
              By nationality
                French
                  Individual jurists -- Continued

1973	Petrus Faber, 1540 or 41-1600 (Table K3)
1974	Fabrot (of Aix), d. 1659 (Table K3)
1976	Antoine Favre (Faber), 1557-1624 (Table K3)
1976.A3A-.A3Z	Individual works. By title, A-Z
1976.A3C63	Codex Fabrianus
1976.A3R37	Rationalia ad pandecta
1976.5	Guillaume Fournier, d. 1584 (Table K3)
1977	Antoine Fumée, 1511-1587 (Table K3)
1978	Jacques Godefrois (Jacobus Gothofredus), 1587-1652 (Table K3)
1980	Denis Godefroy (Dionysius Gotofredus), 1549-1622 (Table K3)
1980.5	Nicolas de Grouchy, 1520-1572 (Table K3)
1982	François Hotman (Hotomanus), 1524-1590 (Table K3)
1982.A3A-.A3Z	Individual works. By title, A-Z
1982.A3A58	Antitribonianus (Table K3)
1983	Louis Le Caron, 1534-1613 (Table K3)
1984	Edmond Mérille, 1579-1647 (Table K3)
1984.A3A-.A3Z	Individual works. By title, A-Z
1984.A3V37	Variantes e Cujacio (Table K3)
1985	Antonius Mornacius, 1554-1619 (Table K3)
1987	Jean Robert, fl. 1569-1582 (Table K3)
1989	Nicolaus Valla, d. 1568 (Table K3)

                Spanish

1990	General works
1992	Collections. Compilations
	Individual jurists
	Individual jurists are listed in alphabetical order
1995	Jerónimo Altamírano, b. 1620 (Table K3)
1997	Francisco de Aruaya, fl. 1625 (Table K3)
2000	Antonio Augustin (Abp. of Tarragon), 1517-1586 (Table K3)
2002	Agostinho Barbosa, 1590-1649 (Table K3)
2003	Antonio Córdoba de Lara, 16th cent. (Table K3)

Sources
  By period
    Post-Justinian periods
      Occident
        Jurists' law. Legistic
          By period
            16th to 18th centuries. Common law in Europe
              By nationality
                Spanish
                  Individual jurists -- Continued

2004	Diego Covarrubias y Leiva, 1512-1577 (Table K3)
2005	Antonio Gómez, b. 1501 (Table K3)
2006	Antonious Goveanus, ca. 1505-1565? (Table K3)
2007	Rodrigo Juárez, 16th/17th cent. (Table K3)
2008	Fernando de Loaces, 1497-1568 (Table K3)
2010	Ramos del Manzano, d. 1638 (Table K3)
2010.5	Antonio de Nebrija, 1444?-1522 (Table K3)
2011	Antonio Padilla y Meneses, 16th cent. (Table K3)
2012	Antonio Pérez, 1583-1622 (Table K3)
2014	Antonio Picardo y Vinuesa, 1565-1631 (Table K3)
2016	Quintadueñas (Table K3)
2018	Retes, d. 1676 (Table K3)
2020	Tomás (Table K3)
2022	Vazquez (Table K3)

                Italian

2030	General works
2032	Collections. Compilations
	Individual jurists
	Individual jurists are listed in alphabetical order
2034	Battista Aimo, 16th cent. (Table K3)
2035	Silvestro Aldobrandini, 1499-1558 (Table K3)
2035.3	Bernardino Alfani, 1534-1590 (Table K3)
2036	Giuseppe Altogradi, fl. 1701 (Table K3)
2037	Antonio Amato, d. 1653 (Table K3)
2037.5	Giovanni Vincenzo d'Anna, 16th cent. (Table K3)
2037.8	Giovanni d'Arnono, fl. 1524-1534 (Table K3)
2038	Francesco Baronio, d. 1679 (Table K3)
2040	Niccolo Belloni, fl. 1542-1547 (Table K3)
2042	Giacomo Beni, fl. 1584 (Table K3)
2042.5	Christoph Besold, 1577-1638 (Table K3)

Sources
  By period
    Post-Justinian periods
      Occident
        Jurists' law. Legistic
          By period
            16th to 18th centuries. Common law in Europe
              By nationality
                Italian
                  Individual jurists -- Continued

2042.8	Giovanni Francesco Bonavoglia, d. 1611 (Table K3)
2042.9	Eligio Caffarello, fl. 1590-1605 (Table K3)
2043	Girolamo Cagnoli, 1490?-1551 (Table K3)
2043.5	Giacomo Caimo, 1609-1679 (Table K3)
2044	Vincenzo Carocci, 16th/17th cent. (Table K3)
2045	Giuseppe Lorenzo Maria de Casaregi, 1675-1737 (Table K3)
2047	Giulio Claro, 1525-1575 (Table K3)
2049	Hippolytus a Collibus, 1561-1612 (Table K3)
2049.5	Antonio Maria Corasi, fl. 1570 (Table K3)
2051	Tiberio Deciani, 1508?-1581 (Table K3)
2053	Onofrio Donadio, 1630-1656 (Table K3)
2053.5	Andrea Fachinei, d. 1607 (Table K3)
2054	Prospero Farinacci, 1554-1618 (Table K3)
2055	Emilio Ferretti, 1489-1552 (Table K3)
2055.5	Giacomo Gallo, 1544-1688 (Table K3)
2056	Ferrante Gargiaria (Table K3)
2056.3	Girolamo Garzano, 16th cent. (Table K3)
2057	Alberico Gentili, 1552-1608 (Table K3)
2057.A3D53	Dialogi sex de veteris juris interpretibus (Table K3)
2059	Scipione Gentili, 1563-1616 (Table K3)
2060	Francesco Giovanetti, d. 1586 (Table K3)
2060.3	Tommaso Grammatico 1473-1556 (Table K3)
2060.5	Gianvincenzo Gravina, 1664-1718 (Table K3)
2061	Paulus Leonius, fl. 1550-1584 (Table K3)
2062	Ottavio Livelli, d. 1634 (Table K3)
2063	Giovanni Battista de Luca, 1614-1683 (Table K3)
2063.2	Giasone dal Maino, 1435-1519 (Table K3)
2063.3	Marco Mantova Benavides, 1489-1582 (Table K3)
2063.35	Paolo Manuzio, 1512-1574 (Table K3)

Sources
  By period
    Post-Justinian periods
      Occident
        Jurists' law. Legistic
          By period
            16th to 18th centuries. Common law in Europe
              By nationality
                Italian
                  Individual jurists -- Continued

2063.5	Antonio Massa, 16th cent. (Table K3)
2064	Giacomo Menochio, 1532-1607 (Table K3)
2064.3	Lodovico Montalto, d. ca. 1533 (Table K3)
2064.5	Sebastiano Monticello (Table K3)
2064.8	Tobia Nonio, 1528-1570 (Table K3)
2065	Giulio Pace, 1550-1635 (Table K3)
2066	Prospero Pasetti, fl. 1575 (Table K3)
2066.5	Lorenzo Ridolfi, fl. 1395-1439 (Table K3)
2066.6	Ippolito Riminaldi, 1520-1589 (Table K3)
2066.8	Gianfrancesco Riva di San Nazarro, d. 1535 (Table K3)
2066.9	Carlo Sigonio, 1524?-1584 (Table K3)
2067	Giovanni Battista Staibano (Table K3)
2070	Lelio Torelli, 1489-1576 (Table K3)

              German

2075	General works
2077	Collections. Compilations

                Individual jurists
                  Individual jurists are listed in alphabetical order

2077.4	Johannis Althusius, 1557-1638 (Table K3)
2077.5	Valentinus Arithmaeus, 1560-1620 (Table K3)
2077.6	Joseph Adam Ayblinger, d. 1722 (Table K3)
2078	Heinrich Bocerus, 1561-1630 (Table K3)
2078.2	Johann Samuel Friedrich von Boehmer, 1704-1772 (Table K3)
2079	Justus Henning Böhmer, 1674-1749 (Table K3)
2079.13	Johannes, Borcholten, 1535-1593 (Table K3)
2079.18	Wulff Brocktorff (Table K3)
2079.19	Everard van Bronkhorst, 1554-1627 (Table K3)
2079.2	Johann Brunnemann, 1608-1672 (Table K3)
2080	Benedikt Carpzov, 1595-1666 (Table K3)
2082	Johannes Cöppen (Table K3)
2082.2	Antonius Costanus, 16th cent. (Table K3)

Sources
  By period
    Post-Justinian periods
      Occident
        Jurists' law. Legistic
          By period
            16th to 18th centuries. Common law in Europe
              By nationality
                German
                  Individual jurists -- Continued

2082.3	Iacob Cramer, fl. 1589-1609 (Table K3)
2082.5	Marquand Fehrer, 1565-1614 (Table K3)
2082.7	Christian Heinrich Eckhard, 1716-1751 (Table K3)
2084	Johann Fichard, 1512-1581 (Table K3)
2084.5	Christoph Freisleben, fl. 1544 (Table K3)
2085	Andreas Gail, 1526-1587 (Table K3)
2086	G. Christian Gebauer, 1690-1773 (Table K3)
2087	Johann Friedrich Georgi, 17th cent. (Table K3)
2088	Hubert van Giffen, ca. 1533-1604 (Table K3)
2090	Jan van Giffen (Giphanius) (Table K3)
2092	Justinus Gobler (Goarinus), 1503?-1567 (Table K3)
2093	Gregor (Meltzer) Haloander, 1501-1531 (Table K3)
2093.5	Christian Gottlieb Haubold, 1766-1824 (Table K3)
2094	Johann Gottlieb Heineccius, 1681-1741 (Table K3)
2095	Karl Christop. Hofacker, 1749-1793 (Table K3)
2096	Ferdinand August Hommel, 1697-1765 (Table K3)
2097	Ludwig Julius Friedrich Höpfner, 1743-1797 (Table K3)
2097.5	Joachim Hoppe, 1656-1712 (Table K3)
2098	Laurentius Kirchhoff, d. 1580 (Table K3)
2098.18	Johann Kleinschmidt (Table K3)
2098.19	Melchior Kling, 1504-1571 (Table K3)
2098.2	Andreas Knichen, 1560-1621 (Table K3)
2098.26	Detlev Langenbeck, fl. 1555-1557 (Table K3)
2098.3	Augustin von Leyser, 1683-1752 (Table K3)

Sources
  By period
    Post-Justinian periods
      Occident
        Jurists' law. Legistic
          By period
            16th to 18th centuries. Common law in Europe
              By nationality
                German
                  Individual jurists -- Continued

2099	Nicolaus Christoph Lyncker, 1643-1726 (Table K3)
2099.14	Philipp Matthaeus, 1554-1603 (Table K3)
2099.2	Andreas Mylius, 1649-1702 (Table K3)
2100	Joachim Mynsinger (v. Frundseck), 1514-1588 (Table K3)
2101	Georg Obrecht, 1547-1712 (Table K3)
2102	Johann Oldendorp, 1480-1567 (Table K3)
2103	Modestinus Pistorius, d. 1565 (Table K3)
2104	Friedrich Esaias Pufendorf, 1707-1785 (Table K3)
2106	Nicolaus Reusner, 1545-1602 (Table K3)
2107	Johannes Reichard Scheffer, fl. ca. 1580 (Table K3)
2108	Hieronymus Schurff (Schürpff), 1481-1554 (Table K3)
2108.5	Jeremias Setser, b. 1568 (Table K3)
2108.6	Zacharis Setzer, fl. 1597 (Table K3)
2108.8	Matthias Stephani, 1576-1646 (Table K3)
2109	Fridericus Philippus Strube, 18th cent. (Table K3)
2110	Georg Adam Struve, 1619-1692 (Table K3)
2111	Heinrich Christian Stryk, 1673-1732 (Table K3)
2112	Samuel Stryk, 1640-1710 (Table K3)
2112.3	Bernard Sutholt, fl. 1618-1625 (Table K3)
2112.5	Henricus à Sverin, fl. 1581-1586 (Table K3)
2114	Christian Thomasius, 1655-1728 (Table K3)
2114.5	Hieronymus Treutler, 1565-1607 (Table K3)
2115	Nikolaus Vigel, 1529-1600 (Table K3)
2116	Herman Vultejus, 1565-1634 (Table K3)
2117	Mattaeus Wesenbeck, 1531-1586 (Table K3)
2118	Ulrich Zasius (Zäsi), d. 1535 (Table K3)

                Dutch

2120	General works
2122	Collections. Compilations

KJA

Sources
 By period
  Post-Justinian periods
   Occident
    Jurists' law. Legistic
     By period
      16th to 18th centuries. Common law in Europe
       By nationality
        Dutch -- Continued
         Individual jurists
          Individual jurists are listed in alphabetical order

2122.48	Pieter Cornelis van Brederode, fl. 1585-1593 (Table K3)
2122.5	Herman Cannegeiter, 1723-1804 (Table K3)
2122.7	Arnoldus Corvinus, d. ca. 1680 (Table K3)
2123	Joost de Damhoudere, 1507-1581 (Table K3)
2124	Cornelius van Eck, d. 1732 (Table K3)
2124.5	Hugo Grotius, 1583-1646 (Table K3)
2125	Joachim Hoppers, 1523-1576 (Table K3)
2126	Ulrich Huber, d. 1694 (Table K3)
2128	Gerard Noodt, 1647-1725 (Table K3)
2129	Cornelis van Pijnacker, 1570-1645 (Table K3)
2129.5	Jacob Reyvaert, ca. 1535-1568 (Table K3)
2129.7	Arnoldus Rotgers, 1684-1752 (Table K3)
2130	Antonius Schulting, 1659-1734 (Table K3)
2132	Jan Verstegen, fl. 1665 (Table K3)
2134	Arnoldus Vinnius, 1588-1657? (Table K3)
2136	Joannes Voet, 1647-1713 (Table K3)
2137	Jacobus Voorda, 1698-1768 (Table K3)
2138	Johannes Ortvinus Westenberg, 1667-1737 (Table K3)

    Particular types of contemporary legal literature
     Consilia. Responsa. Legal (advisory) opinions

2145	General works
2147	Collections. Compilations. Selections (Table K22)

      For consilia collections of both Roman and canon law, see KBR2147

2150.A-Z	Individual jurists, A-Z

      Individual jurists are listed alphabetically
      Including individual and collected consilia of an individual author

2150.B3	Bartolo, of Sassoferrato, 1314-1357 (Table K4)
2150.B333	Andrea Barbazza, 1410-1480 (Table K4)
2150.B65	Nicolas de Bohier, 1469-1539 (Table K4)
2150.B66	Giovanni Bolognetti, 1506-1575 (Table K4)

Sources
Particular types of contemporary legal literature
Consilia. Responsa. Legal (advisory) opinions
Individual jurists, A-Z

2150.B87	Antonius de Butrio (Table K4)
2150.C3	Joannes Calderinus, d. 1365 (Table K4)
2150.C3748	Castiglionchio, Lapo da, d. 1381 (Table K4)
2150.D43	Filippo Decio, 1454-1536 or 7 (Table K4)
2150.D57	Dinus, de Mugello, 1254-ca. 1300 (Table K4)
2150.F37	Prospero Farinacci, 1554-1618 (Table K4)
2150.G35	Angelo Gambiglioni, 15th cent. (Table K4)
2150.G88	Juan Gutierrez, d. 1618 (Table K4)
2150.H68	Caspar Heinrich Horn, 1657-1718 (Table K4)
2150.J63	Joannes, de Anania (Table K4)
2150.O43	Oldrado da Ponte, d. 1335 (Table K4)
2150.P388	Paulus, de Castro (Table K4)
2150.P5	Pietro d'Ancarano, 1330-1416 (Table K4)
2150.P65	Lodovico Pontano, 1409-1439 (Table K4)
2150.R35	José Ramón, 17th cent. (Table K4)
2150.R58	Gianfrancesco Riva di San Nazarro, d. 1535 (Table K4)
2150.R673	Giovanni Antonio Rossi, 1489-1544 (Table K4)
2150.R68	Scipione Rovito, 1556-1636 (Table K4)
2150.S36	Joost Schomaker (Table K4)
2150.S67	Giovanni Pietro Sordi, d. 1598 (Table K4)
2150.S73	Paolo Staibano, b. 1543 (Table K4)
2150.S77	Samuel Stryk, 1640-1710 (Table K4)
2150.S79	Johann Stucke, 1587-1653 (Table K4)
2150.U22	Angelo degli Ubaldi, 1328-ca. 1407 (Table K4)
2150.U23	Baldo degli Ubaldi, 1327?-1400 (Table K4)
2150.V65	Ottaviano Volpelli, f. 1572 (Table K4)
2150.W36	Joannes Wamesius, 1524-1590 (Table K4)
2150.W55	Christian Wildvogel, 1644-1728 (Table K4)
2150.Z37	Ulrich Zasius, 1461-1535 (Table K4)

Private legal documents and instruments see KJA670
Decisiones. Quaestiones. Observationes
    For general collections, see KJA1937
    For general comprehensive works on these types of
        materials, see KJA1935
    For decisiones, quaestiones, and observationes relating to a
        particular court or particular jurisdiction, see the subclass
        for the country
Repertoria. Digests. Indexes
    For repertoria relating to collections of court decisions (of one
        or more courts), or collections of law, ordinances, etc., of
        a particular jurisdiction, see the subclass for the country
    For subject indexes to a particular work, see the jurist or title
        in the appropriate period

Sources
Particular types of contemporary legal literature -- Continued
Formularies
For general and comprehensive works on formularies, see
KJA105
For works on libelii, actiones, ordines judicorum, see
KJA2784+
For formularies for trial lawyers, court practice, etc., see the
subclass for the country
Brocardica juris. Proverbia. Regulae juris see KJA100
Paratitla
see the jurist in the appropriate period
Modus legendi abbreviaturas see KJA132
Dictionaria. Vocabularia see KJA56
Popular works
see the jurist in the appropriate period
Casus literature

2151	General works
2152	Collections. Compilations. Selections (General)
	Individual jurists
	see the jurist in the appropriate period and country
2155	Legal education in Rome. Study and teaching
2157	The legal profession in Rome. Jurists
	Philosophy. Roman jurisprudence
2160	General (Table K22)
2162	The concept of law. Jus Romanum sacrum
	For state and religion see KJA3060
2170.A-Z	Concepts applying to several branches of the law, A-Z
2170.A43	Age
2170.D43	Dead bodies
	Cf. KJA2438.R48 Res extra commercium
2170.G66	Good faith
2170.H67	Horses
2170.L44	Legal documents
2170.O38	Oath
2170.S53	Simulation. Simulatio
2170.V57	Vis major
(2175)	The legal profession in Rome. Jurists
	see KJA2157
	Concepts and principles
2180	Jus privatum and jus publicum (Table K22)
2182	Aequitas. Equity (Table K22)
2183	Time immemorial (Table K22)
2185	Quasi-institutes (Table K22)
2186	Fictions (Table K22)
2188	Private international law. Conflict of laws
	Private law and procedure

Private law and procedure -- Continued
2190	General (Table K22)
	Persons
2192	General (Table K22)
	Natural persons
2194	General (Table K22)
	Caput. Status libertatis et civitatis
2196	General (Table K22)
	Slaves
	Including slavery by birth, servitus poenae, and libertus ingratus
2198	General (Table K22)
2200	Manumissio (Table K22)
	Libertini see KJA2206
2202	Peasantry. Colonatus (Table K22)
2204	Cives ingenui (Table K22)
	Including privileged classes, e.g. senators, equestrians, etc.
2206	Restricted classes (Table K22)
	Including freedmen, coloni adscripti, glebae adscripti, infames, intestabiles, etc.
2208	Peregrini (Table K22)
	Including peregrini socii and dediticii
	Latini
	Including Latini veteri, colonarii, and Junianii
2210	General (Table K22)
	Access to citizenship see KJA2955
2211	Jews
2213	Capacity, incapacity, and auctoritas
	Including limited capacity
2213.5.A-Z	Particular persons, A-Z
	Blind see KJA2213.5.P48
	Children under age of puberty see KJA2213.5.I66
	Deaf see KJA2213.5.P48
	Dead persons see KJA2438.R48
	Freemen in mancipatio see KJA2213.5.S53
2213.5.F87	Furiosi. Mente capti. Insane persons. People with mental disabilities
2213.5.I66	Impuberes. Children under age of puberty
	Insane persons see KJA2213.5.F87
	Mente capti see KJA2213.5.F87
2213.5.M56	Minors. Minores viginti quinque annis
	Mulieres see KJA2213.5.W65
	People with mental disabilities see KJA2213.5.F87
2213.5.P48	Physical disabilities, People with
	Including blind and deaf
2213.5.P76	Prodigi. Prodigals

Private law and procedure
Persons
Natural persons
Capacity, incapacity, and auctoritas
Particular persons, A-Z -- Continued
2213.5.S53   Slaves. Freemen in mancipatio
2213.5.W65   Women. Mulieres
Status familiae. Paterfamilias and filius-familias see
KJA2252+
Capitis deminutio
2214   Capitis deminutio maxima. Loss of liberty (Table K22)
Including poena and captivity (Jus postliminii; Lex
Cornelia)
2216   Capitis deminutio media. Loss of status civitatis (Table
K22)
Including banishment and moving to colony
2218   Capitis deminutio minima. Leaving the family kinship
(Table K22)
Including in manum conventio, adoptio, arrogatio, and
emancipato
2220   Consumtio existimationis (Table K22)
Including infamia, criminal sentence, and civil sentence
(actiones ex delictu, contractu, and quasi-contractu)
Juristic persons
Including non-human entities
2222   General (Table K22)
2223   Populus Romanus (Table K22)
2224   Fiscus Caesaris (Imperial treasury) (Table K22)
2225   Municipalities (Municipia. Universitates. Collegia) (Table
K22)
2225.5   Associations (Table K22)
Including guilds, trade associations, etc.
Family law
2227   General (Table K22)
Family structure. Paterfamilias concept
2229   General (Table K22)
2230   Jus vitae necisque of the head of household (Table K22)
2231   Jus vendeni of the head of household (Table K22)
Marriage
2233   General (Table K22)
2233.5   Sponsalia. Betrothal (Table K22)
2234   Matrimonial status (Table K22)
Including form, consent, age, and connubium (capacity to
contract civil marriage)
2235   Manus. Power of husband (Paterfamilias) (Table K22)
2236   Contubernium. Marriage among slaves (Table K22)
2237   Concubinage. Quasi marriage (Table K22)

KJA

	Private law and procedure
	Inheritance. Succession upon death -- Continued
	Delatio hereditatis. Acquisitio hereditatis
2273	General (Table K22)
2274	Heredes domestici. Heredes sui and heredes necessarii (Table K22)
2275	Heredes extranei (or voluntarii) (Table K22)
2276	Repudiatio hereditatis (Table K22)
2278	Hereditas jacens (Table K22)
	Bonorum possessio (Jus honorarium)
	Cf. KJA2290 Intestate succession
2280	General (Table K22)
2282	Interdictum quorum bonorum (Table K22)
2283	Actio ficticia (In favor of creditors of estate) (Table K22)
2285	Hereditatis petitio possessoria (Table K22)
	Intestate succession. Sequence of heirs
2287	General (Table K22)
2289	Jus civile (Table K22)
2290	Praetorian edict (Jus honorarium). Bonorum possessio (Table K22)
2292	Justinian law (Novella 118) (Table K22)
	Testamentary succession
2294	General (Table K22)
	Jus civile
2296	Testamentum publicum (calatis comitiis) (Table K22)
2298	Testamentum per aes et libram. Testamentum in procinctu (Table K22)
	Jus honorarium
2300	Bonorum possessio secundum tabulas (Table K22)
	Justinian law
2400	Ordinary oral or written private will. Testamentum mysticum (Table K22)
2402.A-Z	Types of wills, A-Z
2402.A78	Testamentum apud acta conditum
2402.B54	Testament of blind persons
2402.M54	Testamentum militis
2402.P37	Testamentum parentis inter libros
2402.P48	Testamentum pestis tempore
2402.P74	Testamentum principi oblatum
2402.R87	Testamentum ruri conditum
2404	Appointment of heir. Institutio heredis (Table K22)
2406	Form requirement (Table K22)
2408	Void and voidable wills. Revocation (Table K22)

KJA

	Private law and procedure
	Law of things. Res
	Classes of things, A-Z -- Continued
2438.E57	Entities. Universitatas rerum
2438.F68	Fruits
	Natural fruits see KJA2438.F68
	Personal and real property see KJA2438.R65
2438.R37	Res corporales and incorporales
2438.R48	Res extra commercium (patrimonium)
2438.R55	Res in comercio (patrimonio)
	Res mancipi, nec mancipi see KJA2438.R55
2438.R65	Res mobiles and immobiles. Personal and real property
	Res publicae. Res communes omnium. Res universitatis (Res humani juris) see KJA2438.E57
	Res sacrae, religiosae, sanctae (res divini juris) see KJA2438.R48
	Possession
2440	General (Table K22)
2442	Acquisition and loss of possession (Table K22)
	Possessory actions
2444	General (Table K22)
2446	Interdicta retinendae possessionis (Table K22)
	Including Interdictum uti possidetis and Interdictum utrubi
2448	Interdicta recuperandae possessionis (Table K22)
	Including Interdictum unde vi and Interdictum de precario
	Ownership
	Including personal and real property (res mobiles and immobiles)
2450	General (Table K22)
2452.A-Z	Classes of ownership, A-Z
2452.B65	Bonitary ownership
2452.C65	Co-ownership
2452.D65	Dominium
2452.P47	Peregrine ownership
	Praetorian ownership see KJA2452.B65
	Acquisition and loss of ownership
	Including personal and real property (res mobiles and immobiles)
2454	General (Table K22)
	History
2456	Acquisitiones civiles (Table K22)
	Including mancipatio, in jure cessio, adjudicatio, assignatio, usucapio, etc.
2457	Acquisitiones naturales (Table K22)
	Including traditio, occupatio, etc.

Private law and procedure
Law of things. Res
Ownership
Acquisition and loss of ownership -- Continued
2459   Occupancy. Occupatio (Table K22)
               Including abandoned and derelict things, thesaurus
                 (treasure trove) and lost things
2471   Praescriptio (longti temporis). Usucapio (Table K22)
2472   Accession (Table K22)
           Succession see KJA2270+
2473   Traditio (Table K22)
               Including traditio longo manu, brevi manu, constitutum
                 possessorium, etc.
2474   Dereliction and abandonment (Table K22)
2475   Donatio (Table K22)
               For donatio propter (ante) nuptias see KJA2246
               For mortis causa donatio see KJA2432
         Claims and actions resulting from ownership
2476   General (Table K22)
           Law of adjoining landowners
2477   General (Table K22)
2478   Actio finium regundorum (Table K22)
2479   Actio aquae pluviae arcendae (Table K22)
2480   Operis novi nuntiatio (Table K22)
2481   Cauti damni infecti (Table K22)
      Rights as to the use of another's property. Jura in re
2483   General (Table K22)
         Servitudes
2485   General (Table K22)
           Real servitudes. Servitudes praediorum rusticorum aut
               urbanorum
2487   General (Table K22)
2489.A-Z   Special types, A-Z
2489.B42   Beam or joist support (tigni immittendi)
2489.B84   Building support (oneris ferendi)
2489.D74   Dripping water (Stillicidii vel fluminis recipiendi vel
               non recipiendi)
2489.R53   Rights of pasture (Jus pascendi)
2489.R55   Rights of way (Iter; actus; via)
2489.R57   Rights to water (Aquae ductus; aquae haustus;
               pecoris ad aquam appulsus)
           Watering cattle see KJA2489.R57
         Personal servitudes
2491   General (Table K22)
2493.A-Z   Special types, A-Z
2493.H32   Habitatio
2493.O73   Operae servorum

Private law and procedure
  Law of things. Res
    Rights as to the use of another's property. Jura in re
     Servitudes
      Personal servitudes
       Special types, A-Z -- Continued

2493.P72	Praecarium
2493.U86	Usus
2493.U88	Ususfructus
	Actions
2495	General (Table K22)
2497	Actio confessoria in rem (Table K22)
	Actiones possessoriae see KJA2444+
2500	Superfices (Table K22)
2502	Emphyteusis. Right to use land in perpetuity (Table K22)
	Real securities
2505	General (Table K22)
2506	Fiducia. Transfer of ownership as security (Table K22)
2508	Pignus. Pledge (Table K22)
2510	Hypotheca (Table K22)
2511	Cadaster. Land surveying and surveys (Table K22)
	Obligations
2512	General (Table K22)
	Debtor and creditor
2514	General (Table K22)
2515	Debitum. Obligato. Obligation to perform and liability for enforcement (Table K22)
2517	Plurality of debtors and creditors. Joint obligations (Table K22)
	Including correality and solidarity
	Types of obligations
2520	Civil, praetorian, and natural obligations (Table K22)
	Secured transactions. Security (Personal)
2522	General (Table K22)
	Fiduca cum creditore see KJA2506
	Pignus see KJA2508
	Adstipulatio see KJA2517
2524	Adpromissio. Suretyship (Table K22)
	Including sponsio, fidepromissio, and fideiussio
	Extinction of obligation
2526	General (Table K22)
2527	Solutio. Performance. Payment (Table K22)
	Release. Ipso jure discharge. Actus contrarius
2528	General (Table K22)
2529.A-Z	Special topics, A-Z
2529.A33	Acceptilatio (verbis or literis)
2529.C64	Compensatio. Setoff

Private law and procedure
Obligations
Contracts
Formation of contract -- Continued
Clauses
2548　General (Table K22)
Pactum de non petendo see KJA2529.P32
Arra (Arrha) see KJA2582.A77
2550　Modalities. Conditions (Table K22)
Stipulation see KJA2562
2551　Formalities (Table K22)
Parties to contract
2553　General (Table K22)
Third parties see KJA2596
Void and voidable contracts
2555　General (Table K22)
2556　Error (Table K22)
Including error in negotio, error in persona, error in
corpore, and error in substantia
2558　Innominate contracts. Legal transactions. Transactio
(Table K22)
For secured transactions see KJA2522+
Verbal contracts
2560　General (Table K22)
2562　Stipulatio (Table K22)
Including Usurae faenus (loans), contractual penalties,
mandatum qualificatum (creditum)
For adstipulatio see KJA2517
For adpromissio, fideiussio, and sponsio see
KJA2524
Dotis dictio see KJA2244
2563　Jusjurandum liberti (Table K22)
2564　Written contracts (Table K22)
Including transscriptio a re in personam and transscriptio a
persona in personam
Real contracts
2566　General (Table K22)
Mutuum. Loan of money. Credit
2568　General (Table K22)
2569　Maritime credit. Foenus nauticum (Table K22)
2570　Commodatum. Loan of things (Table K22)
2572　Depositum (Table K22)
Including depositum irregulare, depositum miserabile,
and sequestration
Pignus see KJA2508
2574　Permutatio. Barter (Table K22)
2576　Contractus aestimatorius (Table K22)

Private law and procedure
  Civil procedure. Arbitration. Bankruptcy
    Formulary system of procedure
      Execution
        Particular types of execution, A-Z -- Continued

2762.C48	Cessio bonorum (beneficium competentiae)
2762.D58	Distractio bonorum
2762.M35	Manus injectio
2762.V45	Venditio bonorum

      Particular procedures

2765	General (Table K22)
2768	Interdictum. Interlocutory orders (Table K22)
2770	Missiones in possessionem (Table K22)
2772	Restitutio in integrum (Table K22)

    Cognitio procedure

2780	General (Table K22)
2782	Jurisdiction (Table K22)

      Actions and defenses

2784	General (Table K22)
2786	Prayer in complaint. Libelli (Table K22)
	Including litis denuntiatio, libellus conventionis, etc.
2788	Defenses. Exceptions (Table K22)
	Including libellus contradictionis
2790	Particular proceedings (Table K22)
	e.g. Default proceedings
2793	Litis contestatio (Table K22)
2795	Representation (Table K22)

      Evidence

2797	General (Table K22)
2800	Oath of parties against calumnia (Table K22)
2802	Sentence (Table K22)
2805	Remedies. Appellate procedure (Table K22)
2807	Execution (Table K22)
2812	Bankruptcy (Table K22)
2820	Notaries (Table K22)
2830	Registration. Recording (Table K22)

Public law

2850	General (Table K22)

  Constitutional history

2856	General works

    By period

2860	Kingdom (753-510 B.C.)
2870	Republic (510-31 B.C.)
	Empire
2880	Principate (31 B.C.-284 A.D.)
	Lombard empire
	see KJ

Public law
    Constitutional principles -- Continued
       Organization of the judiciary
          For civil procedure see KJA2700+
          For criminal procedure see KJA3570+

3040	General (Table K22)
	Magistrates. Juries
3045	General (Table K22)
3047.A-Z	Particular procedures, A-Z
3050	Organization of the judiciary in the provinces (Table K22)
3060	State and religion (Table K22)
	Administrative organization and process
3070	General (Table K22)
	Rome
3073	General (Table K22)
3075	Public safety (Table K22)
	Public health
3078	General (Table K22)
3078.5	Burial laws (Table K22)
3080	Public welfare (Table K22)
	Public property see KJA3170+
	Zoning and building laws see KJA3182
	Municipal and local government other than Rome
	Including towns of the Roman provinces
3090	General (Table K22)
3092	Autonomy and self-government (Table K22)
3092.5	Magistrates and imperial officials (Table K22)
	Including Decurions
	Administration of the provinces
3094	General (Table K22)
	Provincial magistrates and imperial officials
	Including proconsules, propraetores, etc., as provincial governors
3096	General (Table K22)
3098	Asian and other eastern Roman provinces (Table K22)
	Including Middle East, Asia Minor, etc.
3099	Western Roman provinces (Table K22)
	e. g. Roman provinces in Gaul
3100	Northern Roman provinces (Table K22)
3101.A-Z	Particular provinces, A-Z
3101.N67	Noricum
3101.P35	Pannonia
3110	Agriculture (Table K22)
	For public land administration see KJA3180+
3120	Regulation of markets (Table K22)
	Including price regulation
3130	Mining. Quarrying (Table K22)

KJA

Regional comparative and uniform law (Europe)
>   Class here treaties between, and comparative works on the law of,
>   two or more countries or intergovernmental organizations in
>   Europe, including works on legislative cooperation, regardless
>   of whether such countries are members of the European
>   Community or European Union, or not
>
>   For the supranational law of the European Community or European
>   Union, i. e. secondary legislation and other legal measures
>   binding upon all member states, see KJE901+
>
>   For comparative works on the law of countries in Europe with the
>   law of countries in other regions, see K

Bibliography
>   For bibliography of special topics, see the topic, e.g. KJC957,
>   Private international law, or applicable Form Division Tables

2   Bibliography of bibliography
3   General bibliography
3.5   Library catalogs. Union lists
3.6   Sales catalogs
3.7   Indexes to periodical articles, society publications,
           collections, etc.
>   For indexes to a particular publication, see the publication

Periodicals
>   For periodicals consisting primarily of informative material
>   (newsletters, bulletins, etc.) relating to a particular subject,
>   see the subject and form division for periodicals
>
>   For law reports, official bulletins or circulars, and official gazettes
>   intended chiefly for the publication of laws and regulations,
>   see the appropriate entries in the text or form division tables
>
>   For periodicals consisting predominantly of legal articles,
>   regardless of subject matter and jurisdiction see K1+
>
>   For indexes to periodical articles see KJC3.7

7   Monographic series

Official gazettes
>   For official gazettes of an individual jurisdiction, see the subclass
>   for the jurisdiction
>
>   For official gazettes of the European Communities see
>   KJE5+

8   Indexes (General)
9   Collections. Compilations

Legislative and executive papers. Documentation of the
European regional organizations see KJE5+

14.A-Z   Intergovernmental congresses and conferences. By name of
                                    the congress, A-Z
                                    Under each:
                                    .xA15   Serials
                                    .xA2   Monographs. By date
                                    Including ad hoc conferences of heads of state
                                    For intergovernmental congresses on a particular subject, see the
                                        subject
                                Legislation
                                    For legislation of a particular jurisdiction, see the subclass for the
                                        jurisdiction
                                    For legislation on a particular branch of the law or subject, see the
                                        branch or subject
                                    For legislation of the European communities see KJE5+

                                    Indexes and tables. By date
                                        For indexes limited to one jurisdiction, see the subclass for the
                                            jurisdiction
27   General
28   Chronological indexes
29   Indexes of translations
30   Summaries. Abridgments. Digests
                                    Statutes
                                        Including statutory orders and administrative regulations
                                    Collections
                                        Including official and private editions, and annotated editions
34   Serials
35   Monographs. By date
36   Codes and related materials
                                Treaties and other international agreements
                                    Class here treaties between countries limited to the region, and
                                        treaties of regional organizations other than the European
                                        Communities, including all bilateral treaties of an organization
                                    For treaties of public international law, see subclass KZ
                                    For treaties between countries in different regions see
                                        K524+
                                    For treaties of COMECON see KJE807.22+
                                    For treaties of the European Communities see KJE917+
                                    Collections. Compilations
                                        Including either multilateral or bilateral treaties, or both, and
                                            related agreements (accessions, successions, amending
                                            agreements, protocols, etc.)
38   General
39.A-Z   Collected treaties of an individual country limited to its
                                            region, and collected treaties of a regional organization.
                                            By country or organization, A-Z

Treaties and other international agreements
    Collections. Compilations -- Continued
      Individual treaties
        see the subject
   Court decisions and related materials. Law reports

40	Several courts
	Particular courts
	Court of Justice see KJE924.2+
	European Court of Human Rights see KJC5132
54	Encyclopedias
56	Dictionaries. Terms and phrases. Vocabularies

        For dictionaries on a particular branch of the law or subject, see
          the branch or subject
        For bilingual and multilingual dictionaries see K52.A+
        For dictionaries on European Community law see
          KJE926.5

58	Legal maxims
59	Form books

        Including graphic materials, blanks, atlases, etc., and early works
        For form books on a particular branch of the law or subject, see
          the branch or subject
   Judicial statistics

61	General works
63.A-Z	By subject, A-Z
	Directories
64	General
64.7.A-Z	By specialization, A-Z
	Trials
64.9	Collections. Compilations
	Criminal trials and judicial investigations
	Collections. Compilations
65	General
67.A-Z	Particular offenses, A-Z
67.M87	Murder
67.P66	Political crimes

      Individual trials
        see the subclass for the country
    War crime trials
      Trials by international military tribunals see KZ1168+
      Trials of aliens by national courts sitting at home or abroad
        see KZ1175+
      Trials of nationals by the courts of their own country
        Trials by the courts of a particular country
          see the subclass for the country
        Trials by courts of countries in different regions see
          KZ1168+

	Relation of law to other topics see K486+
164.A-Z	Works on diverse aspects of a particular subject falling within several branches of the law. By subject, A-Z
164.C65	Computers
	History of law see KJ1+
	Philosophy, jurisprudence, and theory of European law

      For works on the philosophy and doctrine of a particular country
         in Europe, see the subclass of the country
      For works on the legal philosophy of a particular branch of law,
         see the branch
      For works by European authors on the philosophy of law
         and jurisprudence in general see K237+

383	General works
	The concept of law
385	General works
390	Equity. Fairness
393	Law and the state. Legal order. Respect for the law
394	Precedents. Stare decisis
	Legal science
395	History
396	General works
397	Sources of the law
	Law reform see KJC432
	Methodology
403	General works
404	Legal hermeneutics. Interpretation and construction

      Including lacunae in law and judge-made law
    Uniform law development. Law integration
      Including approximation, alignment, harmonization, etc.
      For unification of the law on a particular subject, see the
         subject
      For legal aspects of political integration see KJE5076
      For legal aspects of European economic integration
         see KJE6417

406	General works
406.5	Congresses. Conferences. By date of the congress

      For congresses, conferences, etc. devoted to unification
         or harmonization of the law on a particular subject,
         see the subject

| 406.7 | Organizations and their legal activities. Cooperation |

      For organizations devoted to unification or harmonization
         of law on a particular subject, see the subject, e.g.
         Private international law

| 408 | Semantics |
| 409 | Classification of law |

      For classification of law library holdings see Z697.L4

Philosophy, jurisprudence, and theory of European law --
Continued

Schools of legal theory

411	General works
413	Humanism
	Historical jurisprudence
416	General works
418	Ethnological jurisprudence. Primitive law

                    Class here works on the law of peoples at an early stage of
                      their civilization

                    For works on the primitive law of a particular people, see
                      the subclass for the appropriate country

                    For works on primitive law not limited to Europe see
                      K190+

428	Sociological jurisprudence
430	Jurisprudence of interest (Interessenjurisprudenz)
431	Influence of other legal systems on the law

              e.g. reception of Roman and canon law

432	Law reform and policies
435.A-Z	Concepts applying to several branches of the law, A-Z

              Deadlines see KJC435.T55

435.G66	Good faith
435.P74	Privileges
435.P76	Property

              Including property damage

435.T54	Time immemorial
435.T55	Time periods. Deadlines
435.V57	Vis major
435.W53	Widows
435.W65	Women
436	Intertemporal law. Retroactive law

          Legal systems compared

              Class here comparisons of the legal systems of Europe
              For comparisons of subjects, see the subject
              For works not limited to Europe see K583+

450	General works
	Civil law systems
455	General works
459	Socialist systems of law
(465)	Common law compared with civil law systems

              see K584

(470)	Canon law compared with civil or common law systems

              see KB

Legal systems compared -- Continued

472   Modern legal systems compared with ancient/early legal systems

Class here comparisons of ancient/early legal systems (e.g. Germanic) with more than one modern legal system

For comparisons of the legal system of an individual country with an ancient/early legal system, see the subclass for the country, e.g. KK941

Ancient legal systems compared see KJ147

Regional divisions. Subregions

Class here general works on the law or the legal systems in force within a single subregion of Europe

For works comparing the law on a particular subject see KJC981+

Benelux countries see KJE501+

480   Central Europe (Table K8)

510   Eastern Europe (Table K8)

Northern Europe. Scandinavia

Including Nordisk Domssamling

530   History

For early sources and treatises on a particular topic, see the topic in KJ

For legal historical sources of an individual Scandinavian country, see the subclass for the country

For collections of North Germanic legal sources see KJ694

541-545   General (Table K7)

548   Nordic Council (Table K15)

Transnational legislative cooperation

562   General (Table K8)

564   The Nordic Uniform Law Committee (Table K15)

570   The Nordic Economic Cooperation Committee (Table K15)

574   The Nordic Cultural Commission (Table K15)

Scandinavia see KJC530+

Nordic countries see KJC530+

600   Southeastern Europe. Balkan Peninsula (Table K8)

630   Southern Europe (Table K8)

(650)   Mediterranean Region

Private law, see class K

Water pollution see K3592.93

Public international law see KZ4110.M44

Law of the sea see KZA1688

Private law

Class here works on all aspects of private law

Private law -- Continued
955   History of private law
      Including sources and treaties
956   General (Table K8)
      Private international law
          Class here works on the conflict rules of two or more countries in
             the region, including conflict rules of branches other than
             private law
          For works on the conflict of laws of an individual country, see the
             country
          For conflict of laws between countries in different regions
             see K7000+
          For conflict of laws between the United States and a
             European country see KF416.A+
957   Bibliography
958   Periodicals
          Class here periodicals consisting primarily of informative
             material (Newsletters, bulletins, etc.)
          For periodicals consisting predominantly of legal articles,
             regardless of subject matter and jurisdiction see K1+
959   Monographic series
      Statutes
960   Collections. Compilations
961   Digests. Summaries. Indexes
      Treaties and other international agreements
          Class here treaties between two or more countries in Europe
          Including works containing both treaties and statutes
          For treaties between countries in different regions see
             K7005+
961.5   Collections
          Including multilateral treaties, bilateral treaties, or both
962   General
          Collected treaties of an individual country see K7006
          Individual treaties
             see the subject
963   Encyclopedias
963.5   Dictionaries
964   History
      Law societies see KJC132
965   Congresses. Conferences. By date of congress
967   General works
          Including compends, essays, festschriften, etc.

	Private international law -- Continued
969	Two or more different legal systems in force in the same territory
	Class here works on domestic and/or international conflict of laws of two or more countries in Europe, each with two coexisting legal systems, e.g. secular and Canon, etc.
	For works limited to a particular country, see the subclass for the country
	Regional unification, approximation (alignment), and harmonization
	Class here works on unification of conflict rules (activities and methods)
	For unification of conflict rules relating to a special subject, see the subject
970	General (Table K8)
	The Hague Conference on Private International Law see K7053+
	Conflict rules of the European Communities see KJE972
	Choice of law
971	General (Table K8)
	Points of contact
972	General (Table K8)
972.5	Nationality and domicile as points of contact (Table K8)
973	Locus regit actum (Table K8)
974	Choice of law by the parties. Party autonomy (Table K8)
975	Renvoi (Table K8)
	Limits of application of foreign law
976	General (Table K8)
977	Public policy and order (Table K8)
978	Recognition of foreign penal, revenue, confiscatory and political laws (Table K8)
978.5	Classification. Qualification (Table K8)
979.A-Z	Particular branches and subjects of the law, A-Z
	Subarrange each by Table K12
	Adoption see KJC979.F35
	Arbitral awards see KJC979.P76
	Automobile insurance see KJC979.I58
	Bankruptcy and execution see KJC979.P76
	Capacity see KJC979.P47
	Civil jurisdiction see KJC3795+
979.C65	Commercial agents (Table K12)
979.C655	Commercial papers and negotiable instruments (Table K12)
979.C657	Commercial sales (Table K12)
979.C658	Contracts. Obligations. Debtor and creditor (Table K12)
979.C67	Corporations (Table K12)

Civil law
Concepts and principles
Legal transactions
Void and voidable transactions -- Continued
1066   Part nullity (Table K8)
Agency
1070   General (Table K8)
1072   Unauthorized representation. Falsus procurator (Table K8)
1078   Power of attorney (Table K8)
Mandate
1081   General (Table K8)
1083   Negotiorum gestio (Table K8)
1088   Secured transactions. Security (Table K8)
1089   Fiduciary transactions. Trust and trustee (Table K8)
1091   Conditions (Table K8)
       Including suspensive and resultory conditions
1093   Limitation of action (Table K8)
Exercise of rights. Protection of rights
1096   General (Table K8)
1097   Self-defense (Table K8)
1098   Necessity (Table K8)
Family law. Domestic relations
1100   History
1101-1105   General (Table K7)
Marriage
1121   General (Table K8)
1122   Betrothal (Table K8)
Marriage impediments
1123   General (Table K8)
1124.A-Z   Individual impediments, A-Z
       Subarrange each by Table K12
1124.C65   Consanguinity (Table K12)
1125   Premarital examinations. Marriage banns (Table K8)
1126   Performance of marriage. Civil marriage (Table K8)
Husband and wife. rights and duties
1128   General (Table K8)
1131   Family name (Table K8)
1132   Legal status of married women (Table K8)
Dissolution of marriage. Matrimonial actions
1139   General (Table K8)
1140   Defective and voidable marriage (Table K8)
1146   Divorce (Table K8)
       Including grounds for divorce
1154   Separation (Table K8)

Civil law
Family law. Domestic relations
Marriage
Dissolution of marriage. Matrimonial actions -- Continued
1155   Settlement of claims from defective or dissolved marriages (Table K8)
1159   Quasi-matrimonial relationships. Unmarried cohabitation. Concubinage (Table K8)
1162   Matrimonial property and regime (Table K8)
Consanguinity and affinity
1185   General (Table K8)
1186   Support (Table K8)
Parent and child
1189   General (Table K8)
Legitimate children
1192   General (Table K8)
1200   Parental power (Table K8)
1210   Stepchildren (Table K8)
1212   Adoption (Table K8)
1216   Illegitimate children (Table K8)
Cf. KJC1227 Affiliation. Paternity
Affiliation. Paternity
1226   General (Table K8)
1227   Illegitimate children (Table K8)
1229   Artificial insemination or implantation (Table K8)
Cf. KJC6228 Medical legislation
Guardian and ward
Including guardianship over adults and minors
1232   General (Table K8)
1247   Curatorship (Table K8)
Law of things. Property
1251-1255   General (Table K7)
Right of property
1261   General (Table K8)
1261.5   Social obligation (Table K8)
Possession
1263   General (Table K8)
1264   Possession by virtue of agency (Table K8)
Acquisition and transfer of possession
1265   General (Table K8)
1266   Intent to possess (Table K8)
1267   Brevi manu traditio (Table K8)
1267.5   Constitutum possessorium (Table K8)
1268   Assignment of chose in possession (Table K8)
1269   Possession immemorial (Table K8)
Violation of possession

Civil law
Law of things. Property
Ownership
Claims and actions resulting from ownership -- Continued
1310 Liability of possessor (Table K8)
1312 Rights and defenses of possessor (Table K8)
Real property
1315 General (Table K8)
Public and private restraint on real property
1318 General (Table K8)
Entail see KJC6613
Fideicommissum. Entailed estates of the greater
nobility
1319 General (Table K8)
1320 Inheritance and succession (Table K8)
Acquisition and loss of ownership see KJC1276+
Registration see KJC1410+
Rights incident to ownership of land
1331 General (Table K8)
1332 Air and space above ground (Table K8)
Cf. KJC6920 Aviation
1333 Underground land. Minerals, metals, and other
resources (Table K8)
1334 Riparian rights. Water rights. Underground water
(Table K8)
1335 Animals and fish (Table K8)
Cf. KJC6681 Game laws
Cf. KJC6695+ Fishery laws
Law of adjoining landowners
1337 General (Table K8)
1338.A-Z Special topics, A-Z
1338.N84 Nuisances (Table K12)
Including heat, fumes, smoke, odor, noise, etc.
Types of real property
1340 Condominium. Horizontal property (Table K8)
1342 Ships (Table K8)
Superficies
1344 General (Table K8)
1345.A-Z Special topics, A-Z
1345.R49 Reversion (Table K12)
Rights as to the use and profits of another's land
History
1346 General
Fief see KJC4435.2+
1347 General (Table K8)
Superficies see KJC1344+

KJC

Civil law
Obligations
Delicts. Torts
Liability -- Continued
1665 Liability for torts of others (Respondeat superior
doctrine) (Table K8)
Including master and servant, employer and employee
1666 Exclusion of liability (Table K8)
Including contractual agreement, assumption of risk by
injured party, and tacit (implied) agreement
1667 Strict liability (Table K8)
Individual torts
1668 Violation of freedom (Table K8)
Physical injuries
1670 General (Table K8)
1672 Accidents (Table K8)
For particular types of accidents see
KJC1696.A+; KJC1708
1674 Medical malpractice (Table K8)
1675 Violation of integrity (Table K8)
Including honor, dignity, and reputation
Violation of privacy
1676 General (Table K8)
1678 Secrets (Table K8)
For privacy of communication see KJC1650
1680 Right in one's own picture (Table K8)
1682 Personal data in information retrieval systems (Table
K8)
Including public and private records, registers,
statistics, etc.
1684 Immoral transactions and acts (Table K8)
1688 Products liability (Table K8)
Ultrahazardous activities and occupations
1690 General (Table K8)
1692 Nuclear reactors. Nuclear damage (Table K8)
Sports. Sports fields and installations
1694 General (Table K8)
1696.A-Z Particular torts, A-Z
1696.S54 Skiing accidents (Table K12)
Liability for safe traffic conditions and accidents
1698 General (Table K8)
1700 Railroads and streetcars (Table K8)
1704 Aviation (Table K8)
Automotive transportation and road traffic
1706 General (Table K8)

KJC

Civil law
  Obligations
    Contracts and transactions
      Parties to contract -- Continued

1764	Third parties (Table K8)
	Void and voidable contracts see KJC1062+
	Error see KJC1063
	Breach of contract see KJC1592
	Discharge of contract see KJC1542+
	Individual contracts and transactions
	Sale
1770	General (Table K8)
1772	Risk (Table K8)
1774	Impossibility (Table K8)
	Default
1776	General (Table K8)
1780	Mora accipiendi (Table K8)
1782	Malperformance (Table K8)
	Warranty
1786	General (Table K8)
1790	Defective merchandise (Table K8)
	Liability of manufacturer
1794	General (Table K8)
1796.A-Z	Individual commodities or goods, A-Z
1796.A88	Automobiles (Table K12)
	Modes of sale
	Conditional sale
1802	General (Table K8)
	Retention of ownership and expectancies see KJC1291
1804	Installment plan (Table K8)
1806	Retractive sale (Table K8)
1808	Preemption (Table K8)
1810	Self-service (Table K8)
1812	Atypical or mixed contracts (Table K8)
1814	Exchange. Barter (Table K8)
1816	Donations. Gifts (Table K8)
1818	Aestimatum (Table K8)
	Lease. Landlord and tenant
1820	General (Table K8)
1825	Commercial and industrial property (Table K8)
	Including operating leasing and producer leasing
	Atypical or mixed contracts
1826	Investment leasing (Table K8)
	Including sale-and-lease-back
1840	Fiduciary transactions. Trusts and trustees (Table K8)

Civil law
   Obligations
      Individual contracts and transactions -- Continued
         Contracts of service and labor

1844	General (Table K8)
1846	Independent work. Professions (Table K8)
	Dependent work
1848	General (Table K8)
1849	Servants. Domestics (Table K8)
	Contract for work and labor
1854	General (Table K8)
1855.A-Z	Particular contracts, A-Z
1855.C65	Computer contracts (Table K12)
1855.T7	Transportation contracts (Table K12)
	Including travel contracts and package tours
1859	Security. Liens (Table K8)
1868	Civil companies (Table K8)
1876	Community by undivided shares (Table K8)
1878	Life annuity (Table K8)
1880	Aleatory contracts. Natural obligations (Table K8)
1886	Suretyship (Table K8)
1905	Discovery (Disclosure) (Table K8)
	Commercial law
2041-2045	General (Table K7)
2050	Commercial courts (Table K8)
	Merchant and business enterprise
2061	General (Table K8)
2074	Accounting (Table K8)
	Agency and prokura
2078	General (Table K8)
2079	Commercial agents (Table K8)
2083	Commercial registers (Table K8)
2085	Sale of business enterprise as a whole (Table K8)
2096	Sale (Table K8)
2108	Consignment. Commission merchants (Table K8)
2112	Auctioneers. Auctions (Table K8)
2118	Warehousing (Table K8)
	Freight forwarders and carriers
	For transportation of persons see KJC6897
2121	General (Table K8)
2124	Bill of lading (Table K8)
	Types of carriers
	For regulatory aspects see KJC6868+
2133	Railroads (Table K8)
2138	Trucklines (Table K8)
2142	Airlines (Table K8)

	Commercial law
	Freight forwarders and carriers
	Types of carriers -- Continued
	Carriage by sea see KJC2260+
2147	Commercial liens (Table K8)
	Negotiable instruments. Titles of credit
2150	General (Table K8)
2162	Bills of exchange (Table K8)
2173	Checks (Table K8)
	Stock certificates and bonds see KJC2475+
	Trust investment see KJC2254
	Bills of lading see KJC2124
	Maritime bills of lading see KJC2264
	Warehouse receipts see KJC2118
	Banking. Stock exchange
2188	General (Table K8)
2192.A-Z	Types of banks and credit instutitions, A-Z
2192.B85	Building and loan associations (Table K12)
2192.M67	Mortgage banks (Table K12)
	Banking transactions
2217	General (Table K8)
2222	Contract (Table K8)
	Including standardized terms of contract
2224	Loans. Credits (Table K8)
2227	Suretyship. Guaranty (Table K8)
2230	Deposit banking (Table K8)
2242	Accounts current (Table K8)
2242.5	Collecting of accounts (Table K8)
2243	Noncash funds transfer (Table K8)
	Including electronic funds transfer
	Stock exchange. Capital market. Bourse. Marché des capitaux. Bôrse. Kapitalmarkt
	Including investments
	For foreign investments see KJC6433+
2245	General (Table K8)
2246	Eurobonds (Table K8)
	Stock exchange transactions. Securities
2247	General (Table K8)
2248	Insider trading in securities (Table K8)
	Investment trusts
2250	General (Table K8)
2254	Trust investments (Table K8)
2255	Criminal provisions (Table K8)
	Maritime law
	For regulatory aspects of water transportation, navigation, and pilotage see KJC6927+

	Commercial law
	Maritime law -- Continued
2256	General (Table K8)
2259	Shipmasters (Table K8)
	Affreightment. Carriage of goods at sea and on inland waters
2260	General (Table K8)
2261	Lay days (Table K8)
2263	Freight forwarders (Table K8)
2264	Ocean bills of lading (Table K8)
2265	Charter parties (Table K8)
2266	Act of God (Table K8)
2267	Carriage of passengers at sea (Table K8)
2268	Average (Table K8)
2272	Salvage (Table K8)
2274	Ship creditors. Ship mortgages (Table K8)
2280	Shipbrokers (Table K8)
2282	Ship registers (Table K8)
2283	Maritime courts (Table K8)
	Prize courts see KZ6640+
	Marine insurance
	Including liability insurance
2285	General (Table K8)
2285.5.A-Z	Particular risks, A-Z
2285.5.W37	War risks (Table K12)
2289	Maritime social legislation (Table K8)
	Insurance law
2301-2305	General (Table K7)
	Insurance carriers
	Including cooperatives, mutual companies, etc.
2311	General (Table K8)
2314	State supervision (Table K8)
2320	Insurance contract (Table K8)
	Including risk and limitation
2333	Adjustment of claims (Table K8)
2337	Insurance brokers (Table K8)
	Particular lines of insurance
2339	Life (Table K8)
2350	Health (Table K8)
2356	Accident (Table K8)
	Property
2364	General (Table K8)
2367	Multiple line insurance (Table K8)
2368.A-Z	Particular hazards, A-Z
	Subarrange each by Table K12
2375	Suretyship insurance (Table K8)

Commercial law
Insurance law
Particular lines of insurance -- Continued
2383	Litigation insurance (Table K8)
	Liability insurance
2390	General (Table K8)
2397	Risk and limitation (Table K8)
2423.A-Z	Particular risks, A-Z
2423.A87	Automobiles (Table K12)
2423.A94	Aviation (Table K12)
	Carriage of passengers at sea see KJC2285+
2423.H85	Hunting (Table K12)
2428	Reinsurance (Table K8)
	Business associations
2432	General (Table K8)
	Personal companies. Unincorporated business associations
2435	General (Table K8)
	Contract. Articles of partnership
2435.13	General (Table K8)
2435.14	Partnership de facto (Table K8)
	Partners
2435.3	General (Table K8)
2435.35	Management (Table K8)
	Including voting
2435.65	Termination (Table K8)
2436.A-Z	Particular companies, A-Z
	Subarrange each by Table K12
2446	Joint ventures (Table K8)
	Stock companies. Incorporated business associations
2448	General (Table K8)
2449	Foreign corporations (Table K8)
	Stock corporations
2451-2455	General (Table K7)
2456	Incorporation and promoters (Table K8)
2458	State supervision (Table K8)
2459	Registration and publicity (Table K8)
	Organization and management
2460	General (Table K8)
2461	Director. Executive boards (Table K8)
2463	Board of controllers and supervisors (Table K8)
2467	Liability (Table K8)
	Corporate finance
2468	General (Table K8)
2469	Capital stock (Table K8)
	Securities

Commercial law
  Business associations
    Stock companies. Incorporated business associations
      Stock corporations
        Corporate finance
          Securities -- Continued

2472	General (Table K8)
	Stocks
2475	General (Table K8)
2476	Bearer stock (Table K8)
2479	Common stock (Table K8)
2480	Preferred stock (Table K8)
2482	Dividends and profits (Table K8)
	Bonds
2483	General (Table K8)
2485	Bearer bonds (Table K8)
2486	Convertible bonds (Table K8)
2487	Jouissance share (Table K8)
2489	Trust investments (Table K8)
	Accounting. Financial statements
2491	General (Table K8)
2494	Pension trusts (Table K8)
	Stocks and stockholders' rights
2495	General (Table K8)
2496	Stockholders' meetings (Table K8)
	Including voting and confidential communication
2501	Foreign stockholders (Table K8)
2502	Minority stockholders (Table K8)
	Private companies. Société à responsabilité limitée.
	Gesellschaft mit beschränkter Haftung (GmbH)
2520	General (Table K8)
2522	Incorporations (Table K8)
	Organization and management
2526	General (Table K8)
2527	Directors (Table K8)
2529	Board of controllers and supervisors (Table K8)
2530	Liability (Table K8)
	Company finance
2532	General (Table K8)
2534	Capital stock (Table K8)
	Stocks and stockholders' rights
2544	General (Table K8)
2547	Minority stockholders (Table K8)
2553	Loss of stockholders' rights (Table K8)
	Including leaving or exclusion
	Combinations. Industrial trusts

	Intellectual and industrial property
	Copyright
	Scope of protection
	Performing rights -- Continued
2655.72	Societies and industrial trusts (Table K8)
2655.73	Broadcasting rights (Table K8)
2655.75	Recording devices (Table K8)
	Including phonographs, magnetic recorders, jukeboxes
2655.76	Filming and photographing (Table K8)
2655.78	Translation (Table K8)
2655.8	Employees' copyright (Table K8)
2655.82	Duration and renewal (Table K8)
2655.85	Delicts. Torts (Table K8)
2655.9	Criminal provisions (Table K8)
	Branches of copyright
2660-2660.9	Literary copyright (Table KJ-KKZ11)
2665-2665.9	Musical copyright (Table KJ-KKZ11)
2670-2670.9	Fine art and photography (Table KJ-KKZ11)
	Violation of rights in one's own picture see KJC1680
	Motion pictures see KJC2690+
2678	Designs and models (Table K8)
2685	Prints and labels (Table K8)
	Including works of commercial art, catalogs, sample books, etc.
2690-2690.9	Motion pictures and television shows (Table KJ-KKZ11)
2692.A-Z	Special topics, A-Z
2695	Computer programs (Table K8)
2700	Quasi copyright and neighboring rights (Table K8)
	Author and publisher
	Including the publishing contract
2706	General (Table K8)
2707	Plays and stage productions (Table K8)
2708	Motion pictures (Table K8)
2709	Music (Table K8)
2710	Scientific literature (Table K8)
2712.A-Z	Special topics, A-Z
	Subarrange each by Table K12
2714	Litigation and execution (Table K8)
	Patent law and trademarks
2721-2725	General (Table K7)
2726	Scope of protection (Table K8)
2727	Antitrust aspects (Table K8)
	Patent practices and procedure
2732	General (Table K8)
	Invention
2734	General (Table K8)

	Intellectual and industrial property
	Unfair competition
	Delicts. Torts
	Protected rights, A-Z -- Continued
2827.T72	Trade secrets. Industrial secrets (Table K12)
2828.A-Z	Individual torts, A-Z
2828.B69	Boycott (Table K12)
	Espionage, Industrial see KJC2827.T72
2830	Practice and procedure (Table K8)
	Social legislation
	Class here works on all aspects of social legislation, including labor law, social insurance, and social services
2836	History
2837	Social reform and policies
2838	General (Table K8)
2839	European Social Charter. Charte sociale européenne (Table K8)
	Labor law
	Including works on both labor law and private law as it applies to the labor management relationship
2849	History
	Criticism. Reform see KJC2837
2851-2855	General (Table K7)
	International organization and international bureaus see HD7801
	European Social Charter. Charte sociale européene see KJC2839
2863	Right to work (Table K8)
2869.7	Conflict of laws (Table K8)
	Labor contract and employment
2870	General (Table K8)
2871	Types of employment (Table K8)
	Including permanent, temporary, part-time, etc.
2878	Salaried employees and wage earners (Table K8)
2880	Constitutional rights in employment (Table K8)
2882	Individual labor contract and collective agreement. Liberty of contract (Table K8)
	Formation of contract
2898	General (Table K8)
2901	Clauses and terms (Table K8)
	Parties to contract
2910	General (Table K8)
	Parties to collective bargaining see KJC3082
2911.A-Z	By industry or occupation, A-Z
2911.A25	Actors (Table K12)
	Agricultural laborers see KJC2911.F37

	Labor law
	Labor-management relations
	Employee participation in management
	Industries and trade, A-Z -- Continued
3040.M37	Mass media (Table K12)
	Collective bargaining and labor agreements
3056	General (Table K8)
	General provisions of civil law and public law
3066	Standardized labor conditions (Table K8)
3068	Most favorable wage (Table K8)
3076	Formation of contract (Table K8)
3082	Parties to contract (Table K8)
	For unions see KJC3123
3097.A-Z	By industry or occupation, A-Z
3097.B35	Banks (Table K12)
	Collective labor disputes
3100	General (Table K8)
3102	Arbitration. Conciliation (Table K8)
3104	Strikes and lockouts. Boycotts (Table K8)
	Corporate representation
3118	General (Table K8)
3123	Unions (Table K8)
	Protection of labor
3140	General (Table K8)
	Hours of labor
3145	General (Table K8)
3154.A-Z	By industry or type of employment, A-Z
	Subarrange each by Table K12
	Vacations
3157	General (Table K8)
3165	Holidays (Table K8)
3169.A-Z	By industry or type of employment, A-Z
	Subarrange each by Table K12
3172	Youth labor (Table K8)
	Women's labor
	Including hours of labor
3175	General (Table K8)
3179	Maternal welfare (Table K8)
3182	Home labor (Table K8)
	Labor hygiene and industrial safety
3185	General (Table K8)
3186	Factory inspection (Table K8)
3187.A-Z	By industry or type of labor, A-Z
	Subarrange each by Table K12
3189.A-Z	By machinery, equipment, etc., A-Z
	Subarrange each by Table K12

	Labor law -- Continued
3192.A-Z	Labor law for particular industries, occupations, or types of employment, A-Z
3192.A44	Alien labor (Table K12)
3192.C48	Church employees (Table K12)
3192.M53	Migrant workers (Table K12)
3192.M55	Miners (Table K12)
3195	Labor supply. Manpower control (Table K8)
3211-3215	Labor courts and procedure (Table K7)
	Social insurance
	Social reform and policies see KJC2837
3271-3275	General (Table K7)
3282	Constitutional aspects (Table K8)
3283	Family policy (Table K8)
	Health insurance
3308	General (Table K8)
3319.A-Z	Particular coverages and benefits, A-Z
	Subarrange each by Table K12
	Workers' compensation
	Including occupational diseases
3350	General (Table K8)
3360.A-Z	Particular coverages and benefits, A-Z
	Subarrange each by Table K12
3374.A-Z	By industry or group of workers, A-Z
	Subarrange each by Table K12
	Social security
	Including old age pensions, invalidity and disability pensions, and survivors' benefits
3381-3385	General (Table K7)
3396.A-Z	Particular coverages and benefits, A-Z
	Subarrange each by Table K12
3411.A-Z	By group of beneficiaries, A-Z
3411.A44	Alien laborers (Table K12)
	Housewives see KJC3411.M68
3411.M68	Mothers. Housewives (Table K12)
	Unemployment insurance
3421-3425	General (Table K7)
3426.A-Z	Particular coverages and benefits, A-Z
	Subarrange each by Table K12
3428.A-Z	By industry or group of workers, A-Z
	Subarrange each by Table K12
	Social services. Public welfare
3431-3435	General (Table K7)
3442.A-Z	Particular coverages and benefits, A-Z
	Subarrange each by Table K12
	Social service beneficiaries

Social services. Public welfare
Social service beneficiaries -- Continued

3468	General (Table K8)
3470	The poor and destitute (Table K8)
3473	Older people (Table K8)
3480	Large families (Table K8)

For family planning see KJC3575

People with disabilities
Including people with physical, mental, and emotional
disabilities

3490	General (Table K8)
3492.A-Z	Particular coverages and benefits, A-Z

Subarrange each by Table K12

3496.A-Z	By group of beneficiaries, A-Z

Subarrange each by Table K12

3498	Asocial persons (Table K8)
3502	Evacuated and homeless persons (Table K8)

War-related groups of beneficiaries

3503	General (Table K8)
3506	Refugees. Expelled or forcefully repatriated persons (Table K8)
3525	Prisoners of war and political prisoners (Table K8)
3530	War victims and war invalids (Table K8)

Children. Youth

3556	General (Table K8)
3567	Protection of children in public (Table K8)
3569	Protection of children against obscenity (Table K8)
3570	Abused children (Table K8)
3575	Birth control. Family planning. Population control (Table K8)
3587	Social courts and procedure (Table K8)

Courts and procedure
Administration of justice

3655	General (Table K8)

Judicial statistics see KJC61+
Judicial assistance see KJC3795+
Courts

3666	General (Table K8)

Regular courts

3673	General (Table K8)
3684	Supreme courts. Courts of last resort (Table K8)

Courts of special jurisdiction

3692	General (Table K8)
3693	Consular courts (Table K8)

Other courts of special jurisdiction
see the subject, e.g. KJC3211+, Labor courts; KJC3587,
Social courts, etc.

Public law
   The State -- Continued
4426   Rule of law (Table K8)
4427   Succession of states (Table K8)
4428.A-Z   Special topics, A-Z
                    Subarrange each by Table K12
         Constitutional law
         Constitutional history
                Class here general and comprehensive works on the
                    constitutional development of Europe as a whole
                For non-legal works on constitutional history see JF20+
                For works on the constitutional development of a
                    subregion (e.g., Scandinavia) see KJC530+
                For sources (Constitutions and related material, and
                    other documents) see KJC4442+
4431   General (Table K8, modified)
                Bibliography see KJC4441
         Feudal law
                Class here general and comparative works on feudal law
                For feudal law of an individual country, see the subclass for
                  the country
4432   General (Table K8)
4433   Collections. Compilations (Table K8)
                Individual sources or groups of sources
4434.2   Liber consuetudinum Imperii Romaniae (Table K20b)
4434.5   Libri feudorum (12th century) (Table K20b)
4434.5.A4-.Z4   Annotated editions. Glosses. Commentaries
                    For summula de feudis et beneficiis (Obertus, de
                      Horto) see KJ425
                Feudal institutes
4435   Feudal lord and vassal (Table K8)
                Fief. Beneficium
4435.2   General (Table K8)
4435.5.A-Z   Special topics, A-Z
4435.5.C65   Commendation. Homage (Table K12)
                  Homage see KJC4435.5.C65
4435.55   Feudal capacity (Table K8)
4435.7   Feudal succession (Table K8)
4435.8   Rights of eschat. Compulsory refeoffment (Table K8)
4436   Constitutional reform. Criticism
4441   Bibliography
                Including bibliography of constitutional history
4441.3   Periodicals
                Including gazettes, yearbooks, bulletins, etc.
             Sources

	Constitutional law
	Sources -- Continued
(4442-4443.5)	Treaties and other international agreements establishing and expanding the European Community and European Union
	see KJE
	Other sources
	Including early and modern constitutions and related material
4444	Indexes and tables
4444.4	Collections. Compilations
	Including annotated editions and commentaries
	Decisions. Administrative rulings. Reports
4444.5	Indexes and tables. Digests. By date
4444.52	Serials
4444.53	Monographs. By date
	Yearbooks see KJC4441.3
4444.8	Conferences. Symposia
4444.9	Surveys on legal activities concerning unification, harmonization, cooperation, etc. Annual (official) reports
4445	General works. Treatises
4447	Revision and amending process (Table K8)
5034	Interpretation and construction (Table K8)
	Constitutional principles
5036	General works
5041	Legitimacy (Table K8)
5044	Legality (Table K8)
	Rule of law see KJC4426
5048	Centralization of power (Table K8)
	Separation and delegation of power
5049	General (Table K8)
5051	Incompatibility of offices. Conflict of interests. Ethics in government (Table K8)
5052	Executive privilege (Table K8)
5053	Judicial review of legislative acts (Table K8)
5054	Privileges of classes and particular groups (Table K8)
5054.5	Privileges, prerogatives, and immunities of states or estates (Table K8)
	Sources and relationships of the law
5057	International law and municipal law. Treaties and agreements (Table K8)
5059	Constitutional aspects of international cooperation, membership in supranational organizations, etc. (Table K8)
	Statutory law and delegated legislation
	Including statutory orders and skeleton laws
5063	General (Table K8)

Constitutional law
Sources and relationships of the law
Statutory law and delegated legislation
5066   Retroactivity (Table K8)
5068   Repeal of legislation (Table K8)
5069   Hierarchy of laws (Table K8)
5070   Customary law. Observance (Table K8)
5075   Intergovernmental relations. Jurisdiction (Table K8)
5095   Territory (Table K8)
                    Including boundary disputes
                Foreign relations
5105   General (Table K8)
                    Foreign service see KJC5445.F67
5107   Executive agreements (Table K8)
                    Foreign assistance programs see KJC6435
5110   Neutrality (Table K8)
5112.A-Z   Other topics, A-Z
                    Subarrange each by Table K12
                Individual and state
                Nationality and citizenship
5114   General (Table K8)
5119   Naturalization and immigration (Table K8)
                    For procedure see KJC6044
5120   Expatriation (Table K8)
                    Emigration see KJC6048
                    Statelessness see KJC979.R43
5126.A-Z   Particular groups, A-Z
                    Subarrange each by Table K12
5132   Human rights. Civil and political rights (Table K8)
5135   European Commission of Human Rights (Table K15)
5138   European Court of Human Rights (Table K15)
                Equality before the law. Antidiscrimination
5142   General (Table K8)
5144.A-Z   Groups discriminated against, A-Z
5144.G39   Gays (Table K12)
                    Jews see KJC5144.M56
5144.M56   Minorities (Ethnic, religious, racial) (Table K12)
5144.W65   Women (Table K12)
5146.A-Z   Special topics, A-Z
                    Culture and language see KJC5146.L36
5146.L36   Language and culture
                        For language regulation in general see KJC6265
                Freedom
5149   General (Table K8)
5154   Freedom of expression (Table K8)
5156   Freedom of religion and conscience (Table K8)

Constitutional law
Organs of government
The legislature. Legislative power
Legislative process -- Continued

5364	Lobbying (Table K8)
5369	Legislators (Table K8)

Including immunity, indemnity, incompatibility, etc.
Heads of state and government. Chef de l'Etat

5379	General (Table K8)

Kings and other rulers

5380	General (Table K8)
5381.A-Z	Special topics, A-Z
5381.A23	Abdication (Table K12)

Prerogatives and privileges see KJC5396+

5381.S92	Succession to the crown (Table K12)

Presidents

5392	General (Table K8)
5393.A-Z	Special topics, A-Z
5393.I57	Impeachment (Table K12)

Prerogatives and powers. Privileges

5396	General (Table K8)
5397.A-Z	Special topics, A-Z
5397.T73	Treatymaking power (Table K12)
5397.V47	Veto power (Table K12)
5397.W37	War and emergency power (Table K12)

Form and structure of governments

5407	General (Table K8)

Monarchy

5408	General (Table K8)

Kings, princes, and other rulers see KJC5380+

5409	Nobility. Dynasties (Table K8)

Including dynastic rules, privileges, prerogatives, and
immunities
Representative government. Régime parlementaire

5412	General (Table K8)
5413	Federal government. Federal republic (Table K8)

Including federal and state relations, jurisdiction, and
interstate compacts

5415	Peoples' republic. Socialist state (Table K8)
5416.A-Z	Special topics, A-Z
5416.C32	Cabinet system. Ministerial responsibility (Table K12)
5416.E95	Executive departments. Ministries (Table K12)

Ministerial responsibility see KJC5416.C32
Ministries see KJC5416.E95

5416.S65	Special boards, commissions, bureaus, task forces, etc. (Table K12)

Constitutional law
  Organs of government
    Heads of state and government. Chef de l'Etat
      Form and structure of governments -- Continued
5445.A-Z	Particular branches of government, A-Z
5445.F67	Foreign service (Table K12)
5456	Constitutional courts and procedure (Table K8)
	Economic constitution see KJC6417
5515	Colonial law

    Class here general and comprehensive works on colonial law
    For works on the laws of the colonies or former colonies of a
      particular country, see the subclass for the country
    For works on the law of a particular colony, see the colony or
      successor state
  Secular ecclesiastical law
    Treaties between church and state. Concordats (Catholic
      Church) and contracts (Protestant Church)
      Including related material

5520	Collections. Compilations
5527	General (Table K8)
	Administrative law
5571	General (Table K8)
	Administrative principles
5586	Rule of law (Table K8)
5587	Autonomy. Rulemaking power (Table K8)
	Limitation and freedom of administration
5588	General (Table K8)
	Abuse of administrative power. Ombudsman see KJC5630
	Administrative process
5607	General (Table K8)
5608	Acts of government (Table K8)
	Administrative acts
5610	General (Table K8)
	Judicial review see KJC5647
5630	Ombudsman. Control over abuse of administrative power (Table K8)
	Legal transactions
5631	General (Table K8)
5632	Public contracts. Government contracts. Government purchasing (Table K8)
5647	Administrative courts and procedure. Judicial review (Table K8)
	Indemnification for acts performed by government
5675	General (Table K8)
	Eminent domain. Expropriation

Administrative law
  Indemnification for acts performed by government
    Eminent domain. Expropriation -- Continued

5772	General (Table K8)
5775	Nationalization (Table K8)
5782	Necessity compensation. Compensation for individual sacrifice (Table K8)
5786	Government liability (Table K8)

  Administrative organization

5794	General (Table K8)
5807	Juristic persons of public law (Table K8)

    Administrative departments of the central government

5850	General (Table K8)
5855	Department of the Interior (Table K8)

    Administrative departments of states, provinces, etc.

5866	General (Table K8)

      Local government

5873	General (Table K8)
5875	State supervision (Table K8)
5877	Municipal government (Table K8)

      Supramunicipal corporations and cooperation.
        Transfrontier cooperation

5880	General (Table K8)
5881	Congress of Local and Regional Authorities of Europe (Table K15)
5882	Council of European Municipalities. Conseil des communes d'Europe. Rat der Gemeinden Europas (Table K15)

  Civil service

5932	General (Table K8)

  Labor law
    Including collective labor law

5958	General (Table K8)

    Labor-management relations

5958.3	General (Table K8)
5960	Collective labor disputes. Strikes (Table K8)

  Police and public safety

5977	General (Table K8)

    Organization and administration

5987	General (Table K8)
5988	Licenses, concessions, and permits (Table K8)

    Public safety

6009	General (Table K8)
6010	Weapons. Explosives (Table K8)

      Including manufacturing, import, and trade of firearms and ammunition

	Police and public safety
	Public safety -- Continued
	Hazardous articles and processes
	Including transportation by land
6011	General (Table K8)
6012	Nuclear power. Reactors. Protection against radiation (Table K8)
	Including nuclear waste disposal
	Cf. KJC1692 Delicts
	Control of individuals
6032	General (Table K8)
	Identification and registration
6034	General (Table K8)
6038	Identity cards (Table K8)
6040	Passports (Table K8)
6044	Immigration and naturalization (Table K8)
6048	Emigration (Table K8)
	Particular groups
	Aliens
6050	General (Table K8)
6056	Alien laborers. Migrant workers (Table K8)
6057	Refugees (Table K8)
	Particular activities
6061	Traveling. Tourism (Table K8)
	Social activities
6063	Sports (Table K8)
6065.A-Z	Other, A-Z
6065.G35	Gambling (Table K12)
	Including lotteries, games of chance, etc.
6066.A-Z	Other, A-Z
	Begging see KJC6066.V34
6066.S85	Sumptuary laws (Table K12)
6066.V34	Vagrancy. Begging (Table K12)
	Public property. Domaine public. Public restraint on private property
6068	General (Table K8)
	Government property. Powers and control
6070	General (Table K8)
6071	Records management. Access to public records (Table K8)
	Including data bases and general data protection
	For violation of privacy see KJC1682
6076	Expropriation. Nationalization (Table K8)
	For government-owned business enterprises see KJC2635
	For indemnification see KJC5772+

	Public property. Domaine public. Public restraint on private property -- Continued
	Conservation of natural resources. Environmental planning see KJC6243
6079	Roads and highways (Table K8)
	Water resources
6094	General (Table K8)
6099	Development and conservation of water resources (Table K8)
	Including water registers
	Protection against pollution see KJC6245
6116.A-Z	Particular bodies of water, river basins, etc., A-Z
6116.C65	Lake Constance (Table K12)
6116.D35	Danube River (Table K12)
6117.A-Z	Particular districts, A-Z
	Subarrange each by Table K12
	Shore protection. Coastal zone management see KJC6244
	Public land law. Land use
6127	General (Table K8)
6130	Land reform and land policy legislation (Table K8)
	For agricultural land law see KJC6593+
	Regional planning
6135	General (Table K8)
6138	Ecological aspects (Table K8)
	City planning and redevelopment
6140	General (Table K8)
6145	Zoning (Table K8)
6155	Building laws (Table K8)
	Public health
6172	General (Table K8)
6178	Contagious and infectious diseases (Table K8)
6187.A-Z	Other public health hazards and measures, A-Z
6187.C35	Camping hygiene (Table K12)
6187.R44	Refuse disposal (Table K12)
6191	Drug laws (Table K8)
6202.A-Z	Special topics, A-Z
	Medical legislation
6206	General (Table K8)
	The health professions
6208	Physicians in general (Table K8)
6210.A-Z	Particular branches of medicine, A-Z
6210.A53	Anesthesiologists (Table K12)
6222	Hospitals and other medical institutions or health services (Table K8)
6226	Institutions for the mentally ill (Table K8)

KJC

Medical legislation -- Continued
   Biomedical engineering. Medical technology
     Including human experimentation in medicine and genetic
     engineering

6227	General (Table K8)
6227.5	Transplantation of organs, tissues, etc. (Table K8)
6228	Human reproductive technology (Table K8)

       Including artificial insemination and fertilization in vitro
       Cf. KJC1229 Family law

6229.A-Z	Special topics, A-Z
6229.E95	Euthanasia. Right to die. Living wills (Table K12)
(6229.G45)	Genetics

       see KJC6227
     Living wills see KJC6229.E95
     Medical devices see KJC6229.M42

6229.M42	Medical instruments and apparatus. Medical devices (Table K12)
6229.R43	Records, Medical (Table K12)

       Including hospital records
     Right to die see KJC6229.E95

6236	Veterinary medicine and hygiene (Table K8)
6237	Prevention of cruelty to animals (Table K8)

   Environmental law

6242	General (Table K8)
6242.5	European Council on Environmental Law (Table K8)
6243	Environmental planning. Conservation of natural resources (Table K8)
6244	Shore protection. Coastal zone management (Table K8)
6245	Environmental pollution (Table K8)
6249	Air pollution (Table K8)

     Water and groundwater pollution
       Including drainage, infiltration, and sewage control

6251	General (Table K8)

     Convention for the Protection of the Mediterranean Sea
       against Pollution ("Barcelona Convention") see
       K3592.93.A41976

6252.A-Z	Pollutants, A-Z
6252.R33	Radioactive substances (Table K12)
6253	Noise control (Table K8)
6254	Recycling of refuse (Table K8)

   Wilderness preservation

6255	General (Table K8)
6256	Wildlife conservation (Table K8)

       Including game, birds, and fish
       For game laws see KJC6681
       For fishery laws see KJC6695+

	Cultural affairs
6257	General (Table K8)
6265	Language (Table K8)
	Including regulation of use, purity, etc.
	Education
6266	General (Table K8)
6275	Religion in public schools (Table K8)
	Including religious instruction and exercise of freedom of religion by students and school employees
6300	Vocational education (Table K8)
	Higher education. Universities
6313	General (Table K8)
	Administration. Institutional management in higher education
6314	General (Table K8, modified)
	Intergovernmental congresses and conferences
	Including proceedings, reports, resolutions, final acts, and works on the congress
6314.A3-.A339	Ad hoc congresses of heads of state. By name of the congress (alphabetically)

Under each:
.xA12-.xA199   Serials
.xA3   Monographs. By date

6314.A333	Standing Conference of Rectors and Vice-Chancellors of the European Universities
6317	Entrance requirements (Table K8)
6318	Academic degrees. International recognition (Table K8)
6341	Adult education (Table K8)
	Science and the arts. Research
6344	General (Table K8)
6345	Public policies in research
	Including research in higher institutions
	Public institutions
6346	General (Table K8)
6347.A-Z	Academies. By name, A-Z
6352.A-Z	Branches and subjects, A-Z
	The arts
6353	General (Table K8)
6354	Fine arts (Table K8)
6405	Historic buildings and monuments. Architectural landmarks
	Including vessels, battleships, archaeological sites, etc.
	Economic law
6411-6415	General (Table K7)
6417	Economic constitution (Table K8)
	Government control and policy

	Economic law
	Government control and policy -- Continued
6428	General (Table K8)
6430	Economic cooperation and integration (Table K8)
	Class here general works
	For the European Economic Community see KJC6411+
	For COMECON see KJE801+
	Foreign investment
	Cf. KJE2449 Foreign corporations. Multinational corporations and business enterprises
6433	General (Table K8)
6434	Government guaranties (Table K8)
	Foreign exchange regulations see KJC7095
	International capital movement regulations see KJC7097
6435	Assistance to developing countries (Table K8)
	Economic assistance
6436	General (Table K8)
	Agricultural credits see KJC6638
6442	Prices and price control (Table K8)
	Government business enterprises see KJC2635
6449	Licenses. Concessions (Table K8)
	Competition rules. Control of contracts and combinations in restraint of trade
6456	General (Table K8)
	Horizontal and vertical combinations
6465	General (Table K8)
6467	Corporate consolidation, merger, etc. (Table K8)
	Including fusion control
	Cartels
6471	General (Table K8)
6474.A-Z	Types of cartels, A-Z
6474.E96	Export and import cartels (Table K12)
6478	Exclusive dealing or use arrangements. Requirement contracts (Table K8)
6497	Monopolies. Oligopolies. Antitrust law (Table K8)
	Money, currency, and foreign exchange control see KJC7090+
	Standards. Norms. Quality control
	For standards and grading of agricultural or consumer products, see the product
6554	General (Table K8)
6556	Weights and measures. Containers (Table K8)
	Standardization
6558	General (Table K8)
6559	Engineering standards (Table K8)

Economic law -- Continued

6564   Labeling (Table K8)
             For labeling of particular products, see the product

         Regulation of industry, trade, and commerce

6569   General (Table K8)

6577   Consumer protection (Table K8)

6580   Advertising (Table K8)

         Primary production. Extractive industries

          Agriculture. Forestry. Horticulture. Viticulture

6590   General (Table K8)

           Land reform and agrarian land policy legislation
             Including restraint on alienation of agricultural land

6593   General (Table K8)

6598   Consolidation of landholdings. Commassation (Table K8)

6600   Conservation of agricultural and forestry lands (Table K8)
             Including soil conservation, field irrigation, erosion control

6612   Control of pests and plant diseases. Plant health regulation (Table K8)
             Including ecological aspects

6613   Entail (Table K8)
           Entailed estates of the greater nobility see KJC1319+

          Agricultural contracts

6622   General (Table K8)

6624   Lease of rural property (Table K8)

          Agricultural business enterprises. Corporate structure

6630   General (Table K8)

6636   Cooperatives (Table K8)
             Including producers and marketing cooperatives

          Marketing orders

6637   General (Table K8)

6638   Economic assistance (Table K8)
             Including agricultural credits production and control, price support, etc.

6646   Standards and grading (Table K8)

6648   Importing and stockpiling (Table K8)

6663.A-Z   Industries or products, A-Z
           Eggs see KJC6663.P68

6663.F63   Fodder and grain (Table K12)
           Grain see KJC6663.F63

6663.M54   Milk production (Table K12)

6663.P68   Poultry. Eggs (Table K12)

6663.S45   Sheep farming (Table K12)

6663.T55   Timber industry (Table K12)

Economic law
Regulation of industry, trade, and commerce
Primary production. Extractive industries
Agriculture. Forestry. Horticulture. Viticulture
Industries or products, A-Z -- Continued

6663.W55	Winemaking (Table K12)
6674	Apiculture. Beekeeping (Table K8)
6681	Game laws (Table K8)
	Including ecological aspects
	Fisheries
6695	General (Table K8)
6695.5	Conservation. Ecological aspects (Table K8)
6696.5.A-Z	By high sea region, A-Z
	Subarrange each by Table K12
6697.A-Z	By fish or marine fauna, A-Z
	Subarrange each by Table K12
	Mining. Quarrying
6700	General (Table K8)
6720	Petroleum (Table K8)
	Including offshore petroleum
	Manufacturing industries
	Including light and heavy industries
6739	General (Table K8)
6743.A-Z	Types of manufacture, A-Z
6743.F47	Fertilizer industry (Table K12)
6743.T48	Textile industry (Table K12)
	Food processing industries. Food products
6750	General (Table K8)
6751	Labeling (Table K8)
6752	Purity (Table K8)
	Including regulation of adulteration and additives
6754.A-Z	Particular industries or products, A-Z
	Confectionary industry see KJC6754.S93
6754.S93	Sugar. Sugared goods (Table K8)
	Including the confectionary industry
	Building and construction industry
	For building laws see KJC6155
6786	General (Table K8)
6788	Contracts and specifications (Table K8)
	Including liability
	International trade
6791	General (Table K8)
	Export and import controls
6792	General (Table K8)
	Foreign exchange regulation see KJC7095
	Trade agreements see KJC6791+

Economic law

Regulation of industry, trade, and commerce

International trade

Export and import controls -- Continued

6795.A-Z	Particular products, A-Z
6795.P74	Precious metals (Table K12)
6799	Domestic trade (Table K8)
6800	Wholesale trade (Table K8)
	Retail trade
6802	General (Table K8)
	Conditions of trading
6804	Sunday legislation (Table K8)
6808.A-Z	Modes of trading
	Subarrange each by Table K12
6810.A-Z	Particular products, A-Z
6810.P47	Perfume (Table K12)
6819	Service trades (Table K8)
6830	Artisans (Table K8)
	Energy policy. Power supply
	Including publicly and privately owned public utilities
6848	General (Table K8)
	Particular sources of power
6852	Electricity (Table K8)
6854	Gas. Natural gas (Table K8)
6858	Atomic energy (Table K8)
	For protection from radiation see KJC6012
	For ecological aspects see KJC6252.R33
	Transportation
6868	General (Table K8)
	Road traffic. Automotive transportation
6871-6875	General (Table K7)
	Motor vehicles
6877	General (Table K8)
6878	Registration (Table K8)
6881	Drivers' licenses (Table K8)
	Including driving schools and instructors
6882	Compulsory insurance (Table K8)
	Traffic regulations and enforcement
6885	General (Table K8)
	Traffic accidents see KJC1708
6887	Traffic violations (Table K8)
6893	Highway safety (Table K8)
6897	Carriage of passengers and goods (Table K8)
6903	Railroads (Table K8)
6919	Pipelines (Table K8)
6920	Aviation. Air law (Table K8)

	Transportation -- Continued
6925	Space law (Table K8)
	Water transportation
6927	General (Table K8)
6939	Coastwise and inland shipping (Table K8)
	Communication. Mass media
6946	General (Table K8)
6947	Constitutional aspects. Freedom of communication (Table K8)
	Postal services. Telecommunication
	For intergovernmental congresses and conventions of the Universal Postal Union (UPU) see K4247+
6950	General (Table K8)
6951	Classification of mail. Rates (Table K8)
6957	Airmail (Table K8)
6958	Registered mail (Table K8)
6959.A-Z	Particular services, A-Z
	Subarrange each by Table K12
	Telecommunication
6964	General (Table K8)
6968	Telegraph (Table K8)
6970	Teletype and data transmission systems. Transnational data flow (Table K8)
	For data protection see KJC1682
6972	Telephone (Table K8)
	Radio and television communication
6976	General (Table K8)
6989	Stations. Networks (Table K8)
	Including frequency allocation and licensing
6995	Broadcasting (Table K8)
	Criminal provisions
7000	General (Table K8)
7002	Pirate stations. Illegal operation of a station (Table K8)
	Press law
7005	General (Table K8)
	Freedom of the press and censorship see KJC6947
7012	Journalists. Correspondents (Table K8)
7015	Horizontal and vertical combinations. Concentration (Table K8)
7016	Right to obtain retraction or restatement of acts (or an opportunity to reply) (Table K8)
7018	Press and criminal justice (Table K8)
	Professions
7032	General (Table K8)
7033	Professional associations (Table K8)
	Individual professions

	Professions
	Individual professions -- Continued
	Health professions see KJC6208+
	Lawyers see KJC3770
	Pharmacists see KJC6191
	Veterinarians see KJC6236
7035	Economic and financial advisors (Table K8)
	Engineering and construction professions
7039	Architects (Table K8)
7045.A-Z	Other professions, A-Z
	Subarrange each by Table K12
7047	Professional ethics. Courts of honor (Table K8)
	Public finance
7049	General (Table K8)
	Finance reform and policies
7050	General (Table K8)
	Monetary policies see KJE7098+
	Organization and administration
	Budget. Government expenditures
7076	General (Table K8)
	Accounting
7077	General (Table K8)
7080	Funds administration (Table K8)
	Expenditure control. Auditing
7082	General (Table K8)
7083	Financial courts (Table K8)
	Public debts
	Including war debts
7085	General (Table K8)
	External debts. International loan agreements
7087	General (Table K8)
7088	European Bank for Reconstruction and Development (Table K8)
	International Bank for Reconstruction and Development see K4451
	Money
7090	General (Table K8)
7092	Bank notes. Banks of issue (Table K8)
7093	Gold trading and gold standard (Table K8)
7094	Currency reforms. Revalorization of debts (Table K8)
7095	Foreign exchange regulation (Table K8)
7097	International capital movement regulations (Table K8)
	National revenue
7098	General (Table K8)
	Taxation
7101-7105	General (Table K7)

Public finance
National revenue
Taxation -- Continued

7114	Double taxation (Table K8)
7118	Taxation as a measure of social or economic policy (Table K8)
7127	Taxation of special activities (Table K8)
7128	Tax saving. Tax avoidance (Table K8)
	Tax administration
7130	General (Table K8)
7136	Collection and enforcement (Table K8)
7161.A-Z	Classes of taxpayers or lines of businesses, A-Z
7161.A45	Aliens (Table K12)
7161.F35	Families (Table K12)
	Income tax
7163	General (Table K8)
7169	Taxable income. Exemptions (Table K8)
	Including profits and capital gains
7174	Deductions (Table K8)
7187	Capital investment (Table K8)
7196.A-Z	Classes of taxpayers or lines of businesses, A-Z
	Subarrange each by Table K12
	Corporation tax
7198	General (Table K8)
7200	Nonprofit associations and corporations (Table K8)
7204	Personal companies (Unincorporated business associations) (Table K8)
7207	Cooperative societies (Table K8)
	Stock companies (Incorporated business associations)
7210	General (Table K8)
7237	Corporate reorganization (Table K8)
7257.A-Z	Lines of corporate businesses, A-Z
7257.I57	Insurance (Table K12)
7258	Foreign corporations (Table K8)
7259	Multinational corporations (Table K8)
	Property tax and taxation of capital
7261	General (Table K8)
7262	Real property tax (Table K8)
7264	Estate, inheritance, and gift taxes (Table K8)
7266	Church tax (Table K8)
7267	Capital gains tax (Table K8)
	Surtaxes
7268	General (Table K8)
7268.5	Excess profits tax (Table K8)
	Excise taxes

	Public finance
	National revenue
	Taxation
	Excise taxes -- Continued
7284	General (Table K8)
7285	Sales taxes (Table K8)
	Including turnover tax and value-added tax
7306	Commodities, services, and transactions (Table K8)
	Methods of assessment and collection
	For assessment and collection of a particular tax, see the tax
7308	General (Table K8)
7309	Stamp duties (Table K8)
	Customs. Tariff
	History
	Including customs union movement
7312	General (Table K8)
7313	Customs Union Study Group (Table K8)
	Trade agreements. Individual tariffs
	Including favored nation clause and reciprocity
7315	General (Table K8, modified)
	Intergovernmental congresses and conferences
	By name of the congress
	Contracting parties to the General Agreement on Tariffs and Trade see K4609.5
7316.A-Z	Trade agreements and tariffs limited to a special commodity. By commodity, A-Z
	Subarrange each by Table K12
7318	Customs administration (Table K8)
7346	Tariff preferences. Generalized system of preferences. Preferential treatment (Table K8)
	Criminal provisions see KJC7475+
	State and local finance
7350	General (Table K8)
	Taxation
7358	General (Table K8)
7358.A-Z	Particular taxes, A-Z
7358.B88	Business tax (Table K12)
7358.P64	Poll tax (Table K12)
7358.P75	Property tax (Table K12)
7358.R42	Real property tax (Table K12)
7431-7435	Tax and customs courts and procedure (Table K7)
	Tax and customs crimes and delinquency
7475	General (Table K8)
7495.A-Z	Individual offenses, A-Z
	Subarrange each by Table K12

	Government measures in time of war, national emergency, or economic crisis
7520	General (Table K8)
7521.A-Z	Special topics, A-Z
	Allocations see KJC7521.I53
	Confiscations see KJC7521.E53
7521.E53	Enemy property. Confiscations (Table K12)
7521.I53	Industrial priorities and allocations (Table K12)
	Including economic recovery measures and nationalization
7521.R42	Reconstruction (Table K12)
7521.R48	Restitution (Table K12)
	War debts see KJC7085+
	National defense. Military law
7690	General (Table K8)
	The armed forces
7708	General (Table K8)
7710	Compulsory service (Table K8)
	Including draft and selective services
	Deferment
	Including disqualification and exemptions
7714	General (Table K8)
7716.A-Z	Particular groups, A-Z
7716.C65	Conscientious objectors (Table K12)
7806	Civil defense (Table K8)
	Military criminal law and procedure
7830	General (Table K8)
7860.A-Z	Particular crimes, A-Z
	Subarrange each by Table K12
7900	Military courts (Table K8)
7925	Military discipline (Table K8)
	Criminal law
	History
7962	General works
7964.A-Z	Special topics not otherwise provided for, A-Z
7964.W58	Witchcraft (Table K12)
7967	Reform of criminal law, procedure, and execution (Table K8)
	Including reform of criminal justice administration
	For works limited to a particular subject, see the subject
	Administration of criminal justice see KJC9430+
7971-7975	General (Table K7)
	Philosophy of criminal law
7994	General works
	Theories of punishment and particular schools of thought see KJC8233
7996	Ideological theories of criminal law
	Including Fascism, Nazism, etc.

Criminal law
Punishment -- Continued
Sentencing. Determining the measure of punishment
8304   General (Table K8)
8310   Circumstances influencing measures of penalty (Table K8)
       Juvenile delinquents see KJC9651+
       Causes barring prosecution or execution of sentence
8322   General (Table K8)
8328   Pardon and amnesty (Table K8)
8338   Limitation of actions (Table K8)
       Including exemptions, e.g. in cases of crimes against humanity
       Individual offenses
       Offenses against the person
       Including aggravating circumstances
8356   Homicide (Table K8)
8357.A-Z   Particular offenses, A-Z
8357.D46   Desertion. Exposing persons to mortal danger (Table K12)
8357.E96   Euthanasia (Table K12)
       Exposing persons to mortal danger see KJC8357.D46
8357.S84   Suicide (Table K12)
8377   Crimes against inchoate life (Table K8)
       Including abortion and justified abortion
8384   Crimes against physical inviolability (Table K8)
8385.A-Z   Particular offenses, A-Z
8385.P64   Poisoning (Table K12)
8410   Criminal aspects of surgical and other medical treatment (Table K8)
8411.A-Z   Particular offenses, A-Z
       Subarrange each by Table K12
8490   Violation of personal privacy and secrets
       Offenses against moral order
       Including aggravating circumstances
8550   Sexual crimes (Table K8)
8551.A-Z   Particular offenses, A-Z
       Subarrange each by Table K12
8551.C45   Child sexual abuse. Lewd acts with children or charges (Table K12)
8551.O26   Obscenity. Pornography (Table K12)
       Pornography see KJC8551.O26
8551.P75   Prostitution (Table K12)
8643   Offenses against property (Table K8)
       Including aggravating circumstances

Criminal law
Individual offenses
Offenses against property -- Continued

Offenses against public order and convenience
Including aggravating circumstances

Crimes against the peace of the community
Including terrorism

Crimes affecting traffic

Criminal courts and procedure
For criticism and reform see KJC7967
For works on both criminal law and procedure see
    KJC7971+
History

	Criminal courts and procedure
	History
	Special topics not otherwise provided for, A-Z -- Continued
9400.5.I57	Inquisition (Table K12)
	Ordeal see KJC1018+
9400.5.T67	Torture (Table K12)
9401-9405	General (Table K7)
	Administration of criminal justice
	For criticism and reform see KJC7967
9430	General (Table K8)
	Judicial statistics see KJC61+
	Judicial assistance see KJC3795+
	Criminal policy see KJC8233
	Court organization
9440	General (Table K8)
9455	Courts of assizes. Juries (Table K8)
	Procedural principles
9485	Due process of law (Table K8)
9488	Uniformity of law application. Stare decisis (Table K8)
9494	Accusation principle (Table K8)
9503	Principles of defense. Equality (Table K8)
9504	Publicity and oral procedure (Table K8)
9506	Speedy trial (Table K8)
9520	Denunciation. Informers
	Pretrial procedures
9525	General (Table K8)
9529	Investigation (Table K8)
	For techniques of criminal investigation see HV8073+
	For forensic medicine, chemistry, toxicology, etc. see RA1001+
9538	Public charges by prosecutor (Table K8)
	Compulsory measures against the accused. Securing of evidence
9550	General (Table K8)
9552	Arrest and commitment (Table K8)
	Including preventive detention
9570	Extradition (Table K8)
	Procedure at first instance
9574	General (Table K8)
9576	Jurisdiction (Table K8)
	Including competence in subject matter and venue
	Trial
9595	General (Table K8)
	Evidence
9597	General (Table K8)
9601	Burden of proof (Table K8)

	Criminal courts and procedure
	Procedure at first instance
	Trial
	Evidence -- Continued
	Admission of evidence
9604	General (Table K8)
9616	Electronic listening and recording devices (Table K8)
	Including wiretapping
	Witnesses
9619	General (Table K8)
9622.A-Z	Privileged witnesses (Confidential communication), A-Z
9622.A86	Attorney and client (Table K12)
	Client and attorney see KJC9622.A86
9622.P45	Physicians (Table K12)
9625	Expert testimony (Table K8)
	For forensic medicine, chemistry, psychology, psychiatry, etc. see RA1001+
9636	Testimony of the accused (Table K8)
9639	Circumstantial evidence (Table K8)
	Particular proceedings
9646	Summary proceedings (Table K8)
	Procedure at juvenile courts
9651-9655	General (Table K7)
9656	The juvenile delinquent (Table K8)
9662	Punishment. Correctional or disciplinary measures (Table K8)
	Judicial decisions
9674	General (Table K8)
9698	Res judicata (Table K8)
9701	Court records (Table K8)
	Participation of injured party in criminal procedures
9705	General (Table K8)
9712	Civil suits of victims in connection with criminal proceedings (Table K8)
	Including reparation (compensation to victims of crimes)
9728.A-Z	Particular remedies, A-Z
	Subarrange each by Table K12
9756	Post-conviction remedies (Table K8)
	Execution of sentence
	Criticism and reform see KJC7967
9760	General (Table K8)
9769	Imprisonment (Table K8)
9790	Suspension of punishment (Table K8)
9791	Restitution (Table K8)
9792	Probation. Parole (Table K8)

KJE

	Regional organization other than the European Community or European Union -- Continued
501-549	Benelux Economic Union. Union economique Benelux. Wirtschaftsunion BENELUX, 1958 (Table KJ-KKZ7)
551-599	European Free Trade Association. Association europeenne de libre echange. Europäische Freihandelszone (EFTA), 1960 (Table KJ-KKZ7)
	FINEFTA see KJE551+
601-649	European Economic Area, 1992 (Table KJ-KKZ7)
	Council for Mutual Economic Assistance. Conseil d'assistance economique mutuelle. Rat für Gegenseitige Wirtschaftshilfe (COMECON). Law of socialist economic integration
801	Bibliography
<803>	Periodicals
804	Monographic series
805	Official gazettes
806	Legislative and executive papers. Documentation
	Official acts
807	Indexes and tables
807.2	Collections. Compilations. By date
	Treaties and other international agreements
	Treaties (individual and collections) establishing or expanding the organization see KJE833+
808	Indexes
809	Collections. By date
	Including either multilateral or bilateral treaties or both and including treaties concluded by COMECON with other European regional organizations
	Individual treaties
	see the appropriate subject in KJE
	Legislation and legal matters
	Including decisions, general conditions, recommendations, etc.
810	Indexes and tables
811	Abridgments and digests
	Collections
812	Serials
813	Monographs. By date
	Individual measures
	see the appropriate subject in KJE
814	Court decisions and related materials
	For decisions and materials on a particular subject, see the subject
815	Dictionaries. Encyclopedias
816	Directories

	Regional organization other than the European Community or European Union
	Council for Mutual Economic Assistance. Conseil d'assistance économique mutuelle. Rat für Gegenseitige Wirtschaftshilfe (COMECON). Law of socialist economic integration -- Continued
817	Congresses. Conferences. By date of the congress
	Academies. Institutes. By name, A-Z
818.I56	International Institute of Economic Problems of the World Socialist System
821	General works
	Including compends, essays, festschriften, etc.
	Theory and methodology of socialist economic law and integration
822	General (Table K14)
	Standing congresses, conferences, etc. devoted to economic integration
822.5	Meeting of Representatives of COMECON Member Countries on Legal Questions
	Other meetings
	For other meetings, see the appropriate subject
822.7	Member nations and economic integration
	Comprehensive Program for the Intensification and Improvement of Cooperation and the Development of Socialist Economic Integration of COMECON Member Countries (1971) see KJE833.A351971
	Other meetings
	For other meetings, see the appropriate subject
824	Private law
	Civil law
824.5	General (Table K14)
824.6	Property and socialist property
	Obligations and contracts
825	General (Table K14)
825.2	Nonperformance. Damages (Table K14)
825.5	Banks. Credit (Table K14)
	Intellectual and industrial property
827	General (Table K14)
	Patent law and trademarks
828	General (Table K14)
828.5	Meeting of Heads of Invention Departments of COMECON Member Countries (Table K15)
	Labor law
829	General (Table K14)
829.5	Meetings of Heads of State Labor Agencies of COMECON Member Countries (Table K15)

Regional organization other than the European Community
    Council for Mutual Economic Assistance. Conseil
        d'assistance économique mutuelle. Rat für Gegenseitige
        Wirtschaftshilfe (COMECON). Law of socialist economic
        integration
      Organization law. Constitution of the Council of Mutual
        Economic Assistance
      Other official acts and legal measures
        Regulations and decisions -- Continued
          Collections. Selections
            Including annotated editions

833.A4	Serials
833.A42	Monographs. By date
833.A43<date>	Individual acts (or groups of acts adopted as a whole)

            Arrange chronologically by appending date of original
              enactment or revision of the law to the number
              KJE833.A43 and deleting any trailing zeros
            Under each:

              .xA2   *Working documents. Official*
                                     records. By date
                                      Including reports and
                                        memoranda of factfinding,
                                        advisory, research, and
                                        drafting committees, etc., and
                                        drafts
              .xA7   *Unannotated editions. By date*
                                      Including official editions with or
                                      without annotation
              .xA8-.xZ8   *Annotated editions. Commentaries.*
                                   General works

833.A5	Opinions. Recommendations

           Including action programs, consultations, target studies,
             etc.
      Administrative decisions see KJE833.A9+

833.A7	Court decisions and related materials. Reports
833.A72	Surveys on legal activity concerning unification,

          harmonization, cooperation. Annual (official) reports

833.A8	Conferences. Symposia
833.A9-.Z9	General works. Treatises

      Sources and relationships of the law
        Cf. KJE822+ Theory and methodology
      International cooperation. Membership in international
        organizations, etc.

834	General works
834.5.A-Z	Particular organizations. By name, A-Z

        European Communities see KJE5062.C68

Regional organization other than the European Community or European Union

Council for Mutual Economic Assistance. Conseil d'assistance économique mutuelle. Rat für Gegenseitige Wirtschaftshilfe (COMECON). Law of socialist economic integration

Organization law. Constitution of the Council of Mutual Economic Assistance -- Continued

Intergovernmental relations. Relations between the Council and member states

835	General works
835.3	Accession of new member states

Foreign (External) relations. International cooperation

For treaties and other international agreements, see the appropriate subject

836	General works
836.5	Cooperation of Foreign Ministers. Conferences and meetings

For conferences and meetings on a particular subject, see the subject

837	Treatymaking power

Relations with associated states

838	General works
838.2	Limited participation (Yugoslavia)
838.3	Cooperant status (Finland, Iraq, Mexico)
838.4	Observer status
838.5	Membership in CMEA-affiliated organizations
838.7	Relations with other non-member states. Extra-COMECON relations
838.8	Relations with developing countries

Cf. KJE862 Assistance to developing countries

Organs and institutions of the Council of Mutual Economic Assistance. Institutional framework of socialist economic integration

For individual committees, commissions, and other bodies with jurisdiction limited to a particular subject, see the appropriate subject

839	General works
839.2	Rules governing the language of the organs
839.5	Conference of the First Secretaries of Communist and Workers' Parties, and of the Heads of Government of the CMEA Members Countries

Assembly (Session) of the Council

840	General (Table K15)
840.2	Powers and duties

Executive Committee

Regional organization other than the European Community or
European Union
Council for Mutual Economic Assistance. Conseil
d'assistance économique mutuelle. Rat für Gegenseitige
Wirtschaftshilfe (COMECON). Law of socialist economic
integration
Organs and institutions of the Council of Mutual Economic
Assistance. Institutional framework of socialist
economic integration
Executive Committee -- Continued

841	General (Table K15)
841.5	Powers and duties
841.7	Secretariat (Table K15)
842	Council Committees
842.3	Permanent Commissions of the Council
842.4	Standing conferences. Permanent meetings of the Council

Indemnification for acts performed by government

843	General (Table K14)
843.4	Government liability (Table K14)

    For contractual liability see KJE825.2

Civil service

844	General (Table K14)
844.2	Privileges and immunities (Table K14)
844.3	Appointment (Table K14)
844.4	Conditions of employment (Table K14)
844.6	Remuneration. Allowances (Table K14)
844.8	Retirement (Table K14)

Socialist public property. Public restraint on private
property

846	General (Table K14)

Water resources

847	General (Table K14)
847.5	Meeting of Heads of Water Agencies of COMECON Member Countries (Table K15)

Medical legislation

848	General (Table K14)
849	Veterinary medicine and hygiene (Table K14)

Environmental law

850	General (Table K14)
851	Council for Protection and Improvement of the Environment (Table K15)

Wilderness preservation

852	General (Table K14)
853	Plant protection (Table K14)

Scientific-technical cooperation

Regional organization other than the European Community or
European Union
Council for Mutual Economic Assistance (COMECON). Law
of socialist economic integration
Scientific-technical cooperation -- Continued

854	General (Table K14)
854.2	Committee for Scientific and Technical Cooperation (Table K15)
854.22	International Center of Scientific and Technical Information (Table K15)
854.3	Intergovernmental Commission for Cooperation of Socialist Countries in Computer Technology (Table K15)
854.34	International Laboratory for Strong Magnetic Fields and Low Temperature (Table K15)
854.4	Banach International Mathematics Center (Table K15)
854.55	Center for Heat and Mass Transfer (Table K15)
854.6	Center for Raising the Qualifications of Scientific Cadres in Electron Microscopy (Table K15)
854.8.A-Z	Special topics, A-Z
854.8.O87	Outer space (Table K12)
	Economic law
856	General (Table K14)
	Central planning. Plan coordination
857	General (Table K14)
	Planning agencies and bureaus
857.3	Committee for Cooperation in planning Activities (Table K15)
857.5	Committee for Cooperation in Material-technical supply (Table K15)
858	Long-term target programs of cooperation
859	Concerted plan of multilateral integration measures
	For economic integration in general see KJE822.7
	Investments
	Including foreign investments
860	General (Table K14)
861	International Investment Bank (Table K15)
862	Assistance to developing countries (Table K14)
863	Economic assistance
	Prices and price control
	Class here general works
	For particular industries or products, see the industry or product
864	General (Table K14)
865	Meeting of Heads of Price Departments of COMECON Member Countries (Table K15)

Regional organization other than the European Community or
European Union
Council for Mutual Economic Assistance (COMECON). Law
of socialist economic integration
Economic law -- Continued
Government business enterprises
867 General
869 International Research Institute for Management
Problems (Table K15)
Horizontal and vertical combinations
870 General (Table K14)
871 Joint enterprises. International and multinational
business associations. Branch organizations for
economic cooperation
For individual associations, see the industry
Standards. Norms. Quality control
873 General (Table K15)
873.5 COMECON Institute of Standardization (Table K15)
Particular industries or sectors
Class under each industry or sector works on plan
coordination, trade practices, economic assistance,
and standards
874 Agriculture (Table K14)
Including horticulture and forestry
875 Fisheries (Table K14)
876 Mining (Table K14)
876.9.A-Z Individual resources, A-Z
876.9.P47 Petroleum (Table K12)
Manufacturing industries
877 General (Table K14)
878 Agricultural machinery industry (Table K14)
878.9 International Society for Machines for Vegetable
Growing, Horticulture and Viticulture.
Agromash (Table K15)
879 Automobile industry (Table K14)
880 Chemical industry (Table K14)
880.9 International Economic Association for Chemical
Fibers. Interkhimvolokno (Table K15)
880.92 Organization for Cooperation in Small-Tonnage
Chemical Products (Table K15)
882 Electrical industry (Table K14)
882.9 Central Despatch Administration for Combined
Power Systems (Table K15)

Regional organization other than the European Community or
European Union
Council for Mutual Economic Assistance (COMECON). Law
of socialist economic integration
Economic law
Particular industries or sectors
Manufacturing industries
Electrical industry -- Continued

882.92	International Organization for Economic and Scientific-Technical Cooperation in the Electrical Engineering Industry. Interelektro (Table K15)
883	Iron and steel industry (Table K14)
883.9	Organization for Cooperation in Ferrous Metallurgy (Table K15)
884	Machine industry (Table K14)
884.9	Organization for Cooperation in the Bearing Industry (Table K15)
884.92	Permanent Commission for Machine-Building (Table K15)
885	Nuclear power industry (Table K14)
885.9	Joint Nuclear Research Institute (Table K15)
885.92	International Economic Association for Nuclear Instrument-Building. Interatominstrument (Table K15)
885.93	International Economic Association for the Organization of Cooperation in Production, Deliveries of Equipment, and Rendering Technical Assistance in Building Nuclear Power Stations. Interatomenergy (Table K15)
886	Textile industry (Table K14)
886.9	International Economic Association for the Production of Technological Equipment for the Textile Industry. Interteksti'mash (Table K15)

External trade. Trade with non-member states

887	General (Table K14)

Foreign exchange control see KJE895+
Domestic trade. Intra-COMECON trade

887.5	General (Table K14)
887.7	Meeting of Ministers of Internal Trade of COMECON Member Countries (Table K15)

Transportation

888	General (Table K14)
888.2	Council for Joint Use of Containers in International Transport (Table K15)

Railroads

Regional organization other than the European Community or
European Union
Council for Mutual Economic Assistance (COMECON). Law
of socialist economic integration
Transportation
Railroads -- Continued
888.5   General (Table KJ-KJE13)
888.7   Common Freight Car Pool (Table KJ-KJE15)
888.8   Organization for Railway Cooperation (Table KJ-
KJE15)
Water transportation
889   General (Table K14)
889.3   International Shipowners' Association (Table K15)
889.4   Bureau for the Coordination of the Chartering of
Vessels (Table K15)
Individual waterways, A-Z
889.6.D35   Danube
Including works on the Danube Commission
Communication. Mass media. Information
890   General (Table K14)
Postal services. Telecommunication
891   General (Table K14)
891.2   Organization for Cooperation of Socialist Countries in
Tele- and Postal Communications (Table K15)
891.22   Space Communications Organization. Intersputnik
(Table K15)
Finance. Money
893   General (Table K14)
894   Permanent Commission for Currency and Financial
Questions (Table K15)
Foreign exchange policy. Multilateral payments
895   General (Table K14)
895.2   International Bank for Economic Cooperation (Table
K15)
Budget of the Council for Mutual Economic Assistance
896   General (Table K14)
896.2   Audit Commission (Table K15)
897   Customs. Tariff (Table K14)

KJE

The European Communities. Community law
>Class here supranational European Community or Union law, i. e.
>>secondary legislation and other legal measures binding upon
>>all member states of the European Community or Union
>For comparative works on the law of two or more countries
>>in Europe, including works on legislative cooperation,
>>regardless of whether or not such countries are
>>members of the European Union or European
>>Community see KJC2+

901 Bibliography
>For bibliography of particular subjects, see the subject

<903> Periodicals
>For periodicals consisting primarily of informative material
>>(newsletters, bulletins, etc.) relating to a particular subject,
>>see subject and form division for periodicals
>For law reports, official bulletins or circulars, and official
>>gazettes intended chiefly for the publication of laws and
>>regulations, see the appropriate entries in the text or Form
>>Division Tables
>For periodicals consisting predominantly of legal articles,
>>regardless of subject matter and jurisdiction see K1+

904 Monographic series
Official gazettes
>For gazettes of a particular committee, agency, etc., see the
>>issuing committee, agency, etc.

907 Journal officiel de le communauté européenne du charbon
>et de l'acier (1952-1958)
Official Journal of the European Communities
>Class here all constituent parts of the gazette, as Series L
>>(Legislation), Series C (Information and Notices), and
>>Series S (Supplement) and the Annex (Debates of the
>>European Parliament)

908 English language edition
908.2 Indexes
908.3 French language edition (Journal officiel des
>Communautés européennes)
908.33 Indexes
908.4 German language edition (Amtsblatt der Europäischen
>Gemeinschaften)
908.44 Indexes
Legal materials produced by the European Parliament see
>KJE5390+
Intergovernmental congresses and conferences see
>KJC14.A+
Official acts

The European Communities. Community law
Official acts -- Continued
915 Indexes and tables
Including lists and tables of laws and regulations adopted in
the member states of the Communities in application of
acts adopted by the Communities
916 Collections. Compilations (General)
e.g. Pasetti et al., Code des Communautés Européennes;
Encyclopedia of European Community Law, etc.
Treaties and other international agreements. Secondary
legislation
Class here treaties concluded by organs of the European
Communities
For treaties (individual and collected) establishing and
expanding the European Communities, including
treaties of association see KJE4442.3
917 Indexes and tables
918 Collections
Including either multilateral or bilateral treaties or both (e.
g., Collections of the Agreements concluded by the
European Communities)
Individual treaties
For individual treaties, see the subject
Other secondary legislation
Regulations. Directives. Réglements. Verordnungen.
Richtlinien. Entscheidungen
920 Indexes and tables
920.5 Abridgments and digests
Collections
921 Serials
921.5 Monographs. By date
e.g. Secondary legislation of the European
Communities: Legislation in force on 31 December
1972; Recueil d'actes, etc.
Individual
For individual regulations, etc., see the subject
922 Recommendations. Opinions. Empfehlungen.
Stellungnahmen
922.5 Other legal measures
e.g. action programs, consultations, target studies, etc.
Court decisions and related material. Law reports
Including authorized and private editions, and decisions
relating to the treaties establishing the European
Communities
For decisions (individual or collected) on a particular subject,
see the subject

The European Communities. Community law
  Official acts
    Court decisions and related material. Law reports --
      Continued
      Indexes and tables
        Including indexes of decisions of several states concerning
          the European Communities
        For indexes limited to decisions of one state, see the state

923	General
923.5	Chronological indexes
923.6	Abridgments and digests

        Including digests of decisions of several states concerning
          the European Communities

923.7	Several courts

      Particular courts
        Court of Justice of the European Communities
          Including Court of Justice of European Coal and Steel
            Community, and including Court of First Instance

924.2	Indexes
924.3	Digests. Summaries
924.5	Reports

        European Court of Human Rights decisions see
          KJC5138
        Court of Auditors decisions see KJE7083

925	Official reports and related materials

        For official general reports, memoranda, etc. of a particular
          assembly, agency, etc., see the issuing assembly, agency,
          etc.

925.5	Abridgments and digests. Reporters

        e.g. Common Market Reporter

926	Encyclopedias
926.5	Dictionaries. Terms and phrases

        e.g., European Treaties Vocabulary, European Communities
          Glossary, etc.
        Including unilingual, bilingual, and polyglot dictionaries
        For dictionaries on a particular subject, see the subject

926.7	Form books

        For form books on a particular subject, see the subject
      Directories

927	General
927.3.A-Z	By specialization, A-Z

      Legal research. Legal bibliography
        Including methods of bibliographic research and how to find the
          law

928	General (Table K14)

	The European Communities. Community law
	Legal research. Legal bibliography -- Continued
	Electronic data processing. Information storage and retrieval
929	General (Table K14)
	EURONET see KJE6970.3
929.5	CELEX (Inter-institutional computerized documentation system for Community law)
929.7	PRC (Proposals, Recommendations, and Communications)
929.8	ACTU (Data on documents issued by the Secretariat-General)
929.9	ASMODEE (Automated System for Monitoring Directives Execution)
	Stella programme see KJE6970.5
931	Surveys of legal activity
	Class here status reports concerning unification, approximation, cooperation, and other activities
	The legal profession see KJE3704
932	Law societies and associations. By name
935	Congresses. Conferences. By date of the congress
	For intergovernmental congresses and conferences see KJC14.A+
937	Academies. Institutes. By name
945	Casebooks. Readings
947	General works. Treatises
949	Compends, outlines, etc.
958	Addresses, essays, lectures
	Including single essays, essays of several authors, festschriften, etc.
959.A-Z	Manuals and other works for particular groups of users. By user, A-Z
959.B87	Businessmen. Foreign investors
	Foreign investors see KJE959.B87
959.5.A-Z	Works on diverse aspects of a particular subject falling within several branches of the law. By subject, A-Z
959.5.C65	Computers
	Theory and methodology of uniform law development. Integration of law
	Including alignment, approximation, harmonization, etc.
	For uniform law development in Europe as a whole see KJC2+
960	General (Table K14)
962	Effectiveness and validity of the law
	For implementation and applicability of the law see KJE5087

The European Communities. Community law
Theory and methodology of uniform law development.
Integration of law -- Continued

964	Sources of community law
	Including general works on treaties, secondary legislation, etc.
	Rule of law see KJE5037
965	Interpretation of international and supranational (community) law
966	Organizations and their legal activity
	Constitutional aspects of international cooperation and membership in international organizations see KJE5059
	Community law and municipal law
	Legal aspects of political integration see KJE5076
	Legal aspects of economic integration see KJE6417
	Member nations and integration of law
969	General (Table K14)
970	Member nations' law reform through Community integration
971	Precedence of Community law
971.5	Implementation of Community law by the states
	Including supervision by Community organs and sanctions
972	Conflict of Community law and municipal law (Table K14)
	For branches of the law or subjects, see the branches or subjects in KJE
(974)	Non-member nations and Community law
	see KJE982
	Relation of Community law to other bodies of law see KJE5075+
975	Intertemporal law. Retroactive law
976	Law reform. Criticism
	For member-nations law reform through Community law see KJE970
980	Private law (Table K14)
	Conflict of laws
	Class here works on the conflict rules of nonmember nations and community conflict rules, including conflict rules of branches other than private law
982	General (Table K8)
983.A-Z	Particular branches and subjects of the law, A-Z
983.C58	Citizenship (Table K12)
983.C64	Commercial sales (Table K12)
983.C66	Contracts (Table K12)

	The European Communities. Community law
	Conflict of laws
	Particular branches and subjects of the law, A-Z --
	Continued
983.I58	Insurance (Table K12)
983.I583	Intellectual and industrial property (Table K12)
	Civil law. Droit civil. Bürgerliches Recht
991-995	General (Table K13)
	Family law. Domestic relations
1101-1105	General (Table K13)
	Marriage
1121	General (Table K14)
1159	Quasi-matrimonial relationships. Unmarried cohabitation. Concubinage (Table K14)
1189	Parent and child (Table K14)
	Property. Law of things
1251	General (Table K14)
1261	Right of property (Table K14)
	Ownership
1275	General (Table K14)
	Acquisition and loss of ownership
1276	General (Table K14)
	Contractual acquisition
1289	General
	Conditions
1290	General (Table K14)
1291	Retention of ownership. Réserve de proprieté. Eigentums vorbehalt (Table K14)
	Real property
1315	General (Table K14)
	Types of real property
	Condominium. Horizontal property
1340	General (Table K14)
1340.5	Timesharing (Real estate) (Table K14)
1360	Hypothecation (Table K14)
	Inheritance and succession
1441-1445	General (Table K13)
1457	Heir (Table K14)
	Testamentary succession. Wills
1467	General (Table K14)
1469.A-Z	Types of wills, A-Z
	Subarrange each by Table K12
1471	Appointment of heir (Table K14)
1473	Legitime. Freedom of testation (Table K14)
1476	Legacy. Testamentary burden (Table K14)
1477	Intestate succession (Table K14)

The European Communities. Community law
  Commercial law
    Maritime law. Droit maritime. Seehandelsrecht
      Affreightment. Carriage of goods at sea and on inland
        waters -- Continued

2266	Act of God (Table K14)
2267	Carriage of passengers at sea (Table K14)
2268	Average (Table K14)
2272	Salvage (Table K14)
2280	Shipbrokers (Table K14)
2282	Ship registers (Table K14)
2283	Maritime courts (Table K14)
	Prize courts
	see subclass KZ
	Marine insurance
	Including liability insurance
2285	General (Table K14)
2285.5.A-Z	Particular risks, A-Z
2285.5.W37	War risks (Table K12)
2289	Maritime social legislation (Table K14)
2301	Insurance law. Droit d'assurances.
	Privatversicherungsrecht.
	Versicherungswirtschaftsrecht (Table K14)
	Including regulation of insurance business
	Insurance carriers
2311	General (Table K14)
2314	State supervision (Table K14)
2320	Insurance contracts (Table K14)
2339	Life insurance (Table K14)
2370	Agricultural insurance (Table K14)
2379	Export credit insurance (Table K14)
	Liability insurance
2390	General (Table K14)
2397	Risk and limitation (Table K14)
2423.A-Z	Particular risks, A-Z
2423.A87	Automobiles (Table K12)
	Reinsurance. Réassurance. Rückversicherung
2428	General (Table K14)
2429	State supervision (Table K14)
	Business associations
2432	General (Table K14)
	Right of establishment and freedom to provide services
	see KJE5174
2433	Domicile (Table K14)
	Personal companies. Unincorporated business
	associations

The European Communities. Community law
Commercial law
Business associations
Stock companies. Incorporated business associations --
Continued

2635	Government ownership. Nationalization (Table K14)

For indemnification see KJE5775

Intellectual and industrial property. Propriété intellectuelle et
industrielle. Urheberrecht und gewerblicher Rechtschutz

2636	General (Table K14)

Copyright

2655	General (Table K14)

Authorship

Including multiple authorship and author cooperatives

2655.2	General (Table K14)
2655.22	Anonyms and pseudonyms (Table K14)
2655.23	Intangible property (Table K14)
2655.3	Plagiarism (Table K14)
2655.4	Formalities (Table K14)

Including registration of claim, transfer, licenses, deposit,
and notice

2655.5	Protected works (Table K14)

Including original works, subsequent rights, idea, and title

Scope of protection

2655.6	General (Table K14)
2655.62	Personality rights. Droit moral (Table K14)

Mechanical reproduction

2655.623	General (Table K14)
2655.64	Documentation and dissemination (Table K14)

Including fair use

2655.65	Exhibition (Table K14)

Performing rights

Cf. KJE2700 Quasi copyright

2655.7	General (Table K14)
2655.72	Societies and industrial trusts (Table K14)
2655.73	Broadcasting rights (Table K14)
2655.75	Recording devices (Table K14)

Including phonographs, magnetic recorders, and
jukeboxes

2655.76	Filming and photographing (Table K14)
2655.78	Translation (Table K14)
2655.8	Employees' copyright (Table K14)
2655.82	Duration and renewal (Table K14)
2655.85	Delicts. Torts (Table K14)
2655.9	Criminal provisions (Table K14)

Branches of copyright

The European Communities. Community law
Intellectual and industrial property. Propiete intellectuelle et
industrielle. Urheberrecht und gewerblicher Rechtschutz
Copyright
Branches of copyright -- Continued
Literary copyright

2660	General (Table K14)
	Authorship
	Including multiple authorship and author cooperatives
2660.2	General (Table K14)
2660.22	Anonyms and pseudonyms (Table K14)
2660.23	Intangible property (Table K14)
2660.3	Plagiarism (Table K14)
2660.4	Formalities (Table K14)
	Including registration of claim, transfer, licenses, deposit, and notice
2660.5	Protected works (Table K14)
	Including original works, subsequent rights, idea, and title
	Scope of protection
2660.6	General (Table K14)
2660.62	Personality rights. Droit moral (Table K14)
	Mechanical reproduction
2660.623	General (Table K14)
2660.64	Documentation and dissemination (Table K14)
	Including fair use
2660.65	Exhibition (Table K14)
	Performing rights
	Cf. KJE2700 Quasi copyright
2660.7	General (Table K14)
2660.72	Societies and industrial trusts (Table K14)
2660.73	Broadcasting rights (Table K14)
2660.75	Recording devices (Table K14)
	Including phonographs, magnetic recorders, and jukeboxes
2660.76	Filming and photographing (Table K14)
2660.78	Translation (Table K14)
2660.8	Employees' copyright (Table K14)
2660.82	Duration and renewal (Table K14)
2660.85	Delicts. Torts (Table K14)
2660.9	Criminal provisions (Table K14)
	Musical copyright
2665	General (Table K14)
	Authorship
	Including multiple authorship and author cooperatives
2665.2	General (Table K14)

The European Communities. Community law
Intellectual and industrial property. Propiete intellectuelle et
industrielle. Urheberrecht und gewerblicher Rechtschutz
Copyright
Branches of copyright
Fine art and photography -- Continued

2670.4	Formalities (Table K14)
	Including registration of claim, transfer, licenses, deposit, and notice
2670.5	Protected works (Table K14)
	Including original works, subsequent rights, idea, and title
	Scope of protection
2670.6	General (Table K14)
2670.62	Personality rights. Droit moral (Table K14)
	Mechanical reproduction
2670.623	General (Table K14)
2670.64	Documentation and dissemination (Table K14)
	Including fair use
2670.65	Exhibition (Table K14)
	Performing rights
	Cf. KJE2700 Quasi copyright
2670.7	General (Table K14)
2670.72	Societies and industrial trusts (Table K14)
2670.73	Broadcasting rights (Table K14)
2670.75	Recording devices (Table K14)
	Including phonographs, magnetic recorders, and jukeboxes
2670.76	Filming and photographing (Table K14)
2670.78	Translation (Table K14)
2670.8	Employees' copyright (Table K14)
2670.82	Duration and renewal (Table K14)
2670.85	Delicts. Torts (Table K14)
2670.9	Criminal provisions (Table K14)
	Motion pictures see KJE2690+
2678	Designs and models (Table K14)
2685	Prints and labels (Table K14)
	Including works of commercial art, catalogs, sample books, etc.
	Motion pictures and television shows
2690	General (Table K14)
	Authorship
	Including multiple authorship and author cooperatives
2690.2	General (Table K14)
2690.22	Anonyms and pseudonyms (Table K14)
2690.23	Intangible property (Table K14)

The European Communities. Community law
Intellectual and industrial property. Propiete intellectuelle et
industrielle. Urheberrecht und gewerblicher Rechtschutz
Author and publisher -- Continued

2712.A-Z   Special topics, A-Z
                      Subarrange each by Table K12
2714   Litigation and execution
                  Patent law and trademarks
2721-2725   General (Table K13)
2732   Community patent. Brevet. Patent (Table K14)
2751.A-Z   Patented processes, products, and engineering methods,
                          A-Z
2751.B55   Biotechnology (Table K12)
2751.P55   Plants (Table K12)
2768   European trademark. Marque de commerce.
                          Markenrecht. Markenschutzrecht (Table K14)
                      Licenses
2775   General (Table K14)
2777   Foreign licensing agreements (Table K14)
                              Including technology transfer and know-how agreements
                  Unfair competition see KJE6536
                  Labor law. Droit du travail. Arbeitsrecht
2851-2855   General (Table K13)
                      Labor contract and employment. Contrat du travail.
                      Arbeitsvertrag
2870   General (Table K14)
                          Types of employment
2872   Temporary employment (Table K14)
2875   Subcontracting (Table K14)
2888   Preferential employment (Table K14)
                              Including people with severe disabilities, veterans, etc.
                          Free movement of labor see KJE5170
2922   Dismissal of employees. Licenciement. Kündigung
                              (Table K14)
                          Prohibition of discrimination in employment. Equal
                          opportunity
2942   General (Table K14)
2945.A-Z   Groups discriminated against, A-Z
2945.H35   People with disabilities (Table K14)
2945.W66   Women (Table K14)
                          Wages. Rémunérations. Entlohnung
2950   General (Table K14)
2953   Equal pay for equal work. Égalité des rémunérations
                                  pour un même travail. Gleiches Entgelt bei gleicher
                                  Arbeit (Table K14)

The European Communities. Community law
Labor law. Droit du travail. Arbeitsrecht
Wages. Remunerations. Entlohnung -- Continued

2958	Family allowances. Allocations familiales. Familienzulage (Table K14)
	Housing allowances see KJE3448
2965	Non-wage payments and fringe benefits (Table K14)
	Including pensions
	Labor management relations
2981-2985	General (Table K13)
2991	Works councils (Table K14)
	Including election, organization, parliamentary practice, etc.
2997	Employee participation in management (Table K14)
	Personnel management
3019	General (Table K14)
3022	Occupational training and retraining. Formation et rééducation professionelles. Berufliche Ausbildung und Berufsumschulung (Table K14)
	Including apprenticeship
	Cf. KJE6300+ Vocational education
3056	Collective bargaining and labor agreements (Table K14)
3100	Labor disputes. Strikes. Lockouts (Table K14)
	Trade unions and employer's organizations. Organisations syndicales de travailleurs et d'employeurs. Arbeitgeber- und Arbeitnehmerverbände
3118	General (Table K14)
	Trade unions. Syndicats des salariés. Gewerkschaften
3123	General (Table K14)
3126	European Trade Union Institute (Table K15)
3136	Employers' organizations. Syndicats d'employeurs. Arbeitgeberverbände (Table K14)
	Protection of labor
3140	General (Table K14)
3145	Hours of labor. Heures ouvrables. Arbeitszeit (Table K14)
3157	Vacations. Congés. Urlaub (Table K14)
3172	Youth labor. Travail des mineures. Jugendarbeit (Table K14)
3175	Women labor. Travail des femmes. Frauenarbeit (Table K14)
	Labor hygiene and industrial safety. Hygiène et sécurité de travail. Persönliche und technische Sicherheit. Betriebssicherheit
3185	General (Table K14)
3190	European Industrial Safety Committee (Table K15)
3192.A-Z	Labor law for particular industries or occupations, A-Z

The European Communities. Community law
Labor law. Droit du travail. Arbeitsrecht
Labor law for particular industries or occupations, A-Z

3192.A37	Agricultural and farm laborers (Table K12)
3192.A44	Alien laborers. Travailleurs étrangers. Fremdarbeiter (Table K12)
3192.B35	Banks (Table K12)
3192.C45	Church employees (Table K12)
	Farm laborers see KJE3192.A37
3192.S44	Self-employed (Table K12)

Labor supply. Manpower supply
    Cf. KJE3276 European Social Fund

3195	General (Table K14)
3197	Labor bureaus (Table K14)
3199	Employment agencies (Table K14)
3205	Criminal provisions (Table K14)

Social legislation. Droit social. Sozialrecht
    Cf. KJE5514+ Economic and Social Committee

3271-3275	General (Table K13)
	European Social Charter see KJC2839
3276	European Social Fund (Table K15)
3277	European Foundation for the Improvement of Living and Working Conditions (Table K15)

Social insurance. Assurances sociales.
    Sozialversicherung

3281	General (Table K14)
3308	Health insurance. Assurance maladie. Krankenversicherung (Table K14)

Workers' compensation. Réparation des accidents de
    travail et maladies professionnelles. Gesetzliche
    Unfallversicherung

3350	General (Table K14)
3364	Medical benefits. Rehabilitation (Table K14)

Social security. Sécurité sociale. Soziale Sicherheit.
    Rentenversicherung

3387	General (Table K14)
3391	European Institute of Social Security (Table K15)

Pensions. Pensions. Renten

3398	General (Table K14)
3405	Old age pensions (Table K14)
3407	Disability pensions. Pensions d'invalidité. Invalidenrente. Berufsunfähigkeit (Table K14)
3410	Pension trusts (Table K14)
	Family allowances see KJE2958
	Housing allowances see KJE3448

	The European Communities. Community law
	Social legislation. Droit social. Sozialrecht
	Social insurance. Assurances sociales.
	Sozialversicherung -- Continued
3418	Unemployment insurance. Assurance-chômage.
	Arbeitslosenversicherung (Table K14)
	Social services. Public welfare. Assistance sociale.
	Sozialfürsorge. Sozialhilfe
3431	General (Table K14)
3448	Housing allowances. Allocation de logement.
	Wohnungsgeld (Table K14)
	Family allowances see KJE2958
	Courts and procedure
3655	Administration of justice. The organization of the judiciary.
	Administration de la justice. Justizverwaltung und
	Rechtspflege
	Courts. Cours. Gerichtshöfe
3666	General (Table K14)
3670	Court of First Instance of the European Communities
	(Table K15)
	Court of Justice see KJE924.2+; KJE5461+
	Court of Auditors see KJE7083
3704	The legal profession
	Judicial assistance. Assistance judiciaire. Rechtshilfe
3795	General (Table K14)
3800	Foreign judgments (Conflict of laws) (Table K14)
	Procedure
3802	General (Table K14)
	Procedural principles, A-Z
3832.D83	Due process of law (Table K12)
3846	Parties to action (Table K14)
3896	Actions and defenses (Table K14)
3926	Evidence (Table K14)
	Judicial decisions
3952	General (Table K14)
3954	Injunctions. Arrest (Table K14)
3968	Interlocutory decisions (Table K14)
3982	Advisory opinions (Table K14)
3985	Special procedures (Table K11)
4010	Remedies (Table K14)
	Noncontentious jurisdiction
4044	General (Table K14)
4070	Notaries (Table K14)
4169	Arbitration (Table K14)
	Including commercial arbitration
4169.5	Costs (Table K14)

The European Communities. Community law
Courts and procedure
Insolvency. Faillite et banqueroute. Zahlungseinstellung
4170   General (Table K14)
4175   Execution (Table K14)
4290   Bankruptcy (Table K14)
4431   Public law (Table K14)
Organization law. Constitution of the European Communities
4441   Bibliography
4441.3   Periodicals
Including gazettes, yearbooks, bulletins, etc.
Treaties establishing and expanding the communities.
Basic law
4442   Indexes and tables
4442.3   Collections
4442.5   Proposed treaties. Drafts. By date
4443.3<date>   Individual treaties
Arrange chronologically by appending the date of signature
of the treaty to the number KJE4443.3 and deleting any
trailing zeros. Subarrange each by Table K5
4443.31951   Treaty of Paris, 1951. Treaty establishing the
European Coal and Steel Community (Montan-
Union) (Table K5)
4443.31957   Treaty of Rome, 1957. Treaty establishing the
European Atomic Energy Community (EURATOM)
(Table K5)
4443.319575   Treaty of Rome, 1957. Treaty establishing the
European Economic Community (EEC) (Table K5)
4443.31965   Merger treaty, 1965. Treaty instituting a single Council
and a single Commission of the European
Communities (Table K5)
4443.3197   Treaty of Luxemburg, 1970 (First budgetary treaty)
(Table K5)
4443.31975   Treaty amending certain financial provisions of the
treaties establishing the European Communities
and of the treaty establishing a single Council and a
single Commission of the European Communities,
1975 (Second budgetary treaty) (Table K5)
4443.31983   Solemn Declaration on European Union, 1983
(Stuttgart) (Table K5)
4443.31986   Single European Act, 1986 (Table K5)
4443.31992   Treaty on European Union (1992) (Table K5)
4443.31997   Treaty of Amsterdam, 1997 (Table K5)
4443.32001   Treaty of Nice, 2001 (Table K5)
4443.32004   Treaty Establishing a Constitution for Europe (2004)
(not ratified) (Table K5)

The European Communities. Community law
Organization law. Constitution of the European Communities
Treaties establishing and expanding the communities.
Basic law
Individual treaties -- Continued

4443.4<date> Treaties of accession (adhesion) and association
Arrange chronologically by appending the date of
signature of the treaty to the number KJE4443.4 and
deleting any trailing zeros. Subarrange each by
Table K5

4443.41963 Agreement concerning the association of Turkey,
1963 (Table K5)

4443.41972 Treaty of Brussels, 1972 (Table K5)
Treaty concerning the accession of the Kingdom of
Denmark, Ireland, the Kingdom of Norway, and the
United Kingdom of Great Britain and Northern
Ireland to the European Economic Community and
the European Atomic Energy Community

4443.41979 Treaty concerning the accession of Greece to the
Community, 1979 (Table K5)

4443.41985 Treaty concerning the accession of Spain and
Portugal to the Community, 1985 (Table K5)

4443.41994 Treaty concerning the accession of Norway, Austria,
Finland, and Sweden to the European Union,
1994 (Table K5)

4443.42003 Treaty concerning the accession of the Czech
Republic, Estonia, Cyprus, Latvia, Lithuania,
Hungary, Malta, Poland, Slovenia, and Slovakia
to the European Union, 2003 (Table K5)
Other official acts and legal measures
Regulations and decisions

4443.6 Indexes and tables
4443.8 Abridgements and digests
Collections. Selections
Including annotated editions
4444 Serials
4444.2 Monographs. By date

The European Communities. Community law
Organization law. Constitution of the European Communities
Other official acts and legal measures
Regulations and decisions -- Continued

4444.3\<date\>	Individual acts (or groups of acts adopted as a whole)

Arrange chronologically by appending date of original
enactment or revision of the law to the number
KJE4444.3 and deleting any trailing zeros

Under each:

.A15	*Indexes and tables*
	Legislative documents and related works
.A2	*Collections. Selections. By date*
.A3	*Drafts (Official). By date*
.A32	*Records of proceedings. Minutes of evidence, reports, etc., of the organ and its committees. By date*
	For annual (official) reports, see KJE4444.8
.A4	*Miscellaneous documents. By date*
	Including memoranda, documents of fact-finding, advisory, research, or drafting committees, etc.
	Unannotated editions
	Including official editions with or without annotation
.A5	*Serials*
.A6	*Monographs. By date*
.A7-.Z	*Annotated editions. Commentaries. General works*
4444.4	Recommendations. Opinions

Including action programs, consultations, target studies,
etc.

Administrative decisions. Reports

4444.5	Indexes and tables
4444.52	Serials
4444.53	Monographs. By date
4444.6	Court decisions and related materials. Reports
4444.8	Surveys on legal activities concerning unification, harmonization, cooperation. Annual (Official) reports
4444.85	Dictionaries. Encyclopedias
4444.95	Conferences. Symposia
4445	General works. Treatises

The European Communities. Community law
    Organization law. Constitution of the European Communities
      -- Continued

5034	Interpretation and construction
	Constitutional principles
5037	Rule of law. Rechtsstaatlichkeit
	Separation of powers see KJE5049+
	Constitutional aspects of political integration see KJE5076
	Sovereignty. Equality of states see KJE5078+
	Expansion of the Community see KJE5091
5038	Immunity of states
	Immunity of Community organs see KJE5402
5041	Legitimacy
	Separation of powers. Separation des pouvoirs. Gewaltentrennung
5049	General (Table K14)
5051	Conflict of interests. Incompatibility of offices (Table K14)
	For specific offices, see the office.
5053	Judicial review of legislative acts
	Class here general works
	For procedure see KJE5472
	Sources and relationships of the law
5057	International law and community law. Treaties and agreements (Table K14)
5059	Constitutional aspects of international cooperation and of membership in international organizations (Table K22)
5062.A-Z	Particular organizations and groups of organizations, A-Z
	Including membership, comparative organizational law, and trade agreements
5062.A87	Association of South East Asian Nations (Table K12)
5062.C65	Contracting Parties to the General Agreement on Tariffs and Trade (Table K12)
5062.C68	Council for Mutual Economic Assistance (Table K12)
5062.E25	Economic Commission for Europe (Table K12)
5062.E87	European Free Trade Association (Table K12)
	GATT see KJE5062.C65
	General Agreement on Tariffs and Trade (Organization) see KJE5062.C65
5062.I68	International Labor Organization (Table K12)
5062.L37	Latin American regional organizations (Table K12)
	Organisation for Economic Co-operation and Development see K3824+
5062.O74	Organization of American States (Table K12)

	The European Communities. Community law
	Organization law. Constitution of the European Communities
	Sources and relationships of the law
	Particular organizations and groups of organizations, A-Z
	-- Continued
5062.U55	United Nations Conference on Trade and Development (Table K12)
5062.U56	United Nations Food and Agricultural Organization (Table K12)
	Intergovernmental (Internal) relations. Community and member nations
5075	General works
5076	Constitutional aspects of political integration (Table K14)
	Sovereignty
5078	General works
5080	Delegation of powers by member states to the Community
5086	Jurisdiction and concurring jurisdictions. Competence d'attribution of the EEC
5087	Cooperation of the states
	Accession of new member states. Adhesion. Beitritt
	For accession treaties see KJE4443.4<date>
5089	General works
5090	Procedures and conditions for accession
5091	Legal problems of expansion of the Community
5092.A-Z	By state, A-Z
5094	Community law and state-local relations (Table K14)
5097.A-Z	By state, A-Z
	Foreign (External) relations. International cooperation
	For international agreements on a particular subject, see the subject
	For foreign assistance programs see KJE6435+
5105	General (Table K14)
5105.5	Political cooperation of Foreign Ministers
5106	Treatymaking power (Table K14)
	Relations with associated overseas countries and territories. Pays et territoires d'outre-mer. Uberseeische Lander und Hoheitsgebiete
5108	General (Table K14)
5108.5.A-Z	Individual countries, A-Z
	Subarrange each by Table K12
	Relations with non-member states
5109	General (Table K14)
	African, Caribbean, and Pacific nations
5110	General (Table K14)

KJE

The European Communities. Community law
Organization law. Constitution of the European Communities
Foreign (External) relations. International cooperation
Relations with non-member states
African, Caribbean, and Pacific nations -- Continued

5110.2<date>	Individual agreements
	Arrange chronologically by appending the date of signature of the agreement to the number KJE5110.2 and deleting any trailing zeros. Subarrange each by Table K5
5110.21963	Convention of Yaoundé (I), 1963 (Table K5)
5110.21968	Arusha Agreement (I), 1968 (did not enter into force) (Table K5)
5110.21969	Arusha Agreement (II), 1969 (Table K5)
5110.219695	Convention of Yaoundé (II), 1969 (Table K5)
5110.21975	Convention of Lomé (I), 1975 (Table K5)
5110.21979	Convention of Lomé (II), 1979 (Table K5)
5110.21984	Convention of Lomé (III), 1984 (Table K5)
5110.22	Cotonou Agreement, 2000 (Table K5)
5112.A-Z	Individual regions or countries, A-Z
	e. g.
5112.N53	Nigeria (Table K12)
5113	Relations with state-trading nations. Pays à commerce d'Etat. Staatshandelslander (Table K14)
	Cf. KJE838.7 Council for Mutual Economic Assistance

Individual and Communities
Nationality and citizenship. Nationalité.
Staatsangehörigkeit

5124	General (Table K14)
	Naturalization (Immigration). Emigration see KJE6044
	Passports and identification see KJE6040

Human rights. Civil and political rights. Droits civiques et
libertes publiques. Droits de l'homme.
Menschenrechte. Grundrechte und
Verfassungsgarantien

5132	General (Table K14)
	Convention for the Protection of Human Rights and Fundamental Freedoms see KJC5132
	European Court of Human Rights see KJC5138

Equality before the law. Antidiscrimination in general

5142	General (Table K14)
5144.A-Z	Groups discriminated against, A-Z
5144.G39	Gay men. Lesbians (Table K12)
	Lesbians see KJE5144.G39

The European Communities. Community law
Organization law. Constitution of the European Communities
Individual and Communities
Human rights. Civil and political rights. Droits civiques et
libertes publiques. Droits de l'homme.
Menschenrechte. Grundrechte und
Verfassungsgarantien
Equality before the law. Antidiscrimination in general
Groups discriminated against, A-Z

5144.M56	Minorities (Table K12)
	Including ethnic, religious, racial, and national
5144.W64	Women (Table K12)
5146.A-Z	Special topics, A-Z
	Culture and language see KJE5146.L36
5146.L36	Language and culture
	For language regulation in general see KJC6265

Freedom

5149	General (Table K14)
5156	Freedom of religion. Liberté religieuse. Religionsfreiheit (Table K14)
5170	Free movement of workers. Libre circulation des travailleurs. Freizügigkeit der Arbeitnehmer (Table K14)
5174	Right of establishment and freedom to provide services. Droit d'establissement et la libre prestation des service. Niederlassungsrecht und freier Dienstleistungsverkehr (Table K14)
	Class here general works
	For particular professions or industries see KJE6695+
5175	Free movement of capital. Libre circulation des capitaux. Freier Kapitalverkehr (Table K14)
5177	Free movement of goods. Libre circulation des marchandises. Freier Warenverkehr (Table K14)
5183	Due process of law (Table K14)
5202	Right to asylum (Table K14)
5205	Right to petition (Table K14)
5210	Right to education (Table K14)
5222	Political parties (Table K14)
5240	Other political organizations, pressure groups, etc. (Table K14)
5250	Internal security (Table K14)
	Including control of subversive activities or groups
5267	Initiative and referendum
	Election law

The European Communities. Community law
Organization law. Constitution of the European Communities
Election law -- Continued
5272   General (Table K14)
5279   Suffrage (active and passive) (Table K14)
Election to particular offices
5291   European Parliament
Community institutions and organs
Class here works on institutions and organs of the European
Communities
For organs, institutions, directorates, etc. with jurisdiction
limited to a specific subject, see the subject, e.g.,
KJE6434 European Investment Bank
For European Coal and Steel Community and its
organs see KJE6745+
For EURATOM and its organs see KJE6768+
5305   General (Table K14)
5306   Rules governing the official languages of the organs.
Régime linguistique des institutions. Regelung der
Sprachenfrage für die Organe der Gemeinschaft
(Table K14)
5307   Decision making. Legislative power. Jurisdiction
(General) (Table K14)
Including delegation of powers
Council of the European Communities. Conseil des
Communautés Européennes. Rat der Europäischen
Gemeinschaften
5318   General (Table K15)
5322   President. Representatives. (Table K14)
Including permanent representatives and the Committee
of Permanent Representatives
5326   Association Councils
5328   European Council (Table K15)
Powers and duties
5329   General (Table K14)
5330   Legislative functions (Table K14)
5349   The legislative process (Table K14)
Commission of the European Communities. Commission
des Communautés Européennes. Kommission der
Europäischen Gemeinschaften
5380   General (Table K15)
5382   Association Committees
Powers and duties
5386   General (Table K14)
5389   Supervision of proper implementation of decisions of
the European Community (Table K14)

The European Communities. Community law
Organization law. Constitution of the European Communities
Community institutions and organs -- Continued
European Parliament. Parlement europeen.
Europäisches Parlament
For debates see KJE908+

5390	General (Table K15)
5391	Bureau (Table K15)
	Including President and Vice Presidents
5392.A-Z	Committees and delegations, A-Z
	Subarrange each by Table K12

Joint Meeting of the members of the Consultative
Assembly of the Council of Europe and the
Members of the European Parliamentary
Assembly see KJE139.7.A+

5393	Secretariat. Secretary General (Table K15)
5394	Directorates-General (Table K15)
	Powers and duties
5396	General (Table K14)
5397	Supervision (Table K14)
5399	Budgetary power (Table K14)
5400	Legislative power (Table K14)
5402	Legal status of members. Immunities (Table K14)

European Court of Justice. Cour de justice.
Europäischer Gerichtshof
For court reports see KJE924+

5461	General (Table K15)
5472	Jurisdiction (Table K14)
5472.5	Advocate-General. Avocats généraux. Generalanwalt. (Table K14)
	European Court of Auditors see KJE7083
	Economic and Social Committee
5514	General (Table K15)
5515	Powers and duties (Table K14)
5517	Consultative Committee of the ECSC (Table K15)
	European Investment Bank see KJE6434
5520	Committee of the Regions. Comité des régions. Ausschuss der Regionen (Table K15)
	Administrative law and process
5602	General (Table K14)
5607	Administrative process (Table K14)
	Including enforcement and procedure
5608	Acts of government (Table K14)
	For judicial review see KJE5472
	Administrative acts
5610	General (Table K14)

	The European Communities. Community law
	Administrative law and process
	Administrative acts -- Continued
5621	Defective acts (Table K14)
	For acts of organs see KJE5608
	Public contracts
5632	General (Table K14)
5635.A-Z	Particular contracts, A-Z
5635.D45	Defense contracts. Military procurement (Table K12)
	Military procurement see KJE5635.D45
5640	Ombudsman. Control over abuse of administrative power (Table K14)
	Indemnification for acts performed by government
5765	General (Table K14)
	Eminent domain. Expropriation
5772	General (Table K14)
5775	Nationalization (Table K14)
	Cf. KJE2635 Government business enterprises
	Government liability
5786	General (Table K14)
5789	Administrative and judicial acts (Table K14)
5793	Administrative acts relating to economic control (Table K14)
5794	Administrative organization (Table K8)
	Civil service. Fonction publique. Offentlicher Dienst. Fonctionnaires. Beamten
5932	General (Table K14)
5933	Privileges and immunities (Table K14)
5938	Appointment. Nomination. Ernennung (Table K14)
5939	Conditions of employment. Regime applicable aux fonctionnaires. Beschäftigungsbedingungen (Table K14)
	Remuneration. Allowances. Indemnities. Vergütungen
5949	General (Table K14)
5952	Housing subsidies. Rent subsidies. Allocation de logement. Wohnungsgeld (Table K14)
5953	Cost-of-living adjustments. Travel and moving expenses (Table K14)
5953.2	Family allowances. Allocations familiales. Familienzulage (Table K14)
5953.3	Survivors' benefits (Table K14)
	Retirement. Retraits. Ruhestand
5954	General (Table K14)
5955	Retirement pensions. Pensions. Ruhegehälter (Table K14)
	Police and public safety

The European Communities. Community law
Police and public safety -- Continued

5977	General (Table K14)
	Public safety
6009	General (Table K14)
6010	Weapons. Explosives (Table K14)
	Including manufacturing, import, and trade of firearms and ammunition
	Hazardous articles and processes
6011	General (Table K14)
6012	Nuclear power. Reactors. Protection against radiation. Radioprotection. Strahlenschutzrecht (Table K14)
	Control of individuals
6032	General (Table K14)
6040	Passports (Table K14)
6044	Emigration. Immigration (Table K14)
	Including non-European Union aliens
	Cf. KJE5170 Free movement of workers
	Particular groups
	Aliens
6050	General (Table K14)
6057	Refugees (Table K14)
	Particular activities
	Social activities
6063	Sports (Table K14)
	Public property. Public restraints on private property
6068	General (Table K14)
	Government property. Powers and control
6070	General (Table K14)
6071	Records management. Access to public records (Table K14)
	Including data bases and general data protection
	For violation of privacy see KJE1626
6076	Nationalization. Expropriation (Table K14)
	For government-owned business enterprises see KJE2635
	For indemnification see KJE5775
6094	Water resources (Table K14)
	Public land law. Land use
6132	General (Table K14)
	Regional policy. Politique régionale. Standortpolitik
6135	General (Table K14)
6137	Regional Policy Committee (Table K15)
	Committee of the Regions see KJE5520
6137.5	European Regional Development Fund (Table K15)
6138	Ecological aspects (Table K14)

KJE

The European Communities. Community law
Public property. Public restraints on private property
Public land law. Land use
Regional policy. Politique regionale. Standortpolitik --
Continued

6140	City planning and redevelopment (Table K14)
6155	Building and construction (Table K14)
6160	Public works (Table K14)
	Including public works contracts

Public health. Santé publique. Volksgesundheit

6172	General (Table K14)
6178.A-Z	Public health hazards and measures, A-Z
6178.R43	Refuse disposal (Table K12)

Drug laws

6191	General (Table K14)
6201	Trade regulation. Advertising (Table K14)
6202.A-Z	Other special topics, A-Z
6202.C65	Cosmetics (Table K12)
6202.D75	Drinking water standards (Table K12)
	Environmental pollution see KJE6247+
	Food law see KJE6778+

Medical legislation

6206	General (Table K14)

Biomedical engineering. Medical technology
Including human experimentation in medicine and genetic
engineering

6227	General (Table K8)
6227.5	Transplantation of organs, tissues, etc. (Table K8)
6228	Human reproductive technology (Table K8)
	Including artificial insemination and fertilization in vitro
6229.A-Z	Special topics, A-Z
	Medical devices see KJE6229.M42
6229.M42	Medical instruments and apparatus. Medical devices (Table K12)
6229.R43	Records, Medical (Table K12)
	Including hospital records
6236	Veterinary medicine and hygiene (Table K14)
6237	Prevention of cruelty to animals (Table K14)

Environmental law. Droit de l'environnement. Umweltsrecht

6242	General (Table K14)
6245	Environmental planning. Environmental protection. Conservation of natural resources (Table K14)
	For ecological aspects of regional planning see KJE6138

Environmental pollution

6247	General (Table K14)

	The European Communities. Community law
	Environmental law. Droit de l'environnement. Umweltsrecht
	Environmental pollution -- Continued
6249	Air pollution. Pollution atmospherique.
	Luftverunreinigung (Table K14)
6251	Water pollution. Pollution des eaux.
	Wasserverseuchung (Table K14)
6253	Noise control. Lutte contre le bruit. Lärmbekämpfung
	(Table K14)
6254	Recycling of refuse (Table K14)
6255	Wilderness preservation. Wildlife conservation (Table K14)
	Cultural affairs
6257	General (Table K14)
	Language, National see KJC6265
	Official language of organs of the Community see KJE5306
	Education
	Cf. KJE5210 Right to education
6266	General (Table K14)
6270	Paul Finet Foundation (Table K15)
	Vocational education. Formation professionnelle.
	Berufsschulwesen
	Cf. KJE3022 Occupational training and retraining
6300	General (Table K14)
6301	European Vocational Training Centre (Table K15)
	Higher education. Universities. Enseignement
	superieur. Universites. Hochschulrecht
6313	General (Table K14)
6321	European University Institute (Table K15)
	Science and the arts. Research
6345	General (Table K14)
6348	European Research and Development Committee (Table
	K15)
6352.A-Z	Branches and subjects, A-Z
	European Communities Statistical Office (Eurostat) see
	KJE6352.S83
	European Space Agency see KJE6352.O87
6352.O87	Outer space (Table K12)
	Including the European Space Agency
6352.S83	Statistical services (Table K12)
	Including the European Communities Statistical Office
	(Eurostat)
	The arts
6353	General (Table K14)
6354	Fine arts (Table K14)
6355-6361	Performing arts
6355	General (Table K14)

KJE

The European Communities. Community law
  Cultural affairs
    Science and the arts. Research
      The arts
        Performing arts -- Continued
          Music. Musicians

6357	General (Table K14)
6361	European Community Youth Orchestra (Table K15)
6380	Libraries (Table K14)
6405	Historic buildings and monuments. Architectural landmarks (Table K14)

          Including vessels, battleships, etc.
  Economic law

6411-6415	General (Table K13)
6417	Legal aspects of economic integration

    Government control and policy. Politique économique.
      Wirtschaftslenkung und Wirtschaftspolitik
      For monetary policy see KJE7051+
      For balance of payments see KJE7062

6428	General (Table K14)
6431	Control of economic growth and expansion. Politique de conjoncture. Konjunkturpolitik. Stabilitätskontrolle (Table K14)

      Including business cycles
    Investments. Investissements. Investitionskontrolle
      Including investments within or outside the Community, and
        foreign investments in the Community
      For free movement of capital see KJE5175

6433	General (Table K22)
6434	European Investment Bank. Banque européenne d'investissement. Europäische Investitionsbank (Table K15)

    Assistance to developing countries. Aide à l'étranger.
      Entwicklungshilfe
      Cf. KJE5105+ Foreign relations
      Cf. KJE7346 Tariff preferences

6435	General (Table K14)
6435.5	European Development Fund. Fonds européen de développement. Europäischer Entwicklungsfonds (Table K15)

      Food aid see KJE6606
    Economic assistance within the Community

6436	General (Table K14)
6437	Subsidies. State aid. Subvention ou aides accordées par les États. Von den Staaten bewilligte Subventionen oder Beihilfen (Table K14)

The European Communities. Community law
Economic law
Government control and policy. Politique economique.
Wirtschaftslenkung un Wirtschaftspolitik
Economic assistance within the Community

6438	New community instrument. Ortoli facility
6439	Community loans (Table K14)
6440	Marketing orders. Reglements d'ecoulement. Marktordnungen (Table K14)

Class here general works
For particular marketing orders, see the subject, e.g.,
Agriculture

6442	Prices and price control. Prix et contrôle des prix. Preisrecht und Preisüberwachung (Table K14)

Class here general works
For particular industries or products, see the industry or
product
Government business enterprises see KJE2635
Consumer protection see KJE6577+

6449	Licenses. Concessions (Table K14)
6452	Protection of the law against acts of economic control (Table K14)

For indemnification see KJE5793
Control of contracts and combinations in restraint of
trade. Competition rules. Cartels. Règles de
concurrence. Droit des ententes. Wettbewerbsrecht.
Kartellrecht

6456	General (Table K14)
6459	Application of competition rules external to the communities
6465	Horizontal and vertical combination (Table K14)
6467	Corporate consolidation, merger, etc. (Table K14)
	Cartels
6471	General (Table K14)
6474.A-Z	Types of cartels, A-Z

Subarrange each by Table K12

6478	Exclusive dealing or use agreements (Table K14)
6484	Price maintenance and open price systems (Table K14)

Particular industries, products, etc.
For particular industries, products, etc., see the subject
Monopolies. Oligopolies. Antitrust law
Including government monopolies (Staatliche
Handelsmonopole)
For revenue administration see KJE7305

6497	General (Table K14)

The European Communities. Community law
  Economic law
    Government control and policy. Politique economique.
      Wirtschaftslenkung und Wirtschaftspolitik
      Control of contracts and combinations in restraint of
        trade. Competition rules. Cartels. Regles de
        concurrence. Droit des ententes. Wettbewerbsrect.
        Kartellrecht
        Monopolies. Oligopolies. Antitrust law -- Continued

6503	Market dominance. Position dominante. Marktbeherrschung (Table K14)

6505	Monopolies delegated by the state to others.
	  Monopoles d'État délégués. Von einem Staat auf
	  andere Rechtstrager übertragene Monopole
	  (Table K14)

	Cartel agencies and procedure
6512	General (Table K14)
6517	Registration. Cartel registers (Table K14)
6530	Damage and indemnification (Table K22) Cf. KJE5793 Government liability
6533	Criminal provisions (Table K14)
6535	Small business (Table K14)
6536	Unfair competition. Concurrence déloyale. Unlauterer Wettbewerb (Table K14)
	European trademark. European copyright see KJE2655+
6537	Dumping (Table K14) Cf. KJE7347 Anti-dumping duty
6554	Standards. Norms. Quality control (Table K14)
6564	Labeling (Table K14) For labeling of particiular products see the product
	Regulation of industry, trade, and commerce
6569	General (Table K14)
	Consumer protection. Droit de la consommation. Verbraucherschutz
6577	General (Table K14)
6578	Consumers Consultative Committee (Table K15)
6578.5	European Bureau of Consumer Unions (Table K15)
6580	Advertising. Publicité. Werbewirtschaft (Table K14)

	Agriculture. Agricultural policy. Politique agricole.
	  Agrarpolitik
	  Cf. KJE6778+ Food processing industry

6601-6605	General (Table K13)
6605.8	Mansholt Plan
6606	Foreign agricultural assistance. Food aid (Table K14)
6607	Agricultural Advisory Committees

The European Communities. Community law
Economic law
Regulation of industry, trade, and commerce
Agriculture. Agricultural policy. Politique agricole.
Agrarpolitik -- Continued
6608   European Agricultural Guidance and Guarantee Fund.
Europäischer Ausrichtungs- und Garantiefonds für
die Landwirtschaft (Table K15)
Agricultural monetary policy
6628   General (Table K14)
6629   Green currencies (Table K14)
6629.2   Monetary compensatory amounts (Table K14)
6636   Cooperative societies. Sociétés coopératives.
Genossenschaften (Table K14)
6637   Marketing orders (Table K14)
6651.A-Z   By sector or product, A-Z
6651.F63   Fodder and grain (Table K12)
Grain see KJE6651.F63
6651.W54   Winemaking (Table K12)
Other sectors or industries
6695   Fisheries. Fish industry. Pêcheries. Secteur de la
pêche. Fischerei. Fischwirtschaft (Table KJ-KKZ8)
Energy industry. Energy policy
6698   General (Table K14)
Coal see KJE6715
Nuclear power see KJE6766
Electric utilities see KJE6758
Petroleum industry see KJE6720
Natural gas see KJE6729
6699   Energy consumption (Table K14)
6700   Energy conservation (Table K14)
6702   Alternative energy sources (Table K14)
Mining and quarrying. Exploitation miniere. Industries
extractives. Bergrecht. Hüttenwesen
Including metallurgy
6710   General (Table K14)
6712   Continental shelf (Table K14)
6715   Coal (Table KJ-KKZ8)
For European Coal and Steel Community see
KJE6745+
6720   Petroleum (Table KJ-KKZ8)
6729   Natural gas (Table KJ-KKZ8)
Manufacturing industries
6739   General (Table K14)
6742   Iron and steel industries (Table KJ-KKZ8)

The European Communities. Community law
   Economic law
     Regulation of industry, trade, an commerce
       Other sectors or industries
         Manufacturing industries
           Iron and steel industries -- Continued
             European Coal and Steel Community.
               Communauté européenne du charbon et de
               l'acier. Europäische Gemeinschaft für Kohle
               und Stahl (Montan-Union)
               For treaties establishing and expanding the
                  Community see KJE4443.3<date>

6745	General (Table K14)
6747	Foreign (External) relations (Table K14)
6748	Community institutions and organs (Table K14)
6752	Agricultural machinery industry (Table KJ-KKZ8)
6754	Automobile industry (Table KJ-KKZ8)
6755	Biotechnology industries (Table KJ-KKZ8)
6756	Computer industry (Table KJ-KKZ8)
6758	Electrical industry. Electric utilities (Table KJ-KKZ8)
6760	Fertilizer industry (Table KJ-KKZ8)
6762	Footwear industry (Table KJ-KKZ8)
6763	Machinery industry (Table KJ-KKZ8)
6764	Measurement instruments industry (Table KJ-KKZ8)
6766	Nuclear power industry (Table KJ-KKZ8)

               Cf. KJE6012 Public safety
             European Atomic Energy Community.
               Communauté européenne de l'energie
               atomique. Europäische Atomgemeinschaft
               (EURATOM)
               For treaties establishing and expanding the
                  Community see KJE4443.3<date>

6768	General (Table K14)
6770	Foreign (External) relations (Table K14)
6771	Community institutions and organs (Table K14)
6772	Joint Research Center (Table K15)
6774	Joint European Torus (Table K15)
6776	Textile industry (Table KJ-KKZ8)
6777.A-Z	Other types of manufacture, A-Z
6777.C54	Chemical industry
6777.E44	Electric appliances

          Food processing industries

6778	General (Table K14)
6778.5	Genetically modified foods (Table K14)
6780	Cereal products (Table KJ-KKZ8)
6781	Meat. Meat products (Table KJ-KKZ8)

The European Communities. Community law
Economic law
Regulation of industry, trade, an commerce
Other sectors or industries
Food processing industry -- Continued

6782	Fruits and vegetables (Table KJ-KKZ8)
(6782.5)	Meat
	see KJE6781
6783	Vegetable oils and fats (Table KJ-KKZ8)
6784	Beverages (Table KJ-KKZ8)
6786	Building and construction industry (Table KJ-KKZ8)
	Drugs see KJE6191+

External trade. Commerce extérieur. Aussenhandel
   For free movement of goods, labor, and capital see
      KJE5170
   For right of establishment and freedom to provide
      services see KJE5174
   For foreign exchange control see KJE7059+
   For balance of payments see KJE7062
   For customs administration see KJE7318+

6791	General (Table K14)
6792	Import policy. Politique d'importation. Einfuhrpolitik
	(Table K14)
	Cf. KJE7347 Anti-dumping duties
6794	Export policy. Politique d'exportation. Ausfuhrpolitik
	(Table K14)
6795	Community quotas. Trade protection. Ausfuhrpolitik
	(Table K14)
	Cf. KJE7326 Tariff

Trade agreements with particular organizations see
   KJE5062.A+
Trade agreements with non-member states see
   KJE5105+
Domestic trade. Intra-Community trade. Commerce
   intérieur. Echanges intracommunautaires.
   Binnenhandel. Innergemeinschaftlicher
   Handelsverkehr

6799	General (Table K14)
6800	Wholesale trade. Commerce de gros. Grosshandel
	(Table K14)
6802	Retail trade. Commerce en detail. Einzelhandel (Table
	K14)
	Service trades
6819	General (Table K14)
6825	Travel agencies. Tourist trade (Table K14)
6830	Artisans (Table K14)

The European Communities. Community law
Economic law -- Continued
Energy policy. Power supply
6848   General (Table K14)
Particular sources of power
6852   Electricity (Table K14)
6854   Gas. Natural gas (Table K14)
6858   Nuclear energy (Table K14)
Transportation. Common transportation policy. Transports.
Politique commune des transports. Verkehrsrecht.
Gemeinsame Verkehrspolitik
6868   General (Table K14)
Road traffic. Automotive transportation. Transports
routiers. Strassenverkehr
6871   General (Table K14)
Motor vehicles
6877   General (Table K14)
6878   Registration (Table K14)
6879   Inspection (Table K14)
6881   Drivers' licenses (Table K14)
6883.A-Z   Particular vehicles, A-Z
6883.A37   Automotive vehicles (Table K12)
Traffic regulations and enforcement
6885   General (Table K14)
6887   Traffic violations (Table K14)
Carriage of passengers and goods
6897   General (Table K14)
6900   Goods carriers (Table K14)
6903   Railroads. Chemins de fer. Eisenbahnverkehrsrecht
(Table K14)
6920   Air transport. Transport aérien. Droit aérien. Luftfahrt
(Table K14)
Water transportation. Transports par eau. Schiffahrtsrecht
6927   General (Table K14)
Maritime law see KJE2256+
6939   Coastwise and inland shipping. Navigation intérieure.
Binnenschiffahrtsrecht (Table K14)
Communication. Mass media. Information
6946   General (Table K14)
Postal services. Telecommunication. Postes.
Télécommunication. Post- und Fernmeldewesen
6950   General (Table K14)
Telecommunication
6964   General (Table K14)
Teletype and data transmission systems
Cf. KJE929+ Information storage and retrieval

The European Communities. Community law
Communication. Mass media. Information
Postal services. Telecommunication. Postes.
Telecommunication. Post- und Fernmeldewesen
Telecommunication
Teletype and data transmission systems -- Continued

6970	General (Table K14)
6970.3	Euronet (Table K14)
6970.5	Stella Programme (Table K14)
	Radio and television communication
6976	General (Table K14)
6989	Networks. Stations (Table K14)
6995	Broadcasting (Table K14)
7005	Press law (Table K14)
7010	Information services. Databases (Table K14)
	Professions. Freie Berufe
7032	General (Table K14)
7033	Professional associations (Table K14)
7045.A-Z	Individual professions, A-Z
7045.A84	Auditors (Table K12)
	Construction profession see KJE7045.E53
7045.E53	Engineering and construction professions (Table K12)
7045.T72	Travel agents (Table K12)
	Financial provisions. Dispositions financières.
	Finanzvorschriften
7050	General (Table K14)
	European monetary system. Système monétaire
	europeen. Europäisches Währungssystem
7051	General (Table K14)
7052	European currency unit (Table K14)
7052.5	Euro (Table K14)
7053	European Monetary Cooperation Fund (Table K14)
7054	Monetary Committee. Comité monetaire.
	Währungsausschuss (Table K15)
7055	Committee of Governors of the Central Bank (Table K15)
	Foreign exchange policy. Politique en matière de change.
	Devisenpolitick
7059	General (Table K14)
7060	Exchange rates. Taux de change. Wechselkurse (Table K14)
7062	Balance of payments. Balance des paiements. Zahlungsbilanz (Table K14)
	Budget. Haushaltsplan
	For the budget of an individual institution, see the institution
7076	General (Table K14)

The European Communities. Community law
Financial provisions. Dispositions financieres.
Finanzvorschriften
Budget. Haushaltsplan -- Continued

7078	Budgetary Policy Committee. Comité de politique budgétaire. Ausschuss für Haushaltspolitik (Table K15)
7080	European unit of account. Unité de compte. Rechnungseinheit
	European unit of account is the weighted sum of the currencies of the member states
	Expenditure control. Auditing. Vérification des comptes. Rechnungslegung
	Including expenditures (Dépenses. Ausgaben)
7082	General (Table K14)
7083	Court of Auditors. Cour des comptes. Rechnungshof (Table K15)
7085	Debts. Loans (Table K14)
	Revenue. Recettes. Einnahmen
7098	General (Table K14)
7099	Communities' own resources. Ressources propres aux Communautés. Eigene Mittel der Gemeinschaften (Table K14)
7100	Financial contributions from member states. Contributions financières des États membres. Finanzbeiträge der Mitgliedstaaten (Table K14)
	Taxation. Imposition. Steuerrecht
	For taxation of particular industries or trades, see the industry or trade
7101-7105	General (Table K13)
7114	Double taxation. Double imposition. Doppelbesteuerung (Table K14)
7128	Tax saving. Tax avoidance (Table K14)
7130	Tax administration (Table K14)
	Direct taxation. Impôts directs. Direkte Steuern
7160	General (Table K14)
	Income tax. Impôt sur le revenue. Einkommensteuer
7163	General (Table K14)
	Salaries and wages. Revenu du travail. Lohnsteuer
7184	General (Table K14)
7186	Taxes on civil service remuneration (Table K14)
7187	Capital investment. Securities (Table K14)

The European Communities. Community law
Financial provisions. Dispositions financieres.
Finanzvorschriften
Revenue. Recettes. Einnahmen
Taxation. Imposition. Steuerrecht
Direct taxation. Impots directs. Direkte Steuern
Income tax. Impot sur le revenue. Einkommensteuer
-- Continued
Corporation tax. Impôt sur les sociétés.
Korperschaftsteuer
Class here general works
For taxation of particular industries, see the industry

7198	General (Table K14)
7217	Capital levy. Prélèvement sur le capital. Kapitalabgabe (Table K14)
7267	Capital gains tax. Impôt sur les plus-values. Kapitalertragsteuer. Kapitalrentensteuer (Table K14)

Indirect taxation. Impôts indirects. Indirekte Steuern

7283	General (Table K14)

Excise taxes. Taxes on transactions. Droits
d'accise. Verbrauchs- und Verkshrssteuern
Including taxes on the raising of capital and on
transactions of securities (Kapitalverkehrsteuern)

7284	General (Table KJE13)
7285	Sales tax. Value-added tax. Turnover tax. Taxe à la valeur ajoutée. Impôt sur le chiffre d'affaires. Mehrwertsteuer. Umsatzsteuer (Table K14)
7305	Government monopolies. Monopoles d'État. Staatliche Handelsmonopole (Table K22)

Commodities, services, and transactions not otherwise
provided for

7306	Transportation of persons and goods. Beförderungssteuer (Table K14)

Including international travel
Customs. Tariff. Douanes. Tarifs. Zölle. Zolltarife
For customs or tariff on a particular commodity, see the
industry

7312	General (Table K14)
7313	Common customs tariff. Tarif douanier commun. Gemeinsamer Zolltarif (Table K14)

Customs organization and administration

7318	General (Table K14)
7319	Establishing the customs value. Etablissement de la valeur en douane. Ermittlung des Zollwerts (Table K14)

The European Communities. Community law
Financial provisions. Dispositions financieres.
Finanzvorschriften
Revenue. Recettes. Einnahmen
Customs. Tariff. Douanes. Tarifs. Zolle. Zolltarife
Customs organization and administration -- Continued

7322	Origin of goods (Table K14)
7324	Tariff classification (Table K14)
7326	Tariff quotas. Contingents douaniers. Zollkontingente (Table K14)
7346	Tariff preferences. Generalized system of preferences. Preferential treatment. Mésures de préférence. Vergünstigungen (Table K14)
7347	Antidumping duties (Table K14)
7351	Free ports and zones (Table K14)
7475	Criminal provisions. Tax and customs delinquency (Table K14)
7520	Community measures in time of war, emergency, or economic crisis. Emergency and wartime legislation (Table K14)
7690	Military law. Defense (Table K14)
	Criminal law
7971-7975	General (Table K13)
8643	Offenses against property (Table K14)
	Crimes against the peace of the community Including terrorism
8780	General (Table K14)
8781.A-Z	Particular offenses, A-Z
8781.C75	Criminal societies. Organized crime (Table K12) Organized crime see KJE8781.C75
	Criminal courts and procedure
9401-9405	General (Table K13)
9430	Administration of criminal justice (Table K14)
9485	Due process of law (Table K14)
	Pretrial procedures
9525	General (Table K14)
	Compulsory measures against the accused. Securing of evidence
9550	General (Table K14)
9570	Extradition (Table K14) Including constitutional aspects
	Execution of sentence
9760	General (Table K14)
9796	Criminal registers (Table K14)

1-4999	Albania (Table KJ-KKZ1 modified)
	Administrative law
	Administrative organization
	Administrative and political divisions. Local government
	other than municipal
2935.A-Z	Administrative divisions (Rrethet), A-Z
	Including official gazettes, bylaws, statutory orders,
	regulations, and general works, as well as works on
	specific legal topics
2935.B47	Berat
2935.D52	Dibrë
2935.D87	Durrës
2935.E42	Elabasan
2935.F53	Fier
2935.F54	Gjirokastër
2935.G72	Gramsh
2935.K64	Kolonjë
2935.K67	Korçë
2935.K78	Krujë
2935.K84	Kukës
2935.L49	Lezhe
2935.L52	Librazhd
2935.L88	Lushnjë
2935.M38	Mat
2935.M57	Mirditë
2935.P47	Përmet
2935.P63	Pogradec
2935.P84	Pukë
2935.S27	Sarandë
2935.S54	Shkodër
2935.S58	Skrapar
2935.T47	Tepelenë
2935.T57	Tirana
2935.T76	Tropojë
2935.V55	Vlorë
	Cities
4980	Berat (Table KJ-KKZ5)
4981	Durrës (Table KJ-KKZ5)
4982	Elbasan (Table KJ-KKZ5)
4983	Fier (Table KJ-KKZ5)
4984	Gjirokastër (Table KJ-KKZ5)
4985	Korçë (Table KJ-KKZ5)
4986	Shkoder (Table KJ-KKZ5)
4987	Tirana (Table KJ-KKZ5)
4988	Vlorë (Table KJ-KKZ5)
4990.A-Z	Other cities, A-Z
	Subarrange each by Table KJ-KKZ6

KJG-KKZ

1-499	Andorra (Table KJ-KKZ2 modified)
	Administrative law
	Administrative organization
	Administrative and political divisions. Local government other than municipal
293.5.A-Z	Administrative divisions (Provinces), A-Z
	Including official gazettes, bylaws, statutory orders, regulations, and general works, as well as works on specific legal topics
293.5.A53	Andorra
293.5.C35	Canillo
293.5.E52	Encamp
293.5.M38	La Massana
293.5.O73	Ordino
490.A-Z	Cities
	e. g.
490.A53	Andorre-La-Vieille (Table KJ-KKZ6)
490.C35	Canillo (Table KJ-KKZ6)
490.E52	Encamp (Table KJ-KKZ6)
490.E82	Les Escaldes (Table KJ-KKZ6)
490.M38	La Massana (Table KJ-KKZ6)
490.O83	Ordino (Table KJ-KKZ6)

	Austria
1-4999	General (Table KJ-KKZ1 modified)
	States (Länder)
	Included in this list are modern jurisdictions (Länder) which are subarranged by Table KJ-KKZ3 and historic (extinct) jurisdictions which are subarranged by Table KJ-KKZ4
6001-6099	Burgenland (Table KJ-KKZ3)
6201-6299	Carinthia (Table KJ-KKZ3)
	Kärnten see KJJ6201+
6401-6499	Lower Austria (Table KJ-KKZ3)
	Niederösterreich see KJJ6401+
	Oberösterreich see KJJ7401+
	Österreich ob der Ens see KJJ7401+
6601-6699	Salzburg (Table KJ-KKZ3)
6701-6709	Salzburg (Archdiocese) (Table KJ-KKZ4)
	Steiermark see KJJ6801+
6801-6899	Styria (Table KJ-KKZ3)
7101-7199	Tirol (Table KJ-KKZ3)
7401-7499	Upper Austria (Table KJ-KKZ3)
7601-7699	Vienna (Table KJ-KKZ3)
7801-7899	Vorarlberg (Table KJ-KKZ3)
	Wien see KJJ7601+
	Cities
9851	Bregenz (Table KJ-KKZ5)
9852	Eisenstadt (Table KJ-KKZ5)
9853	Graz (Table KJ-KKZ5)
9854	Innsbruck (Table KJ-KKZ5)
9855	Klagenfurt (Table KJ-KKZ5)
9856	Linz (Table KJ-KKZ5)
9857	Salzburg (Table KJ-KKZ5)
	For Salzburg (Land) see KJJ6601+
9858	St. Pölten (Table KJ-KKZ5)
9859	Vienna (Table KJ-KKZ5)
	Wien see KJJ9859
9860.A-Z	Other cities, A-Z
	e. g.
9860.L45	Leoben (Table KJ-KKZ6)
9860.S73	Steyr (Table KJ-KKZ6)
9860.V54	Villach (Table KJ-KKZ6)
9860.W44	Wels (Table KJ-KKZ6)

KJG-KKZ

BELARUS

Belarus
see KLF1+

1-4999	Belgium (Table KJ-KKZ1 modified)
	Administrative law
	Administrative organization
	Administrative and political divisions. Local government
	other than municipal
2935.A-Z	Administrative divisions (Provinces), A-Z

Including official gazettes, bylaws, statutory orders, regulations, and general works, as well as works on specific legal topics

For provinces before 1830 see KKM5000+

2935.A58	Antwerp
2935.B72	Brabant
2935.B78	Brussels (Region)
2935.E28	East Flanders
2935.F56	Flanders (Region)
2935.H34	Hainaut
2935.J45	Jemappes
2935.L53	Liège
2935.L55	Limbourg
2935.L89	Luxembourg
2935.N35	Namur
2935.W34	Wallonia (Region)
2935.W48	West Flanders
	Cities
4980	Aalst (Alost) (Table KJ-KKZ5)
4981	Antwerp (Anvers) (Table KJ-KKZ5)
4982	Bruges (Brugge) (Table KJ-KKZ5)
4983	Brussels (Table KJ-KKZ5)
4984	Charleroi (Table KJ-KKZ5)
4985	Ghent (Gand) (Table KJ-KKZ5)
4986	Louvain (Leuven) (Table KJ-KKZ5)
4987	Liège (Luik) (Table KJ-KKZ5)
4988	Mons (Bergen) (Table KJ-KKZ5)
4989	Namur (Table KJ-KKZ5)
4990.A-Z	Other cities, A-Z
	Subarrange each by Table KJ-KKZ6
	Autonomous regions
5001-5099	Brussels (Table KJ-KKZ3)
5101-5199	Flanders (Table KJ-KKZ3)
5201-5299	Wallonia (Table KJ-KKZ3)

KJG-KKZ

Bosnia and Hercegovina (1992-)
>Class here works on the Republic of Bosnia and Hercegovina,
>>including historical periods
>For the Kingdom of Serbs, Croats, and Slovenes, 1918-1928
>>(later Kingdom of Yugoslavia, 1929-1945) see KKZ1+
>For Bosnia and Hercegovina (Federated Republic of
>>Yugoslavia) through 1991 see KKZ5001+

8001-8499	General (Table KJ-KKZ2)
8500.A-Z	Cities, A-Z
8500.S37	Sarajevo
8501-8599	Bosnia and Hercegovina (Federation) (Table KJ-KKZ3)

>Class here works on Croat-Muslim Federation created by the
>>Dayton Accords of 1995

8601-8699	Republika Srpska (Table KJ-KKZ3)

>Class here works on the Serb Republic created by the Dayton
>>Accords of 1995

1-4999	Bulgaria (Table KJ-KKZ1 modified)
	Administrative law
	Administrative organization
	Administrative and political divisions. Local government other than municipal
2935.A-Z	Administrative divisions (Okruzi), A-Z
	Including official gazettes, bylaws, statutory orders, regulations, and general works, as well as works on specific legal topics
2935.B54	Blagoevgrad (Pirin Macedonia)
	For Aegean Macedonia (Greece) see KKE1+
	For medieval and modern Macedonia and the Socialist Republic of Macedonia see KKZ5401+
	For ancient Greek Macedonia see KL2+
2935.G32	Gabrovo
2935.K43	Khaskovo
2935.K87	Kurdzhali
2935.K97	Kyustendil
2935.L68	Lovech
2935.M54	Mikhaylovgrad
2935.P39	Pazardzhik
2935.P47	Pernik
2935.P54	Pleven
2935.P56	Plovdiv
2935.R39	Razgrad
2935.R88	Ruse
2935.S48	Shumen
2935.S54	Silistra
2935.S58	Sliven
2935.S65	Smolyan
2935.S68	Sofia
2935.S72	Stara Zagora
2935.T64	Tolbukhin
2935.T87	Turgovishte
2935.V37	Varna
2935.V44	Veliko Turnovo
2935.V53	Vidin
2935.V72	Vratsa
2935.Y35	Yambol
4931-4939	Eastern Rumelia (Table KJ-KKZ4)
	Cities
4980	Burgas (Table KJ-KKZ5)
4981	Pleven (Table KJ-KKZ5)
4982	Plovdiv (Table KJ-KKZ5)
4983	Ruse (Table KJ-KKZ5)
4984	Shumen (Table KJ-KKZ5)
4985	Sliven (Table KJ-KKZ5)

KJG-KKZ

Cities -- Continued
4986	Sofia (Table KJ-KKZ5)
4987	Stara Zagora (Table KJ-KKZ5)
4988	Varna (Table KJ-KKZ5)
4989	Veliko Turnovo (Table KJ-KKZ5)
4990.A-Z	Other cities, A-Z
	e. g.
4990.B55	Blagoevgrad (Table KJ-KKZ5)
4990.G32	Gabrovo (Table KJ-KKZ5)
4990.P47	Pernik (Table KJ-KKZ5)
4990.T64	Tolbukhin (Table KJ-KKZ5)

Corsica
    see KJW1121+

CROATIA (KINGDOM)

Croatia (Kingdom)
see KJM7001+

Croatia (1992-)
> Class here works on Croatia from 1992 on, including historic
>> (defunct) jurisdictions, e.g. Kingdom of Croatia (1102-1918) and
>> Republic of Croatia (1941-1945)
> For the Kingdom of Serbs, Croats, and Slovenes, 1918-1928
>> (later Kingdom of Yugoslavia, 1929-1945) see KKZ1+
> For the People's Republic of Croatia (Federated Republic of
>> Yugoslavia) through 1991 see KKZ5201+

7001-7499	General (Table KJ-KKZ2)
7505.A-Z	Cities, A-Z
7505.Z34	Zagreb

KJG-KKZ

1-499	Cyrpus (Table KJ-KKZ2 modified)
490.A-Z	Cities, A-Z
	e. g.
490.F35	Famagusta (Table KJ-KKZ6)
490.K96	Kyrenia (Table KJ-KKZ6)
490.L37	Larnaca (Table KJ-KKZ6)
490.L55	Limassol (Table KJ-KKZ6)
490.N52	Nicosia (Table KJ-KKZ6)
490.P37	Paphos (Table KJ-KKZ6)

Czechoslovakia (to 1993)
>Class here works on the law of Czechoslovakia until December 31, 1992, as well as its constituent parts, including territories in all time periods

1-4999
General (Table KJ-KKZ1 modified)
Socialist republics. States
>Included in this list are modern jurisdictions (socialist republics) and historic (extinct) jurisdictions

5001-5009   Bohemia (Table KJ-KKZ4)
5051-5149   Czech Socialist Republic (Table KJ-KKZ3)
5201-5209   Moravia-Silesia (Land) (Table KJ-KKZ4)
5211-5219   Moravia (Table KJ-KKZ4)
5251-5259   Ruthenia (Table KJ-KKZ4)
Galicia see KKP4900+
Silesia, Upper see KKP4931+
5261-5269   Slovak Socialist Republic (Table KJ-KKZ3)
5361-5369   Slovakia (Land) (Table KJ-KKZ4)
5371-5379   Subkarpathian Ruthenia (Land) (Table KJ-KKZ4)
Cities
>see the appropriate jurisdiction, Czech Republic, KJP5980+ or Slovakia, KJQ490+
>For historic (defunct) jurisdictions see KJP5001+

KJG-KKZ

Czech Republic (1993-)
Class here works on the law of the Czech Republic from 1993 on

5401-5899	General (Table KJ-KKZ2)
	Cities
5980	Brno (Table KJ-KKZ5)
5981	Cĕské Budĕjovie (Table KJ-KKZ5)
5982	Havirōv (Table KJ-KKZ5)
5983	Hradec Králové (Table KJ-KKZ5)
5985	Liberec (Table KJ-KKZ5)
5986	Olomouc (Table KJ-KKZ5)
5987	Ostrava (Table KJ-KKZ5)
5988	Plzeň (Table KJ-KKZ5)
5989	Prague (Table KJ-KKZ5)
5990.A-Z	Other cities, A-Z
	Subarrange each by Table KJ-KKZ6

1-499   Slovakia (1993-) (Table KJ-KKZ2 modified)
                             Class here works on the law of Slovakia from 1993 on
                             For historic (defunct) jurisdictions, see KJP5001+
                         Cities
490   Bratislava
492   Košice
498.A-498.Z   Other cities, A-Z
498.B35   Banská Bystrica
498.N58   Nitra
498.P73   Prešov
498.T73   Trenčin
498.Z54   Žilina

1-4999	Denmark (Table KJ-KKZ1 modified)
	Administrative law
	Administrative organization
	Administrative and political divisions. Local government other than municipal
2935.A-Z	Administrative divisions (Ämter), A-Z
	Including official gazettes, bylaws, statutory orders, regulations, and general works, as well as works on specific legal topics
2935.B67	Bornholm
2935.F37	Faroe Islands
2935.F73	Frederiksborg
2935.F95	Fyn
	Greenland see KDZ3001+
2935.H64	Holbaek
2935.K62	København (County)
2935.M37	Maribo
2935.N67	Norrejylland
2935.P72	Praesto
2935.R52	Ribe
2935.R55	Ringkøbing
2935.R68	Roskilde
2935.S65	Sønderjylland
2935.S67	Sorø
2935.V44	Vejle
2935.V52	Viborg
4951-4959	Sjælland (Table KJ-KKZ4)
	Cities
4980	Aalborg (Table KJ-KKZ5)
4981	Aarhus (Table KJ-KKZ5)
4982	Copenhagen (Table KJ-KKZ5)
4983	Helsingor (Table KJ-KKZ5)
4984	Kolding (Table KJ-KKZ5)
4985	Odense (Table KJ-KKZ5)
4990.A-Z	Other cities, A-Z
	Subarrange each by Table KJ-KKZ6

1-4999	Estonia (Table KJ-KKZ1 modified)
	Administrative law
	Administrative organization
	Administrative and political divisions. Local government
	other than municipal
2935.A-Z	Administrative divisions. Counties (Maakonnad and
	rajoon), A-Z

Including official gazettes, bylaws, statutory orders,
regulations, and general works, as well as works on
specific legal topics

2935.H37	Harjumaa (Harju maakond)
2935.H55	Hiiumaa rajoon (Hiiu maakond)
2935.I33	Ida-Virumaa (Ida-Viru maakond)
2935.J37	Järvamaa (Järva maakond)
2935.J65	Jõgevamaa (Jõgeva maakond)
2935.L33	Lääne-Virumaa (Lääne-Viru maakond)
2935.L34	Läänemaa (Lääne maakond)
2935.P37	Pärnumaa (Pärnu maakond)
2935.P65	Põlvamaa (Põlva maakond)
2935.R37	Raplama (Rapla maakond)
2935.S33	Saaremaa (Saare maakond)
2935.T37	Tartumaa (Tartu maakond)
2935.V35	Valgamaa (Valga maakond)
2935.V55	Viljandimaa (Viljandi maakond)
2935.V67	Võrumaa (Võru maakond)
	Cities
4975	Pärnu (Table KJ-KKZ5)
4980	Rakvere (Table KJ-KKZ5)
	Reval see KJS4985
4985	Tallinn. Reval (Table KJ-KKZ5)
4990	Valga (Table KJ-KKZ5)
4995.A-Z	Other cities, A-Z
4995.H33	Haapsalu
4995.J64	Jõgeva
4995.J65	Jõhvi
4995.K37	Kärdla
4995.K87	Kuressaare
4995.P35	Paide
4995.P65	Põlva
4995.R37	Rapla
4995.T37	Tartu
4995.V55	Viljandi
4995.V67	Võru

KJG-KKZ

1-4999	Finland (Table KJ-KKZ1 modified)
	Administrative law
	Administrative organization
	Administrative and political divisions. Local government other than municipal
2935.A-Z	Administrative divisions (Lääni), A-Z
	Including official gazettes, bylaws, statutory orders, regulations, and general works, as well as works on specific legal topics
	Åbo-Björneborg see KJT2935.T87
2935.A38	Ahvenanmaa
	Åland see KJT2935.A38
2935.H35	Häme
2935.K48	Keski-Suomi
2935.K85	Kuopio
2935.K95	Kymi
	Kymmene see KJT2935.K95
2935.L38	Lappi
	Lappland see KJT2935.L38
	Mellersta Finland see KJT2935.K48
2935.M54	Mikkeli
	Norra Karelen see KJT2935.P63
	Nyland see KJT2935.U87
2935.O94	Oulu
2935.P63	Pohjois-Karjala
	St. Michel see KJT2935.M54
	Tavastehus see KJT2935.H35
2935.T87	Turku-Pori
	Uleaborg see KJT2935.O94
2935.U87	Uusimaa
2935.V32	Vaasa
	Vasa see KJT2935.V32
	Cities
	Åbo see KJT4989
	Björneborg see KJT4987
	Helsingfors see KJT4983
4983	Helsinki
4984	Kuopio
4985	Lahti
4986	Oulu
4987	Pori
	Tammerfors see KJT4988
4988	Tampere
4989	Turki
	Uleåborg see KJT4986
4990.A-Z	Other cities, A-Z
	Subarrange each by Table KJ-KKZ6

FRANCE

France
see KJV

1-4999	Greece (Table KJ-KKZ1 modified)
	For ancient Greece see JC71+; KL2+
	Administrative law
	Administrative organization
	Administrative and political divisions. Local government other than municipal
2935.A-Z	Administrative divisions (Nomoi), A-Z
	Including official gazettes, bylaws, statutory orders, regulations, and general works, as well as works on specific legal topics
2935.A24	Achaia
2935.A37	Aitōlia kai Akarnania
2935.A73	Argolis
2935.A74	Arkadia
2935.A77	Arta
2935.A78	Attikē
2935.C45	Chalkidikē
2935.C46	Chania
2935.C47	Chios
2935.C73	Crevena
2935.D63	Dōdekanēsa
2935.D72	Drama
2935.E43	Ēlia
2935.E46	Ēmathia
2935.E87	Eurytania
2935.E88 .	Euvoia
2935.E89	Evros
2935.H47	Hērakleio
2935.I55	Iōannina
2935.K36	Karditsa
2935.K37	Kastoria
2935.K38	Kavala
2935.K47	Kephallēnia
2935.K48	Kerkyra
2935.K54	Kilkis
2935.K67	Korinthia
2935.K69	Kozanē
2935.K84	Kykladai
2935.L34	Lakōnia
2935.L37	Laris
2935.L38	Lasithio
2935.L48	Lesvos
2935.L49	Leukas
2935.M34	Magnēsia
2935.N47	Nessēnia
2935.P44	Pellē
2935.P45	Phlōrina

Administrative law
  Administrative organization
    Administrative and political divisions. Local government
      other than municipal
      Administrative divisions (Nomoi), A-Z -- Continued

2935.P46	Phōkis
2935.P47	Phthiōtida
2935.P53	Pieria
2935.P74	Preveza
2935.R48	Rethymno
2935.R63	Rodopē
2935.S25	Samos
2935.S59	Skyros
2935.T45	Thesprōtia
2935.T46	Thessalonikē
2935.T74	Trikala
2935.V64	Voiōtia
2935.X35	Xanthē
2935.Z34	Zakynthos

Cities

4980	Athens (Table KJ-KKZ5)
4981	Canea (Table KJ-KKZ5)
4982	Heraklion (Table KJ-KKZ5)
4983	Iōannina (Table KJ-KKZ5)
4984	Kavala (Table KJ-KKZ5)
4985	Larisa (Table KJ-KKZ5)
4986	Patras (Table KJ-KKZ5)
4987	Piraeus (Table KJ-KKZ5)
4988	Thessaloniki (Table KJ-KKZ5)
4989	Volos (Table KJ-KKZ5)
4990.A-Z	Other cities, A-Z
	Subarrange each by Table KJ-KKZ6

KJG-KKZ

1-4999	Hungary (Table KJ-KKZ1 modified)
	Administrative law
	Administrative organization
	Administrative and political divisions. Local government
	other than municipal
2935.A-Z	Administrative divisions (Megyek), A-Z
	Including official gazettes, bylaws, statutory orders,
	regulations, and general works, as well as works on
	specific legal topics
	Included in this list are modern jurisdictions and historic
	(extinct) jurisdictions
2935.A22	Abaúj-Torna
2935.A48	Alsó Fehér
2935.A72	Arad
2935.A78	Arva
2935.B32	Bács-Bodrog
2935.B33	Bács Kiskun
2935.B37	Baranya
2935.B38	Bars
2935.B44	Békés
2935.B47	Bereg
2935.B48	Beszterce-Naszód
2935.B54	Bihar
2935.B67	Borsod
2935.B68	Borsod-Abaúj-Zemplén
2935.B73	Brassó
2935.C75	Csanád
2935.C76	Csík
2935.C77	Csongrad
2935.E89	Esztergom
2935.F44	Fejér
2935.F63	Fogaras
2935.G65	Gömör és Kishont
2935.G95	Györ
2935.G96	Gyor-Sopron
2935.H34	Hajdú
2935.H35	Hajdú-Bihar
2935.H37	Háromszék
2935.H48	Heves
2935.H65	Hont
2935.H85	Hunyad
2935.J37	Jász-Nagykun-Szolnok
2935.K57	Kisküküllö
2935.K64	Kolozs
2935.K65	Komárom
2935.K73	Krassó-Szörény
2935.L57	Liptó

Administrative law
   Administrative organization
      Administrative and political divisions. Local government
         other than municipal
            Administration divisions (Megyek), A-Z -- Continued

2935.M36	Máramaros
2935.M38	Maros-Torda
2935.M67	Moson
2935.N33	Nagyküküllö
2935.N63	Nógrád
2935.N93	Nyitra
2935.P47	Pest
2935.P48	Pest-Pilis-Solt-Kiskun
2935.P69	Pozsony
2935.S27	Sáros
2935.S65	Somogy
2935.S67	Sopron
2935.S92	Szabolcs
2935.S93	Szabolcs-Szatmár
2935.S94	Szatmár
2935.S95	Szeben
2935.S96	Szepes
2935.S97	Szilágy
2935.S98	Szolnok
2935.S99	Szolnok-Doboka
2935.T45	Temes
2935.T64	Tolda-Aranyos
2935.T65	Tolna
2935.T67	Torontál
2935.T73	Trencsén
2935.T87	Turóc
2935.U35	Ugoosa
2935.U53	Ung
2935.V38	Vas
2935.V48	Veszprém
2935.Z34	Zala
2935.Z45	Zemplén
2935.Z64	Zólyom

Cities

4980	Budapest (Table KJ-KKZ5)
4981	Debrecen (Table KJ-KKZ5)
4982	Eger (Table KJ-KKZ5)
4983	Györ (Table KJ-KKZ5)
4984	Miskolc (Table KJ-KKZ5)
4985	Pécs (Table KJ-KKZ5)
4986	Salgótarján (Table KJ-KKZ5)
4987	Székesfehérvár (Table KJ-KKZ5)

KJG-KKZ

Cities -- Continued
4988	Szombathely (Table KJ-KKZ5)
4989	Veszprém (Table KJ-KKZ5)
4990.A-Z	Other cities, A-Z
	e. g.
4990.B44	Békéscsaba (Table KJ-KKZ6)
4990.H63	Hódmezövásárhely (Table KJ-KKZ6)
4990.K37	Kaposvár (Table KJ-KKZ6)
4990.K42	Kecskemét (Table KJ-KKZ6)
4990.N93	Nyiregyháza (Table KJ-KKZ6)
4990.S94	Szekszárd (Table KJ-KKZ6)
4990.S96	Szolnok (Table KJ-KKZ6)
4990.T37	Tatabánya (Table KJ-KKZ6)

1-499   Iceland (Table KJ-KKZ2 modified)
490.A-Z   Cities, A-Z
                            e. g.
490.R49   Reykjavik (Table KJ-KKZ6)

IRELAND

Ireland
    see KDK21+

Italy
                    For ancient Rome see JC81+; KJA0+
1-4999   General (Table KJ-KKZ1)
                Autonomous regions (Regioni). States
                    Included in this list are modern jurisdictions (regioni) which are
                        assigned Table KJ-KKZ3 , and historic (extinct) jurisdictions
                        which are assigned Table KJ-KKZ4
5001-5099   Abruzzo (Table KJ-KKZ3)
5101-5199   Basilicata (Table KJ-KKZ3)
5201-5209   Belluno (Table KJ-KKZ4)
5211-5219   Bergamo (Table KJ-KKZ4)
5221-5229   Bolzano (Table KJ-KKZ4)
5251-5349   Calabria (Table KJ-KKZ3)
5401-5499   Campania (Table KJ-KKZ3)
5501-5599   Emilia Romagna (Table KJ-KKZ3)
5601-5609   Florence (Republic and Duchy) (Table KJ-KKZ4)
5651-5749   Friuli-Venezia-Giulia (Table KJ-KKZ3)
5851-5949   Lazio (Table KJ-KKZ3)
6001-6099   Liguria (Table KJ-KKZ3)
                    Including the Republic of Genoa and the Ligurian Republic
6151-6249   Lombardy (Table KJ-KKZ3)
                    For Lombard empire see KJ1+
6351-6449   Marche (Table KJ-KKZ3)
                Milan (Duchy) see KKH9853
6551-6649   Molise (Table KJ-KKZ3)
6701-6709   Naples (Kingdom) (Table KJ-KKZ4)
                    Including the Kingdom of the Two Sicilies
6731-6739   Parma and Piacenza (Duchy) (Table KJ-KKZ4)
6741-6749   Papal States (Table KJ-KKZ4)
6751-6849   Piemonte (Table KJ-KKZ3)
6951-7049   Puglia (Table KJ-KKZ3)
                Sardegna see KKH7151+
7151-7249   Sardinia (Table KJ-KKZ3)
7351-7449   Sicily (Table KJ-KKZ3)
                Toscana see KKH7851+
7551-7649   Trentino-Alto Adige (Table KJ-KKZ3)
7651-7659   Trento (Table KJ-KKZ4)
7751-7759   Treviso (Table KJ-KKZ4)
7841-7849   Tuscany (Grand Duchy) (Table KJ-KKZ4)
7851-7949   Tuscany (Table KJ-KKZ3)
8001-8099   Umbria (Table KJ-KKZ3)
8151-8249   Valle d'Aosta (Table KJ-KKZ3)
8351-8449   Veneto (Table KJ-KKZ3)
8501-8509   Venice (Table KJ-KKZ4)
                Cities
9850   Bologna (Table KJ-KKZ5)
                Firenze see KKH9851

KJG-KKZ

Cities -- Continued

9851	Florence (Table KJ-KKZ5)
	For the Duchy and Republic see KKH5601+
9852	Genoa (Table KJ-KKZ5)
	For the Republic of Genoa and the Ligurian Republic see KKH6001+
9853	Milan (Table KJ-KKZ5)
	Including tthe extinct Duchy of Milan
9854	Naples (Table KJ-KKZ5)
9855	Padua (Table KJ-KKZ5)
9856	Palermo (Table KJ-KKZ5)
9857	Rome (Table KJ-KKZ5)
9858	Venice (Table KJ-KKZ5)
	For pre-1797 Republic see KKH8501+
9859	Verona (Table KJ-KKZ5)
9860.A-Z	Other cities, A-Z
	e. g.
9860.B37	Bari (Table KJ-KKZ6)
9860.B73	Brescia (Table KJ-KKZ6)
9860.C33	Cagliari (Table KJ-KKZ6)
9860.C37	Catania (Table KJ-KKZ6)
9860.M47	Messina (Table KJ-KKZ6)
9860.M63	Modena (Table KJ-KKZ6)
9860.R43	Reggio (Table KJ-KKZ6)
9860.R68	Rovereto (Table KJ-KKZ6)
9860.T37	Taranto (Table KJ-KKZ6)
9860.T87	Turin (Table KJ-KKZ6)

Kosovo
>Class here works on the Republic of Kosovo from 2008 on
>For the province of Kosovo of the Socialist Republic of Serbia
>(Yugoslavia) through 1991 see KKZ5801+

9901-9999	General (Table KJ-KKZ3)
9999.5.A-Z	Cities, A-Z
9999.5.P75	Pristina

KJG-KKZ

1-4999	Latvia (Table KJ-KKZ1 modified)
	Administrative law
	Administrative organization
	Administrative and political divisions. Local government other than municipal
2935.A-Z	Administrative divisions. Districts (Rajoni), A-Z
	Including official gazettes, bylaws, statutory orders, regulations, and general works, as well as works on specific legal topics
2935.A39	Aizkraukles rajons
2935.A48	Alūksnes rajons
2935.B35	Balvu rajons
2935.B38	Bauskas rajons
2935.C47	Cēsu rajons
	Daugavpils (Municipality) see KKI4990.D38
2935.D38	Daugavpils rajons
2935.D63	Dobeles rajons
2935.G85	Gulbenes rajons
2935.J45	Jēkabpils rajons
	Jelgava (Municipality) see KKI4990.J45
2935.J46	Jelgavas rajons
	Jūrmala (Municipality) see KKI4990.J87
2935.K73	Krāslavas rajons
2935.K85	Kuldīgas rajons
	Liepāja (Municipality) see KKI4990.L54
2935.L54	Liepājas rajons
2935.L56	Limbažu rajons
2935.L83	Ludzas rajons
2935.M33	Madonas rajons
2935.O37	Ogres rajons
2935.P74	Preiļu rajons
	Rēzekne (Municipality) see KKI4990.R49
2935.R49	Rēzeknes rajons
	Rīga (Municipality) see KKI4987
2935.R54	Rīgas rajons
2935.S35	Saldus rajons
2935.T35	Talsu rajons
2935.T85	Tukuma rajons
2935.V35	Valkas rajons
2935.V36	Valmieras rajons
	Ventspils (Municipality) see KKI4990.V46
2935.V46	Ventspils rajons
	Cities
4987	Rīga (Table KJ-KKZ5)
4990.A-Z	Other cities, A-Z
4990.D38	Daugavpils
4990.J45	Jelgava

Cities
Other cities, A-Z -- Continued
4990.J87 Jūrmala
4990.L54 Liepāja
4990.R49 Rēzekne
4990.V46 Ventspils
Historic (defunct) jurisdictions
4992 Courland (Table KJ-KKZ5)
Including the duchy of Courland

KJG-KKZ

1-499	Liechtenstein (Table KJ-KKZ2 modified)
	Administrative law
	Administrative organization
	Administrative and political divisions. Local government
	other than municipal
293.5.A-Z	Administrative divisions (Communes), A-Z
	Including official gazettes, bylaws, statutory orders,
	regulations, and general works, as well as works on
	specific legal topics
293.5.B37	Balzers
293.5.E82	Eschens
293.5.G35	Gamprin
293.5.M38	Mauren
293.5.P55	Planken
293.5.R83	Ruggell
293.5.S32	Schaan
293.5.S33	Schellenberg
293.5.T73	Triesen
293.5.T74	Triesenberg
293.5.V32	Vaduz
490.A-Z	Cities, A-Z
	e. g.
490.V33	Vaduz (Table KJ-KKZ6)

5001-9999	Lithuania (Table KJ-KKZ1 modified)
	Administrative law
	Administrative organization
	Administrative and political divisions. Local government other than municpal
7935.A-Z	Administrative divisions (Counties and municipalities. Apskritys, rajono savivaldybės, and miesto savivaldybės), A-Z
	Including historic entities (e.g. autonomous regions, oblasts/sritys, etc.) and including official gazettes, bylaws, statutory orders, regulations, and general works, as well as works on specific legal topics
7935.A49	Alytus County
7935.K38	Kaunas County
7935.K53	Klaipėda County
7935.M37	Marijampolė County
	Memel Territory see KKJ7935.K53
7935.P36	Panevėžys County
7935.S53	Šiauliai County
7935.T38	Tauragė County
7935.T45	Telšiai County
7935.U84	Utena County
7935.V55	Vilnius County
9950.A-Z	Cities, A-Z
9950.A49	Alytus
9950.K53	Klaipėda
9950.M37	Marijampolė
9950.V55	Vilnius

KJG-KKZ

1-499   Luxembourg (Table KJ-KKZ2 modified)
                            Administrative law
                            Administrative organization
                            Administrative and political divisions. Local government
                                other than municipal
293.5.A-Z   Administrative divisions, A-Z
                                Including official gazettes, bylaws, statutory orders,
                                    regulations, and general works, as well as works on
                                    specific legal topics
293.5.D53   Diekirch
293.5.G73   Grevenmacher
293.5.L38   Luxembourg
490.A-Z   Cities, A-Z
                            e. g.
490.D54   Differdange (Table KJ-KKZ6)
490.D83   Dudelange (Table KJ-KKZ6)
490.E82   Esch-Alzette (Table KJ-KKZ6)
490.L89   Luxembourg (Table KJ-KKZ6)
490.P48   Petange (Table KJ-KKZ6)

Macedonia (Republic) (1992-)
    For Pirin Macedonia (Blagoevgrad, Bulgaria) see
       KJM2935.B54
    For Aegean Macedonia (Greece) see KKE1+
    For the Republic of Macedonia (Federated Republic of
       Yugoslavia), 1945-1991 see KKZ5401+
    For the ancient Macedonian-Hellenic period see KL4113

501-999	General (Table KJ-KKZ2)
1000.A-Z	Cities, A-Z
1000.S56	Skopje

KJG-KKZ

1001-1499   Malta (Table KJ-KKZ2)

MOLDOVA

Moldova
    see KLM1+

1-499	Monaco (Table KJ-KKZ2 modified)
	Administrative law
	Administrative organization
	Administrative and political divisions. Local government
	other than municipal
293.5.A-Z	Administrative divisions, A-Z
	Including official gazettes, bylaws, statutory orders,
	regulations, and general works, as well as works on
	specific legal topics
293.5.C65	La Condamine
293.5.F65	Fontvieille
293.5.M65	Monaco-Ville
293.5.M66	Monte-Carlo

Montenegro (Kingdom)
see KKL1001+

KJG-KKZ

Montenegro
    Class here works on the Republic of Montenegro from 2006 on,
        including historic (defunct) jurisdictions, e.g. Independent
        Prinicpality (1878) and Kingdom of Macedonia (1910)
    For the State Union of Serbia and Montenegro (2003-2006)
        see KKZ1+
    For the Socialist Republic of Montenegro (Yugoslavia)
        through 1991 see KKZ5501+

1001-1499	General (Table KJ-KKZ2)
1505.A-Z	Cities, A-Z
1505.P63	Podgorica

            Previously Titograd

	Netherlands
1-4999	General (Table KJ-KKZ1 modified)
	Provinces (Provincies). States
	Included in this list are modern jurisdictions (provinces) which are assigned Table KJ-KKZ3 , and historic (extinct) jurisdictions which are assigned Table KJ-KKZ4
5001-5009	Brabant (Duchy) (Table KJ-KKZ4)
5051-5149	Noord-Brabant (Table KJ-KKZ3)
5551-5649	Limburg (Table KJ-KKZ3)
5881-5889	Hainaut (Comté) (Table KJ-KKZ4)
5911-5919	Heinaut (Province of Netherlands) (Table KJ-KKZ4)
6051-6149	Groningen (Table KJ-KKZ3)
6251-6349	Friesland (Table KJ-KKZ3)
6351-6449	Drenthe (Table KJ-KKZ3)
6551-6649	Overijssel (Table KJ-KKZ3)
6651-6749	Flevoland (Table KJ-KKZ3)
7351-7449	Gelderland (Table KJ-KKZ3)
7451-7549	Utrecht (Table KJ-KKZ3)
7851-7949	Noord-Holland (Table KJ-KKZ3)
8351-8449	Zuid-Holland (Table KJ-KKZ3)
8551-8649	Zeeland (Table KJ-KKZ3)
	Cities
9850	Amsterdam (Table KJ-KKZ5)
9851	Breda (Table KJ-KKZ5)
9852	's-Gravenhage (Table KJ-KKZ5)
9853	Groningen (Table KJ-KKZ5)
9854	Haarlem (Table KJ-KKZ5)
9855	's-Hertogenbosch (Table KJ-KKZ5)
9856	Maastricht (Table KJ-KKZ5)
9857	Nijmegen (Table KJ-KKZ5)
9858	Rotterdam (Table KJ-KKZ5)
9859	Utrecht (Table KJ-KKZ5)
9860.A-Z	Other cities, A-Z
	e. g.
9860.A43	Amersfoort (Table KJ-KKZ6)
9860.A63	Apeldoorn (Table KJ-KKZ6)
9860.A75	Arnhem (Table KJ-KKZ6)
9860.A88	Assen (Table KJ-KKZ6)
9860.D67	Dordrecht (Table KJ-KKZ6)
9860.E45	Eindhoven (Table KJ-KKZ6)
9860.E58	Enschede (Table KJ-KKZ6)
9860.K35	Kampen (Table KJ-KKZ6)
9860.L43	Leeuwarden (Table KJ-KKZ6)
9860.L44	Leiden (Table KJ-KKZ6)
9860.M53	Middelburg (Table KJ-KKZ6)
9860.T55	Tilburg (Table KJ-KKZ6)
9860.Z85	Zwolle (Table KJ-KKZ6)

KJG-KKZ

1-4999	Norway (Table KJ-KKZ1 modified)
	Administrative law
	Administrative organization
	Administrative and political divisions. Local government
	other than municipal
2935.A-Z	Administrative divisions (Fylker), A-Z
	Including official gazettes, bylaws, statutory orders,
	regulations, and general works, as well as works on
	specific legal topics
2935.A35	Akershus
2935.A87	Aust-Agder
2935.B87	Buskerud
2935.F55	Finnmark
2935.H33	Hedmark
2935.H67	Hordaland
2935.M67	Møre og Romsdal
2935.N66	Nord-Trøndelag
2935.N67	Nordland
2935.O77	Oppland
2935.O78	Østfold
2935.R63	Rogaland
2935.S64	Sogn og Fjordane
2935.S67	Sør-Trøndelag
2935.T44	Telemark
2935.T75	Troms
2935.V47	Vest-Agder
2935.V48	Vestfold
	Cities
4980	Ålesund (Table KJ-KKZ5)
4981	Bergen (Table KJ-KKZ5)
4982	Bodø (Table KJ-KKZ5)
	Christiania see KKN4984
4983	Drammen (Table KJ-KKZ5)
4984	Oslo (Table KJ-KKZ5)
4985	Stavanger (Table KJ-KKZ5)
4986	Tromsø (Table KJ-KKZ5)
4987	Trondheim (Table KJ-KKZ5)
4990.A-Z	Other cities, A-Z
	e. g.
4990.K74	Kristiansand (Table KJ-KKZ6)
4990.S24	Sandefjord (Table KJ-KKZ6)
4990.S25	Sandnes (Table KJ-KKZ6)
4990.S54	Skien (Table KJ-KKZ6)

1-4999	Poland (Table KJ-KKZ1 modified)
	Administrative law
	Administrative organization
	Administrative and political divisions. Local government
	other than municipal
2935.A-Z	Administrative divisions (Voivodeships), A-Z
	Including official gazettes, bylaws, statutory orders,
	regulations, and general works, as well as works on
	specific legal topics
2935.B52	Biala Podlaska
2935.B53	Bialystok
2935.B54	Bielsko-Biala
2935.B92	Bydgoszcz
2935.C45	Chelm
2935.C53	Ciechanów
	Cracow see KKP2935.K72
2935.C93	Czestochowa
	Danzig see KKP2935.G35
2935.E42	Elblag
2935.G35	Gdańsk
2935.G67	Gorzów
2935.J44	Jelenia Góra
2935.K34	Kalisz
2935.K37	Katowice
2935.K53	Kielce
2935.K65	Konin
2935.K67	Koszalin
2935.K72	Kraków
2935.K75	Krosno
2935.L43	Legnica
2935.L47	Leszno
2935.L63	Lódź
2935.L65	Lomza
2935.L82	Lublin
2935.N68	Nowy Sacz
2935.O47	Olsztyn
2935.O65	Opole
2935.O87	Ostrołeka
2935.P54	Pila
2935.P55	Piotrków
2935.P57	Plock
2935.P68	Poznań
2935.P79	Przemyśl
2935.R33	Radom
2935.R93	Rzeszów
2935.S53	Siedlce
2935.S54	Sieradz

KJG-KKZ

Administrative law
  Administrative organization
    Administrative and political divisions. Local government
      other than municipal
        Administrative divisions (Voivodeships), A-Z -- Continued

2935.S543	Silesia
2935.S55	Skierniewice
2935.S95	Suwalki
2935.S97	Szczecin
2935.T36	Tarnobrzeg
2935.T37	Tarnów
2935.T67	Torun
2935.W34	Walbrzych
2935.W37	Warsaw
2935.W45	Wloclawek
2935.W75	Wroclaw
2935.Z35	Zamosc
2935.Z53	Zielona Góra
4900-4909	Galicia (Table KJ-KKZ4)
4931-4939	Silesia, Upper (Table KJ-KKZ4)
	Cities
	Breslau see KKP4989
	Cracow see KKP4983
4980	Czestochowa (Table KJ-KKZ5)
	Danzig see KKP4981
4981	Gdansk (Table KJ-KKZ5)
4982	Katowice (Table KJ-KKZ5)
4983	Krakow (Table KJ-KKZ5)
4984	Lódz (Table KJ-KKZ5)
4985	Lublin (Table KJ-KKZ5)
4986	Poznán (Table KJ-KKZ5)
	Stettin see KKP4987
4987	Szczecin (Table KJ-KKZ5)
4988	Warsaw (Table KJ-KKZ5)
4989	Wroclaw (Table KJ-KKZ5)
4990.A-Z	Other cities, A-Z
	e. g.
4990.B52	Bialystok (Table KJ-KKZ6)
4990.B53	Bielsko-Biala (Table KJ-KKZ6)
4990.B93	Bydgoszcz (Table KJ-KKZ6)
4990.B97	Bytom (Table KJ-KKZ6)
4990.C48	Chełmno (Table KJ-KKZ6)
4990.C5	Chorzów (Table KJ-KKZ6)
4990.G35	Gdynia (Table KJ-KKZ6)
4990.G53	Gliwice (Table KJ-KKZ6)
4990.K53	Kielce (Table KJ-KKZ6)
4990.N53	Nienadowa (Table KJ-KKZ6)

Cities
Other cities, A-Z -- Continued

4990.R33	Radom (Table KJ-KKZ6)
4990.R83	Ruda Staska (Table KJ-KKZ6)
4990.S67	Sosnowiec (Table KJ-KKZ6)
4990.T67	Torún (Table KJ-KKZ6)
4990.T92	Tychy (Table KJ-KKZ6)
4990.Z32	Zabrze (Table KJ-KKZ6)

1-4999	Portugal (Table KJ-KKZ1 modified)
	Administrative law
	Administrative organization
	Administrative and political divisions. Local government other than municipal
2935.A-Z	Administrative divisions (Distritos), A-Z
	Including official gazettes, bylaws, statutory orders, regulations, and general works, as well as works on specific legal topics
	Including autonomous regions
2935.A53	Angra do Heroísmo
2935.A93	Aveiro
2935.A96	Azores
2935.B44	Beja
2935.B72	Braga
2935.B73	Bragança
2935.C37	Casteló Branco
2935.C64	Coimbra
2935.E85	Evora
2935.F37	Faro
2935.G82	Guarda
2935.L44	Leiria
2935.L57	Lisboa
2935.M33	Madeira
2935.P67	Portalegre
2935.P68	Porto
2935.S25	Santarém
2935.S37	Setúbal
2935.V52	Viana do Castelo
2935.V55	Vila Real
2935.V57	Viseu
	Cities
4980	Braga (Table KJ-KKZ5)
4981	Coimbra (Table KJ-KKZ5)
4982	Evora (Table KJ-KKZ5)
4983	Faro (Table KJ-KKZ5)
4984	Lisbon (Table KJ-KKZ5)
4985	Porto (Table KJ-KKZ5)
4986	Setúbal (Table KJ-KKZ5)
4990.A-Z	Other cities, A-Z
	e. g.
4990.A45	Almada (Table KJ-KKZ6)
4990.A52	Amadora (Table KJ-KKZ6)
4990.B37	Barreiro (Table KJ-KKZ6)
4990.C68	Covilha (Table KJ-KKZ6)
4990.M38	Matosinhos (Table KJ-KKZ6)
4990.M67	Moscavide (Table KJ-KKZ6)

1-4999	Romania (Table KJ-KKZ1 modified)
	Administrative law
	Administrative organization
	Administrative and political divisions. Local government
	other than municipal
2935.A-Z	Administrative divisions (Judets), A-Z

Including official gazettes, bylaws, statutory orders,
regulations, and general works, as well as works on
specific legal topics
Including autonomous regions

2935.A42	Alba
2935.A72	Arad
2935.A73	Arges
2935.B32	Bacău
2935.B53	Bihor
2935.B57	Bistrita-Nasaud
2935.B68	Botosani
2935.B72	Brăila
2935.B73	Brasov
2935.B82	Bucharest
2935.B88	Buzău
2935.C27	Casaş-Severin
2935.C58	Cluj
2935.C65	Constanţa
2935.C68	Cosvasna
2935.D55	Dimboviţa
2935.D64	Dolj
2935.G34	Galati
2935.G67	Gorj
2935.H37	Harghita
2935.H85	Hunedoara
2935.I24	Ialomiţa
2935.I28	Iaşi
2935.I44	Ilfov
2935.M37	Maramureş
2935.M43	Mehedinţi
2935.M87	Mureş
2935.N32	Neamt
2935.O48	Olt
2935.P72	Prahova
2935.S24	Sălaj
2935.S28	Sătu Mare
2935.S52	Sibiu
2935.S82	Suceava
2935.T44	Teleorman
2935.T55	Timiş
2935.T84	Tulcea

KJG-KKZ

	Administrative law
	Administrative organization
	Administrative and political divisions. Local government
	other than municipal
	Administrative divisions (Judets), A-Z -- Continued
2935.V38	Vaslui
2935.V54	Vilcea
2935.V72	Vrancea
4931-4939	Moldavia (Table KJ-KKZ4)

> Class here works on the region of eastern Romania
> For the historical principality of Moldavia see KLM494
> For the Moldavian A.S.S.R. see KLP0+

4951-4959	Transylvania (Table KJ-KKZ4)
4971-4979	Wallachia (Table KJ-KKZ4)
	Cities
4980	Arad (Table KJ-KKZ5)
4981	Bucharest (Table KJ-KKZ5)
4982	Cluj-Napoca (Table KJ-KKZ5)
4983	Constanta (Table KJ-KKZ5)
4984	Craiova (Table KJ-KKZ5)
4985	Galati (Table KJ-KKZ5)
4986	Iasi (Table KJ-KKZ5)
4987	Resita (Table KJ-KKZ5)
4988	Timisoara (Table KJ-KKZ5)
4989	Tirgu Mures (Table KJ-KKZ5)
4990.A-Z	Other cities, A-Z
	e. g.
4990.A42	Alba Iulia (Table KJ-KKZ6)
4990.A43	Alexandria (Table KJ-KKZ6)
4990.B32	Bacău (Table KJ-KKZ6)
4990.B33	Baia Mare (Table KJ-KKZ6)
4990.B58	Bistrita (Table KJ-KKZ6)
4990.B68	Botosani (Table KJ-KKZ6)
4990.B72	Brăila (Table KJ-KKZ6)
4990.B73	Brasov (Table KJ-KKZ6)
4990.B89	Buzău (Table KJ-KKZ6)
4990.D48	Deva (Table KJ-KKZ6)
4990.D76	Drobeta-Turnu Severin (Table KJ-KKZ6)
4990.F78	Focsani (Table KJ-KKZ6)
4990.M53	Miercurea Ciuc (Table KJ-KKZ6)
4990.O72	Oradea (Table KJ-KKZ6)
4990.P52	Piatra Neamt (Table KJ-KKZ6)
4990.P57	Pitesti (Table KJ-KKZ6)
4990.P59	Ploiesti (Table KJ-KKZ6)
4990.R55	Rimnicu Vilcea (Table KJ-KKZ6)
4990.S28	Satu Mare (Table KJ-KKZ6)
4990.S43	Sf. Gheorghe (Table KJ-KKZ6)

Cities
Other cities, A-Z -- Continued
4990.S52	Sibiu (Table KJ-KKZ6)
4990.S58	Slatina (Table KJ-KKZ6)
4990.S59	Slobozia (Table KJ-KKZ6)
4990.S92	Suceava (Table KJ-KKZ6)
4990.T57	Tirgoviste (Table KJ-KKZ6)
4990.T58	Tirgu Jiu (Table KJ-KKZ6)
4990.T84	Tulcea (Table KJ-KKZ6)
4990.V38	Vaslui (Table KJ-KKZ6)
4990.Z34	Zalău (Table KJ-KKZ6)

KJG-KKZ

RUSSIA

Russia
  see KLA1+

1-499	San Marino (Table KJ-KKZ2 modified)
	Administrative law
	Administrative organization
	Administrative and political divisions. Local government other than municipal
293.5.A-Z	Administrative divisions, A-Z
	Including official gazettes, bylaws, statutory orders, regulations, and general works, as well as works on specific legal topics
293.5.A27	Acquaviva
293.5.B67	Borgo Maggiore
293.5.C45	Chiesanuova
293.5.D65	Domagnano
293.5.F33	Faetano
293.5.F55	Fiorentino
293.5.M65	Monte Giardino
293.5.S24	San Marino
293.5.S47	Serravalle

KJG-KKZ

SERBIA (KINGDOM)

Serbia (Kingdom)
see KKS1001+

Serbia (2006-)
>
> Including historic (defunct) jurisdictions, e.g. Kingdom of Serbia (to
> 1918)
>
> For the Kingdom of Serbs, Croats, and Slovenes, 1918-1928
> (later Kingdom of Yugoslavia, 1929-1945) and the State
> Union of Serbia and Montenegro (2003-2006) see KKZ1+
>
> For the Socialist Republic of Serbia (Yugoslavia) through
> 1991 see KKZ5701+

1001-1499	General (Table KJ-KKZ2)
1505.A-Z	Cities, A-Z
1505.B45	Belgrade
1505.N68	Novi Sad

KJG-KKZ

(3001-3499)   Serbia and Montenegro
                          see KKZ1+

	Slovenia (1992-)
	For the Socialist Republic of Slovenia (Yugoslavia) through
	1991 see KKZ6201+
6001-6499	General (Table KJ-KKZ2)
6505.A-Z	Cities, A-Z
6505.L58	Ljubljana

SOVIET UNION

Soviet Union
see KLA1+

	Spain
1-4999	General (Table KJ-KKZ1)
	Autonomous communities and provinces (Provincias)
	Included in this list are modern jurisdictions and historic (extinct) jurisdictions
5051-5059	Alava (Table KJ-KKZ4)
5101-5109	Albacete (Table KJ-KKZ4)
5201-5209	Alicante (Table KJ-KKZ4)
5301-5309	Almeria (Table KJ-KKZ4)
5321-5329	Andalusia (Table KJ-KKZ4)
5341-5349	Aragón (Table KJ-KKZ4)
5361-5369	Asturias (Table KJ-KKZ4)
5401-5409	Avila (Table KJ-KKZ4)
5501-5509	Badajoz (Table KJ-KKZ4)
5601-5609	Baleares (Table KJ-KKZ4)
5651-5659	Barcelona (Table KJ-KKZ4)
5671-5679	Basque country (Table KJ-KKZ4)
5751-5759	Burgos (Table KJ-KKZ4)
5801-5809	Cáceres (Table KJ-KKZ4)
5851-5859	Cádiz (Table KJ-KKZ4)
5861-5869	Canary Islands (Table KJ-KKZ4)
5871-5879	Cantabria (Table KJ-KKZ4)
6001-6009	Castellón (Table KJ-KKZ4)
6031-6039	Castilla-La Mancha (Table KJ-KKZ4)
6051-6059	Castilla-León. Castile (Table KJ-KKZ4)
6071-6079	Catalonia (Table KJ-KKZ4)
6101-6109	Ciudad-Real (Table KJ-KKZ4)
	Communidad Valenciana see KKT8781+
6211-6219	Córdoba (Table KJ-KKZ4)
6311-6319	Coruña (La) (Table KJ-KKZ4)
6331-6339	Cuenca (Table KJ-KKZ4)
6351-6359	Extremadura (Table KJ-KKZ4)
6391-6399	Galicia (Table KJ-KKZ4)
6431-6439	Gerona (Table KJ-KKZ4)
6451-6459	Granada (Table KJ-KKZ4)
6551-6559	Guadalajara (Table KJ-KKZ4)
6651-6659	Guipúzcoa (Table KJ-KKZ4)
6661-6669	Huelva (Table KJ-KKZ4)
6701-6709	Huesca (Table KJ-KKZ4)
6781-6789	Jaén (Table KJ-KKZ4)
6801-6809	Las Palmas de Gran Canaria (Canary Islands) (Table KJ-KKZ4)
6851-6859	León (Table KJ-KKZ4)
7001-7009	Lérida (Table KJ-KKZ4)
7101-7109	Logrono (Table KJ-KKZ4)
7201-7209	Lugo (Table KJ-KKZ4)
7301-7309	Madrid (Table KJ-KKZ4)

KJG-KKZ

	Autonomous communities and provinces (Provincias) -- Continued
7401-7409	Málaga (Table KJ-KKZ4)
7501-7509	Murcia (Table KJ-KKZ4)
7601-7609	Navarra (Table KJ-KKZ4)
7801-7809	Orense (Table KJ-KKZ4)
7901-7909	Oviedo (Table KJ-KKZ4)
8001-8009	Palencia (Table KJ-KKZ4)
	Palmas (Las) see KKT6801+
8031-8039	Pontevedra (Table KJ-KKZ4)
8051-8059	Rioja, La (Table KJ-KKZ4)
8101-8109	Salamanca (Table KJ-KKZ4)
8211-8219	Santa Cruz de Tenerife (Canary Islands) (Table KJ-KKZ4)
8231-8239	Santander (Table KJ-KKZ4)
8331-8339	Segovia (Table KJ-KKZ4)
8431-8439	Sevilla (Table KJ-KKZ4)
8551-8559	Soria (Table KJ-KKZ4)
8571-8579	Tarragona (Table KJ-KKZ4)
	Tenerife see KKT8211+
8671-8679	Teruel (Table KJ-KKZ4)
8681-8689	Toledo (Table KJ-KKZ4)
8701-8709	Valencia (Table KJ-KKZ4)
8781-8789	Valencian Community (Table KJ-KKZ4)
8881-8889	Valladolid (Table KJ-KKZ4)
9001-9009	Vizcaya (Table KJ-KKZ4)
9101-9109	Zamora (Table KJ-KKZ4)
9251-9259	Zaragoza (Table KJ-KKZ4)
	Spanish Overseas Territories and Provinces
	Ifni see KSE601+
	Spanish Sahara see KTN601+
	Spanish West Africa see KTN1+
	Territories Españoles del Golfo de Guinea see KSE1+
	Cities
9850	Alicante (Table KJ-KKZ5)
9851	Barcelona (Table KJ-KKZ5)
9852	Burgos (Table KJ-KKZ5)
9853	Cádiz (Table KJ-KKZ5)
9854	Córdoba (Table KJ-KKZ5)
9855	Granada (Table KJ-KKZ5)
9856	Madrid (Table KJ-KKZ5)
9857	Malaga (Table KJ-KKZ5)
9858	Sevilla (Table KJ-KKZ5)
9859	Valencia (Table KJ-KKZ5)
9860.A-Z	Other cities, A-Z
	e. g.
9860.A45	Almeria (Table KJ-KKZ6)
9860.B32	Badajoz (Table KJ-KKZ6)

Cities
    Other cities, A-Z -- Continued

9860.B33	Badalona (Table KJ-KKZ6)
9860.B37	Baracaldo (Table KJ-KKZ6)
9860.B54	Bilbao (Table KJ-KKZ6)
9860.C37	Cartagena (Table KJ-KKZ6)
9860.C67	Coruña (La) (Table KJ-KKZ6)
9860.E42	Elche (Table KJ-KKZ6)
9860.G54	Gijón (Table KJ-KKZ6)
9860.H67	Hospitalet (Table KJ-KKZ6)
9860.J47	Jérez de la Frontera (Table KJ-KKZ6)
9860.L45	Leon (Table KJ-KKZ6)
9860.M87	Murcia (Table KJ-KKZ6)
9860.O84	Oviedo (Table KJ-KKZ6)
9860.P34	Palma de Mallorca (Table KJ-KKZ6)
9860.P35	Palmas (Las) (Table KJ-KKZ6)
9860.P36	Pamplona (Table KJ-KKZ6)
9860.S22	Sabadell (Table KJ-KKZ6)
9860.S24	Salamanca (Table KJ-KKZ6)
9860.S25	San Sabastián (Table KJ-KKZ6)
9860.S26	Santander (Table KJ-KKZ6)
9860.S82	Sta Coloma de Grammanet (Table KJ-KKZ6)
9860.S83	Sta Cruz de Tenerife (Table KJ-KKZ6)
9860.T37	Tarrasa (Table KJ-KKZ6)
9860.V34	Valladolid (Table KJ-KKZ6)
9860.V53	Virgo (Table KJ-KKZ6)
9860.V57	Vitoria (Table KJ-KKZ6)
9860.Z37	Zaragoza (Table KJ-KKZ6)

KJG-KKZ

1-4999	Sweden (Table KJ-KKZ1 modified)
	Administrative law
	Administrative organization
	Administrative and political divisions. Local government
	other than municipal
2935.A-Z	Independent counties (Län)
	Included in this list are modern jurisdictions and historic
	(extinct) jurisdictions
	Including official gazettes, bylaws, statutory orders,
	regulations, and general works, as well as works on
	specific legal topics
	Including autonomous regions
2935.A48	Älvsborg
2935.B55	Blekinge
2935.G38	Gavleborg
2935.G67	Goteborg and Bohus
2935.G68	Gotland
2935.H34	Halland
2935.J35	Jämtland
2935.J65	Jönköping
2935.K34	Kalmar
2935.K67	Kopparberg
2935.K74	Kristianstad
2935.K75	Kronoberg
2935.M34	Malmöhus
2935.N67	Norrbotten
2935.O73	Örebro
2935.O75	Österogötland
2935.S56	Skane
2935.S58	Skaraborg
2935.S62	Smaland
2935.S63	Södermanland
2935.S74	Stockholm (County)
2935.U66	Uppsala
2935.V35	Värmland
2935.V36	Västerbotten
2935.V37	Västernorrland
2935.V38	Västmanland
	Cities
4980	Boras (Table KJ-KKZ5)
4981	Göteborg (Table KJ-KKZ5)
4982	Kalmar (Table KJ-KKZ5)
4983	Lund (Table KJ-KKZ5)
4984	Malmö (Table KJ-KKZ5)
4985	Stockholm (Table KJ-KKZ5)
4986	Uppsala (Table KJ-KKZ5)
4987	Västeras (Table KJ-KKZ5)

Cities -- Continued

4988	Visby (Table KJ-KKZ5)
4990.A-Z	Other cities, A-Z
	e. g.
4990.F34	Falun (Table KJ-KKZ6)
4990.H34	Halmstad (Table KJ-KKZ6)
4990.H37	Härnösand (Table KJ-KKZ6)
4990.H44	Helsingborg (Table KJ-KKZ6)
4990.J65	Jönköping (Table KJ-KKZ6)
4990.K36	Karlskrona (Table KJ-KKZ6)
4990.K37	Karlstad (Table KJ-KKZ6)
4990.K74	Kristianstad (Table KJ-KKZ6)
4990.L45	Linköping (Table KJ-KKZ6)
4990.L84	Luleą (Table KJ-KKZ6)
4990.N67	Norrköping (Table KJ-KKZ6)
4990.N92	Nyköping (Table KJ-KKZ6)
4990.O88	Ostersund (Table KJ-KKZ6)
4990.S55	Skara (Table KJ-KKZ6)
4990.U43	Umeą (Table KJ-KKZ6)
4990.V38	Växyö (Table KJ-KKZ6)

KJG-KKZ

Switzerland
For periods before 1648 see KK1+
1-4999	General (Table KJ-KKZ1)

Federal republics (Cantons)
5201-5299	Aargau (Table KJ-KKZ3)
5301-5399	Appenzell. Inner-Rhoden (Table KJ-KKZ3)
5401-5499	Appenzell. Ausser Rhoden (Table KJ-KKZ3)
5501-5599	Basel-Stadt (Table KJ-KKZ3)
5601-5699	Baselland (Table KJ-KKZ3)
5701-5799	Bern (Table KJ-KKZ3)
5901-5999	Fribourg (Table KJ-KKZ3)
6101-6199	Geneva (Table KJ-KKZ3)
6301-6399	Glarus (Table KJ-KKZ3)
6401-6499	Graubünden (Table KJ-KKZ3)
6501-6599	Jura (Table KJ-KKZ3)
6601-6699	Lucerne (Table KJ-KKZ3)
6801-6899	Neuchâtel (Table KJ-KKZ3)
6901-6999	Nidwalden (Table KJ-KKZ3)
7101-7199	Obwalden (Table KJ-KKZ3)
7301-7399	Saint Gall (Table KJ-KKZ3)
7401-7499	Schaffhausen (Table KJ-KKZ3)
7501-7599	Schwyz (Table KJ-KKZ3)
7601-7699	Solothurn (Table KJ-KKZ3)
	Tessin see KKW7801+
7701-7799	Thurgau (Table KJ-KKZ3)
7801-7899	Ticino (Table KJ-KKZ3)
	Unterwalden nid dem Wald see KKW6901+
	Unterwalden ob dem Wald see KKW7101+
8101-8199	Uri (Table KJ-KKZ3)
8201-8299	Valais (Table KJ-KKZ3)
8301-8399	Vaud (Table KJ-KKZ3)
	Waadt see KKW8301+
	Wallis see KKW8201+
8401-8499	Zug (Table KJ-KKZ3)
8501-8599	Zürich (Table KJ-KKZ3)

Cities
9980	Basel (Table KJ-KKZ5)
9981	Bern (Table KJ-KKZ5)
9982	Biel (Table KJ-KKZ5)
9983	Geneva (Table KJ-KKZ5)
9984	Lausanne (Table KJ-KKZ5)
9985	Lucerne (Table KJ-KKZ5)
9986	Saint Gall (Table KJ-KKZ5)
9988	Winterthur (Table KJ-KKZ5)
9989	Zürich (Table KJ-KKZ5)
9990.A-Z	Other cities, A-Z
	Subarrange each by Table KJ-KKZ6

1-4999	Turkey (Table KJ-KKZ1 modified)
	Administrative law
	Administrative organization
	Administrative and political divisions. Local government other than municipal
2935.A-Z	Administrative divisions (II), A-Z
	Including official gazettes, bylaws, statutory orders, regulations, and general works, as well as works on specific legal topics
	Including autonomous regions
2935.A32	Adana
2935.A34	Adiyaman
2935.A37	Afyonkarahisar
2935.A38	Agri
2935.A42	Amasya
2935.A53	Ankara
2935.A58	Antalya
2935.A78	Artvin
2935.A98	Aydin
2935.B34	Balikesir
2935.B54	Bilecik
2935.B55	Bingöl
2935.B57	Bitlis
2935.B64	Bolu
2935.B87	Burdur
2935.B88	Bursa
2935.C35	Çanakkale
2935.C66	Çankiri
2935.C67	Çorum
2935.D45	Denizli
2935.D59	Diyarbakir
2935.E34	Edirne
2935.E42	Elâziğ
2935.E78	Erzincan
2935.E79	Erzurum
2935.E84	Eskişehir
2935.G39	Gaziantep
2935.G57	Giresun
2935.G85	Gümüşane
2935.H34	Hakkari
2935.H38	Hatay
2935.H87	Isparta
2935.I24	Içel
2935.I88	Istanbul
2935.I95	Izmir
2935.K37	Kars
2935.K38	Kastamonu

KJG-KKZ

Turkey
  Administrative law
   Administrative organization
    Administrative and political divisions. Local government
     other than municipal
      Administrative divisions (II), A-Z -- Continued

2935.K39	Kayseri
2935.K57	Kirklareli
2935.K58	Kirsehir
2935.K62	Kocaeli
2935.K65	Konya
2935.K88	Kütahya
2935.M34	Malatya
2935.M35	Manisa
2935.M36	Maras
2935.M37	Mardin
2935.M83	Mugla
2935.M88	Mus
2935.N49	Nevsehir
2935.N53	Nigde
2935.O73	Ordu
2935.R59	Rize
2935.S34	Sakarya
2935.S35	Samsun
2935.S53	Siirt
2935.S55	Sinop
2935.S58	Sivas
2935.T44	Tekirdag
2935.T64	Tokat
2935.T73	Trabzon
2935.T85	Tunceli
2935.U73	Urfa
2935.U82	Usak
2935.V35	Van
2935.Y69	Yozgat
2935.Z65	Zonguldak
4951-4959	Cilicia (Table KJ-KKZ4)
4980.A-Z	Towns, villages, etc., A-Z
	e. g.
4980.A37	Adapazari
4980.B49	Beyoglu
4980.C45	Cengilli
4980.K57	Kirikkale
4980.T37	Tarsus

1-4999	Ukraine (Table KJ-KKZ1 modified)
	For Ukraine as a republic of the USSR (1919-1991), see KLP1+
	Administrative law
	Administrative organization
	Administrative and political divisions. Local government other than municipal
2935.A-Z	Administrative divisions (Oblasts), A-Z
	Including official gazettes, bylaws, statutory orders, regulations, and general works, as well as works on specific legal topics
	Including autonomous regions
2935.C45	Cherkas'ka oblast'
2935.C46	Chernihivs'ka oblast'
2935.C47	Cherniveŧs'ka oblast'
2935.D54	Dnipropetrovs'ka oblast'
2935.D66	Doneŧs'ka oblast'
2935.I73	Ivano-Frankivs'ka oblast'
2935.K53	Kharkivs'ka oblast'
2935.K54	Khersons'ka oblast'
2935.K56	Khmel'nyŧs'ka oblast'
2935.K64	Kiev (Oblast')
2935.K67	Kirovohrads'ka oblast'
2935.L84	Luhans'ka oblast'
2935.L86	L'vivs'ka oblast'
2935.M95	Mykolaïvs'ka oblast'
2935.O44	Odes'ka oblast'
2935.P65	Poltavs'ka oblast'
2935.R68	Rivnens'ka oblast'
2935.S86	Sums'ka oblast'
2935.T47	Ternopil's'ka oblast'
2935.V56	Vinnyŧs'ka oblast'
2935.V65	Volyns'ka oblast'
2935.Z35	Zakarpats'ka oblast'
2935.Z37	Zaporiz'ka oblast'
2935.Z55	ZHytomyrs'ka oblast'
	Autonomous republics
4891-4899	Crimea (Table KJ-KKZ4)
	Previously Krymskaĭa oblast'
	Galicia see KKP4900+
	Cities, communities, etc.
4984	Kiev (Table KJ-KKZ5)
4985	Kharkiv (Table KJ-KKZ5)
4986	Odesa (Table KJ-KKZ5)
4988	Simferopol' (Table KJ-KKZ5)
4989	Zaporizhzhia (Table KJ-KKZ5)
4994.A-Z	Other cities, A-Z
	Subarrange each by Table KJ-KKZ6

KJG-KKZ

Vatican City. Stato Pontificio
see KBU4064+

YUGOSLAVIA (KINGDOM) (1918-1945)

Yugoslavia (Kingdom) (1918-1945)
see KKZ1+

Yugoslavia. Serbia and Montenegro (to 2006)
 Class here works on the Socialist Federal Republic of Yugoslavia
  (earlier name Federal People's Republic) from 1956-1991, and
  its short term successor states, the Federal Republic of
  Yugoslavia (1992-2003) and the State Union of Serbia and
  Montenegro (2003-2006)
 Including the period of the Kingdom of Yugoslavia (1918-1945) after
  the demise of the Austro-Hungarian Empire, also known as the
  Kingdom of Serbs, Croats, and Slovenes (1918-1928)

1-4999	General (Table KJ-KKZ1)
	Socialist republics. Autonomous provinces (to 1991)
5001-5099	Bosnia and Hercegovina (to 1991) (Table KJ-KKZ3)
	For the independent sovereign state see KJK8001+
5201-5299	Croatia (to 1991) (Table KJ-KKZ3)
	For the independent sovereign state see KJM7001+
5401-5499	Macedonia (Republic) (to 1991) (Table KJ-KKZ3)
	For the independent sovereign state see KKK501+
5501-5599	Montenegro (to 1991) (Table KJ-KKZ3)
	For the independent sovereign state see KKL1001+
	For the State Union of Serbia and Montenegro see
	KKZ1+
	Serbia (to 1991)
	For the independent sovereign state see KKS1001+
	For the State Union of Serbia and Montenegro see
	KKZ1+
5701-5799	General (Table KJ-KKZ3)
	Provinces
5801-5899	Kosovo (Table KJ-KKZ3)
	For the independent state of Kosovo (2008-) see
	KKH9901+
6001-6099	Vojvodina (Table KJ-KKZ3)
6201-6299	Slovenia (to 1991) (Table KJ-KKZ3)
	For the independent sovereign state see KKS6001+
	Cities
(6980)	Belgrade
	see KKS1505.B45
(6981)	Ljubljana
	see KKS6505.L58
(6982)	Novi Sad
	see KKS1505.N68
	Podgorica see KKL1505.P63
(6983)	Pristina
	see KKH9999.5.P75
(6984)	Sarajevo
	see KJK8500.S37

	Cities -- Continued
(6985)	Skopje
	see KKK1005.S56
(6986)	Titograd
	see KKL1505.P63
(6987)	Zagreb
	see KJM7505.Z34
(6990.A-Z)	Other cities, A-Z

For cities in Bosnia and Hercegovina see KJK8500.A+ ; for cities in Croatia see KJM7505.A+ ; for cities in Kosovo see KKH9999.5.A+ ; for cities in Macedonia (Republic) see KKK1000.A+ ; for cities in Montenegro see KKL1505.A+ ; for cities in Serbia see KKS1505.A+ ; for cities in Slovenia see KKS6505.A+

KJG-KKZ

Bibliography
>> For bibliography of special topics, see the topic
>> For manuals on legal bibliography, legal research, and the
>> use of law books see KJ-KKZ1 47+

2	Bibliography of bibliography
3	General bibliography
4	Library catalogs
4.5	Sales catalogs
5	Indexes to periodical literature, society publications, and collections

>> For indexes to particular publications, see the publication

Indexes to Festschriften see KJ-KKZ1 74

<6>	Periodicals

>> For periodicals consisting primarily of informative material
>> (Newsletters, bulletins, etc.) relating to a special subject, see
>> the subject and Form Division Tables for periodicals
>> For law reports, official bulletins or circulars intended chiefly for the
>> publication of laws and regulations, see appropriate entries in
>> the text or Form Division Tables
>> For periodicals consisting predominantly of legal articles, regardless
>> of subject matter and jurisdiction, see K1+

6.5	Monographic series
7	Official gazettes

State or city gazettes
>> see the issuing state or city
Departmental gazettes
>> see the issuing department or agency

8	Indexes (General)

Legislative documents
>> see class J

9	Other materials relating to legislative history

>> Including recommended legislation; legislation passed and vetoed

Legislation
>> For statutes, statutory orders, regulations, etc., on a particular
>> subject, see the subject
Indexes and tables
>> Class indexes to a particular publication with the publication
>> Including indexes to statutes of several states
>> For indexes limited to one state, see the state

10	General
10.5	Chronological indexes. By date
10.6	Indexes to publisher editions (unannotated and annotated). By date
10.7	Other bibliographical aids
11	Abridgments and digests

Legislation -- Continued
  Statutes
    Including statutory orders and regulations; comparative state
      legislation
    Collections and compilations
      Including official and private editions
12   Serials
13   Monographs. By date
          Including unannotated and annotated editions
        Collected codes
          Class here works consisting of both private and public law
            codes
          For codes on a particular branch of law, see the branch of law
          For works consisting of the civil and commercial codes
            see KJ-KKZ1 475
          For collected public law codes see KJ-KKZ1 2000+
15   General
15.2   Legislative documents
15.4   Enactments
            Class here collections of enactments of several states
            For enactments of an individual state, see the state
            For enactments of a particular code, see the code
15.6   Statute revision commission acts and reports. By date
        Administrative and executive publications
          Including orders in council; proclamations, etc.
          For regulations on a particular subject, see the subject
          For statutory orders and regulations see KJ-KKZ1 12+
17   Serials
17.5   Monographs. By date
17.6   Digests
17.7   Indexes. By date
        Presidential proclamations
          see class J
  Treaties
    Treaties on international public law
      see KZ
    Treaties on uniform law not limited to a region
      see class K
    Treaties on uniform law of the European region
      see KJC and KJE

	Court decisions and related materials. Reports
	Including decisions of national (federal) courts and decisions of two or more states, and national (federal) and state decisions combined
	Class decisions of an individual state, province, etc., with the respective jurisdiction
	For decisions on a particular subject, see the subject
	For civil and commercial decisions combined see KJ-KKZ1 475
	National (Federal) courts
	Constitutional courts see KJ-KKZ1 2620+
18	Highest courts of appeal. Supreme courts. Courts of Cassation (Table K19)
	Lower courts
19	Various courts (Table K19)
	Including highest court and lower courts
	Intermediate appellate courts. National (Federal) courts of appeal
20	Collective (Table K19)
21.A-Z	Particular courts, A-Z
	Courts of first instance. District courts
22	Collective (Table K19)
23.A-Z	Particular courts, A-Z
	State courts
24	Collections (Reports) covering all states or selected states (Table K19)
24.2	Collections (Reports) covering national (federal) decisions and decisions of the courts of two or more states (Table K19)
	Decisions (Reports) of an individual state
	see the state
24.3	Decisions of national (federal) administrative agencies
	For decisions of particular agencies, see the subject
25	Encyclopedias
26	Dictionaries. Words and phrases
	For bilingual and multilingual dictionaries, see K52+
	For dictionaries on a particular subject, see the subject
27	Maxims. Quotations
28	Form books
	Class here general works
	For form books on a particular subject, see the subject
	Judicial statistics
30	General
	Criminal statistics
31	General
31.3	Juvenile crime
32.A-Z	Other. By subject, A-Z

	Judicial statistics
	Other. By subject, A-Z -- Continued
32.D65	Domestic relations. Family law
	Family law see KJ-KKZ1 32.D65
32.L32	Labor law
32.L44	Legal aid
	Directories
33	National and regional
34.A-Z	By state, A-Z
35.A-Z	Local. By administrative district or city, A-Z
36.A-Z	By specialization, A-Z
	Trials
38	General collections
	Criminal trials and judicial investigations
	For military trials see KJ-KKZ1 3770+
	Collections. Compilations
39	General
40.A-Z	Particular offenses, A-Z
40.A78	Arson
40.F73	Fraud
40.M87	Murder
40.P64	Political crimes
40.S49	Sex crimes
	War crimes see KJ-KKZ1 43
41.A-Z	Individual trials. By defendant or best known (popular) name, A-Z
	Including records, briefs, commentaries, and stories on a particular trial
	War crime trials
	Trials by international tribunals see subclass KZ
43	Collections
44.A-Z	Individual trials. By defendant or best known (popular) name, A-Z
	Including records, briefs, commentaries, and stories on a particular trial
	Other trials
45	Collections. Compilations
46.A-Z	Individual trials. By plaintiff, defendant, or best known (popular) name, A-Z
	Including records, briefs, commentaries, and stories on a particular trial
	Legal research. Legal bibliography
	Including methods of bibliographic research and how to find the law
47	General (Table K11)
	Electronic data processing. Information retrieval
47.5	General (Table K11)

	Legal research. Legal bibliography
	Electronic data processing. Information retrieval -- Continued
47.7.A-Z	By subject, A-Z
47.7.A35	Administrative law (Table K12)
47.7.E58	Environmental law (Table K12)
47.7.I56	Insurance law (Table K12)
47.7.J86	Justice, Administration of (Table K12)
48	Systems of citation. Legal abbreviations
48.7	Legal composition and draftsmanship
49	Law reporting
	Legal education
50	General (Table K11)
	Study and teaching
	General works see KJ-KKZ1 50
50.3	Teaching methods (Table K11)
	Including clinical method, case method, etc.
51.A-Z	By subject, A-Z
51.A36	Administrative process (Table K12)
51.C58	Civil procedure (Table K12)
51.C64	Commercial law (Table K12)
51.C66	Constitutional law (Table K12)
51.L33	Labor law (Table K12)
51.P45	Philosopy of law (Table K12)
51.R65	Roman law (Table K12)
51.7	Students' guides
	For introductory surveys of the law see KJ-KKZ1 50
51.8	Teachers' manuals
52	Pre-law school education (Table K11)
52.3	Law teachers (Table K11)
52.4	Law students (Table K11)
	Including sociology and psychology of law students
	Law schools
52.5	General (Table K11)
53.A-Z	Particular law schools. By name, A-Z
	Including constitution and bylaws, statutes, regulations,
	degrees, and general works (history)
	Post-law school education see KJ-KKZ1 1602+
	The legal profession see KJ-KKZ1 1600+

Bar associations. Law societies. Law institutes
>Class here works on individual associations and their activities, e.g.,
>>journals, annual reports, proceedings, incorporating statutes,
>>bylaws, handbooks, and works (history) about the society
>Including courts of honor and disbarment
>For publications of associations on special subjects, see the subject
>For journals devoted to legal subjects, either wholly or in part, see
>>K1+
>For membership directories see KJ-KKZ1 36.A+
>For biography, Collective see KJ-KKZ1 105+
>For biography, Individual see KJ-KKZ1 110.A+

54	General works
	Particular types of organizations
54.3.A-Z	National associations, A-Z
54.5.A-Z	State associations, A-Z

>Class here works on individual associations and their activities,
>>e.g. journals, annual reports, proceedings, incorporating
>>statutes, bylaws, handbooks, and works (history) about the
>>association
>Including courts of honor and disbarment
>For publications of associations on special subjects, see the
>>subject
>For journals devoted to legal subjects, either wholly or in part,
>>see K1+
>For membership directories see KJ-KKZ1 34.A+
>For biography, Collective see KJ-KKZ1 105+
>For biography, Individual see KJ-KKZ1 110.A+

54.7.A-Z	Local associations, lawyers' clubs, etc. By county, city, A-Z

>Class here works on, and journals by individual associations
>>and their activities, e.g. journals, annual reports,
>>proceedings, incorporating statutes, bylaws, handbooks,
>>and works (history) about the association, club, etc.
>Including courts of honor and disbarment
>For publications of associations, clubs, etc. on special subjects,
>>see the subject.
>For journals devoted to legal subjects, either wholly or in part,
>>see K1+
>For membership directories see KJ-KKZ1 35.A+
>For biography, Collective see KJ-KKZ1 105+
>For biography, Individual see KJ-KKZ1 110.A+

Notarial law. Public instruments see KJ-KKZ1 1846+
Public registers. Registration

56	General (Table K11)
	Civil registry see KJ-KKZ1 1854+
	Registration of juristic persons in civil law see KJ-KKZ1 523.5
	Commercial registers see KJ-KKZ1 925+

	Public registers. Registration -- Continued
57	Registration of miscellaneous titles and documents (Table K11)
	Property registration. Registration of pledges
58	General (Table K11)
	Land register see KJ-KKZ1 737+
	Mining registration see KJ-KKZ1 3350+
	Aircraft registration see KJ-KKZ1 935+
	Law societies and institutes see KJ-KKZ1 54+
62	Congresses. Conferences
64.A-Z	Academies. By name of academy, A-Z
68	General works. Treatises
70	Compends, outlines, examination aids, etc.
	Forms, graphic materials, blanks, atlases see KJ-KKZ1 28
72	Popular works. Civics
74	Addresses, essays, lectures
	Including single essays, collected essays of several authors, festschriften, and indexes to festschriften
78.A-Z	Manuals and other works for particular groups of users. By user, A-Z
78.B35	Bankers
78.B86	Businesspeople. Foreign investors
78.E53	Engineers
78.F37	Farmers
	Semantics and language see KJ-KKZ1 92
	Legal symbolism see KJ-KKZ1 94+
	Legal anecdotes, wit and humor
	see K184.4
	Law and lawyers in literature
	see subclasses PB-PH
	Law and art
	see K487.C8
	Law and history
	see K487.C8
80.A-Z	Works on diverse aspects of a particular subject and falling within several branches of the law. By subject, A-Z
80.A53	Animals (Table K12)
80.C65	Computers (Table K12)
80.D63	Dogs (Table K12)
80.H66	Horses (Table K12)
	Legal advertising see KJ-KKZ1 80.N68
80.L46	Letters (Table K12)
80.N68	Notice. Legal advertising (Table K12)
80.S66	Sponsorship (Table K12)
80.T73	Trees (Table K12)
(80.W65)	Women
	see KJ-KKZ1 517.5

	History of law
85	Bibliography
86	Encyclopedias
	Auxiliary sciences
87	General works
88	Genealogy
90	Paleography
92	Linguistics. Semantics
	Archaeology. Symbolism in law
	Class here general works on various manifestations of legal symbolism
94	General works
96.A-Z	By region, A-Z
98	Inscriptions
100	Heraldry. Seals. Flags. Insignia. Armory
	Law and lawyers in literature
	see subclasses PB - PH
	Biography of lawyers
	Collective
105	General
107	Collections of portraits
110.A-Z	Individual, A-Z

Under each:

.xA3	*Autobiography. Reminiscences. By date*
.xA4	*Letters. Correspondence. By date Including individual letters, general collections, and collections of letters to particular individuals*
.xA6	*Knowledge. Concept of law. By date*
	Bibliography see Z8001+
.xA8-.xZ	*Biography and criticism*

120	General works. Treatises
	By period
	Ancient and early, including ancient people in the region
	see KJ
124	Medieval and early modern periods (to ca. 1800)
	For the Frankish empire, see subclass KJ; for the Jus Romanum Medii Aevi, see subclass KJA
	Sources
	For sources of a territory or town, see the appropriate territory or town
	History and studies on sources
	Including methodology (i.e., exegesis, edition of variants, etc.)

KJ-KKZ1

History of law
  By period
    Medieval and early modern periods (to ca. 1800)
      The State and its constitution -- Continued
        Finance. Fiscalat
          Class here works on topics not represented elsewhere in
            the schedule
          For works on the history of other subjects, see the subject

258	General works
260	Camera
263	Crown goods and dynastic house goods
268	Regalia

        Secular ecclesiastical law
          Class here historical works on the relationship of church and
            state
          For historical works on the internal law and government of a
            church, see KB
          Sources
            Including treaties between state and church (concordats
              and contracts)
            For treaties relating to a particular region or state
              (province), see region or state (province)
            For treaties on a particular subject, see the subject

272	Collections. Compilations
273	Individual concordats. By date
(274)	General works
	see 275

          System of church and state relationships

275	General works
	Germanic period
	see KJ
	Carlovingian state church
	see KB, KJ
	State churches and rulers
276	General works
277.A-Z	Special topics, A-Z
277.J87	Jus reformandi
277.P38	Patronage
	Reformation see KJ-KKZ1 277.J87
277.R68	Royal supremacy
	Summepiscopat see KJ-KKZ1 277.R68
	Church finance and estate
278	General works
279	Feudal fiefs. Precariae. Benefices

	History of law
	By period
	Medieval and early modern periods (to ca. 1800) -- Continued
282.A-Z	Private law. Special topics, A-Z
	Class here works on topics not represented elsewhere in the schedule
	For works on the history of other subjects, see the subject
	Judiciary. Court organization and procedure
283	General works
284	Jurisdiction. Jus evocandi
285.A-Z	Particular courts, A-Z
285.E22	Ecclesiastical courts
285.F45	Fehmic courts
285.H65	Courts of honor
285.L38	Courts of last resort
285.M36	Manorial courts
285.M86	Municipal courts
	Procedure
287	General works
288.A-Z	Special topics, A-Z
292.A-Z	Criminal law and procedure. Special topics, A-Z
	Class here works on topics not represented elsewhere in the schedule
	For works on the history of other subjects, see the subject
292.D83	Duellum. Wager of battle
292.H47	Heresy
292.P54	Pillories
	Wager of battle see KJ-KKZ1 292.D83
292.W58	Witchcraft
	Philosophy, jurisprudence, and theory of law
	Class here works on doctrines peculiar to legal institutions of a country
	For works on the philosophy of law in general, see K237+
	For works on the philosophy of a particular branch of law (e.g. constitutional law or criminal law), see the branch
440	General (Table K11)
	The concept of law
	Including the definition of law
442	General works
443	The object of law. Law and justice
	Ethics. Morality of law
444	General works
444.5	Public policy
444.7	Chicanery. Abuse of rights
444.8	Equity. Fairness
445	Law and the state. Legal order. Respect for law

Philosophy, jurisprudence, and theory of law
The concept of law -- Continued
446 Rights and duties. Sanction
446.5 Effectiveness and validity of the law
447 Certainty of law
Cf. KJ-KKZ1 1715 Civil procedure
Cf. KJ-KKZ1 4622 Criminal procedure
447.5.A-Z Other topics, A-Z
Determinism see KJ-KKZ1 447.5.F73
447.5.F73 Free will and determinism
Legal science
448 General works
Sources of law
449 General works
449.3 Customs and observances
449.5 Legislation
Judge-made law see KJ-KKZ1 452
Rule of law see KJ-KKZ1 2020+
Law reform. Criticism see KJ-KKZ1 471
Methodology
451 General works
452 Legal hermeneutics. Interpretation and construction
Including lacunae in law and judge-made law
Semantics see KJ-KKZ1 92
Schools of legal theory
455 General works
457 Natural law
Historical jurisprudence
458 General works
Ethnological jurisprudence. Primitive law
see K190+
Biological interpretation. Legal evolution
see K328
Positivism
459 General works
460 Utilitarianism
Cf. KJ-KKZ1 465+ Sociological jurisprudence
461 Psychological theory of law. Psychoanalytic jurisprudence
Cf. KJ-KKZ1 465.6 Social psychology of law
462 Existentialist legal theory
462.5 Phenomenology of law
Modern political theory of law
463 General works
464 Socialist. Communist
Sociological jurisprudence
465 General works
465.5 Law and public policy

	Philosophy, jurisprudence, and theory of law
	Schools of legal theory
	Sociological jurisprudence -- Continued
465.6	Social psychology of law
466	Social pathology
467	Neo-Kantianism
468	Free-law movement
469	Pluralism in law
470	Influence of other legal systems on the law (Reception)
471	Law reform and policies. Criticism
	Including reform of administration of justice
472.A-Z	Concepts applying to several branches of the law, A-Z
	Abuse of rights see KJ-KKZ1 444.7
	Applicability see KJ-KKZ1 446.5
	Bona fides see KJ-KKZ1 472.G66
	Chicanery see KJ-KKZ1 444.7
472.C65	Concurrent legislation
	Deadlines see KJ-KKZ1 472.T55
472.D65	Dolus
472.E65	Equality
	Equity see KJ-KKZ1 444.8
472.E88	Estoppel
	Cf. KJ-KKZ1 1799 Res judicata
472.F52	Fictions
472.F67	Forfeiture
472.F73	Freedom of conscience
472.G66	Good faith. Reliance
	Legal advertising see KJ-KKZ1 472.N68
472.L44	Legal documents
472.L52	Liability
472.N44	Negligence
472.N68	Notice. Legal advertising
472.O28	Oath
	Ownership see KJ-KKZ1 472.P68
472.P68	Possession. Ownership
472.P73	Presumption
472.P74	Privacy, Right of
472.P76	Property. Property damage
472.P92	Publicity
	Reliance see KJ-KKZ1 472.G66
472.S45	Self-incrimination
472.T55	Time periods. Deadlines
	Validity and applicability of the law see KJ-KKZ1 446.5
472.V58	Vis major
472.W33	Waiver
475	Private law (Table K11)
	Class here works on all aspects of private law

	Private international law. Conflict of laws
	For regional unification of conflict rules, see KJC
	For conflict of laws between the United States and a particular jurisdiction, see KF416
	For works on conflict rules of branches other than private law (e.g. tax law, criminal law, etc.), see the subject
480	General (Table K11)
481	Public order. Public policy. Ordre public (Table K11)
481.5	Classification. Qualification (Table K11)
481.7	Jurisdiction (Table K11)
482	Renvoi (Table K11)
	Points of contact
483	Domicile (Table K11)
483.5	Interlocal (interstate) law (Table K11)
485.A-Z	Particular branches and subjects of the law, A-Z
	Administrative acts see KJ-KKZ1 2735+
	Adoption see KJ-KKZ1 485.F35
	Arbitration see KJ-KKZ1 485.P76
	Author and publisher see KJ-KKZ1 485.P92
	Bankruptcy see KJ-KKZ1 485.P76
	Capacity see KJ-KKZ1 485.P47
	Cartels see KJ-KKZ1 485.C67
485.C65	Commercial agents (Table K12)
485.C655	Commercial papers and negotiable instruments (Table K12)
485.C657	Commercial sales (Table K12)
485.C658	Contracts. Obligations. Debtor and creditor (Table K12)
485.C67	Corporations. Industrial trusts. Cartels (Table K12)
	For procedure in antitrust cases see KJ-KKZ1 3244+
	Criminal law see KJ-KKZ1 3835
	Debtor and creditor see KJ-KKZ1 485.C658
	Decedents' estate see KJ-KKZ1 485.I45
	Divorce see KJ-KKZ1 485.M375
485.E92	Evasion (Table K12)
	Execution see KJ-KKZ1 485.P76
485.F35	Family. Parent and child. Adoption (Table K12)
	Foreign exchange see KJ-KKZ1 3539
	Foreign judgments see KJ-KKZ1 1646
	Illegality see KJ-KKZ1 485.T67
	Incapacity see KJ-KKZ1 485.P47
	Industrial property see KJ-KKZ1 485.I583
	Industrial trusts see KJ-KKZ1 485.C67
485.I45	Inheritance and succession. Decedents' estate (Table K12)
485.I58	Insurance (Table K12)
485.I583	Intellectual and industrial property (Table K12)
	Judicial assistance see KJ-KKZ1 1644
	Justification see KJ-KKZ1 485.T67
485.L45	Limitation of action (Table K12)

	Private international law. Conflict of laws
	Particular branches and subjects of the law, A-Z -- Continued
485.L62	Loans (Table K12)
485.M37	Maritime (commercial) law (Table K12)
485.M375	Marriage. Matrimonial actions. Matrimonial property (Table K12)
	Negotiable instruments see KJ-KKZ1 485.C655
485.N66	Noncontentious jurisdiction (Table K12)
	Obligations see KJ-KKZ1 485.C658
	Parent and child see KJ-KKZ1 485.F35
485.P47	Persons. Capacity. Incapacity (Table K12)
485.P76	Procedure. Arbitral awards. Execution and bankruptcy (Table K12)
485.P78	Property (Table K12)
485.P92	Publishing contract. Author and publisher (Table K12)
485.R43	Refugees (Table K12)
	Social insurance see KJ-KKZ1 1481
485.S8	Statelessness (Table K12)
485.T67	Torts. Illegality. Justification (Table K12)
485.T72	Trademarks (Table K12)
485.T725	Transfer (Table K12)
485.T78	Trusts and trustees (Table K12)
485.U53	Unfair competition (Table K12)
485.U534	Unjust enrichment (Table K12)
485.V46	Vendors and purchasers (Table K12)
487	Intertemporal law. Retroactive law (Table K11)
	Including conflict of laws
	Civil law
491-500	General (Table K9c)
	General principles
	Applicability. Validity of the law
501	General (Table K11)
502	Interpretation. Analogy (Table K11)
	Ethics (Morality of law). Public policy see KJ-KKZ1 444+
	Chicanery and abuse of rights see KJ-KKZ1 444.7
	Equity see KJ-KKZ1 444.8
	Presumption see KJ-KKZ1 472.P73
	Publicity see KJ-KKZ1 472.P92
	Vis major see KJ-KKZ1 472.V58
502.3	Legal status (Table K11)
502.4	Rights (Table K11)
503	Immaterial rights (Table K11)
	Things see KJ-KKZ1 643
	Acts and events
504	General (Table K11)
	Illegal and unlawful acts see KJ-KKZ1 834+
	De facto contracts see KJ-KKZ1 869.6

Civil law

General principles -- Continued

Legal transactions see KJ-KKZ1 858+

Declaration of intention see KJ-KKZ1 860+

Agency. Power of attorney see KJ-KKZ1 861+

Mandate see KJ-KKZ1 864+

Secured transactions see KJ-KKZ1 859

Fiduciary transactions see KJ-KKZ1 733+

Conditions

505	General (Table K11)
505.5	Suspensive conditions and resolutory conditions (Table K11)
506	Retroactivity (Table K11)

Time periods see KJ-KKZ1 472.T55

Limitation of actions

507	General (Table K11)
508	Delay (Table K11)
508.5.A-Z	Special topics, A-Z
508.5.D55	Dilatory and peremptory pleas (Table K12)

Peremptory pleas see KJ-KKZ1 508.5.D55

Exercise of rights. Protection of rights

509	General (Table K11)
509.5	Self-defense (Table K11)

Cf. KJ-KKZ1 3856 Criminal law

509.6	Necessity (Table K11)
510	Assistance in emergencies (Table K11)

Persons

511	General (Table K11)

Natural persons

Personality

512	General (Table K11)

Birth

513	General (Table K11)
513.3	Unborn children. Nasciturus (Table K11)

Death

513.5	General (Table K11)

Missing persons. Presumption of death

513.7	General (Table K11)
514	Declaration and certification of death (Table K11)

Civil register see KJ-KKZ1 1854+

Civil death see KJ-KKZ1 4004

Capacity and incapacity

Including liability

For civil disability see KJ-KKZ1 4004

515	General (Table K11)

Minors. Children

Including human rights of the child

Civil law
Persons
Natural persons
Capacity and incapacity
Minors. Children -- Continued
515.5 General (Table K11)
516 Majority. Declaration of majority (Table K11)
Limited capacity
517 General (Table K11)
517.2.A-Z Special topics, A-Z
Subarrange each by Table K12
517.5 Women (Table K11)
Class here works on legal status in both private and public
law
518 Insane persons. People with mental disabilities (Table
K11)
For institutional care of the mentally ill see KJ-KKZ1
3113
Interdiction see KJ-KKZ1 628+
518.3.A-Z Other, A-Z
518.3.A34 Aged. Older people (Table K12)
Older people see KJ-KKZ1 518.3.A34
518.3.P46 Physical disabilities, People with (Table K12)
518.3.U52 Unborn children. Nasciturus (Table K12)
518.5 Domicile (Table K11)
518.7 Citizenship (Table K11)
For acquisition of citizenship and nationality see KJ-
KKZ1 2430+
For aliens see KJ-KKZ1 3025+
Personality rights
519 General (Table K11)
519.5 Life. Body. Health (Table K11)
Freedom see KJ-KKZ1 842
Name
520 General (Table K11)
520.5 Title of nobility (Table K11)
Including coat of arms
Dignity, honor, and reputation see KJ-KKZ1 842.7+
Privacy see KJ-KKZ1 843+
Intellectual property see KJ-KKZ1 1160+
Protection of personality rights see KJ-KKZ1 835+
Juristic persons of private law
For business corporations see KJ-KKZ1 1050+
For juristic persons of public law see KJ-KKZ1 2875+
521 General (Table K11)
521.3 Personality (Table K11)
521.4 Capacity. Ultra vires (Table K11)

KJ-KKZ1

	Civil law
	Domestic relations. Family law
	Marital property and regime -- Continued
570	Statutory regimes (Table K11)
572	Contractual regimes. Antenuptial contracts (Table K11)
573	Separation of property (Table K11)
574	Community of property (Table K11)
577	Contracts between husband and wife (Table K11)
	For antenuptial contracts see KJ-KKZ1 572
	For husband and wife commercial enterprises (couple-owned enterprises) see KJ-KKZ1 1083.5
578	Property questions arising from unmarried cohabitation (Table K11)
	Marital property register see KJ-KKZ1 1867
579.A-Z	Special topics, A-Z
579.M37	Management and usufruct by spouse (Table K12)
579.V34	Valuation (Table K12)
	Marriage, church, and state
580	General (Table K11)
	Intermarriage
	see KB
582	Secular (civil) marriage law and ecclesiastical law (Table K11)
	Consanguinity and affinity
583	General (Table K11)
584	Support (Table K11)
	Parent and child
587	General (Table K11)
588	Constitutional rights and guaranties (Table K11)
	Including human rights
	Paternity see KJ-KKZ1 616.5
	Legitimate children
	Including children from defective marriages, divorced marriages, legitimized children from subsequent marriages, etc.
590	General (Table K11)
(592)	Human rights of the child
	see KJ-KKZ1 515.5+
593	Citizenship of children (Table K11)
594	Legal status of children during and after divorce (Table K11)
	Including children from void marriages
595	Legitimation of children (Table K11)
	Including declaration of legitimacy and legitimation by subsequent marriage
	Parental power
	For illegitimate children see KJ-KKZ1 616

KJ-KKZ1

	Civil law
	Domestic relations. Family law
	Consanguinity and affinity
	Parent and child
	Legitimate children
	Parental power -- Continued
598	General (Table K11)
600	Equal rights of parents. Mutual agreements (Table K11)
	Custody. Access to children
	Including parental kidnapping
602	General (Table K11)
603	Agency (Table K11)
604	Negligence. Abuse (Table K11)
	Education see KJ-KKZ1 3138+
	Custodial education see KJ-KKZ1 1549+
606	Property management (Table K11)
607	Property power of mother (Table K11)
	Guardianship court see KJ-KKZ1 1874+
608	Stepchildren (Table K11)
	Adoption
609	General (Table K11)
610	Consent of natural parents (Table K11)
	For procedure see KJ-KKZ1 1872
611.A-Z	Special topics, A-Z
611.A36	Adoption of adults (Table K12)
	Inter-country adoption of children see KJ-KKZ1 485.F35
	Illegitimate children
612	General (Table K11)
	Constitutional rights of children see KJ-KKZ1 516
	Citizenship of children see KJ-KKZ1 593
613	Legal status (Table K11)
614	Right of name (Table K11)
615	Inheritance and succession (Table K11)
616	Parental power. Custody (Table K11)
616.5	Affiliation. Paternity (Table K11)
	Illegitimate children
617	General (Table K11)
617.5	Procedure in paternity suits (Table K11)
619	Artificial insemination (Table K11)
	Cf. KJ-KKZ1 3117 Medical legislation
	Cf. KJ-KKZ1 4108 Criminal law
	Guardian and ward
622	General (Table K11)
623	Care for ward. Agency (Table K11)
624	Property management (Table K11)

KJ-KKZ1

KJ-KKZ1

	Civil law
	Property. Law of things
	Real property -- Continued
	Superfices
704	General (Table K11)
704.5.A-Z	Special topics, A-Z
	Subarrange each by Table K12
	Rights as to the use and profits of another's land
706	General (Table K11)
	Fief see KJ-KKZ1 224+
	Superfices see KJ-KKZ1 704+
707	Emphyteusis (Table K11)
	Servitudes
709	General (Table K11)
	Real servitudes
710	General (Table K11)
711.A-Z	Special types, A-Z
711.R54	Right of way (Table K12)
	Way by necessity see KJ-KKZ1 701.W39
	Personal servitudes
713	General (Table K11)
714	Limited personal servitudes (Table K11)
	Including right of habitation
	Usufruct
715	General (Table K11)
715.5.A-Z	Particular, A-Z
715.5.T55	Things (Table K12)
716	Right of pre-emption (Table K11)
	Hypothecation
717	General (Table K11)
	Mortgage. Hypotheca
718	General (Table K11)
719.A-Z	Types of mortgages, A-Z
719.S43	Secured mortgage (Table K12)
720.A-Z	Special topics, A-Z
720.A66	Appurtenances (Table K12)
720.P74	Priority (Table K12)
720.S42	Secondary mortgage market (Table K12)
	Land charge
722	General (Table K11)
723.A-Z	Types of land charges, A-Z
	Subarrange each by Table K12
723.5.A-Z	Special topics, A-Z
	Subarrange each by Table K12
724	Rent charge (Table K11)
	Pledges
726	General (Table K11)

KJ-KKZ1

Civil law
  Property. Law of things
    Pledges -- Continued
      Contractual pledges

727	General (Table K11)
	Pledges of personal property
	Including possessory and nonpossessory pledges
728	General (Table K11)
729.A-Z	Special topics, A-Z
729.A32	Accessory (Table K12)
729.B34	Bailments (Table K12)
729.P74	Priority (Table K12)
	Pledges of rights
730	General (Table K11)
730.5.A-Z	Special topics, A-Z
730.5.B35	Bank deposits (Table K12)
	Bonds see KJ-KKZ1 730.5.S43
730.5.C46	Choses in action (Table K12)
730.5.E86	Expectancies (Table K12)
730.5.S43	Securities. Bonds. Stocks (Table K12)
	Stocks see KJ-KKZ1 730.5.S43
731	Lien or statutory pledge (Table K11)
	Register of pledges
732	General (Table K11)
	Aircraft mortgage see KJ-KKZ1 935.2
	Ship mortgage see KJ-KKZ1 983
	Transfer of ownership as security. Fiduciary transactions
733	General (Table K11)
734	Expectancies (Table K11)
	Cf. KJ-KKZ1 690 Ownership
735.A-Z	Special topics, A-Z
	Subarrange each by Table K12
	Land register and registration
737	General (Table K11)
738	Publicity (Table K11)
	Courts and procedure. Land partition courts
739	General (Table K11)
	Entry
740	General (Table K11)
741	Entry ex officio (Table K11)
	Including injunctions, bankruptcy, judicial sale, hypotheca, etc.
742	Form requirements (Table K11)
743.A-Z	Special topics, A-Z
	Subarrange each by Table K12
744	Remedies (Table K11)
	Effect of registration

	Civil law
	Property. Law of things
	Land register and registration
	Effect of registration -- Continued
745	General (Table K11)
746.A-Z	Special topics, A-Z
746.P74	Priority of rights (Table K12)
758	Cadastral surveys. Cadaster (Table K11)

Class here general works on surveying agencies

For an individual surveying agency of the state or locality, see the state or locality

	Inheritance. Succession upon death
761-770	General (Table K9c)
771	Right of inheritance. Constitutional guaranty
773	Testamentary succession (Table K11)
775	Intestate succession (Table K11)
	Inheritance. Estate
777	General (Table K11)
	Particular estates or parts
	Entail see KJ-KKZ1 3300+
	Fideicommissum see KJ-KKZ1 3304
	Heirs
780	General (Table K11)
781	Acceptance and disclaimer of inheritance (Table K11)
	Joint heirs. Co-heirs
782	General (Table K11)
782.5	Community of heirs (Table K11)
782.7	Distributive share in estate (Table K11)
	Limited and reversionary heir see KJ-KKZ1 786.5
783	Liability. Debts of estate (Table K11)
784	Possessor of an inheritance (Table K11)
	Wills. Testaments
785	General (Table K11)
785.3.A-Z	Individual wills. By testator, A-Z
	Subarrange each by Table K12
785.5	Freedom of testation (Table K11)
785.7.A-Z	Types of wills, A-Z
	e. g.
785.7.J64	Joint will (Table K12)
785.7.M88	Mutual will (Table K12)
	Nuncupative will see KJ-KKZ1 785.7.P74
785.7.P74	Privileged wills (Table K12)
	Including wills of sailors, military personnel, etc.
	Appointment of heir
786	General (Table K11)
786.5	Limited and reversionary heir (Table K11)
786.6	Form requirements (Table K11)

KJ-KKZ1

	Civil law
	Obligations
	Delicts. Torts -- Continued
	Protected rights
834.5	General (Table K11)
	Personality rights
835	General (Table K11)
	Freedom see KJ-KKZ1 842
	Life, body, and health see KJ-KKZ1 519.5
	Name see KJ-KKZ1 520+
	Integrity see KJ-KKZ1 842.7+
	Privacy see KJ-KKZ1 843+
(836)	Privacy of communication
	see KJ-KKZ1 843.3
	Parties to action in torts
837	General (Table K11)
837.5	Principal. Accessories (Table K11)
837.6	Joint tortfeasors (Table K11)
837.7.A-Z	Other, A-Z
	Subarrange each by Table K12
	Illegality
838	General (Table K11)
838.5.A-Z	Justification grounds, A-Z
838.5.C65	Consent of the injured party (Table K12)
838.5.P74	Privilege (Table K12)
838.5.S44	Self-defense. Self-help (Table K12)
	Self-help see KJ-KKZ1 838.5.S44
838.5.S8	Standard of conduct (Table K12)
	Liability
839	General (Table K11)
839.3	Dolus (Table K11)
839.5	Negligence. Aggravated negligence. Foresight (Table K11)
839.7	Liability for the torts of others (Table K11)
	Including Respondeat superior doctrine
840	Exclusion of liability (Table K11)
	Including contractual agreement, assumption of risk by injured part, and tacit (implied) agreement
841	Strict liability (Table K11)
	For strict liability related to particular dangers or risks, see the topic
	Individual torts
842	Violation of freedom (Table K11)
	Physical injuries
842.2	General (Table K11)
842.3	Accidents (Table K11)
	For particular types of accidents see KJ-KKZ1 848+

	Civil law
	Obligations
	Delicts. Torts
	Individual torts
	Physical injuries -- Continued
(842.5)	Malpractice (Medical)
	see KJ-KKZ1 3100.4
842.6	Death by wrongful act (Table K11)
	Violation of integrity
	Including honor, dignity, and reputation
842.7	General (Table K11)
842.8	Libel and slander (Table K11)
	Violation of privacy
	Cf. KJ-KKZ1 4160+ Criminal law
843	General (Table K11)
843.3	Confidential disclosure. Secrets (Table K11)
	Including works on both civil and criminal aspects
843.4	Right in one's own picture (Table K11)
844	Public opinion polls (Table K11)
844.5	Personal data in information retrieval systems (Table K11)
	Including public and private records, registers, statistics, etc.
	Cf. KJ-KKZ1 843.3 Confidential disclosure
	Immoral transactions and acts
845	General (Table K11)
	Abuse of rights in general see KJ-KKZ1 444.7
845.5	Exceptio doli (Table K11)
846	Deceit. Misrepresentations. Forgery (Table K11)
	Breach of contract. Interference with contractual relations see KJ-KKZ1 826
	Enticement see KJ-KKZ1 1257.E58
	Industrial espionage see KJ-KKZ1 1257.E86
846.5	Products liability (Table K11)
	Ultrahazardous activities and occupations
847	General (Table K11)
847.3	Power lines (Table K11)
847.5	Nuclear reactors. Nuclear damages (Table K11)
	Sports. Sport fields or installations
848	General (Table K11)
848.5.A-Z	Particular, A-Z
848.5.S54	Skiing accidents (Table K12)
	Liability for safe traffic conditions and accidents
849	General (Table K11)
849.3	Railroads and streetcars (Table K11)
850	Aviation (Table K11)
	Automotive transportation and road traffic

	Civil law
	Obligations
	Delicts. Torts
	Individual torts
	Liability for safe traffic conditions and accidents
	Automotive transportation and road traffic -- Continued
850.3	General (Table K11)
850.5	Liability for accidents of owner and/or driver (Table K11)
	Cf. KJ-KKZ1 1031+ Liability insurance (Automobiles)
	Liability for safe conditions of streets, highways, public places, etc.
851	General (Table K11)
851.3	Traffic signs (Table K11)
	Violation of official duties
	Cf. KJ-KKZ1 2840+ Government liability
852	General (Table K11)
852.3.A-Z	Special topics, A-Z
	Subarrange each by Table K12
852.5	Liability for environmental damages (Table K11)
	For environmental crimes see KJ-KKZ1 4351.5+
853.A-Z	Other liabilities, A-Z
853.A54	Animals (Table K12)
853.B84	Buildings, Liability for (Table K12)
	Including public buildings
853.C65	Construction sites, Liability for (Table K12)
853.N84	Nuisance (Table K12)
	Playground accidents see KJ-KKZ1 853.S34
	Public buildings see KJ-KKZ1 853.B84
853.S34	School and playground accidents, Liability for (Table K12)
	Unjust enrichment
854	General (Table K11)
854.5	Sine causa. Without cause (Table K11)
854.7	Restitution (Table K11)
855	Unjust enrichment as counterplea (Table K11)
	Contracts and transactions
	For commercial contracts see KJ-KKZ1 911+
	For government contracts see KJ-KKZ1 2754+
858	General (Table K11)
858.3	Liberty of contract. Party autonomy (Table K11)
858.5.A-Z	Types of contracts, A-Z
858.5.A88	Atypical or mixed contracts (Table K12)
858.5.C65	Consensual and real contracts (Table K12)
858.5.O53	Onerous and gratuitous contracts (Table K12)
858.5.O67	Option (Table K12)

KJ-KKZ1

	Civil law
	Obligations
	Contracts and transactions
	Types of contracts, A-Z -- Continued
858.5.P32	Pactum de contrahendo. Preliminary contracts (Table K12)
	Standardized terms of contracts see KJ-KKZ1 872
858.5.U54	Unilateral and bilateral contracts (Table K12)
859	Secured transactions. Security (Table K11)
	Class here general works
	For particular secured transactions, see the transaction, e.g. KJ-KKZ1, 726, Pledge; KJ-KKZ1, 900, Suretyship, etc.
	Fiduciary transactions see KJ-KKZ1 733+
	Declaration of intention
860	General (Table K11)
860.2	Reliance theory. Will theory (Table K11)
860.3	Mental reservation. Simulation (Table K11)
860.4	Silence (Table K11)
	Agency
	Including statutory agency
861	General (Table K11)
	Authorized representation
861.3	General (Table K11)
861.5	To whom it may concern (Table K11)
861.6	Receiving or delivering of declaration (Table K11)
862	Unauthorized representation. Falsus procurator (Table K11)
862.5	Agent for both contracting parties (Table K11)
	Power of attorney
862.7	General (Table K11)
862.8	General discretionary power of attorney (Table K11)
863	Form requirements. Forms (Table K11)
863.3	Expiration and termination. Cancellation (Table K11)
	Mandate
864	General (Table K11)
	Negotiorum gestio
864.3	General (Table K11)
864.5.A-Z	Special topics, A-Z
864.5.A73	Architects (Table K12)
864.5.A88	Attorneys (Table K12)
	Negotiorum gestio without mandate
865	General (Table K11)
865.5.A-Z	Special topics, A-Z
	Subarrange each by Table K12
866	Form requirements. Notice. Time of effectiveness (Table K11)
866.5	Conditions

Civil law
　Obligations
　　Individual contracts and transactions
　　　Lease. Landlord and tenant
　　　　Rights and claims from lease contract -- Continued
880.8　　　　　Rent (Table K11)
　　　　　　　For rent subsidies see KJ-KKZ1 1524.R45
881　　　　　Compensation for improvements by tenant (Table K11)
881.3　　　　　Liens of landlord (Table K11)
882　　　　　Termination of lease (Table K11)
　　　　　　　Including expiration, rescission, and notice
882.3　　　　　Protection of the tenant (Table K11)
　　　　　Lease litigation and execution
　　　　　　Including procedure at regular civil courts and special
　　　　　　　tribunals
883　　　　　General (Table K11)
883.3　　　　　Remedies (Table K11)
883.5　　　　　Eviction. Forced vacating (Table K11)
　　　　　　　Including subtenant
　　　　Types of property
884　　　　　Real property (Table K11)
　　　　　Buildings. Rooms
884.3　　　　　General (Table K11)
884.4　　　　　Commercial space (Table K11)
　　　　　Housing. Apartments
884.5　　　　　General (Table K11)
885　　　　　State policies and planning (Table K11)
　　　　　Public subsidies
　　　　　　Including subsidies for reconstruction
885.5　　　　　General (Table K11)
885.7　　　　　Tax exemptions and deductions for home building
　　　　　　　(Table K11)
886　　　　　Rationing and distribution of housing (Table K11)
　　　　　　For social housing see KJ-KKZ1 887.3
886.3　　　　　Rent control (Table K11)
　　　　　　　Including subtenant
　　　　　Social measures
887　　　　　General (Table K11)
887.3　　　　　Publically subsidized housing (Table K11)
　　　　　　Rent subsidies see KJ-KKZ1 1524.R45
887.4.A-Z　　　　Housing provided for particular groups, A-Z
887.4.Y68　　　　Young adults (Table K12)
888　　　　　Commercial and industrial property (Table K11)
　　　　　　Including operating leasing, producer leasing, etc.
　　　　Atypical or mixed contracts
888.2　　　　　General (Table K11)

	Civil law
	Obligations
	Individual contracts and transactions
	Lease. Landlord and tenant
	Atypical or mixed contracts -- Continued
	Investment leasing
	Including sale-and-lease-back
888.3	General (Table K11)
	Commercial and industrial leasing see KJ-KKZ1 888
	Farm and farm equipment leasing see KJ-KKZ1 3311
888.5	Ground lease (Table K11)
	Fiduciary transactions. Trusts and trustee
889	General (Table K11)
	Charitable trusts see KJ-KKZ1 526+
890	Loan for use. Commodatum (Table K11)
891	Personal loans. Mutuum (Table K11)
	Including secured loans
	Cf. KJ-KKZ1 955+ Commercial law
	Contracts of service and labor. Master and servant
892	General (Table K11)
	Independent work. Professions
892.3	General (Table K11)
892.4.A-Z	Particular professions and services, A-Z
	Architects see KJ-KKZ1 864.5.A73
	Attorneys see KJ-KKZ1 864.5.A88
892.4.B88	Business consultants (Table K12)
892.4.E93	Executives (Table K12)
892.4.P49	Physicians (Table K12)
892.4.P82	Public relations consultants (Table K12)
	Dependent work
892.5	General (Table K11)
892.6	Servants. Domestics (Table K11)
	Employees. Labor contract see KJ-KKZ1 1279+
892.7.A-Z	Particular groups, A-Z
	Subarrange each by Table K12
	Contract for work and labor
893	General (Table K11)
893.3.A-Z	Particular contracts, A-Z
893.3.C65	Computer contracts (Table K12)
893.3.T72	Transportation contracts (Table K12)
	Including travel contracts and package tours
894	Security. Liens (Table K11)
	Brokerage see KJ-KKZ1 929+
895	Reward. Award (Table K11)
	Mandat see KJ-KKZ1 864+

	Commercial law. Commercial transactions
	Commercial sale -- Continued
926.2.A-Z	Particular, A-Z
926.2.C65	Consignation (Table K12)
926.2.D43	Default of buyer (Table K12)
926.2.E43	Emergency sales of perishables (Table K12)
926.2.F87	Futures (Table K12)
926.3.A-Z	Special modes of selling, A-Z
926.3.F73	Franchises (Table K12)
926.3.S76	Stores (Table K12)
926.3.T44	Telephone selling (Table K12)
926.3.T73	Traveling salespeople (Table K12)
	Vending machines see KJ-KKZ1 3420.V45
926.5.A-Z	Particular products or goods, A-Z
926.5.A88	Automobilies (new or used) (Table K12)
926.5.C65	Computers (Table K12)
926.5.P47	Petroleum (Table K12)
	Used automobiles see KJ-KKZ1 926.5.A88
927	Commercial agents (Table K11)
928	Consignment. Commission merchant. Factors (Table K11)
	Brokerage
929	General (Table K11)
929.3.A-Z	Types of brokers, A-Z
929.3.M37	Marriage brokers (Table K12)
929.3.R42	Real estate agents (Table K12)
930	Auctioneers. Auctions (Table K11)
930.3	Warehousing (Table K11)
	Freight forwarders and carriers. Carriage of passengers and goods
931	General (Table K11)
931.2	Liability (Table K11)
931.3	Bill of lading (Table K11)
932	Liens (Table K11)
932.3.A-Z	Other, A-Z
932.3.D44	Delivery (Table K12)
	Types of carriers
	For regulatory (administrative) aspects see KJ-KKZ1 3440+
933	Railroads (Table K11)
933.5	Passenger carriers. Bus lines (Table K11)
934	Trucklines (Table K11)
	Airlines
935	General (Table K11)
935.2	Airline creditors. Aircraft mortgages (Table K11)
935.4	Aircraft registration (Table K11)
	Carriage by sea see KJ-KKZ1 971+
	Commercial instruments see KJ-KKZ1 937+

	Commercial law. Commercial transactions -- Continued
	Commercial liens
936	General (Table K11)
	Freight forwarder liens see KJ-KKZ1 932
	Negotiable instruments. Titles of credit
937	General (Table K11)
937.3	Possession, ownership, and transfer (Table K11)
	Including legitimation and identification
	Bills of exchange
938	General (Table K11)
938.3.A-Z	Special topics, A-Z
938.3.A22	Acceptance (Table K12)
938.3.B52	Blanks (Table K12)
938.3.C52	Clauses (Table K12)
	Contango see KJ-KKZ1 938.3.P76
938.3.E53	Endorsement (Table K12)
938.3.L52	Liability (Table K12)
	Including drawer, acceptor, and endorser
938.3.P39	Payment and return of instrument (Table K12)
938.3.P76	Prolongation. Contango (Table K12)
938.3.P765	Protest (Table K12)
	Return of instrument see KJ-KKZ1 938.3.P39
	Stamp duties see KJ-KKZ1 3643+
	Checks
939	General (Table K11)
939.3.A-Z	Special topics, A-Z
939.3.T73	Traveler's checks (Table K12)
	Letters of credit see KJ-KKZ1 955.6
	Stock certificates and bonds see KJ-KKZ1 1064+
	Trust investments see KJ-KKZ1 965
	Bills of lading (Land transportation) see KJ-KKZ1 931.3
	Maritime bills of lading see KJ-KKZ1 973
	Promissory notes see KJ-KKZ1 902
	Criminal provisions see KJ-KKZ1 4350
	Banking. Stock exchange
940	General (Table K11)
940.3	State supervision (Table K11)
940.4	Accounting. Auditing (Table K11)
	Types of banks and credit institutions
	Banks of issue
941	General (Table K11)
941.3.A-Z	Particular. By name, A-Z
	Subarrange each by Table K12
942.A-Z	Special topics, A-Z
942.C56	Discount policy (Table K12)
942.D57	Discount rate (Table K12)
	Money see KJ-KKZ1 3534+

KJ-KKZ1

Commercial law. Commercial transactions
Banking. Stock exchange
Types of banks and credit institutions -- Continued

942.5	Foreign banks (Table K11)
943	Mortgage banks (Table K11)
	Savings banks
	Including public and private banks
944	General (Table K11)
944.3	State supervision (Table K11)
	Types of savings programs
945	Special premiums (Table K11)
	Investment savings see KJ-KKZ1 961.5+
945.3.A-Z	Special topics, A-Z
	Identification see KJ-KKZ1 945.3.L44
945.3.L44	Legitimation. Identification (Table K12)
945.3.S39	Savings bonds (Table K12)
946	Criminal provisions (Table K11)
947	Building and loan associations (Table K11)
948	Cooperative societies (Table K11)
949	Clearinghouses (Table K11)
950	Warehouses (Table K11)
	Banking transactions
951	General (Table K11)
952	Security of deposits. Insurance (Table K11)
953	Banking secret. Confidential communication (Table K11)
953.5	Liability (Table K11)
954	Contract (Table K11)
	Including standardized terms of contract, and clauses (e.g. storno clause)
	Deposits see KJ-KKZ1 956+
	Loans. Credit
955	General (Table K11)
955.3	Contract (Table K11)
955.4	Interest rate (Table K11)
	For usury see KJ-KKZ1 4268
955.5.A-Z	Special types of loans, A-Z
955.5.C65	Consumer credit. Small loans (Table K12)
	Including credit cards
	Cf. KJ-KKZ1 4263 Credit card fraud
955.5.D63	Documentary credit (Table K12)
	Small loans see KJ-KKZ1 955.5.C65
955.6	Letters of credit
955.7	Suretyship. Guaranty (Table K11)
	Deposit banking
956	General (Table K11)
956.3	Deposits. Custodianship accounts (Table K11)

Commercial law. Commercial transactions
Banking. Stock exchange
Banking transactions
Deposit banking -- Continued

957	Trading of securities (Table K11)
	Including electronic data processing
958	Criminal provisions (Table K11)
959	Discount (Table K11)
960	Account current (Table K11)
960.3	Collecting of accounts (Table K11)
	Noncash funds transfer
	Including electronic funds transfer
961	General (Table K11)
961.3	Bill paying services. Home banking services. Drafts (Table K11)
	Investments
	For tax measures see KJ-KKZ1 3553.3
961.5	General (Table K11)
	Foreign investments see KJ-KKZ1 3202+
	Stock exchange transactions. Securities
962	General (Table K11)
962.5	Stockbrokers (Table K11)
962.6	Insider trading (Table K11)
962.7.A-Z	Particular stock exchanges. By place, A-Z
	Subarrange each by Table K12
	Commodity exchanges. Produce exchanges
962.8	General (Table K11)
962.9.A-Z	Particular commodity exchanges. By place, A-Z
	Subarrange each by Table K12
	Investment trust
963	General (Table K11)
964	Real estate investment trust (Table K11)
965	Trust investments (Table K11)
966	Criminal provisions (Table K11)
	Including money laundering
967	Foreign exchange (Table K11)
	Taxation of banking and stock exchange transactions see KJ-KKZ1 3640.A+
	Maritime law
	For regulatory aspects of water transportation, navigation, and pilotage see KJ-KKZ1 3470+
970	General (Table K11)
970.3	Shipowners. Ship operators (Table K11)
970.4	Shipmasters (Table K11)
	Affreightment. Carriage of goods at sea and inland waters
971	General (Table K11)

KJ-KKZ1

Commercial law. Commercial transactions
  Maritime law
    Affreightment. Carriage of goods at sea and inland waters --
    Continued

972	Freight forwarders (Table K11)
	Including liability
973	Ocean bills of lading (Table K11)
974	Charter parties (Table K11)
975	Act of God. War. Act of government (Table K11)
976	Carriage of passengers at sea and inland waters (Table K11)
	Including carriage of passengers' luggage
977	Liability (Table K11)
	Including maritime torts and collisions at sea
	Average
978	General (Table K11)
979	Havarie grosse (Table K11)
	Special average. Collision at sea
	Cf. KJ-KKZ1 3470+ Water transportation
980	General (Table K11)
980.3	Criminal provisions (Table K11)
	Insurance see KJ-KKZ1 985+
	Salvage. Shipwreck
981	General (Table K11)
981.3	Criminal provisions (Table K11)
	Ship creditors
982	General (Table K11)
983	Bottomry and respondentia. Ship mortgage (Table K11)
983.3	Maritime liens (Table K11)
984	Shipbrokers (Table K11)
984.3	Ship registers (Table K11)
984.5	Maritime courts (Table K11)
	Prize courts
	see KZ6640+
	Marine insurance
985	General (Table K11)
985.3	Contract (Table K11)
	Including standardized terms of contract, policies, etc.
986	Accidents. Average (Table K11)
986.3	Seaworthiness (Table K11)
	Maritime social legislation
	Including legislation for merchant mariners for inland navigation
987	General (Table K11)
	Labor law for merchant mariners
987.5	General (Table K11)
988	Collective labor agreements. Maritime unions (Table K11)
	Labor standards

	Commercial law. Commercial transactions
	Maritime law
	Maritime social legislation
	Labor law for merchant mariners
	Labor standards -- Continued
989	General (Table K11)
990	Hours of labor (Table K11)
991	Wages. Nonwage benefits (Table K11)
992	Vacations (Table K11)
992.5	Labor hygiene and industrial safety (Table K11)
993	Discipline (Table K11)
	Social insurance for merchant mariners
	Including all branches of social insurance
995	General (Table K11)
996	Organization and administration (Table K11)
	Insurance law
	Including regulation of insurance business
998	General (Table K11)
	Insurance carriers
999	General (Table K11)
	Private insurance associations
	Including cooperatives, mutual companies, etc.
1000	General (Table K11)
1001	State supervision (Table K11)
	Including control of restraint of trade
	Contract
	Including standardized terms of contract, and insurance policy
1002	General (Table K11)
1002.3	Parties to contract (Table K11)
	Including third parties, and including respondeat superior doctrine
1002.4	Limitation of risk (Table K11)
1004	Group insurance (Table K11)
1005	Adjustment of claims (Table K11)
1006	Agents. Brokers (Table K11)
	Life insurance
1008	General (Table K11)
1008.3	Contract. Parties to contract (Table K11)
	Including standardized terms of contract, and including third parties
1009	Group insurance (Table K11)
1010	Old age pensions (Table K11)
1011	Survivors' benefits (Table K11)
1013	Health insurance. Medical care insurance (Table K11)
	Accident insurance
1015	General (Table K11)

311

	Commercial law. Commercial transactions
	Insurance law
	Accident insurance -- Continued
1016	Contract. Parties to contract (Table K11)
	Including standardized terms of contract, and including third parties
1016.3.A-Z	Special topics, A-Z
1016.3.T72	Traveler's insurance (Table K12)
1017	Business insurance
	Including bank insurance
	Property insurance
1018	General (Table K11)
1019	Multiple line insurance (Table K11)
	Including home owners insurance
1020.A-Z	Particular hazards, A-Z
	Burglary see KJ-KKZ1 1020.T43
1020.F57	Fire (Table K12)
	Robbery see KJ-KKZ1 1020.T43
1020.T43	Theft. Burglary. Robbery (Table K12)
1020.W38	Water damage (Table K12)
1022.A-Z	Types of property and business, A-Z
	Subarrange each by Table K12
	Suretyship. Guaranty. Title insurance
1024	General (Table K11)
1025	Credit insurance (Table K11)
	Pension trust insurance see KJ-KKZ1 1340
1025.5	Litigation insurance (Table K11)
1026	Mortgage insurance (Table K11)
	Liability insurance
	Including both statutory and private insurance
1027	General (Table K11)
	Contract. Parties to contract
	Including standardized terms of contract, and including third parties
1027.3	General (Table K11)
1027.5	Limitation of risk (Table K11)
1028	Adjustment of claims (Table K11)
	Risks and damages
	Traffic
1030	General (Table K11)
	Automobiles
1031	General (Table K11)
1032	Contract. Parties to contract (Table K11)
	Including standardized terms of contract, and including third parties
1032.3	Adjustment of claims (Table K11)

	Commercial law. Commercial transactions
	Insurance law
	Liability insurance
	Risks and damages
	Traffic -- Continued
1034	Automotive transportation (General) (Table K11)
	Including trucking, bus lines, etc.
1035	Aviation (Table K11)
1036.A-Z	Other special, A-Z
1036.M35	Malpractice (Table K12)
1036.P64	Pollution (Table K12)
1036.P75	Products liability (Table K12)
1038	Reinsurance (Table K11)
	Business associations
1040	General (Table K11)
1041	Constitutional aspects. Interdiction of private business associations (Table K11)
1042	Expropriation and nationalization of business associations (Table K11)
	Personal companies. Unincorporated business associations
	For civil companies see KJ-KKZ1 897+
1043-1043.9	General (Table KJ-KKZ12)
1045-1045.9	Partnership (Table KJ-KKZ12)
1047-1047.9	Limited partnership (Table KJ-KKZ12)
1049-1049.9	Silent partners (Table KJ-KKZ12)
	Stock companies. Incorporated business associations
1050	General (Table K11)
1051	Foreign corporations (Table K11)
	Stock corporations
1052	General (Table K11)
	Incorporation and promoters
1053	General (Table K11)
	Capital see KJ-KKZ1 1062
1053.3	Liability before registration (Table K11)
1053.4	Defective incorporation (Table K11)
1053.5	Domicile (Table K11)
1054	State supervision (Table K11)
1055	Registration and publicity (Table K11)
	Organization and management
1056	General (Table K11)
	Director or executive board
1057	General (Table K11)
1058.A-Z	Special topics, A-Z
1058.C65	Conflict of interests (Table K12)
1058.D57	Dismissal (Table K12)
1058.E43	Election (Table K12)
1058.L33	Liability (Table K12)

Commercial law. Commercial transactions
 Business associations
  Stock companies. Incorporated business associations
   Stock corporations
    Organization and management
     Director or executive board
      Special topics, A-Z -- Continued
       Pensions see KJ-KKZ1 1058.S25
1058.S25   Salaries. Pensions (Table K12)
      Board of controller and supervisors
1059   General (Table K11)
        Employee's representation in management see KJ-
          KKZ1 1370+
       Stockholders' meetings see KJ-KKZ1 1078
       Auditors see KJ-KKZ1 1075.5
1060   Liability. Relationship to third parties (Table K11)
     Corporate finance
1061   General (Table K11)
1062   Capital stock (Table K11)
        Including increase of capital
1063   Corporation ownership of its own stock or stock of other
          corporations (Table K11)
      Securities
1064   General (Table K11)
       Stocks
1065   General (Table K11)
1065.3   Bearer stock (Table K11)
          Including personal share (Inscribed share)
1065.4   Common stock (Table K11)
          Including without par value
1066   Preferred stock (Table K11)
1067   Dividends and profits (Table K11)
       Bonds
1068   General (Table K11)
1069   Bearer bonds (Table K11)
           Including personal bonds (Inscribed bonds)
1070.A-Z   Other, A-Z
1070.C54   Convertible bonds (Table K12)
1070.J68   Jouissance share (Table K12)
1070.M67   Mortgage bonds (Table K12)
1071   Trust investments (Table K11)
     Accounting. Financial statements. Auditing
        Cf. KJ-KKZ1 3562+ Tax accounting
1072   General (Table K11)
1073   Valuation (Table K11)
1074   Corporation reserves (Table K11)

314

Commercial law. Commercial transactions
　　Business associations
　　　Stock companies. Incorporated business associations
　　　　Stock corporations
　　　　　Accounting. Financial statements. Auditing -- Continued
1075　　　　　　Pension trusts (Table K11)
　　　　　　　　Cf. KJ-KKZ1 1340 Labor law
1075.5　　　　Auditors (Table K11)
　　　　　Stocks and stockholders' rights. Stock transfer
1077　　　　　General (Table K11)
1077.5　　　　Disclosure requirements (Table K11)
1078　　　　　Stockholders' meetings (Table K11)
　　　　　　　　Including voting, resolutions, confidential
　　　　　　　　　communications, etc.
1079　　　　　Minority stockholders (Table K11)
1080　　　　　Business report. Rendering of account (Table K11)
1081　　　　　Stockholders' pre-emption rights (Table K11)
1082　　　　　Loss of stockholders' rights (Table K11)
　　　　　　　　Including exclusion or leaving of shareholders and recall
　　　　　　　　　of stocks
　　　　　Types of corporations
　　　　　　Subsidiary and parent companies see KJ-KKZ1 1145
1083　　　　　Family corporations (Table K11)
1083.5　　　　Couple-owned enterprises (Table K11)
1084　　　　　One-person companies (Table K11)
1085　　　　Termination. Dissolution. Liquidation (Table K11)
　　　　　Corporate reorganization see KJ-KKZ1 1147+
　　　　　Consolidation and merger see KJ-KKZ1 1148
1087　　　　Partnership partly limited by shares (Table K11)
　　　　Private company
1090　　　　General (Table K11)
　　　　　Incorporation
1092　　　　　General (Table K11)
　　　　　　Capital see KJ-KKZ1 1102
1093　　　　　Liability before registration (Table K11)
1093.3　　　　Defective incorporation (Table K11)
1094　　　　　Domicile (Table K11)
1095　　　　　Registration and publicity (Table K11)
　　　　　Organization and management
1096　　　　　General (Table K11)
　　　　　　Directors
1097　　　　　　General (Table K11)
1098.A-Z　　　Special topics, A-Z
　　　　　　　Dismissal see KJ-KKZ1 1098.E43
1098.E43　　　Election. Dismissal (Table K12)
1098.L43　　　Legal status. Liability (Table K12)
1099　　　　Board of controllers and supervisors (Table K11)

KJ-KKZ1

Commercial law. Commercial transactions
Business associations
Stock companies. Incorporated business associations
Private company
Organization and management -- Continued
Stockholders' meetings see KJ-KKZ1 1106

1100	Liability (Table K11)
	Company finance
1101	General (Table K11)
1102	Capital stock (Table K11)
	Including increase and decrease
1103	Accounting. Financial statements. Auditing (Table K11)
	Stock and stockholders' rights. Stock transfer
1104	General (Table K11)
1105	Stocks (Table K11)
	Including stock certificates
1106	Stockholders' meetings (Table K11)
	Including voting and resolutions
1107	Control of partners (Table K11)
1108	Succession. Inheritance (Table K11)
1109	Loss of stockholders' rights (Table K11)
	Including exclusion or leaving of stockholders
	Types of private companies
1112	Family corporations (Table K11)
1113	One-person companies (Table K11)
1114	Termination. Dissolution. Liquidation (Table K11)
1116	Multi-national corporation (Table K11)
1117	Colonial companies (History) (Table K11)
	Cooperative societies
1120	General (Table K11)
1121	Incorporation and promoters (Table K11)
1122	Registration and publicity (Table K11)
	Organization and management
1123	General (Table K11)
1124	Executive board (Table K11)
1125	Board of controllers and supervisors (Table K11)
	Membership meetings see KJ-KKZ1 1132
1126	Liability. Limited liability (Table K11)
	Cooperatives' finance
1127	General (Table K11)
1128	Depositors' fund (Table K11)
1129	Accounting. Financial statements. Auditing (Table K11)
	Membership
1131	General (Table K11)
1132	Membership meetings (Table K11)
	Including voting and resolutions
1132.3	Leaving and entering of members (Table K11)

KJ-KKZ1

Intellectual and industrial property
Copyright -- Continued

1160.4	Procedures. Formalities (Table K11)
	Including registration of claim, transfer, licenses, deposit, and notice
1160.5	Protected works (Table K11)
	Including original works, subsequent rights, idea and title
	Scope of protection
1160.6	General (Table K11)
1160.62	Personality rights (Table K11)
	Mechanical reproduction
1160.63	General (Table K11)
1160.64	Documentation and dissemination (Table K11)
	Including fair use
1160.65	Exhibition rights (Table K11)
	Performing rights
	Cf. KJ-KKZ1 1184 Quasi copyright
1160.7	General (Table K11)
1160.72	Societies and industrial trusts (Table K11)
1160.725	Public lending rights (Table K11)
1160.73	Broadcasting rights (Table K11)
1160.75	Recording rights (Table K11)
	Including phonographs, magnetic recorders, and jukeboxes
1160.76	Filming and photographing (Table K11)
1160.78	Translation (Table K11)
1160.8	Employees' copyright (Table K11)
1160.82	Duration and renewal (Table K11)
1160.9	Delicts. Torts (Table K11)
	Branches of copyright
1165-1165.9	Literary copyright (Table KJ-KKZ9)
1170-1170.9	Musical copyright (Table KJ-KKZ9)
1175-1175.9	Fine art and photography (Table KJ-KKZ9)
	Violation of rights in one's own picture see KJ-KKZ1 843.4
	Motion pictures see KJ-KKZ1 1180+
1177	Designs and models (Table K11)
1179	Prints and labels (Table K11)
	Including works of commercial art, catalogs, sample books, etc.
1180-1180.9	Motion pictures and television programs (Table KJ-KKZ9)
1182.A-Z	Special topics, A-Z
	Subarrange each by Table K12
1183	Computer programs. Computer software (Table K11)
1183.5	Databases (Table K11)
1184	Quasi copyright and neighboring rights (Table K11)
	Author and publisher
	Including the publishing contract

	Intellectual and industrial property
	Author and publisher -- Continued
1185	General (Table K11)
1186	Plays and stage productions (Table K11)
1187	Motion pictures (Table K11)
1188	Music (Table K11)
1189	Scientific literature (Table K11)
1190.A-Z	Special topics, A-Z
	Subarrange each by Table K12
1192	Litigation and execution (Table K11)
	International copyright
	see K1414+
	Patent law and trademarks
1194	General (Table K11)
1195	Scope of protection (Table K11)
1197	Relation to antitrust laws (Table K11)
1200	Patent office (Table K11)
	Patent practice and procedure
1202	General (Table K11)
	Invention
	Including priority and novelty
1203	General (Table K11)
1204	Legal status of inventors. Community of inventors (Table K11)
1205	Employees' invention and technological innovation (Table K11)
1206	Claim drafting (Table K11)
	Including collision of patents
1207	Res judicata (Table K11)
1207.3	Fees (Table K11)
1208	Duration and renewal (Table K11)
1209.A-Z	Types of patents, A-Z
	Subarrange each by Table K12
1210.A-Z	Patented products, processes, and engineering methods, A-Z
1210.B56	Biotechnology (Table K12)
1210.D78	Drugs (Table K12)
1210.P55	Plants (Table K12)
1212	Designs and utility models (Table K11)
	Licenses
	Including compulsory licenses and fees
1213	General (Table K11)
1214	Foreign licensing agreements (Table K11)
	Including know-how
	Patent litigation and infringements
1215	General (Table K11)
1216.A-Z	Special topics, A-Z

KJ-KKZ1

Intellectual and industrial property
Unfair competition
Pushing for sales -- Continued
1246 General (Table K11)
1247 Unordered merchandise by mail (Table K11)
Cf. KJ-KKZ1 869.5 Contracts
1248 Special sales (Table K11)
Rebates and premiums
1250 General (Table K11)
1251.A-Z Special topics, A-Z
Subarrange each by Table K12
1252 Price cutting
1253.A-Z By industry or occupation, A-Z
Subarrange each by Table K12
Delicts. Torts
Cf. KJ-KKZ1 834+ Civil law
1255 General (Table K11)
1256.A-Z Protected rights, A-Z
1256.T72 Trade and industrial secrets (Table K12)
1257.A-Z Torts, A-Z
1257.B69 Boycott (Table K12)
1257.B73 Breach of contract. Evasion (Table K12)
1257.B74 Bribery (Table K12)
1257.E58 Enticement (Table K12)
1257.E86 Espionage, Industrial (Table K12)
Evasion see KJ-KKZ1 1257.B73
Industrial espionage see KJ-KKZ1 1257.E86
1258 Practice and procedure (Table K11)
Including arbitration and award
Labor law
Including works on both labor law and social insurance, and private
labor law as it applies to the labor contract and to the labor-
management relationship
Criticism and reform see KJ-KKZ1 1468
1261-1270 General (Table K9c)
1272 Right and duty to work. Constitutional aspects (Table K11)
1273 Ideology and labor law (Table K11)
1274 Politics and labor (Table K11)
1275 Labor policies. Competition and incentives for high
performance (Table K11)
Organization and administration
Class here works on national departments and boards of labor,
national, state and local departments and boards, or
departments and boards of several states or administrative
districts
For departments or boards (several or individual) of an individual
state or administrative district, see the state or district

KJ-KKZ1

	Labor law
	Organization and administration -- Continued
1276	General (Table K11)
1277.A-Z	Particular, A-Z
	Subarrange each by Table K12
1278	Conflict of laws (Table K11)
	Labor contract and employment
1279	General (Table K11)
	Types of employment
1280	Permanent employment (Table K11)
1280.5	Probationary employment (Table K11)
1281	Temporary employment (Table K11)
	Including seasonal work
1282	Double employment (Table K11)
1283	Part-time employment (Table K11)
1284	Supplementary employment (Table K11)
1285	Subcontracting (Table K11)
1286	Constitutional rights in employment (Table K11)
1286.5	Personnel records (Table K11)
	Individual labor contract and collective agreements. Liberty of contract
1287	General (Table K11)
	Working standards see KJ-KKZ1 1382
	Works agreements see KJ-KKZ1 1355
	Principle of most favorable wage rate see KJ-KKZ1 1381
	Freedom of employment and restraint on freedom of employment
1290	General (Table K11)
	Preferential employment
	Including people with severe disabilities, veterans, etc.
1292	General (Table K11)
1293	Sheltered workshops (Table K11)
	Formation of contract
1295	General (Table K11)
1296	State and labor contract (Table K11)
1297.A-Z	Clauses and terms, A-Z
1297.A34	Age limit (Table K12)
1297.C69	Covenants not to compete (Table K12)
1297.O55	On-the-job training (Table K12)
	Operational changes. Relocation of enterprises see KJ-KKZ1 1311
	Standardized labor conditions see KJ-KKZ1 1379+
1299	Formalities (Table K11)
	Including hiring practices and selection
	Parties to contract
1300	General (Table K11)
	Parties to collective bargaining see KJ-KKZ1 1384+

KJ-KKZ1

Labor law

Prohibition of discrimination in employment. Equal opportunity

Particular groups or types of discrimination, A-Z -- Continued

1328.A33	Aged. Older people (Table K12)
1328.A44	Alien laborers (Table K12)
1328.D58	Disabilities, People with (Table K12)
1328.E84	Ethnic groups. Minorities (Table K12)
	Minorities see KJ-KKZ1 1328.E84
	Older people see KJ-KKZ1 1328.A33
	People with disabilities see KJ-KKZ1 1328.D58
1328.R44	Religious discrimination (Table K12)
	Including general works on religion in the workplace
1328.W58	Women (Table K12)
	Wages
1330	General (Table K11)
	Principle of most favored wage rate see KJ-KKZ1 1381
	Types of wages and modes of remuneration
1332	Daywork. Piecework (Table K11)
1333	Incentive wages (Table K11)
	Including bonus system, profit sharing, etc.
1334	Collective wages (Table K11)
1335	Adjustments. Cost-of-living adjustments (Table K11)
1335.5	Family allowances (Table K11)
1336	Overtime payments (Table K11)
	Including night differentials
1336.5	Payment during sick leave or leave of absence (Table K11)
1337	Time, place, and mode of payment (Table K11)
	Nonwage payments and fringe benefits
1338	General (Table K11)
	Pension and retirement plans
1339	General (Table K11)
1340	Pension trusts (Table K11)
	Including insolvency insurance
1341.A-Z	Other, A-Z
1341.S63	Social (welfare) provisions (Table K12)
1343.A-Z	Groups of employees or industries, A-Z
1343.A34	Agricultural laborers (Table K12)
1343.H6	Hotels, restaurants, taverns (Table K12)
	Restaurants see KJ-KKZ1 1343.H6
	Taverns see KJ-KKZ1 1343.H6
1345	Employees' evaluation (Table K11)
	Labor-management relations
1347	General (Table K11)
1348	Constitutional aspects. Private autonomy. Property rights (Table K11)
1349	Political activities. Limitations (Table K11)

Labor law
Labor-management relations -- Continued
Works councils
Including election, organization, parliamentary practice, etc.

1350	General (Table K11)
1352	Works assembly (Table K11)
	Works councils of business concerns see KJ-KKZ1 1370+
1353	Union participation (Table K11)
	Employee participation in management and planning
1354	General (Table K11)
	Constitutional aspects. Property rights see KJ-KKZ1 1348
1355	Works agreements (Table K11)
	Standardized labor conditions see KJ-KKZ1 1379+
	Production tasks
1357	General (Table K11)
1358	Maximum increase of labor productivity (Table K11)
1359	Technological improvements of enterprise. Innovations (Table K11)
1360	Rationalization (Table K11)
	Labor standards and protection of labor
1362	General (Table K11)
1362.5	Profit sharing. Employee ownership (Table K11)
1363	Working hours (Table K11)
1364	Social (welfare) provisions (Table K11)
	Including pension trusts, health insurance, housing, cafeterias, etc.
1365	Employee rules and discipline (Table K11)
	Including procedure and penalties
	Personnel management
1366	General (Table K11)
1367	Hiring. Dismissal. Transfer (Table K11)
	For personnel questionnaires and tests see KJ-KKZ1 1299
1368	Occupational training or retraining (Table K11)
	Including apprenticeship
1369	Economic policies (Table K11)
	Including control of operational changes
	Employee representation on board of controllers and supervisors
	Including unincorporated and incorporated business associations, cooperative societies, industrial trusts, etc.
1370	General (Table K11)
1372.A-Z	Industries, A-Z
	Subarrange each by Table K12
1373	Youth representatives (Table K11)
1374.A-Z	Industries and trades, A-Z
	Subarrange each by Table K12

Labor law
  Labor-management relations
    Employee participation in management and planning --
      Continued
1375   Criminal provisions (Table K11)
          Collective bargaining and labor agreements
1376   General (Table K11)
1377   Constitutional aspects (Table K11)
1378   Standards for conclusion of labor contracts (Table K11)
              Standardized labor conditions
1379   General (Table K11)
1380.A-Z   By industry, A-Z
                  Subarrange each by Table K12
1381   Most favorable wage (Table K11)
1382   Working standards (Table K11)
1383   Formation of contract (Table K11)
              Parties to contract
1384   General (Table K11)
                Unions see KJ-KKZ1 1402+
                Employers' associations see KJ-KKZ1 1406
1386   Validity, applicability, and effectiveness (Table K11)
                  Including planning periods
1387.A-Z   By industry or occupation, A-Z
1387.B36   Banking (Table K12)
1387.B56   Biotechnology industries (Table K12)
1387.C44   Cement industry (Table K12)
1387.C48   Chemical industry (Table K12)
1387.C66   Construction industry (Table K12)
1387.E48   Educational personnel. School personnel (Table K12)
1387.G37   Gas industry (Table K12)
1387.H54   Highway transportation (Table K12)
1387.H67   Hospital and medical personnel (Table K12)
1387.M33   Machinery industry (Table K12)
                Medical personnel see KJ-KKZ1 1387.H67
1387.P75   Printing industry (Table K12)
                School personnel see KJ-KKZ1 1387.E48
1387.S47   Service industries (Table K12)
1387.S82   Stagehands (Table K12)
1387.W38   Water utilities (Table K12)
          Collective labor disputes
1388   General (Table K11)
              Constitutional aspects see KJ-KKZ1 1348
1389   Arbitration. Conciliation (Table K11)
                  Cf. KJ-KKZ1 1464+ Arbitration (Labor courts)
              Strikes and lockouts. Boycott
1390   General (Table K11)
1392   Picketing (Table K11)

Labor law
　Collective labor disputes
　　Strikes and lockouts. Boycott -- Continued
　　　Wildcat strikes. Sympathy strikes. Political strikes
1393　　　　　General (Table K11)
1394　　　　　Damages (Table K11)
1395　　　　　Criminal provisions (Table K11)
1396　　　　　Nonparticipants. Strike breakers (Table K11)
　　Corporate representation
1399　　　General (Table K11)
1400　　　Constitutional aspects. Freedom of coalition (Table K11)
　　　Unions
1402　　　　General (Table K11)
1403　　　　Personality and capacity (Table K11)
1404　　　　Union organization (Table K11)
　　　　　　Including election, legal status, etc. of officers
1406　　　　Employers' associations (Table K11)
　　Protection of labor
1408　　　General (Table K11)
1409　　　Protection of human resource (Table K11)
　　　Hours of labor
　　　　Including night work and Sunday labor
1410　　　　General (Table K11)
1412　　　　Overtime (Table K11)
　　　　Part-time employment see KJ-KKZ1 1283
1413　　　　Shifts (Table K11)
1414.A-Z　　　By industry or type of employment, A-Z
　　　　　　Subarrange each by Table K12
　　　Vacations
1415　　　　General (Table K11)
1416　　　　Constitutional aspects. Right to recreation (Table K11)
1417　　　　Leave of absence (Table K11)
1418　　　　Sick leave (Table K11)
1419　　　　Holidays (Table K11)
1420　　　　Cash compensation and holiday pay (Table K11)
1421.A-Z　　　By industry or type of labor, A-Z
1421.B84　　　　Building and construction industry (Table K12)
1422　　　Child and youth labor (Table K11)
　　　　　Including hours of labor
　　　Women's labor
　　　　Including hours of labor
1424　　　　General (Table K11)
1426　　　　Maternal welfare (Table K11)
1428　　　Home labor (Table K11)
　　　Labor hygiene and industrial safety
　　　　Including safety regulations for equipment
1430　　　　General (Table K11)

	Labor law
	Protection of labor
	Labor hygiene and industrial safety -- Continued
1432	Factory inspection (Table K11)
1433.A-Z	By industry or type of labor, A-Z
1433.A37	Agricultural laborers (Table K12)
1433.A85	Aviation industry (Table K12)
1433.B84	Building and construction industry (Table K12)
1433.C62	Coal trade (Table K12)
1433.E53	Electric power plants. Electric utilities (Table K12)
1433.G37	Gas industry. Gas manufacture (Table K12)
1433.G67	Government employees and laborers (Table K12)
1433.M56	Miners (Table K12)
1433.O32	Office workers (Table K12)
1433.O33	Offshore oil industry (Table K12)
	School employees see KJ-KKZ1 1433.T43
1433.S93	Sugar trade (Table K12)
1433.T43	Teachers. School employees (Table K12)
1433.T68	Tourism (Table K12)
1433.W37	Waterworks (Table K12)
1434.A-Z	By machinery, equipment, etc. A-Z
1434.V54	Video display terminals (Table K12)
1435.A-Z	Labor law for particular industries or occupations, A-Z
1435.A35	Agricultural laborers (Table K12)
1435.A75	Artisans (Table K12)
1435.A76	Artists (Table K12)
	Athletes, Professional see KJ-KKZ1 1435.P76
1435.A84	Aviation industry (Table K12)
1435.B84	Building and construction industry (Table K12)
1435.C45	Chemical industry (Table K12)
1435.C48	Church employees (Table K12)
1435.C55	Clerks (Table K12)
1435.D65	Domestics (Table K12)
	Education see KJ-KKZ1 1435.T43
1435.E93	Executives (Table K12)
1435.H67	Hospital and medical personnel (Table K12)
1435.J88	Journalists (Table K12)
	Medical personnel see KJ-KKZ1 1435.H67
1435.P76	Professional athletes (Table K12)
	Railroads see KJ-KKZ1 3463
1435.S25	Salaried employees (Table K12)
1435.S44	Self-employed (Table K12)
1435.T43	Teachers. Education (Table K12)
1435.T73	Transportation workers (Table K12)
1435.V64	Volunteers (Table K12)
	Labor supply. Manpower control. Manpower planning
1437	General (Table K11)

Labor law
Labor supply. Manpower control. Manpower planning --
Continued
1438.A-Z   Particular agencies, A-Z
Subarrange each by Table K12
1439   Criminal provisions (Table K11)
Labor courts and procedure
Class here works on courts of several jurisdictions
For courts (several or individual) of an individual jurisdiction, see
the jurisdiction
1440   General (Table K11)
1442.A-Z   Particular courts, A-Z
Subarrange each by Table K12
Procedural principles
1443   General (Table K11)
1444   Due process of law (Table K11)
Including frivolous suits
1445   Parties to action (Table K11)
Pretrial procedures
1446   General (Table K11)
1447   Dispute commissions. Grievance boards (Table K11)
Procedure at first instance
1448   General (Table K11)
1450   Jurisdiction (Table K11)
Including competence in subject matter and venue
Actions and defense
1452   General (Table K11)
1454   Judicial review of grievance procedures (Table K11)
1455   Settlement (Table K11)
1457   Evidence. Burden of proof (Table K11)
Judgments. Judicial decisions
1458   General (Table K11)
1459   Res judicata (Table K11)
1460   Remedies. Appellate procedures (Table K11)
1462   Execution (Table K11)
1463   Costs (Table K11)
Arbitration
1464   General (Table K11)
1465.A-Z   By trade or profession, A-Z
Subarrange each by Table K12
Competence conflicts between labor and social courts see
KJ-KKZ1 1569
Social legislation
1468   Social reform and policies
Including all branches of social legislation and labor
1469   General (Table K11)
Social insurance

	Social legislation
	Social insurance -- Continued
	Criticism and reform see KJ-KKZ1 1468+
	Information retrieval and electronic data processing see KJ-KKZ1 47.5+
1472	General (Table K11)
1473	Constitutional aspects. Private autonomy and compulsory insurance (Table K11)
	Organization and administration
	Including insurance carriers
	For national departments and boards of labor and social insurance see KJ-KKZ1 1276+
1474	General (Table K11)
1474.2	Corporate rights and personality (Table K11)
1474.3	Autonomy. Self-government (Table K11)
1474.4	Officials and employees (Table K11)
	Including labor-management relations
	Finance
1474.5	General (Table K11)
1474.6	Accounting and auditing (Table K11)
1474.7	Dues (Table K11)
	Including employers' and employees' contribution
1474.8	State supervision (Table K11)
	Coverage and benefits
1476	General (Table K11)
1478.A-Z	Groups of beneficiaries, A-Z
1478.A34	Agricultural laborers. Farmers (Table K12)
1478.A43	Aliens (Table K12)
	Farmers see KJ-KKZ1 1478.A34
1478.L35	Laborers in foreign countries (Table K12)
	Merchant mariners see KJ-KKZ1 995+
	Miners see KJ-KKZ1 3365
	Railroads see KJ-KKZ1 3463
1478.S44	Self-employed (Table K12)
1478.W65	Women (Table K12)
1479.A-Z	Special subjects applying to all branches of social insurance
1479.C38	Causation (Table K12)
1480	Criminal provisions (Table K11)
1481	Conflict of laws (Table K11)
	Health insurance
	For private health insurance see KJ-KKZ1 1013
	For health insurance plans see KJ-KKZ1 1364
1483	General (Table K11)
1484	Compulsory insurance (Table K11)
	Including exemptions
1485	Right to insurance (Table K11)
1486	Organization and administration (Table K11)

	Social legislation
	Social insurance
	Health insurance -- Continued
1487.5.A-Z	Coverage and benefits, A-Z
	For public employees and officials see KJ-KKZ1 2978.4
1487.5.L65	Long term care. Nursing care (Table K12)
	Nursing care see KJ-KKZ1 1487.5.L65
1487.5.V63	Vocational rehabilitation (Table K12)
1488.A-Z	Groups of beneficiaries, A-Z
	Subarrange each by Table K12
	The medical profession and health insurance
1489	General (Table K11)
1490	Physicians employed by the health administration (Table K11)
1492	Hospitals and pharmacies under contract with the sickness fund (Table K11)
1493	Criminal provisions (Table K11)
	Workers' compensation
	Including occupational diseases
1495	General (Table K11)
1498	Organization and administration (Table K11)
	For merchant mariners see KJ-KKZ1 995+
1500.A-Z	Coverage and benefits, A-Z
	Subarrange each by Table K12
1501.A-Z	Groups of beneficiaries, A-Z
1501.C58	Civil servants (Table K12)
1501.H35	Handicapped. People with disabilities (Table K12)
1502	Criminal provisions (Table K11)
	Social security
	Including old age pensions, invalidity and disability pensions and survivor benefits
	For pensions and retirement plans of private enterprise see KJ-KKZ1 1339+
	Social reform see KJ-KKZ1 1468+
1504	General (Table K11)
1505	Compulsory insurance. Exemptions (Table K11)
1506	Organization and administration
	For merchant mariners see KJ-KKZ1 995+
	For miners see KJ-KKZ1 3365
	Social security taxes see KJ-KKZ1 3585
1508.A-Z	Coverage and benefits, A-Z
1508.C37	Cash benefits (Table K12)
1508.M43	Medical benefits (Table K12)
1508.O35	Occupational disability pensions (Table K12)
1508.O43	Old age pensions (Table K12)
1510.A-Z	Groups of beneficiaries, A-Z
1510.A43	Agricultural laborers. Farmers (Table K12)

KJ-KKZ1

Social legislation
  Social insurance
    Social security
      Groups of beneficiaries, A-Z -- Continued

1510.A45	Alien laborers (Table K12)
1510.B84	Building and construction industry (Table K12)
	Farmers see KJ-KKZ1 1510.A43
1510.P37	Parents (Table K12)
1510.P75	Professionals (Table K12)
1510.S87	Survivors (Table K12)
1510.T83	Transport workers (Table K12)

     Unemployment insurance
      For pension trusts see KJ-KKZ1 1340
      For civil service pensions see KJ-KKZ1 2978.5

1512	General (Table K11)
1513	Compulsory insurance (Table K11)
	Including exemptions
1514	Organization and administration (Table K11)
1516.A-Z	Coverage and benefits, A-Z
1516.U53	Unemployment cash benefits (Table K12)
1518.A-Z	Groups of beneficiaries, A-Z
1518.S44	Self-employed (Table K12)

  Social services. Public welfare
    Criticism and reform see KJ-KKZ1 1468

1520	General (Table K11)
	Organization and administration
1522	General (Table K11)
1523	Practice and procedure (Table K11)
	Including domicile
1524.A-Z	Coverage and benefits, A-Z
1524.E38	Educational assistance and allowances (Table K12)
	Family planning. Family counseling see KJ-KKZ1 3124+
	Infant welfare see KJ-KKZ1 1524.M38
1524.I57	Institutional care (Table K12)
	For old age homes and nursing homes see KJ-KKZ1 3114.O42
1524.M38	Maternal and infant welfare (Table K12)
1524.R45	Rent subsidies (Table K12)
	Social work and social workers
1525	General (Table K11)
1526	Rural social services (Table K11)
	Social service beneficiaries
1528	The poor and destitute (Table K11)
1529	Older people (Table K11)
1530	Pensioners (Table K11)
1531	Large families (Table K11)

Social legislation
   Social services. Public welfare
     Social service beneficiaries -- Continued
      People with disabilities
         Including people with physical, mental, and emotional
           disabilities

1532	General (Table K11)
1533.A-Z	Coverage and benefits, A-Z
1533.R43	Rehabilitation (Table K12)
	Cf. KJ-KKZ1 1293 Sheltered workshops
1534.A-Z	Beneficiaries, A-Z
1534.B54	Blind (Table K12)
1534.D42	Deaf-mute (Table K12)
1534.M45	Mental disabilities, People with (Table K12)
1535	Asocial types (Table K11)
1536	Evacuated and homeless persons (Table K11)
	War-related groups of beneficiaries
1537	General (Table K11)
1538	Refugees. Expelled or forcefully repatriated persons (Table K11)
1539	Prisoners of war and political prisoners. Veterans (Table K11)
1540	Services for war victims and war invalids (Table K11)
	Children. Youth
1542	General (Table K11)
1543	Constitutional aspects (Table K11)
1544	Organization and administration (Table K11)
	Including supervision of juvenile detention homes
	Measures and provisions
1545	General (Table K11)
1546	Protection of children in public (Table K11)
	Including restaurants, taverns, theaters, gambling, etc.
1547	Protection of children against obscenity (Table K11)
1548	Government guardianship (Table K11)
	Custodial education. Collective education
1549	General (Table K11)
1550.A-Z	Particular, A-Z
1550.O75	Orphanages (Table K12)
	Disaster relief see KJ-KKZ1 3037
	Social courts and procedure
	Class here works on courts of several jurisdictions
	For courts (several or individual) of an individual jurisdiction, see the jurisdiction
1552	General (Table K11)
1554.A-Z	Particular courts, A-Z
1554.A65	Appellate courts (Table K12)
1556	Procedural principles (Table K11)

KJ-KKZ1

Social legislation
  Social courts and procedure -- Continued
1557   Parties to action (Table K11)
            Pretrial procedures
1558   General (Table K11)
1559   Administrative remedies (Table K11)
            Procedure at first instance
1560   General (Table K11)
1562   Jurisdiction (Table K11)
                  Including competence in subject matter and venue
1564   Judicial decisions and judgments (Table K11)
1565   Remedies. Appellate procedures (Table K11)
1567   Execution (Table K11)
1568   Costs (Table K11)
            Competence conflicts between administrative, labor, and
                social courts see KJ-KKZ1 2810
1569   Competence conflicts between social and labor courts (Table
                K11)
      Courts and procedure
        The administration of justice. The organization of the judiciary
              Including the administration of criminal justice
          Criticism. Reform see KJ-KKZ1 471
1572   General (Table K11)
            The judiciary and politics see KJ-KKZ1 471
1573   The judiciary and administration (Table K11)
1574   The judiciary and foreign relations (Table K11)
            Organization and administration
                Class here works on national and state departments of justice
                    or departments of justice of several states
                For the departments of justice of an individual state, see the
                    state
1576   General (Table K11)
1577   National department of justice (Table K11)
            Judicial statistics see KJ-KKZ1 30+
            Judicial assistance see KJ-KKZ1 1642+
            Criminal policy see KJ-KKZ1 3950+
            Courts
                Including courts of both criminal and civil jurisdiction
1580   General (Table K11)
              Regular courts
                  Class here works on national (federal) courts and on courts of
                      several jurisdictions
                  For courts (several or individual) of an individual jurisdiction,
                      see the jurisdiction
1582   General (Table K11)
1583   Local courts. Municipal courts. Magistrate courts. Justice
                      of the peace (Lowest courts) (Table K11)

Courts and procedure
  Courts
    Regular courts -- Continued
      Juvenile courts see KJ-KKZ1 4720+
1584   Regional courts. Provincial courts. District courts (Table
                  K11)
1585   Courts of assizes. Justice (Table K11)
                  Including jury room proceedings
1586   Supreme courts of state or republics (Table K11)
              National (Federal) supreme courts. Supreme courts of
                  cassation
1587   General (Table K11)
                Labor courts see KJ-KKZ1 1440+
                Constitutional courts see KJ-KKZ1 2620+
                Finance courts see KJ-KKZ1 3682+
            Courts of special jurisdiction. Special tribunals
1588   General (Table K11)
1589   Consular courts (Table K11)
1589.5   Sharia courts (Table K11)
1590   Competence conflict courts (Table K11)
                    For competence conflicts between administrative,
                        labor, and social courts see KJ-KKZ1 2810
1591   Courts of honor (Table K11)
                    Class here general works
                    For individual courts see KJ-KKZ1 3439; KJ-KKZ1
                        3524
                Other courts of special jurisdiction
                    see the subject, e.g. 1440+, Labor courts; 3770+, Military
                        courts; etc.
1592   Special tribunal within a court (Table K11)
1593.A-Z   Other public bodies with judicial functions, A-Z
                    e. g.
1593.C65   Comrade's courts (Table K12)
1593.M85   Municipal arbitral boards (Table K12)
              Deliberating and voting. Secrecy
1594   General (Table K11)
                Jury room proceedings see KJ-KKZ1 1585
1595   Court decorum and discipline. Conduct of court proceedings.
                  Mass media (Table K11)
1596   Terms of court (Table K11)
1597   Judicial opinions. Advisory opinions (Table K11)
          The legal profession
              Including judicial officers and personnel
1600   General (Table K11)
            Law school education see KJ-KKZ1 50+
            Post-law school education
1602   General (Table K11)

	Courts and procedure
	The legal profession
	Post-law school education -- Continued
1603	Boards and commissions (Table K11)
	Class here general works
	For boards and commissions of a particular state, see the state
1604	Judicial personnel other than lawyers (Table K11)
1605	Nationality and citizenship (Table K11)
1606.A-Z	Minorities, A-Z
	Subarrange each by Table K12
1607	Salaries, allowances, pensions, etc. (Table K11)
	Judges
1610	General (Table K11)
	Women judges see KJ-KKZ1 1606.A+
1612	Independence of judges (Table K11)
1613	Political activity of judges (Table K11)
1614	Ethics and discipline (Table K11)
	Office of the public prosecutor
1615	General (Table K11)
1617	Supervision (Table K11)
1618	Jurisdiction (Table K11)
	Notaries see KJ-KKZ1 1846+
	Auxiliary personnel. Clerk's office
1620	General (Table K11)
	Clerks to the court
1621	General (Table K11)
1623	Business administration. Court records (Table K11)
	For personal data protection in information retrieval systems see KJ-KKZ1 844.5
1624	Bailiffs (Table K11)
	Experts and expert witnesses
1626	General (Table K11)
1627	Medical examiners (Table K11)
	For forensic medicine, see RA1001+
	Practice of law
1629	General (Table K11)
	Litigation insurance see KJ-KKZ1 1025.5
	Attorneys
1630	General (Table K11)
	Admission to the bar see KJ-KKZ1 54+
1631	Legal ethics and etiquette (Table K11)
1632	Attorney and client (Table K11)
	For violation of confidential disclosures see KJ-KKZ1 843.3; KJ-KKZ1 4164
1633	Law office management (Table K11)
	Including secretaries' and clerks' handbooks, manuals, etc.

Courts and procedure
The legal profession
Practice of law
Attorneys -- Continued

1634	Costs (Table K11)
	For in forma pauperis see KJ-KKZ1 1639
	Courts of honor. Disbarment see KJ-KKZ1 54+
1635.A-Z	Special topics, A-Z
1635.A39	Advertising (Table K12)
1635.F74	Freedom of movement (Table K12)
1636	Legal consultants (Table K11)
1637	Procurators (Table K11)
1639	Legal aid. Legal services to the poor. Community legal services (Table K11)
	For public defender see KJ-KKZ1 4630.D43
	Professional associations see KJ-KKZ1 54+
	Judicial assistance
	Including judicial assistance in criminal matters
1642	General (Table K11)
1644	International judicial assistance (Table K11)
1646	Foreign judgments (Conflicts of laws) (Table K11)
	Procedure in general
	Class here works on civil and criminal procedure and works on civil, commercial, and labor procedure combined
1650	General (Table K11)
	Procedural principles
1651	Due process of law (Table K11)
1652	Uniformity of law application. Stare decisis (Table K11)
1653	Publicity and oral procedure (Table K11)
1654	Speedy trial. Court congestion and delay (Table K11)
1654.5.A-Z	Other, A-Z
1654.5.C65	Conflict of judicial decisions (Table K12)
	Estoppel see KJ-KKZ1 1654.5.P74
1654.5.P74	Preclusion. Estoppel (Table K12)
	Parties in action
1655	General (Table K11)
1656	Privileged parties (Table K11)
1657	Litigant. Plaintiff. Defendant (Table K11)
	Pretrial procedures
1660	General (Table K11)
1662.A-Z	Particular, A-Z
1662.S95	Summons, service of process, subpoena, etc. (Table K12)
	Procedure at first instance. Trial
1663	General (Table K11)
1664	Jurisdiction (Table K11)
	Actions and defenses

KJ-KKZ1

Courts and procedure
Procedure in general
Procedure at first instance. Trial
Actions and defenses -- Continued

1666	General (Table K11)
1667.A-Z	Particular, A-Z
	Subarrange each by Table K12
1668	Particular proceedings (Table K11)
	Evidence. Burden of proof
1672	General (Table K11)
1673	Admission of evidence (Table K11)
	Witnesses
1675	General (Table K11)
1676	Privileged witnesses (Confidential communication). Expert testimony (Table K11)
1677.A-Z	Special topics, A-Z
	Subarrange each by Table K12
	Judicial decisions
1679	General (Table K11)
1680.A-Z	Particular decisions, A-Z
	Subarrange each by Table K12
	Remedies
1686	General (Table K11)
1687	Appellate procedures (Table K11)
1689	New trial. Reopening of a case (Table K11)
1690	Execution (Table K11)
1692	Costs. Fees (Table K11)
	Civil procedure
	For works on procedure and practice in general before particular types of courts or individual courts see KJ-KKZ1 1582+
1695	Criticism. Reform (Table K11)
1701-1710	General (Table K9c)
1712	Civil procedure law relating to other branches of the law (Table K11)
	Procedural principles
1714	Due process of law (Table K11)
	Including frivolous suits
1715	Stare decisis (Table K11)
	Prohibition of abuse of legal procedure and chicanery see KJ-KKZ1 444.7
1716	Publicity and oral procedure (Table K11)
	Principles of evidence see KJ-KKZ1 1772
1718	Speedy trial (Table K11)
1719	Truthfulness and falsehood. Discovery (disclosure) (Table K11)
1720	Prejudicial actions (Table K11)

KJ-KKZ1

	Courts and procedure
	Civil procedure
	Procedure at first instance
	Evidence -- Continued
1784	Oath (Table K11)
	Including oath of witnesses and parties
	Judicial decisions
1785	General (Table K11)
	Judgment
1787	General (Table K11)
1788	Judicial discretion (Table K11)
	Including equity
	Types of judgment
1789	Judgments to do, to tolerate, to refrain from doing (Table K11)
1790	Declaratory judgment (Table K11)
1791	Motion to dismiss, and judgment in rem (Table K11)
1793	Agreed judgment (Table K11)
	Judgment by default see KJ-KKZ1 1765
	Decision without trial see KJ-KKZ1 1766
	Dismissal and nonsuit see KJ-KKZ1 1767
1795	Interlocutory decisions (Table K11)
1796	Void judgments and nonjudgments (Table K11)
1797	Form (Table K11)
1798	Mistakes (error) (Table K11)
	Including correction or withdrawal of faulty decision
1799	Res judicata (Table K11)
1800	Court records. Minutes of evidence (Table K11)
	Including clerks' mistakes and corrections
1802	Advisory opinions (Table K11)
	Special procedures
1804	General (Table K11)
1805	Matrimonial actions (Table K11)
1807	Procedures in parent and child cases (Table K11)
	For procedures in guardianship cases see KJ-KKZ1 1874+
1809	Interdiction. Mental competency procedure (Table K11)
1810	Public summons (Table K11)
	Settlement before trial see KJ-KKZ1 1768
1812	Hortatory procedures (Table K11)
1814	Small claims. Procedures before the justice of the peace or magistrate (Table K11)
	Remedies
1816	General (Table K11)
1817	Injunctions. Arrest (Table K11)
1818	Reformatio in peius (Table K11)
1819	Recourse (Table K11)

Courts and procedure
  Civil procedure
    Remedies -- Continued
      Appellate procedure
1822   General (Table K11)
1824   Revision (Table K11)
1825   Cassation (Table K11)
1826   New trial. Reopening of a case (Table K11)
1828   Waiver of appeal (Table K11)
1829   Arbitration (Table K11)
              Including commercial arbitration
          Costs
1830   General (Table K11)
1832   In forma pauperis (Table K11)
        Noncontentious (ex parte) jurisdiction
1834   General (Table K11)
1835   Parties to action (Table K11)
          Procedure
1837   General (Table K11)
1838   Evidence (Table K11)
1839   Decisions (Table K11)
1840   Remedies and special procedures (Table K11)
1842   Res judicata (Table K11)
          Notaries. Notarial practice and procedure
            Class here works on notaries of several jurisdictions
            For notaries (several or individual) of an individual state,
                administrative district, or municipality, see the state, district,
                or municipality
1846   General (Table K11)
1847   Legal instruments. Certification (Table K11)
1848   Costs (Table K11)
          Registration. Recording
            Class here works on registers of several jurisdictions
            For registers (several or individual) of an individual state,
                administrative district, or municipality, see the state, district
                or municipality
1850   General (Table K11)
1852   Publicity (Table K11)
          Civil register
1854   General (Table K11)
            Registration of civil status
1856   General (Table K11)
1857   Family names (Table K11)
1860   Marriage (Table K11)
1862   Birth (Table K11)

Courts and procedure
 Noncontentious (ex parte) jurisdiction
  Registration. Recording
   Civil register
    Registration of civil status -- Continued

1864	Death (Table K11)
	For absence and presumption of death see KJ-KKZ1 513.7+
1865	Aliens. Stateless foreigners (Table K11)
1866	Costs (Table K11)
1867	Register of matrimonial property (Table K11)
	Land registers see KJ-KKZ1 737+
	Ship registers see KJ-KKZ1 984.3
	Commercial registers see KJ-KKZ1 925+
	Business associations see KJ-KKZ1 1055
	Domestic relations procedure
1870	General (Table K11)
1872	Adoption procedures (Table K11)
	Guardianship court
1874	General (Table K11)
	Jurisdiction
1875	General (Table K11)
	Appointment of guardian
1876	General (Table K11)
1877	Co-guardians. Supervisory guardians (Table K11)
1878	Guardians' responsibilities (Table K11)
	Government guardianship see KJ-KKZ1 1548
	Interdiction see KJ-KKZ1 1548
1880	Inheritance (Probate court) procedure (Table K11)
1882	Costs (Table K11)
	Class here general works
	For costs of a particular branch of noncontentious jurisdiction, see the branch
	Insolvency
1885	General (Table K11)
1886	State of insolvency (Table K11)
	Execution
1888	General (Table K11)
	Parties to execution
	Including executors and administration
1890	General (Table K11)
1892	Succession during execution (Table K11)
	Bailiffs see KJ-KKZ1 1624
	Titles for execution
	Including judgments (res judicata), documents of title, etc.
1894	General (Table K11)
1895	Provisional enforcement (Table K11)

Courts and procedure
   Insolvency
      Execution -- Continued
         Procedure in execution

1896	General (Table K11)
1897	Discovery proceedings. Poor debtors oath (Table K11)
	Including inventory
1900	Judicial decisions (res judicata) (Table K11)
	Execution for payment due
1902	General (Table K11)
	Hortatory procedures see KJ-KKZ1 1812
1904	Attachment and garnishment of personal property (Table K11)
	Attachment and garnishment of rights and choses in action
1906	General (Table K11)
1907	Pledges. Expectancies (Table K11)
1908.A-Z	Other, A-Z
1908.B35	Bank deposits (Table K12)
1908.S34	Salaries and wages (Table K12)
	Judicial sale
1909	General (Table K11)
1910	Good faith (Table K11)
1911	Transfer of ownership (Table K11)
1912	Distribution (Table K11)
1913	Detention of debtor (Table K11)
	Poor debtors oath see KJ-KKZ1 1897
	Remedies see KJ-KKZ1 1926+
	Execution in real property
1915	General (Table K11)
1917	Foreclosure sale. Judicial sale. Receivership (Table K11)
	Exemptions and restrictions see KJ-KKZ1 1934+
1919	Enforcement of surrender of goods or documents (Table K11)
1920	Enforcement of acts (commissions or omissions) (Table K11)
1922	Executions against associations, personal companies, and corporations (Table K11)
	Including execution against juristic persons of public law
1924	Injunction. Arrest. Seizure (Table K11)
1925	Astreinte (Fine for debtor's delay) (Table K11)
	Remedies
1926	General (Table K11)
1927	Objections of third party claiming ownership and seeking release (Table K11)
1928	Costs (Table K11)

	Courts and procedure
	Insolvency
	Execution -- Continued
	Protection against abuse of claims enforcement
1930	General (Table K11)
	Moratorium see KJ-KKZ1 1975
1932	Suspension. Accord and satisfaction (Table K11)
1933	Compromise (Table K11)
	Restriction of execution
1934	General (Table K11)
1935	Salaries. Wages. Pensions (Table K11)
1936	Support (Domestic relations) (Table K11)
1937	Minimum income. Beneficium competentiae (Table K11)
1938	Damages. Compensation for unjustified execution (Table K11)
1939.A-Z	Special topics, A-Z
1939.T45	Third parties (Table K12)
	Bankruptcy
1942	General (Table K11)
1943	Court (Table K11)
	Parties to action
1944	General (Table K11)
1945	Referee (Judge) (Table K11)
1946	Debtor and creditor (Table K11)
	Including legal status, liability, etc.
1947	Trustees in bankruptcy. Receivers. Syndics (Table K11)
	Third parties
1948	General (Table K11)
1949	Spouse. Matrimonial property (Table K11)
1950	Insolvent estate (Table K11)
	Including avoidance of transfers, and property not included in the bankrupt estate (exempted property)
	Procedure
1952	General (Table K11)
	Priority of claims
1954	General (Table K11)
1956	Privileged and secured credits (Table K11)
1957.A-Z	Particular secured or privileged credits, A-Z
1957.I57	Insurance claims (Table K12)
1958	Distribution (Table K11)
1959	Composition to end bankruptcy (Table K11)
	Judicial review of voidable transactions
1961	General (Table K11)
	Fraudulent conveyances see KJ-KKZ1 4276
	Effect of bankruptcy on obligations and rights
1963	General (Table K11)

KJ-KKZ1

Courts and procedure
Insolvency
Bankruptcy
Effect of bankruptcy on obligations and rights -- Continued
1964.A-Z   Special topics, A-Z
1964.H95   Hypotheca. Mortgage (Table K12)
1964.I57   Insurance policies (Table K12)
1964.L42   Lease (Table K12)
                    Mortgage see KJ-KKZ1 1964.H95
1964.S35   Sale (Table K12)
1964.W33   Wages (Table K12)
1965   Costs (Table K11)
Debtors' relief
For wartime debtor's relief see KJ-KKZ1 3717
1970   General (Table K11)
Composition to avoid bankruptcy. Deferment of execution
1972   General (Table K11)
1973   Receivership (Table K11)
1974   Corporate reorganization (Table K11)
1975   Moratorium (Table K11)
Costs
Including bookkeeping and accounting
1976   General (Table K11)
1978   Courts (Table K11)
Including witnesses and expert witnesses
Costs in special proceedings or special courts
see the subject, e.g. 1634, Attorneys; 1830, Civil procedure;
1866, Civil registers; 1764, Administrative courts; etc.
1979   Execution. Enforcement (Table K11)
Public law
Class here works on all aspects of public law, including early works
For civics see KJ-KKZ1 72
2000   General (Table K11)
The State
Including philosophy and theory of the state
For non-legal works on political theory, see subclass JC
2010   General (Table K11)
2015   Sovereignty. Potestas (Table K11)
Federalism see KJ-KKZ1 2373
Rule of law
2020   General (Table K11)
Socialist state
2025   General (Table K11)
2030   Democratic centralism (Table K11)
Constitutional law
For works on the constitutional aspects of a subject, see the subject
History see KJ-KKZ1 2101+

	Constitutional law -- Continued
2050	Constitutional reform. Criticism. Polemic
	For works on a particular constitution, see the constitution
2061.2	Bibliography
	Including bibliography of constitutional history
2062	Monographic series
	Sources
	Including early constitutions and related materials
2064	Collections. Compilations. By date
	Including federal sources, federal and state sources, and sources of several states
2064.5<date>	Individual constitutions
	Arrange chronologically by appending the date of adoption to this number and deleting any trailing zeros. Subarrange each by Table K17
2064.6<date>	Individual sources other than constitutions
	Arrange chronologically by appending the date of adoption or issuance to this number and deleting any trailing zeros. Subarrange by main entry
	Court decisions
2066	Indexes. Digests
2066.3	Serials
2066.5	Monographs. By date
2067	Dictionaries (terms and phrases). Encyclopedias
(2067.4)	Form books. Graphic materials. Tables
	see KJ-KKZ1 2070
2069	Congresses. Conferences. Seminars. By date
2070	General works
	Including history, criticism, private drafts, compends, case books, form books, examination aids, popular works, essays, festschriften, etc.
	Constitutional history
	For general works on constitutional history and administration, see subclass JN
	By period
	Early to ca. 1800 see KJ-KKZ1 202+
	From ca. 1800 to most recent constitution
2101	General works
	Constitutional principles
	Rule of law see KJ-KKZ1 2020+
2120	Sovereignty of parliament
2130	Rulers, princes, dynasties
	Including dynastic rules and works on legal status and juristic personality
	Privileges of classes and particular groups see KJ-KKZ1 2290

KJ-KKZ1

Constitutional law
 Constitutional history
  By period
   From ca. 1800 to most recent
    Constitutional principles -- Continued
     Privileges, prerogatives, and immunities of rulers,
      states, or estates see KJ-KKZ1 2300

2160	Sources and relationships of law
	Intergovernmental relations. Jurisdiction
2170	General works
2180	Federal-state (republic), national-provincial controversies. State-state or interprovincial disputes
	Privileges, prerogatives, and immunities of particular states or estates see KJ-KKZ1 2300
2190	Distribution of legislative power. Exclusive and concurrent legislative power. Reservation of provincial legislation
2200.A-Z	Special topics, A-Z
	Class here works on topics not provided for elsewhere
	For the history of a particular subject, see the subject
2220	Interpretation and construction (Table K11)
2230	Amending process (Table K11)
	Constitutional principles
2240	Legitimacy (Table K11)
2250	Legality. Socialist legality (Table K11)
	Rule of law see KJ-KKZ1 2020+
2260	Centralization of powers (Table K11)
	Separation and delegation of powers
2270	General (Table K11)
2275	Conflict of interests. Incompatibility of offices. Ethics in government (Table K11)
	Executive privilege see KJ-KKZ1 2300
2280	Judicial review of legislative acts (Table K11)
2290	Privileges of classes (estates) and particular groups (Table K11)
2300	Privileges, prerogatives, and immunities of rulers, states, or estates (Table K11)
	Sources and relationships of the law
2320	Preconstitutional and constitutional law
2325	International law and municipal law
	Statutory law and delegated legislation
2330	General (Table K11)
2335	Retroactivity (Table K11)
2340	Customary law and observances (Table K11)
2350	Socialist plans (Table K11)
2360	Decrees (individual) (Table K11)

	Constitutional law -- Continued
	Intergovernmental relations. Jurisdiction
2370	General (Table K11)
2373	Federalism (Table K11)
2375	Federal-state (republic), national-provincial controversies. Interstate (Interprovincial, etc.) disputes (Table K11)
2380	Cooperation of states, republics, provinces, etc. (Table K11)
2385	Exclusive and concurring jurisdiction (Table K11)
	Including national (federal) and state (republic, province, etc.) jurisdiction
2390	National (Federal) territory (Table K11)
	Including boundary disputes
2395	National (Federal) capital (Table K11)
	Foreign relations administration
2400	General (Table K11)
	Foreign service see KJ-KKZ1 2608
2410	Executive agreements (Table K11)
	Foreign assistance programs see KJ-KKZ1 3205
2415	Neutrality (Table K11)
2420.A-Z	Other, A-Z
	Subarrange each by Table K12
	Individual and state
2429	General (Table K11)
	Nationality and citizenship
	For rights and status of citizens see KJ-KKZ1 518.7
2430	General (Table K11)
	Immigration. Naturalization
2440	General (Table K11)
	Procedure see KJ-KKZ1 3023
2445	Expatriation (Table K11)
	Emigration see KJ-KKZ1 3024
	Statelessness see KJ-KKZ1 485.S8
2450.A-Z	Particular groups, A-Z
	Subarrange each by Table K12
	Human rights. Civil and political rights. Civic (socialist) duties
2460	General (Table K11)
	Equality before the law. Antidiscrimination in general
2465	General (Table K11)
2467.A-Z	Groups discriminated against, A-Z
2467.G38	Gays (Table K12)
	Jews see KJ-KKZ1 2467.M56
2467.M56	Minorities (Ethnic, religious, racial, and national) (Table K12)
2467.S55	Single people (Table K12)
2467.W65	Women (Table K12)
2468.A-Z	Special subjects, A-Z

KJ-KKZ1

Constitutional law
 Individual and state
  Human rights. Civil and political rights. Civic (socialist)
   duties
   Equality before the law. Antidiscrimination in general
    Special subjects, A-Z -- Continued
     Culture see KJ-KKZ1 2468.L36

2468.L36	Language and culture (Table K12)
	For language regulation in general see KJ-KKZ1 3137.9
	Freedom
2469	General (Table K11)
2470	Freedom of expression (Table K11)
2472	Freedom of religion and conscience (Table K11)
	Freedom of thought and speech
2474	General (Table K11)
2476	Freedom of information (Table K11)
2478	Prohibition of censorship (Table K11)
2480	Right of opposition to government (Table K11)
2482	Freedom of movement (Table K11)
2483	Freedom of assembly, association, and demonstration (Table K11)
2484	Due process of law (Table K11)
2484.5	Right to life (Table K11)
2484.7	Privacy of home (Table K11)
2485	Privacy of communication. Official and private secrets (Table K11)
2485.5	Right to asylum (Table K11)
2485.7	Right to petition (Table K11)
2486	Right to resistance against government (Table K11)
2488	Political parties and mass organizations (Table K11)
	Including subordinate or connected organizations, and pressure groups, etc.
2490	Internal security (Table K11)
	Including control of subversive activities or groups
	Organs of national government. Supreme organs of state power and state administration
	Including federal and state government
2500	General (Table K11)
	The people
2504	General (Table K11)
2505	Initiative and referendum. Plebiscite (Table K11)
	Political parties see KJ-KKZ1 2488
	Election law
2506	General (Table K11)
2508	Contested elections (Table K11)
	The legislature. Legislative power

Constitutional law
    Organs of national government. Supreme organs of state
        power and state administration
        The legislature. Legislative power -- Continued

2510	General (Table K11)
2512	Control of government (Table K11)
2514	Legislative bodies. People's assemblies (Table K11)
	Including legislative bodies with one or two chambers
	Legislative process
	Including parliamentary practice
2516	General (Table K11)
2518	Interpellation (Table K11)
2520	Bill drafting (Table K11)
	Committees and councils
2522	General (Table K11)
2524	Economic councils (Table K11)
2524.5	Voting (Table K11)
2525	Parliamentary minorities (Table K11)
2526	Lobbying (Table K11)
2528	Legislators (Table K11)
	Including immunity, indemnity, incompatibility, etc.
2529	Dissolution (Table K11)
	Heads of state
2530	General (Table K11)
	Kings, princes, and rulers
2532	General (Table K11)
2535.A-Z	Special topics, A-Z
2535.A23	Abdication (Table K12)
2535.D9	Dynastic rules. Legal status of dynasty (Table K12)
2535.E43	Election (Table K12)
	Legal status of dynasty see KJ-KKZ1 2535.D9
2535.S92	Succession to the crown (Table K12)
	Presidents
2540	General (Table K11)
2544.A-Z	Special topics, A-Z
2544.I47	Impeachment (Table K12)
2548	Collective heads of state. State councils. Presidential
	councils (Socialist) (Table K11)
	Prerogatives and powers of the head of state
2550	General (Table K11)
2554	Crown privilege (Table K11)
2558	Treatymaking power (Table K11)
	Including questions of provincial competence to conduct
	foreign relations
2562	Veto power (Table K11)
2564	War and emergency power (Table K11)
	Other supreme organs

Constitutional law
  Organs of national government. Supreme organs of state
      power and state administration
    Heads of state
      Other supreme organs -- Continued
2570   Central People's Committee (Socialist) (Table K11)
2575   Federal Executive Council (Socialist) (Table K11)
2578   The executive branch. Executive power (Table K11)
            Federal Executive Councils see KJ-KKZ1 2575
            Presidium. Presidential councils see KJ-KKZ1 2548
2580   The Prime Minister and the Cabinet (Table K11)
2585   Council of Ministers (Socialist) (Table K11)
2590   Supreme Councils of Control (Socialist) (Table K11)
            Government departments, ministries, and other
                organizations of government
2600   General (Table K11)
            Departments. Ministries
                Class here works on several departments not related to a
                    particular branch of law or subject
                Including subordinate administrative divisions, councils, etc.
                For works on several departments related to a branch of
                    law or subject, as well as individual departments and
                    their regulatory agencies, see the branch of law or
                    subject
2602   General (Table K11)
            Department of State
2604   General (Table K11)
2608   The foreign service (Table K11)
2610   Subordinate regulatory agencies (Table K11)
                Class here works on several agencies
                For an individual agency, see the branch of law or the
                    subject
2612   Special boards, commissions, bureaus, task forces, etc.
                (Table K11)
2613.A-Z   By name, A-Z
                    Subarrange each by Table K12
2614.A-Z   Special topics, A-Z
                    Subarrange each by Table K12
2615   Council of State (Table K11)
2618   The judiciary. Judicial power (Table K11)
            Constitutional courts (tribunals) and procedure
2620   General (Table K11)
2630   Court organization (Table K11)
2640   Procedural principles (Table K11)
2650   Jurisdiction (Table K11)
2660.A-Z   Special topics, A-Z
2660.C65   Constitutional torts (Table K12)

Constitutional law -- Continued

2670	National emblem. Flag. Seal. Seat of government. National anthem (Table K11)
2672	Political oath (Table K11)
2674	Patriotic customs and observances (Table K11)
2676	Decorations of honor. Awards. Dignities (Table K11)
2677	Commemorative medals (Table K11)
	Economic constitution see KJ-KKZ1 3191+
	Colonial law
2680	General (Table K11)
2685.A-Z	Particular, A-Z
2685.A35	Administrative law (Table K12)
2685.T38	Taxation (Table K12)
2685.T73	Trade regulation (Table K12)
	Secular ecclesiastical law
	Class here works on the relationship of state and church, regardless of denomination
	For works on the internal law and government of a church, see KB
	For history see KJ-KKZ1 272+
	Treaties between church and state. Concordats
	Including related material such as court decisions, official reports, memoranda, etc.
	For concordats relating to a particular region or state (province), see the region or state (province)
	For treatises on a particular subject, see the subject
2688	Collections. Compilations
2689	Individual concordats. By date
2690	General (Table K11)
	Constitutional guaranties
2692	General (Table K11)
2693	Freedom of religion. Freedom of worship (Table K11)
2693.5	Religious symbols. Religious articles (Table K11)
2694	Freedom of speech of the clergy (Table K11)
2695	Protection of church property (Table K11)
2697	Separation of church and state. Independence of church (Table K11)
2698	Religious corporations and societies (Table K11)
2699	Faith-based human services (Table K11)
2700	Church autonomy and state supervision (Table K11)
	Administrative law
2711-2720	General (Table K9c)
	Administrative principles
2721	General (Table K11)
2722	Rule of the law (Table K11)
2724	Autonomy. Rulemaking power (Table K11)

Administrative law
Administrative principles -- Continued
2726   Limitation and freedom of administration (Table K11)
                For abuse of administrative power. Ombudsman see KJ-
                    KKZ1 2760
2728   People's participation in administration (Table K11)
            Relationship to other branches of law or subjects
2729   Civil law
            Administrative process
2730   General (Table K11)
2732   Acts of government (Table K11)
            Administrative acts
2735   General (Table K11)
2737   Classification of acts (Table K11)
2739   Defective acts (Table K11)
                Judicial review of administrative acts see KJ-KKZ1 2790
2739.5   Revocation (Table K11)
2740   Recognition of foreign administrative acts (Table K11)
            Legal transactions
2750   General (Table K11)
              Public contracts. Government contracts. Government
                  purchasing
2754   General (Table K11)
2755.A-Z   Special topics, A-Z
2755.C65   Computer contracts (Table K12)
2755.D44   Defense contracts (Table K12)
                  Public works contracts see KJ-KKZ1 3073
2757   Enforcement. Administrative sanctions (Table K11)
2760   Ombudsman. Control over abuse of administrative power
                  (Table K11)
            Administrative courts and procedure
2764   General (Table K11)
2770   Court organization (Table K11)
2780   Procedural principles (Table K11)
2785   Pretrial procedures. Administrative remedies (Table K11)
                Including remonstration, administrative appeals, etc.
2790   Procedure. Judicial decisions. Remedies (Table K11)
                Including judicial review of administrative acts
2795   Execution (Table K11)
2800   Arbitration (Table K11)
2810   Competence conflicts (Table K11)
2812   Costs (Table K11)
            Indemnification for acts performed by government
2820   General (Table K11)
2824   Eminent domain (Table K11)
                Including procedure
            Government liability

	Administrative law
	Indemnification for acts performed by government
	Government liability -- Continued
2840	General (Table K11)
2845	Acts of government (Table K11)
2850	Administrative and judicial acts (Table K11)
2852.A-Z	Other, A-Z
	Reparation see KJ-KKZ1 2852.V52
2852.V52	Victims of crimes, Compensation to. Reparation (Table K12)
	Administrative organization
2858	General (Table K11)
2860	Centralization and decentralization in government (Table K11)
2864	State supervision and enforcement (Table K11)
2866	State apparatus. Interagency relations (Table K11)
2868	Collegial structure (Table K11)
	Juristic persons of public law
2875	General (Table K11)
	Public corporations
2877	General (Table K11)
2880	Regional corporations (Table K11)
	Class here general works
	For local government see KJ-KKZ1 2920+
	For municipal government see KJ-KKZ1 2937+
	For special districts see KJ-KKZ1 2964+
2885	Cooperative societies of public law (Table K11)
	Class here general works
	For particular cooperative societies, see the subject, e.g. Agricultural cooperative societies
2888	Public institutions (Table K11)
	For particular institutions, see the subject
2890	Public foundations (Table K11)
	Cf. KJ-KKZ1 526+ Foundations in civil law
2893	Government business enterprises (Table K11)
	Including government controlled business enterprises
	For particular enterprises, see the subject
	Administrative departments of national government
	Including federal and central government
2898	Department of the Interior (Table K11)
2905	Subordinate regulatory agencies (Table K11)
	For particular agencies, see the subject
	Special councils, commissions, etc.
2910	General (Table K11)
	Ombudsman see KJ-KKZ1 2760
	Administrative departments of the states (Land, cantons, etc.)

	Administrative law
	Administrative organization
	Administrative departments of the states (Land, cantons, etc.) -- Continued
2915	General (Table K11)
2917	Department of the Interior (Table K11)
	Administrative and political divisions. Local government other than municipal
	Including those of centralized national governments or federal governments
2920	General (Table K11)
2923	Self-government and state supervision (Table K11)
2928	Councils, boards, standing commissions (Table K11)
2935.A-Z	Particular administrative districts, counties, regions, etc., A-Z
	Including official gazettes, bylaws, statutory orders, regulations, and general works, as well as works on specific legal topics
	Municipal government
2937	General (Table K11)
2938	Autonomy and rulemaking power (Table K11)
2939	Self-government and state supervision (Table K11)
2940	Municipal territory (Table K11)
	Including boundaries and incorporation
2940.5	Name. Flags. Insignia. Seals (Table K11)
	Constitution and organization of municipal government
2942	General (Table K11)
2943	Legislative branch. Councils and civic associations (Table K11)
	Executive branch. Officers and employees
	Including elected and honorary offices
	For works on the executive branch of an individual municipality, see the municipality
2945	General (Table K11)
2946	Mayor. City director (Table K11)
	Municipal civil service see KJ-KKZ1 2989
2948.A-Z	Special topics, A-Z
	Subarrange each by Table K12
	Municipal economy
2950	General (Table K11)
2952	Property (Table K11)
	Budget see KJ-KKZ1 3656
	Municipal public services
2954	General (Table K11)
	Public utilities
	For regulation of energy industry see KJ-KKZ1 3431+
2955	General (Table K11)

Administrative law
Administrative organization
Municipal government
Municipal public service
Public utilities
Electricity. Gas see KJ-KKZ1 3432+

2956	Water. Sewage (Table K11)
	For ecological aspects see KJ-KKZ1 3131
2958	Trash collection (Table K11)
2960	Public transportation (Table K11)
	Supramunicipal corporation and cooperation
2962	General (Table K11)
	Special districts
	For special districts within a particular state (Land, canton, etc.), see the state (Land, canton, etc.)
2964	General (Table K11)
2965.A-Z	Particular types of districts, A-Z
	Subarrange each by Table K12
	Water districts see KJ-KKZ1 3052.A+
2967	Federation of municipal corporations (Table K11)
	Civil service. Public officials and functionaries
2970	General (Table K11)
2972	Tenure (Table K11)
2973	Official (superior) order (Table K11)
2974	Incompatibility of offices (Table K11)
2975	Appointment and election (Table K11)
	Conditions of employment
2977	General (Table K11)
2978	Discipline (Table K11)
2978.3	Illicit political activities (Table K11)
2978.4	Remuneration. Allowances (Table K11)
2978.5	Retirement. Pensions (Table K11)
2979	Dismissal (Table K11)
	Labor law and collective labor law
2980	General (Table K11)
	Management-labor relations
2982	General (Table K11)
2983	Work councils (Table K11)
2984	Participation of employees in management (Table K11)
2984.5	Collective bargaining and labor agreement (Table K11)
2985	Collective labor disputes. Strikes (Table K11)
2986	Corporate representation (Table K11)
2987	State civil service (Table K11)
	For works on the civil service of an individual state, see the state
2989	Municipal civil service (Table K11)
	For works on the civil service of an individual municipality, see the municipality

Civil service. Public officials and functionaries -- Continued
2990   Civil service of public corporations other than state or
                              municipal (Table K11)
2992   Public officials and functionaries of the economic
                              administration (Socialist) (Table K11)
                      Police and public safety
3000   General (Table K11)
                      Organization and administration
3001   General (Table K11)
3002   Licenses, concessions, permits (Table K11)
                          Police magistrates
                              Including contraventions
3003   General (Table K11)
3004   Procedure. Penalties (Table K11)
3005.A-Z   Particular violations, A-Z
                                  Begging see KJ-KKZ1 3005.V34
3005.V34   Vagrancy. Begging (Table K12)
3006   Police measures (Table K11)
                          Police force
3007   Criminal police (Table K11)
3007.5   Secret service (Table K11)
                                  Including secret police
3008.A-Z   Other police forces, A-Z
                                  Airport police see KJ-KKZ1 3468.35
3008.P75   Private police (Table K12)
                          Public safety
3009   General (Table K11)
3010   Weapons. Explosives (Table K11)
                                  Including manufacturing, import, and trade of firearms and
                                      ammunition
                              Hazardous articles and processes
                                  Including transportation by land
                                  For product safety see KJ-KKZ1 846.5
                                  For transportation by sea see KJ-KKZ1 3472+
3011   General (Table K11)
3012   Nuclear power. Reactors (Table K11)
                                      Including protection from radiation, and including nuclear
                                          waste disposal
                                      Cf. KJ-KKZ1 847.5 Torts
3013   Flammable materials (Table K11)
3014.A-Z   Poisons and toxic substances, A-Z
3014.A82   Asbestos (Table K12)
                                          Herbicides see KJ-KKZ1 3014.P46
3014.P34   Paint (Table K12)
3014.P46   Pesticides. Herbicides (Table K12)
                              Accident control
3015   General (Table K11)

Police and public safety
Public safety
Accident control -- Continued
3015.5.A-Z   Particular, A-Z
         Electric engineering see KJ-KKZ1 3015.5.E43
3015.5.E43   Electric installations. Electric engineering (Table K12)
3015.5.S74   Steam boilers (Table K12)
     Fire prevention and control
3016   General (Table K11)
       Theaters. Auditoriums
3018   General (Table K11)
3019   Motion picture theaters. Safety films (Table K11)
       Flood control see KJ-KKZ1 3050
       Weather bureaus. Meteorological stations see KJ-KKZ1
         3513
     Control of individuals
3022   General (Table K11)
       Identification and registration
         Including registration of residence
3022.2   General (Table K11)
       Registration of birth, marriage, and death see KJ-KKZ1
         1854+
3022.5   Identity cards (Table K11)
3022.7   Passports (Table K11)
3022.9.A-Z   Other, A-Z
         Subarrange each by Table K12
3023   Immigration and naturalization. Procedure (Table K11)
         For citizenship see KJ-KKZ1 2430+
3024   Emigration (Table K11)
         For freedom of movement see KJ-KKZ1 2482
       Particular groups
       Aliens
         Including citizens of European Community countries,
         homeless aliens, and refugees
3025   General (Table K11)
3026   Temporary admission and residence (Table K11)
3026.5   Identification. Registration (Table K11)
3027   Restriction of political activities (Table K11)
3028   Employment. Business enterprise (Table K11)
       Naturalization see KJ-KKZ1 3023
3029   Deportation (Table K11)
         Including deportation of alien criminals
       Minorities (Ethnic, religious, racial)
3031   General (Table K11)
3032.A-Z   Particular groups, A-Z
3032.G96   Gypsies (Table K12)

KJ-KKZ1

	Police and public safety
	Control of individuals -- Continued
3033	Traveling and transit traffic. Tourism (Table K11)
	Including road traffic and traffic on inland waterways
	Control of social activities
3034	General (Table K11)
3034.5	Vacationing (Table K11)
	Including campgrounds, hostels, outdoor swimming facilities, etc.
	Sport activities
3035	General (Table K11)
3035.5	Mass events (Table K11)
3035.7	Corporate representation (Table K11)
3036.A-Z	Particular sports, A-Z
3036.F58	Fishing, Sport (Table K12)
3036.P73	Prizefighting (Table K12)
3036.S57	Skiing (Table K12)
3036.S63	Soccer (Table K12)
3036.T45	Tennis (Table K12)
3036.5.A-Z	Other, A-Z
	e. g.
3036.5.B85	Bullfights (Table K12)
3036.5.D45	Demonstrations. Processions (Table K12)
3036.5.G35	Gambling (Table K12)
	Including lotteries, games of chance, etc.
	Processions see KJ-KKZ1 3036.5.D45
3036.5.T7	Traveling shows (Table K12)
	Including circuses, puppet theaters, air shows, open-air shows, etc.
3036.7.A-Z	Control of other activities, A-Z
3036.7.S85	Sumptuary laws (Table K12)
3037	Disaster control. Disaster relief (Table K11)
	Including emergency management
	Public property. Public restraint on private property
3040	General (Table K11)
	Government property
3040.5	General (Table K11)
3041	Constitutional aspects. Interdiction of private ownership. Socialist theory of government property (Table K11)
	Administration. Powers and control
3041.5	General (Table K11)
3042	Records management. Access to public records (Table K11)
	Including data bases and general data protection

	Public property. Public restraint on private property
	Government property -- Continued
3043	Expropriation. Nationalization (Table K11)
	For eminent domain see KJ-KKZ1 2824
	For government-owned business enterprises see KJ-KKZ1 3217+
3043.5	Res communes omnium. Things in common use (Table K11)
	Environmental planning. Conservation of natural resources see KJ-KKZ1 3129
	Roads and highways
3043.7	General (Table K11)
3044	Interstate and state highways (Table K11)
3044.5.A-Z	Other, A-Z
3044.5.P74	Private paths (Table K12)
3044.7	Common use. Toll (Table K11)
3044.9	Construction and maintenance (Table K11)
	Including regional planning
	Safety see KJ-KKZ1 851+
	Water resources
	Including rivers, lakes, watercourses, etc.
3046	General (Table K11)
3046.5	Common use (Table K11)
3046.7	Water rights (Table K11)
	Cf. KJ-KKZ1 698 Riparian rights in civil law
3047	Abutting property (Table K11)
	Protection against pollution see KJ-KKZ1 3131
	Development and conservation of water resources
3049	General (Table K11)
3050	Flood control (Table K11)
	Including dams and dikes
	Particular inland waterways and channels see KJ-KKZ1 3480.A+
3052.A-Z	Particular bodies and districts. By name, A-Z
	Subarrange each by Table K12
3053	Shore protection. Coastal zone management (Table K11)
3054	Water courts and procedure (Table K11)
3056	National preserves (Table K11)
	Architectural landmarks and historic monuments see KJ-KKZ1 3183
	Continental shelf and its resources see KJ-KKZ1 3347
	Natural resources and mines see KJ-KKZ1 3350+
3056.5.A-Z	Other, A-Z
	Subarrange each by Table K12
	Public land law
3058	Land reform and land policy legislation (Table K11)
	For agricultural land law see KJ-KKZ1 3290+
3058.3	Government constituted homesteads (Table K11)

KJ-KKZ1

Public property. Public restraint on private property
Public land law -- Continued
3058.5 General (Table K11)
Regional planning
3059 General (Table K11)
3060 Ecological aspects (Table K11)
City planning and redevelopment
3062 General (Table K11)
3063 Consolidation of urban land holdings (Table K11)
Including procedure
3064 Zoning (Table K11)
Including procedure
For variances see KJ-KKZ1 3067+
3065 Assessment of utilities (Table K11)
Including sanitation
Building and construction
Including administrative control and procedure
3067 General (Table K11)
3068 Design (Table K11)
3069 Adjoining landowners (Table K11)
3070 Building materials (Table K11)
3071 Building safety and control (Table K11)
3072 Provisions for people with disabilities (Table K11)
Housing see KJ-KKZ1 884.5+
Fideicommissum see KJ-KKZ1 3304
3073 Public works (Table K11)
Including public works contracts
Public health
3075 General (Table K11)
3076 Organization and administration (Table K11)
Class here works on national departments and boards, national,
state, and local departments and boards, or departments and
boards of several states or administrative districts
For departments and boards (several or individual) of an
individual state or administrative district, see the state or
district
Burial and cemetery laws
Including dead bodies and disposal of dead bodies
3078 General (Table K11)
3079 Cremation (Table K11)
Contagious and infectious diseases
3080 General (Table K11)
3082.A-Z Diseases, A-Z
3082.A53 AIDS (Table K12)
3082.C56 Cholera (Table K12)
3082.T82 Tuberculosis (Table K12)
3082.V45 Venereal diseases (Table K12)

	Public health
	Contagious and infectious diseases -- Continued
	Public health measures
	Including compulsory measures
3084	General (Table K11)
	Immunization. Vaccination
3085	General (Table K11)
3086.A-Z	Diseases, A-Z
3086.P65	Poliomyelitis (Table K12)
3086.S62	Small pox (Table K12)
3087	Quarantine (Table K11)
	Eugenics see KJ-KKZ1 3121
	Environmental pollution see KJ-KKZ1 3130+
3088.A-Z	Other public health hazards and measures, A-Z
3088.R43	Refuse disposal (Table K12)
3088.S77	Street cleaning (Table K12)
3089	Drinking water standards. Fluoridation (Table K11)
	Food laws see KJ-KKZ1 3377+
	Drug laws
3090	General (Table K11)
3091	Pharmaceutical products (Table K11)
3092	Drugs of abuse (Table K11)
	Including narcotics and psychopharmaca
3093	Poisons (Table K11)
3094	Pharmacists and pharmacies (Table K11)
3096	Trade regulation. Advertising (Table K11)
	Including consumer protection
3097	Alcohol. Alcoholic beverages. Liquor laws (Table K11)
	For alcoholic beverage industry see KJ-KKZ1 3395+
3097.5	Cosmetics (Table K11)
	Medical legislation
3098	General (Table K11)
3099.A-Z	Public institutions, agencies, and special bureaus. By name, A-Z
	Subarrange each by Table K12
	The health professions
	Class here works on education, licensing, professional representation, ethics, fees, and liability
	For malpractice, see the individual profession
	Physicians
3100	General (Table K11)
3100.4	Malpractice (Table K11)
3101	Dentists. Dental hygienists (Table K11)
3103.A-Z	Other, A-Z
3103.A53	Anesthesiologists (Table K12)
3103.H43	Healers (Table K12)
	Including herbalists, homeopathic physicians, naturopaths

KJ-KKZ1

Medical legislation
The health professions
Other, A-Z -- Continued

3103.P79	Psychologists. Psychotherapists (Table K12)
	Psychotherapists see KJ-KKZ1 3103.P79
3103.R33	Radiologists (Table K12)
	Auxiliary medical professions. Paramedical professions
3104	General (Table K11)
3105	Nurses and nursing (Table K11)
3106	Midwives (Table K11)
3106.5	Opticians (Table K11)
3107	Physical therapists (Table K11)
3108.A-Z	Health organizations. By name, A-Z
3108.R43	Red Cross (Table K12)
	Cf. KJ-KKZ1 3037 Disaster relief
	Hospitals and other medical institutions or health services
3110	General (Table K11)
3111	Health resorts and spas (Table K11)
3112	Blood banks (Table K11)
	Including blood donations
3113	Institutions for the mentally ill (Table K11)
3114.A-Z	Other health organizations, institutions, or services, A-Z
	Abortion clinics see KJ-KKZ1 3125.A25
3114.D39	Day care centers for infants and children (Table K12)
3114.E43	Emergency medical services (Table K12)
	Nursing homes see KJ-KKZ1 3114.O42
3114.O42	Old age homes. Nursing homes (Table K12)
	Including invalid adults
	Biomedical engineering. Medical technology
	Including human experimentation in medicine and genetic
	engineering
3115	General (Table K11)
3116	Transplantation of organs, tissues, etc. (Table K11)
	Including donation of organs, tissues, etc.
	Cf. KJ-KKZ1 4110 Criminal law
3117	Human reproductive technology (Table K11)
	Including artificial insemination and fertilization in vitro
	Cf. KJ-KKZ1 619 Family law
	Cf. KJ-KKZ1 4108 Criminal law
3119.A-Z	Special topics, A-Z
	Subarrange each by Table K12
(3119.C48)	Change of sex
	see KJ-KKZ1 3115+
3119.C57	Circumcision (Table K12)
3119.C65	Confidential communications (Table K12)
	For data protection see KJ-KKZ1 844.5

	Medical legislation
	Special topics, A-Z -- Continued
(3119.E95)	Experiments with the human body
	see KJ-KKZ1 3115+
(3119.G45)	Genetics, Medical
	see KJ-KKZ1 3115+
3119.I54	Informed consent (Table K12)
	Medical devices see KJ-KKZ1 3119.M43
3119.M43	Medical instruments and apparatus. Medical devices (Table K12)
3119.R42	Medical records. Hospital records. Records management (Table K12)
	Disorders of character, behavior, and intelligence
3120	Alcoholism (Table K11)
	Including works on treatment and rehabilitation
3121	Eugenics. Sterilization and castration (Table K11)
	Euthanasia see KJ-KKZ1 4058
	Right to die see KJ-KKZ1 4058
3122	Veterinary medicine and hygiene. Veterinary public health (Table K11)
	Animal protection. Animal welfare. Animal rights
	Including prevention of cruelty to animals
	For animal rights as a social issue see HV4701+
3123	General (Table K11)
3123.2	Animal experimentation and research (Table K11)
	Including vivisection and dissection
3123.3	Slaughtering of animals (Table K11)
3123.4.A-Z	Other special topics, A-Z
	Birth control. Family planning. Population control
	Cf. KJ-KKZ1 4070+ Illegal abortion (Criminal law)
	Cf. KJ-KKZ1 4222 Contraceptive devices (Criminal law)
3124	General (Table K11)
3125.A-Z	Special topics, A-Z
3125.A25	Abortion clinics
	Environmental law
	For civil liability see KJ-KKZ1 852.5
3127	General (Table K11)
3128	Organization and administration (Table K11)
3129	Environmental planning. Conservation of environmental resources (Table K11)
	For ecological aspects of regional planning see KJ-KKZ1 3060
	Environmental pollution
3130	General (Table K11)
3130.5	Air pollution (Table K11)
	Including noxious gases, automobile emissions, tobacco smoking, etc.

	Environmental law
	Environmental pollution -- Continued
3131	Water and groundwater pollution (Table K11)
	Including pollutants and sewage control
	Pollutants
3131.5	General (Table K11)
3132	Radioactive substances (Table K11)
3132.2	Electromagnetic waves (Table K11)
3132.5	Noise (Table K11)
	Including traffic noise, and noise control
	Cf. KJ-KKZ1 701.N84 Property
3133	Recycling of refuse (Table K11)
	Wilderness preservation
	Including natural monuments, parks, and forests
3134	General (Table K11)
3134.5	Constitutional right to recreation (Table K11)
3134.6	Plant protection (Table K11)
	Wildlife conservation
	Including game, birds, and fish
3135	General (Table K11)
	Game laws and hunting see KJ-KKZ1 3337+
	Fishery laws see KJ-KKZ1 3340+
	Land reclamation in mining see KJ-KKZ1 3369
(3136)	Criminal provisions
	see KJ-KKZ1 4351.5+
	Cultural affairs
3137	General (Table K11)
3137.5	Constitutional aspects. Freedom of science and the arts.
	Academic freedom (Table K11)
3137.7	Cultural policy. State encouragement of science and the arts
	(Table K11)
3137.8	Organization and administration (Table K11)
	Class here works on national, state and/or local departments,
	boards, commissions, etc., of cultural affairs
	For the department of cultural affairs of an individual state or
	district, see the state or district
3137.9	National language (Table K11)
	Including regulation of use, purity, etc.
	Education
3138	General (Table K11)
3138.3	Constitutional safeguards. Parental rights (Table K11)
3138.4	Boards and commissions (Table K11)
3138.5	Parent-teacher associations (Table K11)

Cultural affairs
Education -- Continued
School government. School districts
Including curriculum and participation in school government in
general
For parent-teacher associations see KJ-KKZ1 3138.5
For student participation see KJ-KKZ1 3139.9
3138.55   General (Table K11)
3138.6   School discipline (Table K11)
3138.7   Religious instruction (Table K11)
Including public schools and denominational schools, and
concordats
3138.8   Political science (Table K11)
Students
3139   General (Table K11)
3139.3   Constitutional aspects (Table K11)
Including right and duty to education. Freedom of speech
and expression, etc.
3139.4   Compulsory education (Table K11)
3139.9   Student participation in administration (Table K11)
Teachers. School functionaries
For elementary teachers see KJ-KKZ1 3142
For vocational teachers see KJ-KKZ1 3145
For university teachers see KJ-KKZ1 3152
3140   General (Table K11)
3140.4   Constitutional aspects (Table K11)
Including freedom of speech
3140.5   Education and training (Table K11)
Including religious education
3140.7   Tenure, salaries, pensions, etc. (Table K11)
3140.9   Disciplinary power (Table K11)
3140.95   Preschool education (Table K11)
Elementary education
3141   General (Table K11)
3142   Teachers (Table K11)
Education of children with disabilities
3143   General (Table K11)
3143.4   Children with social disabilities (Table K11)
Including orphans, outcasts, paupers, etc.
3143.6   Children with physical disabilities (Table K11)
3143.7   Children with mental disabilities (Table K11)
Vocational education
3144   General (Table K11)
3145   Teachers (Table K11)
Secondary education
3146   General (Table K11)

Cultural affairs
  Education
    Secondary education -- Continued

3146.6.A-Z	Special topics, A-Z
	Subarrange each by Table K12
3146.8.A-Z	Teaching methods and media, A-Z
	Subarrange each by Table K12
	Higher education. Universities
	For legal education see KJ-KKZ1 50+
	For research policies in higher education see KJ-KKZ1 3160
3147	General (Table K11)
3147.3	Constitutional aspects. Numerus clausus (Table K11)
3147.4	Intelligentsia (General) (Table K11)
	Administration. Institutional management
	Including curriculum
3148	General (Table K11)
3148.3	Self-government and autonomy (Table K11)
	Student participation in administration see KJ-KKZ1 3153.5
3149	Disciplinary power and tribunals (Table K11)
3149.5	Degrees (Table K11)
3150.A-Z	Special topics, A-Z
3150.F54	Finance (Table K12)
	Faculties. Institutes
	For law schools see KJ-KKZ1 53.A+
3151	General (Table K11)
3151.3.A-Z	Particular. By place, A-Z
	Subarrange each by Table K12
3152	Teachers (Table K11)
	Including professors (ordinarii, extraordinarii, and emeriti), magisters, etc.
	Students
3153	General (Table K11)
3153.5	Student participation in administration. Student parliament (Table K11)
3153.7	Fellowships. Grants (Table K11)
3153.8	Selection for higher education (Table K11)
3154	Political activities (Table K11)
	Including strikes
3154.3	Student societies (Table K11)
3155.A-Z	Universities. By place, A-Z
	Subarrange each by Table K12

Cultural affairs
Education
Higher education. Universities -- Continued

3156.A-Z   Other schools or institutions of higher education. By place, A-Z
Subarrange each by Table K12
Including colleges or institutes of technology, schools of music, art, drama, etc.
For academies see KJ-KKZ1 3162.A+
Private schools
3157   General (Table K11)
3157.5.A-Z   Types, A-Z
Subarrange each by Table K12
Denominational schools see KJ-KKZ1 3138.7
3158   Adult education (Table K11)
3159   Physical education. Sports (Table K11)
For liability for sports accidents see KJ-KKZ1 848+
Cf. KJ-KKZ1 3035+ Sports activities
3159.5   Science and the arts (Table K11)
For constitutional guaranties see KJ-KKZ1 3137.5
3160   Public policies in research (Table K11)
Including research in higher education
Public institutions
3161   General (Table K11)
3162.A-Z   Academies. By name, A-Z
Subarrange each by Table K12
3163.A-Z   Research institutes. By name, A-Z
Subarrange each by Table K12
3165.A-Z   Branches and subjects
3165.A72   Archaeology (Table K12)
3165.C37   Cartography (Table K12)
Language see KJ-KKZ1 3137.9
Meteorology see KJ-KKZ1 3513
3165.O25   Oceanography (Table K12)
3165.S73   Statistical services (Table K12)
For data protection see KJ-KKZ1 3042
The arts
3168   General (Table K11)
3169   Fine arts (Table K11)
Performing arts
3170   General (Table K11)
3171   Music. Musicians (Table K11)
Theater
For copyright see KJ-KKZ1 1186
3172   General (Table K11)

Cultural affairs
　Science and the arts
　　The arts
　　　Performing arts
　　　　Theater -- Continued

3172.5	Personnel (Table K11)
	Including managerial, performing, and technical staff
	For labor contracts and collective labor agreement
	of stagehands see KJ-KKZ1 1387.S82
3172.7	Playwrights. Contracts (Table K11)
	Motion pictures
3173	General (Table K11)
3173.3	Labor contracts (Table K11)
3173.5	Regulation of industry (Table K11)
	Including trade practice and censorship
3174	Screenwriters. Contracts (Table K11)
	Public collections
3176	General (Table K11)
3177	Archives. Historic documents (Table K11)
	Libraries
3179	General (Table K11)
3180.A-Z	Types of libraries, A-Z
3180.P82	Public (Table K12)
3180.3	Librarians and other library personnel (Table K11)
3180.5	Legal deposit of books (Table K11)
3182	Inter-library loan (Table K11)
	Including national and international loan
3182.2	Criminal provisions (Table K11)
	Cf. KJ-KKZ1 1547 Protection of children against
	obscenity
3182.5	Museums and galleries (Table K11)
3183	Historic buildings and monuments. Architectural landmarks (Table K11)
	Including vessels, battleships, archaeological sites, etc.
3184	Educational, scientific, and cultural exchanges (Table K11)
	Economic law
3190	General (Table K11)
	Economic constitution
3191	General (Table K11)
3192	Theories and concepts (Table K11)
	Including liberalism, national planning (planification), socialist theory of government ownership of resources, industries, distribution systems, etc.

Economic law

Economic constitution -- Continued

3193	Organization and administration (Table K11)

Class here works on national departments and boards of commerce, national, state, and local departments and boards, or departments and boards of several states or administrative districts

For departments and boards (several or individual) of an individual state or administrative district, see the state or district

Government control and policy

3195	General (Table K11)

National planning

3197	General (Table K11)
3198	Planning agencies and bureaus (Table K11)
3199	Planning periods (Table K11)

Including Five-Year Plans, Two-Year Plans, etc.

3199.5	Techniques and methods of planning (Table K11)
3200	Contract systems. Systems of cooperation (Table K11)
3201	Expansion control (Table K11)

Including business cycles

Investments. Investment control

Including foreign investments

3202	General (Table K11)
3203	Funds (Table K11)
3204.A-Z	By industry of project, A-Z
3204.S54	Shipping (Table K12)
3204.T68	Tourist trade (Table K12)
3205	Assistance to developing countries (Table K11)

For tax measures see KJ-KKZ1 3553.5

Economic assistance

3206	General (Table K11)

Subsidies

3207	General (Table K11)
3207.3	Investment credits (Table K11)

Agricultural credits see KJ-KKZ1 3322

3208	Marketing orders (Table K11)

Class here general works

For particular marketing orders, see the subject, e.g. Agriculture

Prices and price control

3210	General (Table K11)
3211.A-Z	Industries, services, or products, A-Z

Subarrange each by Table K12

Price delicts see KJ-KKZ1 4290

3212	Distribution (Table K11)

Money see KJ-KKZ1 3534+

Foreign exchange control see KJ-KKZ1 3538+

	Economic law
	Government control and policy -- Continued
	Industrial priorities, allocations, and circulation
	Including organizations
	For industrial priorities and allocations in wartime see KJ-KKZ1 3720+
3213	General (Table K11)
3214.A-Z	Raw materials, A-Z
	Subarrange each by Table K12
3215.A-Z	Industries or products, A-Z
	Subarrange each by Table K12
	Rationing see KJ-KKZ1 3724+
	Government business enterprises
3217	General (Table K11)
3218	Central administration (Table K11)
	Including local administration
3219.A-Z	By industry, A-Z
	Subarrange each by Table K12
	Control of contracts and combinations in restraint of trade.
	Competition rules
	For unfair competition see KJ-KKZ1 1234+
3220	General (Table K11)
3220.3	Constitutional aspects (Table K11)
3222	Antidiscrimination (Table K11)
	Horizontal and vertical combinations
3223	General (Table K11)
3224	Corporate consolidation, merger, etc. (Table K11)
	Cartels
3225	General (Table K11)
3227.A-Z	Types of cartels, A-Z
	Subarrange each by Table K12
3228.A-Z	Industries, occupations, etc., A-Z
	Subarrange each by Table K12
	For works relating to an individual company see KJ-KKZ1 3248.A+
	Combinations (Socialist)
3229	General (Table K11)
3230.A-Z	By industry, A-Z
	Subarrange each by Table K12
3231	Exclusive dealing or use arrangements. Requirement contracts (Table K11)
3232	Restraint-of-competition clause in labor relations (Table K11)
	Including collective labor agreement clauses
3233	Restraint-of-competition clause in business concern contracts and in articles of incorporation and partnership (Table K11)

                Economic law
                   Government control and policy
                     Control of contracts and combinations in restraint of trade.
                        Competition rules
                        Horizontal and vertical combinations -- Continued

3235	Price maintenance and open price system (Table K11)
3236.A-Z	Industries, products, etc., A-Z
	Subarrange each by Table K12
3237	Licensing contracts (Table K11)
3238	DIN-norms (Table K11)
3239	Standardized forms of contract (Table K11)
	Monopolies. Oligopolies. Antitrust law
	For government monopolies see KJ-KKZ1 3639
3242	General (Table K11)
3243	Market dominance (Table K11)
	Cartel agencies and procedure
3244	General (Table K11)
3245	Jurisdiction (Table K11)
	Including procedures according to EEC-legislation (conflict of laws)
3246	Cartel register (Table K11)
	Including procedure
3247	Damages (Private law) and indemnification (Public law) (Table K11)
	Criminal provisions see KJ-KKZ1 4286+
3248.A-Z	Mergers, cartels, combinations, business concerns, etc., A-Z
	Subarrange each by Table K12
3249	Small business (Table K11)
	Cooperative societies
3250	General (Table K11)
3251.A-Z	By industry, A-Z
	Subarrange each by Table K12
3253	Chambers of commerce (Table K11)
	Boards of trade see KJ-KKZ1 3429.7
	Money, currency, and foreign exchange control see KJ-KKZ1 3534+
	Standards. Norms
	For standards, grading, and quality control of agricultural or consumer products, see the product
3254	General (Table K11)
3255	Quality control (Table K11)
	Weights and measures. Containers
3257	General (Table K11)
3258.A-Z	By instrument, A-Z
	Subarrange each by Table K12
	Standardization

	Economic law
	Standards. Norms
	Standardization -- Continued
3259	General (Table K11)
	Engineering standards
3260	General (Table K11)
3262.A-Z	By material, A-Z
	Subarrange each by Table K12
3263.A-Z	By instrument, A-Z
	Subarrange each by Table K12
	Norms and standards for conservation of raw or scarce
	materials
	Including recycling of refuse (Metal, glass, paper, wood, etc.)
	Cf. KJ-KKZ1 3133 Environmental law
3264	General (Table K11)
3265	Prohibition of industrial use of scarce materials (Table
	K11)
3266.A-Z	By industry or product, A-Z
	Subarrange each by Table K12
	Price norms see KJ-KKZ1 3210+
3268	Labeling (Table K11)
	Class here general works
	For the labeling of particular goods or products, see the good or
	product
	Regulation of industry, trade and commerce
3272	General (Table K11)
3272.5	Constitutional aspects (Table K11)
	Including freedom of trade and commerce
	For freedom of choice of occupation or profession see
	KJ-KKZ1 3515.5
3273	Licensing (Table K11)
3274	State supervision of installations (Table K11)
3276	Consumer protection (Table K11)
	Advertising
3280	General (Table K11)
3282	Trade fairs and expositions (Table K11)
	Including national and international fairs and expositions
3283.A-Z	By industry or product, A-Z
3283.H43	Health services. Medicine (Table K12)
	Medicine see KJ-KKZ1 3283.H43
3283.T62	Tobacco (Table K12)
3284.A-Z	By medium, A-Z
3284.B76	Broadcasting (Table K12)
	Testing of commercial products see KJ-KKZ1 1242
	Primary production. Extractive industries
	Agriculture

Economic law
　　Regulation of industry, trade and commerce
　　Primary production. Extractive industries
　　　Agriculture -- Continued
　　　　Land reform and agrarian land policy legislation.
　　　　　Nationalization
3290　　　　　General (Table K11)
3292　　　　　Restraint on alienation of agricultural land (Table K11)
3293　　　　　Consolidation of landholdings. Commasation (Table
　　　　　　K11)
3295　　　　General (Table K11)
　　　　Organization and administration
　　　　　Class here works on national departments and boards of
　　　　　　agriculture, national, state, and local departments and
　　　　　　boards, or departments and boards of several states or
　　　　　　administrative districts
　　　　　For departments and boards (several or individual) of an
　　　　　　individual state or administrative district, see the state
　　　　　　or district
3296　　　　　General (Table K11)
3297.A-Z　　　Particular organizations, agricultural science and
　　　　　　research institutions, etc. A-Z
　　　　　　　Subarrange each by Table K12
3298　　　　Agricultural technique (Table K11)
3299　　　　Agricultural planning and planning periods (Table K11)
　　　　Entail
3300　　　　　General (Table K11)
3302.A-Z　　　Special topics, A-Z
　　　　　　　Subarrange each by Table K12
3304　　　　Fideicommissum. Entailed estates of the greater nobility
　　　　　　(Table K11)
　　　　Agricultural contracts
3306　　　　　General (Table K11)
　　　　Leasing of rural property. Farm tenancy
　　　　　Class here civil law provisions as well as legislation
　　　　　　aimed at protection and stability for tenancy
3310　　　　　General (Table K11)
3311　　　　Farm equipment leasing (Table K11)
　　　　Agricultural business enterprise
3312　　　　　General (Table K11)
　　　　Corporate structure
3314　　　　　General (Table K11)
3315　　　　　Cartels (Table K11)
3316　　　　　Cooperative societies (Table K11)
　　　　　　　Including producers and marketing cooperatives
3318　　　　Government agricultural enterprises (Table K11)
　　　　　　Including central and local administration

KJ-KKZ1

	Economic law
	Regulation of industry, trade and commerce
	Primary production. Extractive industries
	Agriculture -- Continued
	Marketing orders
3320	General (Table K11)
	Economic assistance
3321	General (Table K11)
3322	Agricultural credits, loans, mortgages, etc. (Table K11)
3323	Production control and quotas. Price support and regulations (Table K11)
	Priorities, allocations, and distribution
3325	General (Table K11)
3325.5.A-Z	By product, commodity,. etc., A-Z
	Subarrange each by Table K12
3325.8	Standards and grading (Table K11)
	Importing and stockpiling
3326	General (Table K11)
	Rationing see KJ-KKZ1 3724+
	Livestock industry and trade
3327	General (Table K11)
3328.A-Z	Particular, A-Z
3328.H67	Horses (Table K12)
3328.R44	Reindeer (Table K12)
3329	Milk production. Dairy farming (Table K11)
3329.5.A-Z	Products, A-Z
3329.5.C47	Cereal products (Table K12)
3329.5.F63	Fodder and grain (Table K12)
	Grain see KJ-KKZ1 3329.5.F63
3329.5.S44	Seeds (Table K12)
3330	Agricultural courts and procedure (Table K11)
3332	Criminal provisions (Table K11)
3333	Viticulture (Table K11)
3334	Apiculture. Beekeeping (Table K11)
3335	Horticulture (Table K11)
	Protection of new plant varieties see KJ-KKZ1 1210.P55
	Forestry
	Including timber laws
3336	General (Table K11)
	Game laws
3337	General (Table K11)
3338	Game leases and licenses (Table K11)
	Fishery
3340	General (Table K11)
3342.A-Z	Particular fish or marine fauna, A-Z
	Subarrange each by Table K12

	Economic law
	Regulation of industry, trade, and commerce
	Primary production. Extractive industries
	Fishery
	Sport fishing see KJ-KKZ1 3036.F58
	Mining and quarrying
	Including metallurgy
3344	General (Table K11)
3345	Constitutional aspects (Table K11)
3346	Organization and administration (Table K11)

Class here works on national departments and boards, national, state, and local departments and boards, or departments and boards of several states or administrative districts

For departments and boards (several or individual) of an individual state or administrative district, see the state or district

3347	Continental shelf and its resources (Table K11)
	Rights to mines and mineral resources
	Including procedure and registration
3350	General (Table K11)
	Public restraint on property rights and positions.
	Government rights see KJ-KKZ1 3345
3352	Adjoining landowners (Table K11)
	Mining industry and finance
3353	General (Table K11)
3354	Economic assistance (Table K11)
3355	Corporations and cooperatives (Table K11)
3356	Government mining enterprises (Table K11)
3357	Planning and planning periods (Table K11)
	Including calculation of reserves
	Social legislation
3359	General (Table K11)
	Labor law for miners
3360	General (Table K11)
3363	Unions (Table K11)
3364	Mine safety regulations. Rescue work (Table K11)
	Including equipment
3365	Social insurance for miners (Table K11)
	Including all branches of social insurance
3366.A-Z	Resources, A-Z
	Including industries
3366.P4	Peat (Table K12)
3366.P47	Petroleum (Table K12)
3366.P74	Precious metals (Table K12)
3367	Subsidences. Earth movement (Table K11)
3368	Eminent domain (Table K11)

KJ-KKZ1

	Economic law
	Regulation of industry, trade and commerce
	Primary production. Extractive industries
	Mining and quarrying -- Continued
3369	Environmental laws. Land reclamation (Table K11)
	Manufacturing industries
	Including heavy and light industries
3372	General (Table K11)
3373.A-Z	Types of manufacture, A-Z
	Appliances industry, Household see KJ-KKZ1 3373.H68
	Energy industry see KJ-KKZ1 3431+
3373.F45	Fertilizer industry (Table K12)
3373.H68	Household appliances industry (Table K12)
3373.M32	Machinery industry (Table K12)
3373.T48	Textile industry (Table K12)
3373.T69	Toy industry (Table K12)
3375	Recycling industries (Table K11)
	Food processing industries. Food products
	Class here works on trade practices, economic assistance, labeling, sanitation and quality inspection
	Including regulation of adulteration and additives
3377	General (Table K11)
3378	Labeling (Table K11)
3379	Purity (Table K11)
	Including regulation of adulteration and food additives
3380	Cereal products (Table K11)
3381	Fruits and vegetables (Table K11)
3382	Confectionary industry (Table K11)
3383	Meat (Table K11)
3384	Poultry products (Table K11)
3386	Egg products (Table K11)
	Dairy products
3388	General (Table K11)
3390	Cheese (Table K11)
3392	Fishery products. Seafood (Table K11)
3393	Oils and fats (Table K11)
	Beverages
3395	Brewing (Table K11)
3397	Winemaking (Table K11)
3398	Distilling (Table K11)
	For taxation see KJ-KKZ1 3640.D58
3399	Mineral waters (Table K11)
3400.A-Z	Related industries, A-Z
	Subarrange each by Table K12
	Building and construction industry
	For building laws see KJ-KKZ1 3067+
3402	General (Table K11)

	Economic law
	Regulation of industry, trade and commerce
	Building and construction industry -- Continued
3403	Contracts and specifications (Table K11)
	International trade
3405	General (Table K11)
3406	Organization and administration (Table K11)
	Export and import controls
	Including foreign trade practice and procedure
3407	General (Table K11)
	Foreign exchange control see KJ-KKZ1 3538+
	Trade agreements see KJ-KKZ1 3646+
	Export trade
3410	General (Table K11)
3410.5	Criminal provisions (Table K11)
3411	Commercial agents for foreign corporations (Table K11)
3413.A-Z	By region or country, A-Z
	e. g.
3413.E87	European Economic Community countries (Table K12)
	Domestic trade
	For consumer protection see KJ-KKZ1 3276
3415	General (Table K11)
3415.5	Organization and administration (Table K11)
3415.6	Planning and planning periods (Table K11)
3416	Wholesale trade. Government wholesale trade (Table K11)
	Retail trade. Government retail trade
	Cf. KJ-KKZ1 3429+ Artisans
3418	General (Table K11)
3419	Conditions of trading (Table K11)
	Including licensing and Sunday legislation
3420.A-Z	Modes of trading, A-Z
	Chain stores see KJ-KKZ1 3420.D46
3420.D46	Department stores. Chain stores (Table K12)
3420.D57	Direct selling (Table K12)
	Fairs see KJ-KKZ1 3420.M37
3420.M34	Mail-order business (Table K12)
3420.M37	Markets. Fairs (Table K12)
	For trade fairs and expositions see KJ-KKZ1 3282
3420.P43	Peddling (Table K12)
3420.V45	Vending machines (Table K12)
3421	Cooperative retail trade (Table K11)
3422.A-Z	Products, A-Z
3422.A88	Automobiles (Table K12)
3422.M48	Metals (Table K12)
	Metals, Precious see KJ-KKZ1 3422.P73
3422.P46	Petroleum. Petroleum products (Table K12)

KJ-KKZ1

Economic law
  Regulation of industry, trade and commerce
    Domestic trade
      Retail trade. Government retail trade
        Products, A-Z -- Continued
3422.P73   Precious metals (Table K12)
                  Second-hand trade
3423   General (Table K11)
3423.5.A-Z   Types of trade, A-Z
3423.5.A82   Auction houses (Table K12)
3423.5.P39   Pawnbrokers (Table K12)
                Service trades
3424   General (Table K11)
                    Old age homes see KJ-KKZ1 3114.A+
3424.5   Hotels, taverns, and restaurants (Table K11)
                      For railroad dining and sleeping cars see KJ-KKZ1
                        3461.3.A+
3425   Travel agencies. Tourist trade (Table K11)
3425.5.A-Z   Other service trades, A-Z
3425.5.A88   Automobile repair shops (Table K12)
3425.5.E45   Employment agencies (Table K12)
3425.5.P74   Private investigators (Table K12)
                Artisans
3426   General (Table K11)
3427   Apprentices (Table K11)
3428   Licensing and registration (Table K11)
                      Including examinations and examination boards, diplomas,
                        etc.
                  Corporate representation
3429   General (Table K11)
3429.3   Cooperative societies (Table K11)
3429.5   Trade associations (Table K11)
3429.7   Boards of trade (Table K11)
3430.A-Z   Crafts, A-Z
                      Subarrange each by Table K12
              Energy policy. Power supply
                  Including publicly and privately owned utilities
3431   General (Table K11)
3431.15   National, state, and local jurisdiction and supervision (Table
                        K11)
3431.2   Planning and conservation (Table K11)
3431.25   Licensing (Table K11)
3431.3   Ratemaking (Table K11)
3431.4   Corporate structure (Table K11)
3431.5   Monopolies and freedom of contract (Table K11)
3431.6   Accounting. Taxation (Table K11)
3431.7   Engineering (Table K11)

	Economic law
	Energy policy. Power supply -- Continued
	Particular sources of power
3432	Electricity (Table KJ-KKZ10)
3433	Gas. Natural gas (Table KJ-KKZ10)
	Water see KJ-KKZ1 2956
3435	Heat. Steam distributed by central plants (Table KJ-KKZ10)
3436	Atomic energy (Table KJ-KKZ10)
	For protection from radiation see KJ-KKZ1 3012
	For ecological aspects see KJ-KKZ1 3132
3437.A-Z	Other sources of power, A-Z
	Subarrange each by Table K12
3438	Courts and procedures (Table K11)
	Including industrial arbitral courts
3439	Business ethics. Courts of honor (Table K11)
	Criminal provisions see KJ-KKZ1 4286+
	Transportation
3440	General (Table K11)
3441	Organization and administration (Table K11)
	Class here works on national departments and boards of transportation, national, state, and local departments and boards, or departments and boards of several states or administrative districts
	For departments and boards (several or individual) of an individual state or administrative district, see the state or district
	Road traffic. Automotive transportation
3442	General (Table K11)
	Motor vehicles
3443	General (Table K11)
3443.5	Registration (Table K11)
3443.7	Inspection (Table K11)
3444	Safety equipment (Table K11)
3445	Drivers' licenses (Table K11)
	Including driving schools and instructors
3446	Compulsory insurance (Table K11)
3447.A-Z	Vehicles, A-Z
3447.A57	Antique and classic cars (Table K12)
3447.T37	Taxicabs (Table K12)
3447.T78	Trucks (Table K12)
	Traffic regulations and enforcement
3448	General (Table K11)
	Traffic violations
	For criminal interference with street traffic see KJ-KKZ1 4384+
3450	General (Table K11)

KJ-KKZ1

	Transportation
	Road traffic. Automotive transportation
	Traffic regulations and enforcement
	Traffic violations
	Driving while intoxicated see KJ-KKZ1 4386
	Hit-and-run drivers see KJ-KKZ1 4390
3451	Unauthorized use of a motor vehicle (Table K11)
3452	Traffic courts and procedure (Table K11)
	Including fines
	Highway safety
3453	General (Table K11)
3454.A-Z	Particular provisions, A-Z
3454.C75	Crossings (Table K12)
3454.T7	Traffic signs (Table K12)
	Carriage of passengers and goods
3455	General (Table K11)
3455.5	Passenger carriers. Bus lines. Taxicabs (Table K11)
	Goods carriers
3456	General (Table K11)
3457	Ratemaking (Table K11)
	Social legislation see KJ-KKZ1 1414.A+
3458	Sunday legislation (Table K11)
	Railroads
3459	General (Table K11)
	Operation of railroads
3460	General (Table K11)
3461	Railroad land. Right-of-way (Table K11)
3461.3.A-Z	Rolling stock and equipment, A-Z
	e. g.
3461.3.D55	Dining cars (Table K12)
3461.3.S43	Sleeping cars (Table K12)
3462	Railroad safety (Table K11)
	Including railroad crossings, etc. and liability
3463	Officials and employees (Table K11)
	Including tenure, salaries, pensions, labor law, etc.
3464	Ratemaking (Table K11)
3464.3	Carriage of passengers and goods (Table K11)
3464.5	Private sidings (Table K11)
3465.A-Z	Kinds of railroads or railways, A-Z
3465.C32	Cable railways (Table K12)
	Private-track railroads see KJ-KKZ1 3465.S42
3465.S42	Secondary railroads. Private-track railroads (Table K12)
3465.S98	Suspended railways (Table K12)
	Criminal provisions see KJ-KKZ1 4382
	Postal services see KJ-KKZ1 3485+
3466	Pipelines (Table K11)
	Aviation. Air law

	Transportation
	Aviation. Air law -- Continued
3467	General (Table K11)
3467.5	Aircraft. Nationality (Table K11)
	For registration see KJ-KKZ1 935.4
3468	Air traffic rules (Table K11)
	Including air safety and airworthiness
3468.3	Airports (Table K11)
3468.35	Airport police (Table K11)
3468.4	Pilots. Flight crews (Table K11)
	Including licensing, wages, etc.
	Liability see KJ-KKZ1 850
	Crimes aboard aircraft see KJ-KKZ1 4396
3469	Space law (Table K11)
	Water transportation
3470	General (Table K11)
	Ships
3471	General (Table K11)
3471.3	Ship's papers (Table K11)
	For registration see KJ-KKZ1 984.3
	Safety regulations
3472	General (Table K11)
3472.3	Fire prevention (Table K11)
3472.4	Ship crews (Table K11)
3472.5.A-Z	Types of cargo, A-Z
3472.5.D35	Dangerous articles (Table K12)
	Navigation and pilotage
3473	General (Table K11)
3474	Rule of the road at sea (Table K11)
3475	Coastwise and inland navigation (Table K11)
	Harbors and ports of entry
3476	General (Table K11)
3476.3.A-Z	By name, A-Z
	Subarrange each by Table K12
	Coastwise and inland shipping
	Including rafting
3478	General (Table K11)
3479	Carriage of passengers and goods (Table K11)
	Cf. KJ-KKZ1 971+ Affreightment (Commercial law)
3480.A-Z	Individual waterways and channels, A-Z
	Subarrange each by Table K12
	Marine labor law see KJ-KKZ1 987+
	Marine insurance see KJ-KKZ1 985+
3480.5	Combined transportation (Table K11)
	Communication. Mass media
3482	General (Table K11)

KJ-KKZ1

Communication. Mass media -- Continued
3483   Constitutional aspects. Freedom of communication.
                      Censorship (Table K11)
3483.3   Policy. Competition between media (Table K11)
                  Postal services. Telecommunications
3485   General (Table K11)
                  Privacy of mail and telecommunication see KJ-KKZ1 3483
3485.5   Organization and administration (Table K11)
                      Class here works on national departments, national, state and
                          local departments and boards of several states or
                          administrative districts
                      For departments and boards (several or individual) of an
                          individual state or administrative district, see the state or
                          district
3485.7   Government monopoly (Table K11)
3485.8.A-Z   Services other than mail, A-Z
                      Money orders see KJ-KKZ1 3485.8.P68
3485.8.P68   Postal notes. Money orders (Table K12)
3485.8.P69   Postal savings (Table K12)
3486   Rates. Postage. Modes of collection (Table K11)
                      Including postage stamps
                  Telecommunication
3487   General (Table K11)
3487.3   Installation and interference (Table K11)
3488   Telegraph (Table K11)
3489   Teletype and data transmission systems (Table K11)
                  Telephone
3490   General (Table K11)
3490.3   Rates (Table K11)
                          Including local and long distance rates
3490.5   Telephone lines (Table K11)
                          Including extensions
                  Radio communication
                      Including radio and television broadcasting
3491   General (Table K11)
                  Freedom of radio communication see KJ-KKZ1 3483
                  Competition between different media see KJ-KKZ1 3483.3
                  Organization and administration
                      Including national and state jurisdiction
3492   General (Table K11)
3492.3   Private and public institutions. State supervision (Table
                      K11)
                  Stations. Networks
                      Including frequency allocations and licensing
3494   General (Table K11)
3494.3   Post monopoly (Table K11)
3494.5   Interference (Table K11)

Communication. Mass media
   Radio communication
      Stations. Networks -- Continued

3494.7	Amateur stations (Table K11)
	Broadcasting
3495	General (Table K11)
3495.5	Cable television (Table K11)
	Programming. Censorship
3496	General (Table K11)
3496.5.A-Z	Programs, A-Z
3496.5.S66	Sports (Table K12)
3497	Labor law (Table K11)
	Including collective labor law
3497.5.A-Z	Stations, A-Z
	Subarrange each by Table K12
	Criminal provisions
3498	General (Table K11)
3498.3	Pirate stations (Table K11)
3498.5	Illegal operation of a station (Table K11)
3499	Illegal reception (Table K11)
	Press law
3500	General (Table K11)
	Freedom of the press and censorship see KJ-KKZ1 3483
3500.3	Right to information (Table K11)
3500.5	Organization and administration. Institutions (Table K11)
	Planning and planning periods
3502	General (Table K11)
3502.A-Z	Types of literature, A-Z
3502.P47	Periodicals (Table K12)
3502.S34	Schoolbooks (Table K12)
	Including all levels of education
	Publishers and publishing
3503	General (Table K11)
3504	Government publishing enterprises (Table K11)
	Including central administration
3504.3	Journalists. Domestic and foreign correspondents (Table K11)
	Including liability
	Bookdealers
3504.5	General (Table K11)
3505	Government enterprises (Table K11)
3506	Right to obtain retraction or restatement of facts by offender (or an opportunity to reply) (Table K11)
3506.3.A-Z	Special topics, A-Z
3506.3.P37	Party press (Table K12)
3506.3.P65	Political advertising (Table K12)
3506.3.R48	Resistance. Underground press (Table K12)

	Professions. Intelligentsia (Socialist)
	Individual professions
	Other professions, A-Z -- Continued
	Book dealers see KJ-KKZ1 3504.5+
	Graphic artists see KJ-KKZ1 3521.P74
	Journalists see KJ-KKZ1 3504.3
	Librarians see KJ-KKZ1 3180.3
	Performing artists see KJ-KKZ1 3170+
3521.P74	Printers. Graphic artists (Table K12)
3521.R4	Real estate agents (Table K12)
	Social workers see KJ-KKZ1 1525+
3521.S95	Surveyors (Table K12)
	Teachers see KJ-KKZ1 3140+
3524	Professional ethics. Courts of honor (Table K11)
	For a particular court of honor, see the profession
	Public finance
	Finance reform and policies
	Cf. KJ-KKZ1 3195+ Government control and policy
3525	General (Table K11)
	Monetary policies see KJ-KKZ1 3534+
3526	General (Table K11)
3526.3	Constitutional aspects (Table K11)
	Organization and administration
	Class here works on national departments or agencies of finance, national, state, and local departments or agencies, or departments and agencies of several states or administrative districts
	For departments and agencies (several or individual) of an individual state or administrative district, see the state or administrative district
	For financial courts see KJ-KKZ1 3682+
3527	General (Table K11)
3527.3.A-Z	Particular national departments and agencies, A-Z
	Subarrange each by Table K12
3527.5	Officers and personnel. Functionaries (Table K11)
	Including tenure, salaries, pensions, etc., and discipline
	Budget. Government expenditures
3528	General (Table K11)
	Constitutional aspects see KJ-KKZ1 3526.3
3528.3	Accounting (Table K11)
	Including central or local organs of national government
	Expenditure control. Auditing
3529	General (Table K11)
3530	National courts of audit (Table K11)
	Public debts. Loans. Bond issues
3531	General (Table K11)
3532	External debts. International loan agreements (Table K11)

	Public finance
	Organization and administration -- Continued
	Revenue see KJ-KKZ1 3540+
3533	Intergovernmental fiscal relations (Table K11)
	Including revenue sharing
	Money
	Including control of circulation
3534	General (Table K11)
3535	Coinage. Mint regulations (Table K11)
3536	Bank notes. Banks of issue (Table K11)
	Class here public law aspects of banks of issue
	For banking law see KJ-KKZ1 940+
3537	Gold trading and gold standard (Table K11)
3537.5	Currency reforms. Revalorization of debts (Table K11)
	Foreign exchange control
3538	General (Table K11)
	Valuta clause and gold clause see KJ-KKZ1 820.3
	Criminal provisions see KJ-KKZ1 4292
3539	Conflict of laws (Table K11)
	National revenue
3540	General (Table K11)
3540.3	Fees. Fines (Table K11)
	Taxation
	Criticism and reform see KJ-KKZ1 3525+
3541-3550	General (Table K9c)
3551	Constitutional aspects (Table K11)
	Including equality
	Double taxation
3552	General (Table K11)
3552.3	Domicile (Table K11)
3552.4.A-Z	Special topics, A-Z
3552.4.F67	Foreign corporations and foreign stockholders (Table K12)
3552.4.M85	Multi-national corporations (Table K12)
	Taxation and tax exemption as a measure of social and economic policy
3553	General (Table K11)
3553.3	Investments (Table K11)
	Including foreign investments
3553.5	Assistance to developing countries (Table K11)
3554	Export sales (Table K11)
3555.A-Z	Classes of taxpayers or lines of business, A-Z
3555.D57	People with disabilities (Table K12)
3555.S78	Students (Table K12)
3556.A-Z	Taxation of particular activities, A-Z
3556.E44	Electronic commerce (Table K12)

	Public finance
	National revenue
	Taxation -- Continued
3557	Tax saving. Tax avoidance (Table K11)
	For tax planning relating to a particular tax, see the tax
	Tax administration. Revenue service
3558	General (Table K11)
	National departments and agencies see KJ-KKZ1 3527.3.A+
	Financial courts see KJ-KKZ1 3682+
	Officers and personnel. Functionaries see KJ-KKZ1 3527.5
3559	Jurisdiction for tax allocation (Table K11)
	Including concurrent taxing powers of national and state government
	Double taxation see KJ-KKZ1 3552+
	Collection and enforcement
3560	General (Table K11)
	Tax accounting. Financial statements
	Including personal companies and stock companies, etc.
	For a particular tax, see the tax
3562	General (Table K11)
3562.5	Tax consultants (Table K11)
3563	Tax returns (Table K11)
3564.A-Z	Special topics, A-Z
	Subarrange each by Table K12
	Administrative acts
3565	General (Table K11)
3566	Assessment (Table K11)
3567	Tax remission. Delay granted for payment (Table K11)
	Administrative remedies see KJ-KKZ1 3683+
	Judicial review see KJ-KKZ1 3685+
3568	Tax auditing (Table K11)
	Cf. KJ-KKZ1 3701 Tax and customs investigation
3569	Default (Table K11)
	Including penalties
	Cf. KJ-KKZ1 3708 Tax and customs delinquency
3569.3	Tax credit (Table K11)
3569.5	Refunds (Table K11)
3570	Execution (Table K11)
	Cf. KJ-KKZ1 3701 Tax and customs investigation
3571.A-Z	Tax treatment of special activities, A-Z
3571.B35	Bankruptcy (Table K12)
3571.C73	Criminal activity (Table K12)
	Including fines and penalties
3571.D58	Divorce (Table K12)

KJ-KKZ1

	Public finance
	National revenue
	Taxation -- Continued
3572.A-Z	Classes of taxpayers or lines of business, A-Z
3572.A37	Agriculture. Horticulture (Table K12)
3572.C65	Construction industry (Table K12)
3572.H43	Health facilities (Table K12)
3572.H65	Homeowners (Table K12)
	Horticulture see KJ-KKZ1 3572.A37
	Income tax
	For state works on federal income tax see Table KJ-KKZ3 86.65
3573	General (Table K11)
3574	Tax planning. Estate planning (Table K11)
3575	Accounting and financial statements (Table K11)
3576	Assessment (Table K11)
3577	Tax returns (Table K11)
	Taxable income. Exemptions
3578	General (Table K11)
3578.5.A-Z	Particular, A-Z
	Capital gains see KJ-KKZ1 3578.5.P75
3578.5.D48	Deferred compensation (Table K12)
3578.5.P75	Profits. Capital gains (Table K12)
3578.5.T38	Tax-exempt securities (Table K12)
	Deductions
3579	General (Table K11)
3579.3	Amortization. Depreciation allowances (Table K11)
3580	Charitable or educational gifts and contributions (Table K11)
3580.5	Church tax (Table K11)
3581	Interest (Table K11)
	Expenses and losses
3582	General (Table K11)
3582.3.A-Z	Kinds of expenses, A-Z
	e. g.
3582.3.B88	Business expenses (Table K12)
3582.3.E38	Educational expenses (Table K12)
3582.3.E58	Entertainment expenses (Table K12)
3582.3.H62	Hobbies (Table K12)
3582.3.R48	Retirement contributions (Table K12)
	Surtaxes see KJ-KKZ1 3624+
	Salaries and wages
	Including fringe benefits, nonwage payments, etc.
3584	General (Table K11)
3585	Social security tax (Table K11)
3586.A-Z	Classes of taxpayers, A-Z
	Subarrange each by Table K12

	Public finance
	National revenue
	Taxation
	Income tax -- Continued
3588	Capital investment (Table K11)
	Including foreign investment
	Cf. KJ-KKZ1 3553+ Taxation as a measure of
	economic policy
3589	Pensions and annuities (Table K11)
3589.3.A-Z	Other sources of income, A-Z
	Commercial leases see KJ-KKZ1 3589.3.L43
3589.3.D35	Damages (Table K12)
3589.3.E88	Extinguishment of debts (Table K12)
3589.3.G36	Gambling gains (Table K12)
3589.3.I44	Illegal income (Table K12)
3589.3.I56	Intellectual property (Table K12)
	Including copyright, patents, and trademarks
3589.3.L43	Leases (Table K12)
	Including commercial leases
3589.3.L54	Life insurance proceeds (Table K12)
3589.3.U87	Usufruct (Table K12)
	Payment at source of income
	Payroll deduction. Withholding tax
3590	General (Table K11)
	Social security tax see KJ-KKZ1 3585
3591.A-Z	Classes of taxpayers or lines of business, A-Z
3591.A43	Agriculture. Forestry. Horticulture (Table K12)
3591.A44	Aliens (Table K12)
3591.A87	Artisans (Table K12)
3591.A88	Artists (Table K12)
3591.E83	Executives (Table K12)
3591.M37	Married couples (Table K12)
3591.M45	Merchant mariners (Table K12)
3591.P75	Professions (Table K12)
3591.T42	Teachers (Table K12)
	Corporation tax
	Including income of business organizations, business
	associations, and individual merchants
3592	General (Table K11)
	Nonprofit associations, nonprofit corporations,
	foundations (endowments), and pension trust funds
3593	General (Table K11)
3593.5.A-Z	Special topics, A-Z
3593.5.T39	Tax avoidance (Table K12)
	Personal companies (Unincorporated business
	associations)
3594	General (Table K11)

Public finance
National revenue
Taxation
Income tax
Corporation tax
Personal companies (Unincorporated business
associations) -- Continued
3594.5.A-Z   Special topics, A-Z
Subarrange each by Table K12
Cooperatives
3595   General (Table K11)
3595.5.A-Z   Special topics, A-Z
Subarrange each by Table K12
Stock companies (Incorporated business associations)
3596   General (Table K11)
3597   Tax accounting. Financial statements (Table K11)
3597.3   Assessment (Table K11)
3598   Tax returns (Table K11)
Taxable income. Exemptions
3599   General (Table K11)
3600.A-Z   Particular, A-Z
3600.C35   Capital stock (Table K12)
3600.D58   Dividends (Table K12)
3600.I58   Inventories (Table K12)
3600.L63   Loans (Table K12)
3600.P75   Profits (Table K12)
3600.R48   Reserves (Table K12)
Deductions
3602   General (Table K11)
3603   Depreciation of property, plant, and equipment
(Table K11)
3604   Pension reserves (Table K11)
Cf. KJ-KKZ1 3593+ Pension trust funds
3605   Charitable, religious, or educational gifts and
contributions (Table K11)
3605.5   Expenses and losses (Table K11)
Surtaxes see KJ-KKZ1 3624+
Corporate reorganization
3606   General (Table K11)
3607   Conversions (Table K11)
3608   Merger, fusion, and consolidation (Table K11)
3609   Liquidation (Table K11)
3610   Limited partnership (Table K11)
3611   Stock corporation (Table K11)
3612.A-Z   Other, A-Z
3612.B87   Business concern, holding company, and industrial
trusts (Table K12)

Public finance
  National revenue
    Taxation
      Income tax
        Corporation tax
          Other, A-Z -- Continued

3612.G68	Government business corporations (Table K12)
3613.A-Z	Lines of corporate business, A-Z
3613.B35	Banks. Credit institutions (Table K12)
3613.C65	Construction industry (Table K12)
	Credit institutions see KJ-KKZ1 3613.B35
3613.I58	Investment trusts. Real estate investment funds (Table K12)
	Real estate investment funds see KJ-KKZ1 3613.I58
3613.S45	Shipping (Table K12)
	Foreign corporations and stockholders
3614	General (Table K11)
	Double taxation see KJ-KKZ1 3552+
	Multi-national corporations
3615	General (Table K11)
	Double taxation see KJ-KKZ1 3552+
	Property tax. Taxation of capital
	For real property tax see KJ-KKZ1 3670+
	Cf. KJ-KKZ1 3663+ Property tax (State and local finance)
3616	General (Table K11)
3617	Taxation valuation (Table K11)
3618	Accounting. Financial statements (Table K11)
3619	Assessment (Table K11)
3620	Taxable property. Exemptions (Table K11)
3621	Estate, inheritance, and gift taxes (Table K11)
3622	Church tax (Table K11)
3623	Capital gain tax (Table K11)
	Development gains tax see KJ-KKZ1 3672
	Surtaxes
3624	General (Table K11)
3625	Excess profits tax (Table K11)
	Including war profits tax
3626	Unjust enrichment tax (Table K11)
	Poll tax see KJ-KKZ1 3680.P65
	Indirect taxation. Excise taxes. Taxes on transactions
3627	General (Table K11)
	Sales tax
3628	General (Table K11)
3629	Accounting (Table K11)
3630	Assessment (Table K11)
3631	Tax returns (Table K11)

	Public finance
	National revenue
	Taxation
	Excise taxes. Taxes on transactions
	Sales tax -- Continued
	Turnover tax
	Including value-added tax
3633	General (Table K11)
3634	Private use. Expenses (Table K11)
3635	Import sales and export sales (Table K11)
	Personal companies and stock companies
3637	General (Table K11)
3638	Municipal corporations (Table K11)
	Particular commodities, services, and transactions see KJ-KKZ1 3640.A+
3639	Government monopolies (Table K11)
	Including monopolies delegated by the state to others
3640.A-Z	Commodities, services, and transactions, A-Z
3640.A42	Alcoholic beverages (General) (Table K12)
3640.B35	Banking transactions (Table K12)
3640.B37	Bars and taverns (Table K12)
3640.B38	Betting (Bookmaking) (Table K12)
3640.B55	Bills of exchange tax (Table K12)
	Bonds see KJ-KKZ1 3640.S42
	Brandy see KJ-KKZ1 3640.L57
	Champagne see KJ-KKZ1 3640.W55
3640.D58	Distilleries (Table K12)
3640.E96	Export-import sales (Table K12)
	Gambling see KJ-KKZ1 3669
3640.H68	Hotels and motels (Table K12)
	Import sales see KJ-KKZ1 3640.E96
3640.L57	Liquors (Table K12)
3640.M38	Matches (Table K12)
	Motels see KJ-KKZ1 3640.H68
3640.M68	Motor fuels (Table K12)
3640.P48	Petroleum (Table K12)
3640.P82	Public utilities (Table K12)
	Real estate transactions see KJ-KKZ1 3670+
	Recycled products see KJ-KKZ1 3640.W36
3640.R47	Restaurants (Table K12)
3640.R48	Retail trade (Table K12)
3640.S42	Securities and bonds (Table K12)
3640.S76	Stock exchange transactions (Table K12)
	Taverns see KJ-KKZ1 3640.B37
3640.T62	Tobacco (Table K12)
3640.T72	Transportation of persons or goods (Table K12)
3640.W36	Waste products. Recycled products (Table K12)

	Public finance
	National revenue
	Taxation
	Excise taxes. Taxes on transactions
	Commodities, services, and transactions, A-Z --
	Continued
3640.W46	Wholesale trade (Table K12)
3640.W55	Wine (Table K12)
	Methods of assessment and collection
	For assessment and collection of a particular tax, see the tax
3642	General (Table K11)
	Stamp duties
3643	General (Table K11)
	Bills of exchange see KJ-KKZ1 3640.B55
	Criminal provisions see KJ-KKZ1 3693+
	Customs. Tariff
	For foreign trade regulations see KJ-KKZ1 3407+
3645	General (Table K11)
	Tables see KJ-KKZ1 3645+
	Trade agreements
3646	General (Table K11)
3647	Favored nation clause (Table K11)
	Customs organization and administration
3648	General (Table K11)
3649	Officers and personnel (Table K11)
	Including tenure, salaries, pensions, etc.
3650	Jurisdiction. Custom territory (Table K11)
	Practice and procedure
	Including remedies and enforcement
3651	General (Table K11)
3651.3	Duty by weight (Table K11)
3652	Custom appraisal (Table K11)
3653.A-Z	Commodities and services, A-Z
3653.A37	Agricultural commodities. Farm products (Table K12)
3653.A57	Aircraft (Table K12)
	Farm produce see KJ-KKZ1 3653.A37
3653.M6	Motor vehicles (Table K12)
3654	Costs. Fees (Table K11)
	Criminal provisions see KJ-KKZ1 3693+
	State and local finance
	For the public finance of an individual state, administrative district, or municipality, see the state or municipality
	Finance reform see KJ-KKZ1 3525+
3655	General (Table K11)
3656	Budget. Expenditure control (Table K11)
	Including accounting and auditing

Public finance

State and local finance -- Continued

3657   Public debts. Loans (Table K11)

3658   Intergovernmental fiscal relations (Table K11)
                    Class here works on local taxes shared by state and locality
                    For state taxes shared by state and national government
                         see KJ-KKZ1 3533

3659   Fees. Fines (Table K11)
                    Including license fees

Taxation

3660   General (Table K11)

3661   Jurisdiction for tax allocation (Table K11)
                    For concurrent taxing powers of national government
                         and states see KJ-KKZ1 3559

          Tax administration see KJ-KKZ1 3558+

          Income tax see KJ-KKZ1 3573+

          Sales, turnover, and value-added taxes see KJ-KKZ1
               3628+

3662   Estate, inheritance, and gift taxes (Table K11)

          Property tax. Taxation of capital
                    Including juristic persons and business enterprises
                    For real property tax see KJ-KKZ1 3670+

3663   General (Table K11)

          Tax valuation

3664   General (Table K11)

3664.5.A-Z   Particular industries or industrial properties, A-Z
                    Subarrange each by Table K12

3665   Accounting. Financial statements (Table K11)

3665.5   Assessment (Table K11)

3665.7   Tax returns (Table K11)

3666   Taxable property (Table K11)

3667   Deductions (Table K11)

3668   Motor vehicles tax (Table K11)

3669   Taxes from gambling tables. Casinos (Table K11)

          Real property tax
                    Including real estate transactions

3670   General (Table K11)

3671   Valuation of real property. Assessment (Table K11)

3672   Capital gains tax (Table K11)
                    Including development gains

3673.A-Z   Properties, A-Z
                    Subarrange each by Table K12

          Business tax

3674   General (Table K11)

3675   Assessment (Table K11)

3676   Tax returns (Table K11)

3677   Taxable income (Table K11)

	Public finance
	State and local finance
	Taxation
	Business tax -- Continued
3678	Deductions (Table K11)
3679.A-Z	Classes of taxpayers or lines of business, A-Z
	Subarrange each by Table K12
3680.A-Z	Other taxes, A-Z
3680.B53	Bicycle tax (Table K12)
3680.P65	Poll tax (Table K12)
	Tax and customs courts and procedure
	Class here works on national courts, national, state and district courts and boards, or courts and boards of several states or administrative districts
	For courts and boards (several or individual) of an individual state or administrative district, see the state or district
3682	General (Table K11)
	Pretrial procedures. Administrative remedies
3683	General (Table K11)
3684	Tax protest (Table K11)
	Procedure at first instance. Judicial review
3685	General (Table K11)
3685.5	Jurisdiction (Table K11)
3686	Actions. Defenses (Table K11)
3687	Evidence (Table K11)
3688	Judicial decisions. Judgments (Table K11)
	Including court records
	Remedies. Means of review
3689	General (Table K11)
3690	Appellate procedures (Table K11)
3691	Special procedures (Table K11)
	Refunds see KJ-KKZ1 3569.5
	Tax credit see KJ-KKZ1 3569.3
	Tax and customs crimes and delinquency. Procedure
3693	General (Table K11)
	Individual offenses
3695	Tax evasion and tax avoidance (Table K11)
3696	Receiving bootleg merchandise (Table K11)
3697	Violation of confidential disclosure (Table K11)
	Including denunciation
	Smuggling of contraband see KJ-KKZ1 3695
3698	Organized smuggling (Table K11)
3699	Forgery of seals, stamps, etc. (Table K11)
	Procedure
	For criminal procedure in general see KJ-KKZ1 4600.9+
	General see KJ-KKZ1 3693
	Pretrial procedures

Public finance
Tax and customs crimes and delinquency. Procedure
Procedure
Pretrial procedure -- Continued

3700	General (Table K11)
3701	Tax and customs investigation (Table K11)
3703	Evidence (Table K11)
3704	Special procedures in criminal tax cases (Table K11)
3705	Amnesty. Pardon (Table K11)
3708	Tax and customs delinquency (Table K11)
	Including faulty accounting and bookkeeping, etc.

Government measures in time of war, national emergency, or
economic crisis

3709	General (Table K11)

Particular measures

3710	Military requisitions from civilians. Requisitioned land (Table K11)
	For damages and compensation see KJ-KKZ1 3727+
3712	Control of property. Confiscations (Table K11)
	Including enemy and alien property
	For damages and compensation see KJ-KKZ1 3727+

Control of unemployment. Manpower control

3714	General (Table K11)
3715	Compulsory and forced labor (Table K11)
3717	Insolvent debtors. Wartime and crisis relief (Table K11)
	For composition and deferment of execution see KJ-KKZ1 1972+
	For moratorium see KJ-KKZ1 1975
	For agricultural credits see KJ-KKZ1 3322
3719	Finances (Table K11)
	For special levies see KJ-KKZ1 3625
	For procurement and defense contracts see KJ-KKZ1 3730+

Industrial priorities and allocations. Economic recovery
measures. Nationalization

3720	General (Table K11)
3721.A-Z	By industry or commodity, A-Z
	Subarrange each by Table K12

Strategic material. Stockpiling

3722	General (Table K11)
3723.A-Z	By commodity, A-Z
3723.P46	Petroleum products (Table K12)

Rationing. Price control

3724	General (Table K11)
3725.A-Z	By commodity, A-Z
	Subarrange each by Table K12
3726	Criminal provisions (Table K11)

                    Government measures in time of war, national emergency, or
                        economic crisis -- Continued
                    War damage compensation
                        Including foreign claims settlement
3727   General (Table K11)
3729.A-Z   Particular claims, A-Z
                        Confiscations see KJ-KKZ1 3729.R47
                        Demontage see KJ-KKZ1 3729.R46
                        Military occupation damages see KJ-KKZ1 3729.R47
3729.P47   Personal damages. Property loss or damages (Table K12)
                    Property loss or damages see KJ-KKZ1 3729.P47
3729.R46   Reparations. Demontage (Table K12)
3729.R47   Requisitions. Confiscations. Military occupation damages
                        (Table K12)
3729.5.A-Z   Particular victims, A-Z
                        Subarrange each by Table K12
                    Military occupation. Procurement
3730   General (Table K11)
3732.A-Z   Particular, A-Z
                        Subarrange each by Table K12
                        Military occupation damages see KJ-KKZ1 3729.R47
                National defense. Military law
                    For emergency and wartime legislation see KJ-KKZ1 3709+
3735   General (Table K11)
3737   Organization and administration. Command (Table K11)
                    The armed forces
3738   General (Table K11)
                    Compulsory service
                        Including draft and selective service
3739   General (Table K11)
                    Deferment
                        Including disqualification
3740   General (Table K11)
3741.A-Z   Particular groups, A-Z
                        e. g.
3741.A44   Aliens (Table K12)
3741.C65   Conscientious objectors (Table K12)
3742   Discharge (Table K11)
3744   Disability pensions. Rehabilitation (Table K11)
3745   Equipment (Table K11)
                        Including weapons, plants, and installations
3746   Hospitals (Table K11)
3747   Postal services (Table K11)
3748.A-Z   Particular branches of service, A-Z
                        Civil guards see KJ-KKZ1 3748.P37
                        Military police see KJ-KKZ1 3748.P37

National defense. Military law
  The armed forces
    Compulsory service
      Particular branches of service, A-Z -- Continued

3748.P37	Paramilitary defense forces. Civil guards. Military police (Table K12)
3749	Auxiliary services during war or emergency (Table K11)
3750	Civil status and rights of military personnel (Table K11)

  Civil defense

3752	General (Table K11)
3753	Air defense. Air raid shelters (Table K11)
3754	Evacuation (Table K11)

    Participation in NATO or Warsaw Pact
      For NATO (General) or Warsaw Pact (General), see subclass KZ

3756	General (Table K11)
3757	Military expenditures and contributions (Table K11)
	Cf. KJ-KKZ1 3710 Military occupation and procurement
3757.5	Foreign armed forces (Table K11)
	Including damages

  Military criminal law and procedure
    Cf. KJ-KKZ1 4470+ Crimes against national defense

3758	General (Table K11)
3758.5	Illegality and justification. Superior orders (Table K11)

    Individual offenses

3760	Desertion (Table K11)
3761	Incitement. Mutiny (Table K11)
3762	Insubordination (Table K11)
3763	Self-mutilation. Malingering (Table K11)
3764	Calumny. Assault on subordinates (Table K11)
3765	Sabotaging weapons, equipment or means of defense (Table K11)
3767.A-Z	Other, A-Z
3767.D7	Draft evasion (Table K12)
	Firearms, Illegal use of see KJ-KKZ1 3767.I45
3767.G38	Guard duty offenses (Table K12)
3767.I45	Illegal use of firearms (Table K12)

    Courts and procedure

3770	General (Table K11)
3771	Procedure in honor cases (Table K11)
3775	Punishment. Execution (Table K11)
3777	Probation and parole (Table K11)
3779.A-Z	Particular trials. By name of defendant, A-Z
	Subarrange each by Table K12

  Military discipline. Law enforcement
    Including all branches of the armed forces

3780	General (Table K11)

	National defense. Military law
	Military discipline. Law enforcement -- Continued
3782	Superior orders. Enforcement of orders (Table K11)
3783	Procedure (Table K11)
3785.A-Z	Other, A-Z
3785.M55	Military maneuvers (Table K12)
	Criminal law
3790	Reform of criminal law, procedure, and execution

> For works limited to a particular subject, see the subject. For works pertaining exclusively to the codes, see the code
> For reform of criminal justice administration see KJ-KKZ1 471

	Administration of criminal justice see KJ-KKZ1 1571.2+
3791-3800	General (Table K9c)
3810	Constitutional aspects (Table K11)
	Philosophy of criminal law
3812	General (Table K11)
	Theories of punishment. Criminal policy see KJ-KKZ1 3950+
3813	Ideological theories of criminal law (Table K11)
3816.A-Z	Special topics, A-Z
	Subarrange each by Table K12
	Relationship of criminal law to other disciplines, subjects or phenomena
3818	Criminal law and society
	Cf. HV6115+ , Social pathology
3819	Criminal law and psychology
	Cf. HV6080+ , Criminal psychology
3821	Interpretation and construction. Legal hermeneutics
3823.A-Z	Terms and phrases, A-Z
3823.F67	Force
	Including force by use of drugs and hypnosis
3823.H64	Honor
	Concepts and principles
3824	General (Table K11)
	Applicability and validity of the law
3825	General (Table K11)
	Nulla poena sine lege. Nullum crimen sine lege
3826	General (Table K11)
3827	Retroactivity. Ex post facto laws (Table K11)
3828	Interpretation. Analogy (Table K11)
3829	Customary law (Table K11)
	Alternative conviction see KJ-KKZ1 4748
	Territorial applicability
3830	General (Table K11)
	Place of commission of crime
3831	General (Table K11)

KJ-KKZ1

Criminal law
  Concepts and principles
    Applicability and validity of the law
      Territorial applicability
        Place of commission of crime -- Continued
(3832)   Press delicts
                  see KJ-KKZ1 3508+
(3833)   Crimes aboard aircraft
                  see KJ-KKZ1 4396
3835   Conflict of laws (Table K11)
      Temporal applicability
3836   General (Table K11)
3837   Intertemporal law (Table K11)
3838   Personal applicability. Immunities (Table K11)
    Criminal offense
3840   General (Table K11)
3841   Trichotomy and dichotomy (Table K11)
                Including felony, misdemeanor, and transgression
3842   Crimes by commission or omission (Table K11)
3844   Crimes aggravated by personal characteristics (Table K11)
      Criminal act
3845   General (Table K11)
3847   Corpus delicti. Fact-pattern conformity (Table K11)
3849   Omission (Table K11)
        Causation
3851   General (Table K11)
3852   Proximate cause (Table K11)
          Forms of the act see KJ-KKZ1 3911.2+
      Illegality. Justification of otherwise illegal acts
3855   General (Table K11)
3856   Self-defense or defense of another (Table K11)
3857   Necessity (Table K11)
          Superior orders see KJ-KKZ1 3900
3859   Duty to act (Legal authority or duty) (Table K11)
        Consent of the injured party
3861   General (Table K11)
3862   Assumption of risk (Table K11)
3863   Presumed consent (Table K11)
3865.A-Z   Other grounds for justification, A-Z
                  Subarrange each by Table K12
3867   Criminal intent. Mens rea (Table K11)
                Including purpose and scienter, dolus, eventualis, actio libera
                  in causa, etc.
        Negligence and wantonness
3874   General (Table K11)
3876   Foresight. Standard of conduct (Table K11)
        Criminal liability. Guilt

Criminal law
  Concepts and principles
    Criminal offense
      Criminal liability. Guilt -- Continued
3878   General (Table K11)
            Capacity
3880   General (Table K11)
              Incapacity and limited capacity
3882   General (Table K11)
3884   Insane persons. People with mental or emotional
                    disabilities (Table K11)
                    Cf. HV6133 Psychopathology and crime
                Minors
3886   General (Table K11)
3888   Infants (Table K11)
3890   Juveniles. Young adults (Table K11)
3892.A-Z   Special topics, A-Z
3892.D58   Distemper (Table K12)
3892.I58   Intoxication (Table K12)
3892.L58   Litigious paranoia (Table K12)
                  Passion see KJ-KKZ1 3892.D58
3895   Criminal liability of juristic persons (Table K11)
3897   Exculpating circumstances (Table K11)
3900   Superior orders and justification or excusation (Table K11)
                Cf. KJ-KKZ1 3758.5 Military criminal law
            Error
3902   General (Table K11)
3904   Error about fact (Table K11)
3906   Error about grounds for justification or excusation (Table
                K11)
3908   Other (Table K11)
                Including error about extenuating circumstances, error in
                  persona, error in objecto, aberratio ictus, etc.
          Forms of the criminal act
            Omission see KJ-KKZ1 3849
            Attempt
3912   General (Table K11)
3913   Intent and preparation (Table K11)
3914   Inherently ineffective act (Table K11)
3917   Active repentance (Table K11)
                Accessory at attempted crime see KJ-KKZ1 3931
            Perpetrators
3920   General (Table K11)
              Principals and accessories
3922   General (Table K11)
3924   Liability of each participant (Table K11)
3925   Co-principals (Table K11)

Criminal law
  Concepts and principles
    Criminal offense
      Forms of the criminal act
        Perpetrators
          Principal and accessories -- Continued

3927	Accessory before the fact (Table K11)
	Including abettor
3929	Accessory after the fact (Table K11)
3931	Accessory at attempted crime (Table K11)
3933	Complicity (Table K11)
3934	Agent provocateur (Table K11)
3936	Juristic persons. Corporations (Table K11)
(3938)	Aggravating and extenuating circumstances
	see KJ-KKZ1 4022+
3940	Compound offenses and compound punishment (Table K11)
	Civil liability for wrongful acts see KJ-KKZ1 834+

Punishment
3946	General (Table K11)
3948	Constitutional aspects (Table K11)

Theory and policy of punishment
3950	General (Table K11)
3952	Retaliation. Retribution (Table K11)
3954	Safeguarding the social and political system (Table K11)
3956	General and special prevention (Table K11)
	Including education, rehabilitation, and resocialization of perpetrator
	Criminal anthropology
	see HV6030+
3960	Criminal sociology (Table K11)
	For non-legal works, see HV6030+

Penalties and measures of rehabilitation and safety
  For juveniles and young adults see KJ-KKZ1 4726+
  For execution of sentence see KJ-KKZ1 4794.2+
3962	General (Table K11)
3964	Capital punishment (Table K11)
	Imprisonment
	Including maximum and minimum terms
3970	General (Table K11)
	Prisons and jails see KJ-KKZ1 4824
	Reformatories see KJ-KKZ1 3986; KJ-KKZ1 4732
3972	Short-term sentence (Table K11)
3974	Sentencing to probation (Punishment without imprisonment). Conditional sentencing (Table K11)
	Including terms of probation, e.g. education and resocialization through labor

	Criminal law
	Punishment
	Penalties and measures of rehabilitation and safety -- Continued
3978	Fines (Table K11)
3980	Reprimand (Table K11)
	Measures entailing deprivation of liberty
3982	General (Table K11)
3984	Commitment to medical or psychiatric treatment (Table K11)
3986	Commitment to nursing or socio-therapeutic institutions (Table K11)
3990	Commitment of addicts to institutions for withdrawal treatment (Table K11)
3992	Protective custody (Table K11)
	Including dangerous or habitual criminals
	Other measures
3995	Protective surveillance (Table K11)
3997	Expulsion (Table K11)
4000	Driver's license revocation (Table K11)
4002	Prohibition against practicing a profession (Table K11)
4004	Loss of civil rights. Infamy. Disfranchisement (Table K11)
4006	Property confiscation (Table K11)
4008	Confiscation and destruction of corpus delicti (Table K11)
4010	Forfeiture (Table K11)
	Sentencing and determining the measure of punishment
4012	General (Table K11)
4016	Fixed and indeterminate sentence (Table K11)
	Juvenile delinquents see KJ-KKZ1 4722
	Circumstances influencing measures of penalty
4020	General (Table K11)
	Aggravating and extenuating circumstances
	Including principals and accessories
4022	General (Table K11)
4024	Recidivism (Table K11)
4026	Detention pending investigation (Table K11)
	Causes barring prosecution or execution of sentence
4030	General (Table K11)
4032	Active repentance (Table K11)
	Pardon and amnesty. Clemency
4034	General (Table K11)
	Suspension of punishment see KJ-KKZ1 4828
	Probation and parole see KJ-KKZ1 4830+
	Limitation of actions
4038	General (Table K11)
4040.A-Z	Crimes exempt from limitation of action, A-Z

KJ-KKZ1

Criminal law
  Punishment
    Causes barring prosecution or execution of sentence
      Limitation of actions
        Crimes exempt from limitation of action, A-Z -- Continued

4040.C74	Crimes against humanity and human rights (Table K12)
4040.T73	Treasonable endangering of the peace (Table K12)
4040.W37	War crimes (Table K12)

          Criminal registers see KJ-KKZ1 4845
          Criminal statistics see KJ-KKZ1 31+
  Individual offenses

4048	General (Table K11)

    Offenses against the person
      Including aggravating circumstances

4049	General (Table K11)

      Homicide

4050	General (Table K11)
4052	Murder (Table K11)
4054	Manslaughter (Table K11)
4056	Killing on request (Table K11)
4058	Euthanasia. Right to die. Living wills (Table K11)
4060	Suicide. Aiding and abetting suicide (Table K11)
4062	Parricide (Table K11)
4064	Infanticide (Table K11)
4065	Negligent homicide (Table K11)
4067	Desertion. Exposing persons to mortal danger (Table K11)

      Crimes against inchoate life. Illegal abortion

4070	General (Table K11)
4072	Justification of abortion. Legal abortion (Table K11)

        Including ethical, social, medical and eugenic aspects
        For birth control and family planning see KJ-KKZ1
         3124+
      Crimes against physical inviolability

4074	General (Table K11)
4076	Battery (Table K11)
4076.5	Stalking (Table K11)
4078	Communicating venereal disease (Table K11)
4080	Failure to render assistance (Table K11)
4082	Abuse of defenseless persons or dependents. Abuse of older people (Table K11)

        For child abuse see KJ-KKZ1 4190
      Consent. Justified assault
        Cf. KJ-KKZ1 3861+ Criminal law concepts

4084	General (Table K11)
4086	Sports injuries (Table K11)

        Cf. KJ-KKZ1 848+ Torts

Criminal law
  Individual offenses
    Offenses against the person
      Crimes against physical inviolability
        Consent. Justified assault -- Continued
          Medical treatment and operations see KJ-KKZ1 4096+

4088	Compound offenses (Table K11)
4090	Poisoning (Table K11)
4092	Dueling (Table K11)
4094	Brawling (Table K11)

          Criminal aspects of surgical and other medical treatment
            Including biomedical engineering and medical technology

4096	General (Table K11)
4100	Malpractice (Table K11)
	Cf. KJ-KKZ1 3100.4 Medical legislation
4102	Treatment without consent (Table K11)
	Euthanasia see KJ-KKZ1 4058
4103	Genetic engineering (Table K11)
4108	Human reproductive technology (Table K11)
	Including artificial insemination, fertilization in vitro, etc.
4110	Transplantation of organs, tissues, etc. (Table K11)
	Including donation of organs, tissues, etc.
4112	Sterilization (Table K11)
4113	Autopsy (Table K11)
	Confidential communication see KJ-KKZ1 4696.A+
	Psychopharmaca damages see KJ-KKZ1 4100

        Crimes against personal freedom

4116	General (Table K11)
	Force see KJ-KKZ1 3823.F67
4118	False imprisonment (Table K11)
4120	Extortionate kidnapping (Table K11)

          Abduction
            Cf. KJ-KKZ1 602+ Parental kidnapping

4125	General (Table K11)
4127	Political abduction (Table K11)
4130	Abduction of a woman without her consent (Table K11)
4132	Abduction of a female minor (Table K11)
4134	Political accusation (Table K11)
4136	Threats of a felonious injury (Table K11)
4138	Duress (Table K11)
4140	Unlawful entry (Table K11)

        Crimes against dignity and honor
          Including juristic persons and families

4143	General (Table K11)
	Honor see KJ-KKZ1 3823.H64
4145	Insult (Table K11)
4147	Defamation (Table K11)

KJ-KKZ1

Criminal law
　Individual offenses
　　Offenses against the person
　　　Crimes against dignity and honor -- Continued
4149　　　　Calumny (Table K11)
4152　　　　Disparagement of memory of the dead (Table K11)
4154　　　　Defamatory statement and truth (Table K11)
4156　　　　Privileged comment (Table K11)
　　　　　　　Including criticism of scientific, artistic, or professional
　　　　　　　　accomplishments
　　　　　　　For press law see KJ-KKZ1 3510.6
　　　　Violation of personal privacy and secrets
　　　　　Cf. KJ-KKZ1 843+ Torts
4160　　　　General (Table K11)
4162　　　　Constitutional aspects (Table K11)
4164　　　　Violation of confidential disclosures by professional
　　　　　　　persons (Table K11)
4166　　　　Opening of letters (Table K11)
4168　　　　Eavesdropping. Wiretapping (Table K11)
　　　Offenses against religious tranquility and the peace of the
　　　　dead
4170　　　　General (Table K11)
4172　　　　Blasphemy (Table K11)
4174　　　　Disturbing a religious observance (Table K11)
4176　　　　Disturbing the peace of the dead (Table K11)
　　　　　　Including cemeteries and funerals
　　　Offenses against marriage, family, and family status
4180　　　　General (Table K11)
4182　　　　Incest (Table K11)
4184　　　　Adultery (Table K11)
4186　　　　Bigamy (Table K11)
(4188)　　　Abduction of a minor from legal custodian. Parental
　　　　　　kidnapping
　　　　　　　see KJ-KKZ1 602+
4190　　　　Abandonment, neglect, or abuse of a child (Table K11)
4192　　　　Breach of duty of support (Table K11)
4194　　　　Breach of duty of assistance to a pregnant woman (Table
　　　　　　K11)
　　　　　Abortion see KJ-KKZ1 4070+
　　　　　Artificial insemination see KJ-KKZ1 4108
4196　　　　Falsification of civil status (Table K11)
　　　Offenses against sexual integrity
4200　　　　General (Table K11)
4202　　　　Rape (Table K11)
　　　　Compelling lewd acts
4203　　　　General (Table K11)

Criminal law
Individual offenses
Offenses against sexual integrity
Compelling lewd acts -- Continued
4204   Lewd acts with persons incapable of resistance (Table K11)
4206   Abduction for lewd acts (Table K11)
4208   Lewd acts with children or charges. Seduction (Table K11)
4210   Lewd acts by persons taking advantage of official position (Table K11)
4212   Lewd acts in institutions (Table K11)
4216   Sodomy. Homosexual acts (Table K11)
4218   Bestiality (Table K11)
4220   Obscenity (Table K11)
                  Including production, exhibition, performance, advertising, etc.
4222   Prostitution and solicitation (Table K11)
                  Pandering and pimping
4224   General (Table K11)
4225   White slave traffic (Table K11)
                  Offenses against private and public property
4230   General (Table K11)
                  Larceny and embezzlement
4234   General (Table K11)
4236   Burglary (Table K11)
4238   Armed theft and theft by gangs (Table K11)
4240   Pilfering (Table K11)
4242   Domestic and family theft (Table K11)
4244   Automobile theft (Table K11)
                      Including automotive vehicles and their unauthorized use
4246   Energy theft (Table K11)
                      Embezzlement
4250   General (Table K11)
4252   Embezzlement in office (Table K11)
4254   Robbery and rapacious theft (Table K11)
4256   Destruction of property and conversion (Table K11)
                      Fraud
4258   General (Table K11)
4260   Fraudulent insurance claims (Table K11)
4262   Fraud by litigation (Table K11)
4263   Credit card fraud (Table K11)
                          Fraudulent bankruptcy see KJ-KKZ1 4276
4264   Extortion (Table K11)
4266   Breach of trust (Table K11)
4268   Usury (Table K11)
                      Defeating rights of creditors

KJ-KKZ1

	Criminal law
	Individual offenses
	Offenses against private and public property
	Defeating rights of creditors -- Continued
4270	General (Table K11)
4272	Defeating rights of pledgee (Table K11)
4274	Defeating execution (Table K11)
4276	Fraudulent bankruptcy (Table K11)
4280	Game and fish poaching (Table K11)
	Aiding criminals in securing benefits
4282	General (Table K11)
4284	Receiving stolen goods (Table K11)
	Offenses against the national economy
4286	General (Table K11)
4290	Violation of price regulations (Table K11)
	Including price fixing, hoarding, discrimination, overselling and underselling prices established by government etc.
4292	Foreign exchange violations (Table K11)
4294	Economic and industrial secrets. Unauthorized possession or disclosure (Table K11)
	Cf. KJ-KKZ1 1257.E86 Industrial espionage
4298	False statements concerning national planning (Table K11)
	Counterfeiting money and stamps see KJ-KKZ1 4346+
	Offenses against public property see KJ-KKZ1 4230+
4300.A-Z	Other, A-Z
	Subarrange each by Table K12
	Tax and customs crimes see KJ-KKZ1 3693+
	Offenses against public order and convenience
	Including aggravating circumstances
	Disrupting the peace of the community
4305	General (Table K11)
4307	Inciting insubordination (Table K11)
4309	Rowdyism. Vandalism (Table K11)
4310	Inciting crime (Table K11)
4312	Rewarding or approving felonies (Table K11)
4314	Criminal societies (Table K11)
4316	Parasitism (Table K11)
4320	Demonstrations and failure to disperse (Table K11)
4322	Inciting acts against minorities (Table K11)
	Threatening the community. Terrorist activities see KJ-KKZ1 4351.5+
4324	Misuse of titles, uniforms, and insignia (Table K11)
	Crimes against security of legal and monetary transactions and documents
4330	General (Table K11)
4332	Evidence (Table K11)
4334	Forgery and suppression of documents (Table K11)

Criminal law
  Individual offenses
    Offenses against public order and convenience
      Crimes against security of legal and monetary transactions
        and documents -- Continued

4338	Forgery and suppression of mechanical records (Table K11)
	Including forgery of sound recordings and electronic data bases
4340	Physical and identifying marks
	Counterfeiting money and stamps
	Including postage stamps
4346	General (Table K11)
4348	Passing counterfeit money (Table K11)
4350	Counterfeiting securities (Table K11)
	Including checks, bills of exchange, etc.
	Customs crimes see KJ-KKZ1 3693+
	Tax evasion see KJ-KKZ1 3695
4351.A-Z	Other, A-Z
4351.B55	Blanks (Table K12)
4351.D57	Displacing boundaries (Table K12)
4351.F34	False certification (Table K12)
4351.F35	False medical certificates (Table K12)
4351.F67	Forgery of art works (Table K12)
4351.M57	Misuse of credentials (Table K12)
	Money orders see KJ-KKZ1 4351.T44
4351.T44	Telegrams. Money orders (Table K12)
	Crimes involving danger to the community. Crimes against the environment. Terrorism
4351.5	General (Table K11)
4352	Common danger (Table K11)
4354	Arson (Table K11)
4356	Causing explosion (Table K11)
	Including explosives and nuclear energy
4358	Misuse of ionizing radiation (Table K11)
4360	Releasing natural forces (Table K11)
	Including flood, avalanche, rockfall, etc.
4362	Dangerous use of poisonous substances (Table K11)
4364	Poisoning wells or soil (Table K11)
4366	Poisoning food, medicine, etc. (Table K11)
4368	Spreading communicable diseases, morbific agents, or parasites (Table K11)
4370	Damaging water and power installations (Table K11)
4372	Impairing industrial safety appliances (Table K11)
4374	Sabotage of essential services, utilities, warning systems, etc. (Table K11)

Criminal law
Individual offenses
Offenses against public order and convenience
Crimes involving danger to the community. Crimes against the environment -- Continued

4376	Causing danger in construction (Table K11)
	Including collapse, faulty gas or electric installation, etc.
4378	Human trafficking. Human smuggling (Table K11)
	Crimes affecting traffic
4380	Dangerous interference with rail, ship, or air traffic
4382	Unsafe operation of a rail vehicle, ship, or aircraft (Table K11)
	Dangerous interference with street traffic
	For minor traffic violations resulting in fines see KJ-KKZ1 3450+
4384	General (Table K11)
4386	Driving while intoxicated (Table K11)
4388	Duress. Constraint (Table K11)
4390	Leaving the scene of an accident. Hit-and-run driving (Table K11)
	Predatory assault on motorists
4392	General (Table K11)
4394	Assault on taxicab drivers (Table K11)
4396	Crimes aboard aircraft. Air piracy (Table K11)
4398	Riots (Table K11)
	Crimes against public health
4400	General (Table K11)
4402	Intoxication (Table K11)
4404	Illicit use of, possession of, and traffic in narcotics (Table K11)
	Communicating venereal diseases see KJ-KKZ1 4078
4406	Gambling (Table K11)
	Including illegal operation of a lottery or games of chance, and participation
	Cf. KJ-KKZ1 3036.5.G35 Police and public safety
	Acts of annoyance to the public see KJ-KKZ1 3005.A+
	Offenses against the government. Political offenses.
	Offenses against the peace
4415	General (Table K11)
	High treason and treason
4417	General (Table K11)
	High treason against the state
	Including national and state (republic, etc.)
4420	General (Table K11)
4422	Preparation of treasonable acts (Table K11)
4424	Treason against the constitution (Table K11)
4426	Assault on the head of state (Table K11)

	Criminal law
	Individual offenses
	Offenses against the government. Political offenses.
	Offenses against the peace
	High treason against the state -- Continued
4428	Inciting treason (Table K11)
4430	Preparation of despotism (Table K11)
4432	Sabotage endangering the state (Table K11)
4434	Undermining the state apparatus (Table K11)
4438	Lese majesty (Table K11)
4440	Disparagement of the state and its symbols. Disparaging constitutional organs (Table K11)
4442	Treasonable espionage (Table K11)
	For publication of official secrets by the press see KJ-KKZ1 3510.7
4444	Subversive activities (Table K11)
4446	Intelligence activities (Table K11)
4448	Propaganda endangering the state (Table K11)
4455	Treasonable endangering of the peace or of international relations (Table K11)
	Including propaganda, planning, preparation, or participation in an aggressive war
	Crimes in connection with election and voting
4458	General (Table K11)
4460	Bribery. Corrupt practices (Table K11)
4462	Coercing (Table K11)
4464	Deceiving voters (Table K11)
4466	Falsifying votes and voting results (Table K11)
4468	Obstructing voting (Table K11)
	Crimes against national defense
4470	General (Table K11)
4473	Sabotaging and depicting means of defense (Table K11)
	Opposition to power of the state
4476	General (Table K11)
4478	Constraining official action or inaction (Table K11)
4480	Prison escape. Mutiny. Freeing prisoners (Table K11)
4482.A-Z	Other forms of opposition, A-Z
4482.D35	Damaging official announcements (Table K12)
	Endangering the administration of justice. Obstruction of justice
4483	General (Table K11)
	False testimony
4484	General (Table K11)
4486	False unsworn testimony (Table K11)
4490	Perjury (Table K11)
4492	False affirmation (Table K11)
4494	Causing false testimony (Table K11)

Criminal law
 Individual offenses
  Offenses against the government. Political offenses.
   Offenses against the peace
   Endangering the administration of justice. Obstruction of
    justice -- Continued

4496	False accusation (Table K11)
4498	Bringing false complaint (Table K11)
4500	Thwarting criminal justice (Table K11)
4502	Failure to report felony. Misprision (Table K11)
4504	Coercion of testimony (Table K11)
4506	Intentional misconstruction by law officers (Table K11)
4507	Prosecuting innocent persons (Table K11)
	Including execution
	Chicanery and abuse of legal process see KJ-KKZ1 444.7
4508	Repressing conflicting interests. Prevarication (Table K11)
4510	Contempt of court (Table K11)
	For contempt of court by the press see KJ-KKZ1 3511
	Receiving stolen goods see KJ-KKZ1 4284
	Assisting in securing benefits see KJ-KKZ1 4282+
	Crimes against the civil service
4514	General (Table K11)
	Corruption
4516	General (Table K11)
4518	Corrupt act by officials. Accepting benefits (Table K11)
	Including omission of official acts
4520	Bribery. Granting benefits to civil servants (Table K11)
4522	Illegal compensation to arbitrators (Table K11)
	Bribery in connection with election see KJ-KKZ1 4460
	Embezzlement see KJ-KKZ1 4252
	Violating official secrecy
4526	General (Table K11)
4528	Disclosing official secrets (Table K11)
4530	Mail and telecommunication (Table K11)
4532.A-Z	Other, A-Z
	Subarrange each by Table K12
	Crimes against humanity
4538	General (Table K11)
4540	Genocide (Table K11)
4543	Crimes against foreign states, supranational institutions, or international institutions (Table K11)
4545	War crimes (Table K11)
	Offenses commited through the mail
4548	General (Table K11)

Criminal law
  Individual offenses
    Offenses committed through the mail
      Obscenity see KJ-KKZ1 4220
      Threats, extortion, and blackmail see KJ-KKZ1 4264
    Business associations criminal provisions see KJ-KKZ1 1153
    Labor law criminal provisions see KJ-KKZ1 1375
    Social insurance criminal provisions see KJ-KKZ1 1502
    Radio communication criminal provisions see KJ-KKZ1
      3498+
    Press law criminal provisions see KJ-KKZ1 3507+
    Tax and customs crimes see KJ-KKZ1 3693+
    Military criminal law see KJ-KKZ1 3758+
  Criminal procedure
    For works on both criminal and civil procedure, including
      codes of both criminal and civil procedure see KJ-KKZ1
      1650+
    For works on both criminal law and criminal procedure,
      including codes of both criminal law and criminal
      procedure see KJ-KKZ1 3790+
    Criticism and reform see KJ-KKZ1 3790

4601-4610	General (Table K9c)
4612	Constitutional aspects (Table K11)
4614	Criminal procedure and public opinion (Table K11)
	Including trial by newspaper
4616	Sociology of criminal procedure (Table K11)
	Including scandals
	Administration of criminal justice see KJ-KKZ1 1571.2+
	Court organization see KJ-KKZ1 1580+
	Procedural principles
4620	Due process of law (Table K11)
4622	Uniformity of law application. Stare decisis (Table K11)
	Prohibition of abuse of legal process. Chicanery see KJ-KKZ1 444.7
4624	Accusation principle (Table K11)
4626	Publicity and oral procedure (Table K11)
4628	Prejudicial actions (Table K11)
	Including all branches of the law
4630.A-Z	Parties to action, A-Z
4630.A25	Accused. Person charged. Defendant (Table K12)
4630.C74	Criminal judge (Table K12)
	Defendant see KJ-KKZ1 4630.A25
4630.D43	Defense attorney. Public defender (Table K12)
	Person charged see KJ-KKZ1 4630.A25
	Public defender see KJ-KKZ1 4630.D43

Criminal procedure
Parties to action, A-Z -- Continued
4630.S73   State prosecutor (Table K12)
                    Class here works on the legal status of the prosecutor in
                        criminal procedure
                    For general works on the office of the public prosecutor
                        see KJ-KKZ1 1615+
4630.S93   Suspect (Table K12)
4630.V52   Victim (Table K12)
                Pretrial procedures
4632   General (Table K11)
4634   Penal report. Charges brought against a person (Table K11)
                Investigation
4636   General (Table K11)
                    Techniques of criminal investigation
                        see HV8073
4638   Examination of the accused (Table K11)
                        Cf. KJ-KKZ1 4679+ Admission of evidence
4640   Preliminary judicial investigation (Table K11)
                Public charges by prosecutor
4642   General (Table K11)
4644   Stare decisis (Table K11)
4646   Summonses, service of process, and subpoena. Wanted
                    notice (Table K11)
4648   Time periods. Deadlines (Table K11)
                Compulsory measures against the accused. Securing of
                    evidence
4650   General (Table K11)
4652   Search and seizure (Table K11)
                        Including search of persons, buildings, institution's records, etc.
4654   Provisional apprehension (Table K11)
                    Detention pending investigation
                        Cf. KJ-KKZ1 4798+ Execution of sentence
4657   General (Table K11)
4659   Bail (Table K11)
                    Extradition
4660   General (Table K11)
4662   Constitutional aspects (Table K11)
                Procedure at first instance
4664   General (Table K11)
4666   Jurisdiction (Table K11)
                        Including competence in subject matter and venue
4668   Action. Complaint (Table K11)
4670   Exclusion and challenge of court members (Table K11)
4672   Plea bargaining (Table K11)
                    Time period and deadlines see KJ-KKZ1 4648
                    Limitation of action see KJ-KKZ1 4038+

	Criminal procedure
	Procedure at first instance -- Continued
	Trial
4673	General (Table K11)
	Evidence
4675	General (Table K11)
4677	Burden of proof (Table K11)
4678	Presumption of innocence (Table K11)
	Admission of evidence
4679	General (Table K11)
4681	Confession. Self-incrimination. Entrapment (Table K11)
4683	Informers. Official secrets (Table K11)
4685	Narcoanalysis, lie detectors, etc. (Table K11)
4687	Physical examination (Table K11)
	Including blood tests, urine tests, etc.
	For forensic medicine, see RA1001+
4689	Electronic listening and recording devices (Table K11)
	Including wiretapping
4690	Previous testimony, police records, etc. (Table K11)
	Witnesses
4692	General (Table K11)
4696.A-Z	Privileged witnesses (confidential communication), A-Z
	Subarrange each by Table K12
4696.P74	Press (Table K12)
4698.A-Z	Other witnesses, A-Z
4698.C45	Children (Table K12)
4698.P64	Police witnesses (Table K12)
4698.S73	State's witnesses. State's evidence (Table K12)
4700	Expert testimony (Table K11)
	For forensic medicine, chemistry, psychology, psychiatry, toxicology, etc. see RA1001+
4702	Testimony of accused (Table K11)
4704	Documentary evidence (Table K11)
4705	Circumstantial evidence (Table K11)
4706	Alibi (Table K11)
4709.A-Z	Other, A-Z
	Subarrange each by Table K12
4710	Arguments of counsel
	Including summation, closing arguments, and oral pleadings
	Particular proceedings
4711	Summary proceedings
	Proceedings against absentee and fugitives
4713	General (Table K11)
4715	Restitutio in integrum (Table K11)
4717	Recourse against decisions of grievance boards (Table K11)

Criminal procedure
  Procedure at first instance
    Trial -- Continued
      Procedure for juvenile delinquency

4720	General (Table K11)
4722	The juvenile delinquent. The young adult perpetrator (Table K11)
4724	Juvenile crime (Table K11)

        Criminal liability and guilt see KJ-KKZ1 3878+
        Punishment. Correctional or disciplinary measures
          Including measures of rehabilitation and safety

4726	General (Table K11)
4728	Custodial education (Table K11)
4730	Judicial orders (Table K11)
4732	Detention homes. Reformatories (Table K11)

          Cf. KJ-KKZ1 4824 Execution of sentence

4734	Punishment without imprisonment (Table K11)

        Execution of sentence see KJ-KKZ1 4794.2+
      Judicial decisions

4736	General (Table K11)

       Judgment

4738	General (Table K11)

        Sentencing and determination of punishment see KJ-KKZ1 4012+

4740	Judicial discretion (Table K11)

         Including opportunity and equity

4744	Acquittal (Table K11)

       Conviction
         Including measures of rehabilitation and safety

4746	General (Table K11)
4748	Alternative conviction (Table K11)
4750	Dismissal. Decision ab instantia (Table K11)

       Probation see KJ-KKZ1 4830+

4752	Void judgments (Table K11)
4753	Correction or withdrawal of faulty decisions (errors) (Table K11)

       Res judicata

4754	General (Table K11)
4756	Ne bis in idem. Constitutional aspects (Table K11)

       Waiver of appeal see KJ-KKZ1 4788

4760	Court records. Minutes of evidence (Table K11)

        Including clerks, translators, and correction of records
     Participation of injured party in criminal procedure

4762	General (Table K11)
4764	Private charge (Table K11)

       Including public interest

4766	Intervention (Table K11)

Criminal procedure
Participation of injured party in criminal procedure -- Continued
4767 Civil suits of victims in connection with criminal proceedings
(Table K11)
Including reparation (Compensation to victims of crimes)
Special procedures
4768 Procedure before the justice of the peace (Table K11)
Commitment of insane criminals see KJ-KKZ1 3986
Procedure in confiscation of corpus delicti see KJ-KKZ1 4008
Other procedures
see the subject, e.g. 3700+, Tax and customs criminal
procedures; 3770+, Military criminal procedure; etc.
Remedies
4770 General (Table K11)
4775 Gravamen (Table K11)
4777 Reformatio in peius (Table K11)
Appellate procedure
4780 General (Table K11)
4786 Cassation (Table K11)
Restitution in integrum see KJ-KKZ1 4715
4788 Waiver of appeal (Table K11)
Post-conviction remedies
4790 General (Table K11)
4792 Reopening a case. New trial (Table K11)
For procedure before constitutional court see KJ-KKZ1
2620+
Execution of sentence
Including execution of sentence of juvenile courts, and including
deportation
For deportation of alien criminals see KJ-KKZ1 3029
Criticism and reform see KJ-KKZ1 3790
4795 General (Table K11)
Capital punishment see KJ-KKZ1 3964
Imprisonment
Class here works on regulation of both prison administration
and prisoners, and works on regulation of detention
pending investigation and short-term sentences
For penalties in general, including imprisonment see KJ-
KKZ1 3962+
4798 General (Table K11)
4800 Administration of penal or correctional institutions (Table
K11)
Including discipline, hygiene, etc.
The prisoner
4810 General (Table K11)
4812.A-Z Particular, A-Z
Dangerous criminals see KJ-KKZ1 3992

KJ-KKZ1

	Criminal procedure
	Execution of sentence
	Imprisonment
	The prisoner
	Particular, A-Z -- Continued
4812.E38	Education of prisoners. Education through labor (Table K12)
	Insane criminals see KJ-KKZ1 3986
4812.J88	Juvenile prisoners (Table K12)
4812.P64	Political prisoners (Table K12)
4820	Labor and industries in correctional institutions (Table K11)
	Including wages
	Rehabilitation and resocialization see KJ-KKZ1 3956
4824	Penal or correctional institutions (Table K11)
	Including prisons, jails, penal colonies, reformatories, juvenile detention homes, etc.
	Pardon, amnesty, and clemency see KJ-KKZ1 4034+
4828	Suspension of punishment (Table K11)
4829	Restitution (Table K11)
	Probation. Parole
	Including conditions
4830	General (Table K11)
4834	Probation and parole for juvenile delinquents (Table K11)
4837	Probation counselor (Table K11)
4840	Remission (Table K11)
4843	Community-based corrections (Table K11)
4845	Criminal registers (Table K11)
	Judicial error and compensation see KJ-KKZ1 2850
	Extradition see KJ-KKZ1 4660+
4850	Costs (Table K11)
	Victimology
4855	General (Table K11)
4857	Children and sexual crimes (Table K11)
	Compensation to victims of crimes see KJ-KKZ1 2852.V52
	Criminology and penology
	see HV6001+

Bibliography
>   For bibliography of special topics, see the topic
>   For manuals on legal research and the use of law books see
>   KJ-KKZ2 4.2+

1   General bibliography
Sales catalogs
1.2   Indexes to periodical literature, society publications, and
collections
>   For indexes to particular publications, see the publication
Indexes to Festschriften see KJ-KKZ2 7
<1.3>   Periodicals
>   For periodicals consisting predominantly of legal articles, regardless
of subject matter and jurisdiction, see K1+
>   For periodicals consisting primarily of informative material
(Newsletters, bulletins, etc.) relating to a special subject, see
the subject and Form Division Tables for periodicals
>   For law reports, official bulletins or circulars intended chiefly for the
publication of laws and regulations, see appropriate entries in
the text or Form Division Tables
1.4   Monographic series
1.5   Official gazettes
State or city gazettes
>   see the issuing state or city
Departmental gazettes
>   see the issuing department or agency
1.6   Indexes (General)
Legislative documents
>   see class J
1.7   Other materials relating to legislative history
>   Including recommended legislation; legislation passed and vetoed
Legislation
>   For statutes, statutory orders, regulations, etc., on a particular
subject, see the subject
1.8   Indexes and tables
>   Class indexes to a particular publication with the publication
>   Including indexes to statutes of several states
>   For indexes limited to one state, see the state
Statutes
>   Including statutory orders and regulations; comparative state
legislation
Collections and compilations
>   Including official and private editions
1.85   Serials
1.9   Monographs. By date
>   Including unannotated and annotated editions

KJ-KKZ2

	Legislation
	Statutes -- Continued
1.94	Collected codes
	Class here works consisting of both private and public law codes
	For codes on a particular branch of law, see the branch of law
	Administrative and executive publications
	Including orders in council; proclamations, etc.
	For regulations on a particular subject, see the subject
	For statutory orders and regulations see KJ-KKZ2 1.85+
1.95	Serials
2	Monographs. By date
	Presidential proclamations
	see class J
	Treaties
	Treaties on international public law
	see subclass KZ
	Treaties on uniform law not limited to a region
	see class K
	Treaties on uniform law of the European region
	see KJC and KJE
	Court decisions and related materials. Reports
	Including decisions of national (federal) courts and decisions of two or more states, and national (federal) and state decisions combined
	Class decisions of an individual state, province, etc., with the law of the respective jurisdiction
	For decisions on a particular subject, see the subject
	For civil and commercial decisions combined see KJ-KKZ2 47.5
	National (Federal) courts
	Constitutional courts see KJ-KKZ2 262+
2.2	Highest courts of appeal. Supreme courts. Courts of Cassation (Table K19)
	Lower courts
2.23	Various courts (Table K19)
	Including highest court and lower courts
	Intermediate appellate courts. National (Federal) courts of appeal
2.24	Collective (Table K19)
2.25.A-Z	Particular courts, A-Z
	Courts of first instance. District courts
2.26	Collective (Table K19)
2.27.A-Z	Particular courts, A-Z
	State courts
2.3	Collections (Reports) covering all states or selected states (Table K19)

	Court decisions and related materials. Reports
	State courts -- Continued
2.33	Collections (Reports) covering national (federal) decisions and decisions of the courts of two or more states (Table K19)
	Decisions (Reports) of an individual state
	see the state
2.4	Decisions of national (federal) administrative agencies
	For decisions of particular agencies, see the subject
2.5	Encyclopedias
2.6	Dictionaries. Words and phrases
	For dictionaries on a particular subject, see the subject
	For bilingual and multilingual dictionaries, see K52+
2.7	Maxims. Quotations
2.8	Form books
	Class here general works
	For form books on a particular subject, see the subject
	Judicial statistics
3	General
3.2	Criminal statistics
3.23.A-Z	Other. By subject, A-Z
3.23.D65	Domestic relations. Family law
	Family law see KJ-KKZ2 3.23.D65
3.23.L44	Legal aid
	Directories
3.3	National and regional
3.33.A-Z	By specialization, A-Z
	Trials
3.4	General collections
	Criminal trials and judicial investigations
	For military trials see KJ-KKZ2 376.7
	Collections. Compilations
3.5	General
3.6.A-Z	Particular offenses, A-Z
3.6.A78	Arson
3.6.F73	Fraud
3.6.M87	Murder
3.6.P64	Political crimes
	War crimes see KJ-KKZ2 3.9
3.7.A-Z	Individual trials. By defendant or best known (popular) name, A-Z
	Including records, briefs, commentaries, and stories on a particular trial
	War crime trials
	Trials by international tribunals
	see subclass KZ
3.9	Collections

KJ-KKZ2

	Trials -- Continued
4	Other trials
	Legal research. Legal bibliography
	Including methods of bibliographic research and how to find the law
4.2	General (Table K11)
	Electronic data processing. Information retrieval
4.3	General (Table K11)
4.4.A-Z	By subject, A-Z
4.4.A35	Administrative law (Table K12)
4.4.E58	Environmental law (Table K12)
4.4.I56	Insurance law (Table K12)
4.4.J86	Justice, Administration of (Table K12)
4.5	Systems of citation. Legal abbreviations
4.55	Surveys of law research
	Class here status reports on current developments in law or legal doctrine
4.6	Legal composition and draftsmanship
	Legal education
5	General (Table K11)
	Law schools
5.3	General (Table K11)
5.4.A-Z	Particular law schools. By name, A-Z
	Including constitution and bylaws, statutes, regulations, degrees, and general works (history)
	The legal profession see KJ-KKZ2 160+
5.5	Bar associations. Law societies. Law institutes
	Class here works on, and journals by, individual societies and their activities, e.g. annual reports, proceedings, incorporating statutes, bylaws, handbooks, and works (history) about the society
	Including courts of honor and disbarment
	For publications of associations on special subjects, see the subject
	For journals devoted to legal subjects, either wholly or in part, see K1+
	For membership directories see KJ-KKZ2 3.33.A+
	For biography, Collective see KJ-KKZ2 10.5+
	For biography, Individual see KJ-KKZ2 11.A+
	Notarial law. Public instruments see KJ-KKZ2 184.6+
	Public registers. Registration
5.53	General (Table K11)
	Civil registry see KJ-KKZ2 185.4+
	Commercial registers see KJ-KKZ2 97.3
	Property registration. Registration of pledges
5.6	General (Table K11)
	Land register see KJ-KKZ2 74.4+
	Mining registration see KJ-KKZ2 335
	Aircraft registration see KJ-KKZ2 98.8

	Law societies and institutes see KJ-KKZ2 5.5
5.8	Congresses. Conferences
5.9.A-Z	Academies. By name of academy, A-Z
6.3	General works. Treatises
6.4	Compends, outlines, examination aids, etc.
	Forms, graphic materials, blanks, atlases see KJ-KKZ2 2.8
6.6	Popular works. Civics
7	Addresses, essays, lectures

Including single essays, collected essays of several authors, festschriften, and indexes to festschriften

7.3.A-Z	Manuals and other works for particular groups of users. By user, A-Z
7.3.B35	Bankers
7.3.B86	Businesspeople. Foreign investors
7.3.E53	Engineers
7.3.F37	Farmers
	Semantics and language see KJ-KKZ2 9.2
	Legal symbolism see KJ-KKZ2 9.4+
	Legal anecdotes, wit and humor
	see K184.4
	Law and lawyers in literature
	see PB - PH
	Law and art
	see K487.C8
	Law and history
	see K487.C8
7.8.A-Z	Works on diverse aspects of a particular subject and falling within several branches of the law. By subject, A-Z
7.8.C65	Computers (Table K12)
7.8.D63	Dogs (Table K12)
7.8.L46	Letters (Table K12)
7.8.R65	Roman law (Table K12)
(7.8.W65)	Women
	see KJ-KKZ2 52.3
	History of law
8.5	Bibliography
8.6	Encyclopedias
	Auxiliary sciences
8.7	General works
8.8	Genealogy
9	Paleography
9.2	Linguistics. Semantics
	Archaeology. Symbolism in law

Class here general works on various manifestations of legal symbolism

9.4	General works
9.6.A-Z	By region, A-Z

	History of law	
	Auxiliary sciences -- Continued	
9.8	Inscriptions	
10	Heraldry. Seals. Flags. Insignia. Armory	
	Law and lawyers in literature	
	see PB - PH	
	Biography of lawyers	
	Collective	
10.5	General	
10.7	Collections of portraits	
11.A-Z	Individual, A-Z	
	Under each:	
	.xA3	*Autobiography. Reminiscences. By date*
	.xA4	*Letters. Correspondence. By date Including individual letters, general collections, and collections of letters to particular individuals*
	.xA6	*Knowledge. Concept of law. By date*
		Bibliography, see Z8001+
	.xA8-.xZ	*Biography and criticism*
12	General works. Treatises	
	By period	
	Ancient and early, including ancient people in the region	
	see KJ	
12.4	Medieval and early modern periods (to ca. 1800)	
	For the Frankish empire, see subclass KJ; for the Jus Romanum Medii Aevii, see subclass KJA	
	Sources	
	For sources of a territory or town, see the appropriate territory or town	
12.5	History and studies on sources	
	Including methodology (i.e., exegesis, edition of variants, etc.)	
12.9	Collections. Compilations	
	Including translations	
	Individual sources or groups of sources	
	Custumals. Coutumes	
13.4	Bibliography	
13.6	Collections. Compilations	
13.8[date]	Individual sources or groups of sources (Table K20b)	
	National (imperial) laws and legislation	
	Including constitutional laws (leges fundamentales)	
14	Collections. Compilations	
14.2	Individual. by date	

History of law
  By period
    Medieval and early modern periods (to ca. 1800)
      Sources
        Individual sources or groups of sources -- Continued
          Royal (imperial) privileges
            Including privileges for particular classes, ecclesiastical
              rulers, courts of justice, etc.

14.4	Collections. Compilations
14.6	Individual. By date
	Royal (imperial) mandates. Decrees. Edicts, etc. of princes and rulers
14.8	Collections. Compilations
15	Individual. By date

          Treaties
           see K524, KZ, etc.
          Court decisions. Cases. Advisory opinions. Dooms.
            Digests

16	Several courts
16.4.A-Z	Particular courts, A-Z
	Law faculties
16.6	Several faculties
16.8.A-Z	Individual faculties. By place, A-Z

          Trials
           Criminal trials and judicial investigations
             Collections. Compilations

17	General
17.2.A-Z	Particular offenses, A-Z
17.2.P64	Political crimes
17.2.W58	Witchcraft
17.4.A-Z	Individual trials. By defendant, or best known (popular) name, A-Z

                Including records, briefs, commentaries, and stories
                  on a particular trial
           Other trials

17.6	Collections. Compilations
17.8.A-Z	Individual trials. By plaintiff, defendant, or best known (popular) name, A-Z

          Contemporary legal literature

18.2	Compends. Digests. Indexes

            Including repertoria, registra, regesta, etc.
           Formularies
             Including ars notarii, rhetorica, etc.

18.4	Collections. Compilations
18.5	Particular clauses and formulae
18.7	Encyclopedic works. Dictionaries
19.2	General works

	History of law
	By period
	Medieval and early modern periods (to ca. 1800)
	Sources
	Individual sources or groups of sources
	Contemporary legal literature -- Continued
19.3	Popular works
19.5	Addresses, essays, lectures
	The State and its constitution
20.2	General works
	The estates and classes
20.4	General works
20.5.A-Z	Special topics, A-Z
20.5.B57	Birth rights
20.5.D94	Dynastic rules
20.5.E62	Equality of birth
	Feudal capacity see KJ-KKZ2 22.8
20.5.P46	Peonage. Slavery
	Slavery see KJ-KKZ2 20.5.P46
(20.77)	State and church
	see KJ-KKZ2 27.5
20.9	Territory
21.2	Foreign relations
	Feudal law
21.3	General works
	Sources
21.4	Collections. Compilations
22[date]	Individual sources (Table K20b)
	Feudal institutes
22.2	Feudal lord and vassal
	Fief
22.4	General works
22.6.A-Z	Special topics, A-Z
22.6.C65	Commendation. Hommage
	Hommage see KJ-KKZ2 22.6.C65
22.8	Feudal capacity
23	Feudal succession
	Rural (peasant) land tenure and peasantry
23.2	General works
23.4	Manorial estates. Lordships. Seigniories
23.8	Leasehold for years and inheritance
	Succession to rural holdings
24.2	General works
24.4	Entail
	Crown and king. Princes and rulers
24.6	General works
25	The court. Court officials and councils

History of law
  By period
    Medieval and early modern periods (to ca. 1800)
      The State and its constitution -- Continued

25.4	Diet. Generale parlamentum. Legislature
25.6	Military organization
	Finance. Fiscalat
	Class here works on topics not represented elsewhere in the schedule
	For works on the history of other subjects, see the subject
25.8	General works
26	Camera
26.3	Crown goods and dynastic house goods
26.8	Regalia
	Secular ecclesiastical law
	Class here historical works on the relationship of church and state
	For historical works on the internal law and government of a church, see KB
	Sources
	Including treaties between state and church (concordats and contracts)
	For treaties relating to a particular region or state (province), see region or state (province)
	For treaties on a particular subject, see the subject
27.2	Collections. Compilations
27.3	Individual concordats. By date
(27.4)	General works
	see KJ-KKZ2 27.5
	System of church and state relationships
27.5	General works
	Germanic period
	see KJ
	Carlovingian state church
	see KB, KJ
27.6	State churches and rulers
27.8	Church finance and estate
28.2.A-Z	Private law. Special topics, A-Z
	Class here works on topics not represented elsewhere in the schedule
	For works on the history of other subjects, see the subject
	Judiciary. Court organization and procedure
28.3	General works
28.7	Procedure

	Philosophy, jurisprudence, and theory of law
	Class here works on doctrines peculiar to legal institutions of a country
	For works on the philosophy of law in general, see K237+
	For works on the philosophy of a particular branch of law (e.g. constitutional law or criminal law), see the branch
44	General (Table K11)
	The concept of law
	Including the definition of law
44.2	General works
44.3	The object of law. Law and justice
44.4	Ethics. Morality of law
44.5	Law and the state. Legal order. Respect for law
44.6	Rights and duties. Sanction
44.7	Certainty of law
	Cf. KJ-KKZ2 462.2 Criminal procedure
	Legal science
44.8	General works
44.9	Sources of law
	Rule of law see KJ-KKZ2 202+
	Law reform. Criticism see KJ-KKZ2 47
45	Methodology
	Schools of legal theory
45.5	General works
45.7	Natural law
	Modern political theory of law
46.3	General works
46.4	Socialist. Communist
46.5	Sociological jurisprudence
46.8	Influence of other legal systems on the law (Reception)
47	Law reform and policies. Criticism
	Including reform of administration of justice
47.2.A-Z	Concepts applying to several branches of the law, A-Z
	Bona fides see KJ-KKZ2 47.2.G66
47.2.C65	Concurrent legislation
	Deadlines see KJ-KKZ2 47.2.T55
47.2.D65	Dolus
47.2.E65	Equality
47.2.E88	Estoppel
	Cf. KJ-KKZ2 179.3 Res judicata
47.2.F52	Fictions
47.2.F67	Forfeiture
47.2.F73	Freedom of conscience
47.2.G66	Good faith. Reliance
	Legal advertising see KJ-KKZ2 47.2.N68
47.2.L44	Legal documents
47.2.L52	Liability

Concepts applying to several branches of the law, A-Z --
Continued

47.2.N44	Negligence
47.2.N68	Notice. Legal advertising
47.2.O28	Oath
	Ownership see KJ-KKZ2 47.2.P68
47.2.P68	Possession. Ownership
47.2.P73	Presumption
47.2.P74	Privacy, Right of
47.2.P76	Property. Property damage
47.2.P92	Publicity
	Reliance see KJ-KKZ2 47.2.G66
47.2.S45	Self-incrimination
47.2.T55	Time periods. Deadlines
47.2.V58	Vis major
47.2.W33	Waiver
47.5	Private law (Table K11)
	Class here works on all aspects of private law
	Private international law. Conflict of laws
	For regional unification of conflict rules, see KJC
	For conflict of laws between the United States and a particular jurisdiction, see KF416
	For works on conflict rules of branches other than private law (e.g. tax law, criminal law, etc.), see the subject
48	General (Table K11)
48.15	Public order. Public policy. Ordre public (Table K11)
48.2	Renvoi (Table K11)
	Points of contact
48.3	Domicile (Table K11)
48.5.A-Z	Particular branches and subjects of the law, A-Z
	Administrative acts see KJ-KKZ2 274
	Adoption see KJ-KKZ2 48.5.F35
	Arbitration see KJ-KKZ2 48.5.P76
	Author and publisher see KJ-KKZ2 48.5.P92
	Bankruptcy see KJ-KKZ2 48.5.P76
	Capacity see KJ-KKZ2 48.5.P47
	Cartels see KJ-KKZ2 48.5.C67
48.5.C65	Commercial agents (Table K12)
48.5.C655	Commercial papers and negotiable instruments (Table K12)
48.5.C657	Commercial sales (Table K12)
48.5.C658	Contracts. Obligations. Debtor and creditor (Table K12)
48.5.C67	Corporations. Industrial trusts. Cartels (Table K12)
	For procedure in antitrust cases see KJ-KKZ2 324.4+
	Criminal law see KJ-KKZ2 383.2
	Debtor and creditor see KJ-KKZ2 48.5.C658
	Decedents' estate see KJ-KKZ2 48.5.I45
	Divorce see KJ-KKZ2 48.5.M375

Private international law. Conflict of laws
   Particular branches and subjects of the law, A-Z -- Continued

48.5.E92	Evasion (Table K12)
	Execution see KJ-KKZ2 48.5.P76
48.5.F35	Family. Parent and child. Adoption (Table K12)
	Foreign exchange see KJ-KKZ2 353.8+
	Foreign judgments see KJ-KKZ2 164.6
	Illegality see KJ-KKZ2 48.5.T67
	Incapacity see KJ-KKZ2 48.5.P47
	Industrial property see KJ-KKZ2 48.5.I583
	Industrial trusts see KJ-KKZ2 48.5.C67
48.5.I45	Inheritance and succession. Decedents' estate (Table K12)
48.5.I58	Insurance (Table K12)
48.5.I583	Intellectual and industrial property (Table K12)
	Judicial assistance see KJ-KKZ2 164.4
	Justification see KJ-KKZ2 48.5.T67
48.5.L45	Limitation of action (Table K12)
48.5.L62	Loans (Table K12)
48.5.M37	Maritime (commercial) law (Table K12)
48.5.M375	Marriage. Matrimonial actions. Matrimonial property (Table K12)
	Negotiable instruments see KJ-KKZ2 48.5.C655
	Obligations see KJ-KKZ2 48.5.C658
	Parent and child see KJ-KKZ2 48.5.F35
48.5.P47	Persons. Capacity. Incapacity (Table K12)
48.5.P76	Procedure. Arbitral awards. Execution and bankruptcy (Table K12)
48.5.P78	Property (Table K12)
48.5.P92	Publishing contract. Author and publisher (Table K12)
48.5.R43	Refugees (Table K12)
48.5.S8	Statelessness (Table K12)
48.5.T67	Torts. Illegality. Justification (Table K12)
48.5.T72	Trademarks (Table K12)
48.5.T725	Transfer (Table K12)
48.5.T78	Trusts and trustees (Table K12)
48.5.U53	Unfair competition (Table K12)
48.5.U534	Unjust enrichment (Table K12)
48.5.V46	Vendors and purchasers (Table K12)
48.7	Intertemporal law. Retroactive law (Table K11)
	Including conflict of laws
	Civil law
49	General (Table K11 modified)
	Federal legislation
49.A25	Indexes and tables. Digests. By date
	Statutes. Statutory orders
	Collections. Selections
	Including annotated editions and commentaries

Civil law
  General
    Federal legislation
      Statutes. Statutory orders
        Collections. Selections -- Continued

49.A27	Serials
49.A28	Monographs. By date

      Individual acts (or groups of acts adopted as a whole)
        Collections see KJ-KKZ2 49.A27+

49.A282-.A29	Codes
49.A29<date>	Individual codes

Arrange chronologically by appending date of original
enactment or revision of the law to this number and
deleting any trailing zeros
Under each:

.xA12-.xA129	*Indexes and tables*
.xA14	*Bills. By date*
.xA32	*Legislative documents and related works. By date*
.xA52	*Text of the code. Unannotated editions. By date*
	Including official editions with or without annotations, and works containing the introductory act and complementary legislation together with the text of the code
	For individual complementary laws, see the subject
.xA6-.xZ8	*Annotated editions. Commentaries. General works*
	Including criticism, private drafts, and commentaries on private drafts
.xZ9	*Amendatory laws. By date of enactment*
	For amendatory laws pertaining to a particular subject, see the subject

Civil law
  General
    Federal legislation
      Statutes. Statutory orders
        Individual acts (or groups of acts adopted as a whole)
          Codes -- Continued

49.A31<date>
            Other individual acts
              Arrange chronologically by appending date of original
                  enactment or revision of the law to this number and
                  deleting any trailing zeros
              Under each:
                    Unannotated editions
                      Including official editions with or
                        without annotations
        .xA2-.xA29   *Serials*
        .xA4   *Monographs. By date*
        .xA6-.xZ8   *Annotated editions. Commentaries.*
                      General works
              Including enactments of national codes by individual
                states, etc.

      General principles

50
        Applicability. Validity of the law
        Ethics (Morality of law). Public policy see KJ-KKZ2 44.4
        Chicanery and abuse of rights see KJ-KKZ2 44.4
        Equity see KJ-KKZ2 44.4
        Presumption see KJ-KKZ2 47.2.P73
        Publicity see KJ-KKZ2 47.2.P92
        Vis major see KJ-KKZ2 47.2.V58

50.3
        Legal status (Table K11)

50.4
        Rights (Table K11)

50.5
        Immaterial rights (Table K11)
        Things see KJ-KKZ2 64.7

50.55
        Acts and events
        Legal transactions see KJ-KKZ2 87.6+
        Declaration of intention see KJ-KKZ2 87.9+
        Agency see KJ-KKZ2 88+
        Mandate see KJ-KKZ2 88.5+
        Secured transactions see KJ-KKZ2 87.8
        Fiduciary transactions see KJ-KKZ2 74.3

50.6
        Conditions
        Time periods see KJ-KKZ2 47.2.T55

50.7
        Limitation of actions

50.8
        Exercise of rights. Protection of rights
      Persons

51
        General (Table K11)
        Natural persons
          Personality

Civil law
  Persons
    Natural persons
      Personality -- Continued

51.2	General (Table K11)
51.3	Birth (Table K11)
	Death
51.5	General (Table K11)
	Missing persons. Presumption of death
51.7	General (Table K11)
51.8	Declaration and certification of death (Table K11)
	Civil register see KJ-KKZ2 185.4+
	Civil death see KJ-KKZ2 400.4
	Capacity and incapacity
	Including liability
51.9	General (Table K11)
52	Minors. Children
	Including human rights of the child
52.3	Women (Table K11)
	Class here works on legal status in both private and public law
52.5	Insane persons. People with mental disabilities (Table K11)
52.55.A-Z	Other, A-Z
52.55.A34	Aged. Older people (Table K12)
	Older people see KJ-KKZ2 52.55.A34
52.55.P46	Physical disabilities, People with (Table K12)
52.55.U52	Unborn children. Nasciturus (Table K12)
52.6	Citizenship (Table K11)
	For acquisition of citizenship and nationality see KJ-KKZ2 243+
	Personality rights
52.7	General (Table K11)
52.9	Name
	Dignity, honor, and reputation see KJ-KKZ2 85.7+
	Privacy see KJ-KKZ2 85.9+
	Intellectual property see KJ-KKZ2 115.2+
	Protection of personality rights see KJ-KKZ2 83.7
	Juristic persons of private law
	For business corporations see KJ-KKZ2 108.9+
	For juristic persons of public law see KJ-KKZ2 287+
53	General (Table K11)
	Associations
53.3	General (Table K11)
53.5	Incorporated society
	Including profit and nonprofit corporations
53.7	Unincorporated society

KJ-KKZ2

Civil law
  Domestic relations. Family law -- Continued
56.8   Quasi-matrimonial relationships. Unmarried cohabitation
       (Table K11)
    Marital property and regime
56.9   General (Table K11)
57   Statutory regimes (Table K11)
57.2   Contractual regimes. Antenuptial contracts (Table K11)
57.3   Separation of property (Table K11)
57.4   Community of property (Table K11)
57.8   Contracts between husband and wife (Table K11)
       For antenuptial contracts see KJ-KKZ2 57.2
58   Property questions arising from unmarried cohabitation
       (Table K11)
     Marital property register see KJ-KKZ2 186.7
58.2   Marriage, church, and state
    Intermarriage
      see KB
    Consanguinity and affinity
58.3   General (Table K11)
     Parent and child
      Paternity see KJ-KKZ2 62+
      Legitimate children
        Including children from defective marriages, divorced
          marriages, legitimized children from subsequent
          marriages, etc.
59   General (Table K11)
(59.2)   Human rights of the child (Table K11)
        see KJ-KKZ2 52
59.4   Legal status of children during and after divorce (Table
        K11)
        Including children from void marriages
59.5   Legitimation of children (Table K11)
        Including declaration of legitimacy and legitimation by
          subsequent marriage
      Parental power
        For illegitimate children see KJ-KKZ2 62+
59.8   General (Table K11)
60   Custody. Access to children (Table K11)
        Including parental kidnapping
      Education see KJ-KKZ2 315.3+
      Custodial education see KJ-KKZ2 154.9
60.3   Stepchildren (Table K11)
      Adoption
61   General (Table K11)
61.5.A-Z   Special topics, A-Z
61.5.A36   Adoption of adults (Table K12)

KJ-KKZ2

	Civil law
	Domestic relations. Family law
	Consanguinity and affinity
	Parent and child
	Adoption
	Special topics, A-Z -- Continued
	Inter-country adoption of children see KJ-KKZ2 48.5.F35
	Illegitimate children
61.8	General (Table K11)
	Constitutional rights of children see KJ-KKZ2 59.2
61.9	Parental power. Custody (Table K11)
	Affiliation. Paternity
62	Illegitimate children (Table K11)
62.3	Artificial insemination (Table K11)
	Cf. KJ-KKZ2 312.8 Medical legislation
	Cf. KJ-KKZ2 410.8 Criminal law
	Guardian and ward
62.5	General (Table K11)
	Guardianship courts see KJ-KKZ2 187.4+
	Government guardianship see KJ-KKZ2 154.8
	Guardianship over minors
62.6.A-Z	Special topics, A-Z
62.6.E38	Education (Table K12)
62.8	Guardianship over adults (Table K11)
	Property. Law of things
63	General (Table K11)
64	Right of property. Constitutional guaranty. Social obligation (Table K11)
64.5	Socialist property. Doctrine (Table K11)
64.7	Things. Classification of things (Table K11)
64.8.A-Z	Types of private property, A-Z
	Subarrange each by Table K12
	Possession
65	General (Table K11)
65.3	Acquisition and transfer of possession (Table K11)
65.5	Violation of possession (Table K11)
	Ownership
65.7	General (Table K11)
	Right of ownership see KJ-KKZ2 64
	Acquisition and loss of ownership
65.8	General (Table K11)
65.9	Accessions (Table K11)
66	Acquisition of fruits and parts of things (Table K11)
66.3	Prescription (Table K11)
66.4	Succession (Table K11)
	Contractual acquisition

Civil law
  Property. Law of things
    Real property
      Ownership
        Rights incident to ownership of land -- Continued
69   General (Table K11)
69.3   Air and space above ground (Table K11)
                      Cf. KJ-KKZ2 346.7+ Aviation
69.4   Underground. Minerals, metals, and other resources
                    (Table K11)
                      Cf. KJ-KKZ2 335 Mining law
69.5   Riparian rights. Water rights. Underground water
                    (Table K11)
69.7   Animals and fish. Game and fishing rights (Table K11)
                      Cf. KJ-KKZ2 333.7+ Game laws
                      Cf. KJ-KKZ2 334+ Fishery laws
              Law of adjoining landowners
70   General (Table K11)
70.3.A-Z   Special topics, A-Z
70.3.B68   Boundaries. Building across boundaries. Party
                      walls (Table K12)
                    Building across boundaries see KJ-KKZ2 70.3.B68
70.3.E29   Eaves-drip (Table K12)
70.3.L54   Light or window rights (Table K12)
                    Mining rights see KJ-KKZ2 335
70.3.N84   Nuisances (Table K12)
                    Overfall see KJ-KKZ2 70.3.O83
70.3.O83   Overhang. Overfall (Table K12)
                    Party walls see KJ-KKZ2 70.3.B68
(70.3.W38)   Water laws
                      see KJ-KKZ2 69.5
70.3.W39   Way by necessity
                    Window rights see KJ-KKZ2 70.3.L54
              Types of real property
70.4   Condominium. Horizontal property (Table K11)
70.5   Superfices (Table K11)
              Rights as to the use and profits of another's land
70.6   General (Table K11)
                  Fief see KJ-KKZ2 22.4+
                  Superfices see KJ-KKZ2 70.5
                Servitudes
71   General (Table K11)
71.3   Real servitudes
71.5   Personal servitudes (Table K11)
71.6   Usufruct (Table K11)
71.7   Right of pre-emption (Table K11)
              Hypothecation

Civil law
  Property. Law of things
    Hypothecation -- Continued
72   General (Table K11)
72.3   Mortgage. Hypotheca (Table K11)
          Land charge
72.5   General (Table K11)
72.7.A-Z   Types of land charges, A-Z
              Subarrange each by Table K12
72.9   Rent charge (Table K11)
          Pledges
73   General (Table K11)
            Contractual pledges
              Pledges of personal property
                Including possessory and nonpossessory pledges
73.3   General (Table K11)
73.5.A-Z   Special topics, A-Z
73.5.A32   Accessory (Table K12)
73.5.B34   Bailments (Table K12)
73.5.P74   Priority (Table K12)
73.7   Pledges of rights (Table K11)
73.9   Lien or statutory pledge (Table K11)
74   Register of pledges (Table K11)
74.3   Transfer of ownership as security. Fiduciary transactions
              (Table K11)
        Land register and registration
74.4   General (Table K11)
74.5   Courts and procedure. Land partition courts (Table K11)
75   Cadastral surveys. Cadaster (Table K11)
              Class here general works on surveying agencies
              For an individual surveying agency of the state or locality, see
                the state or locality
      Inheritance. Succession upon death
76   General (Table K11)
76.5   Testamentary succession (Table K11)
76.7   Intestate succession (Table K11)
        Inheritance. Estate
77   General (Table K11)
            Particular estates or parts
              Entail see KJ-KKZ2 330
              Fideicommissum see KJ-KKZ2 330.4
          Heirs
78   General (Table K11)
78.2   Joint heirs. Co-heirs (Table K11)
          Wills. Testaments
78.5   General (Table K11)
78.6   Appointment of heir (Table K11)

KJ-KKZ2

Civil law
  Inheritance. Succession upon death
    Wills. Testaments -- Continued
78.7   Legacy. Testamentary burden. Distribution of estate
                  (Table K11)
78.8   Executors and administrators (Table K11)
79   Contract of inheritance (Table K11)
79.2   Purchase of inheritance (Table K11)
79.3   Certificate of inheritance. Proof of heirship (Table K11)
              Inheritance tax see KJ-KKZ2 360.5
  Obligations
80   General (Table K11)
              Debtor and creditor. Chose in action and obligation
80.2   General (Table K11)
                Plurality of debtors and creditors. Joint obligations
80.3   General (Table K11)
80.4   Correality and solidarity (Table K11)
80.5   Community of creditors (Table K11)
80.7   Community of debtors (Table K11)
              Types of obligations
80.9   Civil and natural obligations (Table K11)
                  Cf. KJ-KKZ2 95+ Aleatory contracts
81   Obligations to give (Table K11)
                    Including obligation in kind
                    For money obligations see KJ-KKZ2 82
81.3   Transfer and assumption of obligations (Table K11)
              Extinction of obligation
81.5   General (Table K11)
                Performance. Payment
81.7   General (Table K11)
                  Due date of payment. Time of performance
81.8   General (Table K11)
                    Default (mora) see KJ-KKZ2 82.8
81.9   Consignation (Table K11)
                        Including emergency sale of perishables
82   Special rules as to payment of money debts
82.3   Compensation. Set-off (Table K11)
              Nonperformance
                    Including liability and exclusion from liability
82.4   General
82.5   Negligence. Gross negligence (Table K11)
82.7   Impossibility of performance (Table K11)
82.8   Default (Table K11)
              Damages
82.9   General (Table K11)
83   Causation (Table K11)
83.2   Damages for pain and suffering (Table K11)

Civil law
  Obligations -- Continued
  Delicts. Torts
83.5   General (Table K11)
                Protected rights
83.6   General (Table K11)
83.7   Personality rights (Table K11)
                Parties to action in torts
84   General (Table K11)
84.3   Principal. Accessories (Table K11)
84.4   Joint tortfeasors (Table K11)
84.6   Illegality (Table K11)
                Liability
84.7   General (Table K11)
84.8   Exclusion of liability (Table K11)
                  Including contractual agreement, assumption of risk by
                    injured part, and tacit (implied) agreement
84.9   Strict liability (Table K11)
                  For strict liability related to particular dangers or risks, see
                    the topic
                Individual torts
85   Violation of freedom (Table K11)
                Physical injuries
85.2   General (Table K11)
85.3   Accidents (Table K11)
                  For particular types of accidents see KJ-KKZ2 86.9
(85.5)   Malpractice (Medical)
                  see KJ-KKZ2 310.9+
85.6   Death by wrongful act (Table K11)
                Violation of integrity
                  Including of honor, dignity, and reputation
85.7   General (Table K11)
85.8   Libel and slander (Table K11)
                Violation of privacy
                  Cf. KJ-KKZ2 416+ Criminal law
85.9   General (Table K11)
86   Right in one's own picture (Table K11)
86.3   Public opinion polls (Table K11)
86.5   Personal data in information retrieval systems (Table
                  K11)
                  Including public and private records, registers, statistics,
                    etc.
86.6   Immoral transactions and acts (Table K11)
86.7   Deceit. Misrepresentations. Forgery (Table K11)
86.72   Products liability (Table K11)
86.8   Ultrahazardous activities and occupations (Table K11)
86.9   Sports. Sport fields or installations (Table K11)

KJ-KKZ2

KJ-KKZ2

	Civil law
	Obligations
	Individual contracts and transactions -- Continued
96.4	Acknowledgment of debt (Table K11)
96.5	Discovery (Disclosure) (Table K11)
	Commercial law. Commercial transactions
97	General (Table K11 modified)
	Federal legislation
97.A25	Indexes and tables. Digests. By date
	Statutes. Statutory orders
	Collections. Selections
	Including annotated editions and commentaries
97.A27	Serials
97.A28	Monographs. By date
	Individual acts (or groups of acts adopted as a whole)
	Codes
	Collections see KJ-KKZ2 97.A27+
97.A29<date>	Individual codes

Arrange chronologically by appending date of original
enactment or revision of the law to this number and
deleting any trailing zeros

Under each:

.xA12-.xA129	*Indexes and tables*
.xA14	*Bills. By date*
.xA32	*Legislative documents and related works. By date*
.xA52	*Text of the code. Unannotated editions. By date*
	Including official editions with or without annotations, and works containing the introductory act and complementary legislation together with the text of the code
	For individual complementary laws, see the subject
.xA6-.xZ8	*Annotated editions. Commentaries. General works*
	Including criticism, private drafts, and commentaries on private drafts
.xZ9	*Amendatory laws. By date of enactment*
	For amendatory laws pertaining to a particular subject, see the subject

Commercial law
  General
    Federal legislation
      Statutes. Statutory orders
        Individual acts (or groups of acts adopted as a whole)
          Codes -- Continued

97.A31<date>	Other individual acts

           Arrange chronologically by appending date of original
             enactment or revision of the law to this number and
             deleting any trailing zeros
           Under each:
                Unannotated editions
                  Including official editions with or
                    without annotations

.xA2-.xA29	*Serials*
.xA4	*Monographs. By date*
.xA6-.xZ8	*Annotated editions. Commentaries.*
	General works

         Including enactments of national codes by individual
           states, etc.

97.2	Merchant and business enterprise (Table K11)
97.3	Commercial registers
97.5	Commercial sale (Table K11)
97.6	Commercial agents (Table K11)
97.7	Consignment. Commission merchant. Factors (Table K11)
97.8	Brokerage (Table K11)
97.9	Auctioneers (Table K11)
98	Warehousing (Table K11)
	Freight forwarders and carriers. Carriage of passengers and goods
98.2	General (Table K11)
98.25	Liability (Table K11)
98.3	Bill of lading (Table K11)
98.5	Liens (Table K11)
	Types of carriers
98.6	Railroads (Table K11)
98.62	Passenger carriers. Bus lines (Table K11)
98.7	Trucklines (Table K11)
98.8	Airlines (Table K11)
	Carriage by sea see KJ-KKZ2 97.2
	Commercial instruments see KJ-KKZ2 99
	Commercial liens
98.9	General (Table K11)
	Freight forwarder liens see KJ-KKZ2 98.5
99	Negotiable instruments. Titles of credit (Table K11)
99.3	Bills of exchange
	Stamp duties see KJ-KKZ2 363.3+

	Commercial law. Commercial transactions
	Negotiable instruments. Titles of credit
99.4	Checks (Table K11)
	Letters of credit see KJ-KKZ2 100.5
	Stock certificates and bonds see KJ-KKZ2 109.9
	Trust investments see KJ-KKZ2 101.4
	Bills of lading (Land transportation) see KJ-KKZ2 98.3
	Promissory notes see KJ-KKZ2 96.3
	Criminal provisions see KJ-KKZ2 435
99.5	Banking. Stock exchange (Table K11)
	Including regulation of the banking business
	Types of banks and credit institutions
99.6	Banks of issue (Table K11)
99.7	Mortgage banks (Table K11)
99.8	Savings banks (Table K11)
	Including public and private banks
99.9	Building and loan associations (Table K11)
100	Cooperative societies (Table K11)
100.2	Clearinghouses (Table K11)
100.3	Warehouses (Table K11)
	Banking transactions
100.4	General (Table K11)
	Deposits see KJ-KKZ2 100.6
100.5	Loans. Credit (Table K11)
100.55	Letters of credit (Table K11)
100.6	Deposit banking
100.7	Account current (Table K11)
100.8	Noncash funds transfer (Table K11)
	Including electronic funds transfer
	Investments
	For tax measures see KJ-KKZ2 354.3+
100.9	General (Table K11)
	Foreign investments see KJ-KKZ2 320.9
101	Stock exchange transactions. Securities (Table K11)
	Investment trust
101.2	General (Table K11)
101.3	Real estate investment trust (Table K11)
101.4	Trust investments (Table K11)
101.5	Criminal provisions (Table K11)
	Including money laundering
	Taxation of banking and stock exchange transactions see
	KJ-KKZ2 362.4.A+
	Maritime law
	For regulatory aspects of water transportation, navigation,
	and pilotage see KJ-KKZ2 347+
101.6	General (Table K11)
101.7	Shipowners. Ship operators (Table K11)

Commercial law. Commercial transactions
Maritime law -- Continued
101.8   Shipmasters (Table K11)
Affreightment. Carriage of goods at sea and inland waters
101.9   General (Table K11)
102   Freight forwarders (Table K11)
Including liability
102.2   Act of God. War. Act of government (Table K11)
102.4   Carriage of passengers at sea and inland waters (Table K11)
Including carriage of passengers' luggage
Average
102.6   General (Table K11)
102.7   Havarie grosse (Table K11)
102.8   Special average. Collision at sea (Table K11)
102.9   Salvage. Shipwreck (Table K11)
Ship creditors
103   General (Table K11)
103.2   Bottomry and respondentia. Ship mortgage (Table K11)
103.22   Maritime liens (Table K11)
103.3   Ship registers (Table K11)
103.4   Maritime courts (Table K11)
Prize courts
see KZ6640+
103.5   Marine insurance (Table K11)
Maritime social legislation
Including legislation for merchant mariners for inland navigation
103.6   General (Table K11)
Labor law for merchant mariners
103.7   General (Table K11)
103.8   Labor standards (Table K11)
103.9   Discipline (Table K11)
104   Social insurance for merchant mariners (Table K11)
Including all branches of social insurance
Insurance law
Including regulation of insurance business
104.3   General (Table K11)
Life insurance
104.6   General (Table K11)
104.7   Group insurance (Table K11)
104.8   Old age pensions (Table K11)
104.9   Survivors' benefits (Table K11)
105   Health insurance. Medical care insurance (Table K11)
105.3   Accident insurance (Table K11)
Property insurance
105.5   General (Table K11)
105.6   Multiple line insurance (Table K11)
Including home owners insurance

Commercial law. Commercial transactions
Insurance law
Property insurance -- Continued
105.7.A-Z   Particular hazards, A-Z
Burglary see KJ-KKZ2 105.7.T43
105.7.F57   Fire (Table K12)
Robbery see KJ-KKZ2 105.7.T43
105.7.T43   Theft. Burglary. Robbery (Table K12)
105.7.W38   Water damage (Table K12)
105.8.A-Z   Types of property and business, A-Z
Subarrange each by Table K12
Suretyship. Guaranty. Title insurance
106   General (Table K11)
106.3   Credit insurance (Table K11)
106.35   Litigation insurance (Table K11)
106.4   Mortgage insurance (Table K11)
Liability insurance
106.5   General (Table K11)
Risks and damages
Traffic
106.7   General (Table K11)
106.8   Automobiles (Table K11)
106.9   Automotive transportation (General) (Table K11)
Including trucking, bus lines, etc.
107   Aviation (Table K11)
107.3   Reinsurance (Table K11)
Business associations
107.5   General (Table K11)
107.6   Constitutional aspects. Interdiction of private business
associations (Table K11)
107.7   Expropriation and nationalization of business associations
(Table K11)
Personal companies. Unincorporated business associations
For civil companies see KJ-KKZ2 93.9+
108   General (Table K11)
108.3   Partners (Table K11)
108.4   Accounting. Financial statements. Auditing (Table K11)
108.5   Termination. Dissolution. Liquidation (Table K11)
108.6   Partnership (Table K11)
108.7   Limited partnership (Table K11)
108.8   Silent partners (Table K11)
Stock companies. Incorporated business associations
108.9   General (Table K11)
Stock corporations
109   General (Table K11)
109.3   Incorporation and promoters (Table K11)
109.7   Organization and management

KJ-KKZ2

Commercial law. Commercial transactions
 Business associations
  Stock companies. Incorporated business associations
   Stock corporations -- Continued
    Corporate finance

109.8	General (Table K11)
	Securities
109.9	Stocks (Table K11)
110	Bonds (Table K11)
110.3	Stocks and stockholders' rights. Stock transfer (Table K11)
	Types of corporations
110.4	Family corporations (Table K11)
110.5	One-person companies (Table K11)
110.6	Termination. Dissolution. Liquidation (Table K11)
	Corporate reorganization see KJ-KKZ2 113.6+
	Consolidation and merger see KJ-KKZ2 113.7
110.7	Partnership partly limited by shares (Table K11)
	Private company
110.9	General (Table K11)
111	Stock and stockholders' rights. Stock transfer (Table K11)
	Types of private companies
111.4	Family corporations (Table K11)
111.5	One-person companies (Table K11)
111.6	Multi-national corporation (Table K11)
111.7	Colonial companies (History) (Table K11)
	Cooperative societies
112	General (Table K11)
112.3	Membership (Table K11)
	Combinations. Industrial trusts
	For government control see KJ-KKZ2 322+
113	General (Table K11)
113.3	Consortium (Table K11)
113.5	Business concerns (Table K11)
	Corporate reorganization
113.6	General (Table K11)
113.7	Consolidation and merger (Table K11)
	For government control see KJ-KKZ2 322.3
113.8.A-Z	Special topics, A-Z
	Subarrange each by Table K12
	Insolvency and bankruptcy see KJ-KKZ2 194+
	Intellectual and industrial property
115	General (Table K11)
	Copyright
115.2	General (Table K11)

KJ-KKZ2

Intellectual and industrial property
Patent law and trademarks
Licenses -- Continued
120.7   General (Table K11)
120.8   Foreign licensing agreements (Table K11)
                     Including know-how
121   Patent litigation and infringements (Table K11)
121.8   Patent attorneys (Table K11)
                  International uniform law on patents and trademarks
                     see K1501+
                  Trademarks
122   General (Table K11)
122.5   Practice and procedure (Table K11)
              Unfair competition
                  For restraint of trade see KJ-KKZ2 321.8+
123   General (Table K11)
                  Advertising
123.3   General (Table K11)
123.5   Disparagement of goods (Table K11)
                     Including comparative advertising
123.7   Testing of commercial products (Table K11)
                  Pushing for sales
123.8   Unordered merchandise by mail (Table K11)
124   Special sales (Table K11)
124.3   Rebates and premiums (Table K11)
125   Delicts. Torts (Table K11)
                     Cf. KJ-KKZ2 83.5+ Civil law
125.5   Practice and procedure (Table K11)
                     Including arbitration and award
              Labor law
                  Including works on both labor law and social insurance, and private
                     labor law as it applies to the labor contract and to the labor-
                     management relationship
                  Criticism and reform see KJ-KKZ2 146
126   General (Table K11)
126.3   Labor policies. Competition and incentives for high
                     performance (Table K11)
126.4   Organization and administration (Table K11)
                     Class here works on national departments and boards of labor,
                        national, state and local departments and boards, or
                        departments and boards of several states or administrative
                        districts
                     For departments or boards (several or individual) of an individual
                        state or administrative district, see the state or district
                  Labor contract and employment
126.5   General (Table K11)
127   Types of employment

Labor law
    Labor contract and employment -- Continued
127.3   Individual labor contract and collective agreements. Liberty
            of contract (Table K11)
        Freedom of employment and restraint on freedom of
            employment
128   General (Table K11)
128.3   Preferential employment (Table K11)
            Including people with severe disabilities, veterans, etc.
128.5   Formation of contract (Table K11)
128.7   Parties to contract (Table K11)
        Prohibition of discrimination in employment see KJ-KKZ2
            131+
        Extinction of employment
            Cf. KJ-KKZ2 81.5+ Obligation
129   General (Table K11)
129.3   Dismissal and resignation (Table K11)
130   Job security (Table K11)
130.3   Nonperformance (Table K11)
            Cf. KJ-KKZ2 82.4+ Civil law
130.4   Liability (Table K11)
      Prohibition of discrimination in employment. Equal opportunity
131   General (Table K11)
131.3   Wage discrimination. Equal pay for equal work (Table K11)
131.4.A-Z   Groups discriminated against, A-Z
131.4.A33   Aged persons. Older people (Table K12)
131.4.A44   Alien laborers (Table K12)
131.4.D58   Disabilities, People with (Table K12)
131.4.E84   Ethnic groups. Minorities (Table K12)
          Minorities see KJ-KKZ2 131.4.E84
          Older people see KJ-KKZ2 131.4.A33
          People with disabilities see KJ-KKZ2 131.4.D58
131.4.W58   Women (Table K12)
    Wages
132   General (Table K11)
        Types of wages and modes of remuneration
132.3   Incentive wages (Table K11)
           Including bonus system, profit sharing, etc.
132.4   Collective wages (Table K11)
132.5   Adjustments. Cost-of-living adjustments (Table K11)
        Nonwage payments and fringe benefits
133   General (Table K11)
         Pension and retirement plans
133.2   General (Table K11)
133.3   Pension trusts (Table K11)
133.4.A-Z   Groups of employees or industries, A-Z
133.4.A34   Agricultural laborers (Table K12)

KJ-KKZ2

Labor law
 Wages
  Groups of employees or industries, A-Z -- Continued
133.4.H6   Hotels, restaurants, taverns (Table K12)
   Restaurants see KJ-KKZ2 133.4.H6
   Taverns see KJ-KKZ2 133.4.H6
  Labor-management relations
134   General (Table K11)
   Works councils
    Including election, organization, parliamentary practice, etc.
134.3   General (Table K11)
134.4   Works assembly (Table K11)
   Works councils of business concerns see KJ-KKZ2 137
134.5   Union participation (Table K11)
  Employee participation in management and planning
135   General (Table K11)
   Standardized labor conditions see KJ-KKZ2 137.5+
136   Labor standards and protection of labor (Table K11)
136.6   Personnel management (Table K11)
137   Employee representation on board of controllers and
    supervisors (Table K11)
    Including unincorporated and incorporated business
     associations, cooperative societies, industrial trusts, etc.
  Collective bargaining and labor agreements
137.5   General (Table K11)
137.7   Standardized labor conditions (Table K11)
  Collective labor disputes
138   General (Table K11)
   Strikes and lockouts. Boycott
138.3   General (Table K11)
138.5   Wildcat strikes. Sympathy strikes. Political strikes (Table
    K11)
  Corporate representation
139   General (Table K11)
139.3   Unions (Table K11)
139.5   Employers' associations (Table K11)
  Protection of labor
140   General (Table K11)
140.3   Hours of labor (Table K11)
    Including night work and Sunday labor
   Vacations
140.5   General (Table K11)
141   Sick leave (Table K11)
141.3   Holidays (Table K11)
141.5   Child and youth labor (Table K11)
    Including hours of labor

Labor law
  Protection of labor -- Continued
    Women's labor
      Including hours of labor
141.7   General (Table K11)
141.8   Maternal welfare (Table K11)
142   Home labor (Table K11)
142.3   Labor hygiene and industrial safety (Table K11)
               Including safety regulations for equipment
143   Labor supply. Manpower control. Manpower planning (Table K11)
    Labor courts and procedure
      Class her works on courts of several jurisdictions
      For courts (several or individual) of an individual jurisdiction, see the jurisdiction
144   General (Table K11)
144.3   Procedural principles (Table K11)
    Procedure at first instance
144.5   General (Table K11)
144.6   Actions and defense (Table K11)
145   Evidence. Burden of proof (Table K11)
145.3   Remedies. Appellate procedures (Table K11)
145.5   Arbitration (Table K11)
Social legislation
146   Social reform and policies
               Including all branches of social legislation and labor
146.3   General (Table K11)
    Social insurance
      Criticism and reform see KJ-KKZ2 146
146.5   General (Table K11)
147   Organization and administration (Table K11)
               Including insurance carriers
               For national departments and boards of labor and social insurance see KJ-KKZ2 126.4
147.6   Coverage and benefits (Table K11)
    Health insurance
      For private health insurance see KJ-KKZ2 105
148   General (Table K11)
148.3   Compulsory insurance (Table K11)
               Including exemptions
148.4   Organization and administration (Table K11)
148.8.A-Z   Groups of beneficiaries, A-Z
               Subarrange each by Table K12
    Workers' compensation
      Including occupational diseases
149   General (Table K11)
150.A-Z   Groups of beneficiaries, A-Z

KJ-KKZ2

Social legislation
Social insurance
Workers' compensation
Groups of beneficiaries, A-Z -- Continued

150.C58	Civil servants (Table K12)
150.H35	Handicapped. People with disabilities (Table K12)

Social security
Including old age pensions, invalidity and disability pensions and survivor benefits
Social reform see KJ-KKZ2 146

150.4	General (Table K11)
150.6	Compulsory insurance. Exemptions (Table K11)
151	Unemployment insurance (Table K11)

For civil service pensions see KJ-KKZ2 297.8
Social services. Public welfare
Criticism and reform see KJ-KKZ2 146

152	General (Table K11)
152.3	Organization and administration (Table K11)
152.5	Social work and social workers (Table K11)

Social service beneficiaries

152.6	The poor and destitute (Table K11)
152.7	Older people (Table K11)
152.8	Pensioners (Table K11)
152.9	Large families (Table K11)

People with disabilities
Including people with physical, mental, and emotional disabilities

153	General (Table K11)
153.4.A-Z	Beneficiaries, A-Z
153.4.B54	Blind (Table K12)
153.4.D42	Deaf-mute (Table K12)
153.4.M45	Mental disabilities, People with (Table K12)
153.5	Asocial types (Table K11)
153.6	Evacuated and homeless persons (Table K11)

War-related groups of beneficiaries

153.7	General (Table K11)
153.8	Refugees. Expelled or forcefully repatriated persons (Table K11)
153.9	Prisoners of war and political prisoners. Veterans (Table K11)
154	Services for war victims and war invalids (Table K11)

Children. Youth

154.2	General (Table K11)

Measures and provisions

154.5	General (Table K11)
154.6	Protection of children in public (Table K11)

Including restaurants, taverns, theaters, gambling, etc.

Social legislation
Social services. Public welfare
Social service beneficiaries
Children. Youth
Measures and provisions -- Continued

154.7	Protection of children against obscenity (Table K11)
154.8	Government guardianship (Table K11)
154.9	Custodial education. Collective education (Table K11)

Social courts and procedure
Class here works on courts of several jurisdictions
For courts (several or individual) of an individual jurisdiction, see the jurisdiction

155	General (Table K11)
155.4.A-Z	Particular courts, A-Z
155.4.A65	Appellate courts (Table K12)
155.5	Parties to action (Table K11)
156	Procedure at first instance (Table K11)
156.4	Judicial decisions and judgments (Table K11)
156.7	Execution (Table K11)
156.8	Costs (Table K11)

Competence conflicts between administrative, labor, and social courts see KJ-KKZ2 281

Courts and procedure
The administration of justice. The organization of the judiciary
Including the administration of criminal justice
Criticism. Reform see KJ-KKZ2 47

157	General (Table K11)

The judiciary and politics see KJ-KKZ2 47

157.6	Organization and administration (Table K11)

Class here works on national and state departments of justice or departments of justice of several states
For the departments of justice of an individual state, see the state

Judicial statistics see KJ-KKZ2 3+
Judicial assistance see KJ-KKZ2 164+
Criminal policy see KJ-KKZ2 395

Courts
Including courts of both criminal and civil jurisdiction

158	General (Table K11)

Regular courts
Class here works on national (federal) courts and on courts of several jurisdictions
For courts (several or individual) of an individual jurisdiction, see the jurisdiction

158.2	General (Table K11)
158.3	Local courts. Municipal courts. Magistrate courts. Justice of the peace (Lowest courts) (Table K11)

KJ-KKZ2

	Courts and procedure
	Courts
	Regular courts -- Continued
	Juvenile courts see KJ-KKZ2 472+
158.4	Regional courts. Provincial courts. District courts (Table K11)
158.6	Supreme courts of state or republics (Table K11)
	Courts of special jurisdiction. Special tribunals
158.8	General (Table K11)
158.9	Consular courts (Table K11)
159	Special tribunal within a court (Table K11)
159.3.A-Z	Other public bodies with judicial functions, A-Z
	e. g.
159.3.C65	Comrade's courts (Table K12)
159.3.M85	Municipal arbitral boards (Table K12)
	The legal profession
	Including judicial officers and personnel
160	General (Table K11)
	Law school education see KJ-KKZ2 5+
160.4	Judicial personnel other than lawyers (Table K11)
160.5	Nationality and citizenship (Table K11)
160.6.A-Z	Minorities, A-Z
	Subarrange each by Table K12
161	Judges (Table K11)
161.5	Office of the public prosecutor (Table K11)
	Notaries see KJ-KKZ2 184.6+
	Auxiliary personnel. Clerk's office
162	General (Table K11)
	Clerks to the court
162.3	Business administration. Court records (Table K11)
	For for personal data protection in information retrieval systems see KJ-KKZ2 86.5
162.4	Bailiffs (Table K11)
162.6	Experts and expert witnesses (Table K11)
	Practice of law
162.9	General (Table K11)
	Litigation insurance see Table KJ-KKZ1 1025.5
163	Attorneys (Table K11)
163.16	Legal ethics and etiquette (Table K11)
163.3	Legal consultants (Table K11)
163.4	Procurators (Table K11)
	Judicial assistance
	Including judicial assistance in criminal matters
164	General (Table K11)
164.4	International judicial assistance (Table K11)
164.6	Foreign judgments (Conflicts of laws) (Table K11)

Courts and procedure -- Continued
Procedure in general
Class here works on civil and criminal procedure and works on
civil, commercial, and labor procedure combined

165	General (Table K11)
	Procedural principles
165.15	Due process of law (Table K11)
165.5	Parties in action (Table K11)
166	Pretrial procedures (Table K11)
	Procedure at first instance. Trial
166.3	General (Table K11)
166.6	Actions and defenses (Table K11)
166.8.A-Z	Particular proceedings
	Subarrange each by Table K12
	Evidence. Burden of proof
167	General (Table K11)
167.5	Witnesses (Table K11)
167.9	Judicial decisions (Table K11)
168.6	Remedies (Table K11)
169	Execution (Table K11)
169.2	Costs. Fees (Table K11)
	Civil procedure
	For works on procedure and practice in general before particular types of courts or individual courts see KJ-KKZ2 158.2+
169.5	Criticism. Reform (Table K11)
170	General (Table K11 modified)
	Federal legislation
170.A25	Indexes and tables. Digests. By date
	Statutes. Statutory orders
	Collections. Selections
	Including annotated editions and commentaries
170.A27	Serials
170.A28	Monographs. By date
	Individual acts (or groups of acts adopted as a whole)
170.A282-.A29	Codes
	Collections see KJ-KKZ2 170.A27+

                Courts and procedure
               Civil procedure
              General
             Federal legislation
            Statutes. Statutory orders
           Individual acts (or groups of acts adopted as a whole)
          Codes -- Continued

170.A29<date>   Individual codes
            Arrange chronologically by appending date of original
              enactment or revision of the law to this number
              and deleting any trailing zeros
            Under each:

.xA12-.xA129	*Indexes and tables*
.xA14	*Bills. By date*
.xA32	*Legislative documents and related works. By date*
.xA52	*Text of the code. Unannotated editions. By date*
	Including official editions with or without annotations, and works containing the introductory act and complementary legislation together with the text of the code
	For individual complementary laws, see the subject
.xA6-.xZ8	*Annotated editions. Commentaries. General works*
	Including criticism, private drafts, and commentaries on private drafts
.xZ9	*Amendatory laws. By date of enactment*
	For amendatory laws pertaining to a particular subject, see the subject

Courts and procedure
Civil procedure
General
Federal legislation
Statutes. Statutory orders
Individual acts (or groups of acts adopted as a whole)
Codes -- Continued

170.A31<date>   Other individual acts

Arrange chronologically by appending date of original
enactment or revision of the law to this number
and deleting any trailing zeros

Under each:

Unannotated editions
Including official editions with or
without annotations

.xA2-.xA29	*Serials*
.xA4	*Monographs. By date*
.xA6-.xZ8	*Annotated editions. Commentaries.*
	General works

Including enactments of national codes by individual
states, etc.

170.2   Civil procedure law relating to other branches of the law
(Table K11)
Procedural principles

170.4   Due process of law (Table K11)
Including frivolous suits

170.6   Publicity and oral procedure (Table K11)
Parties to action

171   General (Table K11)

171.5   Litigant. Plaintiff. Defendant (Table K11)
Pretrial procedures

172   General (Table K11)

172.3   Time periods. Deadlines (Table K11)

172.5   Suspension of procedure (Table K11)
Procedure at first instance

173   General (Table K11)

173.7   Jurisdiction. Competence in subject matter and venue
(Table K11)

174   Representation. Power of attorney (Table K11)
Lis pendens see KJ-KKZ2 175.6.L58
Res judicata see KJ-KKZ2 175.6.R48
Time periods. Deadlines see KJ-KKZ2 172.3
Actions and defenses

174.5   General (Table K11)
Classification of actions see KJ-KKZ2 178.5+
Defenses and exceptions

175   General (Table K11)

KJ-KKZ2

KJ-KKZ2

Courts and procedure
Noncontentious (ex parte) jurisdiction
Registration. Recording
Civil register
Registration of civil status -- Continued

186.2	Birth (Table K11)
186.4	Death (Table K11)
	For absence and presumption of death see KJ-KKZ2 51.7+
186.5	Aliens. Stateless foreigners (Table K11)
186.6	Costs (Table K11)
186.7	Register of matrimonial property (Table K11)
	Land registers see KJ-KKZ2 74.4+
	Ship registers see KJ-KKZ2 103.3
	Commercial registers see KJ-KKZ2 97.3
	Domestic relations procedure
187	General (Table K11)
187.2	Adoption procedures (Table K11)
	Guardianship court
187.4	General (Table K11)
	Jurisdiction
187.6	Appointment of guardian (Table K11)
	Government guardianship see KJ-KKZ2 154.8
	Interdiction see KJ-KKZ2 154.8
188	Inheritance (Probate court) procedure (Table K11)
188.2	Costs (Table K11)
	Class here general works
	For costs of a particular branch of noncontentious jurisdiction, see the branch
	Insolvency
188.5	General (Table K11)
	Execution
188.8	General (Table K11)
	Parties to execution
	Including executors and administration
189	General (Table K11)
189.2	Succession during execution (Table K11)
	Bailiffs see KJ-KKZ2 162.4
	Titles for execution
	Including judgments (res judicata), documents of title, etc.
189.4	General (Table K11)
189.5	Provisional enforcement (Table K11)
	Procedure in execution
189.6	General (Table K11)
189.7	Discovery proceedings. Poor debtors oath (Table K11)
	Including inventory
190	Judicial decisions (res judicata) (Table K11)

Courts and procedure
Insolvency
Bankruptcy
Procedure
Priority of claims -- Continued
195.7.A-Z   Particular secured or privileged credits, A-Z
195.7.I57   Insurance claims (Table K12)
195.8   Distribution (Table K12)
195.9   Composition to end bankruptcy (Table K12)
Judicial review of voidable transactions
196   General (Table K11)
Fraudulent conveyances see KJ-KKZ2 427.6
Effect of bankruptcy on obligations and rights
196.3   General (Table K11)
196.5   Costs (Table K11)
Debtors' relief
For wartime debtor's relief see KJ-KKZ2 371.7
197   General (Table K11)
Composition to avoid bankruptcy. Deferment of execution
197.2   General (Table K11)
197.3   Receivership (Table K11)
Corporate reorganization
197.5   Moratorium (Table K11)
197.6   Costs (Table K11)
Including bookkeeping and accounting
Public law
Class here works on all aspects of public law, including early works
For civics see KJ-KKZ2 6.6
200   General (Table K11)
The State
Including philosophy and theory of the state
For non-legal works on political theory, see JC
201   General (Table K11)
201.5   Sovereignty. Potestas (Table K11)
Federalism see KJ-KKZ2 237.3
Rule of law
202   General (Table K11)
Socialist state
202.5   General (Table K11)
203   Democratic centralism (Table K11)
Constitutional law
For works on the constitutional aspects of a subject, see the subject
History see KJ-KKZ2 210+
205   Constitutional reform. Criticism. Polemic
For works on a particular constitution, see the constitution
207.A12   Bibliography
Including bibliography of constitutional history

Constitutional law -- Continued

207.A15   Monographic series

Sources

Including early constitutions and related materials

207.A28   Collections. Compilations. By date

Including federal sources, federal and state sources, and sources of several states

207.A3<date>   Individual constitutions

Arrange chronologically by appending the date of adoption to this number and deleting any trailing zeros

Under each:

.xA6	*Texts. Unannotated editions. By date*
.xA7-.xZ5	*Annotated editions. Commentaries. General works*

207.A32<date>   Individual sources other than constitutions

Arrange chronologically by appending the date of adoption to this number and deleting any trailing zeros. Subarrange by main entry

Court decisions

207.A4   Indexes. Digests

207.A5   Serials

207.A6   Monographs. By date

207.A7   Dictionaries (terms and phrases). Encyclopedias

(207.A72)   Form books. Graphic materials. Tables

see KJ-KKZ2 207.A9+

207.A85   Congresses. Conferences. Seminars. By date

207.A9-Z   General works

Including history, criticism, private drafts, compends, case books, form books, examination aids, popular works, essays, festschriften, etc.

Constitutional history

For general works on political institutions and public administration, see JN

By period

From ca. 1800 to most recent constitution

210   General works

Constitutional principles

Rule of law see KJ-KKZ2 202+

212   Sovereignty of parliament

213   Rulers, princes, dynasties

Including dynastic rules and works on legal status and juristic personality

Privileges of classes and particular groups see KJ-KKZ2 229

Privileges, prerogatives, and immunities of rulers, states, or estates see KJ-KKZ2 230

Constitutional law
　　Constitutional history
　　　By period
　　　　From ca. 1800 to most recent constitution
216　　　　　　Sources and relationships of law
　　　　　　Intergovernmental relations. Jurisdiction
217　　　　　　　General works
218　　　　　　　Federal-state (republic), national-provincial
　　　　　　　　controversies. State-state or interprovincial
　　　　　　　　disputes
　　　　　　　Privileges, prerogatives, and immunities of particular
　　　　　　　　states or estates see KJ-KKZ2 230
219　　　　　　　Distribution of legislative power. Exclusive and
　　　　　　　　concurrent legislative power. Reservation of
　　　　　　　　provincial legislation
220.A-Z　　　　　Special topics, A-Z
　　　　　　　　Class here works on topics not provided for elsewhere
　　　　　　　　For the history of a particular subject, see the subject
222　　　　　Interpretation and construction (Table K11)
　　　　　Constitutional principles
224　　　　　　Legitimacy
225　　　　　　Legality. Socialist legality
　　　　　　Rule of law see KJ-KKZ2 202+
226　　　　　　Centralization of powers (Table K11)
　　　　　　Separation and delegation of powers
227　　　　　　　General (Table K11)
227.5　　　　　　Conflict of interests. Incompatibility of offices. Ethics in
　　　　　　　　government (Table K11)
　　　　　　　Executive privilege see KJ-KKZ2 230
228　　　　　　　Judicial review of legislative acts (Table K11)
229　　　　　　Privileges of classes (estates) and particular groups (Table
　　　　　　　K11)
230　　　　　　Privileges, prerogatives, and immunities of rulers, states, or
　　　　　　　estates (Table K11)
　　　　　Sources and relationships of the law
232　　　　　　Preconstitutional and constitutional law
232.5　　　　　International law and municipal law
233　　　　　　Statutory law and delegated legislation (Table K11)
235　　　　　　　Socialist plans (Table K11)
236　　　　　　　Decrees (individual) (Table K11)
　　　　　Intergovernmental relations. Jurisdiction
237　　　　　　General (Table K11)
237.3　　　　　Federalism (Table K11)
237.5　　　　　Federal-state (republic), national-provincial controversies.
　　　　　　　Interstate (Interprovincial, etc.) disputes (Table K11)
238　　　　　　Cooperation of states, republics, provinces, etc. (Table K11)

	Constitutional law
	Intergovernmental relations. Jurisdiction -- Continued
238.5	Exclusive and concurring jurisdiction (Table K11)
	Including national (federal) and state (republic, province, etc.) jurisdiction
239	National (Federal) territory (Table K11)
	Including boundary disputes
239.5	National (Federal) capital (Table K11)
	Foreign relations administration
240	General (Table K11)
	Foreign service see KJ-KKZ2 260.8
241	Executive agreements (Table K11)
	Foreign assistance programs see KJ-KKZ2 321
241.3	Neutrality (Table K11)
242.A-Z	Other, A-Z
	Subarrange each by Table K12
	Individual and state
242.9	General (Table K11)
	Nationality and citizenship
	For rights and status of citizens see KJ-KKZ2 52.6
243	General (Table K11)
	Immigration. Naturalization
244	General (Table K11)
	Procedure see KJ-KKZ2 302.5
244.5	Expatriation (Table K11)
	Emigration see KJ-KKZ2 302.7
	Statelessness see KJ-KKZ2 48.5.S8
245.A-Z	Particular groups, A-Z
	Subarrange each by Table K12
	Human rights. Civil and political rights. Civic (socialist) duties
246	General (Table K11)
	Equality before the law. Antidiscrimination in general
246.5	General (Table K11)
246.7.A-Z	Groups discriminated against, A-Z
246.7.G38	Gays (Table K12)
	Jews see KJ-KKZ2 246.7.M56
246.7.M56	Minorities (Ethnic, religious, racial, and national) (Table K12)
246.7.S55	Single people (Table K12)
246.7.W65	Women (Table K12)
246.8.A-Z	Special subjects, A-Z
	Culture see KJ-KKZ2 246.8.L36
246.8.L36	Language and culture (Table K12)
	Freedom
246.9	General (Table K11)
247	Freedom of expression (Table K11)

KJ-KKZ2

Constitutional law
  Individual and state
    Human rights. Civil and political rights. Civic (socialist)
      duties
      Freedom -- Continued

247.2	Freedom of religion and conscience (Table K11)
	Freedom of thought and speech
247.4	General (Table K11)
247.6	Freedom of information (Table K11)
247.8	Prohibition of censorship (Table K11)
248	Right of opposition to government (Table K11)
248.2	Freedom of movement (Table K11)
248.4	Due process of law (Table K11)
248.6	Right to resistance against government (Table K11)
248.8	Political parties and mass organizations (Table K11)
	Including subordinate or connected organizations, and pressure
	groups, etc.
249	Internal security (Table K11)
	Including control of subversive activities or groups
	Organs of national government. Supreme organs of state
	power and state administration
	Including federal and state government
250	General (Table K11)
	The people
250.4	General (Table K11)
250.6	Election law (Table K11)
	The legislature. Legislative power
251	General (Table K11)
251.2	Control of government (Table K11)
251.4	Legislative bodies. People's assemblies (Table K11)
	Including legislative bodies with one or two chambers
	Legislative process
	Including parliamentary practice
251.6	General (Table K11)
251.8	Interpellation (Table K11)
252	Bill drafting (Table K11)
252.2	Committees and councils (Table K11)
252.4	Voting (Table K11)
252.5	Parliamentary minorities (Table K11)
252.8	Legislators (Table K11)
	Including immunity, indemnity, incompatibility, etc.
	Heads of state
253	General (Table K11)
	Kings, princes, and rulers
253.2	General (Table K11)
253.5.A-Z	Special topics, A-Z
253.5.A23	Abdication (Table K12)

Constitutional law
  Organs of national government. Supreme organs of state
    power and state administration
    Heads of state
      Kings, princes, and rulers
        Special topics, A-Z -- Continued
253.5.D9   Dynastic rules. Legal status of dynasty (Table K12)
253.5.E43   Election (Table K12)
                      Legal status of dynasty see KJ-KKZ2 253.5.D9
253.5.S92   Succession to the crown (Table K12)
                    Presidents
254   General (Table K11)
254.4.A-Z   Special topics, A-Z
                        Subarrange each by Table K12
254.8   Collective heads of state. State councils. Presidential
                      councils (Socialist) (Table K11)
                    Prerogatives and powers of the head of state
255   General (Table K11)
255.4   Crown privilege (Table K11)
255.8   Treatymaking power (Table K11)
                        Including questions of provincial competence to conduct
                          foreign relations
256   Veto power (Table K11)
256.4   War and emergency power (Table K11)
                  Other supreme organs
257   Central People's Committee (Socialist) (Table K11)
257.5   Federal Executive Council (Socialist) (Table K11)
257.7   The executive branch. Executive power (Table K11)
                    Federal Executive Councils see KJ-KKZ2 257.5
                    Presidium. Presidential councils see KJ-KKZ2 254.8
258   The Prime Minister and the Cabinet (Table K11)
258.5   Council of Ministers (Socialist) (Table K11)
259   Supreme Councils of Control (Socialist) (Table K11)
                    Government departments, ministries, and other
                      organizations of government
260   General (Table K11)
                    Departments. Ministries
                        Class here works on several departments not related to a
                          particular branch of law or subject
                        Including subordinate administrative divisions, councils, etc.
                        For works on several departments related to a branch of
                          law or subject, as well as individual departments and
                          their regulatory agencies, see the branch of law or
                          subject
260.2   General (Table K11)
                      Department of State
260.4   General (Table K11)

Constitutional law
Organs of national government. Supreme organs of state
power and state administration
The executive branch. Executive power
Government departments, ministries, and other
organizations of government
Departments. Ministries
Department of State -- Continued

260.8	The foreign service (Table K11)
261	Subordinate regulatory agencies (Table K11)

Class here works on several agencies
For an individual agency, see the branch of law or the
subject

261.2	Special boards, commissions, bureaus, task forces, etc.
261.4.A-Z	Special topics, A-Z

Subarrange each by Table K12

261.6	Council of State (Table K11)
261.8	The judiciary. Judicial power (Table K11)

Constitutional courts (tribunals) and procedure

262	General (Table K11)
263	Court organization (Table K11)
264	Procedural principles (Table K11)
265	Jurisdiction (Table K11)
266.A-Z	Special topics, A-Z
266.C65	Constitutional torts (Table K12)
267	National emblem. Flag. Seal. Seat of government. National anthem (Table K11)
267.2	Political oath (Table K11)
267.4	Patriotic customs and observances (Table K11)
267.6	Decorations of honor. Awards. Dignities (Table K11)
267.7	Commemorative medals (Table K11)

Economic constitution see KJ-KKZ2 320.64+
Colonial law

268	General (Table K11)
268.5.A-Z	Particular, A-Z
268.5.A35	Administrative law (Table K12)
268.5.T38	Taxation (Table K12)
268.5.T73	Trade regulation (Table K12)

Secular ecclesiastical law
Class here works on the relationship of state and church, regardless
of denomination
For works on the internal law and government of a church, see KB
For history see KJ-KKZ2 27.2+

Secular ecclesiastical law -- Continued
Treaties between church and state. Concordats
Including related material such as court decisions, official reports, memoranda, etc.
For concordats relating to a particular region or state (province), see the region or state (province)
For treatises on a particular subject, see the subject

268.8	Collections. Compilations (Table K11)
268.9	Individual concordats. By date (Table K11)
269	General (Table K11)
	Constitutional guaranties
269.2	General (Table K11)
269.3	Freedom of religion. Freedom of worship (Table K11)
269.4	Freedom of speech of the clergy (Table K11)
269.5	Protection of church property (Table K11)
269.7	Separation of church and state. Independence of church (Table K11)
269.8	Religious corporations and societies (Table K11)
270	Church autonomy and state supervision (Table K11)
	Administrative law
272	General (Table K11)
272.2	Administrative principles (Table K11)
	Relationship to other branches of law or subjects
272.7	Civil law
	Administrative process
273	General (Table K11)
273.2	Acts of government (Table K11)
274	Administrative acts (Table K11)
275	Legal transactions (Table K11)
275.4	Public contracts. Government contracts. Government purchasing (Table K11)
275.7	Enforcement. Administrative sanctions (Table K11)
276	Ombudsman. Control over abuse of administrative power (Table K11)
	Administrative courts and procedure
276.4	General (Table K11)
277	Court organization (Table K11)
278	Pretrial procedures. Administrative remedies (Table K11)
	Including remonstration, administrative appeals, etc.
279	Procedure. Judicial decisions. Remedies (Table K11)
	Including judicial review of administrative acts
280	Arbitration (Table K11)
281	Competence conflicts (Table K11)
281.5	Costs (Table K11)
	Indemnification for acts performed by government
282	General (Table K11)

Administrative law
Indemnification for acts performed by government -- Continued
282.4	Eminent domain (Table K11)
	Including procedure
	Government liability
283	General (Table K11)
283.5	Acts of government (Table K11)
284	Administrative and judicial acts (Table K11)
284.15.A-Z	Other, A-Z
	Reparation see KJ-KKZ2 284.15.V52
284.15.V52	Victims of crimes, Compensation to. Reparation (Table K12)
	Administrative organization
285	Centralization and decentralization in government (Table K11)
	Juristic persons of public law
287	General (Table K11)
	Public corporations
287.7	General (Table K11)
288	Regional corporations (Table K11)
	Class here general works
	For local government see KJ-KKZ2 292+
	For municipal government see KJ-KKZ2 293.7+
	For special districts see KJ-KKZ2 297+
288.5	Cooperative societies of public law (Table K11)
	Class here general works
	For particular cooperative societies, see the subject, e.g. Agricultural cooperative societies
288.8	Public institutions (Table K11)
	For particular institutions, see the subject
289	Public foundations (Table K11)
	Cf. KJ-KKZ2 53.8 Foundations in civil law
289.3	Government business enterprises (Table K11)
	Including government controlled business enterprises
	For particular enterprises, see the subject
	Administrative departments of national government
	Including federal and central government
289.8	Department of the Interior (Table K11)
290	Subordinate regulatory agencies (Table K11)
	For particular agencies, see the subject
	Special councils, commissions, etc.
291	General (Table K11)
	Ombudsman see KJ-KKZ2 276
	Administrative departments of the states (Land, cantons, etc.)
291.5	General (Table K11)
291.7	Department of the Interior (Table K11)

Administrative law
Administrative organization -- Continued
Administrative and political divisions. Local government
other than municipal
Including those of centralized national governments or federal
governments
292   General (Table K11)
292.8   Councils, boards, standing commissions (Table K11)
293.5.A-Z   Particular administrative districts, counties, regions, etc., A-Z
Including official gazettes, bylaws, statutory orders,
regulations, and general works, as well as works on
specific legal topics
Municipal government
293.7   General (Table K11)
293.8   Name. Flags. Insignia. Seals (Table K11)
294   Constitution and organization of municipal government
(Table K11)
295   Municipal economy (Table K11)
Municipal public services
295.6   General (Table K11)
Public utilities
For regulation of energy industry see KJ-KKZ2
343.2+
295.8   General (Table K11)
Electricity. Gas see KJ-KKZ2 343.8
296   Water. Sewage (Table K11)
For ecological aspects see KJ-KKZ2 314
296.2   Trash collection (Table K11)
296.5   Public transportation (Table K11)
Supramunicipal corporation and cooperation
296.8   General (Table K11)
Special districts
For special districts within a particular state (Land, canton,
etc.), see the state (Land, canton, etc.)
297   General (Table K11)
297.2.A-Z   Particular types of districts, A-Z
Subarrange each by Table K12
Water districts see KJ-KKZ2 305.8.A+
Civil service. Public officials and functionaries
297.4   General (Table K11)
297.7   Conditions of employment (Table K11)
297.8   Retirement. Pensions (Table K11)
Labor law and collective labor law
298   General (Table K11)
Management-labor relations
298.2   General (Table K11)

Civil service. Public officials and functionaries
Labor law and collective labor law
Management-labor relations -- Continued

298.3	Work councils (Table K11)
298.5	Collective labor disputes. Strikes (Table K11)
298.7	State civil service (Table K11)
	For works on the civil service of an individual state, see the state
298.9	Municipal civil service (Table K11)
	For works on the civil service of an individual municipality, see the municipality
299	Civil service of public corporations other than state or municipal (Table K11)
299.2	Public officials and functionaries of the economic administration (Socialist) (Table K11)

Police and public safety

300	General (Table K11)

Police magistrates
Including contraventions

300.3	General (Table K11)
300.4	Procedure. Penalties (Table K11)
300.5.A-Z	Particular violations, A-Z
	Subarrange each by Table K12

Police force

300.7	Criminal police (Table K11)

Public safety

300.9	General (Table K11)
301	Weapons. Explosives (Table K11)
	Including manufacturing, import, and trade of firearms and ammunition

Hazardous articles and processes
Including transportation by land
For product safety see KJ-KKZ2 86.72
For transportation by sea see KJ-KKZ2 347.3

301.15	General (Table K11)
301.2	Nuclear power. Reactors (Table K11)
	Including protection from radiation, and including nuclear waste disposal
	Cf. KJ-KKZ2 84.7+ Torts
301.3	Flammable materials (Table K11)
301.4.A-Z	Poisons and toxic substances, A-Z
301.4.A82	Asbestos (Table K12)
301.4.P34	Paint (Table K12)

Accident control

301.5	General (Table K11)
301.6.A-Z	Particular, A-Z
	Electric engineering see KJ-KKZ2 301.6.E43
301.6.E43	Electric installations. Electric engineering (Table K12)

	Police and public safety
	Public safety
	Accident control
	Particular, A-Z -- Continued
301.6.S74	Steam boilers (Table K12)
	Fire prevention and control
301.7	General (Table K11)
	Theaters. Auditoriums
301.8	General (Table K11)
301.9	Motion picture theaters. Safety films (Table K11)
	Flood control see KJ-KKZ2 305.7
	Weather bureaus. Meteorological stations see KJ-KKZ2 351.8
	Control of individuals
302	General (Table K11)
	Identification and registration
	Including registration of residence
302.2	General (Table K11)
	Registration of birth, marriage, and death see KJ-KKZ2 185.4+
302.3.A-Z	Other, A-Z
	Subarrange each by Table K12
302.5	Immigration and naturalization. Procedure (Table K11)
	For citizenship see KJ-KKZ2 243+
302.7	Emigration (Table K11)
	For freedom of movement see KJ-KKZ2 248.2
	Particular groups
302.9	Aliens (Table K11)
	Including citizens of European Community countries, homeless aliens, and refugees
303	Minorities (Ethnic, religious, racial) (Table K11)
	Control of social activities
303.3	General (Table K11)
303.4	Vacationing (Table K11)
	Including campgrounds, hostels, outdoor swimming facilities, etc.
	Sport activities
303.5	General (Table K11)
303.6	Mass events (Table K11)
303.7.A-Z	Particular sports, A-Z
303.7.F58	Fishing, Sport (Table K12)
303.7.P73	Prizefighting (Table K12)
303.7.S57	Skiing (Table K12)
303.7.T45	Tennis (Table K12)
303.8.A-Z	Other, A-Z
303.8.B85	Bullfights (Table K12)
303.8.D45	Demonstrations. Processions (Table K12)

KJ-KKZ2

	Police and public safety
	Control of individuals
	Control of social activities
	Other, A-Z -- Continued
303.8.G35	Gambling (Table K12)
	Including lotteries, games of chance, etc.
	Processions see KJ-KKZ2 303.8.D45
303.8.T7	Traveling shows (Table K12)
	Including circuses, puppet theaters, air shows, open-air shows, etc.
	Public property. Public restraint on private property
304	General (Table K11)
	Government property
304.2	Constitutional aspects. Interdiction of private ownership. Socialist theory of government property (Table K11)
	Administration. Powers and control
304.3	General (Table K11)
304.5	Records management. Access to public records (Table K11)
	Including data bases and general data protection
304.6	Expropriation. Nationalization (Table K11)
	For eminent domain see KJ-KKZ2 282.4
	For government-owned business enterprises see KJ-KKZ2 321.7
	Roads and highways
304.7	General (Table K11)
304.8	Interstate and state highways (Table K11)
	Safety see KJ-KKZ2 87.3
	Water resources
	Including rivers, lakes, watercourses, etc.
305	General (Table K11)
	Protection against pollution see KJ-KKZ2 314
	Development and conservation of water resources
305.5	General (Table K11)
305.7	Flood control (Table K11)
	Including dams and dikes
	Particular inland waterways and channels see KJ-KKZ2 348.A+
305.8.A-Z	Particular bodies and districts. By name, A-Z
	Subarrange each by Table K12
306	Shore protection. Coastal zone management (Table K12)
306.5	Water courts and procedure (Table K11)
306.7	National preserves (Table K11)
	Architectural landmarks and historic monuments see KJ-KKZ2 320.4
	Continental shelf and its resources see KJ-KKZ2 334.7
	Public land law

	Public property. Public restraint on private property
	Public land law -- Continued
306.8	Land reform and land policy legislation
	For agricultural land law see KJ-KKZ2 329+
306.85	Government constituted homesteads
306.9	General (Table K11)
	Regional planning
307	General (Table K11)
307.2	Ecological aspects (Table K11)
	City planning and redevelopment
307.3	General (Table K11)
307.5	Zoning (Table K11)
	Including procedure
	For variances see KJ-KKZ2 308+
	Building and construction
	Including administrative control and procedure
308	General (Table K11)
308.2	Adjoining landowners (Table K11)
308.3	Building safety and control (Table K11)
	Fideicommissum see KJ-KKZ2 330.4
308.4	Public works (Table K11)
	Including public works contracts
	Public health
308.5	General (Table K11)
308.8	Burial and cemetery laws (Table K11)
	Including dead bodies and disposal of dead bodies
	Contagious and infectious diseases
308.9	General (Table K11)
309.A-Z	Diseases, A-Z
309.A53	AIDS (Table K12)
309.C56	Cholera (Table K12)
309.T82	Tuberculosis (Table K12)
309.V45	Venereal diseases (Table K12)
	Public health measures
	Including compulsory measures
309.2	General (Table K11)
	Immunization. Vaccination
309.3	General (Table K11)
309.4.A-Z	Diseases, A-Z
309.4.P65	Poliomyelitis (Table K12)
309.4.S62	Smallpox (Table K12)
309.5	Quarantine (Table K11)
	Eugenics see KJ-KKZ2 313
	Environmental pollution see KJ-KKZ2 313.8+
309.7.A-Z	Other public health hazards and measures, A-Z
309.7.R43	Refuse disposal (Table K12)
309.7.S77	Street cleaning (Table K12)

KJ-KKZ2

Public health -- Continued
   Food laws see KJ-KKZ2 337.7+
   Drug laws

310	General (Table K11)
310.2	Pharmaceutical products (Table K11)
310.3	Narcotics (Table K11)
	Including psychopharmaca
310.4	Poisons (Table K11)
310.5	Pharmacists and pharmacies (Table K11)
310.6	Trade regulation. Advertising (Table K11)
	Including consumer protection

Medical legislation

310.8	General (Table K11)

The health professions
   Class here works on education, licensing, professional
     representation, ethics, fees, and liability
Physicians

310.9	General (Table K11)
310.94	Malpractice (Table K11)
311	Dentists. Dental hygienists (Table K11)
311.2.A-Z	Other, A-Z
311.2.A53	Anesthesiologists (Table K12)
311.2.H43	Healers (Table K12)
	Including herbalists, homeopathic physicians, naturopaths
311.2.P79	Psychologists. Psychotherapists (Table K12)
	Psychotherapists see KJ-KKZ2 311.2.P79
311.2.R33	Radiologists (Table K12)

Auxiliary medical professions. Paramedical professions

311.4	General (Table K11)
311.5	Nurses and nursing (Table K11)
311.6	Midwives (Table K11)
311.65	Opticians (Table K11)
311.7	Physical therapists (Table K11)
311.8.A-Z	Health organizations. By name, A-Z
311.8.R43	Red Cross (Table K12)

Hospitals and other medical institutions or health services

312	General (Table K11)
312.2	Blood banks (Table K11)
	Including blood donations
312.3	Institutions for the mentally ill (Table K11)
312.4.A-Z	Other health organizations, institutions, or services, A-Z
	Abortion clinics see KJ-KKZ2 313.5.A25
312.4.D39	Day care centers for infants and children (Table K12)
312.4.E43	Emergency medical services (Table K12)
	Nursing homes see KJ-KKZ2 312.4.O42
312.4.O42	Old age homes. Nursing homes (Table K12)
	Including invalid adults

Medical legislation -- Continued
Biomedical engineering. Medical technology
Including human experimentation in medicine and genetic
engineering
312.5   General (Table K11)
312.7   Transplantation of organs, tissues, etc. (Table K11)
Cf. KJ-KKZ2 411 Criminal law
312.8   Human reproductive technology (Table K11)
Including artificial insemination and fertilization in vitro
Cf. KJ-KKZ2 62.3 Family law
Cf. KJ-KKZ2 410.8 Criminal law
312.9.A-Z   Special topics, A-Z
(312.9.C48)   Change of sex
see KJ-KKZ2 312.5
312.9.C57   Circumcision (Table K12)
312.9.C65   Confidential communications (Table K12)
For data protection see KJ-KKZ2 86.5
(312.9.E95)   Experiments with the human body
see KJ-KKZ2 312.5
(312.9.G45)   Genetics, Medical
see 312.5
312.9.I54   Informed consent (Table K12)
313   Eugenics. Sterilization and castration (Table K11)
Euthanasia see KJ-KKZ2 405.8
Right to die see KJ-KKZ2 405.8
313.2   Veterinary medicine and hygiene. Veterinary public health
(Table K11)
313.3   Animal protection. Animal welfare. Animal rights (Table K11)
Including prevention of cruelty to animals
For animal rights as a social issue see HV4701+
Birth control. Family planning. Population control
Cf. KJ-KKZ2 407+ Illegal abortion (Criminal law)
313.4   General (Table K11)
313.4.A-Z   Special topics, A-Z
313.5.A25   Abortion clinics (Table K12)
Environmental law
313.7   General (Table K11)
Environmental pollution
313.8   General (Table K11)
313.9   Air pollution (Table K11)
Including noxious gases, automobile emissions, tobacco
smoking, etc.
314   Water and groundwater pollution (Table K11)
Including pollutants and sewage control
Pollutants
314.2   General (Table K11)
314.3   Radioactive substances (Table K11)

KJ-KKZ2

	Environmental law
	Environmental pollution
	Pollutants -- Continued
314.5	Noise (Table K11)
	Including traffic noise, and noise control
	Cf. KJ-KKZ2 70.3.N84 Property
314.6	Recycling of refuse (Table K11)
	Wilderness preservation
	Including natural monuments
314.7	General (Table K11)
	Wildlife conservation
	Including game, birds, and fish
314.8	General (Table K11)
	Game laws and hunting see KJ-KKZ2 333.7+
	Fishery law see KJ-KKZ2 334+
	Land reclamation in mining see KJ-KKZ2 336.9
(314.9)	Criminal provisions
	see KJ-KKZ2 435.2+
	Cultural affairs
315	General (Table K11)
315.2	Cultural policy. State encouragement of science and the arts (Table K11)
	Education
315.3	General (Table K11)
	School government. School districts
	Including curriculum and participation in school government in general
315.5	General (Table K11)
315.6	School discipline (Table K11)
	Students
315.7	General (Table K11)
315.8	Compulsory education (Table K11)
316	Teachers. School functionaries (Table K11)
316.3	Elementary education (Table K11)
316.4	Education of children with disabilities (Table K11)
316.5	Vocational education (Table K11)
316.6	Secondary education (Table K11)
	Higher education. Universities
	For legal education see KJ-KKZ2 5+
316.8	General (Table K11)
316.9	Intelligentsia (General) (Table K11)
	Administration. Institutional management
	Including curriculum
317	General (Table K11)
	Student participation in administration see KJ-KKZ2 317.8
317.3.A-Z	Special topics, A-Z

	Cultural affairs
	Education
	Higher education. Universities
	Administration. Institutional management
	Special topics, A-Z -- Continued
317.3.F54	Finance (Table K12)
317.5	Faculties. Institutes (Table K11)
	Students
317.7	General (Table K11)
317.8	Student participation in administration. Student parliament (Table K11)
317.9	Selection for higher education (Table K11)
318	Political activities (Table K11)
	Including strikes
318.2.A-Z	Universities. By place, A-Z
	Subarrange each by Table K12
318.3.A-Z	Other schools or institutions of higher education. By place, A-Z
	Subarrange each by Table K12
	Including colleges or institutes of technology, schools of music, art, drama, etc.
318.5	Private schools (Table K11)
318.6	Adult education (Table K11)
318.7	Physical education. Sports (Table K11)
	For liability for sports accidents see KJ-KKZ2 86.9
	Cf. KJ-KKZ2 303.5+ Sports activities
318.72	Science and the arts (Table K11)
318.8	Public policies in research (Table K11)
	Including research in higher education
318.9	Public institutions (Table K11)
319.A-Z	Branches and subjects
319.A72	Archaeology (Table K12)
319.C37	Cartography (Table K12)
	Meteorology see KJ-KKZ2 351.8
319.O25	Oceanography (Table K12)
319.S73	Statistical services (Table K12)
	For data protection see KJ-KKZ2 304.5
	The arts
319.2	General (Table K11)
319.3	Fine arts (Table K11)
	Performing arts
319.4	General (Table K11)
319.5	Music. Musicians (Table K11)
	Theater
	For copyright see KJ-KKZ2 118.6
319.6	General (Table K11)
319.7	Playwrights. Contracts (Table K11)

KJ-KKZ2

Cultural affairs
Science and the arts
The arts
Performing arts -- Continued
319.8   Motion pictures (Table K11)
Public collections
319.9   General (Table K11)
320   Archives. Historic documents (Table K11)
320.2   Libraries (Table K11)
320.3   Museums and galleries (Table K11)
320.4   Historic buildings and monuments. Architectural landmarks
(Table K11)
Including vessels, battleships, archaeological sites, etc.
320.6   Educational, scientific, and cultural exchanges (Table K11)
Economic law
320.63   General (Table K11)
Economic constitution
320.64   General (Table K11)
320.7   Organization and administration (Table K11)
Class here works on national departments and boards of
commerce, national, state, and local departments and
boards, or departments and boards of several states or
administrative districts
For departments and boards (several or individual) of an
individual state or administrative district, see the state or
district
Government control and policy
320.72   General (Table K11)
320.8   National planning (Table K11)
320.82   Contract systems. Systems of cooperation (Table K11)
320.9   Investments. Investment control (Table K11)
321   Assistance to developing countries (Table K11)
321.2   Economic assistance (Table K11)
321.3   Marketing orders (Table K11)
Class here general works
For particular marketing orders, see the subject, e.g. Agriculture
Prices and price control
321.4   General (Table K11)
Price delicts see KJ-KKZ2 429
321.5   Distribution (Table K11)
Money see KJ-KKZ2 353.55+
Foreign exchange control see KJ-KKZ2 353.8+
321.6   Industrial priorities, allocations, and circulation (Table K11)
Including organizations
For industrial priorities and allocations in wartime see KJ-
KKZ2 372+
Rationing see KJ-KKZ2 372.5+

Economic law
Government control and policy -- Continued

321.7	Government business enterprises (Table K11)
	Control of contracts and combinations in restraint of trade. Competition rules
	For unfair competition see KJ-KKZ2 123+
321.8	General (Table K11)
	Horizontal and vertical combinations
322	General (Table K11)
322.3	Corporate consolidation, merger, etc. (Table K11)
	Cartels
322.5	General (Table K11)
322.7.A-Z	Types of cartels, A-Z
	Subarrange each by Table K12
322.8	Industries, occupations, etc.
	Combinations (Socialist)
323	General (Table K11)
323.3.A-Z	By industry, A-Z
	Subarrange each by Table K12
323.5	Restraint-of-competition clause in business concern contracts and in articles of incorporation and partnership (Table K11)
323.7	Price maintenance and open price system
324	Monopolies. Oligopolies. Antitrust law (Table K11)
	For government monopolies see KJ-KKZ2 362.2
	Cartel agencies and procedure
324.4	General (Table K11)
324.5	Jurisdiction (Table K11)
	Including procedures according to EEC-legislation (conflict of laws)
324.6	Cartel register (Table K11)
	Including procedure
324.7	Damages (Private law) and indemnification (Public law) (Table K11)
	Criminal provisions see KJ-KKZ2 428.6+
324.8.A-Z	Mergers, cartels, combinations, business concerns, etc., A-Z
	Subarrange each by Table K12
325	Cooperative societies (Table K11)
325.3	Chambers of commerce (Table K11)
	Money, currency, and foreign exchange see KJ-KKZ2 353.55+
	Standards. Norms
	For standards, grading, and quality control of agricultural or consumer products, see the product
325.4	General (Table K11)
325.5	Quality control (Table K11)
	Weights and measures. Containers

KJ-KKZ2

Economic law
 Standards. Norms
  Weights and measures. Containers -- Continued
325.7   General (Table K11)
325.8.A-Z   By instrument, A-Z
     Subarrange each by Table K12
   Standardization
325.9   General (Table K11)
    Engineering standards
326   General (Table K11)
326.2.A-Z   By material, A-Z
     Subarrange each by Table K12
326.3.A-Z   By instrument, A-Z
     Subarrange each by Table K12
    Norms and standards for conservation of raw or scarce
     materials
      Including recycling of refuse (Metal, glass, paper, wood, etc.)
      Cf. KJ-KKZ2 314.6 Environmental law
326.5   General (Table K11)
326.6   Prohibition of industrial use of scarce materials (Table
     K11)
    Price norms see KJ-KKZ2 321.4+
327   Labeling (Table K11)
     Class here general works
     For the labeling of particular goods or products, see the good or
      product
   Regulation of industry, trade and commerce
327.2   General (Table K11)
327.6   Consumer protection (Table K11)
    Advertising
328   General (Table K11)
328.2   Trade fairs and expositions (Table K11)
     Including national and international fairs and expositions
   Primary production. Extractive industries
    Agriculture
     Land reform and agrarian land policy legislation.
      Nationalization
329   General (Table K11)
329.2   Restraint on alienation of agricultural land (Table K11)
329.3   Consolidation of landholdings. Commasation (Table
     K11)
329.5   General (Table K11)

Economic law
  Regulation of industry, trade and commerce
  Primary production. Extractive industries
  Agriculture -- Continued
    Organization and administration
      Class here works on national departments and boards of
        agriculture, national, state, and local departments and
        boards, or departments and boards of several states or
        administrative districts
      For departments and boards (several or individual) of an
        individual state or administrative district, see the state
        or district

329.6	General (Table K11)
329.7.A-Z	Particular organizations, agricultural science and research institutions, etc. A-Z
	Subarrange each by Table K12
329.8	Agricultural technique (Table K11)
329.9	Agricultural planning and planning periods (Table K11)
330	Entail (Table K11)
330.4	Fideicommissum. Entailed estates of the greater nobility (Table K11)
	Agricultural contracts
330.6	General (Table K11)
	Leasing of rural property. Farm tenancy
	Class here civil law provisions as well as legislation aimed at protection and stability for tenancy
331	General (Table K11)
331.2	Farm equipment leasing (Table K11)
	Agricultural business enterprise
331.3	General (Table K11)
	Corporate structure
331.4	General (Table K11)
331.6	Cooperative societies (Table K11)
	Including producers and marketing cooperatives
331.8	Government agricultural enterprises (Table K11)
	Including central and local administration
	Marketing orders
332	General (Table K11)
	Economic assistance
332.2	General (Table K11)
332.5	Priorities, allocations, and distribution (Table K11)
	Importing and stockpiling
332.6	General (Table K11)
	Rationing see KJ-KKZ2 372.5+
332.7	Livestock industry and trade (Table K11)
332.9	Milk production. Dairy farming (Table K11)
333	Agricultural courts and procedure (Table K11)

KJ-KKZ2

Economic law
Regulation of industry, trade and commerce
Primary production. Extractive industries
Agriculture -- Continued
333.2   Criminal provisions (Table K11)
333.3   Viticulture (Table K11)
333.4   Apiculture. Beekeeping (Table K11)
333.5   Horticulture (Table K11)
Forestry
Including timber laws
333.6   General (Table K11)
Game laws
333.7   General (Table K11)
333.8   Game leases and licenses (Table K11)
Fishery
334   General (Table K11)
334.2.A-Z   Particular fish or marine fauna, A-Z
Subarrange each by Table K12
Mining and quarrying
Including metallurgy
334.4   General (Table K11)
334.6   Organization and administration (Table K11)
Class here works on national departments and boards,
national, state, and local departments and boards, or
departments and boards of several states or
administrative districts
For departments and boards (several or individual) of an
individual state or administrative district, see the state
or district
334.7   Continental shelf and its resources (Table K11)
335   Rights to mines and mineral resources (Table K11)
Including procedure and registration
Mining industry and finance
335.3   General (Table K11)
335.4   Economic assistance (Table K11)
335.5   Corporations and cooperatives (Table K11)
335.6   Government mining enterprises (Table K11)
335.7   Planning and planning periods (Table K11)
Including calculation of reserves
Social legislation
335.9   General (Table K11)
Labor law for miners
336   General (Table K11)
336.3   Unions (Table K11)
336.4   Mine safety regulations. Rescue work (Table K11)
Including equipment

Economic law
  Regulation of industry, trade and commerce
    Primary production. Extractive industries
     Mining and quarrying
      Social legislation -- Continued

336.5	Social insurance for miners (Table K11)
	Including all branches of social insurance
336.6.A-Z	Resources, A-Z
	Including industries
336.6.P4	Peat (Table K12)
336.6.P47	Petroleum (Table K12)
336.6.P74	Precious metals (Table K12)
336.7	Subsidences. Earth movement (Table K11)
336.8	Eminent domain (Table K11)
336.9	Environmental laws. Land reclamation (Table K11)

    Manufacturing industries
     Including heavy and light industries

337	General (Table K11)
337.5	Recycling industries (Table K11)

     Food processing industries. Food products
      Class here works on trade practices, economic assistance,
       labeling, sanitation and quality inspection
      Including regulation of adulteration and additives

337.7	General (Table K11)
337.8	Labeling (Table K11)
337.9	Purity (Table K11)
	Including regulation of adulteration and food additives
338	Cereal products (Table K11)
338.2	Fruits and vegetables (Table K11)
338.3	Confectionary industry (Table K11)
338.4	Meat (Table K11)
338.5	Poultry products (Table K11)
338.6	Egg products (Table K11)

      Dairy products

338.8	General (Table K11)
339	Cheese (Table K11)
339.2	Fishery products. Seafood (Table K11)
339.3	Oils and fats (Table K11)

      Beverages

339.5	Brewing (Table K11)
339.7	Winemaking (Table K11)
339.8	Distilling (Table K11)
	Cf. KJ-KKZ2 362.4.D58 taxation
339.9	Mineral waters (Table K11)
340.A-Z	Related industries and products, A-Z
	Subarrange each by Table K12

Economic law
  Regulation of industry, trade and commerce -- Continued
  Building and construction industry
    For building laws see KJ-KKZ2 308+

340.2	General (Table K11)
340.3	Contracts and specifications (Table K11)
	International trade
340.5	General (Table K11)
	Export and import controls
	Including foreign trade practice and procedure
340.7	General (Table K11)
	Foreign exchange control see KJ-KKZ2 353.8+
	Trade agreements see KJ-KKZ2 364.3
	Export trade
341	General (Table K11)
341.15	Criminal provisions (Table K11)
341.3.A-Z	By region or country, A-Z
	e. g.
341.3.E87	European Economic Community countries (Table K12)
	Domestic trade
	For consumer protection see KJ-KKZ2 327.6
341.5	General (Table K11)
341.6	Planning and planning periods (Table K11)
341.7	Wholesale trade. Government wholesale trade (Table K11)
	Retail trade. Government retail trade
	Cf. KJ-KKZ2 342.9+ Artisans
341.8	General (Table K11)
341.9	Conditions of trading (Table K11)
	Including licensing and Sunday legislation
342.A-Z	Modes of trading, A-Z
	Chain stores see KJ-KKZ2 342.D46
342.D46	Department stores. Chain stores (Table K12)
	Fairs see KJ-KKZ2 342.M37
342.M34	Mail-order business (Table K12)
342.M37	Markets. Fairs (Table K12)
	For trade fairs and expositions see KJ-KKZ2 328.2
342.P43	Peddling (Table K12)
342.V45	Vending machines (Table K12)
342.2	Cooperative retail trade (Table K11)
342.3	Second-hand trade (Table K11)
	Service trades
342.4	General (Table K11)
	Old age homes see KJ-KKZ2 312.3
342.5	Travel agencies. Tourist trade (Table K11)
	Artisans
342.6	General (Table K11)

	Economic law
	Regulation of industry, trade and commerce
	Artisans -- Continued
342.7	Apprentices (Table K11)
	Corporate representation
342.9	General (Table K11)
343.A-Z	Crafts, A-Z
	Subarrange each by Table K12
	Energy policy. Power supply
	Including publicly and privately owned utilities
343.2	General (Table K11)
	Particular sources of power
343.3	Electricity (Table K11)
343.4	Gas. Natural gas (Table K11)
	Water see KJ-KKZ2 296
343.5	Heat. Steam distributed by central plants
343.6	Atomic energy (Table K11)
	For protection from radiation see KJ-KKZ2 301.2
	For ecological aspects see KJ-KKZ2 314.3
343.7.A-Z	Other sources of power, A-Z
	Subarrange each by Table K12
343.8	Courts and procedures (Table K11)
	Including industrial arbitral courts
343.9	Business ethics. Courts of honor (Table K11)
	Criminal provisions see KJ-KKZ2 428.6+
	Transportation
344	General (Table K11)
	Road traffic. Automotive transportation
344.2	General (Table K11)
	Motor vehicles
344.3	General (Table K11)
344.4	Registration (Table K11)
344.5	Inspection (Table K11)
344.6	Safety equipment (Table K11)
344.7	Drivers' licenses (Table K11)
	Including driving schools and instructors
344.8	Compulsory insurance (Table K11)
	Traffic regulations and enforcement
344.9	General (Table K11)
	Traffic violations
	For criminal interference with street traffic see KJ-KKZ2 438.4+
345	General (Table K11)
	Driving while intoxicated see KJ-KKZ2 438.6
	Hit-and-run drivers see KJ-KKZ2 439
345.2	Traffic courts and procedure (Table K11)
	Including fines

Transportation
  Road traffic. Automotive transportation
    Traffic regulations and enforcement -- Continued

345.3	Highway safety (Table K11)
	Carriage of passengers and goods
345.5	General (Table K11)
345.6	Goods carriers (Table K11)
	Railroads
346	General (Table K11)
	Operation of railroads
346.2	General (Table K11)
346.3	Railroad safety (Table K11)
	Including railroad crossings, etc. and liability
346.4	Carriage of passengers and goods (Table K11)
346.5.A-Z	Kinds of railroads or railways, A-Z
346.5.C32	Cable railways (Table K12)
	Private-track railroads see KJ-KKZ2 346.5.S42
346.5.S42	Secondary railroads. Private-track railroads (Table K12)
346.5.S98	Suspended railways (Table K12)
	Criminal provisions see KJ-KKZ2 438.2
	Postal services see KJ-KKZ2 348.6
346.6	Pipelines (Table K11)
	Aviation. Air law
346.7	General (Table K11)
346.8	Air traffic rules (Table K11)
	Including air safety and airworthiness
	Crimes aboard aircraft see KJ-KKZ2 439.6
	Water transportation
347	General (Table K11)
	Ships
347.2	General (Table K11)
347.3	Safety regulations (Table K11)
	Navigation and pilotage
347.4	General (Table K11)
347.5	Rule of the road at sea (Table K11)
347.6	Coastwise and inland navigation (Table K11)
347.7	Harbors and ports of entry (Table K11)
	Coastwise and inland shipping
	Including rafting
347.8	General (Table K11)
347.9	Carriage of passengers and goods (Table K11)
	Cf. KJ-KKZ2 101.9+ Affreightment (Commercial law)
348.A-Z	Individual waterways and channels, A-Z
	Subarrange each by Table K12
	Marine labor law see KJ-KKZ2 103.6+
	Marine insurance see KJ-KKZ2 103.5
	Communication. Mass media

Communication. Mass media -- Continued

348.2	General (Table K11)
348.3	Constitutional aspects. Freedom of communication. Censorship (Table K11)

Postal services. Telecommunications

348.5	General (Table K11)
348.6	Rates. Postage. Modes of collection (Table K11)
	Including postage stamps

Telecommunication

348.7	General (Table K11)
348.8	Telegraph (Table K11)
348.9	Teletype and data transmission systems (Table K11)
349	Telephone (Table K11)

Radio communications

Including radio and television broadcasting

349.2	General (Table K11)
	Freedom of radio communication see KJ-KKZ2 348.3
349.3	Organization and administration (Table K11)
	Including national and state jurisdiction
349.5	Stations. Networks (Table K11)
	Including frequency allocations and licensing

Broadcasting

349.6	General (Table K11)
349.7	Programming. Censorship (Table K11)
349.8	Labor law (Table K11)
	Including collective labor law
349.9	Criminal provisions (Table K11)

Press law

350	General (Table K11)
	Freedom of the press and censorship see KJ-KKZ2 348.3
350.2	Right to information (Table K11)

Planning and planning periods

350.3.A-Z	Types of literature, A-Z
350.3.P47	Periodicals (Table K12)
350.3.S34	Schoolbooks (Table K12)
	Including all levels of education
350.4	Publishers and publishing (Table K11)
350.6	Bookdealers (Table K11)
350.7.A-Z	Special topics, A-Z
350.7.P37	Party press (Table K12)
350.7.P65	Political advertising (Table K12)
350.7.R48	Resistance. Underground press (Table K12)
	Underground press see KJ-KKZ2 350.7.R48
350.7.Y68	Youth press (Table K12)

Press and criminal justice

350.8	General (Table K11)

Communication. Mass media
  Press law
    Press and criminal justice -- Continued
     Press delicts
      Including works on both press delicts and particular
        procedures
      For criminal procedure in general see KJ-KKZ2 460.4

351	General (Table K11)
	Libel and slander
351.2	General (Table K11)
351.3	Treason by publishing official secrets (Table K11)
	Cf. KJ-KKZ2 444.2 Treasonable espionage
351.5	Contempt of court (Table K11)
351.8	Weather bureau. Meteorological stations (Table K11)
	Professions. Intelligentsia (Socialist)
352	General (Table K11)
	Violation of confidential communication see KJ-KKZ2 416.4
352.2	Professional associations (Table K11)
	For particular professional associations, see the profession
	Individual professions
	Including technical intelligentsia of government industrial
	enterprises; and including education, licensing, liability, etc.
	Health professions see KJ-KKZ2 310.8+
	Pharmacists see KJ-KKZ2 310.5
	Veterinarians see KJ-KKZ2 313.2
	Attorneys see KJ-KKZ2 163
	Economic and financial advisors
352.3	Accountants (Table K11)
352.4	Auditors (Table K11)
	Engineering and construction
352.5	Architects (Table K11)
352.6	Engineers (Table K11)
352.62.A-Z	Other professions, A-Z
	Book dealers see KJ-KKZ2 350.6
	Graphic artists see KJ-KKZ2 352.62.P74
	Librarians see KJ-KKZ2 320.2
	Performing artists see KJ-KKZ2 319.4+
352.62.P74	Printers. Graphic artists (Table K12)
352.62.R4	Real estate agents (Table K12)
	Social workers see KJ-KKZ2 151.9+
352.62.S95	Surveyors (Table K12)
	Teachers see KJ-KKZ2 316
352.7	Professional ethics. Courts of honor (Table K11)
	For a particular court of honor, see the profession
	Public finance
	Finance reform and policies
	Cf. KJ-KKZ2 320.72+ Government control and policy

Public finance

Finance reform and policies -- Continued

352.8 General (Table K11)

Monetary policies see KJ-KKZ2 353.55+

352.9 General (Table K11)

Organization and administration

Class here works on national departments or agencies of finance, national, state, and local departments or agencies, or departments and agencies of several states or administrative districts

For departments and agencies (several or individual) of an individual state or administrative district, see the state or administrative district

For financial courts see KJ-KKZ2 368+

353 General (Table K11)

Budget. Government expenditures

353.2 General (Table K11)

353.3 Accounting (Table K11)

Including central or local organs of national government

353.4 Expenditure control. Auditing (Table K11)

353.45 Public debts. Loans. Bond issues

Revenue see KJ-KKZ2 353.9+

353.5 Intergovernmental fiscal relations (Table K11)

Including revenue sharing

Money

Including control of circulation

353.55 General (Table K11)

353.58 Coinage. Mint regulations (Table K11)

353.6 Bank notes. Banks of issue (Table K11)

Class here public law aspects of banks of issue

For banking law see KJ-KKZ2 99.5

353.7 Gold trading and gold standard (Table K11)

Foreign exchange control

353.8 General (Table K11)

Criminal provisions see KJ-KKZ2 429.2

National revenue

353.9 General (Table K11)

353.93 Fees. Fines (Table K11)

Taxation

Criticism and reform see KJ-KKZ2 352.8+

354 General (Table K11)

354.2 Double taxation (Table K11)

Taxation and tax exemption as a measure of social and economic policy

354.3 General (Table K11)

354.5 Export sales (Table K11)

Public finance
National revenue
Taxation
Taxation and tax exemption as a measure of social and
economic policy -- Continued

354.6.A-Z	Classes of taxpayers or lines of business, A-Z
	Subarrange each by Table K12
354.7.A-Z	Taxation of particular activities, A-Z
	Subarrange each by Table K12
354.8	Tax saving. Tax avoidance (Table K11)
	For tax planning relating to a particular tax, see the tax

Tax administration. Revenue service

355	General (Table K11)
	Financial courts see KJ-KKZ2 368+
	Double taxation see KJ-KKZ2 354.2

Collection and enforcement

355.3	General (Table K11)
355.4	Tax accounting. Financial statements (Table K11)
	Including personal companies and stock companies, etc.
	For a particular tax, see the tax
355.6.A-Z	Special topics, A-Z
	Subarrange each by Table K12

Administrative acts

355.7	General (Table K11)
	Administrative remedies see KJ-KKZ2 368.3+
	Judicial review see KJ-KKZ2 368.5+
356	Tax auditing (Table K11)
356.3	Execution (Table K11)
356.5.A-Z	Classes of taxpayers or lines of business, A-Z
356.5.A37	Agriculture. Horticulture (Table K12)
356.5.C65	Construction industry (Table K12)
356.5.H43	Health facilities (Table K12)
356.5.H65	Homeowners (Table K12)
	Horticulture see KJ-KKZ2 356.5.A37

Income tax

356.6	General (Table K11)
357	Taxable income. Exemptions (Table K11)

Deductions

357.2	General (Table K11)
357.4	Expenses and losses (Table K11)
	Surtaxes see KJ-KKZ2 361.2
357.5	Salaries and wages (Table K11)
	Including fringe benefits, nonwage payments, etc.
357.6	Capital investment (Table K11)
	Including foreign investment
	Cf. KJ-KKZ2 354.3+ Taxation as a measure of economic policy

Public finance
　National revenue
　　Taxation
　　　Income tax -- Continued
357.7　　　　　　　　Pensions and annuities (Table K11)
　　　　　　　　　Payment at source of income
358　　　　　　　　　Payroll deduction. Withholding tax
358.2.A-Z　　　　　Classes of taxpayers or lines of business, A-Z
358.2.A43　　　　　Agriculture.　Forestry.　Horticulture (Table K12)
358.2.A44　　　　　Aliens (Table K12)
358.2.A87　　　　　Artisans (Table K12)
358.2.A88　　　　　Artists (Table K12)
358.2.E83　　　　　Executives (Table K12)
358.2.M37　　　　　Married couples (Table K12)
358.2.M45　　　　　Merchant mariners (Table K12)
358.2.P75　　　　　Professions (Table K12)
358.2.T42　　　　　Teachers (Table K12)
　　　　　　　　Corporation tax
　　　　　　　　　Including income of business organizations, business
　　　　　　　　　　associations, and individual merchants
358.3　　　　　　　General (Table K11)
358.4　　　　　　　Nonprofit associations, nonprofit corporations,
　　　　　　　　　　foundations (endowments), and pension trust funds
358.5　　　　　　　Personal companies (Unincorporated business
　　　　　　　　　　associations) (Table K11)
358.6　　　　　　　Cooperatives (Table K11)
　　　　　　　　　Stock companies (Incorporated business associations)
358.7　　　　　　　　General (Table K11)
359　　　　　　　　　Taxable income.　Exemptions (Table K11)
359.2　　　　　　　Deductions (Table K11)
　　　　　　　　　Surtaxes see KJ-KKZ2 361.2
359.3　　　　　　　Corporate reorganization (Table K11)
359.4　　　　　　　Limited partnership (Table K11)
359.5　　　　　　　Stock corporation (Table K11)
360.A-Z　　　　　　Lines of corporate business, A-Z
360.B35　　　　　　Banks.　Credit institutions (Table K12)
360.C65　　　　　　Construction industry (Table K12)
　　　　　　　　　Credit institutions see KJ-KKZ2 360.B35
360.I57　　　　　　Insurance (Table K12)
360.I58　　　　　　Investment trusts.　Real estate investment funds
　　　　　　　　　　(Table K12)
　　　　　　　　　Real estate investment funds see KJ-KKZ2 360.I58
　　　　　　　　Foreign corporations and stockholders
360.2　　　　　　　General (Table K11)
　　　　　　　　　Double taxation see KJ-KKZ2 354.2
　　　　　　　　Multi-national corporations
360.3　　　　　　　General (Table K11)

Public finance
National revenue
Taxation
Income tax
Corporation tax
Multi-national corporations -- Continued
Double taxation see KJ-KKZ2 354.2

360.4	Property tax. Taxation of capital (Table K11)
	For real property tax see KJ-KKZ2 367+
	Cf. KJ-KKZ2 366.2 Property tax (State and local finance)
360.5	Estate, inheritance, and gift taxes (Table K11)
360.6	Church tax (Table K11)
361	Capital gains tax (Table K11)
	Development gains tax see KJ-KKZ2 367.3
361.2	Surtaxes
	Poll tax see KJ-KKZ2 368+
	Indirect taxation. Excise taxes. Taxes on transactions
361.25	General (Table K11)
	Sales tax
361.3	General (Table K11)
	Turnover tax
	Including value-added tax
361.5	General (Table K11)
361.6	Import sales and export sales (Table K11)
362	Personal companies and stock companies
	Particular commodities, services, and transactions see KJ-KKZ2 362.4.A+
362.2	Government monopolies (Table K11)
	Including monopolies delegated by the state to others
362.4.A-Z	Commodities, services, and transactions, A-Z
362.4.A42	Alcoholic beverages (General) (Table K12)
362.4.B35	Banking transactions (Table K12)
362.4.B37	Bars and taverns (Table K12)
362.4.B38	Betting (Bookmaking) (Table K12)
362.4.B55	Bills of exchange tax (Table K12)
	Bonds see KJ-KKZ2 362.4.S42
	Brandy see KJ-KKZ2 362.4.L57
	Champagne see KJ-KKZ2 362.4.W55
362.4.D58	Distilleries (Table K12)
362.4.E96	Export-import sales (Table K12)
	Gambling see KJ-KKZ2 366.5
362.4.H68	Hotels and motels (Table K12)
	Import sales see KJ-KKZ2 362.4.E96
362.4.L57	Liquors (Table K12)
362.4.M38	Matches (Table K12)
	Motels see KJ-KKZ2 362.4.H68

	Public finance
	National revenue
	Taxation
	Excise taxes. Taxes on transactions
	Commodities, services, and transactions, A-Z --
	Continued
362.4.M68	Motor fuels (Table K12)
362.4.P48	Petroleum (Table K12)
362.4.P82	Public utilities (Table K12)
	Real estate transactions see KJ-KKZ2 367+
	Recycled products see KJ-KKZ2 362.4.W36
362.4.R47	Restaurants (Table K12)
362.4.R48	Retail trade (Table K12)
362.4.S42	Securities and bonds (Table K12)
362.4.S76	Stock exchange transactions (Table K12)
	Taverns see KJ-KKZ2 362.4.B37
362.4.T62	Tobacco (Table K12)
362.4.T72	Transportation of persons or goods (Table K12)
362.4.W36	Waste products. Recycled products (Table K12)
362.4.W46	Wholesale trade (Table K12)
362.4.W55	Wine (Table K12)
	Methods of assessment and collection
	For assessment and collection of a particular tax, see the tax
363	General (Table K11)
	Stamp duties
363.3	General (Table K11)
	Bills of exchange see KJ-KKZ2 362.4.B55
	Criminal provisions see KJ-KKZ2 370+
	Customs. Tariff
364	General (Table K11)
	Tables see KJ-KKZ2 364+
364.3	Trade agreements (Table K11)
364.4	Customs organization and administration
364.5.A-Z	Commodities and services, A-Z
364.5.A37	Agricultural commodities. Farm products (Table K12)
	Farm produce see KJ-KKZ2 364.5.A37
	Criminal provisions see KJ-KKZ2 368+
	State and local finance
	For the public finance of an individual state, administrative district or municipality, see the state or municipality
	Finance reform see KJ-KKZ2 352.8+
365	General (Table K11)
365.3	Fees. Fines (Table K11)
	Including license fees
365.4	Grants-in-aid (Table K11)
	Taxation

KJ-KKZ2

	Public finance
	State and local finance
	Taxation -- Continued
365.5	General (Table K11)
	Income tax see KJ-KKZ2 356.6+
	Sales, turnover, and value-added taxes see KJ-KKZ2 361.2
366	Estate, inheritance, and gift taxes (Table K11)
366.2	Property tax. Taxation of capital (Table K11)
	Including juristic persons and business enterprises
	For real property tax see KJ-KKZ2 367+
366.3	Motor vehicles tax (Table K11)
366.5	Taxes from gambling tables. Casinos (Table K11)
	Real property tax
	Including real estate transactions
367	General (Table K11)
367.3	Capital gains tax (Table K11)
	Including development gains
367.5	Business tax (Table K11)
367.7.A-Z	Other taxes, A-Z
367.7.P65	Poll tax (Table K12)
	Tax and customs courts and procedure
	Class here works on national courts, national, state and district courts and boards, or courts and boards of several states or administrative districts
	For courts and boards (several or individual) of an individual state or administrative district, see the state or district
368	General (Table K11)
	Pretrial procedures. Administrative remedies
368.3	General (Table K11)
368.4	Tax protest (Table K11)
	Procedure at first instance. Judicial review
368.5	General (Table K11)
368.6	Actions. Defenses (Table K11)
369	Evidence (Table K11)
369.3	Judicial decisions. Judgments (Table K11)
	Including court records
	Remedies. Means of review
369.4	General (Table K11)
369.5	Appellate procedures (Table K11)
	Tax and customs crimes and delinquency. Procedure
370	General (Table K11)
	Individual offenses
370.2	Tax evasion and tax avoidance (Table K11)
	Procedure
	For criminal procedure in general see KJ-KKZ2 459.92+
	General see KJ-KKZ2 370

Public finance
Tax and customs crimes and delinquency. Procedure
Procedure -- Continued
370.3   Pretrial procedure (Table K11)
370.5   Evidence (Table K11)
370.6   Amnesty. Pardon (Table K11)
370.7   Tax and customs delinquency (Table K11)
                      Including faulty accounting and bookkeeping, etc.
                 Government measures in time of war, national emergency, or
                 economic crisis
370.9   General (Table K11)
                 Particular measures
371   Military requisitions from civilians. Requisitioned land (Table
                      K11)
                      For damages and compensation see KJ-KKZ2 373+
371.2   Control of property. Confiscations (Table K11)
                      Including enemy and alien property
                      For damages and compensation see KJ-KKZ2 373+
                 Control of unemployment. Manpower control
371.4   General (Table K11)
371.5   Compulsory and forced labor (Table K11)
371.7   Insolvent debtors. Wartime and crisis relief (Table K11)
371.8   Finances (Table K11)
                      For procurement and defense contracts see KJ-KKZ2
                          373.5+
                 Industrial priorities and allocations. Economic recovery
                 measures. Nationalization
372   General (Table K11)
372.2.A-Z   By industry or commodity, A-Z
                      Subarrange each by Table K12
                 Strategic material. Stockpiling
372.3   General (Table K11)
372.4.A-Z   By commodity, A-Z
372.4.P46   Petroleum products (Table K12)
                 Rationing. Price control
372.5   General (Table K11)
372.6.A-Z   By commodity, A-Z
                      Subarrange each by Table K12
372.7   Criminal provisions (Table K11)
                 War damage compensation
                      Including foreign claims settlement
373   General (Table K11)
373.3.A-Z   Particular claims, A-Z
                      Confiscations see KJ-KKZ2 373.3.R47
                      Demontage see KJ-KKZ2 373.3.R46
                      Military occupation damages see KJ-KKZ2 373.3.R47
373.3.P47   Personal damages. Property loss or damages (Table K12)

Government measures in time of war, national emergency, or
economic crisis
War damage compensation
Particular claims, A-Z -- Continued
Property loss or damages see KJ-KKZ2 373.3.P47
373.3.R46   Reparations. Demontage (Table K12)
373.3.R47   Requisitions. Confiscations. Military occupation damages
(Table K12)
373.4.A-Z   Particular victims, A-Z
Subarrange each by Table K12
Military occupation. Procurement
373.5   General (Table K11)
National defense. Military law
For emergency and wartime legislation see KJ-KKZ2 370.9+
374   General (Table K11)
374.3   Organization and administration. Command (Table K11)
The armed forces
374.5   General (Table K11)
Compulsory service
Including draft and selective service
374.6   General (Table K11)
Deferment
Including disqualification
374.7   General (Table K11)
374.8.A-Z   Particular groups, A-Z
e. g.
374.8.A44   Aliens (Table K12)
374.8.C65   Conscientious objectors (Table K12)
375.A-Z   Particular branches of service, A-Z
Civil guards see KJ-KKZ2 375.P37
Military police see KJ-KKZ2 375.P37
375.P37   Paramilitary defense forces. Civil guards. Military police
(Table K12)
375.18   Foreign military bases
Civil defense
375.2   General (Table K11)
375.3   Air defense. Air raid shelters (Table K11)
375.6   Participation in NATO or Warsaw Pact
For NATO (General) or Warsaw Pact (General), see JX
Military criminal law and procedure
Cf. KJ-KKZ2 447+ Crimes against national defense
375.8   General (Table K11)
376   Individual offenses (Table K11)
376.7   Courts and procedure
377   Punishment. Execution (Table K11)
377.5   Probation and parole (Table K11)

	National defense. Military law
	Military criminal law and procedure -- Continued
377.7.A-Z	Particular trials. By name of defendant, A-Z
	Subarrange each by Table K12
	Military discipline. Law enforcement
	Including all branches of the armed forces
378	General (Table K11)
378.2	Superior orders. Enforcement of orders (Table K11)
378.3	Procedure (Table K11)
378.5.A-Z	Other, A-Z
378.5.M55	Military maneuvers (Table K12)
	Criminal law
379	Reform of criminal law, procedure, and execution
	For works limited to a particular subject, see the subject. For works pertaining exclusively to the codes, see the code
	For reform of criminal justice administration see KJ-KKZ2 47
	Administration of criminal justice see KJ-KKZ2 156.92+
379.5	General (Table K11 modified)
	Federal legislation
379.5.A25	Indexes and tables. Digests. By date
	Statutes. Statutory orders
	Collections. Selections
	Including annotated editions and commentaries
379.5.A27	Serials
379.5.A28	Monographs. By date
	Individual acts (or groups of acts adopted as a whole)
379.5.A282-.A29	Codes
	Collections see KJ-KKZ2 379.5.A27+

Criminal law
  General
    Federal legislation
      Statutes. Statutory orders
        Individual acts (or groups of acts adopted as a whole)
          Codes -- Continued

379.5.A29<date>   Individual codes

Arrange chronologically by appending date of original enactment or revision of the law to this number and deleting any trailing zeros

Under each:

.xA12-.xA129	*Indexes and tables*
.xA14	*Bills. By date*
.xA32	*Legislative documents and related works. By date*
.xA52	*Text of the code. Unannotated editions. By date*
	Including official editions with or without annotations, and works containing the introductory act and complementary legislation together with the text of the code
	For individual complementary laws, see the subject
.xA6-.xZ8	*Annotated editions. Commentaries. General works*
	Including criticism, private drafts, and commentaries on private drafts
.xZ9	*Amendatory laws. By date of enactment*
	For amendatory laws pertaining to a particular subject, see the subject

Criminal law
  General
    Federal legislation
      Statutes. Statutory orders
        Individual acts (or groups of acts adopted as a whole)
        Codes -- Continued
379.5.A31<date>   Other individual acts
                                Arrange chronologically by appending date of original
                                  enactment or revision of the law to this number and
                                  deleting any trailing zeros
                                Under each:
                                              Unannotated editions
                                                Including official editions with or
                                                  without annotations
                  .xA2-.xA29   *Serials*
                  .xA4   *Monographs. By date*
                  .xA6-.xZ8   *Annotated editions. Commentaries.*
                                              General works
                                Including enactments of national codes by individual
                                  states, etc.
380   Constitutional aspects (Table K11)
380.2   Philosophy of criminal law (Table K11)
380.6   Relationship of criminal law to other disciplines, subjects or
                    phenomena (Table K11)
381   Interpretation and construction. Legal hermeneutics
                  Concepts and principles
                    Applicability and validity of the law
381.2   General (Table K11)
381.3   Nulla poena sine lege. Nullum crimen sine lege (Table
                      K11)
                    Alternative conviction see KJ-KKZ2 474.8
                    Territorial applicability
382   General (Table K11)
                      Place of commission of crime
382.2   General (Table K11)
(382.3)   Press delicts
                        see KJ-KKZ2 351
(383)   Crimes aboard aircraft
                        see KJ-KKZ2 439.6
383.2   Conflict of laws (Table K11)
383.6   Temporal applicability (Table K11)
383.7   Personal applicability. Immunities (Table K11)
                    Criminal offense
384   General (Table K11)
384.2   Trichotomy and dichotomy (Table K11)
                      Including felony, misdemeanor, and transgression
384.3   Crimes by commission or omission (Table K11)

Criminal law
Concepts and principles
Criminal offense -- Continued
384.4   Crimes aggravated by personal characteristics (Table K11)
Criminal act
384.5   General (Table K11)
384.6   Corpus delicti. Fact-pattern conformity (Table K11)
384.7   Omission (Table K11)
Causation
385   General (Table K11)
385.2   Proximate cause (Table K11)
Forms of the act see KJ-KKZ2 390.92+
Illegality. Justification of otherwise illegal acts
385.5   General (Table K11)
385.6   Self-defense or defense of another (Table K11)
Consent of the injured party
386   General (Table K11)
386.2   Presumed consent (Table K11)
386.5.A-Z   Other grounds for justification, A-Z
Subarrange each by Table K12
386.7   Criminal intent. Mens rea (Table K11)
Including purpose and scienter, dolus, eventualis, actio libera
in causa, etc.
387   Negligence and wantonness (Table K11)
Criminal liability. Guilt
387.5   General (Table K11)
Capacity
387.7   General (Table K11)
Incapacity and limited capacity
388   General (Table K11)
388.2   Insane persons. People with mental or emotional
disabilities (Table K11)
388.3   Minors (Table K11)
388.5.A-Z   Special topics, A-Z
388.5.D58   Distemper (Table K12)
388.5.I58   Intoxication (Table K12)
388.5.L58   Litigious paranoia (Table K12)
Passion see KJ-KKZ2 388.5.D58
388.7   Criminal liability of juristic persons (Table K11)
390   Superior orders and justification or excusation (Table K11)
Cf. KJ-KKZ2 375.8+ Military and criminal law
390.3   Error (Table K11)
Forms of the criminal act
Omission see KJ-KKZ2 384.5+
Attempt
391   General (Table K11)
391.2   Intent and preparation (Table K11)

	Criminal law
	Concepts and principles
	Criminal offense
	Forms of the criminal act
	Attempt -- Continued
391.5	Active repentance (Table K11)
	Accessory at attempted crime see KJ-KKZ2 393
	Perpetrators
392	General (Table K11)
	Principal and accessories
392.2	General (Table K11)
392.5	Co-principals (Table K11)
392.7	Accessory before the fact (Table K11)
	Including abettor
393	Accessory at attempted crime (Table K11)
393.3	Complicity (Table K11)
393.4	Agent provocateur (Table K11)
393.6	Juristic persons. Corporations (Table K11)
(393.8)	Aggravating and extenuating circumstances see KJ-KKZ2 402.2
394	Compound offenses and compound punishment
	Civil liability for wrongful acts see KJ-KKZ2 83.5+
	Punishment
394.6	General (Table K11)
394.8	Constitutional aspects (Table K11)
	Theory and policy of punishment
395	General (Table K11)
395.2	Retaliation. Retribution (Table K11)
395.4	Safeguarding the social and political system (Table K11)
395.6	General and special prevention (Table K11)
	Including education, rehabilitation, and resocialization of perpetrator
	Criminal anthropology see HV6030+
396	Criminal sociology (Table K11)
	Penalties and measures of rehabilitation and safety
	For juveniles and young adults see KJ-KKZ2 472.6+
	For execution of sentence see KJ-KKZ2 479.22+
396.2	General (Table K11)
396.3	Capital punishment (Table K11)
	Imprisonment
	Including maximum and minimum terms
397	General (Table K11)
	Prisons and jails see KJ-KKZ2 482.4
	Reformatories see KJ-KKZ2 398.6
397.2	Short-term sentence (Table K11)

Criminal law
　　Punishment
　　　Penalties and measures of rehabilitation and safety --
　　　　Continued
397.4　　　　Sentencing to probation (Punishment without
　　　　　imprisonment). Conditional sentencing (Table K11)
　　　　　Including terms of probation, e.g. education and
　　　　　resocialization through labor
397.8　　　　Fines (Table K11)
398　　　　Reprimand (Table K11)
　　　　Measures entailing deprivation of liberty
398.2　　　　General (Table K11)
398.4　　　　Commitment to medical or psychiatric treatment (Table
　　　　　K11)
398.6　　　　Commitment to nursing or socio-therapeutic institutions
　　　　　(Table K11)
399　　　　Commitment of addicts to institutions for withdrawal
　　　　　treatment (Table K11)
399.2　　　　Protective custody (Table K11)
　　　　　Including dangerous or habitual criminals
　　　　Other measures
399.5　　　　Protective surveillance
399.7　　　　Expulsion
400　　　　Driver's license revocation
400.2　　　　Prohibition against practicing a profession
400.4　　　　Loss of civil rights. Infamy. Disfranchisement
400.6　　　　Property confiscation (Table K11)
400.8　　　　Confiscation and destruction of corpus delicti (Table K11)
401　　　　Forfeiture (Table K11)
　　　Sentencing and determining the measure of punishment
401.2　　　　General (Table K11)
401.6　　　　Fixed and indeterminate sentence (Table K11)
　　　　Juvenile delinquents see KJ-KKZ2 472.2
　　　　Circumstances influencing measures of penalty
402　　　　General (Table K11)
　　　　Aggravating and extenuating circumstances
　　　　　Including principals and accessories
402.2　　　　General (Table K11)
402.4　　　　Recidivism (Table K11)
402.6　　　　Detention pending investigation (Table K11)
　　　Causes barring prosecution or execution of sentence
403　　　　General (Table K11)
403.2　　　　Active repentance (Table K11)
　　　　Pardon and amnesty. Clemency
403.4　　　　General (Table K11)
　　　　Suspension of punishment see KJ-KKZ2 482.8
　　　　Probation and parole see KJ-KKZ2 483+

Criminal law
  Punishment
    Causes barring prosecution or execution of sentence --
      Continued
      Limitation of actions

403.8	General (Table K11)
404.A-Z	Crimes exempt from limitation of action, A-Z
404.C74	Crimes against humanity and human rights (Table K12)
404.T73	Treasonable endangering of the peace (Table K12)
404.W37	War crimes (Table K12)

      Criminal registers see KJ-KKZ2 485
      Criminal statistics see KJ-KKZ2 3.2
    Individual offenses

404.5	General (Table K11)

      Offenses against the person
        Including aggravating circumstances

404.9	General (Table K11)

      Homicide

405	General (Table K11)
405.2	Murder (Table K11)
405.4	Manslaughter (Table K11)
405.6	Killing on request (Table K11)
405.8	Euthanasia. Right to die. Living wills (Table K11)
406	Suicide. Aiding and abetting suicide (Table K11)
406.2	Parricide (Table K11)
406.4	Infanticide (Table K11)
406.5	Negligent homicide (Table K11)
406.7	Desertion. Exposing persons to mortal danger (Table K11)

      Crimes against inchoate life. Illegal abortion

407	General (Table K11)
407.2	Justification of abortion. Legal abortion (Table K11)

        Including ethical, social, medical and eugenic aspects
      Crimes against physical inviolability

407.4	General (Table K11)
407.5	Stalking (Table K11)
407.6	Battery (Table K11)
407.8	Communicating venereal disease (Table K11)
408	Failure to render assistance (Table K11)
408.2	Abuse of defenseless persons or dependents. Abuse of older people (Table K11)

        For child abuse see KJ-KKZ2 419
      Consent. Justified assault

408.4	General (Table K11)
408.6	Sports injuries (Table K11)

        Cf. KJ-KKZ2 86.9 Torts
      Medical treatment and operations see KJ-KKZ2 409.6+

KJ-KKZ2

Criminal law
　Individual offenses
　　Offenses against the person
　　　Crimes against physical inviolability -- Continued

408.8	Compound offenses (Table K11)
409	Poisoning (Table K11)
409.2	Dueling (Table K11)
409.4	Brawling (Table K11)

　　　Criminal aspects of surgical and other medical treatment
　　　　Including biomedical engineering, medical technology

409.6	General (Table K11)
410	Malpractice (Table K11)
	Cf. KJ-KKZ2 310.9+ Medical legislation
410.2	Treatment without consent (Table K11)
	Euthanasia see KJ-KKZ2 405.8
410.3	Genetic engineering (Table K11)
410.8	Human reproductive technology (Table K11)
	Including artificial insemination, fertilization in vitro, etc.
411	Transplantation of organs, tissues, etc. (Table K11)
	Including donation of organs, tissues, etc.
411.2	Sterilization (Table K11)
411.3	Autopsy (Table K11)
	Confidential communication see KJ-KKZ2 469.6.A+
	Psychopharmaca see KJ-KKZ2 410

　　　Crimes against personal freedom

411.6	General (Table K11)
411.8	False imprisonment (Table K11)
412	Extortionate kidnapping (Table K11)
	Abduction
	Cf. KJ-KKZ2 60 Parental kidnapping
412.5	General (Table K11)
412.7	Political abduction (Table K11)
413	Abduction of a woman without her consent (Table K11)
413.2	Abduction of a female minor (Table K11)
413.4	Political accusation (Table K11)
413.6	Threats of a felonious injury (Table K11)
413.8	Duress (Table K11)
414	Unlawful entry (Table K11)

　　　Crimes against dignity and honor
　　　　Including juristic persons and families

414.3	General (Table K11)
414.5	Insult (Table K11)
414.7	Defamation (Table K11)
414.9	Calumny (Table K11)
415	Disparagement of memory of the dead (Table K11)
415.4	Defamatory statement and truth (Table K11)

Criminal law
  Individual offenses
    Offenses against the person
      Crimes against dignity and honor -- Continued

415.6	Privileged comment (Table K11)
	Including criticism of scientific, artistic, or professional accomplishments
	Violation of personal privacy and secrets
	Cf. KJ-KKZ2 85.9+ Torts
416	General (Table K11)
416.2	Constitutional aspects (Table K11)
416.4	Violation of confidential disclosures by professional persons
416.6	Opening of letters (Table K11)
416.8	Eavesdropping. Wiretapping (Table K11)
	Offenses against religious tranquility and the peace of the dead
417	General (Table K11)
417.2	Blasphemy (Table K11)
417.4	Disturbing a religious observance (Table K11)
417.6	Disturbing the peace of the dead (Table K11)
	Including cemeteries and funerals
	Offenses against marriage, family, and family status
418	General (Table K11)
418.2	Incest (Table K11)
418.4	Adultery (Table K11)
418.6	Bigamy (Table K11)
(418.8)	Abduction of a minor from legal custodian
	see KJ-KKZ1 602+
419	Abandonment, neglect, or abuse of a child (Table K11)
419.2	Breach of duty of support (Table K11)
419.4	Breach of duty of assistance to a pregnant woman (Table K11)
	Abortion see KJ-KKZ2 407+
	Artificial insemination see KJ-KKZ2 410.8
419.6	Falsification of civil status (Table K11)
	Offenses against sexual integrity
420	General (Table K11)
420.2	Rape (Table K11)
	Compelling lewd acts
420.3	General (Table K11)
420.4	Lewd acts with persons incapable of resistance (Table K11)
420.6	Abduction for lewd acts (Table K11)
420.8	Lewd acts with children or charges. Seduction (Table K11)

KJ-KKZ2

Criminal law
Individual offenses
Offenses against sexual integrity
Compelling lewd acts -- Continued
421 Lewd acts by persons taking advantage of official
position (Table K11)
421.2 Lewd acts in institutions (Table K11)
421.6 Sodomy. Homosexual acts (Table K11)
421.8 Bestiality (Table K11)
422 Obscenity (Table K11)
Including production, exhibition, performance, advertising,
etc.
Pandering and pimping
422.4 General (Table K11)
422.5 White slave traffic (Table K11)
Offenses against private and public property
423 General (Table K11)
Larceny and embezzlement
423.4 General (Table K11)
423.6 Burglary (Table K11)
423.8 Armed theft and theft by gangs (Table K11)
424 Pilfering (Table K11)
424.2 Domestic and family theft (Table K11)
424.4 Automobile theft (Table K11)
Including automotive vehicles and their unauthorized use
424.6 Energy theft (Table K11)
Embezzlement
425 General (Table K11)
425.2 Embezzlement in office (Table K11)
425.4 Robbery and rapacious theft (Table K11)
425.6 Destruction of property and conversion (Table K11)
Fraud
425.8 General (Table K11)
426 Fraudulent insurance claims (Table K11)
426.2 Fraud by litigation (Table K11)
426.3 Credit card fraud (Table K11)
Fraudulent bankruptcy see KJ-KKZ2 427.6
426.4 Extortion (Table K11)
426.6 Breach of trust (Table K11)
426.8 Usury (Table K11)
Defeating rights of creditors
427 General (Table K11)
427.2 Defeating rights of pledgee (Table K11)
427.4 Defeating execution (Table K11)
427.6 Fraudulent bankruptcy (Table K11)
428 Game and fish poaching (Table K11)
Aiding criminals in securing benefits

Criminal law
Individual offenses
Offenses against private and public property
Aiding criminals in securing benefits -- Continued
428.2   General (Table K11)
428.4   Receiving stolen goods (Table K11)
Offenses against the national economy
428.6   General (Table K11)
429   Violation of price regulations (Table K11)
Including price fixing, hoarding, discrimination, overselling
and underselling prices established by government etc.
429.2   Foreign exchange violations (Table K11)
429.4   Economic and industrial secrets. Unauthorized possession
or disclosure (Table K11)
429.8   False statements concerning national planning (Table K11)
Counterfeiting money and stamps see KJ-KKZ2 434.6+
Offenses against public property see KJ-KKZ2 423+
430.A-Z   Other, A-Z
Subarrange each by Table K12
Tax and customs crimes see KJ-KKZ2 370+
Offenses against public order and convenience
Including aggravating circumstances
Disrupting the peace of the community
430.5   General (Table K11)
430.7   Inciting insubordination (Table K11)
430.9   Rowdyism. Vandalism (Table K11)
431   Inciting crime (Table K11)
431.2   Rewarding or approving felonies (Table K11)
431.4   Criminal societies (Table K11)
431.6   Parasitism (Table K11)
432   Demonstrations and failure to disperse (Table K11)
432.2   Inciting acts against minorities (Table K11)
Threatening the community. Terrorist activities see KJ-
KKZ2 435.2+
432.4   Misuse of titles, uniforms, and insignia (Table K11)
Crimes against security of legal and monetary transactions
and documents
433   General (Table K11)
433.2   Evidence (Table K11)
433.4   Forgery and suppression of documents (Table K11)
433.8   Forgery and suppression of mechanical records (Table
K11)
Including forgery of sound recordings and electronic data
bases
434   Physical and identifying marks (Table K11)
Counterfeiting money and stamps
434.6   General (Table K11)

KJ-KKZ2

Criminal law
  Individual offenses
    Offenses against public order and convenience
      Crimes against security of legal and monetary transactions
        and documents
        Counterfeiting money and stamps -- Continued

434.8	Passing counterfeit money (Table K11)
435	Counterfeiting securities (Table K11)
	Including checks, bills of exchange, etc.
	Customs crimes see KJ-KKZ2 370+
	Tax evasion see KJ-KKZ2 370.2
435.15.A-Z	Other, A-Z
435.15.B55	Blanks (Table K12)
435.15.D57	Displacing boundaries (Table K12)
435.15.F34	False certification (Table K12)
435.15.F35	False medical certificates (Table K12)
435.15.F67	Forgery of art works (Table K12)
435.15.M57	Misuse of credentials (Table K12)
	Money orders see KJ-KKZ2 435.15.T44
435.15.T44	Telegrams. Money orders (Table K12)

      Crimes involving danger to the community. Crimes against
        the environment. Terrorism

435.2	Common danger (Table K11)
435.4	Arson (Table K11)
435.6	Causing explosion (Table K11)
	Including explosives and nuclear energy
435.8	Misuse of ionizing radiation (Table K11)
436	Releasing natural forces (Table K11)
	Including flood, avalanche, rockfall, etc.
436.2	Dangerous use of poisonous substances (Table K11)
436.4	Poisoning wells or soil (Table K11)
436.6	Poisoning food, medicine, etc. (Table K11)
436.8	Spreading communicable diseases, morbific agents, or parasites. Biological terrorism (Table K11)
437	Damaging water and power installations (Table K11)
437.2	Impairing industrial safety appliances (Table K11)
437.4	Sabotage of essential services, utilities, warning systems, etc. (Table K11)
437.6	Causing danger in construction (Table K11)
	Including collapse, faulty gas or electric installation, etc.

      Crimes affecting traffic

438	Dangerous interference with rail, ship, or air traffic
438.2	Unsafe operation of a rail vehicle, ship, or aircraft (Table K11)
	Dangerous interference with street traffic
	For minor traffic violations resulting in fines see KJ-KKZ2 345+

                       Criminal law
                           Individual offenses
                               Offenses against public order and convenience
                                   Crimes affecting traffic
                                     Dangerous interference with street traffic -- Continued

438.4	General (Table K11)
438.6	Driving while intoxicated (Table K11)
438.8	Duress. Constraint (Table K11)
439	Leaving the scene of an accident. Hit-and-run driving (Table K11)
	Predatory assault on motorists
439.2	General (Table K11)
439.4	Assault on taxicab drivers (Table K11)
439.6	Crimes aboard aircraft. Air piracy (Table K11)
439.8	Riots (Table K11)
	Crimes against public health
440	General (Table K11)
440.2	Intoxication (Table K11)
440.4	Illicit use of, possession of, and traffic in narcotics (Table K11)
	Communicating venereal diseases see KJ-KKZ2 407.8
440.6	Gambling (Table K11)
	Including illegal operation of a lottery or games of chance, and participation
	Cf. KJ-KKZ2 303.8.G35 Police and public safety
	Acts of annoyance to the public see KJ-KKZ2 300.5.A+
	Offenses against the government. Political offenses.
	Offenses against the peace
441.5	General (Table K11)
	High treason and treason
441.7	General (Table K11)
	High treason against the state
	Including national and state (republic, etc.)
442	General (Table K11)
442.2	Preparation of treasonable acts (Table K11)
442.4	Treason against the constitution (Table K11)
442.6	Assault on the head of state (Table K11)
442.8	Inciting treason (Table K11)
443	Preparation of despotism (Table K11)
443.2	Sabotage endangering the state (Table K11)
443.4	Undermining the state apparatus (Table K11)
443.8	Lese majesty (Table K11)
444	Disparagement of the state and its symbols. Disparaging constitutional organs (Table K11)
444.2	Treasonable espionage (Table K11)
	For publication of official secrets by the press see KJ-KKZ2 351.3

KJ-KKZ2

Criminal law
  Individual offenses
    Offenses against the government. Political offenses.
      Offenses against the peace
        High treason against the state -- Continued

444.4	Subversive activities (Table K11)
444.6	Intelligence activities (Table K11)
444.8	Propaganda endangering the state (Table K11)
445.5	Treasonable endangering of the peace or of international relations (Table K11)

          Including propaganda, planning, preparation, or participation in an aggressive war

        Crimes in connection with election and voting

445.8	General (Table K11)
446	Bribery. Corrupt practices (Table K11)
446.2	Coercing (Table K11)
446.4	Deceiving voters (Table K11)
446.6	Falsifying votes and voting results (Table K11)

        Crimes against national defense

447	General (Table K11)
447.3	Sabotaging and depicting means of defense (Table K11)

        Opposition to power of the state

447.6	General (Table K11)
447.8	Constraining official action or inaction (Table K11)
448	Prison escape. Mutiny. Freeing prisoners (Table K11)
448.2.A-Z	Other forms of opposition, A-Z
448.2.D35	Damaging official announcements (Table K12)

        Endangering the administration of justice. Obstruction of justice

448.3	General (Table K11)

         False testimony

448.4	General (Table K11)
448.6	False unsworn testimony (Table K11)
449	Perjury (Table K11)
449.2	False affirmation (Table K11)
449.4	Causing false testimony (Table K11)
449.6	False accusation (Table K11)
449.8	Bringing false complaint (Table K11)
450	Thwarting criminal justice (Table K11)
450.2	Failure to report felony. Misprision (Table K11)
450.4	Coercion of testimony (Table K11)
450.6	Intentional misconstruction by law officers (Table K11)
450.7	Prosecuting innocent persons (Table K11)

         Including execution

        Chicanery and abuse of legal process see KJ-KKZ2 44.4

450.8	Repressing conflicting interests. Prevarication (Table K11)

Criminal law
Individual offenses
Offenses against the government. Political offenses.
Offenses against the peace
Endangering the administration of justice. Obstruction of
justice -- Continued
451   Contempt of court (Table K11)
         For contempt of court by the press see KJ-KKZ2
         351.5
         Receiving stolen goods see KJ-KKZ2 428.4
         Assisting in securing benefits see KJ-KKZ2 428.2+
         Crimes against the civil service
451.4   General (Table K11)
         Corruption
451.6   General (Table K11)
451.8   Corrupt act by officials. Accepting benefits (Table K11)
         Including omission of official acts
452   Bribery. Granting benefits to civil servants (Table K11)
452.2   Illegal compensation to arbitrators (Table K11)
         Bribery in connection with election see KJ-KKZ2 446
         Embezzlement see KJ-KKZ2 425+
         Violating official secrecy
452.6   General (Table K11)
452.8   Disclosing official secrets (Table K11)
453   Mail and telecommunication (Table K11)
453.2.A-Z   Other, A-Z
         Subarrange each by Table K12
         Crimes against humanity
453.8   General (Table K11)
454   Genocide (Table K11)
454.3   Crimes against foreign states, supranational institutions, or
international institutions (Table K11)
454.5   War crimes (Table K11)
         Offenses commited through the mail
454.8   General (Table K11)
         Obscenity see KJ-KKZ2 422
         Threats, extortion, and blackmail see KJ-KKZ2 426.4
         Radio communication criminal provisions see KJ-KKZ2 349.9
         Press law criminal provisions see KJ-KKZ2 350.8
         Tax and customs crimes see KJ-KKZ2 370+
         Military criminal law
         Optional arrangement for libraries using this classification
see KJ-KKZ2 375.8
<455>   General (Table K11)
<455.6.A-Z>   Individual offenses, A-Z
         Subarrange each by Table K12
         Courts and procedure

KJ-KKZ2

Criminal law
  Individual offenses
    Military criminal law
      Courts and procedure -- Continued

<456>	General (Table K11)
<456.5>	Procedure in honor cases (Table K11)
<457>	Punishment. Execution (Table K11)
<458>	Probation and parole (Table K11)
<459>	Military discipline. Law enforcement (Table K11)

Criminal procedure
    For works on both criminal and civil procedure, including
      codes of both criminal and civil procedure see KJ-KKZ2
      165+
    For works on both criminal law and criminal procedure,
      including codes of both criminal law and criminal
      procedure see KJ-KKZ2 379+
Criticism and reform see KJ-KKZ2 379

460	General (Table K11 modified)
	Federal legislation
460.A25	Indexes and tables. Digests. By date
	Statutes. Statutory orders
	Collections. Selections
	Including annotated editions and commentaries
460.A27	Serials
460.A28	Monographs. By date
	Individual acts (or groups of acts adopted as a whole)
460.A282-.A29	Codes
	Collections see KJ-KKZ2 460.A27+

Criminal procedure
  General
    Federal legislation
      Statutes. Statutory orders
        Individual acts (or groups of acts adopted as a whole)
          Codes -- Continued

460.A29<date>
          Individual codes
            Arrange chronologically by appending date of original enactment or revision of the law to this number and deleting any trailing zeros

Under each:	
.xA12-.xA129	*Indexes and tables*
.xA14	*Bills. By date*
.xA32	*Legislative documents and related works. By date*
.xA52	*Text of the code. Unannotated editions. By date*
	Including official editions with or without annotations, and works containing the introductory act and complementary legislation together with the text of the code
	For individual complementary laws, see the subject
.xA6-.xZ8	*Annotated editions. Commentaries. General works*
	Including criticism, private drafts, and commentaries on private drafts
.xZ9	*Amendatory laws. By date of enactment*
	For amendatory laws pertaining to a particular subject, see the subject

	Criminal procedure
	General
	Federal legislation
	Statutes. Statutory orders
	Individual acts (or groups of acts adopted as a whole)
	Codes -- Continued
460.A31<date>	Other individual acts

460.A31<date>   Other individual acts
> Arrange chronologically by appending date of original enactment or revision of the law to this number and deleting any trailing zeros
> *Under each:*

		Unannotated editions
		Including official editions with or without annotations
	.xA2-.xA29	*Serials*
	.xA4	*Monographs. By date*
	.xA6-.xZ8	*Annotated editions. Commentaries. General works*

> Including enactments of national codes by individual states, etc.

460.2	Constitutional aspects (Table K11)
460.4	Criminal procedure and public opinion (Table K11)
	Including trial by newspaper
	Administration of criminal justice see KJ-KKZ2 156.92+
	Court organization see KJ-KKZ2 158+
	Procedural principles
462	Due process of law (Table K11)
462.2	Uniformity of law application. Stare decisis (Table K11)
462.4	Accusation principle (Table K11)
462.6	Publicity and oral procedure (Table K11)
462.8	Prejudicial actions (Table K11)
	Including all branches of the law
463.A-Z	Parties to action, A-Z
463.A25	Accused. Person charged. Defendant (Table K12)
463.C74	Criminal judge (Table K12)
	Defendant see KJ-KKZ2 463.A25
463.D43	Defense attorney. Public defender (Table K12)
	Person charged see KJ-KKZ2 463.A25
	Public defender see KJ-KKZ2 463.D43
463.S73	State prosecutor (Table K12)
	Class here works on the legal status of the prosecutor in criminal procedure
	For general works on the office of the public prosecutor see KJ-KKZ2 161.5
463.S93	Suspect (Table K12)
463.V52	Victim (Table K12)
	Pretrial procedures

Criminal procedure
    Pretrial procedures -- Continued

463.2	General (Table K11)
463.4	Penal report. Charges brought against a person (Table K11)

      Investigation

463.6	General (Table K11)

        Techniques of criminal investigation
          see HV8073

463.8	Examination of the accused (Table K11)

          Cf. KJ-KKZ2 467.9+ Admission of evidence

464	Preliminary judicial investigation (Table K11)

      Public charges by prosecutor

464.2	General (Table K11)
464.4	Stare decisis (Table K11)
464.6	Summonses, service of process, and subpoena (Table K11)
464.8	Time periods. Deadlines (Table K11)

    Compulsory measures against the accused. Securing of
      evidence

465	General (Table K11)
465.2	Search and seizure (Table K11)

        Including search of persons, buildings, institution's records, etc.

465.4	Provisional apprehension (Table K11)

      Detention pending investigation
        Cf. KJ-KKZ2 479.8+ Execution of sentence

465.7	General (Table K11)
465.9	Bail (Table K11)
466	Extradition (Table K11)

    Procedure at first instance

466.4	General (Table K11)
466.6	Jurisdiction (Table K11)

        Including competence in subject matter and venue

466.8	Action. Complaint (Table K11)
467	Exclusion and challenge of court members (Table K11)
467.2	Plea bargaining (Table K11)

      Time periods and deadlines see KJ-KKZ2 464.8
      Limitation of action see KJ-KKZ2 403.8+
      Trial

467.3	General (Table K11)

        Evidence

467.5	General (Table K11)
467.7	Burden of proof (Table K11)

        Admission of evidence

467.9	General (Table K11)
468	Confession. Self-incrimination. Entrapment (Table K11)
468.3	Informers. Official secrets (Table K11)
468.5	Narcoanalysis, lie detectors, etc. (Table K11)

Criminal procedure
Procedure at first instance
Trial
Evidence
Admission of evidence -- Continued
468.7   Physical examination (Table K11)
          Including blood tests, urine tests, etc.
          For forensic medicine, see RA1001+
468.9   Electronic listening and recording devices (Table K11)
          Including wiretapping
469   Previous testimony, police records, etc. (Table K11)
     Witnesses
469.2   General (Table K11)
469.6.A-Z   Privileged witnesses (confidential communication), A-Z
469.6.P74   Press (Table K12)
469.8.A-Z   Other witnesses, A-Z
469.8.S73   State's witnesses. State's evidence (Table K12)
470   Expert testimony (Table K11)
          For forensic medicine, chemistry, psychology, psychiatry,
            toxicology, etc., see RA1001+
470.2   Testimony of accused (Table K11)
470.4   Documentary evidence (Table K11)
470.5   Circumstantial evidence (Table K11)
470.6   Alibi (Table K11)
470.9.A-Z   Other, A-Z
          Subarrange each by Table K12
470.95   Arguments of counsel
          Including summation, closing arguments, and oral pleadings
     Particular proceedings
471   Summary proceedings
     Proceedings against absentee and fugitives
471.3   General (Table K11)
471.5   Restitutio in integrum (Table K11)
471.7   Recourse against decisions of grievance boards (Table
          K11)
     Procedure for juvenile delinquency
472   General (Table K11)
472.2   The juvenile delinquent. The young adult perpetrator
          (Table K11)
472.4   Juvenile crime (Table K11)
     Criminal liability and guilt see KJ-KKZ2 387.5+
     Punishment. Correctional or disciplinary measures
          Including measures of rehabilitation and safety
472.6   General (Table K11)
472.8   Custodial education (Table K11)
473   Judicial orders (Table K11)

Criminal procedure
Procedure at first instance
Trial
Procedure for juvenile delinquency
Punishment. Correctional or disciplinary measures --
Continued
473.2   Detention homes. Reformatories (Table K11)
     Cf. KJ-KKZ2 482.4 Execution of sentence
473.4   Punishment without imprisonment (Table K11)
Execution of sentence see KJ-KKZ2 479.22+
Judicial decisions
473.6   General (Table K11)
Judgment
473.8   General (Table K11)
Sentencing and determination of punishment see KJ-
KKZ2 401.2+
474   Judicial discretion (Table K11)
     Including opportunity and equity
474.4   Acquittal (Table K11)
Conviction
     Including measures of rehabilitation and safety
474.6   General (Table K11)
474.8   Alternative conviction (Table K11)
475   Dismissal. Decision ab instantia (Table K11)
Probation see KJ-KKZ2 483+
475.2   Void judgments (Table K11)
475.3   Correction or withdrawal of faulty decisions (errors) (Table
K11)
Res judicata
475.4   General (Table K11)
475.6   Ne bis in idem. Constitutional aspects (Table K11)
Waiver of appeal see KJ-KKZ2 478.8
476   Court records. Minutes of evidence (Table K11)
     Including clerks, translators, and correction of records
Participation of injured party in criminal procedure
476.2   General (Table K11)
476.4   Private charge (Table K11)
     Including public interest
476.6   Intervention (Table K11)
476.7   Civil suits of victims in connection with criminal proceedings
(Table K11)
     Including reparation (Compensation to victims of crimes)
Special procedures
476.8   Procedure before the justice of the peace (Table K11)
Commitment of insane criminals see KJ-KKZ2 398.6
Procedure in confiscation of corpus delicti see KJ-KKZ2
400.8

KJ-KKZ2

Criminal procedure
   Special procedures -- Continued
   Other procedures
      see the subject, e.g. KJ-KKZ2 376.7, Military criminal
        procedure, etc.
   Remedies

477	General (Table K11)
477.5	Gravamen (Table K11)
477.7	Reformatio in peius (Table K11)

     Appellate procedure

478	General (Table K11)
478.6	Cassation (Table K11)

      Restitutio in integrum see KJ-KKZ2 471.5

478.8	Waiver of appeal (Table K11)

    Post-conviction remedies

479	General (Table K11)
479.2	Reopening a case. New trial (Table K11)

      For procedure before the constitutional court see KJ-
        KKZ2 262+

   Execution of sentence
     Including execution of sentence of juvenile courts
     Criticism and reform see KJ-KKZ2 379

479.5	General (Table K11)

    Imprisonment
      Class here works on regulation of both prison administration
        and prisoners, and works on regulation of detention
        pending investigation and short-term sentences
      For penalties in general, including imprisonment see KJ-
        KKZ2 396.2+

479.8	General (Table K11)
480	Administration of penal or correctional institutions (Table K11)

      Including discipline, hygiene, etc.

481	The prisoner (Table K11)

      Including discipline, hygiene, etc.

481.2.A-Z	Particular, A-Z
481.2.E38	Education of prisoners. Education through labor (Table K12)

      Insane criminals see KJ-KKZ2 398.6

481.2.J88	Juvenile prisoners (Table K12)
481.2.P64	Political criminals (Table K12)
482	Labor and industries in correctional institutions (Table K11)

      Including wages
     Rehabilitation and resocialization see KJ-KKZ2 395.6

482.4	Penal or correctional institutions (Table K11)

      Including prisons, jails, penal colonies, reformatories, juvenile
       detention homes, etc.

Criminal procedure
  Execution of sentence -- Continued
    Pardon, amnesty, and clemency see KJ-KKZ2 403.4+

482.8   Suspension of punishment (Table K11)
    Probation. Parole
      Including conditions
483   General (Table K11)
483.4   Probation and parole for juvenile delinquents (Table K11)
483.7   Probation counselor (Table K11)
484   Remission (Table K11)
485   Criminal registers (Table K11)
  Extradition see KJ-KKZ2 466
486   Costs (Table K11)
  Victimology
487   General (Table K11)
487.4   Children and sexual crimes (Table K11)
  Criminology and penology
    see HV6001+

	See the names of the jurisdictions in the KJ-KKZ schedules (e.g. KJG 0-4990, Albania) for the names of states, provinces, etc., and numbers assigned to them. To determine a subject division for a given table, etc., add the number or numbers in the table for the subject to the basic number for the state, etc. For example, for guilds in the state of Venice, Italy, add 7.2 in Table 4 to the basic number for Venice, KKH8500, to make KKH8507.2
	Including historical (extinct) states
1	Bibliography
<1.2>	Periodicals
	For periodicals consisting predominantly of legal articles, regardless of subject matter and jurisdiction, see K1+
	For periodicals consisting primarily of informative material (Newsletters, bulletins, etc.) relating to a particular subject, see the subject and form division for periodicals
	For law reports, official bulletins or circulars, and official gazettes intended chiefly for the publication of laws and regulations, see the appropriate entries in the text or form division tables
1.4	Monographic series
	Official gazettes
	For departmental gazettes, see the issuing department or agency
	For city gazettes, see the issuing city
1.45	Indexes (General)
1.5	Serials
1.55	Monographs. By date
	Legislative and executive papers (including historical sources)
	see class J
	Legislation
1.6	Indexes and tables. By date
1.7	Abridgments and digests
	Early territorial laws and legislation
	Class here early sources not provided for elsewhere, e.g. custumals, Landfriedensgesetze, Landrechte und Landesordnungen, privileges, edits, mandates, etc.
2	Collections. Compilations
	Individual
	see the subject
	Statutes
	Including statutory orders and regulations
	For statutes, statutory orders, and regulations on a particular subject, see the subject
	Collections and compilations
	Including official and private editions with or without annotations
2.2	Serials
2.3	Monographs. By date

KJ-KKZ3

	Legislation -- Continued
3.3	Codifications and related material
	Class here collections of codes and codifications not limited to a subject
	Including early codifications, and including enactments of codes
	For codes on a subject, see the subject
	Court decisions and related materials
	Including historical sources, and authorized and private collections
	For decisions on a particular subject, see the subject
3.33	Indexes. Digests. Analytical abstracts. By date
	For indexes relating to a particular publication, see the publication
	Several courts
	Class here decisions of courts of several jurisdictions
3.39	Serials
3.4	Monographs. By date
	Particular courts and tribunals
	Including historical courts and tribunals not provided for by subject
3.43	Highest court of appeals. Supreme Court (Table K19)
	Intermediate appellate courts. Courts of appeal
	Including decisions of the only or several intermediate appellate courts of a state and reports of national court of appeals in judicial districts
3.5	Collective (Table K19)
3.6.A-Z	Particular courts, A-Z
	Trial courts
3.7	Collective (Table K19)
4.A-.Z	Particular courts. By city, county, district, etc., A-Z
	Local courts
	Including justices of the peace courts, people's courts, magistrate's courts, etc.
4.2	Collective (Table K19)
4.4.A-Z	Particular courts. By city, etc., A-Z
4.5.A-Z	Other courts. By place or name, A-Z
	Dictionaries. Words and phrases
	see the numbers provided for dictionaries at the national level
	Form books
	see the numbers provided for form books at the national level
	Judicial statistics
5.2	General
5.3	Criminal statistics
	Including juvenile delinquency
5.4.A-Z	Other. By subject, A-Z
	Directories
	see the numbers provided for directories at the national level

	Trials
	see the numbers provided for trials at the national level
	Legal research
	see the numbers provided for legal research at the national level
	Legal education
	see the numbers provided for legal education at the national level
	Bar associations
	see the numbers provided for bar associations at the national level
5.7.A-Z	Manuals and other works for particular groups of users. By user, A-Z
5.7.B87	Businesspeople. Foreign investors
	Foreign investors see KJ-KKZ3 5.7.B87
6	History of law
	For the history of a particular subject (including historical sources), see the subject
	For collections and compilations of sources see KJ-KKZ3 1.6+
7	Law reform. Criticism
	Including reform of general administration of justice
	For reform of criminal justice administration and criminal law see KJ-KKZ3 91+
8	General works
	Including compends, popular works, civics, etc.
11	Private law (Table K11)
	Private international law. Conflict of laws
	For works on conflict rules of other branches of law (e.g. criminal law), see the subject
12	General (Table K11)
	Interlocal (interstate) law see Table KJ-KKZ1 483.5
13.A-Z	Particular branches and subjects of the law, A-Z
	Subarrange each by Table K12
13.2	Intertemporal law. Retroactive law (Table K11)
	Including conflict of laws
	Civil law
13.3	General (Table K11)
	Persons
13.4	General (Table K11)
	Natural persons
13.5	General (Table K11)
	Personality and capacity
	Including incapacity
13.6	General (Table K11)
13.7	Absence and presumption of death (Table K11)
	Civil registers see KJ-KKZ3 38.2.R44
13.8	Citizenship (Table K11)

KJ-KKZ3

	Civil law
	Property -- Continued
	Real property
17	General (Table K11)
	Land registration law see KJ-KKZ3 19.2+
	Public and private restraint on real property
17.2	General (Table K11)
	Zoning laws see KJ-KKZ3 60.5
	Entail see KJ-KKZ3 74.4
	Entailed estates of the greater nobility see KJ-KKZ3 72.5+
17.3	Ownership. Acquisition and loss (Table K11)
	Including contractual acquisition and loss by judicial decree
	Rights incident to ownership of land
17.4	General (Table K11)
17.5	Law of adjoining landowners (Table K11)
17.6.A-Z	Special topics, A-Z
17.6.A57	Air and space above ground (Table K12)
17.6.R56	Riparian rights. Water rights (Table K12)
	Space above ground see KJ-KKZ3 17.6.A57
	Water rights see KJ-KKZ3 17.6.R56
17.7	Superficies (Table K11)
	Rights as to the use and profits of another's land
18	General (Table K11)
18.2	Emphyteusis (Table K11)
18.3.A-Z	Servitudes (real and personal), A-Z
18.3.C65	Conveyance and life annuities (Table K12)
	Life annuities see KJ-KKZ3 18.3.C65
18.4	Rights of preemption (Table K11)
18.5.A-Z	Types of real property, A-Z
	Subarrange each by Table K12
	Hypothecation
18.6	General (Table K11)
18.7	Mortgage. Hypotheca (Table K11)
18.8	Land charge (Table K11)
19	Pledges (Table K11)
	Land register and registration
19.2	General (Table K11)
19.3	Cadastral surveys. Cadasters (Table K11)
19.4.A-Z	Other special topics, A-Z
	Subarrange each by Table K12
	Inheritance. Succession upon death
19.5	General (Table K11)
	Intestate and testamentary succession
	Including wills
19.6	General (Table K11)

KJ-KKZ3

	Commercial contracts and transactions
22.2	General (Table K11)
	Commercial courts see KJ-KKZ3 31.8
22.3	Merchant and business enterprise (Table K11)
	Including firma, good will, accounting, etc.
22.4	Agency (Table K11)
	Including commercial agents
22.5	Commercial registers (Table K11)
22.6	Commercial sale (Table K11)
22.7	Consignment (Table K11)
22.8	Warehousing (Table K11)
	Freight forwarders and carriers see KJ-KKZ3 25+
22.82	Maritime contracts (Table K11)
	Negotiable instruments. Titles of credit
23	General (Table K11)
23.2	Bills of exchange (Table K11)
23.3	Checks (Table K11)
	Stock certificates and bonds see KJ-KKZ3 28.5.S86
23.4.A-Z	Other special, A-Z
	Subarrange each by Table K12
23.5	Criminal provisions (Table K11)
	Banking. Stock exchange
23.6	General (Table K11)
23.7	State supervision (Table K11)
23.8.A-Z	Types of banks and credit institutions, A-Z
23.8.B35	Banks of issue (Table K12)
23.8.M67	Mortgage banks (Table K12)
23.8.S29	Savings banks (Table K12)
24.A-Z	Banking transactions, A-Z
24.A24	Account current (Table K12)
	Credit see KJ-KKZ3 24.L6
24.D45	Deposit banking (Table K12)
24.L6	Loans. Credit (Table K12)
	Investments
24.3	General (Table K11)
24.4	Stock exchange transactions. Securities (Table K11)
	Carriers. Carriage of goods and passengers
	For regulatory aspects of transportation see KJ-KKZ3 82.5+
25	General (Table K11)
	Coastwise and inland shipping see KJ-KKZ3 26
	Bus lines see KJ-KKZ3 83.3.B88
	Railroads see KJ-KKZ3 83.4+
	Airlines see Table KJ-KKZ1 3467+
25.5	Freight forwarders and carriers (Table K11)

	Commercial contracts and transactions
	Carriers. Carriage of goods and passengers -- Continued
25.7.A-Z	Other special topics, A-Z
	Subarrange each by Table K12
26	Maritime law (Table K11)
	Including coastwise and inland shipping, contracts, insurance, etc.
	Insurance
26.5	General (Table K11)
26.8.A-Z	Branches of insurance, A-Z
	Subarrange each by Table K12
26.8.P76	Property insurance
26.85.A-Z	Individual risks and damages, A-Z
	Subarrange each by Table K12
	Business associations
27	General (Table K11)
	Personal companies (Unincorporated business associations)
27.3	General (Table K11)
27.5.A-Z	Special types of companies, A-Z
	Subarrange each by Table K12
	Stock companies (Incorporated business associations)
28	General (Table K11)
28.3.A-Z	Particular types, A-Z
	Subarrange each by Table K12
28.5.A-Z	Special topics, A-Z
	Bonds see KJ-KKZ3 28.5.S86
28.5.S86	Stock certificates. Bonds (Table K12)
28.5.S88	Stocks and stockholder's rights. Stock transfer (Table K12)
28.7.A-Z	Other types of companies, A-Z
	Subarrange each by Table K12
28.8	Cooperative societies (Table K11)
29	Combinations. Industrial trusts (Table K11)
	Including business concerns, consortia, etc.
	Intellectual and industrial property
	Including copyright, patents, trademarks, unfair competition, etc.
29.3	General (Table K11)
29.5.A-Z	Special topics, A-Z
	Subarrange each by Table K12
	Labor law
	Including works on both labor law and social insurance and private labor law as it applies to the labor contract and to the labor-management relationship
	Criticism and reform see Table KJ-KKZ1 1464+
30	General (Table K11)
30.3	Organization and administration (Table K11)
	Including state and local departments and boards

KJ-KKZ3

	Labor law -- Continued
30.4	Labor contract and employment (Table K11)
30.45	Wages (Table K11)
	Labor-management relations
30.5	General works (Table K11)
30.53	Employee participation in management and planning (Table K11)
	Collective bargaining and labor agreements
30.6	General (Table K11)
30.7.A-Z	By industry, occupation, or group of employees, A-Z
	Subarrange each by Table K12
30.7.G67	Government employees (Table K12)
	Collective labor disputes
	Including strikes
30.8	General (Table K11)
31.A-Z	By industry, occupation, or group of employees, A-Z
	Subarrange each by Table K12
31.2	Labor unions (Table K11)
31.3	Employers' associations (Table K11)
	Protection of labor
31.4	General (Table K11)
31.5.A-Z	Special topics, A-Z
31.5.C44	Child labor (Table K12)
	Holidays see KJ-KKZ3 31.5.V32
31.5.H65	Home labor (Table K12)
31.5.H68	Hours of labor (Table K12)
31.5.L32	Labor hygiene and safety (Table K12)
	Leave of absence see KJ-KKZ3 31.5.V32
	Safety equipment see KJ-KKZ3 31.5.L32
	Sick leave see KJ-KKZ3 31.5.V32
31.5.V32	Vacations. Holidays (Table K12)
	Including leave of absence and sick leave
31.5.W35	Women's labor (Table K12)
31.6.A-Z	By industry, occupation, or group of employees, A-Z
31.6.B84	Building and construction industry (Table K12)
31.7	Labor supply. Manpower control (Table K11)
	Including employment agencies
31.8	Labor courts and procedure (Table K11)
	Social legislation
32	Social reform and policies (Table K11)
	Including all branches of social legislation
32.2	General (Table K11)
32.3	Organization and administration (Table K11)
	For department of labor and social affairs see KJ-KKZ3 30.3
	Social insurance

	Social legislation
	Social insurance -- Continued
32.4	General (Table K11)
32.5.A-Z	Branches of social insurance, A-Z
32.5.H42	Health insurance (Table K12)
32.5.S62	Social security (Table K12)
32.5.U53	Unemployment insurance (Table K12)
32.5.W67	Workers' compensation (Table K12)
32.6.A-Z	By industry, occupation, or group of employees, A-Z
32.6.A34	Agricultural laborers. Farmers (Table K12)
	Farmers see KJ-KKZ3 32.6.A34
	Social services. Public welfare
33	General (Table K11)
33.3.A-Z	Services or benefits, A-Z
	Subarrange each by Table K12
33.5.A-Z	Beneficiary groups, A-Z
33.5.A88	Asocial types (Table K12)
33.5.C44	Children (Table K12)
33.5.D58	Disabled (Table K12)
33.5.E43	Elderly (Table K12)
33.5.F35	Families (Table K12)
	Juveniles see KJ-KKZ3 33.5.C44
33.5.P45	Pensioners (Table K12)
33.5.P66	Poor, The (Table K12)
33.5.R43	Refugees (Table K12)
33.5.W37	War (Table K12)
33.6	Disaster relief (Table K11)
33.7	Social courts and procedure (Table K11)
	Courts and procedure
	The administration of justice. The organization of the judiciary
	Administration of criminal justice see KJ-KKZ3 92.39+
	Criticism and reform see KJ-KKZ3 7
34	General (Table K11)
34.2	Organization and administration (Table K11)
	Including state local departments and boards
	Judicial statistics see KJ-KKZ3 5.2+
	Courts
	History
34.3	General (Table K11)
34.4.A-Z	Particular courts, A-Z
34.4.F48	Feudal and servitory courts (Table K12)
	Manorial courts see KJ-KKZ3 34.4.P38
34.4.P38	Patrimonial and manorial courts (Table K12)
	Servitary courts see KJ-KKZ3 34.4.F48
35	General (Table K11)

KJ-KKZ3

	Courts and procedure
	Courts -- Continued
35.2.A-Z	Particular courts and tribunals, A-Z
	Subarrange each by Table K12
35.4.A-Z	Courts of special jurisdiction, A-Z
	For courts of special jurisdiction not listed below, see the subject, e.g. Labor courts, KJ-KKZ3, 31.8; Social courts, KJ-KKZ3, 33.7, etc.
35.4.C68	Courts of honor (Table K12)
35.4.J88	Justices of the peace (Table K12)
	The legal profession
	Including judicial officers and personnel
35.6	General (Table K11)
	Law school education
	see the numbers provided for legal education at the national level
35.7	Judicial personnel other than lawyers (Table K11)
36	Judges (Table K11)
36.2	Office of the public prosecutor (Table K11)
	Notaries see KJ-KKZ3 38.2.N68
36.4	Practice of law (Table K11)
	Including attorneys and legal consultants
36.45	Legal aid. Legal services to the poor. Community legal services (Table K11)
	Judicial assistance
36.5	General (Table K11)
36.6	International judicial assistance (Table K11)
36.7	Foreign judgments (Conflict of laws) (Table K11)
	Judicial review see KJ-KKZ3 54
37	Procedure in general (Table K11)
	Including all branches of law
	Civil procedure
37.2	General (Table K11)
37.3.A-Z	Special procedures, A-Z
37.3.D43	Decision without trial. Summary proceedings (Table K12)
	Summary proceedings see KJ-KKZ3 37.3.D43
37.4	Remedies (Table K11)
37.5	Arbitration (Table K11)
	Including commercial arbitration
	Noncontentious jurisdiction
38	General (Table K11)
38.2.A-Z	Branches of noncontentious jurisdiction, A-Z
	Children (General) see KJ-KKZ3 38.2.D65
	Civil registers see KJ-KKZ3 38.2.R44
38.2.D65	Domestic relations (Table K12)
	Including children (General)

	Courts and procedure
	Noncontentious jurisdiction
	Branches of noncontentious jurisdiction, A-Z -- Continued
38.2.G82	Guardianship court (Table K12)
38.2.I54	Inheritance (Probate) court (Table K12)
	Matrimonial property registers see KJ-KKZ3 38.2.R44
38.2.N68	Notaries (Table K12)
	Probate court see KJ-KKZ3 38.2.I54
	Recording see KJ-KKZ3 38.2.R44
38.2.R44	Registration. Recording (Table K12)
	Including civil registers, registers of matrimonial property, etc.
	Insolvency
38.5	General (Table K11)
38.6	Execution (Table K11)
	Including procedures
	Bankruptcy
38.7	General (Table K11)
38.8.A-Z	Special topics, A-Z
	Subarrange each by Table K12
39	Debtors' relief (Table K11)
39.2	Costs (Table K11)
40	Public law (Table K11)
	Constitutional law
	History
41	General works
	Estates. Classes
42	General works
42.2	Nobility
	Peasantry see KJ-KKZ3 71.4+
42.3.A-Z	Other special topics, A-Z
	Feudal law
43	General works
43.2.A-Z	Special topics, A-Z
43.3	Constitutional reform. Criticism (Table K11)
43.4	General (Table K11)
	Sources
	Including historical sources and related material
43.5	Collections. Compilations
	Constitutions
	Collections see KJ-KKZ3 43.5
43.9<date>	Individual constitutions
	Arrange chronologically by appending the date of adoption to this number and deleting any trailing zeros. Subarrange each by Table K17

KJ-KKZ3

	Constitutional law
	General
	Sources -- Continued
44.2<date>	Individual sources other than constitutions
	Arrange chronologically by appending the date of adoption or issuance to this number and deleting any trailing zeros. Subarrange by main entry
	Intergovernmental relations see Table KJ-KKZ1 2180
44.4.A-Z	Constitutional principles, A-Z
44.4.R85	Rule of law (Table K12)
44.4.S46	Separation of power (Table K12)
45	Territory (Table K11)
45.3	Foreign relations administration (Table K11)
	Individual and state
45.5	General (Table K11)
46	Nationality and citizenship (Table K11)
46.2.A-Z	Particular groups, A-Z
	Subarrange each by Table K12
	Fundamental rights and constitutional guaranties
46.3	General (Table K11)
46.5.A-Z	Individual rights or guaranties, A-Z
46.5.A87	Freedom of assembly, association, and demonstration (Table K12)
46.5.R44	Freedom of religion and conscience (Table K12)
46.7	Civic duties (Table K11)
47	Political parties (Table K11)
47.2.A-Z	Other special topics, A-Z
	Subarrange each by Table K12
	Election law see KJ-KKZ3 48
47.3	Internal security (Table K11)
	Organs of government
47.5	General (Table K11)
	The people
47.6	General (Table K11)
47.8	Initiative and referendum. Plebiscite (Table K11)
48	Election law (Table K11)
	The legislature. Legislative power
48.3	General (Table K11)
48.32	Legislative bodies. People's assembly (Table K11)
	Including bodies with one or two chambers
48.35	Legislative process (Table K11)
	Including parliamentary practice
48.4.A-Z	Special topics, A-Z
	Subarrange each by Table K12
	The head of state
48.42	General (Table K11)

Constitutional law
  Organs of government
    The head of state -- Continued
    Kings. Princes and other rulers
48.5   General (Table K11)
48.6.A-Z   Special topics, A-Z
48.6.B57   Birth rights (Table K12)
48.6.E43   Election (Table K12)
                    Emergency powers see KJ-KKZ3 48.6.W37
48.6.L44   Legislative power (Table K12)
48.6.R43   Regalia (Table K12)
48.6.S92   Succession (Table K12)
48.6.T73   Treatymaking power (Table K12)
48.6.W37   War and emergency powers (Table K12)
                  The executive branch. Executive power
49   General (Table K11)
49.3   Prime minister and cabinet (Table K11)
49.4   The Governor (Table K11)
49.5.A-Z   Other, A-Z
49.5.C42   Chancellery (Table K12)
49.5.C68   Councils (Table K12)
49.5.P74   Privy council (Table K12)
50.A-Z   Executive departments, A-Z
                    Subarrange each by Table K12
                    Class here departments not provided for by subject
50.2.A-Z   Special boards, commissions, bureaus, etc. By name, A-Z
                    Subarrange each by Table K12
                  The judiciary see KJ-KKZ3 92.39+
50.3   Constitutional courts (tribunals) and procedure (Table K11)
              Secular ecclesiastical law
                Treaties between church and state
                    Including concordats (Catholic Church) and contracts (Protestant
                      Church)
                    For treaties on a particular subject, see the subject
50.5   Collections
51   Individual concordats and contracts. By date
51.2   General works
51.3   General (Table K11)
51.4   Constitutional guaranties (Table K11)
51.5   System of church-and-state relationship (Table K11)
51.6   Religious corporations and societies (Table K11)
51.7   Church autonomy and state supervision (Table K11)
52.A-Z   Special topics, A-Z
                  Subarrange each by Table K12
              Administrative law
53.3   General (Table K11)

KJ-KKZ3

	Administrative law -- Continued
	Administrative process
53.4	General (Table K11)
53.5	Administrative acts and enforcement (Table K11)
53.6	Legal transactions and public contracts (Table K11)
54	Administrative courts and procedure (Table K11)
	Including judicial review of administrative acts
	Indemnification for acts performed by government
54.3	General (Table K11)
54.4	Eminent domain (Table K11)
54.5	Government liability (Table K11)
54.6.A-Z	Other special topics, A-Z
	Subarrange each by Table K12
	Administrative organization
55	General (Table K11)
	Executive departments. Ministries see KJ-KKZ3 50.A+
	Administrative and political divisions. Local government other than municipal
55.4	General (Table K11)
56	Supramunicipal corporations or cooperatives (Table K11)
	Municipal government
56.3	General (Table K11)
56.4	Autonomy and self-government. State supervision (Table K11)
56.5	Constitution and organization of municipal government (Table K11)
	Including city mayor, city director, councils, civic associations, elected and honorary officers, etc.
	For works on officers and employees of an individual municipality, see the municipality
56.6	Civil service (Table K11)
	Police and public safety
57	General (Table K11)
57.3	Police magistrates (Table K11)
	Public safety
57.4	General (Table K11)
57.45	Weapons. Explosives (Table K11)
	Including manufacturing, import, and trade of firearms and ammunition
57.5	Hazardous articles and processes (Table K11)
	Control of individuals
57.6	General (Table K11)
57.7	Identification and registration (Table K11)
58.A-Z	Particular groups, A-Z

Police and public safety
  Public safety
    Control of individuals
      Particular groups, A-Z -- Continued
58.A45   Aliens (Table K12)
          Including citizens of European Community countries,
            homeless aliens, and refugees
58.3   Control of social activities (Table K11)
58.4   Disaster control (Table K11)
    Public property. Public restraint on private property
59   General (Table K11)
59.3   Government property. Powers and control (Table K11)
59.35   Res communes omnium. Things in common use (Table K11)
59.4   Roads and highways (Table K11)
      Water resources
        Including rivers, lakes, water courses, etc.
59.5   General (Table K11)
59.6   Water resources development (Table K11)
      State preserves. Forests
60   General (Table K11)
        Wilderness preservation see KJ-KKZ3 63.6
      Architectural and historical monuments see KJ-KKZ3 69
      Public land law
60.2   Land reform and land policy legislation
          For agricultural land law see KJ-KKZ3 73.4+
60.3   General (Table K11)
        Regional planning
60.4   General (Table K11)
60.5   Land use. Zoning. Subdivision (Table K11)
60.6   Building and construction (Table K11)
         Entail see KJ-KKZ3 74.4
         Fideicommissum see KJ-KKZ3 72.6+
    Public health
61   General (Table K11)
61.2.A-Z   Special topics, A-Z
61.2.B87   Burial and cemetery laws (Table K12)
        Cemetery laws see KJ-KKZ3 61.2.B87
61.2.C65   Contagious and infectious diseases (Table K12)
61.2.D78   Drug laws (Table K12)
          Including pharmacists and pharmacies
        Infectious diseases see KJ-KKZ3 61.2.C65
        Pharmacists and pharmacies see KJ-KKZ3 61.2.D78
61.2.R43   Refuse disposal (Table K12)
      Medical legislation
62.3   General (Table K11)

KJ-KKZ3

	Medical legislation -- Continued
62.4.A-Z	The health professions, A-Z
	Subarrange each by Table K12
62.5.A-Z	Auxiliary (paramedical) professions, A-Z
	Subarrange each by Table K12
62.55	Hospitals and other medical institutions or health services (Table K11)
62.6	Veterinary medicine (Table K11)
	Environmental law
63	General (Table K11)
63.3	Environmental planning and conservation of resources (Table K11)
	Environmental pollution
63.4	General (Table K11)
63.5.A-Z	Pollutants
	Subarrange each by Table K12
63.6	Wilderness preservation (Table K11)
	Including plant and wildlife conservation
63.8	Birth control. Family planning. Population control (Table K11)
	Cultural affairs. Cultural policy
64	General (Table K11)
64.3	Organization and administration (Table K11)
	Including subordinate agencies, commissions, councils, boards, etc.
64.4	Language. Regulation of use, purity, etc. (Table K11)
	Education
65	General (Table K11)
65.2	Teachers (Table K11)
65.3	Elementary and secondary education (Table K11)
65.4	Vocational education (Table K11)
66	Higher education (Table K11)
66.4	Private schools (Table K11)
66.5	Adult education. Continuing education (Table K11)
66.6.A-Z	Special topics, A-Z
66.6.B62	Boards. Commissions. Conferences (Table K12)
	Commissions see KJ-KKZ3 66.6.B62
66.6.C65	Compulsory education (Table K12)
	Conferences see KJ-KKZ3 66.6.B62
66.6.P37	Participation in school government (Table K12)
67	Physical education. Athletics (Table K11)
	Science and the arts
67.2	General (Table K11)
67.3.A-Z	Special topics, A-Z
	Academies see KJ-KKZ3 67.3.P82
67.3.P82	Public institutions. Academies (Table K12)
67.3.S72	Statistical services (Table K12)

	Cultural affairs. Cultural policy
	Science and the arts -- Continued
	Public collections
68	General (Table K11)
68.5	Archives (Table K11)
68.6	Libraries (Table K11)
68.7	Museums and galleries (Table K11)
69	Historic buildings and monuments (Table K11)
	Economic law. Regulation of industry, trade, and commerce
70	General (Table K11)
70.3	Economic constitution (Table K11)
70.4	Organization and administration (Table K11)
	Including departments of commerce, and subordinate agencies and courts
70.5	Corporate representation of industry, trade, and commerce. Guilds (Table K11)
	Standards and norms see Table KJ-KKZ1 3254+
	Labelling see Table KJ-KKZ1 3268
71	Licensing. State supervision (Table K11)
71.2	Consumer protection (Table K11)
	Advertising see Table KJ-KKZ1 3280+
	Agriculture
	History
71.3	General works (Table K11)
	Rural (peasant) land tenure and peasantry
71.4	General (Table K22)
71.5	Mark communities. Village communities (Table K22)
	Manorial estates. Seigniories
72	General (Table K22)
72.3.A-Z	Special topics, A-Z
72.3.M35	Manorial serfdom
72.3.S47	Serfs
	Leasehold for years and inheritance
72.5	General (Table K22)
72.55.A-Z	Special topics, A-Z
	Entailed estates of the greater nobility. Fideicommissum
72.6	General (Table K22)
73	Inheritance and succession (Table K22)
73.3	Courts and procedure (Table K22)
	Land reform and agrarian land policy legislation
73.4	General (Table K11)
73.5	Restraint on alienation of agricultural land (Table K11)
73.6	Consolidation of land holdings. Commasation (Table K11)
74	General (Table K11)

KJ-KKZ3

	Economic law. Regulation of industry, trade, and commerce
	Agriculture -- Continued
74.3	Organization and administration (Table K11)
	Including department of agriculture, viticulture, and forestry, and
	subordinate agencies and boards
74.4	Entail (Table K11)
74.5.A-Z	Agricultural industries and trades, A-Z
	Subarrange each by Table K12
74.6.A-Z	Agricultural products, A-Z
	Subarrange each by Table K12
75	Corporate representation. Agricultural societies (Table K11)
75.3	Agricultural courts (Table K11)
75.4	Viticulture (Table K11)
75.5	Apiculture. Beekeeping (Table K11)
76	Horticulture (Table K11)
76.3	Forestry (Table K11)
	Including timber and game laws
77	Fishery (Table K11)
	Mining and quarrying
77.3	General (Table K11)
77.4.A-Z	By resources, A-Z
	Subarrange each by Table K12
	Manufacturing industries
78	General (Table K11)
78.3.A-Z	Types of manufacture, A-Z
	Subarrange each by Table K12
	Food processing industries
78.5	General (Table K11)
78.6.A-Z	By industry, A-Z
78.6.C47	Cereal products (Table K12)
79	Construction and building industry (Table K11)
79.3	International trade (Table K11)
	Domestic trade
79.5	General (Table K11)
79.6	Wholesale trade (Table K11)
79.7	Retail trade (Table K11)
80.A-Z	Modes of trading, A-Z
	Subarrange each by Table K12
80.3.A-Z	Products, A-Z
	Subarrange each by Table K12
80.3.T62	Tobacco (Table K12)
80.4	Second-hand trade (Table K11)
	Including auction houses, pawnbrokers, etc.
80.5.A-Z	Service trades, A-Z
80.5.H66	Hotels, taverns, and restaurants (Table K12)
	Restaurants see KJ-KKZ3 80.5.H66

	Economic law. Regulation of industry, trade, and commerce
	Domestic trade
	Service trades, A-Z -- Continued
	Taverns see KJ-KKZ3 80.5.H66
80.5.T67	Tourist trade (Table K12)
	Artisans
81	General (Table K11)
	Corporate representation
81.15	General (Table K11)
81.2	Guilds. Trade associations (Table K11)
81.3.A-Z	Crafts, A-Z
	Subarrange each by Table K12
	Public utilities. Power supplies
81.5	General (Table K11)
81.6.A-Z	By utility, A-Z
81.6.E43	Electricity (Table K12)
82	Industrial arbitral courts and procedure (Table K11)
82.3	Business ethics. Courts of honor (Table K11)
82.4	Criminal provisions (Table K11)
	Transportation
82.5	General (Table K11)
	Road traffic
82.6	General (Table K11)
82.7	Traffic regulations and enforcement (Table K11)
83	Carriage of goods and passengers (Table K11)
83.3.A-Z	Special topics, A-Z
83.3.B88	Bus lines (Table K12)
	Railroads
	Including carriage of passengers and goods
83.4	General (Table K11)
83.5.A-Z	Special topics, A-Z
	Subarrange each by Table K12
	Pipelines see Table KJ-KKZ1 3466
	Aviation see Table KJ-KKZ1 3467+
	Water transportation. Domestic shipping
	Including carriage of passengers and goods
83.6	General (Table K11)
83.7.A-Z	Special topics, A-Z
	Subarrange each by Table K12
	Communication. Mass media
84	General (Table K11)
84.3	Postal services (Table K11)
84.4	Telecommunication (Table K11)
84.5	Radio communication (Table K11)
84.6	Press law (Table K11)
84.7.A-Z	Special topics, A-Z

KJ-KKZ3

	Professions
85	General (Table K11)
85.3.A-Z	Individual professions, A-Z
	Subarrange each by Table K12
85.4	Professional ethics. Courts of honor (Table K11)
	For a particular court of honor, see the profession
	Public finance
85.5	General (Table K11)
85.6	Organization and administration (Table K11)
86	Budget. Accounting and auditing (Table K11)
	Including courts
86.3	Public debts. Loans (Table K11)
86.4	Money. Coinage (Table K11)
	Including mint regulations
	Taxation
	Including taxes shared by the state and municipality
	For local ordinances and works on the taxation of a particular
	locality or municipality, see the locality or municipality
86.5	General (Table K11)
86.6	Income tax (Table K11)
86.65	Sales tax (Table K11)
86.7	Estate, inheritance, and gift taxes (Table K11)
	Property tax. Taxation of capital
87	General (Table K11)
87.3.A-Z	Special topics, A-Z
	Subarrange each by Table K12
87.4	Taxation of motor vehicles (Table K11)
87.5	Taxes from gambling tables. Casinos (Table K11)
87.6.A-Z	Other, A-Z
87.6.E83	Excise taxes (Table K12)
87.6.R43	Real property tax (Table K12)
	Customs. Tariff
87.7	General (Table K11)
87.8.A-Z	Special topics, A-Z
	Subarrange each by Table K12
88	Tax and customs courts and procedure (Table K11)
	Tax and customs crimes and delinquency see Table KJ-KKZ1
	3693+
	Government measures in time of war, national emergency, or
	economic crisis
88.3	General (Table K11)
88.4.A-Z	Particular measures or claims, A-Z
88.4.I53	Industrial priorities and allocations (Table K12)
	Legislation for economic and social recovery and restitution
89	General (Table K11)
89.3.A-Z	Groups of victims or types of damage, A-Z

KJ-KKZ3

See the names of the jurisdictions in the KJ-KKZ schedules (e.g.
KJG 0-4990, Albania) for the names of states, provinces, etc.,
and numbers assigned to them. To determine a subject
division for a given table, etc., add the number or numbers in
the table for the subject to the basic number for the state, etc.
For example, for guilds in the state of Venice, Italy, add 7.2 in
Table 4 to the basic number for Venice, KKH8500, to make
KKH8507.2

Table KJ-KKZ4 is not to be further subarranged
Including historical (extinct) states

1.A12A-.A12Z	Bibliography
<1.A13>	Periodicals

For periodicals consisting predominantly of legal articles, regardless
of subject matter and jurisdiction, see K1+
For periodicals consisting primarily of informative material
(Newsletters, bulletins, etc.) relating to a particular subject, see
the subject and form division for periodicals
For law reports, official bulletins or circulars, and official gazettes
intended chiefly for the publication of laws and regulations, see
the appropriate entries in the text or form division tables

1.A14A-.A14Z	Monographic series
	Official gazettes

For departmental gazettes, see the issuing department or agency
For city gazettes, see the issuing city

1.A145A-.A145Z	Indexes (General)
1.A15A-.A15Z	Serials
1.A152	Monographs. By date
	Legislative and executive papers (including historical sources)
	see class J
	Legislation
1.A16	Indexes and tables. By date
	Early territorial laws and legislation

Class here early sources not provided for elsewhere, e.g.
custumals, Landfriedensgesetze, Landrechte und
Landesordnungen, privileges, edits, mandates, etc.

1.A17A-.A17Z	Collections. Compilations
	Individual
	see the subject
	Statutes

Including statutory orders and regulations
For statutes, statutory orders, and regulations on a particular
subject, see the subject

Collections and compilations
Including official and private editions with or without annotations

1.A172A-.A172Z	Serials
1.A173	Monographs. By date

KJ-KKZ4-
KJ-KKZ12

	Legislation -- Continued
1.A178A-.A178Z	Codifications and related material
	Class here collections of codes and codifications not limited to a subject
	Including early codifications, and including enactments of codes
	For codes on a subject, see the subject
	Court decisions and related materials
	Including historical sources, and authorized and private collections
	For decisions on a particular subject, see the subject
1.A18	Indexes. Digests. Analytical abstracts. By date
	For indexes relating to a particular publication, see the publication
	Several courts
	Class here decisions of courts of several jurisdictions
1.A185	Serials
1.A19	Monographs. By date
	Particular courts and tribunals
1.A192	Highest court of appeals. Supreme Court
1.A193	Intermediate appellate courts. Courts of appeal
	Including decisions of the only or several intermediate appellate courts of a state and reports of national court of appeals in judicial districts.
1.A194	Trial courts
1.A196A-.A196Z	Other courts. By place or name, A-Z
	Dictionaries. Words and phrases
	see the numbers provided for dictionaries at the national leval
	Form books
	see the numbers provided for form books at the national leval
1.A197A-.A197Z	History of law
	For the history of a particular subject (including historical sources), see the subject
	For collections and compilations of sources see KJ-KKZ4 1.A16+
1.13	Law reform. Criticism
	Including reform of general administration of justice
	For reform of criminal justice administration and criminal law see KJ-KKZ4 9.3+
1.15	General works
	Including compends, popular works, civics, etc.
1.2	Private law
1.22	Private international law. Conflict of laws
	For works on conflict rules of other branches of law (e.g. criminal law), see the subject
	Civil law
1.3	General
1.32	Persons
1.35.A-Z	Other special topics, A-Z

KJ-KKZ4-
KJ-KKZ12

	Commercial contracts and transactions -- Continued
2.28	Maritime contracts
2.3	Negotiable instruments. Titles of credit
	Banking. Stock exchange
2.4	General
2.5	State supervision
2.6.A-Z	Banking transactions, A-Z
2.6.A24	Account current
	Credit see KJ-KKZ4 2.6.L6
2.6.D45	Deposit banking
2.6.L6	Loans. Credit
	Carriers. Carriage of goods and passengers
2.7	General
2.8	Freight forwarders and carriers
2.815	Maritime law
	Including coastwise and inland shipping, contracts, insurance, etc.
	Insurance
2.82	General
2.9.A-Z	Branches of insurance, A-Z
2.95.A-Z	Individual risks and damages, A-Z
3	Business associations
3.2	Intellectual and industrial property
	Including copyright, patents, trademarks, unfair competition, etc.
	Labor law
	Including works on both labor law and social insurance and private labor law as it applies to the labor contract and to the labor-management relationship
3.23	General
3.235	Wages
3.24	Labor-management relations
3.25	Collective labor disputes
	Including strikes
3.26	Protection of labor
3.265.A-Z	By industry, occupation, or group of employees, A-Z
3.265.B84	Building and construction industry
3.27	Labor courts and procedure
	Social legislation
3.3	General
	Social insurance
3.32.A-Z	Branches of social insurance, A-Z
3.32.H42	Health insurance
3.32.S62	Social security
3.32.U53	Unemployment insurance
3.32.W67	Workers' compensation
	Social services. Public welfare

	Courts and procedure
	Civil procedure -- Continued
3.7	Remedies
3.8	Noncontentious jurisdiction
	Insolvency
3.9	General
3.92	Execution
	Including procedures
3.93	Bankruptcy
4	Public law
	Constitutional law
	History
4.18	General works
	Estates. Classes
4.2	General
4.22	Nobility
	Peasantry see KJ-KKZ4 7.25+
4.25.A-Z	Other special topics, A-Z
4.26	Feudal law
4.265	Constitutional reform. Criticism
4.27	General
	Sources
	Including historical sources and related material
4.28	Collections. Compilations
	Constitutions
4.3<date>	Individual constitutions
	Arrange chronologically by appending the date of adoption to this number and deleting any trailing zeros.
	Subarrange by main entry
4.31<date>	Individual sources other than constitutions. By date
	Arrange chronologically by appending the date of adoption or issuance to this number and deleting any trailing zeros.
	Subarranged by main entry
4.32	Foreign relations administration
	Individual and state
4.4	General
	Fundamental rights and constitutional guaranties
4.42.A-Z	Individual rights or guaranties, A-Z
4.42.R44	Freedom of religion and conscience
	Organs of government
4.45	General
	The people
4.46	Election law
4.5	The legislature. Legislative power
	The head of state
4.54	General

Constitutional law
  Organs of government
    The head of state -- Continued

4.55	Kings. Princes and other rulers
	The executive branch. Executive power
4.6	General
4.63.A-Z	Executive departments, A-Z
	Class here departments not provided for by subject
4.64.A-Z	Special boards, commissions, bureaus, etc. By name, A-Z
	The judiciary see KJ-KKZ4 9.42+
4.65	Constitutional courts (tribunals) and procedure

Secular ecclesiastical law
  Treaties between church and state
    Including concordats (Catholic Church) and contracts (Protestant Church)
    For treaties on a particular subject, see the subject

4.7	Collections
4.72.A-Z	Special topics, A-Z
	Administrative law
4.75	General
4.79	Administrative process
4.8	Indemnification for acts performed by government
	Administrative organization
4.82	General
	Executive departments. Ministries see KJ-KKZ4 4.63.A+
	Administrative and political divisions. Local government other than municipal
4.83	General
4.84	Supramunicipal corporations or cooperatives
	Municipal government
4.94	General
4.95	Constitution and organization of municipal government
	Including city mayor, city director, councils, civic associations, elected and honorary officers, etc.
	For works on officers and employees of an individual municipality, see the municipality
5	Civil service
	Police and public safety
5.2	General
	Public safety
5.25.A-Z	Hazards and preventive measures, A-Z
5.25.F57	Fire prevention and control
5.27	Control of individuals
5.3	Control of social activities
	Public property. Public restraint on private property
5.4	General

KJ-KKZ4-
KJ-KKZ12

Public property. Public restraint on private property -- Continued
5.5   Water resources
                                Including rivers, lakes, water courses, etc.
                            State preserves. Forests
5.6   General
                                Wilderness preservation see KJ-KKZ4 6.3
                                Architectural and historic monuments see KJ-KKZ4 6.8
                            Public land law
5.7   General
5.73   Regional planning
5.76   Public health
                            Medical legislation
5.78   General
5.8   Veterinary medicine
                            Environmental law
5.9   General
6   Environmental pollution
6.3   Wilderness preservation
                                    Including plant and wildlife conservation
                            Cultural affairs. Cultural policy
6.4   General
6.415   Language. Regulation of use, purity, etc.
                                Education
6.42   General
6.45   Elementary and secondary education
6.5   Vocational education
6.55   Higher education
6.6   Adult education. Continuing education
                                Science and the arts
6.62   General
                                Public collections
6.7   Archives
6.75   Museums and galleries
6.8   Historic buildings and monuments
                            Economic law. Regulation of industry, trade, and commerce
7   General
7.2   Corporate representation of industry, trade, and commerce.
                                    Guilds
                                Agriculture
                                History
7.23   General works
                                    Rural (peasant) land tenure and peasantry
7.25   General
                                        Manorial estates. Seigniories
7.3   General
7.32.A-Z   Special topics, A-Z

8.57	Professions
	Public finance
8.58	General
	Taxation
	Including taxes shared by the state and municipality
	For local ordinances and works on the taxation of a particular
	locality or municipality, see the locality or municipality
8.6	General
8.63	Property tax. Taxation of capital
8.64	Taxation of motor vehicles
8.66	Taxes from gambling tables. Casinos
8.7.A-Z	Other, A-Z
8.7.R43	Real property tax
8.72	Customs. Tariff
8.73	Tax and customs courts and procedure
	Government measures in time of war, national emergency, or
	economic crisis
8.8	General
8.82	Legislation for economic and social recovery and restitution
	Military law
8.85	General
9	Civil defense
9.2	Military criminal law and procedure
	Criminal law
9.3	General
9.34	Punishment
9.35.A-Z	Individual offenses, A-Z
9.35.L52	Libel and slander
9.35.S49	Sex crimes
	Slander see KJ-KKZ4 9.35.L52
	Criminal courts and procedure
9.4	General
	Administration of criminal justice
9.42	General
9.45	Judicial assistance
9.5	Court organization
9.52	Procedural principles
9.6	Procedure at first instance
9.62	Judicial decisions and remedies
	Execution of sentence
9.7	General
	Imprisonment
9.72	General
9.73.A-Z	Penal institutions, A-Z
9.8.A-Z	Other special, A-Z
9.8.C36	Capital punishment

.A1A-.A1Z	Bibliography
<.A15>	Periodicals
	For periodicals consisting predominantly of legal articles, regardless of subject matter and jurisdiction, see K1+
	For periodicals consisting primarily of informative material (Newsletters, bulletins, etc.) relating to a particular subject, see the subject and form division for periodicals
	For law reports, official bulletins or circulars, and official gazettes intended chiefly for the publication of laws and regulations, see the appropriate entries in the text or form division tables
.A17-.A17Z	Official gazettes
	Including historical sources
	Legislative documents
	Including historical sources
	Cf. JS31, Municipal documents of local governments
.A2A-.A2Z	Serials
.A25	Monographs. By date
.A3	Statutes (national and/or state) affecting cities, etc. By date
	Including historical sources
	Charters (Privileges), ordinances, and local laws
	Including historical sources
.A35A-.A35Z	Indexes
.A4A-.A4Z	Serials
.A45	Collections. By date
.A5	Individual charters or acts of incorporation. By date
	Collections of decisions and rulings
	Including historical sources
.A6A-.A6Z	Serials
.A65	Monographs. By date
	Judicial statistics. Surveys of local administration of justice
.A7A-.A7Z	Serials
.A75A-.A75Z	Monographs
.A8A-.A8Z	Special agencies, courts, or topics, A-Z
	Subarranged by date
	Directories
	see the numbers provided for directories at the national level
	Legal profession
	see the numbers provided for the legal profession at the national level
	Legal aid
	see the numbers provided for legal aid at the national level
	History
	For the history of a particular subject, see the subject
.A85A-.A85Z	Sources
	Class here sources not falling under one of the categories above
.A9-.Z	General works

KJ-KKZ4-
KJ-KKZ12

Particular subjects
    Not to be further subarranged by form
  Private law
    Including civil and commercial law

.12	General

    Domestic relations. Marriage. Parent and child

.13	General
.14.A-Z	Special topics, A-Z

    Property. Law of things. Real property

.15	General
.18	Land register
.19.A-Z	Special topics, A-Z

    Inheritance. Succession upon death

.2	General
.23.A-Z	Special topics, A-Z

    Obligations

.24	General
.25.A-Z	Special topics, A-Z
.26	Merchant and business enterprise
.27	Commercial registers
.28	Banking. Negotiable instruments. Insurance
.29	Business associations

  Labor law. Social insurance. Public welfare

.3	General
.32.A-Z	Particular groups, A-Z
.33.A-Z	Particular agencies, institutions, or courts, A-Z

  Courts and procedure see KJ-KKZ5 .37
  City constitution and government

.34	General
.35	Legislative functions. City council, etc.
	Including elections
.36	Executive functions. Mayor and administrative departments.
	Municipal civil service
	Including elections
.37	Judicial functions. City courts and procedure

  Municipal civil service see KJ-KKZ5 .36
  Police and public safety. Police force

.4	General
.44.A-Z	Particular safety hazards or preventive measures, A-Z
.44.F57	Fire
.46.A-Z	Special topics, A-Z

  Public property. Public restraint on private property

.47	General
.5.A-Z	Special topics, A-Z
	Building see KJ-KKZ5 .5.Z65
	City planning and redevelopment see KJ-KKZ5 .5.Z65
	Housing see KJ-KKZ5 .5.Z65

	Particular subjects
	Public property. Public restraint on private property
	Special topics, A-Z -- Continued
.5.Z65	Zoning. Building. City planning and redevelopment. Housing
	Public health. Medical legislation
.54	General
.55	Burial and cemetery laws
.58.A-Z	Special topics, A-Z
.58.D74	Drinking water
.58.R44	Refuse disposal
.6	Environmental laws
	Cultural affairs
.63	General
.64	Education. Schools. Institutions
.65	Theater. Orchestra
.66	Public collections
.67.A-Z	Historic buildings and monuments, A-Z
.68.A-Z	Special topics, A-Z
	Industry, trade, and commerce
.7	General
.75.A-Z	Artisans, A-Z
.76.A-Z	Professions, A-Z
.78.A-Z	Corporate representation, A-Z
	e. g.
.78.B62	Boards of trade
.78.C42	Chambers of commerce
.78.G55	Guilds
.78.T72	Trade associations
.8	Public utilities
	Public finance
.83	General
.85	Sources of revenue. Taxes, fees, and fines
.86	Offenses (Violation of ordinances) and administration of criminal justice. Correctional institutions
	Supramunicipal corporations and organizations
	see KJ-KKZ3 56

KJ-KKZ4-
KJ-KKZ12

.xA-.xZ	Legislation. By main entry, A-Z
.x2	Decisions. Rulings
.x3	General works
	Including comprehensive works and works on specific legal topics

For organizations limited by subject, see the subject in KJC, e.g.
KJC5138 European Commission of Human Rights
For works on official acts or legal measures on a particular subject,
see the subject in KJC

1	Bibliography
<3>	Periodicals

For periodicals consisting predominantly of legal articles, regardless
of subject matter and jurisidiction, see K1+
For periodicals consisting primarily of informative material
(newsletters, bulletins, etc.) relating to a particular subject, see
the subject and form division for periodicals
For law reports, official bulletins or circulars, and official gazettes
intended chiefly for the publication of laws and regulations, see
the appropriate entries in the text or form division tables

4	Monographic series
5	Journals. Official gazettes
<6>	Legislative and executive papers. Documentation
6.2	Intergovernmental congresses and conferences
	see KJC14+

Non-governmental congresses see KJ-KKZ7 17
Official acts

8	Indexes and tables
9	Collections. Compilations
9.2	Treaties and other international agreements
	see KJC

Treaties (individual and collections) establishing and
expanding the regional organization see KJ-KKZ7 23.A25+
Legislation and legal measures
Including conclusions, resolutions, recommendations, decisions,
opinions, etc.

10	Indexes and tables
11	Abridgments and digests
	Collections
12	Serials
13	Monographs. By date
13.2	Individual
	see the appropriate subject in KJC
14	Court decisions and related material. Law reports
	For decisions and materials on a particular subject, see the subject
15	Dictionaries. Encyclopedias
16	Directories
17	Congresses. Conferences. By date of the congress
	For intergovernmental congresses, see KJC14+
21	General works
	Including compends, essays, festschriften, etc.
	Organization law

Organization law -- Continued

23.A12	Bibliography
23.A15	Periodicals
	Including gazettes, yearbooks, bulletins, etc.
	Monographic series see KJ-KKZ7 23.A9+
	Treaties establishing and governing the organization. Primary law
23.A25	Indexes and tables
23.A3	Collections
	Including either multilateral or bilateral treaties or both
23.A35<date>	Multilateral treaties (Table K6)
	Arrange chronologically by appending date of signature of the treaty to .A35 and deleting any trailing zeros
23.A43A-.A43Z	Bilateral treaties. By organization (country) used as main entry, and date of signature of the treaty
	For bilateral treaties relating to a multilateral treaty, see 23.A35[date] in this table and .xZ4-.xZ59 in Table K6
	Other official acts and legal measures
	Regulations and decisions
23.A436	Indexes and tables
23.A438	Abridgements and digests
	Collections. Selections
23.A44	Serials
23.A442	Monographs. By date
23.A45<date>	Individual acts (or groups of acts adopted as a whole)
	Arrange chronologically by appending the date of original enactment or revision of the law to this number and deleting any trailing zeros
	Under each:
	.A2 *Working documents. Official records. By date*
	Including reports and memoranda of factfinding, advisory, research, and drafting committees, etc., and drafts
	.A7 *Unannotated editions. By date*
	Including official editions with or without annotation
	.A8-.Z8 *Annotated editions. Commentaries. General works*
23.A5	Opinions. Recommendations
	Including action programs, consultations, target studies, etc.
	Administrative decisions see KJ-KKZ7 23.A9+
23.A7	Court decisions and related materials. Reports

Organization law -- Continued

23.A72   Surveys on legal activity concerning unification, harmonization,
                   cooperation. Annual (official) reports
23.A8   Conferences. Symposia
23.A9-.Z9   General works. Treatises
25   Constitutional principles
                Foreign (External) relations. International cooperation
                   Including membership in international organizations
26   General (Table K14)
26.2   United Nations
                       see JZ5003.A+
26.4   Relations with other European regional organizations
                       For relations with the European Economic Community, see
                          KJE5060+
26.6   Relations with non-member states
                Intergovernmental (Internal) relations and cooperation.
                   Relations with member states
28   General (Table K14)
28.5   Jurisdiction
28.7   By state, A-Z
                Organs of the organization
29   General works
30   Rules governing the official language of the organ
                   Election law
32   General (Table K14)
32.5.A-Z   Election to a particular office, A-Z
32.7.A-Z   Expert committees and subcommittees, A-Z
36   Powers and duties (Table K14)
                   Legislative organ. Parliamentary assembly
38   General (Table K15)
38.5   Standing committee
39.A-Z   Ordinary committees and subcommittees, A-Z
39.5   Powers and duties (Table K14)
39.7.A-Z   Joint committees. Interparliamentary (Consultative) councils,
                        A-Z
39.9.A-Z   Joint services, A-Z
                   Courts of justice. Tribunals
                        For court reports see KJ-KKZ7 14
40   General (Table K15)
40.3   Jurisdiction (Table K14)
                Civil service
42   General (Table K14)
43   Incompatibility of offices (Table K14)
43.5   Privileges and immunities (Table K14)
43.6   Appointment (Table K14)

Civil service -- Continued
43.8   Conditions of employment (Table K14)
                    Including discipline
44   Remuneration. Allowances (Table K14)
45   Retirement (Table K14)
46   Collective labor law (Table K14)
48   Finance. Budget (Table K14)
(49)   Other topics
                    see the subject in KJC

0	General (Table K14)
	Legal activities concerning integration, harmonization, and approximation see KJ-KKZ8 0
0.2	Right of establishment and freedom to provide services (Table K14)
	Common policy
0.3	General (Table K14)
0.4	Marketing orders (Table K14)
0.5	Competition rules (Table K14)
	Finance
0.52	General (Table K14)
0.6	Economic assistance. Production aid (Table K14)
0.62	Price policy. Prices (Table K14)
0.7	Import levy. Import licenses (Table K14)
0.72	Export levy. Export licenses. Export report refunds (Table K14)
0.8	Standards and grading. Quality inspection. Labeling. Sanitation (Table K14)
0.82	Trade with third countries. Extra-community relations (Table K14)
0.9	Conservation. Ecological aspects (Table K14)

0	General (Table K11)
	Authorship
	Including multiple authorship and author cooperatives
0.2	General (Table K11)
0.22	Anonyms and pseudonyms (Table K11)
0.23	Intangible property (Table K11)
0.3	Plagiarism (Table K11)
0.4	Procedures. Formalities (Table K11)
	Including registration of claim, transfer, licenses, deposit, and notice
0.5	Protected works (Table K11)
	Including original works, subsequent rights, idea and title
	Scope of protection
0.6	General (Table K11)
0.62	Personality rights (Table K11)
	Mechanical reproduction
0.63	General (Table K11)
0.64	Documentation and dissemination (Table K11)
	Including fair use
0.65	Exhibition rights (Table K11)
	Performing rights
0.7	General (Table K11)
0.72	Societies and industrial trusts (Table K11)
0.725	Public lending rights (Table K11)
0.73	Broadcasting rights (Table K11)
0.75	Recording rights (Table K11)
	Including phonographs, magnetic recorders, and jukeboxes
0.76	Filming and photographing (Table K11)
0.78	Translation (Table K11)
0.8	Employees' copyright (Table K11)
0.82	Duration and renewal (Table K11)
0.9	Delicts. Torts (Table K11)

0	General (Table K11)
0.15	National, state, and local jurisdiction and supervision (Table K11)
0.2	Planning and conservation (Table K11)
0.25	Licensing (Table K11)
0.3	Ratemaking (Table K11)
0.4	Corporate structure (Table K11)
0.5	Monopolies and freedom of contract (Table K11)
0.6	Accounting. Taxation (Table K11)
0.7	Engineering (Table K11)

KJ-KKZ4-
KJ-KKZ12

0	General (Table K8)
	Authorship
	Including multiple authorship and author cooperatives
0.2	General (Table K8)
0.22	Anonyms and pseudonyms (Table K8)
0.23	Intangible property (Table K8)
0.3	Plagiarism (Table K8)
0.4	Formalities (Table K8)
	Including registration of claim, transfer, license, deposit, and notice
0.5	Protected works (Table K8)
	Including original works, subsequent rights, idea, and title
	Scope of protection
0.6	General (Table K8)
0.62	Personality rights. Droit moral (Table K8)
	Mechanical reproduction
0.623	General (Table K8)
0.64	Documentation and dissemination (Table K8)
	Including fair use
0.65	Exhibition (Table K8)
	Performing rights
0.7	General (Table K8)
0.72	Societies and industrial trusts (Table K8)
0.73	Broadcasting rights (Table K8)
0.75	Recording devices (Table K8)
	Including phonographs, magnetic recorders, jukeboxes
0.76	Filming and photographing (Table K8)
0.78	Translation (Table K8)
0.8	Employees' copyright (Table K8)
0.82	Duration and renewal (Table K8)
0.85	Delicts. Torts (Table K8)
0.9	Criminal provisions (Table K8)

KJ-KKZ4-
KJ-KKZ12

A

Accidents
Civil law: KJC1672, KJ-KKZ1 842.3,
KJ-KKZ2 85.3
Labor contract and employment
liability: KJC2940
Liability: KJ-KKZ1 1324
Marine insurance: KJ-KKZ1 986
Accompanying marks (Trademarks):
KJ-KKZ1 1221.A25
Accord and satisfaction (Insolvency
procedures): KJ-KKZ1 1932, KJ-
KKZ2 193.2
Account current: KJ-KKZ1 960, KJ-
KKZ2 100.7, KJ-KKZ3 24.A24, KJ-
KKZ4 2.6.A24
Accountants: KJ-KKZ1 3517, KJ-KKZ2
352.3
Accounting
Banking: KJ-KKZ1 940.4
Business concerns: KJ-KKZ1 1142
Business enterprise: KJC2074,
KJE2074
Cooperative societies: KJ-KKZ1 1129
Courts and procedure: KJ-KKZ2
197.6
Courts and proceedings: KJ-KKZ1
1976+
Energy policy: KJ-KKZ1 3431.6
Merchant and business enterprise:
KJ-KKZ1 923+
Merchant and business enterprise):
KJ-KKZ3 22.3
Personal companies: KJ-KKZ2 108.4
Private company: KJ-KKZ1 1103
Property tax: KJ-KKZ1 3618
Public finance: KJ-KKZ1 3528.3, KJ-
KKZ2 353.3, KJ-KKZ3 86
Sales tax: KJ-KKZ1 3629
Social insurance: KJ-KKZ1 1474.6
State and local property tax: KJ-KKZ1
3665
State finance: KJ-KKZ1 3656
Stock companies: KJE2491+
Stock corporation: KJC2491+
Stock corporations: KJ-KKZ1 1072+

Accounting, Faulty
Tax and customs delinquency: KJ-
KKZ1 3708
Accounting, Faulty (Tax and customs
delinquency): KJ-KKZ2 370.7
Accounting statements (Income tax):
KJ-KKZ1 3575
Accounts current: KJC2242
Accusatio (Criminal court procedure):
KJA3540.A24
Accusation (Criminal procedure):
KJA3584
Accusation principle (Criminal
procedure): KJ1000, KJ-KKZ1 4624,
KJ-KKZ2 462.4
Accused, The
Criminal procedure: KJ-KKZ1
4630.A25, KJ-KKZ2 463.A25
Achievement of purpose (Extinction of
obligation): KJ-KKZ1 823.5.A34
Acknowledgment of debt (Contracts and
obligations): KJ-KKZ1 903, KJ-KKZ2
96.4
Acquisitio hereditatis: KJA2273+
Acquisition and loss of nationality and
citizenship: KJA2932
Acquisition and loss of ownership
Property: KJ857+, KJA2454+,
KJC1276+, KJE1276+, KJ-KKZ1
655+, KJ-KKZ2 65.8+, KJ-KKZ3
16.7
Real property: KJ-KKZ1 688+, KJ-
KKZ2 68.8
Acquisition and loss of possession:
KJA2442
Acquisition and transfer of possession:
KJ-KKZ1 648+, KJ-KKZ2 65.3
Acquisition bona fide: KJC1297, KJ-
KKZ1 672, KJ-KKZ2 67.2
Acquisition of estate (Testamentary
succession): KJA2412+
Acquisition of legacy: KJA2424
Acquisition of possession (Property):
KJC1265+
Acquisition of real property: KJ866+
Acquisitiones (Civiles): KJA2456
Acquisitiones (Naturales): KJA2457

Administration of criminal justice:
KJA3525+, KJC9430+, KJE9430, KJ-
KKZ1 1571.2+, KJ-KKZ2 156.92+, KJ-
KKZ3 92.39+, KJ-KKZ4 9.42+
Administration of customs: KJC7318
Administration of government property:
KJ-KKZ1 3041.5+, KJ-KKZ2 304.3+
Administration of justice: KJC3655+,
KJE3655+, KJ-KKZ1 1571.2+, KJ-
KKZ2 156.92+, KJ-KKZ3 33.9+, KJ-
KKZ4 3.38+
Administration of public property:
KJA3170+
Administration of the provinces:
KJA3094+
Administrative acts: KJE5610+, KJ-
KKZ1 2735+, KJ-KKZ3 53.5
Government liability: KJE5789, KJ-
KKZ1 2850, KJ-KKZ2 284
Economic control: KJE5793
Taxation: KJ-KKZ1 3565+, KJ-KKZ2
355.7+
Administrative appeals (Courts and
procedure): KJ-KKZ1 2785, KJ-KKZ2
278
Administrative courts and procedure:
KJC5647, KJ-KKZ1 2764+, KJ-KKZ2
276.4+, KJ-KKZ3 54
Administrative law: KJC5571+,
KJE5602+, KJ-KKZ1 2711+, KJ-KKZ2
272+
Administrative organization: KJA3070+,
KJC5794+, KJE5794, KJ-KKZ3 55+,
KJ-KKZ4 4.82+
Administrative power, Control over
abuse of: KJE5640
Administrative process: KJC5607+,
KJE5602+, KJE5607, KJ-KKZ1
2730+, KJ-KKZ2 273+
Administrative regulations (Regional
law): KJC34+
Administrative remedies
Administrative courts and procedure:
KJ-KKZ1 2785, KJ-KKZ2 278
Social courts and procedure: KJ-
KKZ1 1559

Administrative remedies
Tax and customs courts and
procedure: KJ-KKZ1 3683+, KJ-
KKZ2 368.3+
Administrative sanctions: KJ-KKZ1
2757, KJ-KKZ2 275.7
Admission of evidence
Civil procedure: KJ-KKZ1 1775+, KJ-
KKZ2 177.5
Courts and procedure: KJ-KKZ1 1673
Criminal courts and procedure: KJ-
KKZ1 4679+, KJ-KKZ2 467.9+
Criminal procedure: KJC9604+
Adoption
Conflict of laws: KJ-KKZ1 485.F35,
KJ-KKZ2 48.5.F35
Domestic relations: KJ-KKZ3 16
Family law: KJ844, KJA2254+,
KJC1212, KJ-KKZ1 609+, KJ-KKZ2
61+
Marriage impediments: KJ-KKZ1
544.5.A36, KJ-KKZ2 54.6.A36
Private international law: KJC979.F35
Adoption of adults: KJ-KKZ1 611.A36,
KJ-KKZ2 61.5.A36
Adoption procedures: KJC4126, KJ-
KKZ1 1872, KJ-KKZ2 187.2
Adpromissio: KJA2524
Adult education: KJC6341, KJ-KKZ1
3158, KJ-KKZ2 318.6, KJ-KKZ3 66.5,
KJ-KKZ4 6.6
Adulteration of food: KJC6752
Adulterium
Criminal law: KJA3468.A38
Adultery: KJ-KKZ1 4184, KJ-KKZ2
418.4
Marriage impediments: KJ-KKZ1
544.5.A38, KJ-KKZ2 54.6.A38
Adults (Guardianship): KJC1232+
Advertising: KJE6580
Attorneys: KJ-KKZ1 1635.A39
Drug laws: KJE6201, KJ-KKZ1 3096,
KJ-KKZ2 310.6
Obscenity: KJ-KKZ1 4220, KJ-KKZ2
422
Regulation: KJC6580, KJ-KKZ1
3280+, KJ-KKZ2 328+

Beschäftigungsbedingungen
  Civil service: KJE5939
Bestiality: KJ-KKZ1 4218, KJ-KKZ2
  421.8
Betriebssicherheit: KJE3185+
Betrothal: KJA2233.5, KJC1122, KJ-
  KKZ1 543, KJ-KKZ2 54.3
Bettering (Defects of goods sold): KJ-
  KKZ1 876
Betting
  Aleatory contracts: KJ-KKZ1 899.3,
    KJ-KKZ2 95.3
  Excise taxes: KJ-KKZ1 3640.B38, KJ-
    KKZ2 362.4.B38
Beverages (Industry regulation): KJ-
  KKZ1 3395+, KJ-KKZ2 339.5+
Bicameral legislative bodies: KJC5317
Bicycle tax: KJ-KKZ1 3680.B53
Bigamy: KJA3468.B53, KJ-KKZ1 4186,
  KJ-KKZ2 418.6
  Marriage impediments: KJ-KKZ1
    544.5.E94, KJ-KKZ2 54.6.E94
Bill drafting: KJC5354
Bill drafting (Legislative process): KJ-
  KKZ1 2520, KJ-KKZ2 252
Bill of lading: KJ-KKZ1 931.3, KJ-KKZ2
  98.3
Bill of lading (Freight forwarders and
  carriers): KJC2124
Bill paying services (Noncash funds
  transfer): KJ-KKZ1 961.3
Bills of exchange: KJC2162, KJ-KKZ1
  938+, KJ-KKZ2 99.3 , KJ-KKZ3 23.2
  Counterfeiting securities: KJ-KKZ1
    4350, KJ-KKZ2 435
Bills of exchange tax (Excise taxes):
  KJ-KKZ1 3640.B55, KJ-KKZ2
  362.4.B55
Bills of lading, Ocean: KJE2264
Binnenhandel: KJE6799+
Binnenschiffahrtsrecht: KJE6939
Biological terrorism: KJ-KKZ2 436.8
Biomedical engineering
  Criminal law: KJ-KKZ1 4096+, KJ-
    KKZ2 409.6+

Biomedical engineering
  Medical legislation: KJC6227+,
    KJE6227+, KJ-KKZ1 3115+, KJ-
    KKZ2 312.5+
Biotechnology
  Patent law: KJC2751.B56,
    KJE2751.B55
Biotechnology industries: KJE6755
Biotechnology industries (Collective
  bargaining): KJ-KKZ1 1387.B56
Biotechnology (Patent law): KJ-KKZ1
  1210.B56
Birds (Conservation): KJ-KKZ1 3135+,
  KJ-KKZ2 314.8+
Birth: KJ796, KJ-KKZ1 513+, KJ-KKZ2
  51.3
  Civil register: KJ-KKZ1 1862, KJ-
    KKZ2 186.2
Birth control: KJ-KKZ1 3124+, KJ-KKZ2
  313.4+
Birth rights
  Kings and other rulers: KJ-KKZ3
    48.6.B57
  The estates and classes: KJ-KKZ1
    205.B57, KJ-KKZ2 20.5.B57
Blanks (Legal documents)
  Bills of exchange: KJ-KKZ1
    938.3.B52
  Crimes against legal transactions: KJ-
    KKZ1 4351.B55, KJ-KKZ2
    435.15.B55
Blasphemy: KJ-KKZ1 4172, KJ-KKZ2
  417.2
Blind persons
  Capacity and incapacity:
    KJA2213.5.P48
  Social services: KJ-KKZ1 1534.B54,
    KJ-KKZ2 153.4.B54
Blood banks: KJ-KKZ1 3112, KJ-KKZ2
  312.2
Blood covenant: KJ158.B55
Blood donations: KJ-KKZ1 3112, KJ-
  KKZ2 312.2
Blood tests
  Civil procedure: KJ-KKZ1 1776
  Criminal procedure: KJ-KKZ1 4687,
    KJ-KKZ2 468.7

Bus lines
  Liability insurance: KJ-KKZ1 1034,
    KJ-KKZ2 106.9
Business administration (Court clerks):
  KJ-KKZ1 1623, KJ-KKZ2 162.3
Business associations: KJC2432+,
  KJE2432+, KJ-KKZ1 1040+, KJ-KKZ2
  107.5+
Business concerns: KJC2613, KJ-KKZ1
  1140+, KJ-KKZ2 113.5, KJ-KKZ3 29
  Corporation tax: KJ-KKZ1 3612.B87
Business cycles: KJE6431, KJ-KKZ1
  3201
Business enterprises: KJC2061+,
  KJE2061+
  Aliens: KJ-KKZ1 3028
  Property tax: KJ-KKZ1 3663+, KJ-
    KKZ2 366.2
Business ethics: KJ-KKZ3 82.3
Business ethics (Economic law): KJ-
  KKZ1 3439, KJ-KKZ2 343.9
Business expenses (Income tax
  deductions): KJ-KKZ1 3582.3.B88
Business names: KJ-KKZ1 922
Business report (Stocks and
  stockholders' rights): KJ-KKZ1 1080
Business tax
  Public finance: KJC7196.A+
  State and local finance:
    KJC7358.B88, KJ-KKZ1 3674+, KJ-
    KKZ2 367.5
Businessmen (Community law):
  KJE959.B87
Businesspeople
  Manuals for: KJ-KKZ3 5.7.B87
Byzantine Empire (Source of Roman
  law): KJA1350+
Byzantine law: KJA0+

C

Cabinet system, Government:
  KJC5416.C32
Cable railways: KJ-KKZ1 3465.C32,
  KJ-KKZ2 346.5.C32
Cable television: KJ-KKZ1 3495.5

Cadaster: KJA2511, KJC1437, KJ-
  KKZ1 758, KJ-KKZ2 75, KJ-KKZ3
  19.3
Cadastral surveys: KJC1437, KJ-KKZ1
  758, KJ-KKZ2 75, KJ-KKZ3 19.3
Cafeterias (Labor standards and
  protection of labor): KJ-KKZ1 1364
Calculation of reserves (Mining and
  quarrying: KJ-KKZ2 335.7
Calculation of reserves (Mining and
  quarrying): KJ-KKZ1 3357
Calumnia
  Roman law: KJA3435
Calumny: KJ-KKZ1 4149, KJ-KKZ2
  414.9
  Military criminal law and procedure:
    KJ-KKZ1 3764
Camera (Finance): KJ-KKZ1 260, KJ-
  KKZ2 26
Campgrounds (Public safety): KJ-KKZ1
  3034.5, KJ-KKZ2 303.4
Camping hygiene (Public health):
  KJC6187.C35
Campus Martius: KJ767
Cancellation
  Extinction of debt: KJ-KKZ1
    823.5.W58
Cancellation of power of attorney: KJ-
  KKZ1 863.3
Capacity
  Capacity and disability
    Civil law (Natural persons): KJ-
      KKZ1 515+, KJ-KKZ2 51.9+
  Capacity and incapacity
    Comparative law
      Criminal liability: KJ-KKZ1 3880+,
        KJ-KKZ2 387.7+
    Juristic persons: KJ-KKZ1 521.4
  Feudal capacity: KJC4435.55
  Private international law: KJ-KKZ1
    485.P47, KJ-KKZ2 48.5.P47
Capacity and incapacity
  Comparative law: KJC1016+
    Criminal liability: KJC8132
  Germanic law: KJ800+
  Private international law: KJC979.P47
  Roman law: KJA2213

Common use
  Water resources: KJ-KKZ1 3046.5
Communauté européenne de l'energie
  atomique: KJE6768+
Communauté européenne du charbon
  et de l'acier: KJE6745+
Communicating (Transmitting) venereal
  disease: KJ-KKZ1 4078, KJ-KKZ2
  407.8
Communication: KJC6946+, KJE6946+,
  KJ-KKZ1 3482+, KJ-KKZ2 348.2+, KJ-
  KKZ3 84+, KJ-KKZ4 8.52+
  Council for Mutual Economic
    Assistance: KJE890+
Communio pro partibus indivisis:
  KJA2609
Communist theory of law: KJ-KKZ1
  464, KJ-KKZ2 46.4
Communities (Germanic law): KJ812+
Community by undivided shares:
  KJA2609, KJC1876
Community law: KJE901+
Community law and municipal law:
  KJE969+
Community legal services: KJ-KKZ1
  1639
Community loans: KJE6439
Community of creditors: KJ-KKZ1
  813.7, KJ-KKZ2 80.5
Community of debtors: KJ-KKZ1 813.9,
  KJ-KKZ2 80.7
Community of heirs: KJ-KKZ1 782.5
Community of inventors: KJ-KKZ1 1204
Community of property (Marital property
  and regime): KJ-KKZ1 574, KJ-KKZ2
  57.4
Community quotas
  External trade: KJE6795
Company finance (Private companies):
  KJC2532+, KJ-KKZ1 1101+
Comparative advertising: KJ-KKZ1
  1238, KJ-KKZ2 123.5
Comparative organization law:
  KJE5062.A+
Compelling lewd acts: KJ-KKZ1 4203+,
  KJ-KKZ2 420.3+
Compensatio: KJA2529.C64

Compensatio
  Civil procedure: KJA2752
Compensation
  Defects of goods sold: KJ-KKZ1
    876.3
  Extinction of obligation: KJC1566, KJ-
    KKZ1 822.9, KJ-KKZ2 82.3
Compensation for improvements by
  tenants: KJ-KKZ1 881
Compensation for individual sacrifice
  (Government indemnification):
  KJC5782
Compensation for maintenance and
  improvement: KJ-KKZ1 822
Compensation for unjustified execution:
  KJ-KKZ1 1938
Compensation to victims of crimes
  (Criminal procedure): KJ-KKZ1
  2852.V52
Compensatory damages to injured party
  (Criminal procedure): KJ-KKZ1
  2852.V52
Competence
  Social and labor courts: KJ-KKZ1
    1569
Competence conflict courts: KJ-KKZ1
  1590
Competence conflicts
  Administrative courts and procedure:
    KJ-KKZ1 2810, KJ-KKZ2 281
Competence d'attribution
  Intergovernmental relations: KJE5086
Competence in subject matter and
  venue
  Civil procedure: KJ-KKZ1 1737+, KJ-
    KKZ2 173.7
  Criminal courts: KJ-KKZ2 466.6
  Criminal courts and procedure:
    KJC9576, KJ-KKZ1 4666
  Labor courts and procedure: KJ-KKZ1
    1450
  Social courts and procedure: KJ-
    KKZ1 1562
Competition and incentives for high
  performance: KJ-KKZ1 1275, KJ-
  KKZ2 126.3

Constitutional rights
  Recreation: KJ-KKZ1 3134.5
Constitutional rights and guaranties
  Parent and child: KJ-KKZ1 588
Constitutional safeguards (Education):
  KJ-KKZ1 3138.3
Constitutional torts: KJ-KKZ2 266.C65
Constitutiones principum: KJA390+
Constitutum possessorium
  Acquisition and transfer of possession:
    KJC1267.5, KJ-KKZ1 649.5
  Contractual acquisition: KJC1295, KJ-
    KKZ1 670.5
  Property: KJ-KKZ1 649.5
Constraining official action or inaction
  (Opposition to power of the state): KJ-
  KKZ1 4478, KJ-KKZ2 447.8
Constraint (Crimes affecting traffic): KJ-
  KKZ1 4388, KJ-KKZ2 438.8
Construction and maintenance (Roads
  and highways): KJ-KKZ1 3044.9
Construction industry
  Collective bargaining: KJ-KKZ1
    1387.C66
  Corporation tax: KJ-KKZ1 3613.C65,
    KJ-KKZ2 360.C65
Construction laws
  Regional policy: KJE6155
Construction sites, Liability for: KJ-
  KKZ1 853.C65
Consular courts: KJC3693, KJ-KKZ1
  1589, KJ-KKZ2 158.9
Consular-senatorial proceedings
  (Roman law): KJA3555
Consular tribunate: KJA2992
Consulate: KJA2992
Consumer credit: KJ-KKZ1 955.5.C65
Consumer goods: KJA2438.C65
Consumer protection: KJC6577,
  KJE6577+, KJ-KKZ1 3276, KJ-KKZ2
  327.6
  Drug laws: KJ-KKZ1 3096, KJ-KKZ2
    310.6
  Regulation of industry, trade, and
    commerce: KJ-KKZ3 71.2
Consumers Consultative Committee:
  KJE6578

Consumptibles: KJA2438.C65
Consumtio existimationis: KJA2220
Contagious and infectious diseases:
  KJC6178, KJ-KKZ1 3080+, KJ-KKZ2
  308.9+, KJ-KKZ3 61.2.C65
Containers: KJC6556
Containers (Economic law): KJ-KKZ1
  3257+, KJ-KKZ2 325.7+
Contango (Bills of exchange): KJ-KKZ1
  938.3.P76
Contempt of court: KJ-KKZ1 4510, KJ-
  KKZ2 451
  Libel and slander: KJ-KKZ1 3511, KJ-
  KKZ2 351.5
Contested elections: KJ-KKZ1 2508
Continental shelf: KJ-KKZ1 3347, KJ-
  KKZ2 334.7
Contingents douaniers: KJE7326
Continuing education: KJ-KKZ3 66.5,
  KJ-KKZ4 6.6
Contract systems (Government control
  and policy): KJ-KKZ1 3200, KJ-KKZ2
  320.82
Contracts
  Accident insurance: KJ-KKZ1 1016
  Automobiles: KJ-KKZ1 1032
  Banking transactions: KJC2222, KJ-
    KKZ1 954
  Civil law: KJC1720+, KJE1640
  Conflict of laws: KJE983.C66, KJ-
    KKZ1 485.C658, KJ-KKZ2
    48.5.C658
  Insurance law: KJ-KKZ1 1002+
  Liability insurance: KJ-KKZ1 1027.3+
  Life insurance: KJ-KKZ1 1008.3
  Loans: KJ-KKZ1 955.3
  Motion pictures: KJ-KKZ1 3174
  Personal companies: KJC2435.13+
  Private international law:
    KJC979.C658
  Private law and procedure: KJA2542+
  Protestant church: KJ-KKZ3 51
  Standardized terms, policies, etc: KJ-
    KKZ1 985.3
  Theater: KJ-KKZ1 3172.7, KJ-KKZ2
    319.7

Contracts and combinations in restraint of trade, Control of: KJ-KKZ1 3220+, KJ-KKZ2 321.3

Contracts and specifications (Building and construction industry): KJ-KKZ1 3403, KJ-KKZ2 340.3

Contracts and transactions (Civil law): KJ-KKZ1 858+, KJ-KKZ2 87.6+, KJ-KKZ3 20.8+

Contracts between husband and wife: KJ-KKZ1 577, KJ-KKZ2 57.8

Contracts for work and labor: KJ-KKZ1 893+, KJ-KKZ2 93.6

Contracts of inheritance: KJC1480, KJ-KKZ1 790+, KJ-KKZ2 79, KJ-KKZ3 19.7
  Community law: KJE1480

Contracts of service and labor: KJC1844+, KJ-KKZ1 892+, KJ-KKZ2 93+, KJ-KKZ3 21.8+, KJ-KKZ4 1.84+

Contracts through correspondence, telephone, teletype or wire: KJ-KKZ1 869.4

Contractual acquisition
  Personal property: KJC1289+, KJ-KKZ1 666+, KJ-KKZ2 66.5+
  Real property: KJ-KKZ1 688+, KJ-KKZ2 68.8

Contractual agreement excluding liability: KJC1666, KJ-KKZ1 840, KJ-KKZ2 84.8

Contractual discharge
  Extinction of obligation: KJC1575

Contractual discharge (Extinction of obligation): KJ-KKZ1 823.5.C65

Contractual penalties: KJC1747, KJ-KKZ1 870.5

Contractual pledges: KJC1383, KJ-KKZ1 727+, KJ-KKZ2 73.3+

Contractual regimes (Marital property and regime): KJ-KKZ1 572, KJ-KKZ2 57.2

Contractus aestimatorius: KJA2576

Contrat du travail: KJE2870+

Contributions financières des États membres
  Community law: KJE7100

Contributory and comparative negligence (Damages): KJ-KKZ1 832.5

Control of contracts
  Economic law: KJE6456+

Control of government: KJC5315, KJ-KKZ1 2512, KJ-KKZ2 251.2

Control of individuals (Public safety): KJC6032+, KJE6032+, KJ-KKZ1 3022+, KJ-KKZ2 302+, KJ-KKZ3 57.6+, KJ-KKZ4 5.27

Control of partners (Private company): KJ-KKZ1 1107

Control of property (Government measures): KJ-KKZ1 3712, KJ-KKZ2 371.2

Control of social activities (Public safety): KJ-KKZ1 3034+, KJ-KKZ2 303.3+, KJ-KKZ3 58.3, KJ-KKZ4 5.3

Control of unemployment: KJ-KKZ1 3714+, KJ-KKZ2 371.4+

Control over abuse of administrative power: KJ-KKZ1 2760, KJ-KKZ2 276

Contrôle des banques
  State supervision: KJE2189

Contrôle des prix: KJE6442

Contubernium: KJA2236

Convention of Lome (I), 1975: KJE5110.21975

Convention of Lome (II), 1979: KJE5110.21979

Convention of Yaoundé, 1963: KJE5110.21963

Conversions (Corporate reorganization tax): KJ-KKZ1 3607

Convertible bonds: KJC2486, KJ-KKZ1 1070.C54

Conveyance and life annuities (Real property): KJ-KKZ1 898.5, KJ-KKZ2 94.3, KJ-KKZ3 18.3.C65

Conviction (Criminal procedure): KJ-KKZ1 4746+, KJ-KKZ2 474.6+

Cooperative retail trade (Domestic trade): KJ-KKZ1 3421, KJ-KKZ2 342.2

Cooperative societies: KJE2565, KJ-KKZ1 1120+, KJ-KKZ2 112+

Corpus Iuris Civilis: KJA1062.2+

Correality and solidarity: KJA2517, KJC1505

Correality and solidarity (Plurality of debtors and creditors): KJ-KKZ1 813+, KJ-KKZ2 80.4

Correction of faulty decisions
Civil procedure: KJC3976, KJ-KKZ1 1798
Criminal procedure: KJ-KKZ1 4753, KJ-KKZ2 475.3

Correction of records (Criminal procedure): KJ-KKZ1 4760, KJ-KKZ2 476

Correctional institutions
Administration of: KJ-KKZ1 4800, KJ-KKZ2 480
Criminal procedure: KJ-KKZ1 4824, KJ-KKZ2 482.4

Correctional measures
Criminal procedure: KJ-KKZ1 4726+, KJ-KKZ2 472.6+
Juvenile courts: KJC9662

Correspondence, Contracts through: KJC1737

Correspondents (Press law): KJC7012

Corrupt acts by officials: KJ-KKZ1 4518, KJ-KKZ2 451.8

Corrupt practices (Crimes in connection with election and voting): KJ-KKZ1 4460, KJ-KKZ2 446

Corruption
Crimes against the civil service: KJ-KKZ1 4516+, KJ-KKZ2 451.6+
Offenses against the government: KJA3390.C67

Cosmetics
Public health: KJE6202.C65, KJ-KKZ1 3097.5

Cost-of-living adjustments (Civil service): KJE5953, KJ-KKZ1 1335, KJ-KKZ2 132.5

Costs: KJC4172, KJE4169.5
Attorneys: KJ-KKZ1 1634
Bankruptcy: KJ-KKZ1 1965, KJ-KKZ2 196.5

Costs
Civil procedure: KJ-KKZ1 1830+, KJ-KKZ2 183+
Civil register: KJ-KKZ1 1866, KJ-KKZ2 186.6
Courts and procedure: KJ-KKZ1 1976+, KJ-KKZ2 197.6, KJ-KKZ3 39.2
Criminal procedure: KJ-KKZ1 4850, KJ-KKZ2 486
Customs: KJ-KKZ1 3654
Execution: KJ-KKZ1 1928, KJ-KKZ2 192.9
Labor courts and procedure: KJ-KKZ1 1463
Noncontentious jurisdiction: KJ-KKZ1 1882, KJ-KKZ2 188.2
Notaries: KJ-KKZ1 1848, KJ-KKZ2 184.8
Remedies: KJ-KKZ1 1692
Social courts and procedure: KJ-KKZ1 1568, KJ-KKZ2 156.8

Cotonou Agreement, 2000: KJE5110.22

Council for Mutual Economic Assistance: KJE801+

Council of Europe, 1949: KJE101+

Council of European Municipalities: KJC5882

Council of State: KJ-KKZ1 2615, KJ-KKZ2 261.6

Council of the European Communities: KJE5318+

Councils
Central government: KJ-KKZ3 49.5.C68
Legislature: KJC5359+
Municipal government: KJ-KKZ1 2943, KJ-KKZ3 56.5, KJ-KKZ4 4.95

Counterclaim (Defenses): KJ-KKZ1 1756.S48, KJ-KKZ2 175.6.S48

Counterfeiting: KJA3390.C69

Counterfeiting money and stamps (Crimes against legal transactions): KJ-KKZ1 4346+, KJ-KKZ2 434.6+

Counterfeiting securities: KJ-KKZ1 4350, KJ-KKZ2 435

Criminal offense: KJA3350+, KJC8054+

Criminal police: KJ-KKZ1 3007, KJ-KKZ2 300.7

Criminal procedure: KJ-KKZ1 4600.9+, KJ-KKZ2 459.92+
Medieval and early modern periods: KJ-KKZ1 292.A+

Criminal procedure and public opinion: KJ-KKZ1 4614, KJ-KKZ2 460.4

Criminal provisions
Agriculture: KJ-KKZ1 3332, KJ-KKZ2 333.2
Banking transactions: KJ-KKZ2 101.5
Business associations: KJ-KKZ1 1153
Collision at sea: KJ-KKZ1 980.3
Commercial law: KJC2255, KJ-KKZ1 966
Copyright: KJE2655.9
Fine arts: KJE2670.9
Literary copyright: KJE2660.9
Motion pictures: KJE2690.9
Musical copyright: KJE2665.9
Television shows: KJE2690.9
Deposit banking: KJ-KKZ1 958
Economic law: KJ-KKZ3 82.4, KJ-KKZ4 8.35
Health insurance: KJ-KKZ1 1493
Labor law: KJE3205
Labor-management relations: KJ-KKZ1 1375
Libraries: KJ-KKZ1 3182.2
Radio and television communication: KJC7000+
Radio communication: KJ-KKZ1 3498+, KJ-KKZ2 349.9
Rationing: KJ-KKZ1 3726, KJ-KKZ2 372.7
Salvage: KJ-KKZ1 981.3
Savings banks: KJ-KKZ1 946
Social legislation: KJ-KKZ1 1480
Wildcat strikes: KJ-KKZ1 1395

Criminal registers: KJC9796, KJE9796, KJ-KKZ1 4845, KJ-KKZ2 485, KJ-KKZ3 91.6

Criminal societies: KJE8781.C75, KJ-KKZ1 4314, KJ-KKZ2 431.4

Criminal sociology: KJ-KKZ1 3960, KJ-KKZ2 396

Criminal statistics: KJ-KKZ1 31+, KJ-KKZ2 3.2, KJ-KKZ3 5.3

Criminal tax cases, Special procedures in: KJ-KKZ1 3704

Criminal trials: KJ-KKZ1 39+, KJ-KKZ2 3.5+
Roman law: KJA127+

Crossings (Highway safety): KJ-KKZ1 3454.C75

Crown goods and dynastic house goods: KJ-KKZ1 263, KJ-KKZ2 26.3

Crown privilege: KJ-KKZ1 2554, KJ-KKZ2 255.4

Culpa
Criminal law: KJA3354
Obligations: KJC1582+, KJ-KKZ1 824.5+

Culpa in contrahendo: KJC1588, KJ-KKZ1 825.5

Culpa lata: KJA2531

Culpa levis: KJA2532

Cultural affairs: KJC6257+, KJE6257+, KJ-KKZ3 64+, KJ-KKZ4 6.4+

Cultural exchanges: KJ-KKZ1 3184, KJ-KKZ2 320.6

Cultural policy: KJ-KKZ1 3137.7, KJ-KKZ2 315.2, KJ-KKZ3 64+, KJ-KKZ4 6.4+

Curatorship
Domestic relations: KJ-KKZ3 16.4
Family law: KJA2267
Guardian and ward: KJC1247, KJ-KKZ1 629+

Curatorship for helpless (frail) adults: KJ-KKZ1 630

Curic Rhaetia: KJ575+

Currency: KJA3160

Currency reforms (Public finance): KJC7094, KJ-KKZ1 3537.5

Curriculum (Higher education): KJ-KKZ1 3148+, KJ-KKZ2 317+

Custodial education
Children: KJ-KKZ1 1549+, KJ-KKZ2 154.9

Custodial education
  Juvenile delinquency: KJ-KKZ1 4728,
    KJ-KKZ2 472.8
Custodianship accounts (Deposit
  banking): KJ-KKZ1 956.3
Custody
  Parental power of legitimate children:
    KJ-KKZ1 602+, KJ-KKZ2 60
Custody of illegitimate children: KJ-
  KKZ1 616
Custom and observance (Sources of
  law): KJ-KKZ1 449.3
Custom territory: KJ-KKZ1 3650
Customary law
  Constitutional law: KJC5070
  Criminal law: KJ-KKZ1 3829
Customary law and observances: KJ-
  KKZ1 2340
Customs: KJ783+, KJC7312+,
  KJE7312+
  Administration of public property:
    KJA3210
  National revenue: KJ-KKZ1 3645+,
    KJ-KKZ2 364+, KJ-KKZ3 87.7+, KJ-
    KKZ4 8.72
Customs courts: KJC7431+
Customs crimes and delinquency:
  KJC7475+
Customs organization and
  administration: KJ-KKZ1 3648+, KJ-
  KKZ2 364.4
Customs union movement: KJC7312+
Customs value, Establishing the:
  KJE7319

D

Dairy farming: KJ-KKZ1 3329, KJ-KKZ2
  332.9
Dairy products (Industry regulation): KJ-
  KKZ1 3388+, KJ-KKZ2 338.8+
Damage
  Monopolies: KJE6530
Damages: KJ906, KJA2616,
  KJC1610+, KJ-KKZ1 828+, KJ-KKZ2
  82.9+, KJ-KKZ3 20.2+

Damages
  Defects of goods sold: KJ-KKZ1
    876.3
  Foreign armed forces: KJ-KKZ1
    3757.5
  Government control and policy: KJ-
    KKZ1 3247, KJ-KKZ2 324.7
  Income tax: KJ-KKZ1 3589.3.D35
  Liability of possessor: KJ-KKZ1 679
  Protection against abuse of claims
    enforcement: KJ-KKZ1 1938
  Wildcat strikes: KJ-KKZ1 1394
Damages as counterplea: KJ-KKZ1
  832.7
Damages for pain and suffering:
  KJC1627, KJ-KKZ1 831+, KJ-KKZ2
  83.2
Damaging official announcements: KJ-
  KKZ1 4482.D35, KJ-KKZ2 448.2.D35
Damaging power installations: KJ-KKZ1
  4370, KJ-KKZ2 437
Damaging water installations: KJ-KKZ1
  4370, KJ-KKZ2 437
Damnum injuria datum: KJA2627
Dams: KJ-KKZ1 3050, KJ-KKZ2 305.7
Dangerous articles (Ship cargo): KJ-
  KKZ1 3472.5.D35
Dangerous criminals (Protective
  custody): KJ-KKZ1 3992
Dangerous interference with air traffic:
  KJ-KKZ1 4380, KJ-KKZ2 438
Dangerous interference with rail traffic:
  KJ-KKZ1 4380, KJ-KKZ2 438
Dangerous interference with ship traffic:
  KJ-KKZ1 4380, KJ-KKZ2 438
Dangerous interference with street
  traffic: KJ-KKZ1 4384+, KJ-KKZ2
  438.4+
Dangerous use of poisonous
  substances: KJ-KKZ1 4362, KJ-KKZ2
  436.2
Danube River
  Water resources: KJC6116.D35
Data bases
  Access to (Government control):
    KJC6071

Decurions
  Non-Roman municipal government:
    KJA3092.5
Deductions
  Business tax: KJ-KKZ1 3678
  Income tax: KJC7174, KJ-KKZ1
    3579+, KJ-KKZ2 357.2+
  Property tax: KJ-KKZ1 3667
  Stock companies: KJ-KKZ1 3602+,
    KJ-KKZ2 359.2
Defamation (Criminal law): KJ-KKZ1
  4147, KJ-KKZ2 414.7
Defamatory statement and truth
  (Criminal law): KJ-KKZ1 4154, KJ-
  KKZ2 415.4
Default
  Civil procedure: KJC3864
  Civil proceedings: KJA2790
  Obligations: KJA2539, KJC1603, KJ-
    KKZ1 827.6, KJ-KKZ2 82.8
  Sale contracts: KJC1776+, KJ-KKZ1
    874.5, KJ-KKZ2 89.77
  Taxation: KJ-KKZ1 3569
Default and restitution (Civil procedure):
  KJ-KKZ1 1731
Default judgment: KJ-KKZ1 1765, KJ-
  KKZ2 176.5
Default of buyer: KJ-KKZ1 926.2.D43
Defeating rights of creditors: KJ-KKZ1
  4270+, KJ-KKZ2 427+
Defeating rights of pledgee: KJ-KKZ1
  4272, KJ-KKZ2 427.2
Defective administrative acts: KJE5621,
  KJ-KKZ1 2739
Defective incorporation
  Private company: KJ-KKZ1 1093.3
  Stock corporations: KJ-KKZ1 1053.4
Defective marriage: KJC1140, KJ-KKZ1
  555+, KJ-KKZ2 55.5+
Defective merchandise (Sale contracts):
  KJC1790
Defects of goods sold (Warranty): KJ-
  KKZ1 875.5+
Defendant
  Courts and procedure: KJ-KKZ1 1657
  Criminal procedure: KJ-KKZ1
    4630.A25, KJ-KKZ2 463.A25

Defense
  Community law: KJE7690
  Defense attorney: KJ-KKZ1 4630.D43,
    KJ-KKZ2 463.D43
  Defense contracts: KJE5635.D45
Defenses
  Tax and customs courts and
    procedure: KJ-KKZ1 3686, KJ-
    KKZ2 368.6
Defenses and exceptions (Civil
  procedure): KJ-KKZ1 1755+, KJ-
  KKZ2 175+
Deferment
  Military service: KJC7714+
Deferment from compulsory service:
  KJ-KKZ1 3740+, KJ-KKZ2 374.7+
Deferment of execution (Debtor's relief):
  KJ-KKZ1 1972+, KJ-KKZ2 197.2+
Deferred compensation (Taxable
  income): KJ-KKZ1 3578.5.D48
Deficere (Offenses against the
  government): KJA3390.D44
Definition of law: KJ-KKZ1 442+, KJ-
  KKZ2 44.2+
Degrees (Administration of higher
  education): KJ-KKZ1 3149.5
Delatio hereditatis: KJA2273+
Delay (Civil law): KJ-KKZ1 508
Delay granted for payment (Taxation):
  KJ-KKZ1 3567
Delegatio passiva and activa (Extinction
  of obligation): KJA2529.N68
Delegation of powers
  Community institutions and organs:
    KJE5307
Delegation of powers by member states
  to the Community: KJE5080
Deliberation (Courts): KJ-KKZ1 1594+
Delicts: KJ922+, KJA2612+, KJC1640+,
  KJ-KKZ1 834+, KJ-KKZ2 83.5+, KJ-
  KKZ3 20.4+, KJ-KKZ4 1.72
  Copyright: KJC2655.85, KJE2655.85
    Literary copyright: KJE2660.85
    Motion pictures: KJE2670.85,
      KJE2690.85
    Musical copyright: KJE2665.85
    Television shows: KJE2670.85

Delicts
  Intellectual and industrial property:
    KJ-KKZ1 1160.9, KJ-KKZ2 115.9
  Unfair competition: KJC2826+, KJ-
    KKZ1 1255+, KJ-KKZ2 125
Delictuous infamy: KJA3630.D45
Delivery
  Carriage of passengers and goods:
    KJ-KKZ1 932.3.D44
Democracy
  Public law: KJC4425.5
Democratic centralism: KJ-KKZ1 2030,
  KJ-KKZ2 203
Demonstratio: KJA2722
Demonstrations
  Police and public safety: KJ-KKZ1
    3036.5.D45, KJ-KKZ2 303.8.D45
Demonstrations and failure to disperse:
  KJ-KKZ1 4320, KJ-KKZ2 432
Demontage (War damage
  compensation): KJ-KKZ1 3729.R46,
  KJ-KKZ2 373.3.R46
Denominational schools (Religious
  instruction): KJ-KKZ1 3138.7
Dental hygienists: KJ-KKZ1 3101, KJ-
  KKZ2 311
Dentists: KJ-KKZ1 3101, KJ-KKZ2 311
Denunciation
  Criminal procedure: KJC9520
Denunciation (Tax and customs
  procedure): KJ-KKZ1 3697
Department of State: KJ-KKZ1 2604+,
  KJ-KKZ2 260.4+
Department of the Interior: KJC5855
Department stores: KJ-KKZ1 3420.D46,
  KJ-KKZ2 342.D46
Dependent work (Contracts):
  KJC1848+, KJ-KKZ1 892.5+, KJ-
  KKZ2 93.5
Deportation
  Aliens: KJ-KKZ1 3029
  Execution of sentence: KJ-KKZ1
    4794.2+
  Roman law penalties: KJA3620.D47
Deposit
  Contracts and transactions: KJ-KKZ1
    896, KJ-KKZ2 93.8

Deposit
  Copyright: KJC2655.4, KJE2655.4,
    KJ-KKZ1 1160.4, KJ-KKZ2 115.5
  Fine arts: KJE2670.4
  Literary copyright: KJE2660.4
  Motion pictures: KJE2690.4
  Musical copyright: KJE2665.4
  Television shows: KJE2690.4
Deposit banking: KJC2230, KJ-KKZ1
  956+, KJ-KKZ2 100.6, KJ-KKZ3
  24.D45, KJ-KKZ4 2.6.D45
Depositors' fund (Cooperatives'
  finance): KJ-KKZ1 1128
Deposits (Banking): KJ-KKZ1 956.3
Depositum irregulare (Contracts and
  obligations): KJ-KKZ1 896
Depositum (Real contracts): KJA2572
Depreciation allowances (Income tax
  deductions): KJ-KKZ1 3579.3
Depreciation of property, plant, and
  equipment (Stock companies
  deductions): KJ-KKZ1 3603
Deprivation of liberty, Measures
  entailing (Criminal law): KJ-KKZ1
  3982+
Deprivation of liberty, Measures of
  (Criminal law): KJ-KKZ2 392.2+
Dereliction: KJA2474, KJC1302
Dereliction and abandonment
  (Ownership): KJ-KKZ1 673, KJ-KKZ2
  67.3
Derivative possession (Property): KJ-
  KKZ1 647.D47
Desertion: KJC8357.D46, KJ-KKZ1
  4067, KJ-KKZ2 406.7
  Military criminal law and procedure:
    KJ-KKZ1 3760, KJ-KKZ2 376
Designation
  Roman Empire: KJA2885.D47
Designs and models
  Copyright: KJC2678, KJE2678, KJ-
    KKZ1 1177, KJ-KKZ2 117.7
  Patent law: KJC2753, KJ-KKZ1 1212,
    KJ-KKZ2 120.6
Destitute
  Social services: KJC3470

Eaves-drip (Law of adjoining
  landowners): KJ-KKZ1 701.E29, KJ-
  KKZ2 70.3.E29
Eavesdropping (Violation of personal
  privacy): KJ-KKZ1 4168, KJ-KKZ2
  416.8
Ecclesiastical courts: KJ-KKZ1 285.E22
Echanges intracommunautaires:
  KJE6799+
Ecological aspects
  Fisheries: KJC6695.5
  Game laws: KJC6681
  Pest and plant disease control:
    KJC6612
  Public land law: KJE6138
  Regional planning: KJC6138, KJ-
    KKZ1 3060, KJ-KKZ2 307.2
Economic and financial advisors:
  KJC7035, KJ-KKZ1 3517+, KJ-KKZ2
  352.3+
Economic and industrial secrets:
  KJC2827.T72, KJ-KKZ1 4294, KJ-
  KKZ2 429.4
Economic assistance
  Government control and policy: KJ-
    KKZ1 3206+, KJ-KKZ2 321.2
  Marketing orders: KJ-KKZ1 3321+,
    KJ-KKZ2 332.2+
  Mining industry and finance: KJ-KKZ1
    3354, KJ-KKZ2 335.4
Economic Commission for Europe:
  KJE5062.E25
Economic constitution: KJC6417, KJ-
  KKZ1 3191+, KJ-KKZ2 320.64+, KJ-
  KKZ3 70.3
Economic control, Protection of the law
  against acts of: KJE6452
Economic cooperation and integration:
  KJC6430
  COMECON: KJE856+
  European Economic Community:
    KJC6411+
Economic councils: KJ-KKZ1 2524
Economic councils (The legislature):
  KJC5360
Economic crises
  Community measures: KJE7520

Economic crisis dismissal: KJ-KKZ1
  1305
Economic growth and expansion,
  Control of: KJE6431
Economic integration: KJE6417
Economic interest groupings:
  KJE2598+
Economic law: KJC6411+, KJE6411+,
  KJ-KKZ1 3190+, KJ-KKZ2 320.63+,
  KJ-KKZ3 70+, KJ-KKZ4 7+
  Council for Mutual Economic
    Assistance: KJE856+
Economic measures
  Community law: KJE7520
Economic policies
  Employee participation: KJ-KKZ1
    1369
Economic policy (Taxation): KJC7118
Economic recovery measures,
  Government: KJ-KKZ1 3720+, KJ-
  KKZ2 372+
Edicta magistratum: KJA285+
Education: KJC6266+, KJE6257+, KJ-
  KKZ1 3138+
  Children with disabilities: KJ-KKZ1
    3143+, KJ-KKZ2 316.4
  Criminal law punishment: KJ-KKZ1
    3956, KJ-KKZ2 395.6
  Guardianship over minors: KJ-KKZ1
    625.5.E38, KJ-KKZ2 62.6.E38
  Labor law: KJ-KKZ1 1435.T43
  Prisoners: KJ-KKZ1 4812.E38, KJ-
    KKZ2 481.2.E38
  Probation sentence: KJ-KKZ1 3974,
    KJ-KKZ2 397.4
Education and training (Teachers): KJ-
  KKZ1 3140.5
Education, Right to
  Civil and political rights: KJE5210
Educational assistance and allowances:
  KJ-KKZ1 1524.E38
Educational exchanges: KJ-KKZ1 3184,
  KJ-KKZ2 320.6
Educational expenses (Income tax
  deductions): KJ-KKZ1 3582.3.E38

Family name
  Civil register: KJ-KKZ1 1857, KJ-
    KKZ2 185.7
Family planning: KJ-KKZ1 3124+, KJ-
  KKZ2 313.4+
Family policy (Social insurance):
  KJC3283
Family structure: KJA2229+
Family theft: KJA3446
  Larceny and embezzlement: KJ-KKZ1
    4242, KJ-KKZ2 424.2
Famous and notorious trademarks:
  KJC2775
Farm equipment leasing: KJ-KKZ1
  3311, KJ-KKZ2 331.2
Farm laborers
  Labor law: KJE3192.A37
Farm products
  Tariff: KJ-KKZ1 3653.A37
Farm tenancy: KJ-KKZ1 3310+, KJ-
  KKZ2 331+
Farmers
  Manuals for: KJ-KKZ1 78.F37, KJ-
    KKZ2 7.3.F37
Fascism (Criminal law theories):
  KJC7996
Faulty gas installations: KJ-KKZ1 4376,
  KJ-KKZ2 437.6
Favored nation clause: KJ-KKZ1 3647
Federal and state government (Organs
  of national government): KJ-KKZ1
  2500+, KJ-KKZ2 250+
Federal Executive Council (Socialist):
  KJ-KKZ1 2575, KJ-KKZ2 257.5
Federal government
  Administrative department: KJ-KKZ1
    2898+, KJ-KKZ2 289.8+
  Constitutional law: KJC5413
Federal republic
  Constitutional law: KJC5413
Federal-state controversies: KJ-KKZ1
  2180, KJ-KKZ1 2375, KJ-KKZ2 218
Federal-state (Republic) controversies:
  KJ-KKZ2 237.5
Federalism: KJ-KKZ1 2373, KJ-KKZ2
  237.3

Federation of municipal corporations:
  KJ-KKZ1 2967
Fees (Administration of public property):
  KJA3210
Fehde: KJ982.F48
Fehmic courts: KJ-KKZ1 285.F45
Fellowships for students: KJ-KKZ1
  3153.7
Felony: KJ-KKZ1 3841, KJ-KKZ2 384.2
Fertilization in vitro
  Criminal law: KJ-KKZ1 4108
  Medical legislation: KJC6228,
    KJE6228, KJ-KKZ1 3117, KJ-KKZ2
    312.8
Fertilization in vitro, etc
  Criminal law: KJ-KKZ2 410.8
Fertilizer industry: KJC6743.F47,
  KJE6760
Festuca: KJ868
Feud (Criminal law and procedure):
  KJ982.F48
Feudal and servitory courts: KJ-KKZ3
  34.4.F48, KJ-KKZ4 3.42.F48
Feudal capacity: KJ-KKZ1 228, KJ-
  KKZ2 22.8
Feudal fiefs (Church finance and
  estate): KJ-KKZ1 279
Feudal institutes: KJC4435+, KJ-KKZ1
  221+, KJ-KKZ2 22.2+
Feudal law: KJ-KKZ1 213+, KJ-KKZ2
  21.3+, KJ-KKZ3 43+, KJ-KKZ4 4.26
Feudal lord and vassal: KJC4435, KJ-
  KKZ1 222, KJ-KKZ2 22.2
Feudal succession: KJ-KKZ1 230, KJ-
  KKZ2 23
Fictions: KJ-KKZ1 472.F52, KJ-KKZ2
  47.2.F52
Ficucia (Real securities): KJA2506
Fideicommissum
  Real property: KJC1319+, KJ-KKZ1
    3304, KJ-KKZ2 330.4, KJ-KKZ3
    72.6+, KJ-KKZ4 7.45+
Fideiussio: KJA2524
Fideiussor: KJ914.A+
Fidepromissio: KJA2524
Fides (Contracts): KJC1730

Foreign investments
  Income tax: KJ-KKZ1 3588
  Taxation and tax exemption: KJ-KKZ1
  3553.3
Foreign investors
  Community law: KJE959.B87
  Manuals for: KJ-KKZ3 5.7.B87
Foreign judgments
  Conflict of laws: KJC3800, KJE3800,
  KJ-KKZ1 1646, KJ-KKZ2 164.6, KJ-
  KKZ3 36.7
  Criminal courts and procedure: KJ-
  KKZ3 93.4
Foreign licensing agreements:
  KJC2757, KJE2777, KJ-KKZ1 1214,
  KJ-KKZ2 120.8
  Trademarks: KJC2793, KJ-KKZ1
  1230
Foreign military bases: KJ-KKZ2 375.18
Foreign relations: KJA3320+,
  KJC5105+, KJE5105+
  Council for Mutual Economic
  Assistance: KJE836+
  European Atomic Energy
  Commission: KJE6770
  European Coal and Steel Community:
  KJE6747
  Medieval and early modern periods:
  KJ-KKZ1 212, KJ-KKZ2 21.2
Foreign relations administration
  Constitutional law: KJ-KKZ1 2400+,
  KJ-KKZ2 240+
  Medieval and early modern periods:
  KJ-KKZ3 45.3, KJ-KKZ4 4.32
Foreign service: KJ-KKZ1 2608, KJ-
  KKZ2 260.8
Foreign stockholders: KJC2501
  Corporation tax: KJ-KKZ1 3614+
  Double taxation: KJ-KKZ1 3552.4.F67
Foreign trade practice: KJ-KKZ1 3407+,
  KJ-KKZ2 340.7+
Foresight
  Delicts: KJ-KKZ1 839.5
  Negligence and wantonness:
  KJC8126, KJ-KKZ1 3876

Forestry: KJC6590+, KJ-KKZ1 3336+,
  KJ-KKZ2 333.6+, KJ-KKZ3 76.3, KJ-
  KKZ4 7.64
  Income tax: KJ-KKZ1 3591.A43, KJ-
  KKZ2 358.2.A43
  Regalia: KJ786.F67
Forestry lands, Conservation of:
  KJC6600
Forests: KJ-KKZ3 60+, KJ-KKZ4 5.6+
  Wilderness preservation: KJ-KKZ1
  3134+
Forfeiture
  Criminal law: KJC8251.F67, KJ-KKZ1
  4010, KJ-KKZ2 401
Forfeiture of property: KJA3630.F67
Forgery
  Delicts: KJ-KKZ1 846, KJ-KKZ2 86.7
  Mechanical records: KJ-KKZ2 433.8
  Offenses against property: KJA3456+
Forgery of art works: KJ-KKZ1
  4351.F67, KJ-KKZ2 435.15.F67
Forgery of documents: KJ-KKZ1 4334,
  KJ-KKZ2 433.4
Forgery of mechanical records: KJ-
  KKZ1 4338, KJ-KKZ2 433.8
Forgery of seals: KJ-KKZ1 3699
Forgery of sound recordings and
  electronic data bases: KJ-KKZ1 4338,
  KJ-KKZ2 433.8
Forgery of stamps: KJ-KKZ1 3699
Form
  Judgment: KJ-KKZ1 1797
  Matrimonial status: KJA2234
  Testamentary succession: KJA2406
Form requirements
  Contracts and transactions: KJ-KKZ1
  866
  Courts and procedure: KJ-KKZ1 742
  Power of attorney: KJ-KKZ1 863
  Wills: KJ-KKZ1 786.6
Formalities
  Contracts: KJA2551, KJC1760, KJ-
  KKZ1 872.5
  Copyright: KJC2655.4, KJE2655.4,
  KJ-KKZ1 1160.4, KJ-KKZ2 115.5
    Fine arts: KJE2670.4, KJE2670.5

Hortatory procedures (Civil procedure): KJ-KKZ1 1812, KJ-KKZ2 181.2

Horticulture: KJC6590+
  Income tax: KJ-KKZ1 3591.A43, KJ-KKZ2 358.2.A43

Horticulture (Regulation): KJ-KKZ1 3335, KJ-KKZ3 76, KJ-KKZ4 7.63
  Taxation: KJ-KKZ1 3572.A37, KJ-KKZ2 356.5.A37

Hospital and medical personnel (Collective bargaining): KJ-KKZ1 1387.H67

Hospital personnel
  Labor law: KJ-KKZ1 1435.H67

Hospital records: KJC6229.R43, KJE6229.R43, KJ-KKZ1 3119.R42

Hospitals: KJC6222
  Contract with the sickness fund: KJ-KKZ1 1492
  Medical legislation: KJ-KKZ1 3110+, KJ-KKZ2 312+
  The armed forces: KJ-KKZ1 3746

Hostage (Contracts): KJ914.H68

Hostels (Public safety): KJ-KKZ1 3034.5, KJ-KKZ2 303.4

Hostes Populi Romani: KJA3280+

Hotels and motels
  Excise taxes: KJ-KKZ2 362.4.H68
  Industry regulation: KJ-KKZ1 3424.5, KJ-KKZ3 80.5.H66
  Wages: KJ-KKZ1 1343.H6, KJ-KKZ2 133.4.H6

Hotels and Motels
  Excise taxes: KJ-KKZ1 3640.H68

Hours of labor: KJC3145+, KJE3145, KJ-KKZ1 1410+, KJ-KKZ2 140.3, KJ-KKZ3 31.5.H68
  Child and youth labor: KJ-KKZ1 1422, KJ-KKZ2 141.5
  Merchant mariners: KJ-KKZ1 990
  Women: KJC3175+
  Women's labor: KJ-KKZ1 1424+, KJ-KKZ2 141.7+

Household appliances industry
  Manufacturing industry: KJ-KKZ1 3373.H68

Household (Marriage bond): KJ-KKZ1 548

Housewives (Social security): KJC3411.M68

Housing
  Labor standards and protection of labor: KJ-KKZ1 1364
  Lease: KJ-KKZ3 21.5+, KJ-KKZ4 1.82+

Housing allowances
  Social services: KJE3448

Housing courts (Leasing contracts): KJ-KKZ3 21.4

Human experimentation in genetic engineering
  Medical legislation: KJC6227+, KJE6227+, KJ-KKZ1 3115+, KJ-KKZ2 312.5+

Human experimentation in medicine
  Medical legislation: KJC6227+, KJE6227+, KJ-KKZ1 3115+, KJ-KKZ2 312.5+

Human reproductive technology: KJC6228, KJ-KKZ1 4108
  Criminal law: KJ-KKZ2 410.8
  Medical legislation: KJE6228, KJ-KKZ1 3117, KJ-KKZ2 312.8

Human rights: KJE5132+
  Constitutional law: KJC5132
  Parent and child: KJ-KKZ2 59.2

Human rights of the child
  Capacity and incapacity: KJ-KKZ2 52
  Capacity and incpacity: KJ-KKZ1 515.5+

Human smuggling: KJC8855, KJ-KKZ1 4378

Human trafficking: KJC8855, KJ-KKZ1 4378

Humanism: KJC413

Hunno: KJ764.C45

Hunting
  Liability insurance: KJC2423.H85

Husband and wife: KJ825+, KJC1128+
  Civil law: KJ-KKZ1 547+, KJ-KKZ2 55.2+

Husband and wife, Contracts between: KJ-KKZ1 577, KJ-KKZ2 57.8

International Center of Scientific and Technical Information: KJE854.22
International cooperation: KJE5105+
International fairs: KJ-KKZ1 3282, KJ-KKZ2 328.2
International institutions, Crimes against: KJ-KKZ1 4543, KJ-KKZ2 454.3
International judicial assistance: KJ-KKZ1 1644, KJ-KKZ2 164.4, KJ-KKZ3 36.6
  Administration of criminal justice: KJ-KKZ3 93.3
International Labor Organization: KJE5062.I68
International Laboratory for Strong Magnetic Fields and Low Temperature: KJE854.34
International law and municipal law: KJC5057, KJ-KKZ1 2325, KJ-KKZ2 232.5
International loan agreements: KJ-KKZ1 3532
International recognition (Higher education): KJC6318
International relations: KJE5057+
International trade: KJC6791+, KJ-KKZ1 3405+, KJ-KKZ2 340.5+, KJ-KKZ3 79.3, KJ-KKZ4 7.8
International travel
  Taxation: KJE7306+
Interpellation (Legislative process): KJC5352, KJ-KKZ1 2518, KJ-KKZ2 251.8
Interpleader (Civil procedure): KJ-KKZ1 1763, KJ-KKZ2 176.3
Interpretation and construction of law: KJ-KKZ1 452
  Applicability and validity of the law (Criminal law): KJ-KKZ1 3828
  Civil law: KJ-KKZ1 502
  Constitutional law: KJ-KKZ1 2220, KJ-KKZ2 222
  Criminal law: KJ-KKZ1 3821, KJ-KKZ2 381
Interpretation of international law: KJE965

Interregnum (Magistracies): KJA2983
Interstate and state highways: KJ-KKZ1 3044, KJ-KKZ2 304.8
Interstate (Interprovincial, etc.) disputes: KJ-KKZ1 2375, KJ-KKZ2 237.5
Intertemporal law: KJC436, KJE975, KJ-KKZ1 487, KJ-KKZ2 48.7, KJ-KKZ3 13.2
Intertiatio (Germanic law): KJ1024
Intertiation (Germanic law): KJ1024
Intervention
  Civil procedure: KJ-KKZ1 1762, KJ-KKZ2 176
Intervention of injured party (Criminal procedure): KJ-KKZ1 4766, KJ-KKZ2 476.6, KJ-KKZ2 476.7
Intestability (Criminal law): KJA3630.I58
Intestate succession: KJA2287+, KJC1477
  Community law: KJE1477
Intestate succession (Inheritance): KJ-KKZ1 775, KJ-KKZ2 76.7, KJ-KKZ3 19.6+
Intoxication
  Criminal law: KJ-KKZ1 4402, KJ-KKZ2 440.2
  Criminal liability: KJ-KKZ1 3892.I58, KJ-KKZ2 388.5.I58
Intra-Community trade: KJE6799+
Invalid adults (Medical legislation): KJ-KKZ1 3114.O42, KJ-KKZ2 312.4.O42
Invalidenrente (Social security): KJE3407
Invalidity and disability pensions: KJC3381+
Invention
  Patent law: KJC2734+
  Patent practice and procedure: KJ-KKZ1 1203+, KJ-KKZ2 120.3
Inventory
  Insolvency: KJ-KKZ1 1897, KJ-KKZ2 189.7
  Merchant and business enterprise: KJ-KKZ1 923+
  Taxable income: KJ-KKZ1 3600.I58

Investigations
  Criminal courts and procedure:
    KJC9529
  Pretrial procedures: KJ-KKZ1 4636+,
    KJ-KKZ2 463.6+
Investissements (Government control):
  KJE6433+
Investitionskontrolle (Government
  control): KJE6433+
Investitura: KJ868
Investment control (Government control
  and policy): KJ-KKZ1 3202+, KJ-
  KKZ2 320.9
Investment credits (Economic law): KJ-
  KKZ1 3207.3
Investment trusts: KJC2250+,
  KJE2250+, KJ-KKZ1 963+, KJ-KKZ2
  101.2+
  Corporation tax: KJ-KKZ1 3613.I58,
    KJ-KKZ2 360.I58
Investments
  Commercial law: KJC2245+, KJ-
    KKZ1 961.5+, KJ-KKZ2 100.9+
  Council for Mutual Economic
    Assistance: KJE860+
  Government control: KJE6433+, KJ-
    KKZ1 3202+, KJ-KKZ2 320.9
  Tax and tax exemption: KJ-KKZ1
    3553.5
Ipso jure discharge: KJA2528+
Iron and steel industries: KJE6742
Italian jurists (16th to 18th centuries):
  KJA2030+
Italici: KJA2955
Ius gentium (Roman law): KJA3320+

J

Jails: KJ-KKZ1 4824, KJ-KKZ2 482.4
Jews
  Discrimination against (Constitutional
    law): KJC5144.M56
Job security (Extinction of employment):
  KJC2926+, KJ-KKZ1 1310+, KJ-KKZ2
  130
Joinder of actions: KJ-KKZ1 1752
Joinder of parties: KJ-KKZ1 1759

Joint and several obligation (Plurality of
  debtors and creditors): KJ-KKZ1
  813.5
Joint committees of the Council of
  Europe: KJE139.7.A+
Joint European Torus: KJE6774
Joint heirs: KJA2417+, KJ-KKZ1 782+,
  KJ-KKZ2 78.2
Joint obligations: KJA2517, KJC1505
Joint possession (Property): KJ-KKZ1
  647.J64
Joint Research Center (Nuclear power
  industry): KJE6772
Joint tortfeasors: KJ-KKZ1 837.6, KJ-
  KKZ2 84.4
Joint ventures
  Business associations: KJ-KKZ1
    1139
  Personal companies: KJC2446,
    KJE2446
Joint will: KJ-KKZ1 785.7.J64
Jouissance share: KJC2487
  Securities: KJ-KKZ1 1070.J68
Journalists: KJC7012, KJ-KKZ1 3504.3
  Labor law: KJ-KKZ1 1435.J88
Judex qui litem suam facit: KJA2634
Judge-made law: KJC404, KJ-KKZ1
  452
Judges: KJC3716+, KJC3716, KJ-KKZ1
  1610+, KJ-KKZ2 161
  Bankruptcy proceedings: KJ-KKZ1
    1945
  Parties to action: KJ-KKZ1 1726
  Political activity of: KJ-KKZ1 1613
  The legal profession: KJ-KKZ3 36,
    KJ-KKZ4 3.5
Judgments
  Civil procedure: KJC3956+, KJ-KKZ1
    1787+, KJ-KKZ2 178.3+
  Courts and procedures: KJ968
  Criminal procedure: KJA3600+, KJ-
    KKZ1 4738+, KJ-KKZ2 473.8+
  Labor courts and procedure: KJ-KKZ1
    1458+
  Tax and customs courts and
    procedure: KJ-KKZ1 3688, KJ-
    KKZ2 369.3

Judiciary, The, and administration: KJ-KKZ1 1573

Judiciary, The, and foreign relations: KJ-KKZ1 1574

Judicis postulationem, Legis actio per: KJA2716.J83

Jugendarbeit: KJE3172

Jukeboxes
  Copyright: KJC2655.75, KJE2655.75
    Fine arts: KJE2670.75
    Literary copyright: KJE2660.75
    Motion pictures: KJE2690.75
    Musical copyright: KJE2665.75
    Television shows: KJE2690.75
  Recording rights: KJ-KKZ1 1160.75

Jura in re (Law of things): KJA2483+

Juries: KJ1026, KJA3045+, KJC9455

Juris jurandi in principem formulae: KJA664

Jurisdiction
  Civil procedure: KJA2782
  Community law
    Community institutions and organs: KJE5307
    Intergovernmental relations: KJE5086
  Comparative law
    Civil procedure: KJC3872
    Private international law: KJC3795+
  Conflict of laws: KJ-KKZ1 481.7
  Constitutional courts: KJ-KKZ1 2650, KJ-KKZ2 265
  Constitutional history: KJ-KKZ1 2170+, KJ-KKZ2 217+
  Constitutional law: KJ-KKZ1 2370+, KJ-KKZ2 237+
  Court of: KJ-KKZ1 1588+
  Courts and procedure: KJ-KKZ1 1664
    Civil procedure: KJ-KKZ1 1737+, KJ-KKZ2 173.7
  Courts of: KJ-KKZ2 158.8+
  Criminal courts and procedure: KJC9576
  Criminal procedure: KJA3592
  Customs: KJ-KKZ1 3650
  Guardianship court: KJ-KKZ1 1875+, KJ-KKZ2 187.6+

Jurisdiction
  History of law: KJ-KKZ1 284
  Labor courts and procedure: KJ-KKZ1 1450
  Procedure at first instance: KJ-KKZ1 3685.5
    Criminal procedure: KJ-KKZ1 4666, KJ-KKZ2 466.6
  Public prosecutor: KJ-KKZ1 1618
  Social courts and procedure: KJ-KKZ1 1562
  The Senate (Roman law): KJA3037

Jurisdiction for tax allocation: KJ-KKZ1 3661

Jurisprudence: KJ-KKZ1 440+, KJ-KKZ2 44+

Jurisprudence of European law: KJC383+

Jurisprudence of interest: KJC430

Juristic acts: KJC1050

Juristic persons: KJA2222+, KJC3847, KJ-KKZ1 521+, KJ-KKZ2 53+
  Civil procedure: KJC3847, KJ-KKZ1 1723
  Criminal law: KJ-KKZ1 3936, KJ-KKZ2 393.6
  Offenses against the person: KJ-KKZ2 414.3+
  Offenses against the persons: KJ-KKZ1 4143+
  Property tax: KJ-KKZ1 3663+, KJ-KKZ2 366.2
  Public law: KJC5807, KJ-KKZ1 2875+, KJ-KKZ2 287+
    Execution for payment due: KJ-KKZ1 1922, KJ-KKZ2 192.5

Juristic persons of private law (Civil law): KJC1030+, KJ-KKZ3 14.2+

Jurists
  Jurists' law: KJA798+
  Legal profession: KJA2157

Jurists' law: KJA690+, KJA1568+

Jury and jury procedure: KJA3536+

Jury room procedure: KJ-KKZ1 1585

Jus: KJA690+

Jus civile
  Intestate succession: KJA2289

Legislation
  Council for Mutual Economic
    Assistance: KJE810+
  Maritime social legislation: KJ-KKZ1
    987+, KJ-KKZ2 103.6+
  Sources of law: KJ-KKZ1 449+
  The Senate (Roman law): KJA3037
Legislative bodies: KJC5317, KJ-KKZ1
  2514, KJ-KKZ2 251.4
Legislative branch (Municipal
  government): KJ-KKZ1 2943
Legislative papers of the European
  Communities: KJE915+
Legislative power: KJC5310+,
  KJE5307, KJ-KKZ1 2510+, KJ-KKZ2
  251+, KJ-KKZ3 48.3+
Legislative process: KJA2976,
  KJC5349+, KJ-KKZ1 2516+, KJ-KKZ2
  251.6+, KJ-KKZ3 48.35
Legislators: KJC5369, KJ-KKZ1 2528,
  KJ-KKZ2 252.8
Legislature: KJC5310+
Legislature, The: KJ-KKZ1 2510+, KJ-
  KKZ2 251+, KJ-KKZ3 48.3+
Legistic: KJA1568+
Legitimacy
  Constitutional principles: KJE5041
Legitimacy (Constitutional law):
  KJC5041, KJ-KKZ1 2240, KJ-KKZ2
  224
Legitimate children: KJC1192+, KJ-
  KKZ1 590+, KJ-KKZ2 59+
Legitimation
  Declaration of: KJ-KKZ1 595, KJ-
    KKZ2 59.5
  Savings banks: KJ-KKZ1 945.3.L44
Legitimation and identification
  Negotiable instruments: KJ-KKZ1
    937.3
Legitimation by subsequent marriage:
  KJ-KKZ1 595, KJ-KKZ2 59.5
Legitimation of children: KJ-KKZ1 595,
  KJ-KKZ2 59.5
Legitimation of concubinate children by
  subsequent marriage: KJA2257
Legitime
  Community law: KJE1473

Lenocinium (Criminal law):
  KJA3468.L45
Lesbians
  Discrimination against: KJE5144.G39
Lese majesty: KJC9021.L48, KJ-KKZ1
  4438, KJ-KKZ2 443.8
Letters: KJ-KKZ1 80.L46, KJ-KKZ2
  7.8.L46
Letters of credit: KJ-KKZ1 955.6, KJ-
  KKZ2 100.55
Lewd acts by persons taking advantage
  of official position: KJ-KKZ1 4210, KJ-
  KKZ2 421
Lewd acts in institutions: KJ-KKZ1
  4212, KJ-KKZ2 421.2
Lewd acts with children or charges:
  KJC8551.C45, KJ-KKZ1 4208, KJ-
  KKZ2 420.8
Lewd acts with persons incapable of
  resistance: KJ-KKZ1 4204, KJ-KKZ2
  420.4
Lex Cornelia: KJA2629
Liability: KJ-KKZ1 931.2
  Banking transactions: KJ-KKZ1 953.5
  Bills of exchange: KJ-KKZ1 938.3.L52
  Business concerns: KJ-KKZ1 1143
  Capacity and incapacity: KJ800+
  Consensual contracts: KJA2582.L52
  Cooperative societies: KJ-KKZ1 1126
  Damages: KJ-KKZ1 828.5
  Debtor and creditor: KJ-KKZ1 1946
  Delicts: KJA2614, KJ-KKZ1 839+, KJ-
    KKZ2 84.7+
  Director or executive board (Stock
    corporations): KJ-KKZ1 1058.L33
  Directors (Private company): KJ-
    KKZ1 1098.L43
  Freight forwarders: KJ-KKZ1 972, KJ-
    KKZ2 102
  Heirs: KJ-KKZ1 783
  Incorporated society: KJ-KKZ1 524
  Journalists: KJ-KKZ1 3504.3
  Labor contract and employment:
    KJC2938+, KJ-KKZ1 1322+
  Maritime law: KJ-KKZ1 977
  Obligations: KJA2530+
  Press delicts: KJ-KKZ1 3510

INDEX

Losses
  Stock companies income tax
    deductions: KJ-KKZ1 3605.5
Lost income
  Damages: KJC1620
Lost profits: KJ-KKZ1 830
Lost property: KJ-KKZ1 657
Lotteries
  Aleatory contracts: KJ-KKZ1 899.5,
    KJ-KKZ2 95.5
  Police and public safety: KJ-KKZ1
    3036.5.G35
Lower classes: KJA2944+
Luftfahrt: KJE6920
Luftverunreinigung
  Community law: KJE6249
Lutte contre le bruit
  Community law: KJE6253

M

Machinery industry
  Collective bargaining: KJ-KKZ1
    1387.M33
  Manufacturing industry: KJ-KKZ1
    3373.M32
  Regulation: KJE6763
Magic (Criminal law and procedure):
  KJ985.W58
Magistrate (Civil procedure): KJ-KKZ1
  1814, KJ-KKZ2 181.4
Magistrate courts (Courts and
  procedure): KJ-KKZ1 1583, KJ-KKZ2
  158.3
Magistrates
  Non-Roman municipal government:
    KJA3092.5
Magnetic recorders
  Copyright: KJE2655.75
    Fine arts: KJE2670.75
    Literary copyright: KJE2660.75
    Motion pictures: KJE2690.75
    Musical copyright: KJE2665.75
    Television shows: KJE2690.75
Magnetic recorders (Copyright):
  KJC2655.75

Magnetic recorders (Copyright)(: KJ-
  KKZ1 1160.75
Mail
  Classification of: KJC6951
  Violating official secrecy: KJ-KKZ1
    4530, KJ-KKZ2 453
Mail-order business
  Trade regulation: KJ-KKZ1 3420.M34,
    KJ-KKZ2 342.M34
Maior domus: KJ764.M34
Majority (Capacity and incapacity):
  KJ802+, KJ-KKZ1 516
Mala fide possessor
  Liability of: KJ-KKZ1 678+, KJ-KKZ2
    67.8
  Rights and defenses of: KJ-KKZ1
    680+, KJ-KKZ2 68
Malingering (Military criminal law and
  procedure): KJ-KKZ1 3763
Malo ordine tenure (Germanic law):
  KJ956
Malperformance (Sale contracts):
  KJC1782
Malpractice
  Criminal law: KJ-KKZ1 4100, KJ-
    KKZ2 410
  Insurance law: KJ-KKZ1 1036.M35
Malpractice, Medical (Civil law): KJ-
  KKZ2 85.5
Management
  Personal companies: KJC2435.35
Mandate (Legal transactions):
  KJC1081+, KJ-KKZ1 864+, KJ-KKZ2
  88.5+
Mandatum: KJA2590
Mannitio: KJ947
Manorial courts: KJ-KKZ1 285.M36, KJ-
  KKZ3 34.4.P38, KJ-KKZ4 3.42.P38
Manorial estates: KJ-KKZ1 234+, KJ-
  KKZ2 23.4, KJ-KKZ3 72+, KJ-KKZ4
  7.3+
Manpower control: KJC3195, KJ-KKZ1
  1437+, KJ-KKZ2 143, KJ-KKZ3 31.7
  Government measures: KJ-KKZ1
    3714+, KJ-KKZ2 371.4+
Manpower planning: KJ-KKZ1 1437+,
  KJ-KKZ2 143

Mass media
  Courts: KJ-KKZ1 1595
Mass organizations (Constitutional law):
  KJ-KKZ1 2488, KJ-KKZ2 248.8
Master and servant: KJC1665, KJ-
  KKZ1 892+, KJ-KKZ2 93+
Matches (Excise taxes): KJ-KKZ1
  3640.M38, KJ-KKZ2 362.4.M38
Maternal welfare
  Social services: KJ-KKZ1 1524.M38
  Women's labor: KJC3179, KJ-KKZ1
    1426, KJ-KKZ2 141.8
Matrimonial actions: KJA2238+,
  KJC1139+, KJ-KKZ1 555+, KJ-KKZ2
  54.4+, KJ-KKZ3 15.5, KJ-KKZ4 1.46
  Civil procedure: KJ-KKZ1 1805, KJ-
    KKZ2 180.5
  Private international law: KJ-KKZ1
    485.M375, KJ-KKZ2 48.5.M375
Matrimonial property
  Bankruptcy: KJ-KKZ1 1949
  Private international law: KJ-KKZ1
    485.M375, KJ-KKZ2 48.5.M375
  Registration of: KJC4117, KJ-KKZ3
    38.2.R44
Matrimonial property and regime:
  KJ832+, KJC1162, KJ-KKZ3 15.6, KJ-
  KKZ4 1.5
Maximum terms of imprisonment
  (Criminal law): KJ-KKZ1 3970+, KJ-
  KKZ2 397+
Mayor (Municipal government): KJ-
  KKZ1 2946, KJ-KKZ3 56.5, KJ-KKZ4
  4.95
Means of review (Tax and custom
  courts and procedure): KJ-KKZ1
  3689+, KJ-KKZ2 369.4+
Measurement instruments industry:
  KJE6764
Measures of punishment and cruelty
  (Criminal law): KJC8304+
Meat
  Regulation: KJE6781
Meat industry (Regulation): KJ-KKZ1
  3383, KJ-KKZ2 338.4
Meat products industry
  Regulation: KJE6781

Mechanical reproduction
  Copyright: KJC2655.623+, KJ-KKZ1
    1160.63+
  Fine arts: KJE2670.623+
  Literary copyright: KJE2655.623+,
    KJE2660.623+
  Motion pictures: KJE2690.623+
  Musical copyright: KJE2665.623+
  Television shows: KJE2690.623+
Medical aspects of justification of
  abortion: KJ-KKZ1 4072, KJ-KKZ2
  407.2
Medical benefits
  Social security: KJ-KKZ1 1508.M43
  Workers' benefits: KJE3364
Medical care insurance: KJ-KKZ1 1013,
  KJ-KKZ2 105
Medical devices: KJC6229.M42,
  KJE6229.M42, KJ-KKZ1 3119.M43
Medical engineering
  Medical legislation: KJE6227+
Medical examiners: KJ-KKZ1 1627
Medical institutions: KJC6222
Medical instruments and apparatus:
  KJC6229.M42, KJE6229.M42, KJ-
  KKZ1 3119.M43
Medical legislation: KJC6206+,
  KJE6206+, KJ-KKZ1 3098+, KJ-KKZ2
  310.8+
  Council for Mutual Economic
    Assistance: KJE848+
Medical personnel
  Labor law: KJ-KKZ1 1435.H67
Medical profession and health
  insurance: KJ-KKZ1 1489+
Medical records: KJC6229.R43,
  KJE6229.R43, KJ-KKZ1 3119.R42
Medical technology
  Criminal law: KJ-KKZ1 4096+, KJ-
    KKZ2 409.6+
  Medical legislation: KJC6227+, KJ-
    KKZ1 3115+, KJ-KKZ2 312.5+
Medicine
  Advertising: KJ-KKZ1 3283.H43
Medicines
  Patent law: KJC2751.M44
Mehrwertsteuer: KJE7285

Money orders
  Crimes against legal transactions: KJ-KKZ1 4351.T44, KJ-KKZ2 435.15.T44
  Postal services: KJ-KKZ1 3485.8.P68
Monopoles d'État
  Taxation: KJE7305
Monopoles d'État délégués: KJE6505
Monopolies: KJE6530
  Competition rules: KJC6497, KJE6497+, KJ-KKZ1 3242+, KJ-KKZ2 324
  Energy policy: KJ-KKZ1 3431.5
Mora
  Obligations: KJA2539
Mora accipiendi: KJA2582.M67, KJC1780, KJ-KKZ1 874.5, KJ-KKZ2 89.77
Moral rights (Intellectual and industrial property): KJ-KKZ1 1157
Morality of law: KJ-KKZ1 444+, KJ-KKZ2 44.4
Moratorium (Debtors' relief): KJ-KKZ1 1975, KJ-KKZ2 197.5
Morgincap: KJ834
Mortgage: KJ-KKZ1 718+, KJ-KKZ2 72.3, KJ-KKZ3 18.7
  Bankruptcy: KJ-KKZ1 1964.H95
Mortgage banks: KJ-KKZ1 943, KJ-KKZ2 99.7
Mortgage insurance: KJ-KKZ1 1026, KJ-KKZ2 106.4
Mortis causa (Immoral transactions): KJ-KKZ1 868+, KJ-KKZ2 89.3
Most favorable wage: KJC3068, KJ-KKZ1 1381
Mothers (Social security): KJC3411.M68
Motion picture theaters (Fire prevention and control): KJ-KKZ1 3019, KJ-KKZ2 301.9
Motion pictures: KJ-KKZ1 3173+, KJ-KKZ2 319.8
  Author and publisher: KJC2708, KJE2708, KJ-KKZ1 1187, KJ-KKZ2 118.7

Motion pictures
  Copyright: KJC2690+, KJE2690+, KJ-KKZ1 1180+, KJ-KKZ2 118
Motion to dismiss (Civil procedure): KJ-KKZ1 1791
Motor fuels (Excise taxes): KJ-KKZ1 3640.M68, KJ-KKZ2 362.4.M68
Motor vehicles: KJC6877+, KJE6877+, KJ-KKZ1 3443+, KJ-KKZ1 3668, KJ-KKZ2 344.3+, KJ-KKZ2 366.3
  Tariff: KJ-KKZ1 3653.M6
Mulieres
  Capacity and incapacity: KJA2213.5.W65
Multilateral treaties
  Council for Mutual Economic Assistance: KJE833.A25+
Multilateral treaties (Council for Mutual Economic Assistance): KJE833.A35<date>
Multinational corporations
  Corporation tax: KJ-KKZ1 3615+, KJ-KKZ2 360.3+
  Double taxation: KJ-KKZ1 3552.4.M85
  Stock companies: KJE2449, KJ-KKZ1 1116, KJ-KKZ2 111.6
  Taxation: KJC7259
Multiple authorship
  Copyright: KJE2655.2+, KJ-KKZ1 1160.2+, KJ-KKZ2 115.3
    Fine arts: KJE2670.2+
    Literary copyright: KJE2660.2+
    Motion pictures: KJE2690.2+
    Musical copyright: KJE2665.2+
    Television shows: KJE2690.2+
Multiple line insurance: KJC2367, KJ-KKZ1 1019, KJ-KKZ2 105.6
Mundium: KJ834
Municipal arbitral boards: KJ-KKZ1 1593.M85, KJ-KKZ2 159.3.M85
Municipal corporations: KJ-KKZ1 3638
Municipal courts: KJ-KKZ1 1583, KJ-KKZ2 158.3
  Medieval and early modern periods: KJ-KKZ1 285.M86

N

Neuroses (Damages): KJ-KKZ1
831.5.N48
Neutrality (Foreign relations): KJC5110,
KJ-KKZ1 2415, KJ-KKZ2 241.3
New Community instrument (Economic
assistance): KJE6438
New trial
Civil procedure: KJC4024, KJ-KKZ1
1826, KJ-KKZ2 182.6
Courts and procedure: KJ-KKZ1 1689
Criminal procedure: KJ-KKZ1 4792,
KJ-KKZ2 479.2
Newspaper court reporting: KJ-KKZ1
3507.3
Nexum (Contracts): KJA2543
Niederlassungsrecht
Community law: KJE5174
Night differentials: KJ-KKZ1 1336
Night work: KJ-KKZ1 1410+, KJ-KKZ2
140.3
Nobility: KJC5409
Estates: KJ-KKZ3 42.2, KJ-KKZ4
4.22
Noise
Environmental pollutants: KJ-KKZ1
3132.5, KJ-KKZ2 314.5
Land ownership: KJ-KKZ1 701.N84,
KJ-KKZ2 70.3.N84
Noise control: KJC6253, KJE6253, KJ-
KKZ1 3132.5, KJ-KKZ2 314.5
Nominatio judicis: KJA2722
Nomination
Civil service: KJE5938
Non-European Union aliens: KJE6044
Non-member nations and integration of
law: KJE982+
Non-wage payments
Labor law: KJE2965
Noncash funds transfer: KJC2243, KJ-
KKZ1 961+, KJ-KKZ2 100.8
Noncash payments (Money debts):
KJC1561
Noncontentious (ex parte) jurisdiction:
KJ-KKZ1 1834+, KJ-KKZ2 183.4+
Noncontentious jurisdiction: KJC4044+,
KJE4044+, KJ-KKZ1 485.N66, KJ-
KKZ3 38+, KJ-KKZ4 3.8

Noncontentious jurisdiction
Judicial assistance: KJC3795+
Nonjudgments: KJ-KKZ1 1796
Nonparticipants (Collective labor
disputes): KJ-KKZ1 1396
Nonperformance: KJA2530+
Labor contract and employment:
KJC2930, KJ-KKZ1 1315+, KJ-KKZ2
130.3
Obligations: KJ906, KJC1580+,
KJE1580+, KJ-KKZ1 824+, KJ-KKZ2
82.4+, KJ-KKZ3 20.2+
Nonpossessory pledges of personal
property: KJ-KKZ1 728+, KJ-KKZ2
73+
Nonprofit associations
Taxation: KJC7200
Nonprofit associations (Corporation tax):
KJ-KKZ1 3593+, KJ-KKZ2 358.4
Nonprofit corporations (Corporation tax):
KJ-KKZ1 3593+, KJ-KKZ2 358.4
Nonwage benefits (Maritime law): KJ-
KKZ1 991
Nonwage payments
Income tax deductions: KJ-KKZ1
3584+, KJ-KKZ2 357.5
Labor law: KJ-KKZ1 1338+, KJ-KKZ2
133+
Nordisk Domssamling (Comparative
law): KJC530+
Norms
Conservation of raw or scarce
materials: KJ-KKZ1 3264+, KJ-
KKZ2 326.5+
Economic law: KJC6554+, KJE6554,
KJ-KKZ1 3254+, KJ-KKZ2 325.4+
Notaries
Noncontentious jurisdiction: KJE4070
Notaries (Noncontentious jurisdiction):
KJ-KKZ1 1846+, KJ-KKZ2 184.6+, KJ-
KKZ3 38.2.N68
Notice: KJ-KKZ1 80.N68, KJ-KKZ1
472.N68, KJ-KKZ2 47.2.N68
Contracts and transactions: KJ-KKZ1
866
Copyright: KJC2655.4, KJE2655.4,
KJ-KKZ1 1160.4, KJ-KKZ2 115.5

Notice
  Copyright
    Fine arts: KJE2670.4
    Literary copyright: KJE2660.4
    Motion pictures: KJE2690.4
    Musical copyright: KJE2665.4
    Television shows: KJE2690.4
  Termination of lease: KJ-KKZ1 882,
    KJ-KKZ2 90.8
Novatio (Extinction of obligation):
  KJA2529.N68
Novation: KJC1569
  Extinction of obligation: KJ-KKZ1
    823.5.N68
Novelty (Patent practice and procedure):
  KJ-KKZ1 1203+, KJ-KKZ2 120.3
Noxious gases: KJ-KKZ1 3130.5, KJ-
  KKZ2 313.9
Nuclear damage (Torts): KJC1692, KJ-
  KKZ1 847.5
Nuclear energy
  Criminal law: KJ-KKZ1 4356, KJ-
    KKZ2 435.6
  Economic law: KJE6858
Nuclear power industry: KJE6766
  Regulation: KJE6012
Nuclear power (Public safety):
  KJC6012, KJE6012, KJ-KKZ1 3012,
  KJ-KKZ2 301.2
Nuclear reactors
  Public safety: KJC6012
  Torts: KJC1692, KJ-KKZ1 847.5
Nuclear reactors (Public safety): KJ-
  KKZ1 3012, KJ-KKZ2 301.2
Nuisance
  Liability: KJ-KKZ1 853.N84
Nuisances
  Claims and actions resulting from
    ownership: KJ-KKZ1 676, KJ-KKZ2
    67.6
  Land ownership: KJC1338.N84
  Landownership: KJ-KKZ1 701.N84,
    KJ-KKZ2 70.3.N84
Nulla poena sine lege: KJC8026+, KJ-
  KKZ1 3826+, KJ-KKZ2 381.3
Nullum crimen sine lege: KJ-KKZ1
  3826+, KJ-KKZ2 381.3

Numerals (Trademarks): KJC2769
Numerus clauses (Higher education):
  KJ-KKZ1 3147.3
Nurses and nursing: KJ-KKZ1 3105,
  KJ-KKZ2 311.5
Nursing care
  Health insurance: KJ-KKZ1
    1487.5.L65
Nursing homes: KJ-KKZ1 3114.O42,
  KJ-KKZ2 312.4.O42

O

Oath: KJA2170.O38, KJ-KKZ1
  472.O28, KJ-KKZ2 47.2.O28
  Civil procedure: KJ-KKZ1 1784
  Courts and procedure: KJ960
  Criminal procedure: KJ1016
  Private law: KJ804.O38
Oath of parties against calumnia:
  KJA2800
Oath of witnesses: KJ-KKZ1 1784
Object at issue: KJ-KKZ1 1748
Object of law: KJ-KKZ1 443, KJ-KKZ2
  44.3
Objection of third party claiming
  ownership and seeking release: KJ-
  KKZ1 1927
Obligatio: KJA2515
Obligation in kind: KJ-KKZ1 814.5, KJ-
  KKZ2 81
Obligation to perform and liability for
  enforcement: KJA2515
Obligations
  Civil law: KJ-KKZ1 801+, KJ-KKZ2
    80+
  Community law: KJE1491+
  Comparative law: KJC1491+
  Germanic law: KJ898+
  Law (Conflict of laws): KJ-KKZ1
    485.C658, KJ-KKZ2 48.5.C658
  Roman law: KJA2512+
Obligations to do or to refrain from
  doing: KJ-KKZ1 815
Obligations to give: KJ-KKZ1 814.5, KJ-
  KKZ2 81

667

Pharmaceutical products: KJ-KKZ1
3091, KJ-KKZ2 310.2
Pharmacists and pharmacies: KJ-KKZ1
3094, KJ-KKZ2 310.5, KJ-KKZ3
61.2.D78
Phenomenology of law: KJ-KKZ1 462.5
Philosophy
Roman law: KJA2160+
Philosophy of law: KJC383+, KJ-KKZ1
440+, KJ-KKZ2 44+
Criminal law: KJC7994+, KJ-KKZ1
3812+, KJ-KKZ2 380.2
European law: KJC383+
Legal education: KJ-KKZ1 51.P45
Phonographs
Copyright: KJE2655.75
Fine arts: KJE2670.75
Literary copyright: KJE2660.75
Motion pictures: KJE2690.75
Musical copyright: KJE2665.75
Television shows: KJE2690.75
Phonographs (Copyright): KJC2655.75,
KJ-KKZ1 1160.75
Photographing
Copyright: KJE2655.76, KJE2655.78
Fine arts: KJE2670.76
Literary copyright: KJE2660.76
Motion pictures: KJE2690.76
Musical copyright: KJE2665.76
Television shows: KJE2690.76
Photographing (Copyright):
KJC2655.76, KJ-KKZ1 1160.76
Photography
Copyright: KJE2670+
Photography (Copyright): KJ-KKZ1
1175+, KJ-KKZ2 117.5
Physical and identifying marks: KJ-
KKZ1 4340, KJ-KKZ2 434
Physical disabilities, People with
Capacity and incapacity: KJ-KKZ1
518.3.P46, KJ-KKZ2 52.55.P46
Physical education: KJ-KKZ1 3159, KJ-
KKZ2 318.7
Physical examination
Civil procedure: KJ-KKZ1 1776
Criminal procedure: KJ-KKZ1 4687,
KJ-KKZ2 468.7

Physical injuries
Civil law: KJC1670+, KJ-KKZ1
842.2+, KJ-KKZ2 85.2+
Private law: KJA2629
Physical therapists: KJ-KKZ1 3107, KJ-
KKZ2 311.7
Physicians: KJC6208, KJ-KKZ1
892.4.P49, KJ-KKZ1 892.4.P82
Health administration employees: KJ-
KKZ1 1490
Privileged witnesses: KJC9622.P45
Picketing (Strikes and lockouts): KJ-
KKZ1 1392
Piecework (Wages): KJ-KKZ1 1332
Pignoris capionem, Legis actio:
KJA2716.P53
Pignus (Roman law): KJA2508
Pilfering: KJ-KKZ1 4240, KJ-KKZ2 424
Pillories: KJ-KKZ1 292.P54
Pilots: KJ-KKZ1 3468.4
Pipelines (Railroads): KJ-KKZ1 3466,
KJ-KKZ2 346.6
Pipelines (Transportation): KJC6919
Piracy
Offenses against public safety:
KJA3463.5.P57
Pirate radio stations: KJC7002, KJ-
KKZ1 3498.3
Place of commission of crime:
KJC8036+, KJ-KKZ1 3831+, KJ-KKZ2
382.2+
Place of payment (Wages): KJ-KKZ1
1337
Plagiarism: KJC2655.3, KJ-KKZ1
1160.3
Copyright: KJE2655.3
Fine arts: KJE2670.3
Literary copyright: KJE2660.3
Motion pictures: KJE2690.3
Musical copyright: KJE2665.3
Television shows: KJE2690.3
Plaintiff (Parties to action): KJ-KKZ1
1657
Civil procedure: KJ-KKZ1 1725+, KJ-
KKZ2 171.5
Planning agencies and bureaus:
KJE857.3+, KJ-KKZ1 3198

Political cooperation of foreign ministers: KJE5105.5

Political crimes (Criminal trials): KJ-KKZ1 40.P64, KJ-KKZ2 3.6.P64

Political criminals (Imprisonment): KJ-KKZ2 481.2.P64

Political integration
Constitutional aspects: KJE5076

Political laws, Foreign (Recognition of): KJC978

Political oath: KJ-KKZ1 2672, KJ-KKZ2 267.2

Political offenses: KJ-KKZ1 4415+, KJ-KKZ2 441.5+

Political organizations, Non-party
Constitutional law: KJE5240

Political parties (Constitutional law): KJC5222, KJE5222, KJ-KKZ1 2488, KJ-KKZ2 248.8

Political prisoners
Social services: KJC3525

Political prisoners (Imprisonment): KJ-KKZ1 4812.P64

Political prisoners (Social services): KJ-KKZ1 1539, KJ-KKZ2 153.9

Political rights
Constitutional law: KJC5132, KJE5132+

Political science (Education): KJ-KKZ1 3138.8

Political strikes: KJ-KKZ1 1393+, KJ-KKZ1 1393, KJ-KKZ2 138.5

Political theory of law: KJ-KKZ1 463+, KJ-KKZ2 46.3+

Politics and labor: KJ-KKZ1 1274

Politique agricole: KJE6601+

Politique commune des transports
Community law: KJE6868+

Politique de conjuncture
Community law: KJE6431

Politique d'exportation: KJE6794

Politique d'importation: KJE6792

Politique économique
Community law: KJE6428+

Politique en matière de change
Community law: KJE7059+

Politique régionale
Public land use: KJE6135+

Poll tax: KJC7358.P64, KJ-KKZ1 3680.P65, KJ-KKZ2 367.7.P65

Pollutants
Environmental pollution: KJ-KKZ1 3131.5+, KJ-KKZ2 314.2+
Water and groundwater pollution: KJ-KKZ1 3131, KJ-KKZ2 314

Pollution
Insurance law: KJ-KKZ1 1036.P64

Pollution atmospherique
Community law: KJE6249

Pollution des eaux
Community law: KJE6251

Poor
Social services: KJC3470

Poor debtors oath: KJ-KKZ1 1897, KJ-KKZ2 189.7

Poor, The (Social services): KJ-KKZ1 1528, KJ-KKZ2 152.6, KJ-KKZ3 33.5.P66

Population control: KJ-KKZ1 3124+, KJ-KKZ2 313.4+

Populus Romanus
Constitutional principles: KJA2910
Juristic persons: KJA2223

Ports of entry: KJ-KKZ1 3476+, KJ-KKZ2 347.7

Portuguese jurists (6th to 15th centuries): KJA1870+

Position dominante
Monopolie: KJE6503

Positive interest (Damages): KJA2616

Positivism: KJ-KKZ1 459+

Possession: KJ855+, KJA2440+, KJC1263+, KJ-KKZ1 472.P68, KJ-KKZ2 47.2.P68, KJ-KKZ3 16.6
Narcotics: KJ-KKZ1 4404, KJ-KKZ2 440.4
Negotiable instruments: KJ-KKZ1 937.3
Property: KJ-KKZ1 646+, KJ-KKZ2 65+
Real property: KJ865.2+, KJ866+
Rights (Property): KJ-KKZ1 647.P67

Publicity and registration
Courts and procedure: KJ-KKZ1
1852, KJ-KKZ2 185.2
Private company: KJ-KKZ1 1095
Stock corporations: KJ-KKZ1 1055
Publicity (Criminal procedure): KJ-KKZ2
462.6
Publicly subsidized housing: KJ-KKZ1
887.3
Publishers and publishing
Press law: KJ-KKZ1 3503+, KJ-KKZ2
350.4
Publishing contract: KJ-KKZ2 118.5+
Publishing contracts: KJ-KKZ1 1185+
Publishing contract: KJC2706+
Author and publisher: KJE2706+
Private international law: KJ-KKZ1
485.P92, KJ-KKZ2 48.5.P92
Punishment
Criminal law: KJ980+, KJC8230+, KJ-
KKZ1 3946+, KJ-KKZ2 394.6+, KJ-
KKZ3 91.4+, KJ-KKZ4 9.34
Determination of punishment:
KJA3604+, KJ-KKZ1 4012+, KJ-
KKZ2 401.2+
Inequality of punishment: KJA3608
Juvenile courts: KJC9662
Juvenile delinquency procedure: KJ-
KKZ1 4726+, KJ-KKZ2 472.6+
Military criminal law: KJ-KKZ1 3775,
KJ-KKZ2 377
Punishment without imprisonment: KJ-
KKZ1 3974, KJ-KKZ2 397.4
Juvenile delinquency procedure: KJ-
KKZ1 4734, KJ-KKZ2 473.4
Puppet theaters (Public safety): KJ-
KKZ1 3036.5.T7, KJ-KKZ2 303.8.T7
Purchase of inheritance: KJ-KKZ1 792,
KJ-KKZ2 79.2
Purgative oath
Courts and procedure: KJ960
Criminal procedure: KJ1016
Purgo (Contracts): KJ914.S87
Purity
Food processing: KJC6752
Purity (Food processing industries): KJ-
KKZ1 3379, KJ-KKZ2 337.9

Purpose and scienter (Criminal intent):
KJ-KKZ1 3867, KJ-KKZ2 386.7
Pushing for sales (Unfair competition):
KJ-KKZ1 1246+, KJ-KKZ2 123.8+

Q

Quaestio (Criminal court procedure):
KJA1937
Quaestiones (Roman law): KJA1937
Quaestorship: KJA3006
Qualification
Conflict of laws: KJ-KKZ1 481.5
Limits of application of foreign law:
KJC978.5
Quality control
Economic law: KJE6554
Quality control (Economic law):
KJC6554+, KJ-KKZ1 3255, KJ-KKZ2
325.5
Quality marks: KJ-KKZ1 1221.Q34
Quarantine: KJ-KKZ1 3087, KJ-KKZ2
309.5
Quarrying: KJA3130, KJC6700+,
KJE6710+, KJ-KKZ3 77.3+, KJ-KKZ4
7.66
Quasi-contracts (Obligations):
KJA2602+
Quasi copyright: KJC2700, KJ-KKZ1
1184, KJ-KKZ2 118.4
Quasi copyright and neighboring rights:
KJE2700
Quasi-delicts: KJA2632+
Quasi-institutes: KJA2185
Quasi marriage: KJA2237
Quasi-=matrimonial relationships:
KJE1159
Quasi-matrimonial relationships:
KJC1159, KJ-KKZ1 568, KJ-KKZ2
56.8
Quotas
Tariff
Customs: KJE7326

R

Refugees
  Control of
    Public safety: KJE6057
  Private international law:
    KJC979.R43, KJ-KKZ1 485.R43,
    KJ-KKZ2 48.5.R43
  Public safety: KJ-KKZ3 58.A45
  Social services: KJC3506
  Social services to: KJ-KKZ1 1538,
    KJ-KKZ2 153.8, KJ-KKZ3 33.5.R43,
    KJ-KKZ4 3.34.R43
Refunds (Tax collection): KJ-KKZ1
  3569.5
Refuse disposal: KJC6187.R44,
  KJE6178.R43, KJ-KKZ1 3088.R43,
  KJ-KKZ2 309.7.R43, KJ-KKZ3
  61.2.R43
Regalia
  Finance: KJ783+, KJ-KKZ1 268, KJ-
    KKZ2 26.8
  Kings and other rulers: KJ-KKZ3
    48.6.R43
Regalia metallorum et salinarum:
  KJ937
Regelung der Sprachenfrage für die
  Organe der Gemeinschaft (European
  Communities): KJE5306
Régime applicable aux fonctionnaires
  Civil service: KJE5939
Régime linguistique des institutions (The
  European Communities): KJE5306
Régime parlementaire (Constitutional
  law): KJC5412+
Regional comparative and uniform law:
  KJC2+
Regional courts: KJ-KKZ1 1584, KJ-
  KKZ2 158.4
Regional divisions (Comparative law):
  KJC479.2+
Regional planning
  Public land law: KJC6135+, KJ-KKZ1
    3059+, KJ-KKZ2 307+, KJ-KKZ3
    60.4+, KJ-KKZ4 5.73
  Roads and highways: KJ-KKZ1
    3044.9
Regional Policy Committee: KJE6137

Regional policy (Public land law):
  KJE6135+
Regional public corporations: KJ-KKZ1
  2880, KJ-KKZ2 288
Register of marital property: KJ-KKZ2
  186.7
Register of matrimonial property: KJ-
  KKZ1 1867
Register of pledges: KJ-KKZ1 732+,
  KJ-KKZ2 74
Registered mail: KJC6958
Registers
  Violation of privacy: KJC1682,
    KJE1626, KJ-KKZ1 844.5, KJ-KKZ2
    86.5
Registration
  Cooperative societies: KJ-KKZ1 1122
  Effect of (Land registration): KJ-KKZ1
    745+
  Incorporated society: KJ-KKZ1 523.5
  Noncontentious jurisdiction: KJ-KKZ1
    1850+, KJ-KKZ2 185+
  Noncontentious jurisdiction): KJ-KKZ3
    38.2.R44
  Public registers: KJ-KKZ1 56+, KJ-
    KKZ2 5.53+
  Stock companies: KJC2459
Registration of aliens: KJ-KKZ1 3026.5
Registration of artisans: KJ-KKZ1 3428
Registration of civil status
  (Noncontentious jurisdiction): KJ-
  KKZ1 1856+, KJ-KKZ2 185.6+
Registration of copyright claim:
  KJC2655.4, KJE2655.4, KJ-KKZ1
  1160.4, KJ-KKZ2 115.5
  Fine arts: KJE2670.4
  Literary copyright: KJE2660.4
  Motion pictures: KJE2690.4
  Musical copyright: KJE2665.4
  Television shows: KJE2690.4
Registration of individuals: KJC6034+,
  KJ-KKZ1 3022.2+, KJ-KKZ2 302.2+,
  KJ-KKZ3 57.7
Registration of motor vehicles:
  KJC6878, KJE6878, KJ-KKZ1 3443.5,
  KJ-KKZ2 344.4

Ruling classes: KJA2935+
Rural land tenure: KJ742+, KJ-KKZ1 232+, KJ-KKZ2 23.2+, KJ-KKZ3 71.4+
Rural social services: KJ-KKZ1 1526

S

Sabotage
  Treason: KJ-KKZ1 4432, KJ-KKZ2 443.2
Sabotage and depicting means of defense: KJ-KKZ1 4473, KJ-KKZ2 447.3
Sabotage of essential services, utilities, warning systems, etc: KJ-KKZ1 4374, KJ-KKZ2 437.4
Sabotage of weapons, equipment or means of defense: KJ-KKZ1 3765
Sacral acts (Magistracies): KJA2987
Sacramento, Legis actio: KJA2716.S23
Sacrilegium and Peculatus (Roman law): KJA3444
Sacrilegium (Offenses against the government): KJA3390.S23
Safeguarding the social and political system (Criminal law punishment): KJ-KKZ1 3954, KJ-KKZ2 395.4
Safety equipment (Road traffic): KJ-KKZ1 3444, KJ-KKZ2 344.6
Safety films (Fire prevention and control): KJ-KKZ1 3019, KJ-KKZ2 301.9
Safety measures: KJA3630.A+, KJC8250+
Safety regulations
  Equipment
    Industrial safety: KJ-KKZ1 1430+, KJ-KKZ2 142.3
    Ships: KJ-KKZ1 3472+, KJ-KKZ2 347.3
Sala (Real property): KJ873
Salaried employees
  Labor law: KJC2878, KJ-KKZ1 1435.S25

Salaries
  Attachment and garnishment of rights and choses in action: KJ-KKZ1 1908.S34, KJ-KKZ2 190.8.S34
  Customs organization: KJ-KKZ1 3649
  Income tax: KJE7184+, KJ-KKZ1 3584+, KJ-KKZ2 357.5
  Public finance: KJ-KKZ1 3527.5
  Railroad officials and employees: KJ-KKZ1 3463
  Restriction of execution: KJ-KKZ1 1935
  Stock corporations: KJ-KKZ1 1058.S25
  Teachers: KJ-KKZ1 3140.7
  The legal profession: KJ-KKZ1 1607
Sale
  Bankruptcy: KJ-KKZ1 1964.S35
  Commercial contracts and transactions: KJ-KKZ3 22.6, KJ-KKZ4 2.22
  Commercial law: KJC2096
  Consensual contracts: KJA2580+
  Contracts and transactions: KJC1770+, KJE1690+, KJ-KKZ1 874+, KJ-KKZ2 89.75+, KJ-KKZ3 20.9+, KJ-KKZ4 1.73
Sale after approval: KJ-KKZ1 878.S24, KJ-KKZ2 89.9.S24
Sale-and-lease-back: KJC1826, KJ-KKZ1 888.3+, KJ-KKZ2 92.4+
Sale in kind: KJ-KKZ1 878.S25, KJ-KKZ2 89.9.S25
Sale of business enterprise as a whole: KJC2085, KJE2085, KJ-KKZ1 925.5
Sale on approval: KJ-KKZ1 878.S26, KJ-KKZ2 89.9.S26
Sales tax: KJC7285, KJE7285, KJ-KKZ1 3628+, KJ-KKZ2 361.3+, KJ-KKZ3 86.65
Salland (Real property): KJ873
Salvage
  Maritime law: KJC2272, KJE2272, KJ-KKZ1 981+, KJ-KKZ2 102.9
Sample books
  Copyright: KJC2685
  Fine arts: KJE2685

Self-mutilation (Military criminal law and procedure): KJ-KKZ1 3763

Self-service (Modes of sale): KJC1810, KJ-KKZ1 878.S44, KJ-KKZ2 89.9.S44

Semantics
Germanic law: KJ170
History of law: KJ77, KJC408, KJ-KKZ1 92, KJ-KKZ2 9.2

Senate (Roman law): KJA3035+

Senatores: KJA2942

Senators, Tribunals for (Roman law): KJA3560

Sentence
Civil procedure: KJA2802
Criminal procedure: KJ1032

Sentencing
Criminal law: KJC8304+

Sentencing to probation: KJ-KKZ1 3974, KJ-KKZ2 397.4

Separation
Marriage: KJ-KKZ1 565, KJ-KKZ2 56.5
Marriage law: KJC1154

Séparation des pouvoirs (Community law): KJE5049+

Separation of church and state: KJ-KKZ1 2697, KJ-KKZ2 269.7

Separation of powers (Constitutional law): KJC5049+, KJE5049+, KJ-KKZ1 2270+, KJ-KKZ2 227+, KJ-KKZ3 44.4.S46

Separation of property (Marital property and regime): KJ-KKZ1 573, KJ-KKZ2 57.3

Sequence of heirs: KJA2287+

Servants
Contract for service and labor: KJ-KKZ1 892.6
Contracts for service and labor: KJ-KKZ3 21.9, KJ-KKZ4 1.9
Contracts for work and labor: KJC1849

Service industries
Collective bargaining: KJ-KKZ1 1387.S47

Service industries (Cooperative societies): KJ-KKZ1 1133.S47

Service marks (Trademarks): KJ-KKZ1 1221.S47

Service of process (Pretrial procedure)
Criminal procedure: KJ-KKZ1 4646, KJ-KKZ2 464.6

Service of process (Pretrial procedures)
Civil procedure: KJ-KKZ1 1729
Courts and procedure: KJ-KKZ1 1662.S95

Service trades: KJC6819, KJE6819+

Service trades (Industry regulation): KJ-KKZ1 3424+, KJ-KKZ2 342.4+

Services (Excise taxes): KJC7306

Servitudes
Law of things: KJA2485+
Real property: KJ879+, KJC1348+, KJ-KKZ1 709+, KJ-KKZ2 71+

Servitus poenae (Slaves): KJA2198+

Servus poenae (Roman law penalties): KJA3620.S42

Set-off
Civil procedure: KJ-KKZ1 1756.S48, KJ-KKZ2 175.6.S48
Extinction of obligation: KJA2529.C64, KJC1566, KJ-KKZ1 822.9, KJ-KKZ2 82.3

Settlement
Labor courts and procedure: KJ-KKZ1 1455

Settlement before trial: KJC3923, KJ-KKZ2 176.8

Settlement before trial (Civil procedure): KJ-KKZ1 1768

Settlement of claims from defective or dissolved marriages: KJC1155, KJ-KKZ1 567, KJ-KKZ2 56.7

Severe disabilities, People with
Preferential employment: KJ-KKZ1 1292+, KJ-KKZ2 128.3

Sewage control (Water and groundwater pollution): KJC6251+, KJ-KKZ1 3131, KJ-KKZ2 314

Sewage (Public utilities): KJ-KKZ1 2956, KJ-KKZ2 296

Sex crimes
Criminal law: KJ-KKZ4 9.35.S49
Criminal trials: KJ-KKZ1 40.S49

Suretyship: KJ914.S87, KJA2524, KJC1886, KJ-KKZ1 900+, KJ-KKZ2 95.8
  Insurance law: KJC2375, KJ-KKZ1 1024+, KJ-KKZ2 106+
Surgical and other medical treatment, Criminal aspects of: KJ-KKZ1 4096+, KJ-KKZ2 409.6+
Surrender of goods or documents (Insolvency procedure in execution): KJ-KKZ1 1919, KJ-KKZ2 192
Surtaxes: KJC7268+, KJ-KKZ1 3624+, KJ-KKZ2 361.2
Surveys, Legal
  European Communities: KJE931
Survivors
  Social security: KJ-KKZ1 1510.S87
Survivors' benefits: KJC3381+, KJE5953.3, KJ-KKZ1 1011, KJ-KKZ2 104.9
Suspect, The (Criminal procedure): KJ-KKZ1 4630.S93, KJ-KKZ2 463.S93
Suspended railways: KJ-KKZ1 3465.S98, KJ-KKZ2 346.5.S98
Suspension
  Insolvency claims enforcement: KJ-KKZ1 1932, KJ-KKZ2 193.2
  Labor contract and employment: KJ-KKZ1 1305
Suspension of procedure (Civil procedure): KJ-KKZ1 1732, KJ-KKZ2 172.5
Suspension of punishment (Criminal courts and procedure): KJC9790, KJ-KKZ1 4828, KJ-KKZ2 482.8
Suspensive conditions: KJ-KKZ1 505.5
  Civil law: KJC1091
Symbolims
  Roman law: KJA78
Symbolism in law: KJ78, KJ172+, KJ-KKZ1 94+, KJ-KKZ2 9.4+
Sympathy strikes: KJ-KKZ1 1393+, KJ-KKZ1 1393, KJ-KKZ2 138.5
Syndicats d'employeurs: KJE3136
Syndicats des salariés: KJE3123+
Syndics (Bankruptcy): KJ-KKZ1 1947
Syndodalis conventus: KJ767

System of citation: KJC83
Système monétaire europeen: KJE7051+
Systems of citation: KJA132
Systems of cooperation (Economic law): KJ-KKZ1 3200

T

Tacit (implied) agreements (Exclusion of liability): KJC1666, KJ-KKZ1 840, KJ-KKZ2 84.8
Tarif douanier commun: KJE7313
Tariff: KJC7312+, KJE7312+, KJ-KKZ1 3645+, KJ-KKZ2 364+, KJ-KKZ3 87.7+, KJ-KKZ4 8.72
Taux de change
  Community law: KJE7060
Taverns
  Excise taxes: KJ-KKZ1 3640.B37, KJ-KKZ2 362.4.B37
  Industry regulation: KJ-KKZ1 3424.5, KJ-KKZ3 80.5.H66
  Protection of children in public: KJ-KKZ1 1546, KJ-KKZ2 154.6
  Wages: KJ-KKZ1 1343.H6, KJ-KKZ2 133.4.H6
Tax accounting: KJ-KKZ1 3562+, KJ-KKZ2 355.4
  Stock companies: KJ-KKZ1 3597
Tax administration: KJC7130+, KJE7130, KJ-KKZ1 3558+, KJ-KKZ2 355+
Tax allocation, Jurisdiction for: KJ-KKZ1 3559
Tax and customs courts and procedure: KJ-KKZ1 3682+, KJ-KKZ2 368+, KJ-KKZ3 88, KJ-KKZ4 8.73
Tax and customs crimes and delinquency: KJ-KKZ1 3693+, KJ-KKZ2 370+
Tax and customs delinquency: KJ-KKZ1 3708, KJ-KKZ2 370.7
Tax and customs investigation: KJ-KKZ1 3701
Tax auditing: KJ-KKZ1 3568, KJ-KKZ2 356

Voting

Cooperative societies: KJ-KKZ1 1132

Courts: KJ-KKZ1 1594+

Crimes in connection with: KJ-KKZ1 4458+, KJ-KKZ2 445.8+

Private company: KJ-KKZ1 1106

Stockholders' meetings: KJC2496, KJE2496, KJ-KKZ1 1078

The legislature: KJ-KKZ1 2524.5, KJ-KKZ2 252.4

W

Wadia

Law of things: KJ885+

Obligations: KJ914.W33

Wage discrimination: KJC2943, KJ-KKZ1 1327, KJ-KKZ2 131.3

Wage earners: KJC2878

Wager of battle

Courts and procedure: KJ964.D83

Criminal law and procedure: KJ-KKZ1 292.D83

Wages: KJC2950+, KJE2950+, KJ-KKZ1 1330+, KJ-KKZ2 132+, KJ-KKZ3 30.45, KJ-KKZ4 3.235

Attachment and garnishment of rights and choses in action: KJ-KKZ1 1908.S34, KJ-KKZ2 190.8.S34

Bankruptcy: KJ-KKZ1 1964.W33

Community law: KJE2950+

Income tax: KJE7184+

Comparative law: KJC2950+

Labor standards and protection of labor: KJC3008

Income tax deductions: KJ-KKZ1 3584+, KJ-KKZ2 357.5

Labor standards: KJ-KKZ1 991

Pilots: KJ-KKZ1 3468.4

Restriction of execution: KJ-KKZ1 1935

Währungsausschuss

Community law: KJE7054

Waiver: KJ-KKZ1 472.W33, KJ-KKZ2 47.2.W33

Waiver of appeal

Civil procedure: KJ-KKZ1 1828

Waiver of appeal

Criminal procedure: KJ-KKZ1 4788, KJ-KKZ2 478.8

Wanted notice (Pretrial criminal procedures): KJ-KKZ1 4646, KJ-KKZ2 464.6

War: KJA3328

Affreightment: KJ-KKZ1 975, KJ-KKZ2 102.2

Social services: KJ-KKZ3 33.5.W37, KJ-KKZ4 3.34.W37

War and emergency powers: KJC5397.W37, KJ-KKZ1 2564, KJ-KKZ2 256.4, KJ-KKZ3 48.6.W37

War crime trials: KJC68.2+, KJ-KKZ1 42.2+, KJ-KKZ2 3.72+, KJ-KKZ2 3.9

War crimes: KJ-KKZ1 4545, KJ-KKZ2 454.5

Exemption from limitation of action: KJ-KKZ1 4040.W37, KJ-KKZ2 404.W37

War damage compensation (Government measures): KJ-KKZ1 3727+, KJ-KKZ2 373+

War debts (Public finance): KJC7085+

War-related groups of beneficiaries (Social services): KJC3503+, KJ-KKZ1 1537+, KJ-KKZ2 153.7+

War risks

Maritime law: KJE2285.5.W37

War risks (Marine insurance): KJC2285.5.W37

War victims

Social services: KJC3530

War victims and war invalids (Social services): KJ-KKZ1 1540, KJ-KKZ2 154

Warandia (Contracts): KJ912+

Warehouses (Banking): KJ-KKZ1 950, KJ-KKZ2 100.3

Warehousing: KJC2118, KJ-KKZ1 930.3, KJ-KKZ2 98, KJ-KKZ3 22.8

Warranty

Consensual contracts: KJA2582.W37

Contracts: KJ-KKZ1 875+, KJ-KKZ2 89.8

Sale contracts: KJC1786+

Wildlife conservation
  Environmental law: KJE6255
Will theory (Contracts): KJ-KKZ1 860.2
Wills: KJC1467+, KJ-KKZ1 785+, KJ-
  KKZ2 78.5+, KJ-KKZ3 19.6+
  Community law: KJE1467+
  Sailors: KJ-KKZ1 785.7.P74
Window rights (Law of adjoining
  landowners): KJ-KKZ1 701.L54, KJ-
  KKZ2 70.3.L54
Wine
  Excise taxes: KJ-KKZ1 3640.W55,
    KJ-KKZ2 362.4.W55
  Marks of origin: KJC2779
Winemaking: KJC6663.W55,
  KJE6651.W54, KJ-KKZ1 3397, KJ-
  KKZ2 339.7
Wiretapping: KJ-KKZ1 4168, KJ-KKZ2
  416.8
  Criminal procedure: KJC9616
Wirtschaftslenkung and
  Wirtschaftspolitik
  Community law: KJE6428+
Wirtschaftsunion BENELUX, 1958:
  KJE501+
Witchcraft
  Criminal law and procedure:
    KJ985.W58, KJ-KKZ1 172.W58, KJ-
    KKZ1 292.W58, KJ-KKZ2 17.2.W58
  History of criminal law: KJC7964.W58
Withdrawal
  Civil procedure: KJ-KKZ1 1753
  Extinction of obligation: KJ-KKZ1
    823.5.W58
Withdrawal of faulty decisions (Civil
  procedure): KJ-KKZ1 1798
Withdrawal of faulty decisions (Criminal
  procedure): KJ-KKZ1 4753, KJ-KKZ2
  475.3
Withholding tax: KJ-KKZ1 3590+, KJ-
  KKZ2 358
Without cause (Unjust enrichment): KJ-
  KKZ1 854.5
Witness
  Criminal procedure: KJ1016, KJ-
    KKZ2 469.2+

Witnesses
  Civil procedure: KJ-KKZ1 1777+, KJ-
    KKZ2 177.7+
  Court costs: KJ-KKZ1 1978
  Courts and procedure: KJ960, KJ-
    KKZ1 1675+, KJ-KKZ2 167.5
  Criminal procedure: KJC9619+, KJ-
    KKZ1 4692+
Wohnungsgeld
  Civil service: KJE5952
  Social services: KJE3448
Women: KJC435.W65, KJ-KKZ1 517.5
  Capacity and incapacity:
    KJA2213.5.W65, KJC1019, KJ-
    KKZ1 517.5, KJ-KKZ2 52.3
  Discrimination against
    Constitutional law: KJC5144.W65,
      KJE5144.W64, KJ-KKZ1
      2467.W65, KJ-KKZ2 246.7.W65
    Labor law: KJE2945.W66, KJ-KKZ1
      1328.W58, KJ-KKZ2 131.4.W58
    Social insurance: KJ-KKZ1 1478.W65
Women's labor: KJC3175+, KJE3175,
  KJ-KKZ1 1424+, KJ-KKZ2 141.7+, KJ-
  KKZ3 31.5.W35
Wood, Recycling of: KJ-KKZ1 3264+,
  KJ-KKZ2 326.5+
Work and labor, Contract for:
  KJC1854+
Work councils: KJC2991
  Civil service: KJ-KKZ1 2983, KJ-
    KKZ2 298.3
Workers' compensation: KJC3350+,
  KJE3350+
Workers' compensation (Social
  insurance): KJ-KKZ1 1495+, KJ-KKZ2
  149+, KJ-KKZ3 32.5.W67, KJ-KKZ4
  3.32.W67
Working hours: KJ-KKZ1 1363
Working standards (Collective
  bargaining): KJ-KKZ1 1382
Works agreements (Employee
  participation): KJC3001
Works assembly (Labor-management
  relations): KJ-KKZ1 1352, KJ-KKZ2
  134.4

GPO U.S. GOVERNMENT PRINTING OFFICE: 2008–340–014/60018